*SEC Regulation
Outside the United States*

SEC Regulation Outside the United States

Fifth Edition

Edited by Mark Berman

Published by Risk Books, a Division of Incisive Financial Publishing Ltd

Haymarket House
28–29 Haymarket
London SW1Y 4RX
Tel: +44 (0)20 7484 9700
Fax: +44 (0)20 7484 9800
E-mail: books@riskwaters.com
Sites: www.riskbooks.com
www.incisivemedia.com

© 2005 the Editor and the named Authors, all rights fully reserved.

ISBN 1 904339 54 9

British Library Cataloguing in Publication Data
A catalogue record for this book is available from the British Library

Managing Editor: Laurie Donaldson
Development Editor: Steve Fairman
Copy Editor: Andrew John
Senior Designer: Rebecca Bramwell

Typeset by Mizpah Publishing Services, Chennai, India

Printed and bound in Spain by Espacegrafic, Pamplona, Navarra

Conditions of sale
All rights reserved. No part of this publication may be reproduced in any material form whether by photocopying or storing in any medium by electronic means whether or not transiently or incidentally to some other use for this publication without the prior written consent of the copyright owner except in accordance with the provisions of the Copyright, Designs and Patents Act 1988 or under the terms of a licence issued by the Copyright Licensing Agency Limited of 90, Tottenham Court Road, London W1P 0LP.

Warning: the doing of any unauthorised act in relation to this work may result in both civil and criminal liability.

Every effort has been made to ensure the accuracy of the text at the time of publication, this includes efforts to contact each author to ensure the accuracy of their details at publication is correct. However, no responsibility for loss occasioned to any person acting or refraining from acting as a result of the material contained in this publication will be accepted by the copyright owner, the editor, the authors or Incisive Media Plc.

This book is current as at August 1 2005 and represents the personal views of the Editor and the Authors and not their organisations or colleagues. Reasonable care has been taken in the preparation of this book, but this book is not specific legal advice on which persons may rely. No responsibility can be or is accepted for any omissions, errors or for any loss sustained by any person placing reliance on its contents.

Contents

	List of Contributors	vii
1	The US Federal Securities Laws and the Securities and Exchange Commission *Mark Berman* Threadneedle Asset Management Limited	1
2	US-Registered Offers *Ottilie L Jarmel* Shearman & Sterling LLP	15
3	Private Placements, Regulation S and Related Developments *Richard M Kosnik; Gene Kleinhendler* Jones Day; Gross, Kleinhendler, Hodak, Halevy, Greenberg & Co.	129
4	Financial Information: Accounting and Disclosure *Abigail Arms* Shearman & Sterling LLP	183
5	US/European Cross-Border M&A: Regulatory Framework and Recent Developments *Scott Simpson* Skadden Arps LLP	281
6	Fund Managers, Investment Advisers and Funds *Barry P Barbash; Simon FT Cox* Shearman & Sterling LLP; Norton Rose	333
7	Broker–Dealer Regulation *Mark Berman; Steven F Gatti* Threadneedle Asset Management Limited; Clifford Chance US LLP	401
8	Developments in International Regulation and Enforcement *Michael D Mann, William P Barry* Richards Spears Kibbe and Orbe LLP	479
9	Enforcement of US Securities Laws *Colleen P Mahoney* Skadden Arps LLP	609
	Index	725

DEDICATION

In memory of Linda Quinn who helped make this book and many SEC developments possible.

ACKNOWLEDGEMENTS

The Authors and the Editor wish to acknowledge the efforts of the following persons, without whom this book may not have been possible: Lynn Hiestand, Michal Berkner, Lorenzo Corte and Christian Pilkington of Skadden Arps; Karina Lengler, Benjamin Allworth and Phyllis Stoller of Shearman & Sterling; Russell King of Norton Rose; Einat Meisel of Gross Kleinhendler; Micah Nessan of Jones Day; Stacey Becker, Megan Gordon and Carol Thomas of Clifford Chance; and Hannah, Zoë and Katie B.

List of Contributors

Abigail Arms is a partner with Shearman & Sterling LLP. She advises domestic and international investment banking and corporate clients on capital markets, derivatives and securities law matters. Ms. Arms served in several capacities in the Division of Corporation Finance of the Securities and Exchange Commission from 1984–1997. She participated in a number of Division initiatives to streamline the capital-raising regulatory framework, including the elimination of pricing amendments, universal shelf and Rule 144A. Ms. Arms was a member of Chairman Levitt's Disclosure Simplification Task Force, which published its report in March 1996.

Barry P Barbash is a partner with Shearman & Sterling LLP and heads the firm's asset management practice group. His practice includes advising financial services company clients on a wide range of transactions and regulatory matters. For five years prior to joining Shearman & Sterling, he served as director of the Securities and Exchange Commission Division of Investment Management, in which capacity he had responsibility for the US mutual fund industry, US and non-US investment managers and US based or sponsored private funds.

William P Barry is an attorney with Richards Spears Kibbe & Orbe LLP. His practice focuses on securities enforcement and white collar criminal representation, as well as corporate compliance issues. Mr. Barry received his BA from Wesleyan University in 1991 and his JD from George Washington University Law School in 1995. From 1995–1996, Mr. Barry was law clerk to the Honorable Truman A. Morrison III, District of Columbia Superior Court.

Mark Berman is counsel in the Legal, Compliance & Audit Group of Threadneedle Asset Management Limited, and advises on hedge fund legal, corporate governance and AML issues and regulatory matters. He has counselled multi-national banks and investment firms on compliance, electronic trading and international regulatory matters. From 1985 to 1990, he was a lawyer with the Divisions of Corporation Finance and Market Regulation at the Securities and Exchange Commission where he worked on domestic and international disclosure and trading practices issues. Mr Berman, who has lectured on law and regulation at the London

Business School, is a member of the Advisory Council of the SEC Historical Society.

Simon FT Cox is a partner in Norton Rose's corporate finance department and works on a wide range of UK and international securities, mergers and acquisitions and financial services projects, with an emphasis on collective investment and emerging and transition markets. He qualified with Norton Rose and has been a partner since 1988. Simon is a member of the Securities Institute, the IBA and the City of London Solicitors Company.

Steven F Gatti is of counsel at Clifford Chance. His practice concentrates on financial services regulatory counselling, securities enforcement, securities litigation and white-collar defence. He specialises in complex civil and administrative matters arising under the US securities laws and regulations and internal investigations, strategic counselling to broker–dealers and other financial services companies and has extensive experience in defending global financial institutions in multi-jurisdictional investigations and litigation before the Securities and Exchange Commission, the National Association of Securities Dealers Regulation, Inc., The New York Stock Exchange, Inc., other self-regulatory organisations as well as state regulatory authorities.

Ottilie L Jarmel is counsel in the Capital Markets practice group of Shearman & Sterling. She has worked on a variety of public and private financing transactions for both domestic and non-US corporations and advises issuers on their ongoing compliance obligations under US securities laws, including the Sarbanes–Oxley Act, corporate governance, securities offering reforms, securities and electronics (including online offerings and websites), Regulation FD, SEC accounting issues, Rule 10b5-1 trading plans and Regulation M-A.

Gene Kleinhendler is a managing partner with Gross Kleinhendler Hodak Halevy Greenberg & Co. Prior to that he was an attorney at the Securities and Exchange Commission. He directs his firm's Technology and Venture Law group and led the development and expansion of these practice fields during the 1980s and 1990s. He counsels mature technology companies in complex international transactions, securities law matters, and financing and corporate reorganisation and has also represented the interest of his clients in securities litigation in several jurisdictions. He is a co-author of "ISR International Securities Regulation, Israel Section", published by Oceana Publications, Inc. and was a committee member on the Israel Securities Authority Committee for Dual Listing Requirements.

LIST OF CONTRIBUTORS

Richard M Kosnik is a partner with Jones Day. He heads the New York Office securities practice and coordinates the integration of Jones Day's US and international capital markets efforts. He has managed a broad range of transactions and projects representing financial institutions, US issuers, and non-US issuers from numerous jurisdictions, including equity and debt securities offerings into the US public and private markets, tender offers for equity and debt securities, and the establishment of a variety of ADR programmes. Mr Kosnik served for four years as head of the Office of International Corporation Finance in the SEC's Division of Corporation Finance. He was in charge of the international corporate finance program and was responsible for overseeing the review of all public offerings by non-US issuers in the United States and rulemaking initiatives and interpretive policies in international corporate finance, including all matters relating to Rule 144A and Regulation S.

Colleen P Mahoney heads the firm's securities enforcement and compliance practice of Skadden Arps. She represents corporations and their officers, directors and employees in Securities and Exchange Commission and other law enforcement investigations, as well as in federal court securities litigation. Also, Ms. Mahoney assists management and boards of directors performing internal investigations. She advises public companies, financial services firms and financial institutions on preventive and remedial measures before and after securities-related issues arise. She also counsels clients on issues in the emerging field of consumer financial regulation. Ms. Mahoney joined Skadden, Arps after 15 years at the Securities and Exchange Commission, where she served as acting general counsel, and deputy director of the Division of Enforcement between 1994 and 1998. She was executive assistant to the chairman of the SEC in 1993. She also was the Division of Enforcement's chief counsel between 1990 and 1993. Ms. Mahoney joined the Commission in 1983 in the litigation section of the Office of the General Counsel. During her tenure at the SEC, Ms. Mahoney helped manage a civil law enforcement program that initiated more than 400 new cases a year.

Michael D Mann is a partner in the law firm of Richards Spears Kibbe & Orbe LLP, focusing on international securities regulation and enforcement and the cross-border conduct of business. He regularly represents public companies, their audit committees, officers and directors in connection with their compliance with US regulatory requirements, including the Sarbanes–Oxley Act. From 1989 to 1996, Mr. Mann served as the first director of the SEC's Office of International Affairs. He also served as associate director in the SEC's Division of Enforcement.

Scott Simpson is a partner at Skadden Arps. Mr Simpson specialises in cross-border merger and acquisition transactions, including contested takeovers, he has also been involved in a variety of corporate finance transactions. Mr Simpson was profiled in 1992 in The American Lawyer in connection with his representation of the Polish Government, and featured by The American Lawyer in 2000 as one of 12 notable American transaction lawyers. The Daily Deal, based on independent market data, has ranked Mr Simpson among the top transaction lawyers in Europe in 2002 and 2003.

1

The US Federal Securities Laws and the Securities and Exchange Commission

Mark Berman
Threadneedle Asset Management Limited

The Securities and Exchange Commission (SEC or Commission) is the US federal agency charged with administering and enforcing the US federal securities laws.

The Commission was established in 1934 by the US Congress (Congress) under the Securities Exchange Act of 1934 that, like the Securities Act of 1933, had the 1929 stock market crash as its catalyst. Unlike regulators in other nations, no US governmental entity administers or oversees the SEC. It is an independent agency, operating under the Executive branch of government.

This chapter outlines the SEC's principal operating divisions, shows how the Commission exercises its jurisdiction and states how the SEC Staff (Staff or SEC Staff) operates. It summarises key terms used throughout this book, including the definition of the term "security".

SOURCES OF SECURITIES LAWS AND THE LEGISLATIVE AND JUDICIAL FRAMEWORK

The Commerce Clause of the US Constitution authorises the Congress, the Legislative branch of the federal government, to pass laws that govern commerce among states and between states and other nations. Laws take effect when signed by the President of the United States, the head of the Executive branch of government.

The federal courts, the judicial branch of the federal government, construe laws and resolve controversies.[1] These courts may overturn a federal statute as being unconstitutional. These courts may also declare invalid a SEC rule if it contravenes an intent of Congress, if the rule was not adopted pursuant to statutory authority or if the SEC exceeded its deference in adopting a rule. Indeed, the US courts have been a significant in helping shape the US securities laws. This is evidenced by cases that define the term "security" and "tender offer", that clarify when conduct is actionable as trading on the basis of material nonpublic information and violative of the anti-fraud provisions of the key acts and that provide the so-called "private rights of action".

By comparison, in the United Kingdom (UK) there is no written constitution and no separation of branches of government. Subject to single a provision of the Human Rights Act 1998, the UK Parliament has the unlimited power to create, alter and repeal law. In the exercise of its powers Parliament has passed, among other laws, the Companies Acts 1985 and 1989, Part V Criminal Justice Act 1993, Part VII Proceeds of Crime Act 2002 and the Financial Services and Markets Act 2000 (FSMA).

The FSMA creates a statutory regime for carrying on financial services and delegates authority in a hierarchical scheme via HM Treasury to the Financial Services Authority (FSA). The FSA adopts rules under the FSMA and the Regulated Activities Order to regulate the carrying on of a "regulated activity".

THE US FEDERAL SECURITIES LAWS

The events of 1929 and the ensuing years were the focus of Congressional hearings, which led to the enactment of the Securities Act of 1933 and, one year later, the Securities Exchange

---

1   The US federal court system is divided into three levels: US district courts hear cases in the first instance; circuit courts of appeals entertain appeals; and the Supreme Court of the United States of America hears (US Supreme Court) final appeals. For example, a case will start in the US District Court for the Southern District of New York, go on appeal to the Court of Appeals for the Second Circuit and end up before the US Supreme Court. Examples of cases heard by the US Supreme Court involving "splits among the circuits" (ie, two or more circuit courts have taken a different position on a matter and a single position is sought) are *Landreth Timber Co v. Landreth*, 471 U.S. 681 (1985) (Landreth) (the sale of business controversy) and *Reves v Ernst & Young*, 494 U.S. 56, reh'g denied, 494 U.S. 1092 (1990) (Reves) (when a promissory note could be a security). Other cases are noted throughout this book. The federal system operates in parallel with the court systems of the 50 US states and the District of Columbia.

Act of 1934. In shaping the first of these acts, the Congress was faced with the decision of what regulatory philosophy the act should fulfil. The operating models that it considered were a "fraud act" with strict enforcement measures (then in place in New York), "merit regulation" and "disclosure", based loosely on the then-in-force UK Companies Act. The approach that prevailed was disclosure. The basic philosophy of the federal securities laws was then, and it is today, full and fair disclosure. They also provide express statutory civil liability and anti-fraud/manipulation provisions. Sections in each law make any person who wilfully violates it subject to the penalty of a fine or imprisonment, or both.

The federal securities laws with which the SEC is concerned are as follows.

- *Securities Act of 1933* (Securities Act): this provides for the disclosure and registration of distributions of securities, including shares of investment companies, and exemptions from registration.
- *Securities Exchange Act of 1934* (Exchange Act): this act covers exchanges and over-the-counter (OTC) markets, brokers and dealers, civil violations and insider dealing (and certain criminal law violations), trading and sales practices, capital adequacy and customer protection, purchases of securities on credit, periodic reporting requirements, proxy regulation and issuer and third-party tender offers.
- *Public Utility Holding Company Act of 1935* (PUHCA): this provides for the establishment of public utility holding companies.
- *Trust Indenture Act of 1939* (TIA): this law governs public offers of debt (bonds and debentures) including the form of the governing trust deed.
- *Investment Company Act of 1940* (1940 Act): under this act, investment companies register shares for offers (or seek exemptions from registration) and the SEC governs aspects of investment-company structure and management.
- *Investment Advisers Act of 1940* (Advisers Act): this regulates investment advisers.

These laws are often amended from time to time. Examples of laws that have been passed that amend the US federal securities laws include the Private Securities Litigation Reform Act of 1995, the Gramm–Leach–Bliley Act of 1999 and the Sarbanes–Oxley Act of

2002. In this way, the US federal securities laws remain not only true to their original structure, which have lasted for more than 70 years with relatively little fundamental change, but reflect current developments.

THE SECURITIES AND EXCHANGE COMMISSION
The role and structure of the SEC

The Commission is a bipartisan, independent federal administrative agency under the Executive branch of the US Government. It consists of five commissioners, each of which is appointed by the President subject to the advice and consent of the US Senate (Senate), and one of which serves as chairman. Each commissioner serves a five-year term. The SEC is charged with the administration and enforcement of the federal securities laws. It also gives advice to the US federal courts in corporate re-organisation proceedings under the US bankruptcy laws.

The SEC as a commission meets in one of two ways. It holds public meetings to debate matters such as rule adoptions and revisions, interpretations of the federal securities laws and other matters. It also meets in private to deliberate on investigations and disciplinary and enforcement matters.

The Commission is authorised to retain Staff to administer and enforce the federal securities laws, adopt rules and regulations which have the force of law (or to further an intent of Congress or pursuant express statutory say so), issue interpretative releases and file *amicus* briefs with US courts on matters related to its jurisdiction. The SEC is staffed by lawyers, accountants, investigators, examiners, financial analysts and other professionals. The SEC comprises operating divisions and offices. Its headquarters are located in Washington, DC and it has operating centres in other locations throughout the US.

Operating divisions and offices

Division of Corporation Finance. This division administers the disclosure requirements and policies behind the federal securities laws (primarily under the Securities Act and portions of the Exchange Act, and the rules and regulations thereunder), issuer tender offers and advisory transactions, registration statements, beneficial ownership reports and proxy materials.

Division of Market Regulation. This division oversees the Exchange Act, the exchanges and the OTC markets, self-regulatory organisations, broker–dealer registration and activities, capital adequacy, trading practices and sales activities, settlement and transfer agent activities, books and records requirements, and other related matters.

Division of Investment Management. This division administers the 1940 Act, the Advisers Act and PUHCA, investment companies and adviser registration and regulation.

Office of the General Counsel. This office is responsible for advising on legislation, ethics and litigation, adjudication, appellate advocacy and bankruptcy.

Office of Compliance Inspections and Examinations. This office schedules, conducts and coordinates inspections/examinations for exchanges, broker–dealers, investment companies, transfer agents and clearing agencies to ensure compliance with the federal securities laws and SEC rules.

Division of Enforcement. This division and its "CyberForce" group investigate alleged breaches of, and secures the enforcement with, the federal securities laws.

Other SEC offices include Internet Enforcement, International Affairs, the Secretary, Filings and Information Services, Economic Analysis, Legislative Affairs, Administrative Law Judges, the Chief Accountant, Investor Education and Assistance, the Inspector General and Public Affairs, Policy Evaluation and Research. The SEC's Regional offices (New York, Boston, Atlanta, Chicago and Los Angeles) are concerned with enforcement matters.

Operations, rule-making, policy and enforcement
Rule-making
The Staff researches and prepares rule-making proposals with supporting materials for submission to the SEC. Proposals are made to adopt new rules or to amend, consolidate or rescind existing rules or regulations. If the SEC wishes to consider a proposal, it is considered in a public meeting. If the SEC approves the proposal, it is then published in the Federal Register for public comment. Under the Administrative Procedures Act, the SEC must consider public comments received. The Staff prepares a comment summary and

submits recommendations to the SEC itself. The proposal is then calendared for action. If the SEC approves the proposal, it is published in the Federal Register and comes into force upon publication or within a stated time frame. Proposed and final rules and their proposing and adopting releases, respectively, may be found on the SEC's website, which is www.sec.gov.

Guidance, no-action positions, interpretations and advocacy
The Staff provides guidance and derogations as follows.

The *no-action letter* process permits the public and industry practitioners to obtain the informal views of the Staff on interpretations of the federal securities laws – a process that is particularly helpful in the absence of SEC rule-making or other formal guidance. Responses to requests for no-action, and the requests themselves, are generally made publicly available, although confidential treatment is available in specified circumstances to protect against premature disclosure of a business transaction. While no-action positions are not binding on the SEC (and will not even insulate the recipient from private suits), they have precedential effect. Although in general only the recipient of the response can rely on a no-action letter directly, third parties generally derive comfort from them, particularly if the issue raised and the surrounding facts are materially similar to those addressed in the no-action letter and the Staff has made explicit the basis of its position.

Interpretative letters contain express interpretations or analyses by the Staff of laws or rules based on a specific factual situation. Recent interpretations include issues such as whether a particular instrument was a security, or whether certain types of transactions by corporate directors fell within the ambit of the SEC's rules under Section 16 of the Exchange Act. Interpretations do not bind the Commission.

The Staff also provides *exemptive relief*. The Staff acts pursuant to delegated authority to issue an exemption from the operation of the securities laws and/or the rules thereunder as regards a particular transaction. It is a statement of law and may be relied upon solely by the grantee. Exemptions have been issued for specific transactions and also for classes of transactions.

In litigation that involves important determinations under the federal securities laws, the Staff will file briefs as *amicus curiae*, advocating the SEC's position.

The staff also issues Legal Bulletins, Staff Accounting Bulletins, Q&A Releases and Telephone Interpretations, all of which may be found on the SEC's website.

Enforcement

To ensure the smooth operation of the federal securities laws, the Staff will conduct investigations, impose statutory sanctions, revoke broker–dealer registrations and conduct administrative actions under its jurisdiction. If it uncovers evidence of criminal conduct, it will refer the matter to the US Department of Justice (DOJ) for appropriate action.

Staff members of the Division of Enforcement investigate possible securities laws violations and make recommendations to the Commission regarding enforcement actions. Only the five-person Commission, however, can authorise the bringing of an enforcement action.

SEC oversight authority

The SEC is authorised by the Exchange Act to oversee the US securities markets, exchanges and OTC markets and industry participants.

In addition to the SEC, the principal securities regulatory agencies in the United States are the National Association of Securities Dealers, Inc (NASD), the Municipal Securities Rule Making Board and the major stock exchanges, each of which is operated subject to SEC oversight and whose rules are subject to SEC approval.

The NASD was established in 1938 as the self-regulatory agency of the US securities industry. Unlike the New York Stock Exchange (NYSE), which is registered with the SEC under the Exchange Act, the NASD is not an exchange. In 1996, as part of a settlement of administrative proceedings commenced by the SEC and in response to a report initiated by the NASD itself, the NASD was reorganised into two major operating subsidiaries: NASD Regulation, Inc (NASDR), an independent subsidiary of the NASD; and the National Association of Securities Dealers Automated Quotation system (NASDAQ).[2] The principal objective was to separate the regulation

---

2   NASDAQ is comprised of the NASDAQ National Market®, which includes nearly 3,900 larger, actively traded NASDAQ securities, and the NASDAQ SmallCap Market, for securities of issuers that are smaller and/or less highly capitalised.

of broker–dealers from the operation of NASDAQ. The mission of NASDR is "to regulate securities markets for the ultimate benefit and protection of the investor". It pursues this mission through, *inter alia*, the education, testing and registration of securities professionals, periodic examination of member securities firms to determine compliance with law and regulation, continuous surveillance of the markets operated by NASDAQ and review of underwriting arrangements for new issues (including the fairness of underwriting compensation). NASDR administers the NASD Conduct Rules.

Like the NASD, the national stock exchanges govern certain conduct of their member firms in addition to regulating trading on the exchange itself and promulgating criteria for listing. Through their listing criteria and listing agreements, the exchanges and NASDAQ impose a variety of corporate governance requirements on listed companies, affecting such matters as board composition, shareholder approval for certain transactions, proxy procedures, information dissemination to shareholders and the public, and certain notices and disclosures to the exchanges themselves.

JURISDICTION
What is a security?
The SEC exercises its jurisdiction over *securities*. It manifests its control over: public offers and private placements of securities, exempt securities and exempt transactions under the Securities Act; secondary market activities under the Exchange Act; public offers of debt securities under the TIA; the packaging of securities in the guise of mutual funds and investment companies under the 1940 Act; and advice on funds and investment companies via the Advisers Act.

The Securities Act (Section 2(1)) and Exchange Act (Section 3(a)(10)) definitions of the term "security" are similar. Both definitions include notes, stocks, shares, bonds, debentures, evidence of indebtedness, certificates of interest and participations in profit-sharing arrangements. In *Tcherepnin v. Knight*,[3] the US Supreme Court held that the definitions of security in the Securities Act and the Exchange Act were "virtually identical". Accordingly, the US courts and the SEC will treat the two definitions as being identical

---

3   389 U.S. 332 (1967) (*Tcherepnin*).

when required to construe the terms or apply the law. The US Supreme Court has held that Congress adopted a "broad definition of 'security', sufficient to encompass virtually any instrument that might be sold as an investment."[4]

The US federal courts have determined that, while some instruments are securities under the US federal securities laws, others are not.

The instruments that have been judicially determined to *be* securities (other than common stock, bonds and other obvious types of securities) include investment contracts, participations in orange groves, certain types of participatory condominiums and co-op (housing) leases, short-term uncollateralised notes, "commodities pools" that pool the funds of investors to invest in commodities futures contracts and certificates of deposit (CDs) programmes established and sold by SEC-registered broker–dealers.

For example, the court in *Gary Plastic Packaging Corp v. Merrill Lynch, Pierce, Fenner & Smith, Inc*,[5] found that a brokered CD programme where investors bought packaged CDs gave rise to "investment contracts" and was a security because "a significant portion of the customer's investment" depended on the managerial and financial expertise of the broker–dealer. In other instances, courts reviewing activities involving CDs reached a different conclusion. In *Marine Bank v. Weaver*,[6] the US Supreme Court held that a certificate of deposit issued by a federally regulated US bank was not a security under Section 2(1) of the Securities Act, because its repayment was "virtually guaranteed" by the Federal Deposit Insurance Corporation. In *Wolf v. Banamex*,[7] a CD issued by a Mexican bank was held not to be a security.

The US courts have adopted a number of tests to help determine whether certain instruments would be deemed to be a security. These include the following.

❑ "*Investment contracts*": an investment of funds in a common enterprise with an expectation of profits derived from the efforts of others would be deemed to be a security under Securities Act

---

[4] *SEC v. Edwards* 124 S.Ct. 892, 894 (2004) (Edwards), citing Reves, 494 U.S. 56, 61.
[5] 756 F.2d 240 (2nd Cir. 1985).
[6] 455 U.S. 551 (1982).
[7] 739 F.2d 1458 (7th Cir. 1984), *cert denied*, 469 U.S. 1108 (1985).

Section 2(1). See *SEC v. W.J. Howey & Co* (interests in citrus groves deemed to be a security);[8] *SEC v. Koscot Interplanetary, Inc* (pyramid promotion scheme deemed to be a security);[9] *United Housing Foundation, Inc v. Forman* (shares in cooperative deemed to be a security);[10] and *International Brotherhood of Teamsters v. Daniels* (non-contributory, compulsory pension plan not a security).[11]

- The *"family resemblance" test*: a note is presumed to be a security.
- The *"sale of business" controversy*: under this line of cases, the sale of a business by the sale of all of it shares and the passing control to the purchaser may be deemed to be a security.[12]

Other investments have been held by the courts or interpreted by the SEC *not* to be securities. These include certain partnership interests, non-contributory compulsory pension plans, insurance products, commercial loans (as long as the loan is for commercial purposes and is not investment in nature, and was not widely distributed) and, as noted above, federally regulated bank certificates of deposits.

Determining whether an instrument is or is not a security is not as simple as seeing if its namesake appears in the two sections cited above, or reviewing the terms of the instrument. Court decisions have made it clear that the context in which an instrument is offered, sold or resold may be determinative and it is important to remember that the definitions of "security" in both of the acts cited above are preceded by the words "unless the context otherwise requires . . .".

What are these tests and how do courts apply them?

The *Howey* test has been widely used to cover many types of schemes, for example, a "virtual stock market" website where investors could "part with their money" in a gaming format might be a security. The court in *SEC v. SG Ltd*[13] held that the site met the four *Howey* factors and overturned the lower District Court ruling

---

8   328 U.S. 293 (1946) *Howey*.
9   497 F.2d 473 (5th Cir. 1974).
10 421 U.S. 837 (1975).
11 439 U.S. 551 (1979).
12 *See* Landreth.
13 265 F.3d 42 (1st Cir. 2001).

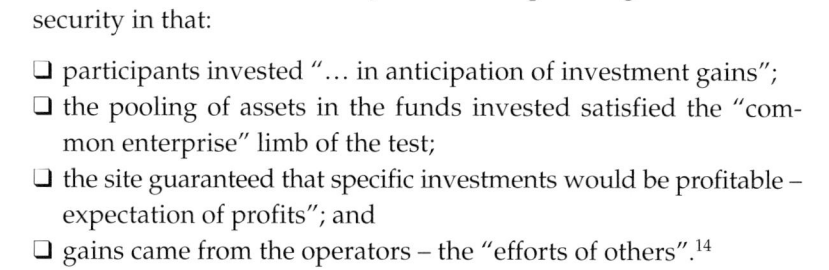

THE US FEDERAL SECURITIES LAWS AND THE SECURITIES AND EXCHANGE COMMISSION

that the venture more closely resembled gambling rather than a security in that:

❑ participants invested "… in anticipation of investment gains";
❑ the pooling of assets in the funds invested satisfied the "common enterprise" limb of the test;
❑ the site guaranteed that specific investments would be profitable – expectation of profits"; and
❑ gains came from the operators – the "efforts of others".[14]

Howey was cited as controlling in *Edwards*, which involved the sale and leaseback of payphones to the public via independent distributors. The seller of the payphones, ETS Payphones Inc. (ETS), agreed that the payphones would be leased back from the purchaser for a fixed monthly payment – and a more than 10% annual return. The SEC brought an enforcement action after ETS filed for bankruptcy protection, alleging that the "sale and leaseback" programme was an investment contract and that in offering the programme ETS violated the registration provisions of the Securities Act and the antifraud provisions of the US federal securities laws. The case reached the US Supreme Court, which held that, under *Howey*, the programme was an investment contract. In holding that the fixed monthly payment constituted profits "coming from the efforts of others" under the four-part *Howey* investment contract test, the *Edwards* court dismissed the seller's argument that the programme was not an investment contract and a security because the programme offered a fixed return. The Court held that under the investment contract analysis "[n]o distinction can be drawn between fixed and variable rate returns",[15] that either fixed or variable rates of return were profits under the *Howey* test and that profits in the sense of income or return are what investors seek on their investment, not the profits of the scheme itself.

As regards promissory notes, in *Reves* the US Supreme Court articulated a number of factors to be used to help determine whether a "note" or a "loan" would be a security. The *Reves* Court

---

14 See *Albanese v Florida National Bank of Orlando*, 823 F.2d 408, 411 (11th Cir. 1987) (holding that the "efforts of others" is determined by considering how much, if any, control investors had over the operator of the business or scheme that they looked to to generate returns).
15 Edwards, 124 S.Ct. at 895.

held that there is a reputable presumption that a note would be a security, but it also identified types of notes that would not be deemed to be securities including notes delivered in financing, short-term notes secured by accounts receivables and notes evidencing loans by banks for operating purposes. The Court stated that it may not be easy to make a meaningful inquiry into whether a note resembled one of the non-security instruments and it articulated four factors to be used to help determine whether a note fits into this category or was otherwise a security. The factors are (1) the motivation prompting the transaction, (2) the plan of distribution, (3) the reasonable expectations of the investing public and (4) other factors (the presence of a regulatory scheme, etc). Thus, the following were or were not deemed to be securities under *Reves*.

❏ promissory notes issued to customers in return for personal loans were deemed to be a security (*Stoiber v. SEC*).[16] The factors that this court said were to be examined were (1) motivation to encourage the transaction, (2) distribution plan, (3) reasonable expectation of investors and (4) existence of regulatory scheme that would make the application of the federal securities law unnecessary.

❏ promissory notes issued to induce an individual to make a loan to a company were not securities, because they were not widely traded and were collateralised (*Bass v. Janney Montgomery Scott, Inc*).[17]

❏ A promissory note was not a security, because it paid less than the prime interest rate and issuance by a high-risk venture indicated that it was not an investment instrument. A reasonable person would not expect to profit from its paying below market interest, no public distribution of its interest and the investing public would not expect federal securities laws to apply to it (*Jeanne Piabert S.A. v. Sefrioui*).[18]

❏ A promissory note was a security, under the *Reves* test, where the above four elements were present and the note in question was due and payable in 365 days and that the unpaid principal would be converted into common stock (*Leemon v. Burns*).[19]

---

16 161 F.3d 745 (D.C. Cir 1998).
17 210 F.3d 577 (6th Cir. 2000).
18 (9th Cir. 2000).
19 175 F.3d 551 (S.D.N.Y. 2001).

The risk of selling an instrument that one does not think is a security but which actually turns out to be is significant, because if an exemption is not properly established, it could involve the issuer and underwriters in an offer that has violated Section 5 of the Securities Act – the basic registration provision. In certain instances, it could subject the issuer, underwriters, accountants and lawyers to civil liability under the Securities Act and the Exchange Act, as well as claims under state or local laws.

Derivatives, options and futures

A single stock put or call option is a security under the US federal securities laws. So, an option on a securities index is also a security. However, an option on an interest rate is not a security, as would be an option on a currency that was not listed on a US exchange. A commodity, as defined in the US Commodity Exchange Act (CEA), is not a security and falls outside the SEC's remit. What, then, is the treatment of futures, single-stock futures or discretionary accounts?

The language of these acts and developments in the US securities, derivatives and commodities markets led to confusion over where and how new products could be sold and traded, and who was to regulate these markets. It is clear that the SEC exercises its jurisdiction over the securities and the securities options markets, and the US Commodities Trading Futures Commission (CFTC) controls the commodities markets. Historically, the CFTC and the SEC regulated a separate set of instruments and, under the "Johnson–Shad" accord, adopted a hands-off approach as regards certain instruments. This changed with the adoption of the Commodity Futures Modernization Act of 2000 which, in addition to revising the CEA and undoing the Johnson–Shad accord, lifted a 25-year-old ban on single-stock futures to permit these instruments and "narrow-based security indices" not only to be traded on US exchanges, but to be jointly regulated by the FCTC and the SEC.

Now, single-stock futures, narrow-stock index futures and certain swap agreements are both securities *and* futures under the Commodity Futures Modernization Act. Section 2A of the Securities Act states that the Section 2(1) definition of the term security "does not include … any non-security-based swap agreement (as defined in Section 206C of the Gramm–Leach–Bliley Act) … [and] any security-based swap agreement (as defined in Section 206B of the

Gramm–Leach–Bliley Act"). The SEC has limited oversight authority over equity-based swaps. Requirements for margin levels, listing standards and other key trading provisions are governed equally by the SEC and the CFTC. Futures on broad-based indices are now regulated by CFTC.

A discussion of the interstices of securities–derivatives–commodities regulation is beyond the scope of this book. However, it is important to note that a non-US broker, dealer or bank that proposes to offer or provide a secondary market in hybrid instruments (including derivatives) to US persons must consider the application not only of the US federal securities laws, but also the commodities laws and the rules and regulations of the exchanges and markets where these instruments may trade.

2

US-Registered Offers

Ottilie L Jarmel[1]
Shearman & Sterling LLP

Over time, the international capital markets have undergone profound changes. Technology, coupled with deregulation and the opening of capital markets around the world, has made the internationalisation of the world's securities markets a reality. In the 1990s, investors and issuers accessed securities markets around the world as never before. Cross-border acquisitions using stock as acquisition currency became a key factor in the internationalisation of companies' shareholder bases. Investors sought to diversify their portfolios and companies sought low-cost capital wherever it could be found. Issuers use the securities markets as a source of capital. By the end of 2003, US holdings of foreign securities reached approximately US$3,152 billion, an increase of 36% from 2001. As of January 2005, foreign holdings of US securities were approximately US$4.5 trillion and nearly half of all equity securities traded in the United States.

Reflecting the size and strength of the US securities markets, international companies have dramatically increased their participation in the US markets. As of year-end 2004, 460 non-US companies from 47 countries were listed on the New York Stock Exchange (NYSE), representing approximately 16.6% of the companies listed, and approximately 10.5% of the trading volume on the NYSE.

---

1 The author dedicates this chapter to the late Linda Quinn, friend, colleague and co-author for too few years; mentor still. Ms. Quinn co-authored earlier editions of this chapter.

Access to the US securities market has proven important to large international companies and to governments seeking to privatise major government enterprises, where the size of offers and expected ongoing capital needs require sizeable equity investments. Smaller hi-tech companies have also found the United States to be an important source of capital, with its deep and sophisticated venture capital market and an equity market receptive to these developing growth companies. In addition, in the US capital markets many foreign companies have found "currency" in the form of listed stock available for acquisitions in the United States.

The SEC, the US exchanges and NASDAQ have welcomed the internationalisation of the US securities markets and have undertaken to make it easier for non-US issuers to enter the US capital markets.

The Sarbanes–Oxley Act of 2002 (SOX), with its imposition of additional regulatory and administrative requirements (in particular, Section 404, which requires an audit of internal controls), has caused non-US companies with a US listing to reconsider the benefits of listing in the United States.[2] Companies entering the US markets have always had to make a cost-benefit analysis as to whether they considered a US listing was worth the initial and ongoing reporting pursuant to SEC disclosure requirements. SOX has now shifted the balance of such cost-benefit analysis. The cost of compliance with SOX Section 404 particularly in the initial stages and increased audit fees on an ongoing basis has led many foreign private issuers[3] to re-evaluate their need for SEC registration and a

---

2 *See* Jim Bartos & Peter King, Shearman & Sterling LLP: "SEC deregistration A growing trend", PLC (April 2005), available at www.practicallaw.com/5-200-545.

3 A "foreign private issuer" is defined in Rule 405 under the Securities Act as any foreign issuer other than a foreign government except an issuer meeting the following conditions: (a) more than 50% of the outstanding voting securities of such issuer are held of record either directly or through voting trust certificates or depositary receipts by residents of the United States; and (b) any of the following: (i) the majority of the executive officers or directors are US citizens or residents; (ii) more than 50% of the assets of the issuer are located in the United States; or (iii) the business of the issuer is administered principally in the United States. The test for calculating US ownership for purposes of the definition of "foreign private issuer" is the same as the test in Exchange Act Rule 12g3–2(a), which requires issuers to look through the record ownership of banks, broker-dealers or other nominee holders to determine the residence of the account holder. Issuers are also required to count shares of voting securities beneficially owned by residents whether derived from beneficial ownership reports publicly filed or from information otherwise provided to the issuer.

US listing. While terminating a listing or quotation is simple, deregistering and suspending SEC reporting obligations can be a challenging process.

DEREGISTRATION

Former SEC Chairman William Donaldson noted his expectation that the SEC will examine the issue of deregistration by foreign private issuers and consider a rule proposal before the end of 2005. Donaldson acknowledged that US federal securities laws and regulations on deregistration were designed many years ago, before there was much in the way of cross-border listings.

In March 2005, 11 European organisations submitted a proposal to the SEC to simplify deregistration. The organisations represent most of the largest publicly held companies in Europe, including more than 100 that are listed in the United States. The organisations proposed two alternatives.

The first would focus on US investor protection after deregistration, as opposed to the level of US holdings, whether based on trading volume or the number of US shareholders. In particular, companies required to satisfy International Financial Reporting Standards (IFRS) and report under standards adopted by the International Organisation of Securities Commissions (IOSCO) would be allowed to deregister as long as their US share trading volume is below 5% of their worldwide volume and provided that they: (i) provide certain narrative and financial statement disclosure; (ii) maintain a highly liquid home trading market; and (iii) provide US retail investors a cost-free mechanism to sell their shares where permitted under local law, either through a tender offer or through a brokerage facility providing for sales on the home market during a six-month period following deregistration. In addition, at least 55% of the company's worldwide trading volume would have to be on a single non-US market. Under the second alternative, deregistration would be permitted if 10% or less of the company's shares were held in the United States, if 10% or less of the company's shareholders were in the United States or if the company had fewer than 3,000 shareholders. (Under current SEC rules, a non-US company may only deregister if it has fewer than 300 shareholders in the United States, which is difficult to establish because most European shares are held through intermediaries and it is hard to ascertain the number of shareholders.) Qualified institutional buyers (QIBs), employees and directors would not be counted in the US holder thresholds.

Both alternatives would eliminate the current requirement that a company reinstate its registration if the number of US shareholders increases above 300 after deregistration.

The SEC has indicated its receptivity to deregistration reform. Donaldson, speaking in London in January 2005, said "While the [deregistration] rules were designed to protect investors, we should seek a solution that will preserve investor protections without inappropriately designing the US capital market as one with no exit".[4]

SARBANES–OXLEY

SOX was brought in to law in response to the corporate scandals of many US companies – Enron, WorldCom, Adelphia, HealthSouth, Tyco, Global Crossing and Cendant. Provisions of SOX have now been used against many non-US companies – Parmalat, Vivendi, Hollinger, Ahold, Adecco, TV Azteca, Royal Dutch Shell and others. SOX makes no distinction between US issuers and foreign private issuers listed in the United States. The disclosure requirements are generally the same for US and foreign issuers; the auditor oversight and independence provisions apply to all accounting firms, including all US and non-US accounting firms that audit non-US public companies required to file financial statements with the SEC; and the audit committee rules, while reflecting some accommodation for foreign issuers, nevertheless, apply and have had far-reaching consequences for the internal corporate governance structures and practices of foreign reporting companies.

As discussed in more detail in Chapters 4 and 5, and elsewhere in this book, SOX generally applies to US and non-US issuers that have securities registered with the SEC or are required to file reports under the Exchange Act, including non-US issuers filing annual reports on Form 20-F. It also applies to any issuer that has filed a registration statement under the Securities Act that is not yet effective. It does not apply to issuers who merely furnish information to the SEC under Rule 12g3–2(b) of the Exchange Act.

---

4   Speech by former SEC Chairman William H Donaldson: US Capital Markets in the Post-Sarbanes–Oxley World: Why Our Markets Should Matter to Foreign Issuers, London, England (25th January 2005), available at www.sec.gov/news/speech/spch012505whd.htm.

The key provisions of SOX are actually contained in the law itself, but many of the SOX provisions were brought into force by SEC rulemaking, including through the listing standards of such self-regulatory organisations as the NYSE and NASDAQ. While foreign issuers and other international constituencies were unusually vocal in the SEC rule-making process and urged the SEC to use its exemptive authority in connection with SOX's application to foreign issuers, the SEC Staff has stated in public remarks that the SEC does not view itself as having the latitude to use its exemptive authority in connection with legislation that was enacted "with unmistakable clarity of purpose" so recently, and many provisions of SOX give the SEC little or no latitude as regards the ability to carve out exemptions for non-US issuers. The SEC has, nonetheless, reaffirmed its keen interest in continuing to attract foreign issuers to the US markets and has pledged substantial support to foreign issuers who seek to register or list their securities in the United States. Although there are no wholesale exemptions under the rules, the SEC has remained attuned to potential conflicts with home country laws and regulatory practices and will seek to interpret the new requirements in keeping with its history of accommodation.

BASIC US REGULATORY SCHEME
Companies offering their securities to the public in the United States, whether or not they are incorporated in the United States, must register the securities with the SEC under the Securities Act. The Securities Act governs the offer and sale of securities and is designed to promote full and fair disclosure about the issuer of the securities and the offer transaction. Its basic operative provisions are the registration and prospectus delivery requirements of Section 5, the exemptions from registration in Sections 3 and 4, the liability provisions of Sections 11 and 12 relating to material misstatements contained in registration statements and prospectuses, the controlling person liability provisions of Section 15 and the anti-fraud prohibitions of Section 17.

If the securities are to be listed on the NYSE, the American Stock Exchange (AMEX) or another US exchange or traded on NASDAQ, they must also be registered under the Exchange Act. Registration under either the Securities Act or the Exchange Act will subject the company to ongoing public reporting obligations under the Exchange Act.

Companies, including non-US issuers that are subject to Exchange Act reporting under Section 15(d) or that have securities registered under Section 12 of the Exchange Act, are also subject to the Foreign Corrupt Practices Act (*see* Chapter 8). This law makes it a criminal offence to engage in corrupt practices with respect to foreign officials – that is, bribes to foreign government officials or political parties to help obtain, retain or direct business. It also requires companies to maintain accurate books and records and internal accounting controls.

Companies that publicly offer debt securities also need to comply with the requirements of the TIA, which requires debt securities to be issued under a trust indenture conforming to the requirements of the law.

Non-US companies entering the US securities markets need to consider the 1940 Act. The 1940 Act primarily governs the offer and sale of securities by, and the regulation of, mutual funds, unit trusts and similar types of issuers. Due to the broad scope of the definition of the term "investment company", the 1940 Act can often be a troubling area for non-US companies, especially those that maintain large investment portfolios or hold a significant minority position in other companies. Since compliance with the 1940 Act is not a practical option, it is important to identify possible issues arising under this Act at an early stage in the offer process.

A non-US company also needs to assess whether it would be classified as a passive foreign investment company (PFIC) under US tax law. As discussed in more detail in Chapter 6, a non-US company may be classified as a PFIC if it meets either of two tests, one based on the extent of passive income, the other on the extent of gross assets producing passive income. If it is classified as a PFIC, holders of shares in the United States would be subject to an onerous tax regime. The NYSE modified its policy against listing the US securities of a PFIC. In 1998, Orix Corporation, a Japanese issuer, was permitted to list, but was required to provide special disclosure regarding the potential tax consequences of its PFIC status in its annual report and registration statement on Form 20-F because the SEC believed the risk was great that shareholders would be surprised by the tax treatment of the shares under PFIC rules.

Each of the individual states within the United States has its own securities laws (known as blue sky laws) that require registration with state agencies of securities offered within the state's borders. Under federal legislation enacted in 1996, securities listed on or senior to securities listed on the NYSE or AMEX or quoted on NASDAQ are exempt from registration under state law.

The NYSE, AMEX and NASDAQ also impose their own rules on listed companies, which address a broad range of matters relating to disclosure, the issuance of securities and the rights of security holders. Certain accommodations have been made, however, for governance policies and practices of non-US companies that are in accordance with their home market laws and practices.

Statutory framework under the Securities Act
The US federal securities laws are intended to protect investors by ensuring the availability of material information necessary to make informed investment decisions. The Securities Act requires that detailed information be provided to purchasers concerning the issuer and the securities offered for sale, and that all offers and sales of securities be registered with the SEC unless an exemption from registration is available. Exemptions from registration are provided for specified types of securities, for example, commercial paper, insurance policies, and US bank and thrift securities or securities guaranteed by such banks or thrifts. Certain transactions are also exempt – most notably, transactions by persons other than an issuer, underwriter or dealer, non-public offers or private placements, exchanges of securities of the same issuer where no special solicitation compensation is paid, specified offers by private issuers not exceeding US$1 million annually and limited small offers of up to US$5 million. Sales of securities by affiliates are generally treated as comparable to sales by the company under the Securities Act for purposes of determining the need to register the transaction.

Under the Securities Act, a registered offer may be divided into three stages. The first stage is the period after a company decides to make a public offer and prior to the filing of the registration statement with the SEC (pre-filing period). The second stage is the period after the filing of the registration statement and prior to its effectiveness (pre-effective period or waiting period). The final stage is the period after the registration statement becomes effective (post-effective period).

Section 5 of the Securities Act governs what activity is required or permissible in each stage. It reads as follows:

(a) Unless a registration statement is in effect as to a security, it shall be unlawful for any person, directly or indirectly – (i) to make use of any means or instruments of transportation or communication in interstate commerce or of the mails to sell such security through the use or medium of any prospectus or otherwise; or (ii) to carry or cause to be carried through the mails or in interstate commerce, by any means or instruments of transportation, any such security for the purpose of sale or for delivery after sale. (b) It shall be unlawful for any person, directly or indirectly – (i) to make use of any means or instruments of transportation or communication in interstate commerce or of the mails to carry or transmit any prospectus relating to any security with respect to which a registration statement has been filed under this Act, unless such prospectus meets the requirements of Section 10; or (ii) to carry or cause to be carried through the mails or in interstate commerce any such security for the purpose of sale or for delivery after sale, unless accompanied or preceded by a prospectus that meets the requirements of sub-Section (a) of Section 10. (c) It shall be unlawful for any person, directly or indirectly, to make use of any means or instruments of transportation or communication in interstate commerce or of the mails to offer to sell or offer to buy through the use or medium of any prospectus or otherwise any security, unless a registration statement has been filed as to such security, or while the registration statement is the subject of a refusal order or stop order or (prior to the effective date of the registration statement) any public proceeding or examination under Section 8.

The current regulatory framework under Section 5, which was substantially modified under the SEC's recently adopted securities offering reforms, is as follows: in general, no offers – oral or written – to sell the securities may be commenced until after a registration statement containing the prescribed disclosures is filed with the SEC, and no sales may take place until after the registration statement is declared effective. A prospectus complying with Section 10(a) of the Securities Act must be delivered to the purchaser of the security. Failure to comply with the registration and prospectus delivery requirements gives the purchaser of the security a right to rescind the purchase for up to one year following the offer. Violation of the registration and prospectus delivery requirements may also trigger an enforcement action by the SEC.

Scope of the New Rules

In June 2005, the SEC adopted, for the first time in decades, significant reforms to the Securities Act in the guise of securities offering reforms (2005 Reforms).[5] These changes were intended to liberalise the registration procedures and communications rules for securities offerings in the United States. The new rules will become effective on 1 December 2005. The new rules, according to the Adopting Release, represent "constructive, incremental changes" in the US regulatory structure and the offering process rather than introducing a far-reaching new system. The SEC believes that its objectives can be best achieved by further integration of Securities Act and Exchange Act disclosure and adjustments in the current registration system.

The reforms involve four main areas:

❑ Communications related to registered securities offerings;
❑ Registration and other procedures in the offering and capital formation processes;
❑ Delivery of information to investors, including delivery through access and notice, and timeliness of that delivery; and
❑ Liability of issuers and underwriters.

The reforms do not address unregistered offerings, such as those under Regulation D, Rule 144A or Regulation S, or integration issues. Nor do they apply to registered business combinations.[6]

Categories of Issuers

The new offering and communications framework looks largely to the status of the issuer. The new rules establish a new category of issuer, known as a "well-known seasoned issuer". The most liberalising aspects of the 2005 Reforms (namely, automatic shelf registration) are available only to these issuers, who have a reporting history under the Exchange Act and, according to the Commission, are presumptively the most widely followed in the marketplace.[7]

---

5   Securities Act Release 8591 (19th July 2005) (Adopting Release). This Chapter does not address the application of US securities law, or the 2005 Reforms, to asset-backed issuers.
6   Reforms for business combination transactions were adopted in 1999. *See* Regulation of Takeovers and Security Holder Communications, Release No. 33–7760 (22nd October 1999).
7   According to the Adopting Release, in 2004, well-known seasoned issuers, who represented approximately 30% of listed issuers, accounted for about 95% of US equity market capitalisation. They have accounted for more than 96% of the total debt raised in registered offerings over the past eight years by issuers listed on a major exchange or equity market. These issuers, accordingly, represent the most significant amount of capital raised and traded in the United States.

A **well-known seasoned issuer** is an issuer that is required to file reports under Section 13(a) or Section 15(d) of the Exchange Act and that meets the following requirements as of the date on which its status as a well-known seasoned issuer is determined: (i) the issuer must meet the registrant requirements of Form S-3 or Form F-3; (ii) the issuer, as of a date within 60 days of its eligibility determination date, either (X) has a worldwide market value of its outstanding voting and non-voting common equity held by non-affiliates of US$700 million or more;[8] or (Y) has issued in the last three years at least US$1 billion aggregate principal amount of non-convertible securities, other than common equity, in primary offerings for cash, not exchange, registered under the Securities Act; and (iii) the issuer is not an ineligible issuer.

Other issuers are defined as follows:

A **non-reporting issuer** is an issuer that is not required to file reports pursuant to Section 13 or 15(d) of the Exchange Act, regardless of whether it is filing such reports voluntarily.

An **unseasoned issuer** is an issuer that is required to file reports pursuant to Section 13 or 15(d) of the Exchange Act, but does not satisfy the requirements of Form S-3 or Form F-3 for a primary offering of its securities.

A **seasoned issuer** is an issuer that is eligible to use Form S-3 or Form F-3 to register a primary offering of securities.

Many foreign private issuers will qualify as well-known seasoned issuers. For these foreign private issuers, the offering and publicity reforms will be welcome. However, it is unlikely that the reforms alone will affect a company not yet registered with the Commission in its cost/benefit analysis as to the strategic benefits versus the compliance and cost burdens of being listed in the United States and of being an SEC registrant.

Foreign private issuers that are well-known seasoned issuers should find the offering reforms to be beneficial and may be influenced as to whether to include the United States in an offering on a

---

[8] To determine whether an issuer meets the US$700 million public float threshold, the issuer will calculate its public float in the same manner that it calculates its public float for purposes of determining Form S-3 or F-3 eligibility. The determination of public float is based on a public trading market. Therefore, an entity with US$700 million of common equity securities outstanding but not trading in any public trading market would not be a well-known seasoned issuer based on the market capitalization threshold test.

registered basis by the new automatic shelf registration process. Most foreign private issuers have not had universal shelves in place and at the time of an international offering have always faced uncertainty as to the US time schedule and the effect of a potential SEC review. Since the change in review policy which no longer permits a confidential filing, and then withdrawal of that filing if there is a review decision, many foreign private issuers have excluded the United States or, if the securities are eligible, only included the United States on a Rule 144A basis, rather than face the potential scheduling and other difficulties consequent on a review decision at the time of an offering. For well-known seasoned issuers, the automatic shelf procedure removes these uncertainties. As the Adopting Release points out, foreign private issuers that are well-known seasoned issuers may particularly find the automatic shelf procedure attractive in rights offerings, where sales in the rights offering may take place immediately upon filing of the registration statement. The announcement of the offering to different markets may also thereby be more easily coordinated.

Pre-filing period
The Securities Act's restrictions on offers and sales during the pre-filing period also restrict communications that could condition the market for the securities. The SEC interprets the term "offer" broadly to include any communication that conditions the market for, or arouses public interest in, the securities, even if the offer is not mentioned. Such a communication during the pre-filing period may constitute an illegal offer of securities under Section 5, and is commonly referred to as "gun-jumping".

As originally enacted, a fundamental premise of the Securities Act was that investment decisions should be based principally on a prospectus that meets the disclosure requirements of Section 10 of the Securities Act. Over the last 20 years, the SEC, through its integrated disclosure system, has increasingly relied on the continuous reporting system under the Exchange Act to provide investors with the information necessary to make an informed investment decision. Notwithstanding the evolution of the integrated disclosure system, the SEC until 2005 continued to maintain the basic prohibitions on market conditioning and offers outside the prospectus and information incorporated therein. However, recent changes to the Exchange Act reporting process, designed to produce more timely and extensive disclosures and greater scrutiny by the Commission of those reports, have led to the SEC's recent liberalization of communications during the offer process, as described below.

The 2005 Reforms will permit, pursuant to newly adopted safe harbours, prior to the filing of the registration statement, (i) reporting issuers and non-reporting issuers to release regularly released factual information; (ii) reporting issuers to release regularly released forward-looking information; (iii) well-known seasoned issuers to communicate orally or in writing within the 30-day period prior to the filing of the registration statement (subject to filing written statements with the SEC); and (iv) all issuers to communicate freely more than 30 days prior to filing, provided the communication does not reference a securities offering that is or will be the subject of a registration statement.

These pre-filing safe harbours (discussed in detail below) will not be available to underwriters and other offering participants, who remain subject to the prohibition under Section 5 on all offers, oral and written, prior to the filing of a registration statement.

Pre-effective or waiting period

Once a registration statement is filed, the securities covered by the registration statement may be offered, but not sold, to the public.[9] Currently, there is no restriction on oral offer communications, although they remain subject to liability for false or misleading statements under Section 12(a)(2) of the Securities Act and anti-fraud prohibitions. Meetings with potential investors (road shows) are permitted once the registration statement is filed. Written offer communications may only be made by means of a prospectus complying with Section 10 of the Securities Act. The prospectus used at this stage, termed a preliminary prospectus or "red herring", is filed as part of the registration statement. A red herring is so named because of the legend (once required to be printed in red) on the cover page stating that the registration statement has been filed with the SEC but has not become effective, and that the securities

---

9 The basic distinction between the definitions of an "offer" and a "sale" is that no money or anything of value may pass in an offer, but a sale does involve money or value. As part of its reform of its tender offer regulatory regime, the SEC adopted Rule 162(a) under the Securities Act to permit tenders of securities prior to the effectiveness of a registration statement on Form S-4 or F-4 filed in connection with a registered exchange offer.

may not be sold and offers to purchase may not be accepted prior to the time the registration statement becomes effective. This, too, will change when the 2005 Reforms become effective.

The 2005 Reforms permit, during the pre-effective period: (i) reporting issuers and non-reporting issuers to disseminate regularly released factual information; (ii) reporting issuers to disseminate regularly released forward-looking information; and (iii) all issuers and other offering participants to use "free writing prospectuses" subject to certain conditions. In addition, a broader category of routine communications regarding the issuer and the offering will be permitted to be made as part of a Rule 134 notice.

A Rule 134 notice, a publication with limited information – somewhat more than Rule 135 announcements, including the name of the managing underwriters and persons from whom a prospectus may be obtained – is also permitted during the waiting period. (Rule 134 also permits solicitation of indications of interest provided that the solicitation is preceded or accompanied by a preliminary prospectus). Rule 134 has been amended by the 2005 Reforms to permit publication of a broader category of information.

For first-time SEC filers not previously required to file reports pursuant to Section 13(a) or 15(d) of the Exchange Act, underwriters must deliver copies of the preliminary prospectus to any person who is expected to receive a confirmation of sale, at least 48 hours prior to the sending of the confirmation (ie, 48 hours prior to pricing), pursuant to Rule 15c2–8 under the Exchange Act.

The preliminary prospectus may omit specific information that depends on the pricing of the offer, which generally occurs at or after the time the registration statement is made effective, as well as the names of the members of the underwriting syndicate other than the lead or managing underwriters. This information can be provided in a final prospectus that is filed with the SEC, either in an amendment prior to effectiveness of the registration statement or more commonly after effectiveness pursuant to Securities Act Rule 430A.

The pricing information omitted from the registration statement must be included in a final prospectus filed with the SEC within two business days of the earlier of the price being set and the distribution of the prospectus to the public. The final prospectus can be used and filed without further SEC action. If pricing occurs more than 15 business days after effectiveness, a post-effective amendment to the registration statement will be required. This amendment will be subject to SEC Staff review.

Post-effective period and prospectus delivery requirements
Historically, during the post-effective period, written sales materials (in addition to the prospectus) could always be used as long as purchasers received a final prospectus (with all of the information completed, including the price and the terms of the securities) with or prior to delivery of the sales materials. As a matter of practice, however, corporate issuers generally did not use written materials other than the prospectus.

In all registered public offers, a final prospectus must be delivered prior to or with the earlier of written confirmation of sale and delivery of the security. In the case of initial public offers (IPOs), dealers, whether or not participating in the distribution, are subject to prospectus delivery requirements for purchases of securities from them for a period of 25 days if the securities are listed on a US exchange or traded on NASDAQ, or 90 days for other securities. The period runs from the later of the date the securities were first offered to the public and the date of effectiveness of the registration statement. The requirements are set forth in Rule 174 under the Securities Act. These prospectus delivery requirements effectively limit the publication of research during the prospectus delivery period.

The 2005 Reforms permit, during the post-effective period, (i) reporting issuers and non-reporting issuers to disseminate regularly released factual information; (ii) reporting issuers to disseminate regularly released forward-looking information; and (iii) non-reporting and unseasoned issues to use free writing prospectuses, provided they are accompanied or preceded by a statutory final prospectus. The communications reforms are discussed below.

As part of its 2005 Reforms, the Commission has acknowledged that the current final prospectus delivery requirements do not adequately serve the goal of timely delivery of information to investors, but instead result in the final prospectus being delivered long after the purchase commitment has been made and the resulting contract of sale has been executed. Moreover, because a final prospectus must accompany or precede a confirmation, current prospectus delivery requirements also result in delays in sending the confirmation, which impede market clearance and settlement objectives.

The Commission has, thus, adopted an **access equals delivery** model for delivery of a final prospectus. Under new Rule 172(b), the final prospectus delivery obligation will be deemed satisfied without physical delivery of the prospectus to investors as long the issuer either files a final statutory prospectus with the Commission within the required Rule 424 prospectus filing timeframe or makes a good faith and reasonable effort to file such a prospectus within that timeframe.[10]

Communications under the 2005 Reforms
Statutory and regulatory restrictions on offering activities prior to and during the registration process, and the anomalies of the oral/written distinction, have made it difficult for issuers to distinguish between permitted and prohibited market communications, particularly in light of the significant advancements in technology, which have rendered the statutory framework increasingly unworkable. Recognizing the market's demand for more timely corporate disclosure and the ability of issuers to capture, process, and disseminate that information, the reforms seek to integrate the role technology plays in informing the markets and investors about important corporate information and developments, and attempt to draw clearer boundaries between communications that are permitted and those that are not.

Companies and other offering participants often limit their ordinary course market communications unnecessarily when contemplating or conducting a public offering, concerned that improper soliciting activities – "gun-jumping" – might delay their offering and result in a loss of market opportunity.[11]

Liability for information will be analysed at the time the investment decision is made by an investor, which typically occurs at the time an investor's indication of interest is confirmed, not, as today,

---

[10] Rule 172 covers only delivery of final prospectuses. In the Adopting Release, the Commission noted that the "access equals delivery" model is not, in their view, appropriate for preliminary prospectus delivery obligations in initial public offerings and thus the existing requirement in Exchange Act Rule 15c2–8(b) that preliminary prospectuses be delivered in IPOs remains in effect.

[11] *See* Corporate Publicity and discussion of gun-jumping, *infra*.

at the closing of an offering. Accordingly, all material information will need to be available or conveyed (either orally or in writing) to a potential investor at the time the investor makes an investment decision. Inclusion of new or correcting material information in a later dated prospectus will not correct for any disclosure deficiency that existed at the earlier time of the investment decision.

Due to enhanced requirements for Exchange Act reporting, increased SEC Staff scrutiny of such reports, the increased role of technology in disseminating information and broader access to such information, the SEC's initiatives liberalise written communications outside the statutory prospectus.

Other catalysts for reform include the proliferation of offerings of increasingly complex securities as to which the Commission believes written communications, such as detailed descriptions of the securities and the offerings, would benefit investors; and the continuing trend towards globalisation of securities markets and multinationalisation of issuers, which necessitates a regulatory framework that accommodates more flexible communications.

The Commission's reforms reflect its belief that investors and the market will benefit from access to greater communications so long as investor protection is maintained through the appropriate Securities Act liability standards for materially deficient disclosures in prospectuses and oral communications.

In brief, the 2005 Reforms will generally permit greater freedom in communications during the offering process, based on the status of the issuer and its reporting history.

The new rules regarding communications retain the oral/written distinction at the heart of Section 5, but add new definitions of "written communication" and "graphic communication" to resolve the ambiguities created by the proliferation of electronic communications.

"A written communication" (defined in Rule 405) is any communication that is written, printed, or television or radio broadcast (regardless of the transmission means), or a graphic communication (newly defined, below). Live, real-time communications to a live audience, including those transmitted by graphic means, are excluded from the definition. All communications that fall outside that definition are oral communications, including for purposes of liability under Section 12(a)(2) of the Securities Act.

"Graphic communication" (defined in Rule 405) includes all forms of electronic media, including, but not limited to, audiotapes, videotapes, facsimiles, CD-ROM, electronic mail, Internet *websites*, substantially similar messages widely distributed (rather than individually distributed) on telephone answering or voice mail systems, computers, computer networks and other forms of computer data compilation. The definition does not include a communication that originates live, in real-time to a live audience and does not originate in recorded form or otherwise as a graphic communication, even if it is transmitted through graphic means.

Communications Treated as Written:

- E-mails;
- Faxes;
- Electronic *website* postings;
- Electronic road shows;
- Broadly disseminated or "blast" voice mail messages;
- Live telephone calls or video or webcast conferences that are recorded by or on behalf of the originating party and then transmitted;
- Live telephone calls or video or webcast conferences that are recorded by the recipient and then retransmitted by the recipient;
- Live telephone calls or video or webcast conferences that are transmitted other than live and in real-time;
- Slides and other graphic visual aids used at a live meeting;
- A communication that is a television or radio broadcast, regardless of the transmission means (whether cable or Internet), and whether or not live (for example, a live business news program broadcast by traditional means or on cable).
- Media reports or media interviews conducted live as part of a television program, regardless of how the television signal is transmitted – whether over the airwaves, or through cable, satellite, or Internet – or how it is received by the recipient, whether via a television set or a computer.

Communications Treated as Oral:

- Live telephone call, even if recorded by the recipient;
- Individual telephone voice mail messages from live telephone calls;

SEC REGULATION OUTSIDE THE UNITED STATES

- Live telephone calls (through whatever means by which they are transmitted, including the Internet);
- Live, in-person road shows to a live audience;
- Live, real-time road shows to a live audience that are transmitted graphically;
- Live, real-time road shows to a live audience that are transmitted to an "overflow room";
- Live, real-time communications that are transmitted by graphic means to a live audience;
- Webcasts or video conferences that originate live and in real-time at the time of transmission and are transmitted through video conferencing facilities or are webcast in real-time to a live audience.

Free Writing Prospectuses

The new rules characterise many communications that today may constitute illegal offers or illegal writings under the Securities Act as a new form of permissible written communication called a "free-writing prospectus". A free writing prospectus (defined in Rule 405) is a written communication made by an issuer or other offering participant that is not a statutory prospectus and that constitutes an "offer" of securities[12]. While free writing prospectuses are not subject to requirements on content, other than a legend (discussed below), the information may not conflict with the information in the registration statement, including Exchange Act reports incorporated by reference into the registration statement. The Adopting Release affirms that disclaimers of accuracy, responsibility or liability are impermissible in free writing prospectuses.[13]

In all cases, use of a free writing prospectus will be conditioned on it being filed with the SEC on or before the date of first use and

---

12 Free writing prospectuses would not include communications that fit within any other safe harbour, eg, those made in compliance with Rule 134 or 135, new Rule 168 or 169 for regularly released factual business and forward-looking information, or the research safe harbours of Rules 137, 138 and 139.

13 Examples of impermissible legends or disclaimers that will cause the materials not to be permissible free writing prospectuses or not to be effective as to any purchaser for liability purposes include: (i) disclaimers regarding accuracy or completeness or reliance by investors; (ii) statements requiring investors to read or acknowledge that they have read or understand the registration statement; (iii) language indicating that the communication is neither a prospectus nor an offer to sell or a solicitation of an offer to buy; and (iv) for information required to be filed with the Commission, statements that the information is confidential.

on the inclusion of a legend indicating, among other things, when the statutory prospectus can be accessed, or by providing the URL for the SEC *website* (EDGAR) or a hyperlink to the statutory prospectus. In some cases, a free writing prospectus must be preceded or accompanied by the statutory prospectus.

A free writing prospectus will, like oral communications and other prospectuses used today, be subject to disclosure liability under Section 12(a)(2) of the Securities Act. It will not be subject to liability under Section 11 of the Securities Act, unless the issuer makes the free writing prospectus a part of the registration statement, such as by filing the free writing prospectus as an exhibit to an Exchange Act report that is incorporated by reference into the registration statement.

The free writing prospectus system will allow issuers and underwriters to use e-mail and other forms of written communications to convey offering-related information to potential investors, information that today is often not communicated at all or is communicated only orally due to the existing restrictions on the use of most written communications other than the preliminary and final statutory prospectuses. For example, under the SEC's 2005 Reforms, underwriters will be able to e-mail offering-related information, such as preliminary term sheets and other selling materials, to potential investors without violating the registration and prospectus requirements of the Securities Act. Because their use of free writing prospectuses will be subject to disclosure liability under Section 12(a)(2), underwriters will likely develop compliance procedures to control the content of any material their employees disseminate and the number of individuals authorised to disseminate free writing to investors.

Website *offers*

An offer on an issuer's *website* or hyperlinked to a third party's *website* from the issuer's *website* will be considered a written offer by the issuer and, unless exempt, will be a free writing prospectus subject to the conditions of Rule 433. The same is true of information contained on a third party *website* hyperlinked from the issuer's *website*. Hyperlinks from a third party *website* to an issuer's *website* may also be a free writing prospectus of the third party with regard to the issuer's securities, depending on the facts and circumstances.

Under the new rules, any hyperlink contained within a written communication used to offer an issuer's securities, whether in the issuer's or any other offering participant's *website*, will be considered part of that written communication.

Historical information on websites
Historical information relating to an issuer will not be considered a current offer of the issuer's securities and, therefore, will not be a free writing prospectus, if that historical information is separately identified as such and located in a separate section of the issuer's *website* containing historical information, such as an archive. The use of That historical information will become a current offer if it is incorporated by reference into or otherwise included in a prospectus, or otherwise used or referred to (by hyperlink or otherwise) in connection with the offering.

New Communications Safe Harbours
30-Day Bright-Line Exclusion for All Issuers
The 2005 Reforms amended Rule 163A to codify existing SEC Staff practice and permit all issuers to communicate at any time up to 30 days before the filing of a registration statement without violating the gun-jumping provisions so long as (i) the communication is made by or on behalf of the issuer, (ii) the communication does not reference a securities offering and (iii) the issuer takes reasonable steps to prevent further distribution or publication of the information during the 30 days immediately before filing of the registration statement.

The 30-day bright-line exclusion will be available only to the issuer and will not cover communications made by any other offering participant, including underwriters and dealers.

Safe Harbours for Regularly Released Factual Business Information and Forward-Looking Information
The SEC has adopted two non-exclusive safe harbours from the gun-jumping provisions, for continuing ordinary course business communications.

The first safe harbour (Rule 168) will permit a reporting issuer (ie, well-known seasoned issuers, seasoned issuers and unseasoned issuers, but not voluntary filers), as well as asset-backed issuers and certain non-reporting foreign private issuers to continue to disseminate regularly released factual business information[14] and forward-looking[15] information at any time during the registered offering process.

A second safe harbour (Rule 169) will permit a non-reporting issuer (an IPO issuer or voluntary filer) to continue to disseminate regularly released factual business information[16] (but not forward-looking information) that is intended for use by persons other than in their capacity as investors or potential investors, such as customers and suppliers.

While the Rule 168 safe harbour, for reporting issuers, covers forward-looking information, the Rule 169 safe harbour does not. The SEC was concerned with the lack of such information, or history, in the marketplace and the possibility that forward-looking information would be used for purposes of conditioning the market for the issuer's securities. Both safe harbours will be, however, available to all eligible issuers, including non-reporting issuers.

Information is considered regularly released if the issuer has previously released or disseminated the same type of information in the ordinary course of its business, and the release or dissemination is consistent in timing, manner, and form with the issuer's similar past release or dissemination of such information. The method of releasing or disseminating the information also must be consistent in material respects with prior practice (ie, the information must be provided by the same employees who historically have provided such information).

---

14 Under Rule 168, "factual business information" is defined as: (i) factual information about the issuer, its business or financial developments, or other aspects of its business; (ii) advertisements of, or other information about, the issuer's products or services; and (iii) dividend notices. The definition was modified from the proposal to make clear that factual business information may be communicated within the safe harbour by including it in any report or material filed with, furnished to, or submitted to the SEC.

15 "Forward-looking information" includes: (i) projections of the issuer's revenues, income (loss), earnings (loss) per share, capital expenditures, dividends, capital structure, or other financial items; (ii) statements about management's plans and objectives for future operations, including those relating to the issuer's products or services; (iii) statements about the issuer's future economic performance, including statements of known material trends and uncertainties contemplated by MD&A; and (iv) any underlying assumptions.

16 Under Rule 169, "factual business information" is defined as: (i) factual information about the issuer, its business or financial developments, or other aspects of its business; and (ii) advertisements of, or other information about, the issuer's products or services.

While there is no specified minimum time period to satisfy the regularly released element, the issuer must have some track record of releasing the particular type of information. One prior release, according to the Adopting Release, could establish this track record. The safe harbour is intended to cover not only scheduled releases of information, but also communications, such as product advertising and product release information or earnings guidance changes, that are made on an unscheduled or episodic basis, provided that the issuer has previously provided such communications containing factual business and forward-looking information in that manner.

Pre-Filing Free Writing for Well-Known Seasoned Issuers Only
New Rule 163 exempts well-known seasoned issuers[17] and those communicating on their behalf from the Section 5 restrictions on pre-filing offers, oral and written. These pre-filing free writing prospectuses are permitted, provided they are appropriately legended and filed with the Commission promptly when and if the issuer files a registration statement.[18] Filing is not required if the information has previously been filed with or furnished to the Commission. In view of the new automatically effective shelf registration process, well-known seasoned issuers usually will likely have a registration statement on file that they can use for any of their registered offerings. Consequently, it will be unusual for well-known seasoned issuers to need to avail themselves of the Rule 163 (pre-filing offering) exemption.

Post-Filing Free Writing for All Issuers
The 2005 Reforms expand the types of written offering-related communications that may be made by the issuer and any offering participants after the filing of the registration statement. New Rule 164 permits any issuer to use a free writing prospectus after filing a registration statement subject to certain conditions set forth in new Rule 433.

---

[17] The Rule 163 exemption is not available to communications involving registered business combination transactions or communications in offerings by registered investment companies or business development companies.
[18] *See* Rule 163. For the text of the legend, *see* Rule 163(b)(1).

US-REGISTERED OFFERS

In the case of non-reporting and unseasoned issuers, the ability to use a free writing prospectus would be conditioned (in addition to filing and use of a legend) upon it being preceded or accompanied by the statutory prospectus (eg, by hyperlink, not merely by referring to its availability) where:

❏ the free writing prospectus is prepared by or on behalf of[19] or used or referred to by an issuer or prepared by or on behalf of or used or referred to by other offering participants;
❏ consideration has been or will be given by the issuer or an offering participant for the dissemination (in any format) of the free writing prospectus, including any published article, publication or advertisement; or
❏ Securities Act Section 17(b) requires disclosure that consideration has been or will be given by the issuer or an offering participant for any activity described therein in connection with the free writing prospectus.[20]

Once the required statutory prospectus is sent or given to an investor, additional free writing prospectuses could be provided without having to send or give an additional statutory prospectus unless there were material changes in the most recent statutory prospectus from the prospectus provided, in which event the most recent statutory prospectus would need to be sent or given to an investor prior to or along with the additional free writing prospectus.[21]

In the case of well-known seasoned issuers and seasoned issuers, a free writing prospectus may be used any time after a registration statement is filed, provided that it is filed and contains a legend stating that the issuer has filed a registration statement, including a prospectus, with the SEC, that investors should read the prospectus and other filed documents, which are available free

---

19 Rule 433(h) provides that a written communication or information is prepared or provided by or on behalf of a person if the person or an agent or representative of the person authorises the communication or information or approves the communication or information before it is used. An offering participant other than the issuer shall not be an agent or representative of the issuer solely by virtue of its acting as an offering participant.
20 Securities Act Section 17(b) generally requires persons who make statements describing an issuer's securities to disclose the receipt (and the amount) of consideration given, directly or indirectly, by an issuer, underwriter, or dealer in exchange for making the statements.
21 In an IPO, the price range must be included to constitute a statutory prospectus.

from EDGAR or which may be obtained by calling a toll-free telephone number. The legend may contain an e-mail address, through which the statutory prospectus may be requested.[22]

Once the required statutory prospectus is sent or given to an investor, additional free writing prospectuses may be provided without having to send or give an additional statutory prospectus unless there are material changes in the most recent statutory prospectus.

Free Writing for Underwriters and Other Offering Participants
Free writing prospectuses prepared by other offering participants, including underwriters, dealers, affiliates, selling security holders unaffiliated with the issuer and others acting on their behalf, do not have to be filed unless they are distributed by such persons in a manner reasonably designed to achieve broad unrestricted dissemination, such as where the underwriter includes a free writing prospectus on an unrestricted *website*, provides a hyperlink from an unrestricted *website* to information that would be a free writing prospectus, or sends out a press release regarding the issuer or the offering that is a free writing prospectus. Free writing prospectuses sent directly to customers of an offering participant, without regard to number, would not be considered broadly disseminated.

On the other hand, free writing prospectus posted on a *website* with access restricted to customers would not require filing; nor would an e-mail sent by an underwriter to its customers, regardless of the number of customers, or to other members of the selling group.

A free writing prospectus prepared by an offering participant other than the issuer, such as a member of the underwriting syndicate, for its own use, even one based on information provided by an issuer but that does not itself contain issuer information,[23] is not required to be filed with the SEC but will be subject to the record retention requirement (discussed below). If the free writing prospectus contains issuer information that is not already included or incorporated in the prospectus or a filed free writing prospectus,

---

[22] With respect to published articles, the legend requirement would be satisfied by filing the published article with the SEC as a free writing prospectus and including the legend in the filed copy.

[23] "Issuer Information" is defined in Rule 433(h) to mean information about the issuer or its securities that has been provided by or on behalf of the issuer.

the issuer information, not necessarily the free writing prospectus itself, must be filed by the issuer.

Corporate publicity
The restrictions on publicity under the Securities Act have been construed by the SEC to apply to news stories that are based on communications by participants in the offer. As a result, non-US companies have historically excluded US journalists from press conferences, interviews and other forums during the pendency of an offer. In response to complaints by the US news media about such treatment, the SEC adopted a new rule to permit offshore press contacts by foreign private issuers and their representatives such as underwriters and public relations firms.

Special provisions have been made in Rule 135e for non-US companies. As discussed in Chapter 3, Rule 135e permits certain press contacts outside the United States by foreign private issuers, referred to as offshore press contacts. Offshore press contacts, whether through interviews, meetings or press releases, if done in accordance with the safe harbour, will not be deemed an offer for the purposes of Section 5, even where such contacts result in a news story printed or broadcast in the United States. However, if such publicity is inconsistent with the disclosure in the prospectus, the SEC Staff is likely to require that the company address the subject of the publicity in the prospectus.

Rule 135e offers no protection for press contacts made in the United States by a foreign private issuer. The Rule defines the conditions under which issuers and selling security holders, and their representatives, may provide US journalists with access to offshore press conferences, offshore press interviews and written materials released offshore without risk of violation of the registration provisions of Section 5. Rule 135e clarifies that providing US journalists, print or broadcast, with access to offshore press activities in connection with an offer by a non-US issuer will not be deemed an "offer" for the purposes of Section 5, "directed selling efforts" for the purposes of Regulation S or "general solicitation" or "general advertising" for the purposes of the Regulation D private placement exemption, provided that the conditions of Rule 135e are met.

Rule 135e only affects the registration requirements under Section 5. Anti-fraud and other civil liability provisions with respect to written and oral material misstatements or omissions continue to apply to offshore press activities.

Concerned about offshore publicity flowing back into the United States, the SEC Staff takes a stringent approach and requires issuers to include in their prospectuses publicity including pre-deal research released offshore that has become accessible in the United States, particularly if it contains forward-looking information, notwithstanding the applicability of the Rule 135e safe harbour or Regulation S. Thus, while offshore publicity by a non-US issuer in connection with a concurrent offshore offering may be exempt from the registration requirements of Section 5 (and, thus, from US publicity restrictions), it may, nonetheless, end up subject to Section 11 prospectus liability.

An issuer is permitted to make a public announcement of a proposed public offer during the pre-filing period. The SEC recognises that an offer may be a material development that should be disclosed to shareholders and the trading markets. Rule 135 permits an issuer (but not an underwriter), prior to the filing of a registration statement, to publish limited information about an offer, including: the name of the issuer; the title, amount and terms of the securities; the amount of the offer; whether the offer is to be made to existing security holders; the anticipated time of the offer; the manner and purpose of the offer (without identifying the underwriters); and additional details in the case of a rights offer, an exchange offer or an offer to employees. Inclusion of any information other than that specifically permitted precludes reliance on the Rule.

Sanctions for gun-jumping can be disruptive to the offer process. Where the SEC believes certain disclosures have had the effect of conditioning or arousing interest in the market, the SEC may require a "cooling-off" period (which can be as long as several months, although it is generally shorter) so that the effect of the public disclosure can dissipate. More typically, the SEC may request that an issuer disclose in its prospectus the information contained in any materials made public in violation of the rules and, in a number of cases, has required inclusion of a risk factor discussing the potential rescission rights available to investors arising out of the violation. In addition to enforcement actions brought by the SEC, gun-jumping may result in private suits for rescission under Section 12(a)(1) of the Securities Act.

In April 2004, *Playboy* ran an interview with the founders of Google one week before the registration statement for Google's IPO was originally filed. The *Playboy* article, over which Google had no control, was published in August during the offering process. As a result of the publication, the SEC Staff required Google to include the text of the entire article as an appendix to Google's registration statement – typically the SEC Staff forces companies to include only those statements that are market-conditioning – and to include a risk factor in the prospectus indicating that the article may involve a possible gun-jumping violation under Section 5 of the Securities Act. The SEC did not require the offering to be delayed.

Salesforce.com, Inc. faced worse sanctions. For a *single day* in May 2004 its CEO allowed a reporter to accompany him while the company was "in registration". Subsequently, the CEO was quoted in a *New York Times* article that included optimistic statements about the company. The SEC imposed a 30-day cooling-off period and required Salesforce.com to add a risk factor in its prospectus indicating that the article may be held to be gun-jumping in violation of the Securities Act and that the company could be required to repurchase the securities sold in the offering.

Responding to concerns that it had been overly zealous in citing issuers for gun-jumping based on corporate publicity, the SEC Staff announced in 2001 a general policy that it would not raise gun-jumping issues with respect to corporate communications made more than 45 days prior to filing of the registration statement unless it found the publicity to be egregious. (As further discussed above, the SEC's 2005 Reforms codify the SEC Staff position and provide a *30-day* bright-line exclusion under which all issuers will be able to communicate more than 30 days before the filing of a registration statement without risk of violating the gun-jumping prohibitions of Section 5 as long as: (i) the communication was made by or on behalf of the issuer; (ii) the communication did not reference a securities offering; and (iii) the issuer took reasonable steps within its control to prevent further distribution or publication of the information during the 30 days immediately before the filing of the registration statement.)

Media Publications As Free Writing Prospectuses

The Commission states in the Adopting Release that it wants "to encourage the role of the media as an important communicator of information" but does "not want issuers and offering participants to avoid responsibility for their offering or marketing efforts by using the media." New Rule 433(f) thus permits media publications, but subjects them to disclosure liability under Securities Act Section 12(a)(2) and, in certain cases, filing with the Commission.

Where an issuer or any offering participant provides information (orally or in writing) about the issuer or the offering to the media that constitutes an offer, the media publication of that information in any format will constitute a free writing prospectus of the issuer or offering participant. Prior to filing the registration statement, media publications will continue to be impermissible offers and gun-jumping violations, unless they relate to well-known seasoned issuers. The new rules thus provide a safe harbour for such information for all issuers except well-known seasoned issuers as to whom such communications would be permitted.

Where the issuer or offering participant prepares, pays for, or gives consideration for the preparation, publication or dissemination of or uses or refers to a published article, television or radio broadcast, or advertisement, the issuer or other offering participant will have to satisfy the conditions to the use of any other free writing prospectus of that offering participant at the time of the publication or broadcast.

In the case of non-reporting and unseasoned issuers, the publication will have to be preceded or accompanied by a statutory prospectus, which will effectively prohibit such issuers and other participants in such issuers' offerings from engaging in infomercials or other broadcast ads about issuers or their securities or offerings that include information beyond that permitted by the Rule 134 safe harbour. In the case of seasoned issuers, the most recent statutory prospectus must be on file and the issuer or other offering participant will have to file the free writing prospectus on or before the date of first use.

Independent media publications (where the issuer and other offering participants are not affiliated with the media, but provide, authorise or approve the information contained in the media piece and the publication is not paid for by the issuer or other offering participants) must be filed by the issuer or other offering participant with the appropriate legend within four business days after the issuer or offering participant becomes aware of its publication or first broadcast. While the media piece will not have to be preceded or accompanied by the statutory prospectus, a registration statement will need to be on file and a statutory prospectus will need to be available for all issuers other than well-known seasoned issuers. The media will have no filing or other obligations under the new rules.

Under the 2005 Reforms, the *Playboy* article on Google would be regarded as an independent media free writing prospectus and would be required to be filed by Google, with the appropriate legend, within four business days after Google or another offering participant became aware of its publication. While the article would not have had to have been preceded or accompanied by the statutory prospectus, a registration statement would have had to have been on file and a statutory prospectus would have had to have been available for all issuers other than well-known seasoned issuers. *Playboy* would not have had any filing or other obligation.

Road Shows

Road shows are an integral part of a securities offer and may be conducted once the registration statement is filed with the SEC–during the waiting period. Road shows are viewed as oral offer communications and thus are permitted during the waiting period. In addition to marketing the specific securities being offered, road shows help the issuer develop strong and ongoing investor interest in the company. A road show in connection with a global offer usually consists of a series of meetings lasting from several days to several weeks, at which management makes presentations to potential investors and provides them with the opportunity to ask questions. Road shows commonly include one-on-one meetings between key management and major potential institutional investors, and are subject to the same regulatory regime as the more traditional group presentations.

The principal securities law issue implicated by road shows has been to assure that written materials are not used at the road show in a manner to cause them to be viewed as non-conforming written prospectuses, which, until the 2005 Reforms, were prohibited during the waiting period. Equally important, the presentation itself could not be communicated in a fashion that would convert the oral presentation into a Section 2(a)(10) prospectus – a written communication or communication by radio or television. For these reasons, slides, graphs, other written visual aids and audio and video tapes may be used, but are not distributed (except perhaps in one-on-one meetings, in which case they are retrieved).

In the United States, radio or television broadcasts in connection with an offer are treated as written communications for the purposes of Section 5 and, therefore, are subject to restrictions during the offer process. Until recently, this largely foreclosed the use of electronic communications to conduct road shows. However, reflecting the SEC's policy of encouraging the use of electronic media to communicate with investors, the SEC Staff issued no-action letters in the context of registered equity offers permitting the electronic broadcast of a road show over a private network to a subscriber base and authorising the transmission of a password-protected road show over the Internet. In each case, the SEC sought to ensure that viewers: (a) are limited to the category of investors traditionally invited to road shows; (b) have available to them, and appreciate the importance of, the filed prospectus; (c) do not have unlimited opportunities to view the road show; and (d) do not have the ability to tape the road show or distribute it. The SEC Staff did not articulate a legal theory, but stated that it would not recommend enforcement action on the grounds that the road shows constitute an illegal prospectus. These letters will be rescinded upon effectiveness of the 2005 Reforms, on 1 December 2005, when new rules concerning electronic road shows come into force.

Under the 2005 Reforms, electronic road shows, defined as road shows that do not originate live, in real-time to a live audience and that are graphically transmitted, in connection with registered offerings will be considered written communications and, therefore, free writing prospectuses. Electronic road shows will be permitted (without many of the conditions currently imposed by the electronic road show no-action letters) if the issuer satisfies certain conditions for use of a free writing prospectus. Issuer participation or involvement in a road show would make the road show an "issuer free writing prospectus".

Under the 2005 Reforms, an electronic road show or script will not be subject to filing, except for material issuer information[24] not previously included or incorporated by reference in the registration statement or in a filed free writing prospectus related to the offering, so long as the issuer:

- ❏ makes at least one version of a *bona fide* electronic road show[25] readily available electronically to any potential investor at the same time as the electronic version; and
- ❏ files any issuer free writing prospectus or material issuer information used at an electronic road show (other than the road show itself).

Electronic road shows involving a non-reporting or unseasoned issuer would be subject to the condition that the issuer's statutorily compliant prospectus accompany or precede the electronic road show, for example, by hyperlink.

The SEC does not require the filing of any material issuer information provided at an electronic road show.

The materials presented as part of these road shows, such as slides or PowerPoint® presentations, will similarly not be graphic communications required to be filed unless they are separately transmitted as graphic communications. As a result, live communications, such as live road shows transmitted electronically (whether to an overflow room or another city), will not be considered graphic communications and thus not free writing prospectuses. However, they will be treated as oral communications and will be subject to liability under Securities Act Section 12(a)(2) and the anti-fraud provisions.

Registration statements and Form 20-F
Form 20-F
Securities Act registration is accomplished by filing a registration statement with the SEC. A registration statement consists of the

---

24 "Issuer Information" is defined in Rule 433(h) to mean information about the issuer or its securities that has been provided by or on behalf of the issuer.
25 A "bona fide electronic road show" is a version that contains a presentation by an issuer's management and that covers the same general areas regarding the issuer, its management and the securities being offered as the other version; it need not address all of the same subjects, provide the same information as the other electronic versions or provide an opportunity for questions and answers, even if other electronic versions do.

prospectus, which is distributed to investors, and other information that is not distributed to investors but may be reviewed by the SEC and is publicly available, including exhibits consisting of material contracts of the issuer and other documents. A non-US company that meets the definition of a "foreign private issuer" will generally use registration forms specially designed for non-US issuers. The principal forms now used are Forms F-1, F-2, F-3 and F-4;[26] the choice of form depends on the status of the issuer and the type of transaction. The forms differ principally in the amount of information that must be set forth in the prospectus and that which may be incorporated by reference from documents on file with the SEC. All foreign private issuers are required to submit their registration statements and reports on Form 20-F and Form 6-K to the SEC electronically via the SEC's EDGAR. A first-time foreign private issuer will register on Form F-1, which requires all information to be included in the prospectus. Sizeable companies that have been registered and have timely filed reports under the Exchange Act for a year, including an annual report on Form 20-F, are eligible to use more abbreviated forms that allow incorporation by reference. These forms are not boilerplate forms to be filled in, but are to be used as a guide in the preparation of the registration statement. The disclosure requirements applicable to the prospectus are prescribed by such forms and are extensive. The specific disclosure requirements are incorporated by reference principally from Form 20-F and to a limited extent Regulation S-K.

Form 20-F is specifically designed for foreign private issuers to register securities and provide annual reports under the Exchange Act. The disclosures required by Form 20-F are modified somewhat from those required of US issuers to accommodate certain home country practices. For example, disclosures about executive compensation in Form 20-F are far less detailed than those required of US companies. Form 20-F requires, *inter alia*, a description of the general development of the company's business over the last five years, as well as a description of principal products and services, principal markets and method of distribution, the status of new products or services requiring substantial future investment and special characteristics of the company's industry that may affect

---

26 In the 2005 Reforms, the SEC has rescinded Forms F-2 and S-2.

future financial performance. Where appropriate, significant risk factors relating to the company's national environment must be disclosed. In addition, a discussion of management's analysis of the results of operations, financial condition and liquidity of the issuer and material trends, uncertainties and contingencies, quantitative and qualitative disclosures about market risk sensitive instruments and disclosure about executive officers and directors are required.

Form 20-F also prescribes the financial statements to be furnished. The financial statements to be included must be presented on a consolidated basis and include: (a) audited balance sheets as at the end of each of the two most recent fiscal years; (b) audited income statements for each of the three fiscal years preceding the date of the most recent balance sheet; (c) audited statements of changes in the financial position or statements of cash or funds flow for each of the three fiscal years preceding the date of the most recent balance sheet; and (d) in certain cases, unaudited interim statements. In addition, certain "pro forma" financial information may be required for certain business combinations, dispositions of a significant portion of a business by sale, abandonment or distribution to shareholders, or acquisitions of real estate operations or properties of significant size.

Critical accounting policies. In addition to the required financial statements, companies are also required to include disclosure regarding their critical accounting policies in their Management's Discussion and Analysis (MD&A). Chapter 7 contains detailed discussion of MD&A requirements. In 2001, reflecting concern for the quality and transparency of companies' financial reporting, the SEC issued "cautionary advice" to issuers regarding disclosure of critical accounting policies.[27] The SEC defined critical accounting policies as those "most important to the portrayal of the company's financial condition and results, and that require management's most difficult, subjective or complex judgments". Central to the cautionary advice is the SEC's tenet that "even a technically accurate application of generally accepted accounting principles (GAAP) may nonetheless fail to communicate important information if it is not accompanied by appropriate and clear analytic disclosures to facilitate an investor's understanding of the company's financial

---

[27] Securities Act Release 8040 (12th December 2001).

status, and the possibility, likelihood and implication of changes in the financial and operating status".

In 2002, the SEC proposed rules that would codify its 2001 guidance.[28] As of the date of this book, the rules had not yet been adopted. The proposed rules would require disclosure concerning critical accounting estimates made by companies in applying their accounting policies. It would also require disclosure regarding the initial adoption of new accounting policies that would have a material impact on a company's financial presentation (unless it resulted solely from new accounting literature issued by a recognised accounting standard setter). An accounting estimate would be considered critical and would be required to be disclosed if it meets two tests: (i) the estimate requires the company to make assumptions regarding matters that are highly uncertain at the time the estimate is made; and (ii) it must be the case that different estimates that the company reasonably could have used, or changes in the accounting estimate that are reasonably likely to occur from period to period, would have a material impact on the presentation of the company's financial condition, changes in financial condition or results of operations.

The proposed rules would apply to foreign private issuers and would potentially be more burdensome for foreign issuers whose primary financial statements are presented on a basis other than US GAAP, such as home country GAAP or in accordance with International Accounting Standards and IFRS[29] issued by the IASC and IASB. Under its proposal, the SEC would require these issuers to address critical accounting estimates both with respect to the primary financial statements and with respect to their reconciliation to US GAAP, whether the reconciliation is under Item 17 or Item 18 of Form 20-F. (The requirements relating to presentation of financial statements are discussed later.) Similarly, foreign private issuers would be required to provide the proposed MD&A disclosure about the initial adoption of accounting policies as it pertains to their primary financial statements, but would also be required to take into account the reconciliation to US GAAP. The new disclosures would be provided under Item 5 of Form 20-F, "Operating and Financial Review and Prospects".

---

28 Securities Act Release 8098 (10th May 2002).
29 Securities Act Release 7801 (6th February 2000).

Although foreign private issuers are not required to report on a quarterly basis and are exempt from US proxy and information statement disclosure requirements, they are required to file an annual report on Form 20-F and a current report on Form 6-K. Unless a foreign private issuer files a registration statement that is required to include interim financial statements and related MD&A disclosure, it would not be required to update the proposed MD&A disclosure more frequently than annually, on Form 20-F. The SEC will, nonetheless, encourage foreign private issuers to disclose voluntarily on Form 6-K any newly identified critical accounting estimates and any other material changes to the most recent MD&A disclosure. The SEC also indicated that, if a non-US regulator were to adopt the proposed MD&A requirements, the SEC would expect foreign private issuers in that jurisdiction to provide the updated information on Form 6-K.

Independent auditor. The audited financial statements are required to be audited by an independent auditor in accordance with United States generally accepted auditing standards (GAAS). It is critical that an international accounting firm that is expert in the rules of the SEC be engaged to prepare the financial statements. Due to the SEC's rigorous requirements with regard to the independence of auditors, certain companies may even find it necessary to retain new auditors to satisfy SEC independence requirements. Under SEC rules, independence of the accountants requires independence in appearance as well as in substance. The SEC and the American Institute of Certified Public Accountants have extensive rules and guidelines on independence matters. In general, an accountant must not, during the period of his professional engagement, have any direct financial interest or any material indirect financial interest in the company. Nor may the accountant serve as a promoter, underwriter, voting trustee, director, officer or employee of his or her client.

Over recent years, the SEC has developed rules intended to promote the independence of auditors. Among the SEC's many concerns is that an auditor's independence will be impaired where it performs appraisal or valuation services or any service involving a fairness opinion for an audit client and it is reasonably likely that the results would be material to the audit client's financial statements or would end up being audited by the auditor. The SEC suggests that, when an accountant ends up reviewing his or her own work during a financial statement audit, the auditor who has appraised a significant asset or liability during the year is less likely to question his or her own work at the end of the year. In addition, where an auditor has assisted in the development of financial projections, he or she may develop a mutuality of interest with the audit client in meeting those projections.

In keeping with these concerns, the SEC adopted rules under SOX to strengthen auditor independence and require additional disclosure by companies about the services provided to them by their independent accountants.[30] As discussed in Chapter 4, the rules: clarify the scope of non-audit services prohibited to be performed by a company's outside auditor; specify audit committee pre-approval requirements in respect of audit and non-audit services; require that critical accounting policies and other material written communications between management and registered audit firms be reported to a company's audit committee; require mandatory rotation of certain audit partners, as well as a "time-out" period after that, with the timing of each depending on the partner's involvement in the audit; address auditor conflicts of interest arising from audit partner compensation and employment by issuer clients; and require disclosures of information related to audit and non-audit services provided by, and fees paid to, a company's outside auditor.

To further protect the integrity of the audit process and the resulting financial statements, the SEC also adopted rules under SOX that would supplement existing rules prohibiting officers and directors of a company from improperly influencing the conduct of audits.[31]

SOX created a new body, the Public Company Accounting Oversight Board (PCAOB), to oversee the audit profession. The PCAOB adopted, as interim Rule 3600T, Independence Standards Board (ISB) Standard No 1, which requires auditors of US and non-US registrants alike to provide audit committees with a letter on an annual basis disclosing any matters or relationships between the auditor and the client that may affect the auditor's independence

---

30 Securities Act Release 8183 (28th January 2003).
31 Exchange Act Release 46685 (18th October 2002).

(known as the ISB letter). The ISB letter should discuss not only all matters relevant to the firm in the local jurisdiction, but also to its affiliates overseas. The SEC has been particularly concerned with lack of disclosure by US companies that have international operations audited by a foreign affiliate of a US firm. For this reason, audit committees in any jurisdiction should be encouraged to ask the engagement partner if appropriate steps have been taken to ensure the auditor's independence on a global basis.

The SEC requires non-US issuers to comply with US independence rules. The SEC's independence rules conflict with those in a number of countries, especially in Europe where various regulatory authorities actually call for the accountant to issue a report regarding the consideration to be exchanged in a non-monetary transaction, such as a stock-for-stock merger. In such countries, it may be necessary for the audit client to retain a different auditing firm to audit the financials.

Presentation of financials. Foreign private issuers registering securities with the SEC may either present financial statements prepared in accordance with US GAAP and Regulation S-X under the Securities Act, or present consolidated financial statements prepared in accordance with their home country's accounting principles or with international accounting standards, together with a discussion of the material differences between US GAAP and the accounting principles used and a quantitative reconciliation of such differences to US GAAP. The requirement to reconcile the financial statements is intended to assure that US investors have information about non-US issuers comparable with that required of US companies. There are two types of reconciliation specified by Items 17 and 18 of Form 20-F. Item 17 requires reconciliation only of the difference in the measurement items, including income statement and balance sheet amounts. Item 18 requires a full reconciliation, which would include all supplemental disclosure required by US GAAP and Regulation S-X in the footnotes to the financial statements, such as full industry segment and geographic data. Compliance with Item 18 is required in any offer registered under the Securities Act, except an offer of non-convertible investment-grade securities. A non-US issuer may use Item 17 if it is simply listing its securities on a US stock exchange or NASDAQ, or for the purposes of its annual report. A large majority of non-US companies choose to provide a reconciliation rather than preparing US GAAP financials. Foreign private issuers may use whatever reporting currency they deem appropriate in the registration statement.

Under the leadership of IASB, IFRS has become widely recognised by preparers and users of financial statements over recent years. As a result, numerous non-US issuers are switching from their home country accounting principles to IFRS. In addition, an increasing number of jurisdictions around the world are adopting or incorporating IFRS as their basis of accounting, as a result of which a large number of issuers will switch to IFRS from their Previous GAAP.[32] In April 2005, the SEC again amended Form 20-F,[33] to provide a one-time accommodation for eligible foreign private issuers adopting IFRS (voluntarily or by mandate) for the first time, prior to or for the first financial year starting on or after 1st January 2007, to file financial statements prepared in accordance with IFRS for only the two most recent financial years. Based on previous SEC rules, when changing their basis of accounting to IFRS, foreign private issuers were required to provide audited financial statements prepared in accordance with IFRS for the three most recent financial years. The accommodation, which is set forth as new General Instruction G to Form 20-F and is effective as of 19th May 2005, also requires certain disclosures relating to: (i) any exceptions from IFRS on which a foreign private issuer relies; and (ii) the reconciliation from its previous basis of accounting to IFRS.

Foreign private issuers will be eligible for the accommodation if:

❑ they are "first-time adopters" and adopt IFRS prior to or for their first financial year starting on or after 1st January 2007;
❑ they state that their financial statements comply with IFRS and are not subject to any qualification relating to the application of IFRS as issued by the IASB; and
❑ their independent auditors opine, without qualification, on compliance with IFRS.

---

[32] The term "Previous GAAP" refers to the basis of accounting that a first-time adopter uses immediately before adopting IFRS.
[33] Securities Act Release 8567 (12th April 2005).

Foreign private issuers adopting IFRS for the first time will be able to take advantage of the accommodation and exclude IFRS financial statements for the third financial year from:

❑ a registration statement if (i) the most recent audited financial statements required by Form 20-F are for the 2007 financial year or an earlier financial year and (ii) the audited financial statements for the most recent financial year are prepared in accordance with IFRS; and
❑ an annual report on Form 20-F if (i) the annual report relates to the 2007 financial year or an earlier financial year and (ii) the audited financial statements for the financial year to which the annual report relates are prepared in accordance with IFRS.

The amendments retain the requirements under Items 17(c) and 18 of Form 20-F regarding the reconciliation of financial statement items to US GAAP. Foreign private issuers relying on the accommodation will not be required to present condensed US GAAP financial information; however, they will continue to be required to provide an audited reconciliation of the two years of IFRS financial statements to US GAAP. Such audited reconciliation must be included as a note to the audited financial statements.

For a fuller discussion of the accommodation, *see* Chapter 4 and Securities Act Release 8567 (dated 12th April 2005).

Non-GAAP financial measures. When preparing financial statements and other financial information for use in the company's report on Form 20-F for inclusion in an earnings release, companies are now required to consider carefully their use of non-GAAP financial measures. In 2003, the SEC adopted rules regulating the use of non-GAAP financial measures, as directed by Section 401 of SOX.[34] The rules include a new disclosure regulation, Regulation G, which requires public reporting companies that disclose or release non-GAAP financial measures to include, in that disclosure or release, a presentation of the most directly comparable GAAP financial measures and a reconciliation of the differences between the disclosed non-GAAP financial measures and the most directly comparable GAAP financial measures. If the non-GAAP financial

---

34 Securities Act Release 8176 (22nd January 2003).

measure is released orally or by telephone, webcast, broadcast or other similar means, the company is permitted to provide the required accompanying information by posting it on its *website* and disclosing during its presentation the location and availability of that information.

Regulation G applies to foreign issuers, subject to a limited exception. Specifically, the requirements of Regulation G do not apply to public disclosure of a non-US GAAP financial measure by a non-US issuer if: (i) the securities of the issuer are listed or quoted on a securities exchange or inter-dealer quotation system outside the United States; (ii) the non-GAAP financial measure is not derived from or based on a measure calculated and presented in accordance with US GAAP; and (iii) the disclosure is made by or on behalf of the issuer outside the United States, or is included in a written communication that is released by or on behalf of the issuer outside the United States. The SEC stated in the Regulation G adopting release that the exception for foreign issuers should continue to apply where: (i) a written communication is released in the United States as well as outside the United States, as long as the communication is released in the United States contemporaneously with or after the release outside the United States and is not otherwise targeted at persons located in the United States; (ii) foreign or US journalists or other third parties have access to the information; (iii) the information appears on one or more *website*s maintained by the issuer, as long as the *website*s, taken together, are not available exclusively to, or targeted at, persons located in the United States; and/or (iv) following the disclosure or release of the information outside the United States, the information is submitted to the SEC in a Form 6-K.

For information filed with the SEC, the new rules include requirements that are more extensive and detailed than Regulation G. In particular, filings with the SEC (including registration statements) that include non-GAAP financial measures must also include: (i) a presentation, of equal or greater prominence, of the most directly comparable financial measures calculated and presented in accordance with GAAP; (ii) a reconciliation (by schedule or other clearly understandable method) of the differences between the non-GAAP financial measures used with the most directly comparable measure calculated in accordance with GAAP; (iii) a statement disclosing the reasons why the company's management believes that presentation of the non-GAAP financial measures provides useful information to investors; and (iv) to the extent material, a statement disclosing any additional purposes for which the company's management uses the non-GAAP financial measures. In addition, the new rules prohibit in filings with the SEC the inclusion of certain types and methods of presentation of non-GAAP financial measures and the use of certain exclusions or adjustments in non-GAAP financial measures.

Other Form 20-F requirements. In addition to the financial statements described above, selected financial data is required to be presented for the preceding five fiscal years and, if interim financial statements are included, should be updated for any such interim periods. This includes net sales or operating revenues, income from continuing operations, income from continuing operations per common share, total assets, long-term obligations and redeemable preferred stock, and cash dividends declared per common share. A company may decide to include more items or information for a longer period of time. In addition, a five-year history of exchange rates and dividends is required to be presented.

The SEC permits first-time foreign private issuers registering with the SEC to reconcile only the latest two fiscal years and any interim financial period shown, both in the financial statements and in the selected financial data. For first-time registrants using US GAAP financial statements, issuers only have to provide two-year rather than three-year income and cashflow statements if the financial statements are presented in accordance with US GAAP.[35]

Form 20-F also requires disclosure about market risk sensitive instruments such as derivative financial instruments, derivative commodity instruments and other financial instruments. Item 9A of Form 20-F requires disclosure outside the financial statements of both quantitative and qualitative information about the market risks inherent in such instruments if either: (a) the fair value of such instruments is material as at the end of the latest fiscal year; or (b) the potential near-term loss in future earnings, fair value or cash-flow from reasonably possible changes in market rates or prices would be material.

---

[35] Securities Act Release 7983 (June 2001).

The narrative qualitative disclosure would describe, to the extent material, the company's primary market risk exposures, how they are managed and whether they have changed in the most recently completed fiscal year or are expected to change in the future. The quantitative disclosure would be presented using, at the company's option, one of three approaches: (i) a table that includes information on the fair value of the instruments and expected cashflows for five years (or the contract terms and maturity dates from which future cashflows can be estimated); (ii) a sensitivity analysis that uses hypothetical changes in interest rates and prices to project potential losses in earnings, fair values or cashflows; or (iii) a VAR analysis that projects such potential losses based on the likelihood of different types of market movements.

Detailed information is also required in the footnotes to financial statements about the methods used to account for derivative transactions. Foreign private issuers providing reconciliation in accordance with Item 17 of Form 20-F would not be subject to this footnote disclosure requirement. However, they may have an independent obligation to provide information regarding their accounting policies for derivatives in their MD&A.

In addition to the disclosure specified in Form 20-F, the registration forms applicable to foreign private issuers also require disclosure about the terms of the offer based on the requirements in Regulation S-K. Regulation S-K sets forth the SEC's disclosure requirements applicable to the non-financial statement portions of filings under the Securities Act and Exchange Act for US companies. Non-US companies that do not qualify as foreign private issuers would generally provide disclosures as specified in Regulation S-K rather than Form 20-F.

Form 20-F incorporates in their entirety the international disclosure standards endorsed by IOSCO.[36] The IOSCO international disclosure standards replaced most of the non-financial statement disclosure requirements of Form 20-F and made conforming changes to registration statements for foreign private issuers under the Securities Act. The SEC believes that, as recast, Form 20-F will serve as "an 'international passport' to the world's capital markets", enabling issuers to use a single non-financial statement

---

[36] Securities Act Release 7637 (2nd February 1999).

disclosure document to raise capital and list their securities in multiple jurisdictions. While the IOSCO standards were substantively comparable to the old Form 20-F, the amendments do modify many requirements. As a result, issuers have found the amended Form 20-F to have some unanticipated changes. The amendments to Form 20-F did not affect market risk disclosures under Item 9A or Item 17 or 18 financial statement reconciliation requirements.

The amended Form 20-F requires expedited updating of financial statements included in a Securities Act registration statement. Thus, financial statements contained in a registration statement under the Securities Act or Exchange Act may be no older than 15 months at the time of the offer or listing (ie, the effective date of the registration statement) or, in the case of a foreign private issuer registering its IPO, 12 months at the time of filing unless the issuer is offering securities in the United States for the first time and is already public in its home country or the host country permits older financial statements to be used.

The SEC will waive the 12-month requirement if the issuer can represent that no jurisdiction outside the United States imposes the 12-month requirement and that the requirement would be impracticable or would impose undue hardship.

The issuer will be required to include interim financial statements (including US GAAP reconciliation) covering at least the first six months of the issuer's fiscal year if the date of a registration statement is more than nine months after the end of the issuer's last fiscal year. The interim financials may be unaudited. In addition to accelerating the updating of financial statements, Item 8 also expands the required balance sheets to three fiscal years, unless the registrant is not required to provide the earliest of the three years by a jurisdiction outside the United States.

Disclosure and liability – general issues
In addition to the specific requirements called for by the various forms, disclosure documents are required to include all additional material information necessary to make the statements therein not misleading even if such information is not required by a specific line item. Information is generally considered to be "material" if there is a substantial likelihood that a reasonable investor would attach importance to it in determining whether to purchase or sell

the security. Issuers are liable for a materially misleading registration statement unless they can show the investor knew that the information was wrong. Underwriters are also responsible for the adequacy of the disclosure in the registration statement. If the documents are found to be misleading, an underwriter will be liable to the purchasers of the securities unless the underwriter can show that, after reasonable investigation, the underwriter reasonably believed that the statements were true and that there were no material omissions. This is commonly referred to as the "due diligence defence" and is discussed in the following. Damages are typically measured as the difference between the amount paid for the security and the value of the security at the time the claim for damages is made. It is not generally necessary for the claiming investor to show that the damages were caused by the misstatement, although damages may be reduced if the issuer proves that the decline in value was caused by factors other than the misstatement.

A Securities Act registration statement is signed by the issuer, its principal executive, financial and accounting officers, a majority of its board of directors and its authorised representative in the United States. Those responsible for the registration statement – the issuer, its accountants, underwriters, named experts, directors (whether or not they have signed) and specified officers – are also responsible for any information in the Exchange Act periodic reports incorporated by reference (a fuller discussion of the liabilities to which such persons are subject is given in the following).

Today, the SEC has an additional mechanism to take enforcement action against the company officials that it finds responsible for inadequate disclosure. Under new officer certification rules enacted pursuant to Section 302 of SOX, a company's principal executive officer (CEO) and principal financial officer (CFO), or persons performing similar functions, are required to certify the disclosure in the company's annual report on Form 20-F.[37] (The form of the certification, which is set forth in the general instructions to Form 20-F, is reproduced in Chapter 4.) Any officer who provides a false certification is potentially subject to SEC action for violation of Section 13(a) or 15(d) of the Exchange Act or Sections 11 and 12(a)(2) of the Securities Act (in the event the report containing the certification is incorpo-

---

[37] Rules 13a-14 and 15d-14 under the Exchange Act.

rated by reference into a registration statement under the Securities Act) and to SEC and private actions for violation of Section 10(b) of the Exchange Act and Rule 10b-5 thereunder. The Section 302 certification requirements do not apply to reports on Form 6-K.

Reports on Form 20-F must also be accompanied by a second certification, pursuant to Section 906 of SOX, which amended the US criminal code.[38] With respect to each periodic report containing financial statements filed by a company with the SEC pursuant to Section 13(a) or 15(d) of the Exchange Act, the company's CEO and CFO must certify that the report fully complies with the requirements of the Exchange Act and that the information contained in the report fairly presents, in all material respects, the financial condition and results of operations of the company. Officers who knowingly provide a false certification are liable for a fine of up to US$1 million and/or a prison term of up to 10 years. The penalty is increased to US$5 million and/or 20 years for a wilful violation.

Although the law does not expressly exclude reports on Form 6-K, securities law practitioners have taken the position that Form 6-K should not be viewed as subject to the Section 906 certification requirement for several reasons. First, the law applies only to periodic reports "filed" under the Exchange Act and, unless specifically incorporated by reference into a registration statement, reports on Form 6-K are "furnished" or "submitted" to the SEC.[39] Second, Forms 6-K are not generally understood to be periodic reports for purposes of the Exchange Act. Finally, in light of the lack of clarity of the legislation and the arguments for asserting that Section 906 does not apply to Form 6-K reports, it is unlikely that the criminal authorities would choose to prosecute a failure to file a certification with Form 6-K unless and until the obligation is clarified by the appropriate governmental authorities. The SEC indicated that it does not intend to provide guidance with respect to compliance with Section 906, given that it is a criminal statute and administered by the US Attorney General.

Potential disclosure liability. In a case of considerable significance for registered non-US issuers, prior to SOX the SEC brought an

---

[38] 18 U.S.C. Section 1350.
[39] A document that is *filed* carries with it liability under Exchange Act Section 18. A document that is *furnished* does not.

administrative cease and desist action against Sony Corporation and the director and general manager of its Capital Market and Investor Relations Division for violations of the laws and regulations governing annual and interim reports filed with the SEC.[40] The SEC found that interim earnings press releases, filed under cover of Form 6-K as well as the MD&A contained in both Sony's annual report to shareholders and its Form 20-F annual report, "made inadequate disclosures about the nature and extent of Sony Pictures' net losses and their impact on the consolidated results Sony was reporting". The *Sony* action is significant, particularly in light of the limited number of cases the SEC has previously brought against reporting foreign private issuers and in its application of Rule 12b-20 under the Exchange Act to a registrant's home country disclosures furnished to the SEC on Form 6-K. SEC registrants are required by Exchange Act Rule 12b-20 to not only include all information expressly required in the report but also "such further material information, if any, as may be necessary to make the required statements, in the light of the circumstances under which they are made, not misleading" in any reports filed with the SEC.

Foreign private issuers are exempted from the quarterly and current reporting requirements applicable to domestic registrants. In place of such reports, these non-US registrants are required to furnish to the SEC under cover of Form 6-K material information made available to investors voluntarily or pursuant to home country or stock exchange rules. The *Sony* action makes clear, however, that notwithstanding the SEC's reliance on home country disclosures of non-US registrants to provide interim information to US investors, the SEC expects such reports to be as forthcoming about the company and its financial condition and results of operations as is required in the Forms 10-Q and 8-K reports of US issuers. Where it believes that this is not the case, as evidenced by the *Sony* action, the SEC is prepared to take enforcement action, not only against the company but also against those company officials it finds responsible for the inadequate disclosure.

In the cease and desist order against Sony, the SEC obtained a court-ordered US$1 million penalty from the company and required,

---

[40] Litigation Release 15832 (5th August 1998) (*Sony*).

among other things, specified disclosure procedures to be followed in the future. Sony was required to have its outside accountants examine its 1998 MD&A disclosures in both its annual report to shareholders and its Form 20-F annual report pursuant to the newly issued Statement on Auditing Standards No 86 – Amendment to Statement on Auditing Standards No 72, Letters for Underwriters and Certain Other Requesting Parties (March 1998).[41] In addition, Sony was required to implement procedures to assure that its chief financial officer is the principal official responsible for assuring the accuracy of Sony's public financial disclosures and their compliance with applicable legal and accounting requirements.

SEC Staff Accounting Bulletin 99 – SEC guidance on materiality
The SEC has published guidance with respect to assessing materiality in connection with the preparation of financial statements.[42] Public comments by the SEC Staff make clear the SEC's intention that the guidance applies to all disclosures by companies to the public. SEC Staff Accounting Bulletin 99 (SAB 99) was issued to address the burgeoning practice of earnings management, which former SEC Chairman Arthur Levitt criticised as "a misuse [of] the concept of materiality". It was prompted by Levitt's call for "guidance that emphasises the need to consider qualitative, not just quantitative, factors of earnings".

According to the SEC Staff, SAB 99 "does not create new standards or definitions for materiality". Rather, it develops existing concepts of materiality under the accounting literature (which calls for viewing the facts in the "surrounding circumstances) and US Supreme Court dicta (which speak of evaluating the "total mix" of information made available to investors), and reiterates the importance of "factual context" and "qualitative" factors in assessing the significance of an item to users of financial statements.

---

41 *See* Auditing Standards Board, SSAE No 8, "Management's Discussion and Analysis". In performing an SSAE 8 review, accountants are required to form an opinion or provide negative assurance with respect to whether: (a) the MD&A satisfies applicable SEC rules and regulations; (b) historical financials have been accurately derived in all material respects from the issuer's financial statements; and (c) the issuer's underlying information and assumptions provide a reasonable basis for the disclosure. A significant element of the accountant's review is consideration of management's methodology for the preparation of the MD&A and evaluation of the effectiveness of the issuer's internal controls.
42 SEC Staff Accounting Bulletin No 99 – Materiality, Release SAB 99 (12th August 1999).

Citing the customary "rule of thumb" that an item falling below a 5% threshold is not material in the absence of egregious circumstances, the SEC Staff clarified that, while such rules of thumb may have a place in initial assessments of materiality, "exclusive reliance on this or any age or numerical threshold has no basis in the accounting literature or the law".

To illustrate that a per cent test alone is not defensible, SAB 99 lists qualitative factors that could render material a quantitatively small misstatement of a financial statement item and asks whether the misstatement:

- arises from an item capable of precise measurement or whether it arises from an estimate and, if so, the degree of imprecision inherent in the estimate;
- masks a change in earnings or other trends;
- hides a failure to meet analysts' consensus expectations for the enterprise;
- changes a loss into income or vice versa;
- concerns a segment or other portion of the registrant's business that has been identified as playing a significant role in the registrant's operations or profitability;
- affects the registrant's compliance with regulatory requirements;
- affects the registrant's compliance with loan covenants or other contractual requirements;
- has the effect of increasing management's compensation – for example, by satisfying requirements for the award of bonuses or other forms of incentive compensation; or
- whether the misstatement involves concealment of an unlawful transaction.

A 2005 SEC enforcement action demonstrates the continued importance of qualitative materiality factors. In June 2005, the SEC filed a complaint against Huntington Bancshares, Inc., its CEO, former CFO and former controller.[43] The complaint alleged that Huntington's 2001 and 2002 financial statements used improper accounting to materially inflate earnings. In assessing the materiality of the alleged improper accounting practices, the SEC focused on qualitative materiality factors. The SEC quoted SAB 99 for the

---

43 Litigation Release 19243 (2nd June 2005).

proposition that qualitative factors may cause a misstatement of an item in a financial statement of a quantitatively small amount to be material. While the increases in reported operating earnings resulting from the accounting misstatement may have been quantitatively small (less than 5% in each year), they were material because they enabled Huntington to meet or exceed Wall Street analysts' earnings per share (EPS) expectations and to meet internal EPS targets that determined the bonuses of senior management, a factor specifically identified in SAB 99. Without admitting or denying the allegations in the complaint, Huntington consented to pay a penalty of US$7.5 million.[44]

Disclosure of activities in OFAC-sanctioned countries – enhanced scrutiny

In a May 2001 letter to a US Congressman, the then-acting Chair of the SEC outlined new SEC initiatives to enhance disclosures by SEC-registered foreign issuers of their business activities with countries or persons subject to US sanctions. While the letter was issued in response to concern raised by the Congressman with respect to business activities in Sudan, the SEC's response letter takes issue with foreign issuers who do business with governments, entities or individuals subject to US economic sanctions administered by the United States Treasury Department's Office of Foreign Asset Control (OFAC).

The US federal securities laws are intended to protect investors by ensuring the availability of material information necessary to make informed investment decisions. The SEC's announcement compels foreign issuers to reconsider the scope of their disclosures. On the grounds that activity otherwise prohibited for US companies would be "significant to a reasonable investor's decision about whether to invest in that company", the SEC advised that its SEC Staff would:

❑ target for review all registration statements filed by foreign companies with material dealings in sanctioned countries;

---

[44] The CEO, former CFO and former controller agreed to disgorge bonuses, and pay pre-judgement interest and penalties in the amounts of US$667,609, US$415,215, and US$51,660, respectively. In addition, the controller consented to a suspension from appearing or practicing before the Commission for two years and the CFO consented to an undertaking that he will not act as an officer or director of a public company for five years.

- ❏ undertake a more detailed review of foreign companies' material business activities that would implicate US sanctions laws if undertaken by US persons and assure that investors are provided adequate disclosure about a company's business with or in such countries; and
- ❏ aim to increase sanctions-related enforcement by bringing to OFAC's attention disclosures implicating any of the sanctions programs.

Currently, OFAC oversees an extremely diverse and fragmented sanctions regime that spans various countries, programs and "specially designated nationals" (SDNs) and with whom US companies are prohibited from conducting business. (The sanctions do not apply to foreign companies.) Certain activities may be prohibited in one country but not another, even though, at some level, OFAC considers each to be a "sanctioned country". As of April 2005, OFAC-sanctioned countries included Afghanistan (Taliban ruled), Angola (UNITA), the Western Balkans, Burma, Cuba, Iran, Iraq, Liberia, Libya, North Korea, Sierra Leone, Sudan, Syria and Zimbabwe. Among the activities prohibited at that time were trade, investment, financial transactions and supporting public projects. In addition to the increased likelihood of SEC Staff review, the SEC's letter and attached memorandum from the Director of the Division of Corporation Finance, the SEC group responsible for review of filings, suggest that the SEC Staff may apply a broader view of materiality with respect to doing business with OFAC-sanctioned parties on the ground that a reasonable investor would likely find it significant. The Director undertook to have the SEC review Staff:

"seek information from foreign registrants about their material business in countries on OFAC's sanctions list and their business relationships with countries, governments or entities on those lists. This type of disclosure would make available to investors additional information about situations on which the proceeds of an offering could – however indirectly benefit countries, governments, or entities that, as a matter of US foreign policy, are off limits to US companies".

The Director also noted the potential need for such issuers to disclose material risks of US imposed sanctions as well as any material risk that "public opposition to the company would have a materially adverse effect on the operations of the company".

A disclosure may be as basic as general business relationships and projects that are material to the issuer, or as complex as how the proceeds of an offering could, however indirectly or remotely, benefit a "sanctioned country" or other entity subject to US economic sanctions.

Foreign issuers are advised to consider a number of important implications:

- foreign issuers should be prepared for enhanced scrutiny by OFAC, through its review of disclosures made in SEC filings, and by the SEC;
- notwithstanding the SEC's focus on financial materiality, proponents of the disclosure may argue that the phrase "material information" has been extended to include the politically sensitive activity of business dealings with sanctioned countries, and that, under this formulation, materiality should, in this context, include non-financial considerations;
- the new disclosure burden will likely have the practical effect of shifting the burden to foreign issuers to explain why a given business dealing is not material;
- foreign issuers' interpretation of OFAC's regulations will now be under significantly greater scrutiny by investment banks and others in the securities offering and registration process; historically, OFAC's determinations were made exclusively by a company and not second-guessed by anyone; and
- enhanced disclosure scrutiny may be a first step by lawmakers and interest groups seeking to expand the reach of US sanctions to include foreign companies subject to the reporting requirements of the Exchange Act, as is the case with the FCPA.

Disclosure of status as voluntary filer under the Exchange Act
The SEC is including a new box on the cover page of Forms 10-K and 20-F to be checked by an issuer if it is filing reports voluntarily. The box is for informational purposes only; an issuer's filing obligation will be unaffected by an incorrectly checked box. The disclosure is intended to make investors and other market participants aware that an issuer is a voluntary filer and may cease to file Exchange Act reports without notice at any time and for any reason. In addition, the new communications and procedural rules

will not treat voluntary filers as reporting issuers or seasoned issuers. Voluntary filers desiring treatment as reporting issuers are encouraged to register a class of their securities under the Exchange Act.

Preparation of the registration statement
Registration Statement
The preparation of a registration statement generally starts as soon as a decision is made to conduct a public offer. The preparation of the prospectus contained in a registration statement involves gathering information, both financial and non-financial, concerning the company and its operating environment. For a first-time issuer, an English language annual report or Euromarket offer circular, if any, can form a basis from which to start. In certain cases, particularly where there is a need to obtain US GAAP financial information audited in accordance with US GAAS, information gathering may take a considerable amount of time. For first-time issuers, it usually takes several months to prepare the registration statement. If a company has previously registered securities, preparation time will be much less.

Drafting a prospectus involves determining how to market the company's securities and ensuring that the information furnished to the SEC and to the market is full, fair and correct. For many companies, the SEC registration statement will also constitute the most comprehensive disclosure document about the company. Hence, the company's presentation of itself and its strategic position in its US prospectus will also be important to its home securities markets and its other constituencies, such as employees, customers and competitors. Certain parts of the prospectus are relatively straightforward due to their technical nature, such as the description of the securities and of the offer. Others are by their nature more judgmental, particularly the MD&A.

Shelf Registration
Preparation of the registration statement for a non-US company's IPO in the United States can take three to four months (or possibly longer) from the decision to proceed. Follow-on offers by the same company will benefit, of course, from the work that has gone before. To the extent the company becomes eligible to use Form

F-3,[45] which permits the incorporation by reference of much information from the company's Exchange Act filings, the time frame can be compressed to as little as one week depending on such factors as whether the SEC determines to review the filing and whether the managing underwriters determine to pre-market the issue. SEC review of a registration typically takes 30–45 days. The SEC has an informal policy of expediting reviews to accommodate non-US issuers' time schedules, particularly in the case of global offers. Even under optimal circumstances, a "traditional" registered offer, in the absence of shelf registration, necessitates the loss of some timing flexibility and, potentially, of windows of market opportunity. The 2005 Reforms, particularly the introduction of automatic shelf registration for well-known seasoned issuers and other shelf registration reforms (discussed below), are intended to increase efficiency and permit large issuers to access the market with minimal (or no) regulatory delays.

A non-US issuer eligible to use Form F-3 may use the shelf registration procedure under Securities Act Rule 415 to register a specified aggregate dollar amount of securities in advance and issue the registered securities from time to time thereafter (referred to as delayed shelf registration). This allows a company to take advantage of market opportunities to offer securities to the public at short notice. The company has considerable flexibility under this procedure as it does not have to specify in the registration statement the specific amount of each class of securities it will offer pursuant to the registration statement. Shelf registration reduces the lead time required for SEC-registered offers to near zero, at least in theory, by front-end loading the process of prospectus preparation as well as the review of such information by the SEC Staff. The shelf prospectus that is delivered to each purchaser comprises a "base" prospectus containing or incorporating by reference disclosures regarding the issuer, as well as a general plan (or alternative plans) of offer, and a "prospectus supplement", which contains information regarding the specific offer, including transaction terms. The base prospectus incorporates by reference the issuer's most current Exchange Act

---

45 Form F-3 eligibility for equity offers generally requires that the issuer have a public float of at least US$75 million, have been subject to the reporting requirements of the Exchange Act for at least 12 months prior to the filing, have filed a Form 20-F annual report and have timely filed its required Exchange Act filings.

annual report and other specified Form 6-K reports on an ongoing basis and in this fashion should remain up-to-date at all times.[46] The base prospectus is included in a registration statement that is declared effective by the SEC. The prospectus supplement containing transaction terms is prepared at the time of the offer and does not require prior review by the SEC. The amount of securities that may be shelf-registered is limited to an amount the issuer reasonably expects to offer and sell within two years of the registration statement's effective date. The SEC defers to the company's judgement in this regard. Securities remaining unsold on the shelf may continue to be offered and sold beyond the two-year period.[47]

The SEC introduced shelf registration in 1982. Although shelf registration was available for equity as well as debt securities from its inception, many issuers were initially uncomfortable registering large amounts of equity on a shelf basis for fear of the so-called "market overhang" perception – that is, that the market might discount the price of the issuer's outstanding stock for the dilution which would occur upon issuance of the shelf-registered securities. Since the early 1990s, the fear of market overhang appears to have dissipated somewhat and equity shelf "takedowns" have become somewhat more common. In 1992, the SEC introduced the concept of "universal shelves" (permitting the registration of a dollar-equivalent amount of securities without designating the specific form of such securities) and in 1994 extended the availability of universal shelves to non-US issuers. Universal shelves are still not available for secondary offers.

Currently, an issuer that wants to take full opportunity of shelf registration will have to file an annual report on Form 20-F early, by

---

[46] To the extent material developments occur after the issuer's most recent Exchange Act filing, such information may be included in the prospectus by means of a submission on Form 6-K, which can then be incorporated by reference in the Securities Act registration statement and base prospectus, or can be included in a "Recent Developments" section of the prospectus supplement, or both. Form 6-Ks are not automatically incorporated by reference into a Form F-2, F-3 or F-4 registration statement. The issuer has to incorporate specific Form 6-Ks into the registration statement.

[47] As the non-refundable filing fee is payable at the outset and is based on a percentage of the amount to be registered (currently 0.0001177 (US$117.70 per million) times the estimated maximum offer proceeds), it is in the issuer's economic self-interest to make a good faith estimate of the amount to be placed on the shelf. The rate is expected to decrease to 0.0001070 in October 2005 (US$107 per million).

the end of three months after the close of its fiscal year, to meet timing requirements for financial statements in the registration statement. If the annual report is not filed until due (six months after fiscal year-end), the shelf registration will not be usable until the Form 20-F is filed.

Revised Registration Process Under the 2005 Reforms
Due to enhanced requirements for Exchange Act reporting, the increased role of technology in disseminating information, and broader access to such information, the SEC has determined it appropriate to adopt initiatives to build on the current system but streamline the registration process for most categories of issuers. The new rules provide incremental improvements in the existing shelf registration system and, while modernising the registration process for all issuers, provide the greatest flexibility for well-known seasoned issuers.

The SEC has adopted several revisions to the registration process under Rule 415. The new rules will eliminate for shelf-eligible offerings, other than business combination and continuous offering transactions, the current requirement to register only that amount of securities an issuer intends to offer within the next two years. While issuers will be allowed to register any amount of securities, because of the open-ended nature of the automatic shelf registration statement, the new rules require issuers to file new shelf registration statements every three years. An automatic shelf registration statement will not be able to be used after three years. Issuers will be able to carry forward to the new shelf registration statement any unused securities and unused fees paid on the old shelf registration statement.

The modifications to Rule 415 also (i) expand the type of information that primary shelf-eligible issuers and automatic shelf issuers may omit at effectiveness from a base prospectus in delayed offerings and later include in a prospectus supplement, Exchange Act report incorporated by reference into the base prospectus, or a post-effective amendment; and (ii) eliminate at-the-market offering restrictions to permit seasoned issuers to conduct at-the-market offerings of equity securities without identifying an underwriter in their registration statement and without a volume limitation.

Automatic shelf registration for well-known seasoned issuers only

In addition to the changes to the shelf registration process discussed above, well-known seasoned issuers will be permitted to register unspecified amounts of different classes of securities on a Form F-3 registration statement that will become automatically effective upon filing. The automatic shelf registration statement can be used for all primary and secondary offerings except those in connection with business combination transactions or exchange offers.

A well-known seasoned issuer will have to evaluate its eligibility to use the automatic shelf procedures on the initial filing date and reassess its eligibility at the time of each updated prospectus required by Section 10(a)(3).

Because enhanced Exchange Act reporting is at the core of the SEC's recent rulemaking philosophy, the new rules establish an incentive for accelerated filers to resolve outstanding SEC Staff comments on their Exchange Act reports in a timely manner by requiring all accelerated filers to disclose, in their annual reports on 20-F, any unresolved SEC Staff comments received 180 days before the issuer's last fiscal year-end that the issuer believes are material. This could have the effect of causing well-known seasoned issuers to accede to Staff comments to avoid having to publicly disclose the substance of an unresolved comment.

Since the amount of securities covered by an automatically effective shelf registration statement will be an unspecified amount, the new rules provide that filing fees can be paid in advance or on a pay-as-you-go basis.

Automatically effective shelf registration statements and post-effective amendments thereto will become effective automatically upon filing, without SEC Staff review.

A well-known seasoned issuer will be permitted to register on an automatically effective shelf registration statement an unspecified amount of securities to be offered, without indicating whether the securities will be sold in primary offerings or secondary offerings on behalf of selling security holders.

A well-known seasoned issuer will be able to add new classes of securities or securities of an eligible subsidiary to an automatically effective shelf registration statement at any time before the sale of those securities.

Certain issuers are ineligible for well-known seasoned issuer status and, therefore, may not use automatic shelf registration. Known as ineligible issuers (defined in Rule 405), these issuers are, as of the relevant date of determination:[48]

❑ Reporting issuers who are not current[49] in their Exchange Act reports, *other than* reports required solely pursuant to certain Items under Form 8-K (which exclusion does not apply to foreign private issuers);
❑ Issuers who are or during the prior three years were or any of their predecessors were:
  – blank check companies;
  – shell companies (other than business combination related shell companies);
  – penny stock issuers;
  – limited partnerships offering and selling their securities other than through a firm commitment underwriting;
  – issuers who have filed for bankruptcy or insolvency during the past three years, except those that have filed an annual report with audited financial statements after emergence from bankruptcy;[50]

---

[48] Eligibility, in most cases, is not determined at the time of reliance on the new rules for each free writing prospectus, but rather at the commencement of an offering and will not result in a change of status during an offering. As adopted, eligibility determinations will be made: (i) if the offering is registered pursuant to Rule 415 (the shelf registration rule), the earliest time after the filing of the registration statement covering the offering at which the issuer, or in the case of an underwritten offering the issuer or another offering participant, makes a bona fide offer, including without limitation through the use of a free writing prospectus, in the offering; or (ii) otherwise at the time of filing of a registration statement covering the offering.

[49] Under the definition as adopted, an issuer must be current, but not necessarily timely, in its required filings under the Exchange Act for the past twelve months or such shorter period that the issuer is subject to the Exchange Act reporting requirements.

[50] Commenters were concerned that an involuntary bankruptcy disqualification could disadvantage issuers because a creditor could cause an issuer to be ineligible simply by filing an involuntary bankruptcy petition against the issuer. In response to commenters' concerns, the definition of "ineligible issuer" under Rule 415 provides that ineligibility based on an involuntary bankruptcy filing arises on the earlier of (i) 90 days after the date of filing of an involuntary petition (if the case was not earlier dismissed) or (ii) the conversion of the case to a voluntary proceeding under federal bankruptcy or state insolvency laws. As a result, issuers will not immediately be considered ineligible because an involuntary bankruptcy petition has been filed.

- issuers who have been or are the subject of refusal or stop orders under the Securities Act during the past three years, or are the subject of a pending proceeding under Securities Act Section 8 or Section 8A; or
- issuers who, or whose subsidiaries at the time they were subsidiaries of the issuer, have been convicted of any felony or misdemeanour described in certain provisions of the Exchange Act, have been found to have violated the anti-fraud provisions[51] of the federal securities laws, or have been made the subject of a judicial or administrative decree or order (including a settled claim or order) prohibiting certain conduct or activities regarding the anti-fraud provisions of the federal securities law during the past three years.

Dealing with the SEC
Accommodations for US issuers

Over time, the SEC has undertaken a number of initiatives to facilitate the entry of overseas companies into the US public securities markets. These efforts reflect the SEC policy of encouraging overseas companies' participation in the US capital markets. The SEC's goal is to provide US investors with the broadest possible range of investment opportunities, internationally as well as in the United States, and to enhance the attractiveness of the US securities markets. These initiatives have included:

❏ streamlining reconciliation requirements to allow first-time registrants to provide financial information on a US basis for only two years;
❏ allowing updating of financial statements generally on a home-country basis;
❏ the elimination of quarterly reports;
❏ exemptions from proxy rules, insider reporting and short-swing profit recovery provisions;

---

51 The Commission narrowed the class of disqualifying violations in response to commenters' concern that the disqualifying violations were too broad and should be limited to violations of the anti-fraud provisions, not any provision of the federal securities laws.

❏ aggregate executive compensation disclosure rather than individual disclosure, if permitted in an issuer's home country;
❏ permitting the use of international accounting standards for cashflow statements, operations in hyperinflationary economies and specific aspects of business combinations;
❏ in certain instances, confidential reviews of disclosure documents; and
❏ expedited review schedules to meet the needs of non-US companies.

In addition, the SEC has provided accommodations on a case-by-case basis to address a company's specific problems. While SOX does not contain any exemption for non-US issuers, and while the SEC is unwilling to compromise where investor protection is concerned, the SEC recognises that cross-border listings frequently require issuers to navigate duplicative or even contradictory regulations in different jurisdictions, which places an unnecessary burden on issuers and investors.

The SEC's rules relating to audit committees contain an exception for companies domiciled in these jurisdictions that would allow employees who are not officers of a company to sit on the audit committee. This enables the issuers with dual board systems to comply with both sets of law while ensuring that independent directors can communicate directly with auditors without management interference.

Other accommodations provided by the SEC in the wake of SOX include the following:

❏ an exemption for non-GAAP communications outside the United States, even where those communications reach the United States, so as not to interfere with the home country practices regarding how foreign companies communicate with investors in non-US markets;
❏ under SOX, all audit firms, including non-US audit firms, providing significant audit services for US-listed issuers, are required to be registered and inspected by the PCAOB. Due to potential conflicts with foreign privacy laws and blocking statutes, the PCAOB has modified the information required to be provided by foreign firms during the registration process. In

addition, the PCAOB is seeking to collaborate with counterparts in Europe and elsewhere in developing its oversight role vis-à-vis non-US audit firms; and

❑ an extension of the compliance date for the SEC rules adopted under Section 404 of SOX for non-US issuers by one year. Non-US issuers are required to include in their annual reports on Form 20-F: (i) a management report on their internal control over financial reporting; and (ii) an accompanying attestation report from their independent auditor beginning with their annual reports for fiscal years ending on or after 15th July 2006. For calendar-year companies, the reports will first be required to be included in annual reports for the year end 2006, due to be filed in 2007.

The SEC's sensitivity in this area is expected to continue.

SEC review – responding to SEC comments
Registration statements and Form 20-F annual reports filed with the SEC are subject to review and comment by the SEC Staff. The registration statements of all first-time filers are reviewed. Other filings are reviewed on a selective basis. The selection is based on a number of factors, including the extent to which features of the securities or the offer are unusual, recent developments affecting the issuer or its industry, the financial condition of the company or a change in the company's outside auditors. The decision as to whether a filing will be reviewed is left to the SEC review Staff who will generally inform an issuer within several days of filing whether or not the filing will be reviewed.

Registration statements are public when filed. To address non-US issuers' concerns about the review process, the SEC has allowed these companies to submit registration statements in draft form for review. The drafts are not public; this allows the company to respond to comments and make any necessary changes to the registration statement prior to its official public filing. The confidential submission to the SEC Staff of a draft registration statement does not start the waiting period, as discussed above. Marketing of the offer, therefore, could not begin until the official public filing. However, in 2001, the SEC Staff announced that it would no longer routinely provide confidential review of disclosure documents for reporting foreign private issuers. The change in review policy was simply announced in an outline published by the SEC Staff of the Division of Corporation Finance without explanation or solicitation of public comment. Now, except in unusual circumstances, the SEC Staff will no longer allow confidential treatment for foreign private issuers already public in the United States either by virtue of having registered a transaction under the Securities Act or having registered securities under the Exchange Act. Confidential treatment will generally only be available for an issuer's initial registration with the SEC. The SEC Staff indicated, however, that it would consider on a case-by-case basis whether home country practices warrant confidential review for issuers already public in the United States.

The review Staff in the SEC's Division of Corporation Finance is organised by industry, which helps develop SEC Staff expertise, and is comprised of attorneys, accountants and, to a lesser extent, financial analysts. The review is conducted to determine compliance with the disclosure requirements of the securities laws, including compliance of the financial statements with applicable accounting standards. The review is not an audit or verification of the truthfulness, completeness or accuracy of the information. The SEC does not assess or pass on the merits of the securities or the terms of the transaction. Under the US federal securities laws, it is the investor, not the government, who determines the merits of the investment.

If the SEC Staff believes that information is incomplete, unclear or not in compliance with the disclosure requirements, or has questions about the information presented, it will issue comments on the registration statement. The SEC Staff may also ask for supplemental information to help it evaluate the disclosures. The supplemental information may be provided on a private basis, but may lead to a request by the SEC Staff for additional disclosure in the registration statement. The issuer must respond satisfactorily to all of the SEC Staff's concerns before the SEC will declare the registration statement effective. The comments may require amendment of the document. Any such amendment must be filed with the SEC as a pre-effective amendment. Once the comments are resolved, the registration statement is ready to be declared effective. Pursuant to rules relating to acceleration of effectiveness, such effectiveness may take place on a day and at a time requested by the issuer.

Where there are difficult or novel legal or accounting questions, the SEC Staff encourages issuers to consult with them prior to making a filing. If deemed appropriate by the issuer, the SEC Staff will have a pre-filing meeting with the issuer and its advisers. These meetings are private and issuers are not committed to filing a registration statement to explore issues with the SEC Staff on a pre-filing basis.

The SEC Staff introduced a new policy in connection with its review of Securities Act and Exchange Act registrations involving non-US audit firms that are affiliated with US firms. The SEC Staff will now request confirmation that the US affiliated firm has been involved with the filing in accordance with internal policies of the US firm, as well as the identification of the US personnel involved. The SEC Staff expects these representations to be made in the initial transmittal letter sent with the registration statement.

Confidential treatment

A registration statement filed with the SEC is a public document. Historically, the SEC has permitted companies to request confidential treatment of certain information filed under the Securities Act and the Exchange Act where public disclosure of the information would result in competitive harm. Confidential treatment has commonly been sought for specific provisions of contracts. SEC rules require companies to file publicly all material contracts except for most contracts entered into in the ordinary course of business.

Most information for which confidential treatment is sought falls within the US Freedom of Information Act (FOIA) exemption that covers trade secrets and privileged or confidential commercial or financial information. The SEC typically grants confidential treatment with respect to contractual terms deemed by a company to be of particular sensitivity with respect to its competitive position, such as royalty payments, license fees, product specifications and product costs and pricing, provided such information has not otherwise been previously publicly disclosed, for example in a press release, the prospectus or another report publicly filed with the SEC, other governmental authority or stock exchange. In general, information that is required to be disclosed by a specific line item must be disclosed, even if it is confidential.

Requests for confidential treatment are typically submitted to the SEC in the form of a letter at the time the registration statement or report containing the exhibit is filed or the draft registration statement is submitted for review. The information for which confidential treatment is requested must be omitted from the registration statement and prospectus when filed; if it is mistakenly included in the public filing, the SEC may not be able to grant confidential treatment. The issuer must provide the omitted information privately to the SEC Staff as part of its confidential treatment request. SEC Staff Legal Bulletin No 1 (28th February 1997) states details on filing requests for confidential treatment.

Foreign issuers should contact the Office of International Corporate Finance at the SEC in advance of submitting draft registration statements and ensure that the documents are complete in all material respects at the time of first submission, unless special arrangements have been made in advance with the Office of International Corporate Finance.

While registration statements are public when filed, SEC Staff comment letters and filer responses were, until recently, only released by the SEC pursuant to individual requests under FOIA. However, in response to an increasing number of FOIA requests, and citing a desire to "expand the transparency of the comment process", the SEC announced that it will make available on its *website*, after 12th May 2005, the SEC Staff comment letters and filer responses made after 1st August 2004.[52]

SEC Staff comment letters and filer responses will not be released until at least 45 days after the completion of a staff review. The review period will be regarded as complete upon resolution of all issues relating to a filing review. For these purposes, a review will be regarded as complete even if the filer has agreed to make changes in a future filing, but has not yet done so.

More than ever, companies should give careful consideration to their responses to SEC comment letters. While companies are not permitted to seek confidential treatment of SEC Staff comment letters, they may request, where appropriate, that any sensitive information whose disclosure might result in competitive harm be kept confidential pursuant to Rule 83 of FOIA.

Where there is a Rule 83 request for confidential treatment, the SEC plans to make only the redacted versions of response letters (paper copy of the response letter that excludes the confidential

---

[52] *See* SEC, Confidential Treatment Procedure under Rule 83 and Press Release 2004–89 (24th June 2004).

information) available to the public. However, requests by the public for access to those portions of a response letter for which confidential treatment was requested may still be made under FOIA.

The SEC indicated it will begin asking all companies whose filings are chosen for review to make a representation in writing (a Tandy representation) that they will not use the SEC Staff comment process as a defence in securities-related litigation. In making such announcement, the SEC noted that neither the request by the SEC nor the representation by the company should be construed as confirming that there is or is not an inquiry or investigation involving the filer.

Liability and due diligence
Liability

If a Securities Act registration statement, when it becomes effective, contains an untrue statement of a material fact or omits to state a material fact required to be stated therein or necessary to make the statements therein not misleading, the issuer, any person who signs the registration statement (the chief executive, financial and accounting officers of the issuer and their authorised representatives in the United States), every director (whether or not they signed it), every underwriter of the offer and, as to such part, any accountant, engineer or other expert who has with his or her consent been named as having prepared or certified a part of the registration statement will be subject to civil liability under Section 11 of the Securities Act.

Each of these persons, other than the issuer, may avoid liability if he can prove that, after reasonable investigation, he had reasonable grounds to believe, and did believe, that the statements in the registration statement were true and that there was no omission to state a material fact required to be stated therein or necessary to make the statements therein not misleading. Further, to the extent that parts of the registration statement are certified by experts (other than such person), as to those parts he or she only needs to prove that he or she had no reasonable grounds to believe and did not believe that there was a misstatement or omission. Any defendant, including the issuer, may avoid liability by proving that the purchaser at the time of acquisition of the security knew of the untruth or omission.

An action under Section 11 can only be brought by persons who acquired securities covered by the registration statement, whether directly from the issuer or in the secondary market. The extent of the liability is, in general, the difference between the amount paid for the security (not exceeding the public offer price) and either (a) the market price of the security at the time the suit is brought or (b) the price at which the security was disposed of before the suit. Damages may be reduced to the extent that the defendant can show that the loss in value is caused by reasons other than the misstatement or omission.

In addition, under Section 12 of the Securities Act, a purchaser in a public offer may recover losses from any person who sold such purchaser the security by means of a prospectus or oral communication that included an untrue statement of a material fact or omitted to state a material fact necessary in order to make the statements therein, in light of the circumstances under which they were made, not misleading unless the seller can prove that he did not know, and in the exercise of reasonable care could not have known, of the untruth or omission. Under Section 12(a)(2), the purchaser's claim is against the seller of the security. "Seller" has been interpreted by the US courts more broadly than simply the person who passes title to the purchaser and would include a person who solicits the purchaser and is motivated at least in part by a desire to serve his non-financial interests or those of the securities owner. Liability is for rescission or for damages if the security is no longer owned. As in the case of Section 11 liability, the defendant may avoid liability by proving that the purchaser knew of the misstatement or omission. Likewise, damages may be reduced to the extent the defendant can show that the loss of value was caused by reasons other than the misstatement or omission.

Under Section 15 of the Securities Act, any person found to control a person liable under Section 11 or 12 is jointly and severally liable to the same extent as the controlled person unless the controlling person had no knowledge of or reasonable ground to believe in the existence of the facts by reason of which the liability of the controlled person is alleged to exist. The term "control" is defined in Rule 405 under the Securities Act as "the possession, direct or indirect, of the power to direct or cause the direction of the management and policies of a person, whether through ownership of voting securities, by contract, or otherwise".

Section 17(a) of the Securities Act prohibits the use of any device, scheme or artifice to defraud or to make a misleading statement in the sale of the securities. Section 17 claims are brought by the SEC, not private parties.

The Exchange Act also contains a broad anti-fraud liability provision, Section 10(b), which applies to the purchase or sale of securities. Rule 10b-5 thereunder states that "in connection with the purchase or sale of any security, it is unlawful for any person, directly or indirectly, to make any untrue statement of a material fact or to omit to state a material fact necessary in order to make the statements made, in light of the circumstances under which they were made, not misleading". Liability under Rule 10b-5 requires proof of "scienter" or knowledge of the statement's misleading nature on the part of the person making it, or at least a reckless disregard for its accuracy and completeness. This liability extends not only to documents filed with the SEC, but also to public statements made by a company, for example, in a press release.

A company is responsible for any public statement made by its directors, officers and others that the market can reasonably assume are speaking on behalf of the company. If the statements are materially incorrect or misleading, the company may be liable. Thus, for example, responses by a company spokesperson to press inquiry about a market rumour, such as a pending acquisition or possible profit warning, must be accurate unless the company chooses not to answer the inquiry. The SEC has indicated that a "no comment" answer is the same as silence and should not give rise to liability.[53]

In *Carnation*, the SEC made clear that there is no defence to liability based on the spokesmen's lack of knowledge of the true facts. Carnation Company entered into preliminary negotiations with Nestle, SA concerning a possible acquisition by Nestle of Carnation. During the course of the negotiations, rumours concerning the acquisition circulated in the market, resulting in unusual activity in the Carnation stock. In the midst of these negotiations, however, Carnation issued public statements denying the existence of the negotiations and denying knowledge of reasons for the unusual stock activity. In an investigative report alleging that certain of such

---

[53] *In the Matter of Carnation Company*, Exchange Act Release 22214 (8th July 1985) (*Carnation*).

public statements were false and misleading in violation of Section 10(b) of the Exchange Act and Rule 10b-5 thereunder, the SEC provided guidance regarding the disclosure requirements of Rule 10b-5:

❑ liability for fraudulent misrepresentation is "triggered whenever the issuer speaks, regardless of whether the issuer is trading in its securities or is otherwise required to disclose material facts";
❑ accuracy and completeness in disclosure whenever issuers make public statements is vital to the integrity of the marketplace; and
❑ "any person responsible" for a material misstatement "may be liable under the federal securities laws".

Thus, the SEC cautioned that it would take enforcement action against issuers who voluntarily comment on takeover rumours and unusual market activity in their stock, but do not include all material facts necessary to make the public comments not materially misleading. This would, for instance, preclude a company from stating falsely that it is not aware of any explanation for unusual market activity.

In 2000, the SEC sued E.ON, a German company with American Depositary Receipts (ADRs) listed on the NYSE, for misleading denials of merger negotiations.[54] The action involved misleading merger denials made by a German company, in compliance with German law, about a transaction that took place wholly within Germany. Emphasising that the US securities laws extend beyond US borders, the SEC stated that the action "reminds foreign issuers trading on US markets that they remain subject to [US] fraud laws even when speaking abroad" – see Chapter 8 for a detailed discussion of this case.

In taking its position, the SEC stated that the German company violated Rule 10b-5 by deliberately issuing materially false and misleading merger denials at a time when the merger negotiations were material. Certain of the denials were drafted in English for publications such as *The Wall Street Journal*, which published them in the United States. The SEC stated that, while it recognises that disclosure practices and laws regarding the existence of merger negotiations may differ among jurisdictions, there is no safe harbour

---

54 *In the matter of E.ON AG*, Exchange Act Release 43372 (28th September 2000).

for foreign issuers from violations of the anti-fraud provisions of the US securities laws if US jurisdictional requirements are met (as they were here, where the company had ADRs trading on a US exchange). In the SEC's view, misleading corporate statements serve to erode investor confidence in the market and "thereby reduce liquidity, to the detriment of investors and issuers alike".[55]

For securities law purposes, spokespersons include any person that investors and the market could reasonably believe spoke for the company, including executives, directors and employees. Company designation of a person as a spokesperson is not a prerequisite for liability.

Under the federal securities laws, a statement, while literally true, can still be found misleading and therefore violative of the law if it misleads an investor because it is a half-truth, or is deliberately confusing or important implications are not explained. Once a company makes a public statement, whether voluntary or compulsory, it has a duty under Section 10(b) and Rule 10b-5 thereunder to disclose sufficient information so that the statement is not "false or misleading or … so incomplete as to mislead". The Supreme Court gave this description of materiality in a proxy contest, a standard that has become applicable for general disclosure purposes.

An omitted fact is material if there is a substantial likelihood that a reasonable shareholder would consider it important in deciding how to vote. This standard does not require proof of a substantial likelihood that disclosure of the omitted fact would have caused the reasonable shareholder to change their vote. What the standard does contemplate is a showing of a substantial likelihood that, under all the circumstances, the omitted fact would have assumed actual significance in the deliberations of the reasonable shareholder. Put another way, there must be a substantial likelihood that the disclosure of the omitted fact would have been viewed by the reasonable investor as having significantly altered the "total mix" of information made available.[56]

In March 2005, the SEC issued an investigative report under the Exchange Act to highlight potential liability of issuers under the Exchange Act for false or misleading disclosures regarding material

---

55 See *Carnation* at 1030.
56 See *Northway*.

contractual provisions, such as representations, whether described in, or in agreements appended to, an SEC filing. The Titan Corporation entered into a merger agreement in September 2003, in which it made a representation that, to its knowledge, neither the company nor its subsidiaries, nor any director, officer, agent or employee had taken any action that would cause the company or any of its subsidiaries to be in violation of the Foreign Corrupt Practices Act. The proxy statement was filed with the SEC and sent to Titan's shareholders, and the merger agreement, containing the representation, was filed as an exhibit to the proxy statement. The SEC took the position that while the representation in the merger agreement was not made to Titan's shareholders, the inclusion of the representation in the proxy statement filed with the SEC constituted a disclosure to investors. The SEC further stated that while Titan properly disclosed the civil and criminal Foreign Corrupt Practices Act investigation in its proxy statement, "depending on the context in which the disclosure is made..., a reasonable investor could conclude [from reading the merger agreement] that the statements made in the representation describe the actual state of affairs and the information could be material".[57] The *Titan* case is discussed in more detail in Chapter 8.

If an agreement that contains a materially misleading representation (or other contractual provision) is filed with the SEC as an exhibit, is incorporated by reference into a filed document, or is summarised in a filed document, the filed document will itself be misleading unless the company discloses additional material information – such as material facts contradicting or qualifying the representation – necessary to make the disclosure of the representation not misleading. The failure to disclose such further additional material information, if negligent, would result in a violation of Exchange Act Section 14(a) and Rule 14a-9 and, if it involved scienter, a violation of Exchange Act Section 10(b) and Rule 10b-5.

Representations, typically considered matters of private contract, may now have implications beyond risk allocation between the parties, although the SEC Staff has said orally that *Titan* does not stand for the proposition that investors can always rely on representations in merger agreements. The SEC has warned that

---

[57] Exchange Act Release 51238 (1st March 2005).

general disclaimers regarding the material accuracy and completeness of disclosure may not be sufficient where there is material information contradictory to representations made. However, the SEC Staff has stated orally that it would not object to a general or specific cautionary statement to the effect that representations are not assertions of fact; the sufficiency of a disclaimer would depend on the facts and circumstances.

It is customary for the issuer to indemnify the underwriters against any liability arising from a misstatement in or omission from the registration statement or prospectus (other than a misstatement or omission with respect to certain limited information supplied by the underwriters regarding the plan of distribution of the securities and other underwriting matters). Some courts have found such contractual indemnity unenforceable in situations where the underwriters have failed to establish their due diligence defence, as discussed below. The SEC requires an undertaking or disclosure in the registration statement with respect to indemnification provisions.

Due diligence investigation
Section 11(c) of the Securities Act states that reasonable investigation and reasonable grounds for belief will be judged by the standard of reasonableness required of a prudent person in the management of their own property. The SEC has enumerated considerations that affect reasonableness, including the type of issuer, security, person and offer, and whether such person's reliance on officers and employees was justified in light of their duties.

The "reasonable investigation" referred to in Section 11 is known as a "due diligence" investigation. Due to its importance in defending the parties to an offer (other than the issuer) from liability, the due diligence investigation is a fundamental aspect of the offer process. A due diligence investigation is conducted by the lead underwriter or underwriters on behalf of the underwriting syndicate, by the underwriters' counsel, as the underwriters' agent, and by the issuer's counsel. Due diligence takes place throughout the entire registration process. There are no statutory guidelines regarding the conduct of a due diligence investigation; however, a practice has developed that includes certain standard procedures. In the course of the investigation, the parties meet with the issuer's senior management and may visit the issuer's main sites, speak with the issuer's principal customers and suppliers, and speak with the issuer's auditors. The drafting sessions at which the prospectus is discussed and revised by representatives of all parties are often used as a forum for discussion of substantive disclosure issues with appropriate company representatives. Counsel will conduct a corporate check, which involves a careful examination of the issuer's material contracts, relations with governmental authorities, reports from auditors and other experts, indebtedness and other major commitments, legal proceedings and minutes of meetings of shareholders, the board of directors and key committees. A corporate check is also likely to be conducted on any material subsidiary of the issuer.

Shelf registration has gone a long way to improving companies' timely access to the capital markets on a SEC-registered basis. On the other hand, shelf registration has raised investment banking concerns regarding the "gate-keeping" role of underwriters and other professionals with regard to their due diligence obligations for disclosure.[58] For example, an underwriter who has not participated in the preparation of incorporated Exchange Act reports may nevertheless be liable for misstatements in those documents when they form part of a registration statement for a US offer. There are real questions as to how an underwriter satisfies the "reasonable investigation" burden it must sustain in establishing its due diligence defence in the context of a shelf offer for which it has received only hours' notice.[59] While these concerns are no longer new, they have taken on a special urgency in the context of full-sized equity shelf takedowns, "bought" deals, "spot secondaries" and "overnight" deals.[60] The long-lived bull market of the 1990s impelled issuers and their underwriters to explore the outermost horizons of the shelf concept.

---

58 *See*, for example, the Report of the Advisory Committee on the Capital Formation and Regulatory Processes (24th July 1996) and Securities Act Release 7314 (25th July 1996).
59 *See* Rule 176 under the Securities Act.
60 A "bought" deal occurs when an underwriter commits to purchase the issuer's securities at a fixed price before any pre-marketing has occurred; the underwriter accepts the pricing risk without the benefit of market solicitations. A "spot secondary" and an "overnight deal" describe shelf takedowns on behalf of the issuer or selling shareholders conducted on little or no notice to the underwriter or the market. Such transactions are marketed nearly exclusively to institutions in large "blocks".

The underwriters normally receive additional support for their due diligence defence through letters provided by counsel and accountants. Counsel for both the issuer and the underwriters will normally be required to give a letter to the underwriters stating that their investigation has not revealed any material misstatements or omissions in the registration statement. These are commonly called "disclosure opinions" or "10b-5 opinions". Accountants will be expected to provide "comfort letters" regarding financial information contained in the prospectus.

The comfort letter provides "comfort" with respect to, *inter alia*, financial information in the registration statement that is not covered by the auditor's report included, or incorporated by reference, in the registration statement. It should be noted that an auditor's report, together with the financial statements certified by the report, constitutes part of the registration statement that has been "expertised". As to such expertised portions, an underwriter can establish a due diligence defence under Section 11 without the "reasonable investigation" required for other parts of the registration statement. Therefore, other things being equal, underwriters gain more protection by having a statement covered by the auditor's report than by the comfort letter.

Although it is not required under US securities law, a comfort letter is universally requested by underwriters as part of their due diligence. The accounting profession has adopted standards that provide for the conditions under which the letter may be delivered and the contents of a model comfort letter.

In a recent case having potentially far-reaching consequences for underwriter due diligence, a US federal district court issued a ruling denying summary judgement to the underwriters of WorldCom's 2000 and 2001 public debt offerings.[61] The case has been hailed as the most important due diligence decision in years. The decision makes clear that:

❏ financial statements covered by audit opinions qualify as "expertised" information; financial statements covered by comfort letters do not; comfort letters do not "expertise any portion of the registration statement that is otherwise non-expertised";

---

61 *In re WorldCom, Inc. Securities Litigation*, 346 F. Supp. 2d 628 (S.D.N.Y. 2004).

- while underwriters may rely on audit opinions incorporated into a registration statement for purposes of Section 11, they may not rely on unaudited financial information or comfort letters in presenting a due diligence defence; and
- underwriters' reliance on audited financial statements may not be blind – where "red flags" regarding the reliability of an audited financial statement emerge, mere reliance on an audit will not be sufficient to protect against Section 11 liability.

The underwriters contended that they were entitled to summary judgement on their affirmative defences of reliance and due diligence because they were entitled to rely on the accountant's audits and comfort letters. They argued that they had no duty to investigate the reliability of the accountants' audits or to make any inquiry regarding the accuracy of WorldCom's statement of its assets. The court denied the underwriters' motions for summary judgement and ordered that the matter proceed to trial. While the underwriters have since settled, the court's summary judgement decision raises issues as to the nature and extent of underwriters' due diligence obligations and how underwriters may appropriately satisfy their due diligence defence.

The court found that, in assessing the reasonableness of a due diligence investigation, the underwriters' receipt of a comfort letter is important evidence, but is not sufficient by itself to establish a due diligence defence. The court also noted that there were questions of fact as to whether the underwriters conducted a reasonable investigation, namely: (i) the cursory nature of their inquiries; (ii) their failure to go behind any of the almost formulaic answers given to questions; and (iii) their failure to inquire into issues prominent in their own internal evaluations of WorldCom's financial condition and in the financial press, in particular their own internal downgrades of WorldCom's credit rating and certain swap transactions they undertook to limit their credit exposure. Quoting a prominent due diligence case from the 1970s, the court stated: "[t]acit reliance on management assertions is unacceptable; the underwriters must play devil's advocate".[62] The court went on to say that, given the "enormity" of the offerings and the general

---

[62] *Feit v. Leasco Data Processing Equip. Corp.*, 332 F. Supp. 544, 582 (E.D.N.Y. 1971).

deterioration in WorldCom's financial situation, these were red flags that warranted a more probing investigation.

WorldCom also raises the question of whether due diligence can ever be adequate to satisfy an underwriter's due diligence obligation in rapidly executed offerings. The court noted that in December 1998, the SEC stated that it "expressly rejected the consideration of competitive timing and pressures when evaluating the reasonableness of an underwriter's investigation". Former SEC Chairman Donaldson also said recently: "The advent of shelf registration over twenty years ago, with time pressure issues akin to those facing market participants today, raised similar concerns regarding due diligence. ... But the basic principles continue to apply. How they apply may be a more nuanced question, especially for a well-known issuer and particularly so for one the underwriter regularly follows. In the end you must decide whether, in a compressed time frame, you have the ability to bring to bear your business, legal and financial knowledge of the issues and general acumen in order to conduct the inquiry into the issuer's business and prospects that the due-diligence defence demands – and that your accounts expect".[63]

The 2005 Reforms, which provide for more rapid execution of offerings by large seasoned issuers, do not provide any guidance on whether an underwriter's due diligence defence has been met in the context of these offerings. *WorldCom's* heightened due diligence standards may undermine the benefits of automatic shelf and cause less creditworthy issuers to continue to rely for certain offerings eg, high-yield debt and convertible securities, on the Rule 144A market.

Projections and other forward-looking information
Disclosure of forward-looking information, such as projections of earnings and other financial items, management plans and objectives and future economic performance, is recognised by the SEC as especially valuable to investors in making informed investment decisions and thus encouraged, but generally not required, to be disclosed. Despite its desirability and importance, companies and

---

[63] Speech by former Chairman William H. Donaldson: Remarks before the Bond Market Association, New York (20th April 2005), available at www.sec.gov/news/speech/spch042005whd.htm.

underwriters typically are reluctant to make such disclosure due to a significant risk of private securities fraud litigation if it turns out to be incorrect or misleading. The safe harbour for forward-looking information in Section 27A of the Securities Act added by the Private Securities Litigation Reform Act of 1995 is intended to encourage the voluntary disclosure of forward-looking information by protecting SEC-registered and reporting issuers from liability for forward-looking statements. The safe harbour protects the issuer if either: (a) the forward-looking statement is identified as such and is accompanied by meaningful cautionary statements identifying important factors that could cause actual results to differ materially from those projected; or (b) the plaintiff cannot prove that the person making the statement had actual knowledge that it was false or misleading (or, if made by a business entity, that the statement was made by or with the approval of an executive officer who had actual knowledge that it was false or misleading). The safe harbour applies to oral as well as written forward-looking statements. It enables companies to bring oral statements made by issuers and their officers, directors and employees, including those made at road shows and analysts' meetings, within the safe harbour if: (a) the statement is identified as such; (b) the statement includes caution that actual results could differ materially from those projected; and (c) reference is made to a "readily available" written document indicating the factors that could cause actual results to differ.

The safe harbour is not available for, *inter alia*, IPOs, financial statements or tender offers.

Marketing the offer: *websites*, publicity and road shows
As discussed above, US securities laws impose significant restrictions on publicity that conditions the market for a proposed registered offer. The US regulatory scheme differs from that of many jurisdictions outside the United States where the customary practice is to broadly disseminate publicity as a means of generating investor interest and where disseminating offer documents and other publicity about an offer through traditional means or, increasingly, through a company's *website* is not uncommon. This difference in practice presents heightened difficulties in global offers.

The difference in publicity practices between US and non-US issuers raises significant uncertainties as to how *website*s may be used for publicity purposes in the context of a global offer, particularly in light of the blurring of geographical boundaries by the Internet.

Publication of information on a *website*, if found to condition the market or offer for sale the securities covered by the registration statement, could constitute an offer or a non-conforming prospectus and would be subject to the same restrictions during the offer as any other written communication. Information on *website*s is viewed by the SEC as a written communication and thus subject to the same restrictions as any other written communication during the offer period. For these reasons, attention needs to be paid to all *website* communications during an offer.

While non-US issuers typically regard publication of information on their *website*s as conduct outside the United States, such publication may be viewed as a communication issued into the United States, rather than as offshore activity.

The SEC has published an interpretive release on the use of *website*s in connection with offshore sales of securities.[64] The Web Site Release outlines the SEC's views as to when *website* postings of offer or solicitation material are offers in the United States that must be registered under Section 5 of the Securities Act and when such postings would not be deemed to be activity taking place in the United States. However, the SEC specifically stated that the guidance principally applies to foreign private issuers. It does not apply when a non-US issuer is conducting a registered offering in the United States or to offerings by US issuers.

The basic principle underlying the SEC's interpretation is that *website* communications not targeted at the United States should be viewed as activity outside the United States. The guidance in the Web Site Release provides that an offshore Internet offer made by a non-US offeror would not be viewed by the SEC as targeted at the United States if:

❏ the *website* includes a prominent disclaimer making it clear that the offer is directed only to countries other than the United States;

---

[64] Securities Act Release 7516 (23rd March 1998) (Website Release).

❑ the offeror and underwriters implement procedures that are reasonably designed to guard against sales to US persons in the offshore offer; and
❑ the issuer is not engaged in a US-registered offering.

The adequacy of measures will depend on the facts and circumstances, and can be satisfied through different means, some of which are discussed in the Website Release.

Non-US issuers generally may rely on procedures to protect against sales to US persons and the use of disclosures to make clear that the offer is not being made in the United States. Even in the absence of sales in the United States, the SEC will take enforcement action whenever it believes that fraudulent or manipulative Internet activities have originated in the United States or placed US investors at risk.

If the non-US offeror is undertaking a private offer in the United States at the same time as it is conducting an offshore offer using an Internet solicitation, the SEC suggests that additional procedures should be implemented to protect against the Internet communications resulting in the solicitation of investors in the exempt offer. The offeror is urged to take steps to preclude persons responding to the offshore Internet offer from participating in the exempt private offer or to ensure that access to the posted offer materials is limited to viewers who first provide information indicating residence outside the United States. The Web Site Release makes clear, however, that "any investor solicited by the issuer or underwriter prior to or independent of the *website* posting could participate in the private offer, regardless of whether the investor may have viewed the posted offshore offer materials". These would allow participants in an exempt offer to rely on a procedure that simply assures that sales are only made to those they solicited directly.[65] The Internet posting should only relate to the offshore offer.

The SEC offers no guidance, only words of caution, to non-US offerors in connection with offers that include a registered US tranche.

The SEC suggests a need for stricter procedures for offers by US issuers due to their substantial contacts with the United States and

---

65 *See* Website Release, footnote 28.

the likelihood that their securities, even if initially offered and sold offshore, will flow back into the United States. These include password protections under which persons seeking access to the Internet offer would have to demonstrate that they are not US persons before being issued a password for the site.

Where a US-registered offer takes place concurrently with an unregistered offshore Internet offer, the SEC restricts the making of offers prior to the filing of the registration statement. Accordingly, to avoid gun-jumping concerns under Section 5, premature posting of offer information (beyond that permitted in accordance with the safe harbour of Rule 135), even if targeted exclusively at non-US persons, must not take place. However, the SEC offers little guidance as to the appropriate procedures that should be undertaken in this context.

If, despite the issuer's implementation of reasonable procedures, a US person circumvents such procedures and buys the securities, this would not, in and of itself, cause the SEC to consider the offer to be targeted at US persons as long as the issuer did not have reason to believe the buyer was a US person (although the specific offer and sale could still violate Section 5). However, frequent circumventions may cause the reasonableness of the procedures to be questioned. Nonetheless, the individual transaction may violate Section 5 and subject the issuer to liability.

In addition, precautions of the nature described above will not safeguard solicitations that appear by their content to be targeted at US persons; for example, if the solicitation includes a discussion of the US tax advantages of the investment, it is likely to be viewed as being targeted at the United States.

The SEC has provided interpretative guidance as to the application of the federal securities laws to Internet postings by foreign private issuers in connection with tender and exchange offers, business combinations and rights offers.[66] The guidance in the 1999 Internet Release imposes far stricter guidelines (eg, restricted access) for avoiding US jurisdiction in the case of tender and exchange offers or rights offerings.

Information posted on a *website*, whether in the context of an offer or otherwise, may be construed as a corporate communication

---

66 *See* Securities Act Release 7759 (22nd October 1999) (1999 Internet Release).

upon which the trading market may depend and, therefore, as to which a company may have potential liability. *Website* communications will be evaluated in this context whether or not they are intended for such purpose and whether they are related to product, marketing, business or financial information.

An offer on an issuer's *website* or hyperlinked to a third party's *website* from the issuer's *website* will be considered a written offer by the issuer and, unless exempt, will be a free writing prospectus subject to the conditions of Rule 433. The same is true of information contained on a third party *website* hyperlinked from the issuer's *website*. Hyperlinks from a third party *website* to an issuer's *website* may also be a free writing prospectus of the third party with regard to the issuer's securities, depending on the facts and circumstances.

Under the 2005 Reforms, any hyperlink contained within a written communication used to offer an issuer's securities, whether in the issuer's or any other offering participant's *website*, will be considered part of that written communication.

Companies are now being advised to put in place procedures while in registration to assure that no information that can be viewed as conditioning the market for their securities in violation of Section 5 is disseminated over their *website*s and that any information that is posted, particularly any information commenting on the offer, is consistent with the legal requirements described above. In general, companies should not establish a new *website* or materially expand the scope of an existing *website* during the pendency of an offer, particularly in the case of an IPO or unseasoned issuer. All *website* communications should be reviewed before being posted, dated, evaluated for continued accuracy and relevance, and removed or clearly achieved as they become stale or irrelevant. They should not contain hype regarding current or anticipated financial performance or any hyperlinks from a posted prospectus.

Under Rule 163A(a), issuers and their underwriters and dealers will be required to take all reasonable steps within their control to prevent redistribution or republication during the 30-day period prior to filing of a registration statement of communications that were posted at a point in time in which they could freely communicate. With the new safe harbour, such communications need not be removed from their *website*s (or from a third party *website* on their behalf) and will not, as a result of being posted, be treated as having been republished during such period.

Historical information relating to an issuer will not be considered a current offer of the issuer's securities and, therefore, will not be a free writing prospectus if that historical information is separately identified as such and located in a separate section of the issuer's *website* containing historical information, such as an archive. The use of that historical information will become a current offer if it is incorporated by reference into or otherwise included in a prospectus, or otherwise used or referred to (by hyperlink or otherwise) in connection with the offering.

While the new rules address particular situations in which information retained on a *website* will not be considered a free writing prospectus, other information located on or hyperlinked to a *website* might similarly not be considered a current offer of the issuer's securities and, therefore, not a free writing prospectus, where it can be demonstrated that the information was published previously. For example, certain information that, while not contained in a separate section of an issuer's *website*, is dated or otherwise identified as historical information and is not referred to in connection with the offering activities may not be a current offer, depending on the particular facts and circumstances.

In 2000, the SEC published its fourth interpretive release[67] addressing the securities law issues raised by the use of electronic media and offering clarifying guidance as to liability for hyperlinking. The EM Release makes clear that the envelope theory was intended to help issuers and financial intermediaries meet SEC delivery requirements and that the fact that information appears on the same menu or is hyperlinked to the same *website* on which a mandated disclosure document is posted does not in and of itself cause such information to be deemed part of the solicitation or offer, unless the hyperlink is contained in the mandated disclosure document itself.

The SEC provided guidance and suggested factors to be considered in determining when the principle of "adoption" (ie, explicit or implicit endorsement or approval of the information) should apply to hyperlinked information. These factors include: (a) the

---

67 *See* Securities Act Release 7856 (28th April 2000) (EM Release).

context of the hyperlink (mandated disclosure, offer to sell or hyperlinked information supporting or supported by statements of the issuer or intermediary); (b) the risk of confusion about the source of the information (through framing or inlining of information, or by not indicating when the reader is leaving one site and accessing information on another site); and (c) the selectivity of the hyperlinked information (hyperlinks used selectively depending on the specific information included on the third party's site).

The SEC also suggested precautions that issuers can take to avoid being considered to have adopted the hyperlinked information. Such precautions include: (i) having an intermediate screen that clearly and prominently indicates when the reader is leaving the issuer's or intermediary's *website* and that the information that follows is not the issuer's or the intermediary's, (ii) posting a clear and prominent disclaimer of responsibility for and endorsement of the hyperlinked information that precedes or accompanies access to the hyperlinked information (although the SEC has cautioned that disclaimers are not conclusive), and (iii) employing techniques that allow investors to view both the issuer's site and the hyperlinked site contemporaneously.

Research and the role of securities analysts
Research reports
Research reports by broker-dealers have been recognised by the SEC and the markets as contributing to the efficiency of the capital markets by synthesising and analysing information. However, they can be problematic for a company in registration. First, the distribution of research reports during an offer raises the risk that recipients will claim they relied on the research rather than on the prospectus in making an investment decision. This increases the risk of liability based on the report, in part because the research is not written with the same attention to liability concerns as the prospectus. Second, as communications that may be viewed as market conditioning, or written communications that may be viewed as prospectuses not complying with the statutory requirements of Section 10, research reports in connection with a proposed offer of securities represent a risk of violating the "gun-jumping" prohibitions and prospectus requirements of Section 5. Third, research reports represent a risk of violating the trading restrictions

of Regulation M under the Exchange Act as a prohibited inducement to purchase during a distribution. Finally, the publication of research reports in the United States could constitute an offer in the United States, which would be inconsistent with the offshore transaction requirement and the restrictions on directed selling efforts in Regulation S, depending on the facts and circumstances. Similarly, public distribution of research reports may raise publicity concerns that could preclude reliance on a private placement exemption or resales under Rule 144A.

Some of these risks may be reduced by the observance of a blackout period (during which the effect of the research may dissipate) for some time before and during the offer when distribution of research reports by syndicate members anywhere in the world would be prohibited. Although the practice of employing "blackout periods" lacks a statutory basis, it is used in a number of global offers.

The SEC has adopted three safe harbours under the Securities Act – Rules 137, 138 and 139 – to address the problems associated with the distribution of research reports in connection with registered offers. These rules apply both prior to and after the filing of the registration statement. Each contains specific conditions for reliance. Generally, Rules 137, 138, and 139 describe circumstances in which a broker or dealer may publish research constituting an offer around the time of a registered offering without violating the Section 5 prohibitions on pre-filing offers and impermissible prospectuses.

Also, Regulation M (discussed in the following and in detail in Chapter 7) permits reliance on Rules 138 and 139 during a distribution of securities – whether registered or exempt.

In international and global offers, securities are frequently offered in jurisdictions in which the customary practice is to broadly disseminate research as a means of generating investor interest. This difference in practices raises significant legal issues regarding the permissible extent of the distribution of research reports. In the event that the offer does not qualify for the SEC safe harbours, research is typically distributed on a limited basis outside the United States by non-US underwriters to non-US persons under procedures designed to protect against indirect distribution into the United States.

SEC 2005 Reforms for research
Recognizing the ongoing flow of information in the marketplace and acknowledging the benefits to investors provided by uninterrupted research and the recent regulatory reforms implemented to address abuses in the area (eg, the mandated structural separation between a firm's analysts and investment bankers and requirement to disclose potential conflicts of interests), the SEC has made measured revisions to the research safe harbour under Securities Act Rules 137, 138 and 139. The revisions will permit dissemination of research around the time of an offering under a broader range of circumstances. In each case, the expanded safe harbours will not be available for research relating to ineligible issuers.

The new rules define "research report" as a written communication that includes information, opinions, and recommendations with respect to securities of an issuer or an analysis of a security or an issue whether or not it provides information reasonably sufficient upon which to base an investment decision. Note that the definition of "research report" in Regulation AC requires that the research report contain information sufficient upon which to make an investment decision and does not cover information, opinions, and recommendations about an issuer or its securities. Under the new definition as adopted, it is possible that an industry report, for example, will constitute a research report, but fall outside the definition under Regulation AC.

Rule 137
Rule 137, which allows the publication of research by non-participating brokers or dealers in the regular course of business, has been expanded to cover non-reporting companies. Rule 137 will continue to be available only to brokers and dealers who are not participating in the registered offering of the issuer's securities; have not received compensation from the issuer, its affiliates, or participants in the securities distribution, among others, in connection with the research report; and publish or distribute the research report in the regular course of business. The SEC has clarified the compensation language in Rule 137 to provide that the prohibition on compensation applies to compensation for the particular research report.

Rule 138

Rule 138 permits a broker or dealer participating in a distribution of an issuer's common stock and similar securities to publish or distribute research that is confined to that issuer's fixed income securities, and vice versa, if it publishes or distributes that research in the regular course of its business.

Rule 138 has been expanded to cover all reporting companies that are current in their periodic Exchange Act reports on Form 10-K, 10-Q and 20-F at the time of reliance on the exemptions, rather than only issuers who are Form S-3 or Form F-3 eligible, as was previously the case. In response to commenters' suggestions, the Commission has also expanded Rule 138 as it applies to foreign private issuers to allow reliance on the safe harbour by broker-dealers publishing or distributing research reports on non-reporting foreign private issuers that either have had equity securities traded on a designated offshore market or have a US$700 million worldwide public float.[68]

The new rules eliminate the "reasonable regularity" requirement, but adds the condition that the broker or dealer have previously published or distributed research reports in the regular course of its business on the same type of securities that is the subject of the report. The Adopting Release clarifies that this condition does not mean that the broker or dealer must have a history of publishing research reports about the particular issuer or its securities. If a broker or dealer begins publishing research about a different type of security around the time of a public offering of an issuer's security and does not have a history of publishing research on those types of securities, the Commission is concerned that such publication or distribution might be a way to provide information about the publicly offered securities in order to circumvent the provisions of Section 5 and the newly adopted free writing rules.

Rule 139

Rule 139 permits a broker or dealer participating in a distribution of securities by a seasoned issuer or by certain non-reporting

---

[68] Prior to the reforms, Rule 138 required that a foreign private issuer's securities be traded on a designated offshore securities market for at least twelve months. Rule 138 has been amended to specify that this requirement relates to the issuer's equity securities. Also, because the reforms eliminate Forms S-2 and F-2, Rule 138 has been revised to eliminate the reference to those forms.

foreign private issuers to publish research concerning the issuer or any class of its securities, if that research is in a publication distributed with reasonable regularity in the normal course of its business. Rule 139 also provides a safe harbour for industry reports covering smaller seasoned issuers, if the broker or dealer complies with restrictions on the nature of the publication and the opinion or recommendation expressed in that publication.

While a research report published or distributed by a broker or dealer may not be considered an offer by the broker or dealer under Rule 139, an issuer hyperlinking to that research report would not be able to rely on Rule 139. Rather, the research report would be a free writing prospectus of the issuer and the conditions of proposed Rule 433, including the filing requirements, would have to be satisfied.

1. Issuer-Specific, Focused Reports – Rule 139(a)

Prior to the 2005 Reforms, the Rule conditioned eligibility for the safe harbour on the size of the issuer's public float, reporting history or, in the case of foreign private issuers, trading history on a designated offshore market (as defined in Regulation S), and on the investment banking firm's publication of such research in the normal course of business and with reasonable regularity. The eligibility requirements remain unchanged except, consistent with the amendments to Rule 138, they have been expanded to cover a broader category of non-reporting foreign private issuers[69] as well as certain majority owned subsidiaries of Form S-3 or Form F-3 eligible issuers.[70]

In a change from the proposal, the Commission has retained the requirement that a broker or dealer publish or distribute the research report in the regular course of its business, but has eliminated the requirement that the report be published with reasonable regularity. Nonetheless, the amended Rule requires that the broker or dealer must have distributed or published at least one research report about the issuer or its securities, or have distributed or

---

69 A non-reporting foreign private issuer must either have its equity securities be traded on a designated offshore securities market for at least twelve months or have a US$700 million worldwide public float.
70 The reforms change the existing eligibility standards for the use of Form S-3 and Form F-3 and allow majority-owned subsidiaries to use Form S-3 and Form F-3 under the same circumstances in which majority-owned subsidiaries may be well-known seasoned issuers.

published at least one such report following discontinuation of the coverage. This requirement is intended to ensure that the most important element of the "reasonable regularity" requirement is retained, namely that the report initiating (or re-initiating) coverage of an issuer not benefit from an exemption under Rule 139.

Amended Rule 139 does not require any minimum time period for the broker or dealer to have distributed or published research reports, only that the particular broker or dealer have initiated or re-initiated coverage. In addition, the amendment does not require that the previously published or distributed research report cover the same securities that are the subject of the registered offering.

2. *Industry Reports – Rule 139(b)*
Believing that there is little risk that a regularly issued industry report will be issued to condition the market for a security, the Commission has eliminated the requirement that an industry report not contain a more favourable recommendation than the one made in the last report published by the broker or dealer – a condition which can, effectively, control the recommendation being made and constrain the broker or dealer from publishing what may be a legitimate change in opinion. The Commission is not requiring that the research report include any prior recommendations regarding the issuer or its securities. However, the research respect will have to contain similar types of information about the issuer or its securities as contained in prior reports. As with current Rule 139(b), an industry research report could not cover non-reporting companies in registration, or voluntary filers.

The SEC has codified in its 2005 Reforms interpretive guidance with respect to the publication of research reports complying with the safe harbours under Rules 138 and 139 in the context of a Regulation S or Rule 144A offer. Brokers and dealers may publish and distribute research reports complying with Rule 138 or Rule 139 without such reports being deemed directed selling efforts for purposes of Regulation S, or being viewed as making an offer to non-QIBs in violation of the requirement under Rule 144A that offers as well as sales only be made to QIBs.

Regulation AC
Over the past few years, the integrity of research reports has come into question due to a number of highly publicised incidents

involving research analysts' conflicts of interest. To promote the integrity of research reports and investor confidence in the recommendations contained in those reports, the SEC adopted Regulation Analyst Certification (Regulation AC) in 2003.[71] Regulation AC requires certification by research analysts that the views and opinions they express in research reports and public appearances accurately reflect their personal views about the subject securities and issuers. Analysts would also have to disclose whether they received compensation for their specific recommendations or views. Broker-dealers would be required to make, keep and maintain records of research analyst certifications and disclosures in connection with public appearances.

Regulation AC contains a narrow exception for foreign persons that are located outside the United States and are not associated with a registered broker-dealer that prepares research on foreign securities and provides it to major US institutions in the United States. In these instances, the foreign person is excepted from the requirements of Regulation AC. In addition, in the case of a research analyst employed outside the United States by a foreign person located outside the United States, Regulation AC only applies to public appearances while the research analyst is physically present in the United States.

Regulation AC is similar to the SRO rules recently enacted by the United States, for example NASD and NYSE, to govern member broker-dealer communications and address research analysts' conflicts of interest. Regulation AC, however, imposes different requirements and is broader in its scope and application. Regulation AC applies to both debt and equity securities, while the SRO rules apply only to equity securities. Regulation AC applies to brokers, dealers and certain associated persons, which may also include investment advisers and others that prepare research reports, all of whom, in the SEC's view, should be subject to core standards of integrity, rather than only "associated persons of a member" (in the case of the SRO rules) or "associated persons of a registered broker or dealer" (in the case of SOX). However, while the certification requirements of Regulation AC apply only to the research analyst or analysts primarily responsible for the content of a research

---

[71] Securities Act Release 8193 (20th February 2003).

report (ie, junior analysts are not required to certify), the SRO rules cover junior analysts because the concerns those provisions seek to address (eg, trading ahead of research reports) exist with respect to all analysts associated with a member firm and those persons who report to analysts.

Communications with analysts
Financial analysts are recognised as an important means by which the investment community can learn about a company. They have been viewed by the SEC as essential to facilitating the flow of information to the marketplace and facilitating the integrated disclosure system embodied in the Exchange Act. Since their views are among the total mix of information publicly available and considered by market professionals and investors, their initiatives have long been held to enhance market efficiency in pricing.

In general, it is permissible for companies to educate analysts by means of publicly disclosed historical information, or facts that are generally known, including information relating to market forces affecting their businesses. In the late 1990s, the SEC voiced strong concerns about selective disclosure of material non-public information – disclosure to some, but not to the public generally – stating its view that the practice is unethical and unfair to investors.

Indeed, former SEC Chairman Levitt urged the Division of Enforcement to bring actions based on such practices. While no cases were brought, reflecting the difficulty for the SEC in articulating a cause of action under then-current law, the SEC in December 1999 published for comment, and in August 2000 adopted, Regulation FD,[72] which expressly prohibits selective disclosure (discussed in the following). Selective disclosure also raises significant investor relations concerns and, in certain cases, may result in violations of insider trading laws.

Corporate communications with analysts also entail other risks. A company risks entangling itself with an analyst's report by some measure of participation in its preparation. In such a case, the company may be viewed as having adopted the statements in the report as its own and, thus, may be liable under Exchange Act Rule 10b-5 for any statements that are false or misleading, or may be

---

[72] Securities Act Release 7881 (15th August 2000).

found to have taken on a duty to update the information contained in the report.

Neither the SEC nor the courts have provided clear guidance as to what constitutes entanglement sufficient to justify attribution of an analyst's statements to a company. It is possible that a company could entangle itself: by making a statement to the analyst that is directly quoted in the report; by providing non-public information to an analyst that the analyst uses in the report; by distributing the report; by commenting on or editing the report; by approving the final version of the report; or by confirming, or guiding, an analyst's earnings estimate. Nonetheless, public companies do conduct at least some level of dialogue with the analyst community, and a number review and comment on drafts of an analyst's research report for factual accuracy. Companies may also be found to assume responsibility for analyst reports after their publication. Sending out a research report or hyperlinking to a report on a *website* may be viewed as endorsement of the report's content and thus legal adoption of the information.

Regulation FD
The SEC's adoption of Regulation FD appears to be having as significant a consequence on the communications practices of public companies in the United States as any recent regulatory action. Failure to comply with Regulation FD constitutes a reporting violation and subjects an issuer to an SEC enforcement action, which has caused great concern and changes in disclosure practices in the United States. While foreign private issuers and foreign governments are exempt from Regulation FD, the SEC has warned that selective disclosure of material, non-public information by a non-US issuer to a financial analyst or any other third party could constitute "tipping", which can give rise to a violation of the US federal insider trading laws. Also, selective disclosure may run afoul of public disclosure policies of the US exchanges on which an issuer's securities are listed.

Under Regulation FD, US public companies intentionally making selective, non-confidential disclosures of material, non-public information (oral or written) to specified securities market professionals and investors are required to contemporaneously announce such information publicly. Public disclosure may be made: (a) by means of filing or furnishing the information with the SEC; or (b) by another method or combination of methods reasonably designed to effect broad non-exclusionary distribution. Whether a particular disclosure method satisfies this standard will depend on the facts and circumstances, including the company's traditional practices for publicly disclosing information.

What has proved most troublesome is the SEC's view that earnings guidance, including non-public confirmation by the company of its own guidance or of the "street's" consensus estimates, is disclosure of material information that would violate Regulation FD if not made public.

The SEC could bring an administrative action seeking a cease-and-desist order, or a civil action seeking an injunction and/or civil monetary penalties. Since Regulation FD expressly states that the failure to make a disclosure required "solely" by Regulation FD does not create liability under Exchange Act Rule 10b-5, the issuer should not be subject to private liability for failure to comply with Regulation FD. The issuer would, however, remain open to potential liability for "tipping" and insider trading under Rule 10b-5 under a "duty to correct" or "duty to update" theory, or for entanglement or adoption. Issuers also face the risk of liability under Rule 10b-5 for Regulation FD disclosures that are misleading or because of misstatements or omissions.

Based on its discussion in the release adopting Regulation FD, the SEC seemed likely to take a far-reaching view of material, non-public information in assessing the need for enforcement action with respect to a public company's private conversations with institutional investors, market professionals and analysts, especially any communications that could be characterised as earnings guidance. The SEC also made clear that, in assessing a company's intent with regard to a selective disclosure, it would consider in any enforcement action whether the company has an appropriate policy and generally adheres to it. The SEC further cautioned the companies that providing earning guidance raises a substantial risk of liability under Regulation FD and must be handled strictly in accordance with both Regulation FD as well as the company's internal disclosure policies. With regard to assessing the materiality of a confirmation of earnings guidance, the SEC established that a company should consider whether the confirmation itself conveys any information beyond the original forecast and whether that additional information is material. The primary factors to be considered are:

❑ how much time has passed since the most recent public guidance was given;
❑ where the company is in its earning cycle; and
❑ whether anything important has happened in the interim between the initial estimate and the confirmation that would likely cause a reasonable investor to question the continued accuracy of the initial estimate.

Indeed, the SEC went on to demonstrate the far reach of Regulation FD in its first enforcement actions under the rule. In 2002, the SEC instituted three settled enforcement actions and issued one report of investigation under Regulation FD.[73] In determining the materiality of the information imparted selectively to the analysts in these cases, the SEC not only looked at the type of information disclosed, but also at the effect of the communication. In *Raytheon*, the SEC cited as support for its decision the fact that analysts responded by lowering their estimates after the company's CFO held one-on-one conference calls with them to discuss quarterly earnings per share guidance, despite the fact that only annual earnings per share guidance had been disclosed at an earlier investor conference. Similarly, in *Secure Computing*, the SEC noted the significant increase in the share price and trading volume of the company's stock that occurred on the same day as the company's CEO informed two portfolio managers and two institutional investors about a significant contract prior to the issuance of a press release announcing the contract.

More recently, in March 2005, the SEC settled its first Regulation FD enforcement action involving a reaffirmation of earnings by an issuer and issued its first Regulation FD administrative order against a director of investor relations.[74] In *Flowserve*, the CEO and director of investor relations met privately with analysts from four investment firms. In response to a question from an analyst about

---

[73] *In the Matter of Raytheon Company and Franklin A. Caine,* Exchange Act Release 46897 (25th November 2002); *In the Matter of Secure Computing Corporation and John McNulty;* Exchange Act Release 46895 (25th November 2002); *In the Matter of Siebel Systems, Inc.,* Exchange Act Release 46896 (25th November 2002); *Report of Investigation in the Matter of Motorola Inc.,* Exchange Act Release 46898 (25th November 2002).
[74] Litigation Release 19154 (24th March 2005).

Flowserve's earnings guidance for the year, the CEO reaffirmed the previously disclosed full-year earnings guidance. Contrary to Flowserve's disclosure policy that earnings guidance is effective at the date given and may only be updated in a public announcement, neither the CEO nor the director of investor relations mentioned this policy to the analysts; nor did the director of investor relations caution the analysts prior to the meeting that there were topics that should not be discussed with the CEO. The following day, an analyst who attended the meeting issued a report stating that Flowserve reaffirmed its earnings guidance. The next day, Flowserve's stock closed approximately 6% higher than on the previous day and the trading volume increased almost 50%. After the market closed that day, Flowserve filed a current report on Form 8-K stating the contents of the conversation with the analysts and, further, that the company was not comfortable at that point projecting more than marginal earnings improvement in 2003, unless markets started to improve. The day after filing the Form 8-K, Flowserve's stock closed at the same closing price as the day before and trading volume decreased by nearly 25%. The SEC cited as support for its allegation the fact that: (i) the Form 8-K was filed more than 53 hours after the conversation with the analysts and nearly 26 hours after the issuance of the analyst's report; (ii) Flowserve had violated its own disclosure policy, which mandated a specific response to questions regarding the company's level of "comfort" with its previously announced earnings guidance; and (iii) Flowserve, a calendar-year company, reaffirmed its guidance 42 days before the end of its fiscal year, and nearly a full month after its last public reaffirmation in its Form 10-Q. Without admitting or denying the SEC's allegations, Flowserve and its CEO consented the entry of a final judgement that required Flowserve to pay a US$350,000 civil penalty and its CEO to pay a US$50,000 civil penalty. Flowserve, its CEO and its director of investor relations also consented to the SEC's issuance of a cease-and-desist order.[75]

In light of these enforcement actions, it appears that the SEC is broadly defining the concept of material, non-public information – not limiting its enforcement actions to selective disclosure of

---

75 *In the Matter of Flowserve Corporation, C. Scott Greer, and Michael Conley*, Exchange Act Release 51427 (24th March 2005).

earnings guidance *per se*, and taking into account how analysts respond to the communication, as well as movements in stock price and trading volume. The SEC is also sending a message that investor-relations personnel have a serious compliance role.

2005 Amendments to Regulation FD

The 2005 Reforms amended the exemptions to Regulation FD in order to except the following communications, made in connection with a registered securities offering, from the range of prohibited selective disclosures of material, non-public information:

- a registration statement filed under the Securities Act, including the prospectus;
- a free writing prospectus used after filing of the registration statement or a communication falling within the exception to the definition of prospectus contained in clause (a) of Securities Act Section 2(a)(10);
- any other Section 10(b) prospectus;
- a notice permitted by Rule 135 or 134; or
- an oral communication made in connection with the registered securities offering after filing of the registration statement.

Communications made during or in connection with a registered offering and not contained in the list of exceptions above, for example, the publication of regularly released factual business information or regularly released forward-looking information or pre-filing communications, will continue to be subject to Regulation FD.

In addition, the new rules narrow the types of registered offerings eligible for the Regulation FD exclusion to (i) those involving capital formation for the account of the issuer and (ii) underwritten offerings that are both an issuer capital formation and a selling security holder offering. The existing exclusion for registered business combination transactions will remain.

Previously, Regulation FD applied to offerings of the types described in Rule 415(a)(1)(i) through (vi).[76] Rule 415(a)(1)(i)

---

[76] The types of offerings under these provisions of Rule 415 are delayed or continuous offerings that are: (1) securities to be offered or sold solely by or on behalf of selling security holders other than the issuer or its subsidiaries; (2) securities offered pursuant to dividend or interest reinvestment plans or an employee benefit plan of the issuer; (3) securities to be issued upon the exercise of outstanding options, warrants or rights; (4) securities to be issued upon conversion of other outstanding securities; (5) securities pledged as collateral; and (6) securities registered on Form F-6.

provides for offerings by selling security holders. The new rules amend Regulation FD to clarify that, as to such offerings (where the registered offering also includes a registered offering, whether or not underwritten, for capital formation purposes for the account of the issuer), Regulation FD does *not* apply unless the issuer's offering is included for the purpose of evading Regulation FD. This is intended to prevent *de minimis* participation by an issuer in what is otherwise entirely a selling security holder offering for the purpose of excluding communications in the offering from the application of Regulation FD.

For purposes of Regulation FD, communications made in reliance on the Rule 163A 30-day bright-line safe harbour will be deemed not made in connection with a registered securities offering and, thus, will be subject to Regulation FD.

Regulation M

Regulation M governs the trading of securities by participants where there is a "distribution" at least part of which occurs in the United States. It restricts issuers and "distribution participants" from bidding for, purchasing or inducing others to bid for or purchase securities during a distribution, subject to certain exceptions and conditions. Distributions can include exempt as well as registered offers.

Regulation M, which is discussed in detail in Chapter 7, became effective in 1997 and replaced the "Trading Practices Rules"[77] that had been criticised as an overly technical and overly inclusive effort to address potential market manipulation during the course of an offer – and in large part were in direct conflict with the legal requirements of some non-US jurisdictions. In general, Regulation M is more tailored to the realities of modern trading markets than its predecessor's rules, focusing restrictions on activities with greater potential for abuse, and removing restrictions from activities with little or no potential for abuse. In this context, it is important to keep in mind that Section 9 of the Exchange Act makes unlawful any activity, whether prohibited by Regulation M or not, which is intended to have, or has, the effect of market manipulation.

---

[77] Former Exchange Act Rules 10b-6, 10b-6A, 10b-7 and 10b-8.

Regulation M will be applied extra-territorially with respect to any SEC-registered offer. Thus, the inclusion of a publicly offered US tranche in any global offer will invoke the restrictions of Regulation M with respect to all aspects of the global offer. This may have important consequences for the distribution of research (which may be considered an "inducement" to bid for or purchase securities) and market-making activities by underwriters, as well as for purchases by the issuer and its affiliates.

Regulation M imposes different purchase restrictions on an issuer and selling shareholders, on the one hand, and distribution participants (underwriters and prospective underwriters, brokers, dealers and others who are participating or have agreed to participate in a distribution), on the other. An important exception to the trading restrictions is provided for large issuers with actively traded securities – the so-called "ADTV" exception. The ADTV exception is available to distribution participants but not to the issuer or its affiliates.[78] If Regulation M applies, the restrictions commence on the latest of: (a) one business day prior to pricing of securities with an ADTV of at least US$100,000 and a public float of at least US$25 million; (b) five business days prior to pricing of all other securities; and (c) the date on which the affected person becomes a distribution participant. The restrictions cease at the completion of each participant's distribution (generally, at pricing).

As was generally the case with its predecessor Trading Practices Rules, Regulation M does not apply to investment-grade non-convertible debt, preferred stock or asset-backed securities, or to exempt offers in the United States made exclusively to QIBs under Rule 144A.[79]

Stabilisation is permitted if conducted in accordance with Rule 104 of Regulation M. In general, Rule 104 is designed to assure that the issuer and distribution participants follow the independent market price. There are no general exemptions to Rule 104, except for offers made solely to QIBs under Rule 144A.

---

[78] Issuer-affiliates acting as a distribution participant may also avail themselves of the ADTV exception, provided that such distribution participant maintains written policies and procedures designed to prevent the flow of information to the financial services affiliate, and provided that certain other safeguards and restrictions are observed. See Rule 101 of Regulation M.

[79] This exception does not extend, however, to offers made to institutional accredited investors who are not QIBs.

The SEC has proposed to amend Regulation M and these amendments would change certain of the key figures noted above – in particular, the threshold for the ADTV test. The amendments are discussed in more detail in Chapter 7.

Continuous reporting under the Exchange Act – beneficial ownership reports

Periodic reports

A non-US issuer considering a global offer that includes an SEC-registered tranche must appreciate that the US disclosure obligations do not terminate with the offer. Becoming a public company in the United States[80] requires the non-US issuer to enter the continuous reporting system under the Exchange Act. Annual reports on Form 20-F, including financial statements reconciled to US GAAP, must be filed within six months after the end of each fiscal year. The information required annually on Form 20-F updates most of the information originally required in a Securities Act or Exchange Act registration statement.

Non-US issuers must submit interim reports on Form 6-K. Form 6-K requires information which is: (a) made public pursuant to home-country law; (b) filed with a non-US stock exchange and made public by such exchange; or (c) distributed or required to be distributed to the issuer's security holders. While Form 6-K requires the submission of information deemed "material", some issuers choose to file all of the above-described information on Form 6-K to avoid having to make case-by-case judgements. Interim financial statements contained in Form 6-K submissions need not be reconciled to US GAAP. However, to the extent the issuer may later want to incorporate such interim financial statements in a Securities Act registration statement relating to a public offer of equity or non-investment-grade debt or preferred securities, such interim financial statements may have to be so reconciled for inclusion in the registration statement. Specifically, if such

---

80 An issuer becomes a public company upon the effectiveness of a registration statement under the Securities Act or Exchange Act (debt or equity). *See* Exchange Act Section 15(d). An issuer's reporting obligations under the Exchange Act continue indefinitely until the issuer has fewer than 300 US security holders and has successfully withdrawn its listing from all national securities exchanges, at which time it may apply to cease its reporting obligations with the SEC. *See* Exchange Act Section 12(g)(4) and Rule 12d2–2(d) thereunder.

interim reports are necessary to meet the requirement that the financial statements included in the registration statement directly or through incorporation be of a date not more than 10 months from the sale, reconciliation will be required. In addition, Rule 3–19(f) of Regulation S-X may require reconciliation of certain other significant items included in the interim financial information. A number of non-US issuers reconcile their interim reports rather than wait to reconcile them in connection with a specific offer to allow them to take full advantage of the shelf registration process. Finally, all Exchange Act reports must be in the English language. Exhibits or other documents filed with such reports in a foreign language generally must be accompanied by an English summary, version or translation.[81]

In addition to the liabilities discussed above, for disclosure deficiencies made in connection with an offer, an issuer may have independent liability for its ongoing Exchange Act reports. Exchange Act Section 18(a) imposes liability for material misstatements or omissions contained in any "filed" Exchange Act report (such as the annual report on Form 20-F) on any person who makes or causes to be made such misstatements or omissions. (No such liability attaches to materials that are "furnished" to the SEC.) It is a defence to such liability to show that the statement was made in good faith and without knowledge that the statement was false or misleading. Information on Form 6-K is not deemed filed for the purposes of Section 18 unless specifically incorporated by reference into a filed document.

A designation of an issuer's security on NASDAQ, or a listing on the NYSE or AMEX, subjects the issuer to the additional reporting requirements of those markets and constitutes an independent predicate for being subject to the continuous reporting requirements of the Exchange Act.[82] Both the NYSE and NASD require listed companies to furnish security holders with annual reports containing financial statements. The NYSE's listing agreement generally requires that annual reports be furnished no later than three months after the end of the issuer's fiscal year. However, the NYSE

---

81 Exceptions to this requirement include offer materials for non-US offers for which no English translation, version or summary is otherwise available.
82 *See* Exchange Act Sections 12(b) and 12(g), NYSE Listed Company Manual section 103.02 and NASD Rule 4320(a).

typically agrees, on a case-by-case basis, to allow a longer period but not more than six months, if necessary, to parallel home country requirements. While the NYSE also requires listed companies to furnish quarterly financial reports to security holders, the NYSE will permit semi-annual reporting if such reporting is consistent with the law and practice of the issuer's home country. NASDAQ rules do not require quarterly reporting. NASDAQ rules require an annual report to be furnished a "reasonable period of time prior to the company's annual meeting of shareholders".[83] Both the NYSE and NASDAQ expect listed companies to promptly disclose any material information or developments concerning the issuer to the public.

Beneficial ownership reports
The Exchange Act requires that holders of more than 5% of a class of voting equity securities listed in the United States file reports of such ownership with the SEC. Beneficial ownership reports are intended to put both investors and the listed company's management on notice of possible changes in the control of a listed company. The obligation to file beneficial ownership reports applies whether or not the relevant share purchases are made in the United States. Therefore, if any of a company's shareholders at the time of a company's listing of its equity shares hold more than 5% of the equity shares of the company, such shareholders would be required to file a Schedule 13D or 13G, as discussed in the following, with the SEC.

Beneficial ownership reports are either "long form" (Schedule 13D) or "short form" (Schedule 13G). Schedule 13D is a detailed form that must be filed within 10 days after an acquisition of securities which increases the acquiror's holdings to greater than 5% of the outstanding shares. Schedule 13D must contain detailed information including, *inter alia*, the identity and background of the acquiror, the source of funding for the listed purchases and the acquiror's plans with respect to the listed company. Schedule 13D must be promptly amended whenever there is a material change in the information presented, including, *inter alia*, a change in ownership representing 1% or more of the class of listed securities.

---

83 NASD Rule 4460(b)(1).

Schedule 13G is a short form for reporting beneficial ownership requiring information only as to the identity of the shareholder and the number of shares beneficially owned. Schedule 13G may be used by institutional shareholders who own more than 5% of the class of listed shares and who acquired their shares in the ordinary course without any intent to influence the control of the listed company. Likewise, a holder of more than 5% of a class of equity securities at the time the securities are registered under the Exchange Act may use Schedule 13G; any increases in the position thereafter will require a filing on Schedule 13D. Schedule 13G must be amended annually within 45 days after the end of the calendar year to report any changes in the information provided. In addition, institutional investors using Schedule 13G must file amendments within 10 days after the end of the first month that such person's beneficial ownership exceeds 10% of a class of equity securities, and thereafter within 10 days of the end of any month in which such person's beneficial ownership increases or decreases by more than 5%.

The SEC permits "passive investors" beneficially owning less than 20% of a class of listed shares to report ownership on Schedule 13G (instead of Schedule 13D) under certain circumstances. If the greater-than-5% investor certifies that it has acquired and holds the securities without the purpose or effect of changing or influencing the control of the issuer and as long as the investor holds less than 20% of the class, it may now report ownership on Schedule 13G instead of Schedule 13D. Such investors, however, are subject to more timely filing requirements than would otherwise be the case for Schedule 13G. Initial filings on Schedule 13G for "passive investors" are due within 10 calendar days after the 5% threshold has been reached (instead of 45 calendar days after the calendar year-end), and thereafter "promptly" upon crossing the 10% threshold and again with every additional 5% change (up or down). Finally, upon crossing the 20% level, the "passive investor" will be required to file on Schedule 13D within 10 calendar days and may neither acquire more of that class of securities nor vote its securities until 10 calendar days after such Schedule 13D filing is made. Similarly, if an investor ceases to have a passive intent, it must file on Schedule 13D within 10 calendar days and is also subject to a 10 calendar-day "cooling-off period" before being able to vote its securities or make further purchases.

Submission of reports

Foreign private issuers are required to submit their disclosure documents, including periodic and beneficial ownership reports, to the SEC electronically via EDGAR. The SEC will make exceptions for (and permit paper filings of): (i) glossy annual reports to shareholders if the sole purpose of the Form 6-K is to furnish a copy to the SEC; and (ii) materials other than press releases that are being furnished to the SEC on Form 6-K, provided that they are not required to be, and have not been, distributed to security holders and, if they contain material information including disclosure of annual audited or interim consolidated financial results, they have already been filed with the SEC through EDGAR. Offering circulars and prospectuses pertaining solely to non-US offerings are not required to be filed on Form 6-K if the material information contained in them is otherwise included in a Form 6-K, Form 20-F or other filing.

NASD and exchange regulations of offers and listed companies

In addition to the SEC, the principal securities regulatory agencies in the United States are the NASD and the major national stock exchanges, or self regulatory organisations (SROs), each of which operates subject to SEC oversight and each of whose rules are subject to SEC approval. Non-US issuers must consider the application of the rules of the NASD and the exchanges not only when they make a global offer with an SEC-registered tranche, but also with respect to ongoing obligations.

NASD Regulation administers the NASD Conduct Rules that include the Free-Riding and Withholding Interpretation[84] and the Corporate Financing Rule.[85] The Free-Riding and Withholding Interpretation prohibits any member firm from failing to make a bona fide distribution of securities at the public offer price in any public offer of securities which trade at a premium to the public offer price in the secondary market. In other words, the NASD requires that member firms may not hold onto "hot" issues in a public offer for the member firms' own benefit; instead, they must permit the investing public the opportunity to purchase such securities and

---

[84] NASD Conduct Rule 2110–1.
[85] NASD Conduct Rule 2710.

enjoy the benefit of any price appreciation. The Interpretation further requires member firms participating in syndicate arrangements with non-member foreign broker-dealers to obtain their written agreement to comply with the Interpretation. Issuer-directed sales (eg, securities reserved for employees, customers or suppliers) are also subject to the Interpretation. The Corporate Financing Rule also sets forth the process by which new issues are submitted to and reviewed by the NASD Staff to determine the fairness of the underwriting arrangements.

Like the NASD, the national stock exchanges govern certain conduct of their member firms in addition to regulating trading on the exchanges themselves and promulgating criteria for listing. For example, the NYSE prohibits member firms from making recommendations (including the publication of research) on companies "controlled" by the member firms.[86]

Through their listing criteria and listing agreements, the exchanges and NASDAQ impose a variety of corporate governance requirements on listed companies, affecting such matters as board composition, shareholder approval for certain transactions, proxy procedures, information dissemination to shareholders and the public, and certain notices and disclosures to the exchanges themselves.

American Depositary Receipts

General

A foreign private issuer planning to enter the US securities markets must consider whether to offer its own securities directly to potential investors or to offer them through the establishment of an ADR programme. Most foreign private issuers raising equity capital in the United States have done so through the sale of shares represented by ADRs (also called ADSs). ADRs are transferable receipts representing ownership of shares in a non-US issuer. ADRs are most frequently issued for common (ordinary) or preferred (preference) shares of foreign issuers, although they can be used for debt securities. Each ADR may represent one share, a fraction of a share or multiple shares of the foreign issuer, in order to compensate for the difference in pricing levels between the US market and foreign markets.

---

[86] NYSE Rule 312(g).

ADRs are issued in registered form, normally by a US commercial bank acting as the depositary, against the deposit of the issuer's shares with a custodian bank usually in the issuer's home country (as agent for the depositary). The depositary is empowered to transfer ownership of the ADRs from investor to investor on its own record books, but continues to be the registered holder of the underlying securities. When requested by the holders, ADRs can be exchanged at any time for the underlying security.

Ownership of ADRs offers the US security holder a number of advantages over ownership of foreign shares. First, ADRs offer ease of transfer because the underlying securities need not be physically transferred to the United States (which also facilitates arbitrage between the US and non-US markets), since transfers are performed on the depositary's books. Second, the depositary collects dividends and converts them into US dollars for distribution to ADR holders. Finally, the depositary is also responsible for distributions other than cash dividends and may, for example, sell subscription rights for shares not registered in the United States and distribute the proceeds to ADR holders, thereby giving such holders the benefits of distributions such as rights offers, which they may not be entitled to receive directly. Essentially, investors in ADRs have substantially the same rights and privileges as owners of the underlying shares.

It should be emphasised that an ADR programme itself is only a bookkeeping system. Without a formal offer of an issuer's securities, the establishment of an ADR programme will not increase the equity of the issuer, nor will it necessarily increase the number of shareholders. What it will do is make it easier for investors in the United States to invest in the securities of the issuer.

Application of US securities laws
The SEC considers ADRs separate "securities" from the securities that they represent. Where ADRs represent newly issued shares or shares distributed by a statutory underwriter (as defined in the Securities Act), registration under the Securities Act is required unless an exemption, such as the private placement exemption, is available. Accordingly, a foreign private issuer making an IPO that includes a US tranche in an ADR form must generally arrange for the filing of a registration statement (on Form F-6) with the SEC for

the issuance of the ADRs and a registration statement (typically on Form F-1) with respect to the underlying securities. Once ADRs are registered, the foreign private issuer may have a reporting obligation if the requirements for exemption are not met.

For ADRs representing previously issued shares, limited disclosure is required under the Securities Act and the extent to which the foreign issuer is involved depends on whether the ADR programme is sponsored or unsponsored. While the sale of such ADRs does not produce additional capital for the foreign issuer, it does increase that company's visibility in the US market, which could be helpful if the issuer later seeks to raise capital in the United States through a registered public offer or private placement of shares.

There are two types of ADR programmes: (a) programmes initiated by an interested US broker-dealer or depositary bank for the securities of a Rule 12g3–2(b)-exempt issuer,[87] but otherwise without the cooperation of the issuer (unsponsored ADR programme); and (b) programmes initiated by or with the cooperation of the issuer itself (sponsored ADR programme).

Unsponsored ADR programme

An unsponsored ADR programme is initiated by US broker-dealers or depositary banks who conclude that there is sufficient market interest to warrant trading in the shares of a foreign issuer in the United States. The broker-dealer or bank then approaches the issuer to determine whether the issuer has any objection to the establishment of an unsponsored ADR programme. If there is no objection, the broker-dealer or bank asks the issuer to request an exemption from registration under the Exchange Act pursuant to Rule 12g3–2(b) and, after the establishment of such exemption, a

---

[87] Rule 12g3–2(b) under the Exchange Act provides an exemption from the registration requirements of the Exchange Act for foreign private issuers who would otherwise be subject to such registration requirements because its securities were held "of record" by more than 500 persons in the United States. To be eligible for such exemption, an issuer must "furnish" to the SEC certain information the issuer has made public pursuant to home-country law, or filed with any stock exchange on which its securities are listed, or distributed to shareholders. A key distinction between "furnishing" such information to and "filing" it with the SEC is that the furnishing of such information does not subject the issuer to potential liability under Section 18 of the Exchange Act for misleading statements in documents filed with the SEC under the Exchange Act. The issuer, nonetheless, retains potential liability under Rule 10b-5 and Section 17 of the Securities Act for such "furnished" information.

registration statement on Form F-6 (with the form of ADR attached) will be filed by the broker-dealer or bank with the SEC. The issuer is not involved or responsible. Form F-6 principally requires only a description of the ADRs. No issuer-related information is required.

Registration of ADRs on Form F-6 does not impose reporting obligations on an issuer. However, in order for the ADR depositary to use Form F-6 to register the ADRs, the issuer must either be a registered and reporting company under the Exchange Act or have obtained an exemption from registration under Rule 12g3–2(b) by agreeing to supply home-country reports in lieu of Exchange Act reports to the SEC on an ongoing basis. Once the F-6 registration statement is cleared by the SEC and becomes effective, shares of the issuer are deposited with the custodian and ADRs are issued in the United States. After an issuer has perfected a Rule 12g3–2(b) exemption, there is nothing to prevent more than one depositary from setting up unsponsored ADR programmes. However, multiple programmes can result in substantial costs in connection with the subsequent development of a sponsored ADR programme because of the requirement to consolidate the securities trading in the respective unsponsored ADR programmes.

In an unsponsored ADR programme, the depositary has no legal relationship with the issuer. Instead, the depositary's relationship is solely with the holder of the ADR and is recorded in the receipt itself. Depositaries thus exercise discretion as to whether to solicit proxies from ADR holders for matters submitted to a vote by shareholders and they do not vote shares without proxies. However, while issuers incur no expenses in connection with an unsponsored ADR programme (expenses are borne by the ADR holders), they have no control over the programme either.

If a foreign private issuer desires to list the ADRs on the NYSE or AMEX, or to have them quoted on NASDAQ, it must sponsor the ADR facility and also register the underlying securities under the Exchange Act. Thereafter, foreign private issuers must comply with the full ongoing reporting obligations of the Exchange Act.

Sponsored ADR programme
A sponsored ADR programme is formally initiated by the company itself and can, but need not, coincide with an IPO or listing in the

United States. The decision to initiate a programme and incur the costs of its administration turns on a number of factors, including, in particular, how the company wishes to treat its ADR holders. A sponsored ADR programme will enhance the dividend yield to ADR holders if the company pays certain fees otherwise subtracted by the depositary. In this regard, and in the absence of transfer fees payable by the holder, an ADR holder is treated equally with the company's other shareholders. In addition, when a company designates a single depositary, it has greater control over the market for its shares.

In establishing a sponsored ADR programme, the issuer designates a single depositary and enters into a standard-form deposit agreement with it. This forms a legal relationship between the issuer and the depositary, and dictates the services the depositary will offer ADR holders and the rights of the ADR holders. Some of the depositary's functions include the issuance of ADRs against the deposit of the underlying shares, the maintenance of transfer books, the forwarding of interim and annual reports and notices of meetings, and the payment of dividends. The ADR holder's rights include the right to collect dividends and the right to vote. In addition, ADR holders must be entitled to surrender their ADRs in exchange for the underlying shares at any time, subject to certain narrow regulatory exceptions.

The Form F-6 for a sponsored ADR programme is also relatively simple although, because of the company's cooperation in the programme, it requires the issuer, its principal officers and a majority of its board of directors to sign the registration statement. As with other Securities Act registration statements, officers or directors, as signatories to the Form F-6, are exposed to liability under the Securities Act for material misstatements or omissions.

If the issuer implements a sponsored ADR programme, the SEC requires the issuer to arrange for the unsponsored facilities to be terminated. This usually requires the issuer or the depositary of the sponsored facility to pay the cancellation or withdrawal fees incurred by the depositaries of the unsponsored facilities.

Form F-6 registration statements for both unsponsored and sponsored ADR programmes are reviewed by the SEC Staff and declared effective like any other registration statement. Only after "effectiveness" may the securities of the issuer be deposited with a custodian of the depositary and ADRs issued for trading in the United States.

It is important to note, however, that the establishment of a sponsored ADR programme will not subject a company to the provisions of SOX. SOX only applies to an issuer that has securities registered under Section 12 of the Exchange Act that is required to file reports under Section 15(d) of the Exchange Act or that files or has filed a registration statement that has not yet become effective under the Securities Act. First, as stated above, the registration of ADRs on Form F-6 does not impose any Exchange Act reporting obligations on a company as long as it has obtained, and is furnishing information to the SEC pursuant to, a Rule 12g3–2(b) exemption. In addition, a company that files a registration statement on Form F-6 would not be considered an "issuer" that has filed a registration statement that has not yet become effective because the F-6 only registers the ADRs, not the underlying securities, and the issuer of the ADRs for purposes of the Securities Act is the legal entity created by the agreement for the issuance of the ADRs.

Offers and sales to employees

Rule 701 permits companies not subject to the reporting requirements of the Exchange Act to offer and sell securities to their employees (including US employees of non-US issuers) without having to file a Securities Act registration statement, under the conditions described in the following. These conditions are principally that the offers and sales of securities are pursuant to a written compensatory benefit plan (such as an employee stock ownership plan (ESOP)) or pursuant to a written compensation contract, and that the dollar amount of securities offered or sold in any 12-month period in no event exceeds a specified amount.

Under Rule 701, the maximum amount of securities that may be sold in a year is the greatest of: (a) US$1 million; (b) 15% of total assets; or (c) 15% of outstanding shares. The SEC does not count offers in calculating the limit, but does require specific disclosure to be given to the employee investors if the aggregate sales price or amount of securities sold during any consecutive 12-month period exceeds US$5 million. The required disclosure would include certain financial information that need not be audited unless audited statements are available. The financial information must be reconciled to US GAAP. Non-reporting foreign private issuers are required to provide the same disclosure as non-reporting domestic issuers if sales under Rule 701 exceed US$5 million in a 12-month period.

In amending Rule 701 in 1999, the SEC stated that when, and if, it accepts international accounting standards or guidelines for filing and reporting purposes, it will further amend Rule 701 to allow these standards to satisfy the Rule's financial statement disclosure obligations for foreign private issuers. In any case, foreign private issuers making smaller offers may continue to use "home country" reports to satisfy the anti-fraud standards. However, those making offers in excess of US$5 million will have to provide the newly required disclosure, which includes unaudited financial statements reconciled in accordance with US GAAP.

Every issuer contemplating the use of employee stock options must consider the effects of the recent enforcement action brought against Google and its counsel.[88] The SEC charged Google and its general counsel with violating Securities Act Section 5 by failing to register more than US$80 million in employee stock options that it sold over a 12-month period prior to its IPO. Google was required to register the options or provide detailed financial information. Google did neither, and the repercussions included not only the enforcement action but also damage to Google's reputation.

Global offers
Syndicate structure – underwriting arrangements and documentation

A global offer by a non-US issuer may be divided along geographic lines into two (or possibly more) tranches, each with its own syndicate of underwriters and all led by a "global coordinator". Over the past several years, there has been a trend towards the use of a single global syndicate, a structure that is common in circumstances in which the US tranche is relatively small or in which there are few US underwriters and marketing activity in the United States is limited. This section addresses global offers in which the US tranche (which often includes Canada) is registered with the SEC. In such

---

[88] *In the Matter of Google, Inc. and David C. Drummond*, Securities Act Release 8523 (13th January 2005) (*Google*).

offers, the non-US tranches may or may not be fully registered with the SEC, depending on factors discussed below.

Offers are commonly underwritten by financial intermediaries – in the United States, broker-dealers that are NASD member firms. The marketing and underwriting process in the United States has evolved around the registration requirements of the Securities Act and is based on the concept of "selling securities" – as opposed to practices employed in other countries. In the United States, the underwriter typically commits to purchase the securities only at the end of the waiting period and sells the securities immediately following the pricing. During the waiting period, the underwriters solicit indications of interest from potential investors – a practice referred to as "book building". Sales may only be made after the registration statement is declared effective. This is in contrast to offers in other jurisdictions, like the traditional domestic UK offer which is premised on inviting subscriptions and where pricing occurs at the beginning of the offer process and the underwriters commit to purchase at that price and bear the market risk throughout the offer period. Typically, in such case, the underwriters lay off such risk through sub-underwritings to institutional investors – a practice that is not easily accommodated under US securities laws. Underwritings proceed in the United States on either of two bases – firm commitment or best efforts. On a best-efforts basis, more common in offers of smaller, newer companies, the underwriter is not committed to buy the security and the issuer remains at risk for the success of the offer.

Most firm-commitment underwritings include an over-allotment option (sometimes referred to as a "green shoe"), under which the company or the selling shareholders or both grant an option, typically for 30 days, to the underwriters to purchase additional shares on terms identical to those on which the original shares are sold for the purpose of covering syndicate short sales. NASD rules limit the over-allotment option to 15% of the number of securities in a firm-commitment offer. The option enables the underwriters to over-allot the shares they are purchasing from the company in order to create market demand and to satisfy this demand either through securities purchased in the market for syndicate account or through exercise of the over-allotment option.

Each regional syndicate enters into an underwriting agreement with the issuer, specifying the terms on which the securities will be purchased and sold. Each underwriting agreement will, in addition to establishing the quantity and purchase price of the securities to be purchased by the respective syndicate, provide for closing and settlement mechanics. Each underwriting agreement will also include: (a) representations by the issuer to the syndicate relating to the issuer's business and financial condition, the accuracy of the registration statement and prospectus, and certain other matters; (b) certain covenants of the issuer principally designed to facilitate the public offer; (c) indemnity of the underwriters by the issuer for liabilities arising from actual or alleged misstatements contained in the registration statement or prospectus; and (d) conditions to closing, including, importantly, the condition that each tranche of the global offer has simultaneously closed and certain "force majeure" provisions. The obligation of the underwriters to purchase the securities may be several or may be joint and several, depending on the applicable market. It is customary in many non-US offers for the obligation to be joint and several. In US-registered offers, the obligation is several and not joint.[89] Under the Securities Act, an underwriter is liable under Section 11 only to the extent of securities underwritten by it.

Each regional syndicate is governed by an agreement among underwriters (sometimes called an agreement among managers with respect to the non-US tranches). The agreement among underwriters appoints a regional lead manager and establishes a mechanism for allocating selling concessions (albeit in a remarkably oblique manner). The agreement among underwriters will give the regional lead manager limited powers of attorney to execute documents on behalf of the syndicate (such as the underwriting agreement and the agreement among syndicates), and generally to coordinate the activities of the syndicate. The regional lead manager may or may not be affiliated with the global coordinator.

All of the regional syndicates enter into an agreement among syndicates (sometimes called an intersyndicate agreement or an orderly marketing agreement) that establishes the geographic selling regions and the applicable selling restrictions, and

---

[89] Subject to a "step-up" provision that typically requires non-defaulting underwriters to purchase securities of a defaulting underwriter up to a specified amount (usually 10% of the entire tranche).

appoints the global coordinator. The global coordinator is typically given sole authority: to conduct stabilising activities on behalf of the global underwriters; to over-allot and to exercise the over-allotment (or green shoe) option (if any); and to permit sales between syndicates in response to global demand for the securities. The global coordinator will also have the authority to control publicity and research generated by any underwriter relating to the global offer or to the issuer. Finally, the global coordinator may receive additional compensation for its role as global coordinator in the form of a *praecipuum* or portion of the underwriting discount.

The intersyndicate agreement often requires members of one syndicate to contribute to losses incurred by members of other syndicates according to their respective underwriting commitments. The agreement may limit contribution to the amount underwritten and sold by the particular underwriter's syndicate or, where there is a single global syndicate, to the amount sold within the particular underwriter's selling region.

As stated above, when the US tranche of a global offer for a non-US issuer is SEC-registered, it may be feasible not to register a substantial portion of the offer conducted outside of the United States, thereby saving the issuer SEC registration fees and preserving the argument that Section 11 liability does not attach to such non-US tranches. To accomplish this result, the non-US tranches of the global offer must be conducted in accordance with Regulation S. The registration statement for the US tranche should make clear that it only covers offers and sales of securities in the global offer that are initially made in the United States, plus any additional amount necessary to cover resales back into the United States (flowback) within the restricted period of Regulation S. The additional amount registered to cover flowback is typically 10–15% of the non-US offer, although if there exists or is expected to develop a substantial US market for the issuer's securities, a larger proportion (up to 100%) should be registered. Even where the entire global offer is registered with the SEC because of flowback concerns, it may be possible to reduce Section 11 liability exposure with respect to the non-US sales by conducting offers and sales with respect to the non-US tranches in accordance with Regulation S and making clear that the registration statement does not extend to initial sales outside the United States.[90]

Registration and prospectus delivery requirements
In connection with global equity offers involving an SEC-registered tranche, the syndicate arrangements usually permit securities to be transferred from one regional syndicate to another in response to demand in the various markets. Accordingly, part of or the entire international offer is typically registered with the SEC to permit such shares to be sold in the United States.

While the offer restrictions described previously will apply to the public offer in the United States, they should not apply to any offer conducted outside the United States in accordance with Regulation S (*see* Chapter 3). However, US underwriters often prefer uniform compliance by the various syndicates with certain restrictions. The US underwriters may wish each syndicate to observe the Securities Act restrictions on the timing of offers and sales in connection with the international tranches so that the international underwriters do not gain a marketing advantage from earlier offers and sales, or from their use of written sales material that the US underwriters are not permitted to distribute. In addition, premature secondary market trading in one market could adversely affect the distribution as a whole.

Delivery of the non-US prospectus is permitted but not required to be made outside the United States. Each underwriter generally agrees in the underwriting agreement to establish its own delivery procedures in compliance with local law. However, the non-US prospectus will typically contain a legend to the effect that dealers effecting transactions in the United States may be required to deliver the US prospectus until a certain date, depending on the application of Rule 174 discussed above.

Rule 174, as currently in effect, sets an aftermarket delivery period of 25 days after effectiveness for IPOs that are listed on an exchange or quoted on NASDAQ. (The period is 40 or 90 days for other IPOs.) The 2005 Reforms amend Rule 174 to provide that during the aftermarket period, dealers can rely on Rule 172, the "access equals delivery" rule, to satisfy any aftermarket delivery obligations.

---

90 Corresponding differentiation should also be made in the offer document used for the Regulation S tranches.

Resales in the United States of registered international shares would require delivery of the US prospectus under certain circumstances.

Circumscribing Section 11 liability
In order to eliminate any rights that purchasers outside the United States might have under Section 11 of the Securities Act in respect of the international offer, often the non-US tranches are not registered for sale outside the United States except to the extent necessary to cover: (a) that portion of the offer expected to be offered and sold in the United States; and (b) an additional amount necessary to cover potential flowback into the United States – the amount of which will depend on the jurisdiction of the dominant market for the securities, the sizes of the respective offers and the extent to which the intersyndicate agreement provides for reallocation of securities in the non-US tranches into the US offer. The amount to be registered in the United States should be determined with the lead manager and global coordinator shortly before the registration statement becomes effective. In light of the risk that unregistered shares resold into the United States may taint an entire offer due to the inability to trace the specific shares sold in excess of the registered amount, it is inadvisable to under-register shares in the United States.

A number of changes may be made to the registration statement and prospectus to enhance protection from Section 11 liability. These changes represent a judgement that variations between the registration statements and offer documents for the US registered offer and non-US unregistered offer will highlight their distinct US legal consequences. The registration statement should indicate that the amount of shares registered also includes any shares initially offered or sold outside the United States that are thereafter sold or resold in the United States, and that offers and sales of shares outside the United States are being made pursuant to Regulation S and are not covered by the registration statement. A separate offer document should be used for any non-US offer. It may be called an "offer circular" to distinguish it from the US prospectus. To the extent that different offer circulars may be used in several countries simultaneously, it is critical to coordinate their drafting. Although the offer circular used with respect to an international tranche need not comply as to form with the requirements under the Securities Act, it is generally prudent, in order to reduce the risk of liability for all participants, that the disclosure be substantively identical to that contained in the US prospectus and that discrepancies be avoided.

To avoid discrepancies in substantive information that could give rise to disclosure liabilities, the non-US offer circular will be nearly identical to the prospectus filed with the registration statement. The principal exceptions would be: (a) the cover page and inside cover page in certain technical respects regarding SEC legends and syndicate territorial restrictions; (b) the plan of distribution or underwriting section; and (c) if necessary or useful, a non-US tax section. The key is to indicate that offers and sales outside the United States are being made pursuant to Regulation S and are not covered by the registration statement that is in effect for offers and sales in the United States. To emphasise that the offer circular is not a part of the registration statement, neither the offer circular nor those pages that differ from the prospectus would be filed with the registration statement. Eliminating the delivery of a US prospectus in the international transaction should also help minimise the possibility of Section 11 liability.

While these precautions do not eliminate the potential that Section 12(a)(2) and Rule 10b-5 claims will be available to purchasers, the exposure to US issuers and underwriters may be limited under Section 11 if there is no proof that non-US investors relied on the US prospectus.

3

Private Placements, Regulation S and Related Developments

Richard M Kosnik; Gene Kleinhendler

Jones Day; Gross, Kleinhendler, Hodak,
Halevy, Greenberg & Co.

In this chapter, we discuss certain exemptions from registration under the Securities Act for offers and sales of securities, outline the history, structure and applications of Regulation S and related rules, summarise Rule 144A, touch on resales of restricted securities and discuss the recent evolution of this regulatory framework. In particular, we focus on the manner in which the implementation of Regulation S and related rules represent an attempt by the SEC to adapt to the globalisation of the capital markets by allowing some flexibility to issuers wishing to conduct offers and sales of securities outside of the US. We also discuss how perceived abuses of Regulation S on the part of some issuers led the Commission to amend Regulation S in 1998, the effect of which is to diminish its usefulness to US domestic issuers legitimately applying Regulation S, but not to non-US issuers.

PRIVATE PLACEMENTS AND THE SECURITIES ACT

As discussed in Chapter 2, Section 5 of the Securities Act provides that no offer may be made to the public unless a registration statement has been filed with the SEC, and that no sales of securities may be made until the registration on file with the SEC has been declared effective. Section 3 of the Securities Act provides exemptions for certain types of securities, and Section 4 exempts certain transactions from registration.

In particular, issuers offer and sell securities without registration under the Securities Act and may do so by conducting private placements of those securities in reliance upon exemptions from registration afforded by Section 4(2) of the Securities Act, or by Regulation D there under.

Private placements made in reliance upon Section 4(2) of the Securities Act or Regulation D offer a number of advantages to issuers compared with offerings of securities registered under the Securities Act. First, the transaction costs associated with a private placement, such as accounting, legal and printing expenses, are generally lower than in a registered public offering. Second, the issuer in a private placement has greater control over the timing of the issuance of the securities than it would if it were subject to the SEC registration process, primarily due to the absence of a need for SEC staff review of the offering document. Third, unlike an issuer in a registered offering, a private placement issuer generally does not become subject to continuing obligation requirements under the Exchange Act by virtue of the offering. In addition, an issuer that is not subject to continuing obligations and that conducts a private placement will generally avoid becoming subject to the corporate governance and other requirements of SOX. Finally, the absence of specific SEC-mandated disclosure in a private placement affords more flexibility to issuers in preparing offering documentation. In particular, financial statements included in a private placement offering document are not required to be prepared in accordance with, or reconciled to, US GAAP.

As described in greater detail below, private placements made in reliance on Section 4(2) of the Securities Act or Regulation D also have a number of disadvantages. For example, private placements are subject to various limitations, such as restrictions relating to the number and nature of offerees and the manner in which the offering may be made, and the securities received in such private placements are "restricted securities" under Rule 144 under the Securities Act.

Section 3(b)
Section 3(b) of the Securities Act allows the Commission to promulgate rules and regulations adding particular classes of securities to the securities exempt under Section 3 of the Securities Act if the amount of the securities being sold is so small or the nature of the

offerings is so limited that it is not in the public interest or necessary for the protection of investors to subject the offer and sale of such securities to the registration requirements of the Securities Act. However, pursuant to Section 3(b), the Commission may not exempt offers and sales of securities where the aggregate offering price exceeds US$5 million. The Commission has adopted several small offering rules, including: rules providing exemptions for conditional small issuances of securities in which issuers may test the market for potential investor interest prior to the filing of required offering documents with the Commission and the delivery of those documents to investors (Regulation A); offers and sales of securities pursuant to certain compensatory benefit plans (Rule 701); and limited unregistered offers and sales of securities (Rules 504 and 505 of Regulation D).

Section 4(2)
Section 4(2) of the Securities Act provides that the registration provisions of Section 5 of the Securities Act shall not apply to "transactions by an issuer not involving any public offering". The Securities Act does not define the phrase "public offering", as a result, the conditions required to ensure an offer complies with Section 4(2) have developed out of a mixture of case law and market practice, which have grown and evolved since the adoption of Section 4(2). The determination as to whether a particular offer and sale of securities will qualify for the Section 4(2) exemption is fact sensitive. In making such a determination, counsel will consider a number of factors, each of which will be given in its own particular weight depending on the facts and circumstances. In addition, counsel will impose a number of conditions intended to ensure that the initial offer is made in a limited, private manner and that the restricted securities do not flow into the US public markets, each of which conditions will be tailored to the particular offer. The following is a list of several of these factors and conditions that may be considered in a private placement of securities.

Nature of security
Important factors are whether debt or equity securities are being offered and, importantly, whether the class of securities being

offered is traded in a public market in the United States or, if not, whether there is a significant amount of US market interest in those securities.

Form of security
It is important that holders of privately placed securities be aware of their "restricted" nature. Counsel will consider the degree to which the securities must be separately identifiable from other securities of the same class which may trade in the US public markets and the means of achieving separate identification, such as requiring issuance of securities in physical form, use of legends on physical certificates and separate CUSIP and ISIN numbers for restricted securities.

Method of offer
A Section 4(2) private placement must be made in a way that ensures that any offer of the securities is not made to the public. In general, the issuer and the distribution participants will be prohibited from broadly publishing the offer (e.g. no advertisements soliciting offers to purchase), any offer document will be legended and its distribution will be strictly limited, and only a limited number of potential purchasers who meet specified eligibility criteria may be contacted.

Nature of offerees
Offers and sales in private placements must be made to individuals and entities that have the capability of evaluating the particular investment and bearing the investment risks (see the discussion under Regulation D regarding non-accredited investors). It is not uncommon in US private placements, particularly in placements to non-QIBs, for investors to confirm in writing factors such as their status (e.g. QIB or institutional accredited investor), their ability to bear the risk of the investment and their agreement to abide by the applicable resale restrictions.

Number of offerees
Private offers may only be made to a limited number of offerees. The number of permitted offerees may vary greatly from offer to offer, depending on the particular facts and circumstances.

Available information
The offerees in a private placement must have access to or possess the information that would enable such offerees to make an informed investment decision. In general, this information includes financial statements, information concerning the issuer's business, financial condition, results of operations, property and management.

Resale restrictions
By their nature, restricted securities obtained by investors in private placements may not be freely resold to investors in the United States public markets. In general, resales of restricted securities will be allowed in the United States in limited circumstances (e.g. only to QIBs in accordance with Rule 144A) or outside the United States in accordance with Regulation S.

Regulation D
Regulation D provides a safe harbour from the registration requirements of the Securities Act for offers and sales of securities by issuers that comply with the provisions of the regulation. Offers of securities which comply with the provisions of Regulation D applicable to offers and sales of large amounts of securities (Rule 506) are deemed to be "transactions not involving any public offering within the meaning of Section 4(2) of the [Securities] Act". Rule 504 of Regulation D permits private placements of securities with a value of up to US$1 million. Rule 505 of Regulation D also permits private placements of securities, but with a limit of US$5 million on the aggregate offering price.

Rule 506 of Regulation D, which applies to offers and sales of securities with no limitation, imposes a number of conditions, the most important of which are the following.

- Manner of offer: the securities may not be offered or sold by means of any form of general solicitation or general advertising.
- Nature of purchasers: each purchaser which is not an accredited investor, either alone or with its "purchaser representative" (as defined in Regulation D), must be capable of evaluating the merits and risks of the investment. An "accredited investor" is defined in Regulation D to include certain financial institutions, trusts, partnerships, directors and executive officers of the issuer, and high net-worth individuals.

- Number of purchasers: there may be no more than 35 purchasers of the securities who are not accredited investors.
- Information requirement: if a sale is made to a non-accredited investor, information specified in the Rule must be furnished to the investor. The required information that is to be delivered is generally substantially the same information that the issuer would disclose in a registration statement filed with the Commission. In light of the anti-fraud provisions of the federal securities laws, issuers extending offers to both non-accredited and accredited investors generally provide accredited investors with the same information required to be made available to non-accredited investors.
- Resale restrictions: securities acquired in an offer made in reliance on Rule 506 of Regulation D are restricted securities. The issuer is required to exercise reasonable care to ensure that the purchasers of the securities are not underwriters (as defined in Section 2(11) of the Securities Act). Regulation D notes that reasonable care will be demonstrated if the issuer inquires as to whether the purchaser is acquiring the securities for itself or for other persons, and gives written disclosure that the securities have not been registered under the Securities Act and cannot be resold unless they are registered or an exemption from registration is available.

Accredited investors

"Accredited Investor" is defined in Regulation D Rule 501 as any one of the institutions enumerated in the rule and any individual who satisfies one of two "financial" tests. The enumerated institutions include banks, savings and loan associations, brokers and dealers, investment companies and business development companies. Under the "financial" tests individuals must have:

- an individual net worth, or joint net worth with that person's spouse, at the time of his purchase in excess of US$1 million; or
- an individual income in excess of US$200,000 in each of the two most recent years or joint income with that person's spouse in excess of US$300,000 in each of those years and a reasonable expectation of reaching the same income level in the current year.

Both non-US and US companies rely on the private placement exemptions afforded by Regulation D and Section 4(2) to offer and sell their securities without having to register those offers and sales with the SEC under Section 5 of the Securities Act. However, these exemptions do not work in isolation from requirements imposed by other US federal securities laws. For example, non-US investment companies offering their securities or units to US investors in Regulation D offerings or Section 4(2) private placements must coordinate their activities to ensure that they avail themselves of exemptions under the 1940 Act to avoid being classified as an investment company and having to register with the SEC under Section 7 of the 1940 Act. As discussed in more detail in Chapter 6, the safe harbour under Rule 506 of Regulation D is used by non-US investment companies seeking to avail themselves of the exemption provided by Section 3(c)(1) of the 1940 Act. However, use of Regulation D may be more limited when a non-US investment company seeks to rely on the exemption provided by Section 3(c)(7) of the 1940 Act, since that exemption requires that all investors be "qualified purchasers" – a standard that is higher than and different from the definition of accredited investor under Regulation D. In addition, any non-US issuer that wishes to use Regulation D must also ensure that the entity contacting potential US investors is a registered broker–dealer under the Exchange Act, or is undertaking activities that do not require such registration. In many cases, entities making such contacts attempt to structure their activities to comply with the safe harbour afforded by Exchange Act Rule 15a-6 (see Chapter 7 for more information).

REGULATION S

Issuers wishing to offer and sell securities without registration under the Securities Act may also do so outside the United States in transactions that do not require such registration. Offers and sales of securities that do not involve the use of US jurisdictional means are not subject to the application of the registration requirements of the Securities Act. However, as it is often unclear whether there have been US contacts in an offshore offer sufficient to result in the application of the registration requirements of the Securities Act, many issuers and distributors rely upon the Regulation S safe harbour in making offers and sales.

Genesis of Regulation S

International offers of debt and equity securities by non-US issuers involving concurrent unregistered offers outside the United States and private placements in the United States have grown enormously in the past 10 years. This increase in activity has resulted from the growing need for capital by non-US issuers operating in developed and developing markets as well as increased demand on the part of US institutional investors for securities of non-US issuers as those investors seek to diversify their portfolios and improve investment returns. This growth in cross-border capital formation has been supported by important regulatory developments, such as the adoption of Rule 144A[1] and Regulation S[2] in 1990.

The implementation of Regulation S reflects the adoption by the SEC of a "territorial" approach to the regulation of non-US securities offerings. The SEC recognised that uncertainties over the extraterritorial reach of the registration requirements of the Securities Act had led to the development of unduly complex procedures to assure that the Securities Act did not apply to certain offers. In addition, many non-US issuers preferred to avoid any contact with US markets and investors in order to prevent what they perceived to be the extraterritorial application of the US securities laws. The result of this was that US investors were often excluded, to their detriment, from a number of international securities offers.

In adopting Regulation S, the Commission recognised that, while the registration of securities offers is intended to protect investors (whether US or non-US nationals) purchasing securities in the US capital markets, it would not be appropriate to exercise its jurisdiction by requiring Securities Act registration in the case of non-US offers with limited involvement or contact with the United States. The Commission took a territorial approach to the registration requirements of Section 5 of the Securities Act when it adopted Regulation S. However, it clearly noted that its position was *not* that it did not have jurisdiction over the types of offers which would qualify for the Regulation S safe harbour, but rather that it was deciding, at that time, not to exercise that jurisdiction. In

---

1   Securities Act Release 6862 (23 April 1990).
2   *See* Securities Act Release 6863 (24 April 1990) and Rules 901 to 905, including the Preliminary Notes.

addition, while the SEC liberalised its position with respect to the application of the registration requirements of the Securities Act, it did not retreat from its much broader application of the anti-fraud provisions of the US federal securities laws.

While the adoption of Regulation S represented a departure from its earlier position, not surprisingly the Commission did not go so far as to adopt the doctrine of "mutual recognition" or "reciprocal regulation" (under which non-US issuers, when conducting securities offers in the United States, would be held to the registration and disclosure standards of their home jurisdictions), in light of the fact that the registration and disclosure standards in markets outside the United States in many cases vary dramatically from, and are much less stringent than, those of the US federal securities laws.

As discussed in greater detail below, in response to perceived abuses of Regulation S the SEC amended Regulation S in 1998 and retreated to some degree from its earlier territorial approach to the application of the registration requirements of the Securities Act to offers and sales of securities outside the United States.

Regulation S relies on a territorial approach, but as the US federal securities laws do not work in isolation from one another, in the totality of a transaction one must balance the territorial approach of Regulation S and the scope of the safe harbour exemption it provides against, for example, the broad definition of solicitation that is employed by the SEC's Division of Market Regulation in evaluating the scope of the Exchange Act, or the reach of the exemptions found in Sections 3(c)(1) and 3(c)(7) of the 1940 Act – or the registration and anti-fraud provisions of the Advisers Act.

Operation of Regulation S

Offers made outside the United States may or may not be subject to the registration requirements of the Securities Act, depending on a number of factors. Uncertainty with respect to the application of the registration statement requirements for offshore offers led the Commission to issue a release[3] in the 1960s, which provided guidance with respect to the application of the registration requirements to certain types of offshore transactions. While Release 4708 and numerous related no-action letters provided guidance to

---

3   Securities Act Release 4708 (9 July 1964) (Release 4708).

market participants, they did not address all types of transactions and, as a result, created uncertainty and discomfort for many market participants.

The Commission adopted Regulation S in order to address the concerns of market participants arising in the context of offshore transactions, and to replace Release 4708 and the substantial body of no-action letters that the Staff issued in this regard.

Regulation S provides a safe harbour with respect to the application of the registration requirements of Section 5 to offers and sales of securities conducted outside the United States. As mentioned above, Regulation S was intended to provide greater clarity to the application of the registration requirements of the Securities Act to offers and sales of securities outside the United States and, as a result, eliminate uncertainty regarding the application of the registration requirements of the Securities Act to certain offers made outside the United States which existed prior to the adoption of Regulation S. Regulation S was an important development from a US regulatory perspective because it represented an attempt by the Commission to deal with the increasing globalisation of the world's securities markets in a way which continued to provide for the protection of US investors without unnecessarily complicating or impeding the ability of issuers to raise capital outside the United States. With this regulation, the Commission demonstrated a willingness to modify its regulations to adapt to a global marketplace and ensure that it was not unnecessarily extending the reach of US securities regulation into non-US securities markets.

For the large part, Regulation S has been remarkably successful, particularly in allowing non-US issuers to conduct offers inside and outside the United States with greater certainty as to the application of the registration requirements of the Securities Act. This greater certainty has encouraged non-US issuers to include US investors in their global offers through the use of Rule 144A. In that regard, issuers and market participants have made extensive use of Regulation S in structuring primary and secondary issues of securities in markets inside and outside the US through private placements of Rule 144A-eligible "restricted securities" (*see* below). As a result, Regulation S, together with Rule 144A (which was intended to facilitate the trading of restricted securities among large institutional investors in the US market), have been important contributors

PRIVATE PLACEMENTS, REGULATION S AND RELATED DEVELOPMENTS

to the development of the global securities markets and the US private placement market, and have also contributed, indirectly, to encouraging non-US issuers to enter into the US public market.

Outline of Regulation S

The following is a description of Regulation S and some of its most important features, including the 1998 amendments. Among other items, as discussed in greater detail below, the 1998 amendments added new Rule 905, classifying equity securities of US issuers sold in reliance on Regulation S as restricted securities within the meaning of Rule 144 and lengthening the period during which sales of such securities are restricted from 40 days to one year. Apart from the tighter restrictions on equity securities of US issuers, these amendments have had relatively little effect on the basic requirements and conditions of Regulation S.

Threshold requirement

Regulation S (Securities Act Rules 901 to 905) is not available for "any transaction or series of transactions that, although in technical compliance with [Regulation S], is part of a plan or scheme to evade the registration provisions of the [Securities] Act".[4]

Preliminary Note 2 is an important and valuable part of Regulation S because it allows the Commission to provide objective criteria with respect to the safe harbour provisions, which gave the market some degree of certainty, without having to provide detailed exceptions or exclusions from the regulation, which might have diminished the utility of the regulation. Over the last few years, members of the Commission and the Staff have indicated their belief that Preliminary Note 2 may not be as effective a deterrent to impermissible transactions as originally intended, and the 1998 amendments significantly modify the application of the Regulation S safe harbour to offers and sales of equity securities by US issuers.

General Statement (Rule 901)

Rule 901 of Regulation S ("General Statement") provides that "[f]or the purposes only of [s]ection 5 of the Securities Act . . . the terms

---

[4] Regulation S, Preliminary Note 2.

"offer," "offer to sell," "sell," "sale," and "offer to buy" shall be deemed . . . not to include offers and sales that occur outside the United States".[5]

The General Statement may be relied upon by an issuer conducting an offer or a person reselling a security outside the United States but, given the lack of specificity with respect to what constitutes an offer or sale outside the US, most issuers and market participants prefer to rely upon the detailed safe harbours provided by Rule 903 (Issuer Safe Harbour) or Rule 904 (Resale Safe Harbour), each of which is discussed in greater detail below.

The general conditions

Two general conditions apply to each of the Issuer and Resale Safe Harbours.

Offshore transaction requirement. Rule 902(h) defines the term "offshore transaction". Under it, an offer or sale of securities is offshore and need not be SEC-registered if two conditions are satisfied. First, the offer is not made to a person in the United States. Second, at the time the buy order is originated, the buyer is outside the United States, or the seller and any person acting on its behalf reasonably believes that the buyer is outside the United States; or for purposes of: (a) the Issuer Safe Harbour – the transaction is executed in, on or through a physical trading floor of an established foreign securities exchange that is located outside the United States; or (b) the Resale Safe Harbour – the transaction is executed in, on or through the facilities of a designated offshore securities market[6] and neither the seller nor any person acting on its behalf knows that the transaction has been pre-arranged with a buyer in the United States.

---

5 "United States" is defined in Rule 902(l) as "[T]he United States of America, its territories and possessions, any State of the United States, and the District of Columbia".

6 Under Rule 902(b), the following are "designated offshore securities markets": the Eurobond market, as regulated by the International Securities Market Association; the European Association of Securities Dealers Automated Quotation; and the stock exchanges of Alberta, Alexandria, Amsterdam, Australia, Berlin, Bermuda, Euronext Brussels SA/NV, Cairo, Copenhagen, Frankfurt, Helsinki, Hong Kong, Ireland, Istanbul, Johannesburg, Korea, London, Luxembourg, Madrid, Mexico, Milan, Montreal, Oslo, Paris, Singapore, Stockholm, Tokyo, Toronto, Valencia, Vancouver, Warsaw and Zurich. The SEC is empowered under Rule 902 to designate other foreign securities exchanges or non-exchange markets as designated offshore securities markets, and has recently extended the designation to the stock exchanges of Prague, Taiwan and Vienna.

PRIVATE PLACEMENTS, REGULATION S AND RELATED DEVELOPMENTS

No directed selling efforts. In addition, each of the Issuer and Resale Safe Harbours require that no directed selling efforts be made in the United States by an issuer, distributor or any of their affiliates. The term "directed selling efforts" is defined in Rule 902(c)(1) to mean "any activity undertaken for the purpose of, or that could reasonably be expected to have the effect of, conditioning the market in the United States for any of the securities being offered in reliance on . . . Regulation S". The Rule provides exceptions for advertisements which are required to be published under US or foreign law (Rule 902(c)(3)(i)), tombstone advertisements, subject to certain conditions (Rule 902(c)(3)(iii)), visits of investors to facilities located in the United States (Rule 902(c)(3)(iv)), distribution in the United States of quotations through certain broker–dealer quotation systems (Rule 902(c)(3)(v)), publications of notices that comply with Rule 135 or Rule 135(c) (Rule 902(c)(3)(iv)) and providing US journalists with access to meetings held, and press-materials released, outside the United States in accordance with Rule 135(e) (Rule 902(c)(3)(vii)).

Issuer Safe Harbour (Rule 903)

The Issuer Safe Harbour establishes three categories of transactions involving offers and sales of securities. In addition to the two General Conditions that apply to each of the three categories, additional restrictions specific to each category are imposed. In general, the additional conditions imposed under Category 3 of the Issuer Safe Harbour are more burdensome than those imposed under Category 2, which in turn are more burdensome than those imposed under Category 1.

Category 1 (Rule 903(b)(1)). Category 1 requires compliance with the two General Conditions, but does not impose any additional requirements. Offers and sales of the following are eligible under Category 1:

❑ offers and sales of securities of a foreign issuer[7] that reasonably believes at the commencement of the offer there is no "substantial

---

7 Rule 902(e) defines "foreign issuer" to mean any issuer other than a domestic issuer (i.e. a "foreign government" or a "foreign private issuer" as defined in Rule 405 under the Securities Act). Excluded from this definition is an issuer which has more than 50% of its outstanding voting securities held of record either directly or through voting trust certificates or depositary receipts by residents of the US and: (a) the majority of the executive officers or

US market interest"[8] in the class of equity securities being offered or, in the case of debt securities, the debt securities of the issuer or, in the case of warrants and convertible securities, the securities to be purchased upon exercise, or the convertible or the underlying securities;
- ❏ securities offered and sold in an overseas directed offer;[9]
- ❏ securities backed by the full faith and credit of a foreign government; or
- ❏ securities offered and sold to employees of the issuer or its affiliates pursuant to an employee benefit plan established and administered in accordance with the law of a country other than the United States, and customary practices and documentation of such country.

Category 2 (Rule 903(b)(2)). Category 2 may be used for offers and sales of equity securities of non-US issuers which are reporting under the Exchange Act or, if the securities are debt securities of a reporting issuer, or of a non-reporting, non-US issuer. In addition to requiring compliance with the two General Conditions, Category 2 also requires the following:

- ❏ "offering restrictions"[10] must be implemented;

---

directors of the issuer are US citizens or residents; (b) more than 50% of the assets of the issuer are located in the United States; or (c) the business of the issuer is administered principally in the United States.

[8] Rule 902(j) sets forth the tests for equity and debt securities to be applied in determining whether there exists a "substantial US market interest". The test with respect to equity securities focuses upon the size of the US public markets for the class of the issuer's equity securities being offered and the volume of US trading compared with offshore trading. The test with respect to debt securities focuses upon the amount of debt held by US persons and the number of US security holders.

[9] Rule 903(b)(1)(ii) defines an "overseas directed offering" to include offers of securities directed into a single country other than the United States to the residents thereof and that is made in accordance with local laws, customary practices and documentation.

[10] Rule 902(g) sets forth a detailed definition of the phrase "offering restrictions". In general, the Regulation S offer restrictions require that: (a) distributors agree in writing that all offers and sales of securities prior to the end of the applicable distribution compliance period be made only in accordance with Regulation S or in registered or exempt transactions; and (b) all offer materials and documents used prior to the expiration of the applicable distribution compliance period state that the securities have not been registered under the Securities Act and may not be offered or sold in the United States or to a US person (other than distributors) other than in a transaction registered or exempt from registration under the Securities Act.

- ❏ the offer or sale, if made prior to the expiration of a 40-day "distribution compliance period",[11] may not be made to or for the account or benefit of a US person; and
- ❏ each distributor selling securities to a distributor, dealer or person receiving a selling concession, fee or other remuneration in respect of the sale of securities must notify the purchaser that it is subject to the same restrictions on offers and sales that apply to a distributor.

Category 3 (Rule 903(b)(3)). Category 3 is used for offers or sales of securities that are not covered by Categories 1 or 2. This category includes, for example, offers or sales of equity securities of reporting and non-reporting US issuers and equity securities of non-reporting foreign issuers where there is a substantial US market interest in those securities. In addition to compliance with the two General Conditions, Category 3 requires the following:

- ❏ "offering restrictions" are implemented;
- ❏ in the case of debt securities, a 40-day distribution compliance period is imposed and the securities are represented upon issuance by a temporary global security which is not exchangeable for definitive securities until the expiration of the 40-day distribution compliance period and, for persons other than distributors, only upon certification of beneficial ownership of the securities by a non-US person or a US person who purchased securities in a transaction that is exempt from registration under the Securities Act;
- ❏ in the case of equity securities, a one-year distribution compliance period and the following conditions are imposed:
  (a) the purchaser (other than a distributor) certifies that (i) it is not a US person and is not acquiring the securities for the account or benefit of a US person or (ii) it is a US person who

---

[11] Rule 902(f) defines "distribution compliance period" to mean a period that commences on the later of the date on which the securities were first offered to persons other than distributors in reliance on Regulation S or the date of closing of the offer and ends at the expiration of the applicable period specified in Rule 903(b)(2) or (3). All offers and sales by a distributor of an unsold allotment or subscription are deemed to be made during the distribution compliance period. Rule 902(f) imposes additional conditions relating to the calculation of the distribution compliance period for continuous offers of securities, including non-convertible debt securities and warrants.

purchased the securities in a transaction that is exempt from registration under the Securities Act;

(b) the purchaser (other than a distributor) agrees to resell the securities only in accordance with Regulation S or in a transaction that is registered or exempt from registration under the Securities Act;

(c) a legend is placed upon the securities of domestic issuers to the effect that transfer is prohibited except in accordance with Regulation S; and

(d) the issuer is required to refuse to register any transfer of securities that is not made in accordance with Regulation S; and

❑ each distributor selling securities to a distributor, dealer or person receiving a selling concession, fee or other remuneration prior to the expiration of the applicable distribution compliance period must notify the purchaser that it is subject to the same restrictions on offers and sales that apply to a distributor.

Resale Safe Harbour (Rule 904)

The Resale Safe Harbour is available for offers and sales of securities by any person other than the issuer, a distributor, any of their respective affiliates or any person acting on their behalf. An officer or director who is an affiliate for reasons other than solely as a result of holding such position may not make use of the Resale Safe Harbour. In addition to imposing the two General Conditions, the Resale Safe Harbour requires the following:

❑ if a dealer or person receiving a selling concession, fee or other remuneration in respect of the securities being offered or sold sells a security before the end of any applicable distribution compliance period, neither the seller nor any person acting on its behalf knows that the offeree or buyer is a US person and, if the seller or any person acting on its behalf knows that the purchaser is a dealer or a person receiving a selling concession, fee or other remuneration in respect of the securities being sold, the purchaser is notified that the securities may be offered and sold during the applicable distribution compliance period only in accordance with Regulation S or in a transaction that is registered or exempt from the registration requirements of the Securities Act;

PRIVATE PLACEMENTS, REGULATION S AND RELATED DEVELOPMENTS

❏ an officer or director permitted to rely upon the Resale Safe Harbour may not receive a selling concession, fee or other remuneration in connection with the offer or sale of a security, other than the usual and customary broker's commission that would be received by a person executing the transaction as agent.

The Regulation S Resale Safe Harbour has frequently been used in conjunction with Rule 144A and thereby contributed to improving cross-border liquidity for securities of non-US issuers offered in Regulation S and Rule 144A offers. Purchasers of Rule 144A securities can rely on the Resale Safe Harbour to resell restricted Rule 144A securities into the generally more liquid offshore home market for the securities. In addition, during any applicable Regulation S distribution compliance period, purchasers of Regulation S securities which may be limited in their ability to resell those securities into the US public markets may resell them to large institutional buyers in the United States using Rule 144A.

Before the 1998 Regulation S amendments, all restricted securities sold in a *bona fide* Resale Safe Harbour transaction were eligible for resale into the United States. Under the Regulation S amendments, however, equity securities of US issuers are not only subject to more extensive offer restrictions under Regulation S, but are now also classified as restricted securities under Rule 144. As a result, equity securities of US issuers sold in a *bona fide* Regulation S Issue Safe Harbour transaction may not be freely resold into the United States and resales of restricted equity securities of US issuers outside the United States in accordance with the Resale Safe Harbour will not change the restricted nature of those securities. Equity securities of non-US issuers and debt securities of US and non-US issuers were not affected by the Regulation S amendments and, as a result, they are treated, and may be resold, as was permitted by Regulation S prior to the amendments.

REGULATION S AND THE POTENTIAL FOR ABUSE
Regulation S flexibility

Despite the general acceptance and use of Regulation S, there are aspects of the regulation that, in practice, present difficulties for issuers, underwriters and their lawyers attempting to apply the regulation. While Regulation S has objective standards that apply to particular matters, it contains certain more subjective elements that are more difficult to apply in practice. For example, an issuer, an underwriter and other parties acting on their behalf cannot undertake activities which might "condition" the US market for the securities which are to be offered and sold outside the United States in accordance with Regulation S. It is difficult in certain circumstances to determine whether a particular activity might so condition the market. This issue is even more difficult where the activity in question may be an accepted or expected activity in the issuer's home jurisdiction.

Uncertainties such as these created difficulties for the SEC, which was faced with the challenge of attempting to draft a regulation that provides some degree of certainty with respect to its application, but is not so rigid as to inhibit legitimate activities in markets outside the United States. By necessity the Commission structured a degree of flexibility into Regulation S and since its adoption it has promulgated additional regulations directed at addressing various practical difficulties faced by issuers and intermediaries seeking to rely on the regulation. The flexibility built into Regulation S, however, has raised concerns and presented difficulties for the Commission.

Problem transactions

After the adoption of Regulation S in 1990, the Commission and its Staff attempted to assist issuers and market participants in addressing difficulties that they faced in making use of the regulation. However, at the same time the Commission became more concerned about the potential abuse of Regulation S by US reporting companies. The SEC and its Staff monitored the use of the regulation and expressed concern from time-to-time regarding perceived abuses of the regulation by market participants. In April 1994, a Congressional sub-committee requested that the SEC investigate these potential abuses and determine whether Regulation S should be eliminated or substantially modified. The developments and market activities that have raised concerns regarding the use of Regulation S have included the following.

Misunderstanding of the regulation

In some cases, market participants may simply be unclear about the requirements of Regulation S, particularly the 40-day distribution compliance period in Category 2. While securities sold in *bona fide* Regulation S transactions may be eligible, in theory, for resale into the US public markets on the day after the end of the distribution compliance period, some market participants may be marking the passage of time and losing sight of the fact that not only must the original offer and sale be made in a *bona fide* Regulation S offer, but each and every subsequent resale must have its own exemption from Securities Act registration. Preliminary Note 2 to Regulation S and the spirit of the Regulation must be carefully considered by purchasers of Regulation S securities contemplating resales of those securities into the United States.

Certain Category 2 offers
The most difficult Regulation S issues that have arisen and concerned the Commission and its Staff, particularly before the adoption of the 1998 amendments to Regulation S, have been in the context of Category 2 offers of equity securities by issuers reporting under the Exchange Act where those securities are listed or quoted, and trade primarily in the United States. When the primary trading market that is generally the most liquid and efficiently priced for securities offered in a Regulation S offer is the United States, there is an increased likelihood that resales of those securities will be made in the United States. This issue is made more difficult by the fact that the securities sold in the Regulation S offer may be sold at a discount to the price in the US public market (due to the distribution compliance period), which further increases the possibility of resales in the United States. In some transactions, the discount can be substantial (eg, between 20 and 40% less than the current public market price), significantly increasing the temptation for purchasers in a Regulation S offer to: (a) sell in the US public markets before the expiration of the distribution compliance period; (b) purchase Regulation S securities and enter into transactions that may lay off the economic risk prior to the end of the distribution compliance period; or (c) purchase securities in the Regulation S offer with the intent of selling in the US public markets after the end of the distribution compliance period. This was a particular concern of the Commission and Staff when Category 2 offers and sales of equity securities of reporting US issuers were subject to a 40-day restricted period rather than the current one-year distribution compliance period.

Short sales

The short selling of securities in the US market during the course of a Regulation S offer raises various issues. The Commission, its Staff and members of Congress noted reports that in some Regulation S offers purchasers may be shorting securities into the US market with the intent of covering those positions with Regulation S securities, which in many cases are sold offshore at prices that represent a significant discount to the price for the security in the US public markets. US public market prices for securities can drop substantially when significant short selling takes place and Regulation S securities flow into the United States to cover those short positions. These sales may be interpreted as indirect unregistered distributions of securities in the United States that do not comply with the provisions of Regulation S.

Fraudulent transactions

As with any rule or regulation, there have been persons who have made use of Regulation S to support transactions that are clearly fraudulent.

In 1994, the Commission adopted Securities Act Rule 135c in an attempt to assist US and non-US issuers making offers and sales of equity securities in accordance with either Regulation S or private placement exemptions to meet their disclosure obligations to the US public market regarding the proposed offer without running afoul of selling efforts and general solicitation prohibitions. With Rule 135c, the Commission may have believed that it would not only be able to assist reporting issuers in meeting their disclosure obligations to investors in the US public market, but also, indirectly, that the Rule might assist in addressing the problem of Regulation S offers of equity securities by reporting issuers, in that significant Regulation S sales would be reported. Such reporting would not only provide important information to investors in the US public market, but would also give the Commission a trail to follow in policing perceived abuses of Regulation S. While Rule 135c was helpful to some extent, its wider utility was limited in that it permitted, but did not require, issuers to disclose unregistered offers and sales of securities.

As the use of Regulation S expanded after its adoption, the SEC became concerned about the application of Regulation S in certain transactions. As this concern grew, the Staff began to informally express their worries through discussions with market participants and at conferences and other speaking engagements, frequently suggesting that if the abuses did not subside then action might have to be taken to amend the regulation. Early in 1995, the SEC stepped up its attempt to convince the market of the seriousness of its concern regarding Regulation S abuses by bringing enforcement actions against persons who, in the Commission's view, sought to evade the registration requirements of the Securities Act through purported Regulation S offers that were in effect US distributions of securities (see Chapter 9).

In June 1995, the Commission continued with its program of influencing the market into compliance with Regulation S by issuing an interpretative release relating to Regulation S in which it stated its views regarding the perceived abuses of Regulation S and asked for comments regarding the use of the regulation and whether amendments were necessary.[12] This more formal expression of the Commission's views appears to have been an attempt to reinforce the statements that the Commission's Staff had been making to the market for several years and to convince the market that the Commission was serious about amending the regulation, which could limit its usefulness, if the perceived abuses did not stop.

In October 1996, in a further attempt to address the perceived abuse of Regulation S by certain US issuers reporting under the Exchange Act, the Commission adopted amendments to the Exchange Acts periodic reporting forms for US issuers requiring disclosure of unregistered equity offers. The October 1996 amendments required US companies to report sales of equity securities under Regulation S on Form 8-K within 15 days of occurrence and all other unregistered sales of equity securities in their quarterly 10-Q reports and, in respect of sales in the last quarter of a fiscal year, their annual report on Form 10-K. With this step, the SEC appears to have been attempting to heighten the level of its oversight of the use of the Regulation S market by reporting US issuers and its leverage over those companies, since the Commission could take action against an issuer for the failure to file required Exchange Act reports, which in practice is easier than proving a Regulation S violation. This has

---

[12] Securities Act Release 7190 (27 June 1995).

been overtaken by changes brought about by SOX that have shortened the time period within which to file a Form 8-K.

These actions by the SEC and its Staff appear to have been an attempt to "influence" US issuers to not abuse Regulation S in order to avoid having to amend the regulation to prevent or restrict its use by those issuers. Apparently, these various actions did not adequately address the Commission's concerns regarding Regulation S abuses, as in early 1997 the Commission proposed significant amendments which would greatly restrict the availability of the benefits of the regulation to US and certain non-US reporting issuers.

Early in 1998, the Commission adopted a modified version of the original proposed amendments, which significantly reduced the benefit of Regulation S for US issuers offering and selling equity securities, but, unlike the original proposal, did not substantially change the application of Regulation S to non-US issuers.

While no rule or regulation will necessarily stop people from committing securities fraud, if Regulation S is facilitating such fraud there will be pressure to amend the regulation to clarify or restrict its application. Such concerns led the Commission to adopt the 1998 amendments to Regulation S. Perceived abuses in the future may result in additional amendments to the regulation.

The regulatory challenge in a global market

The difficulties encountered by the SEC and by market participants that relate to Regulation S are, in a large part, an outgrowth of the expansion of the global securities markets and present a challenge to all parties to find a means of addressing the difficulties presented without creating a regulatory structure which would inhibit the productive, free operation of the global securities markets and discourage non-US issuers from accessing the US capital markets. Regulation S was the first significant attempt by the Commission to institute a flexible approach to regulating cross-border capital markets activity which could have an impact on the US capital markets, and reflected an appropriate balance between US regulatory needs and the need of the global markets to operate without the weight of unnecessary regulation. This balance has not only contributed to the growth of capital markets activity outside the United States, but has also encouraged non-US issuers to access the US capital markets.

A broader and more fundamental issue underlying these difficulties relating to Regulation S is how the Commission can and should regulate capital raising activities of US and non-US issuers in a global market environment that is not only fundamentally different from that which existed when the most significant US federal securities laws were enacted early in the 20th century, but also from the global market environment at the time Regulation S was adopted. Many of the US securities laws and regulations in effect today were written or adopted at a time when communication and the delivery of information across international borders was inefficient, cross-border capital raising and trading activities were limited and, in most cases, the physical location of activity was determinative of the impact upon US investors and the US market. In this environment, securities laws and regulations focused on the use of "US jurisdictional means" as the trigger for their application and prohibited or regulated specified activities within the jurisdiction of the US as the means of achieving a particular regulatory purpose. Activities outside the United States were not generally regulated because their potential effect on the US markets was limited given the existing environment. The difficulty for the SEC and other regulators around the world is how to apply or adapt their existing regulatory schemes to a global capital market environment where information flows and large volumes of securities-related activities take place as easily across borders as within individual jurisdictions.

The ultimate direction taken by the Commission in addressing the perceived abuses of Regulation S by a comparatively small number of market participants may have a significant impact upon global securities markets. Whether the SEC addresses the growing complexity of regulating in an expanding global securities market by continuing with, and building upon, the territorial approach to regulation, or whether it shifts to an approach that extends the reach of Commission regulation to unduly interfere with legitimate activities in markets outside the United States, may have a marked effect on the evolution of international capital markets.

AMENDMENTS TO REGULATION S
Proposed Amendments
In February 1997, the Commission increased its pressure on issuers that were perceived to be abusing Regulation S by issuing a release

proposing certain amendments to Regulation S (Proposed Amendments) to "stop abusive practices in connection with equity offers purportedly made in reliance on Regulation S".[13] From the text of the proposing release, it appeared that the Commission felt it had no choice but to propose these rather restrictive amendments to end what it regarded as egregious abuses.

Summary

The Proposed Amendments would not have affected the availability of the Regulation S safe harbour for offers of debt securities by US and non-US issuers, regardless of the US reporting status of the issuer or the level of trading of its debt or equity securities in the US markets. The main focus of the Proposed Amendments was on offers of equity securities of US issuers that are reporting in the United States or whose securities are of substantial interest to investors in the United States, which is the context in which the Commission believed the most serious problems arise. In addition, the Commission proposed to subject to the Proposed Amendments' broader restrictions equity securities of foreign private issuers where the "principal market" for those securities is in the United States. It is interesting to note that the SEC proposed to include equity securities of non-US issuers, even though they conceded in the release that they are not aware of widespread abuses involving non-US issuers. While the Commission stated that it believed the potential for abuse exists with respect to equity securities of non-US issuers, any proposal to amend Regulation S in this way should be based on clear evidence of significant abuses, since the imposition of restrictions upon non-US issuers will have a significant negative effect on the willingness of non-US issuers to enter the US public markets.

It is also interesting to note that under the Proposed Amendments, the Commission did not propose to eliminate the availability of Regulation S for offers of equity securities of US issuers and non-US issuers, where the principal market for their securities is in the United States. The Commission stated that the abuses identified to date did not warrant such elimination, but by making such a statement the Commission clearly was signalling to the market that the Staff would consider further tightening of the regulation if the level

---

13 Securities Act Release 7392 (20 February 1997).

of abuse grew. The result under the Proposed Amendments was in effect to create an offshore private placement exemption for US and certain non-US issuers with requirements that fall somewhere between the traditional Section 4(2) or Regulation D private placement exemption, and the less restrictive Regulation S safe harbour.

Application to US and non-US issuers
The Proposed Amendments would have applied with respect to the equity securities[14] of any US issuer and the equity securities of any non-US issuer if it has its "principal market in the United States".

Under the Proposed Amendments, a non-US issuer would have its principal market in the United States if "more than 50% of all trading in such class of securities took place in, on or through the facilities of securities exchanges and inter-dealer quotation systems in the United States in the shorter of the issuer's prior fiscal year or the period since the issuer's incorporation".[15]

The Commission stated that the Proposed Amendments would apply to equity securities of non-US issuers since it believed there was the potential for abuse of Regulation S where the principal trading market for those securities is in the United States. It is curious that the Commission would propose to include equity securities of non-US issuers, rather than requesting comment regarding the possibility of such inclusion, given that the Commission itself noted that such abuse relating to equity securities of non-US issuers is not as evident as in the case of US issuers. In fact, in the release relating to the Proposed Amendments the Commission did not cite any evidence of such abuse.

The Commission's proposed basis on which to include equity securities of non-US issuers within the coverage of the Proposed Amendments was quite broad. Commentators noted, for example, that the proposed definition of "principal market in the United States" would cover a large number of non-US issuers. As discussed below, the result would have been that a large number of

---

14 "Equity securities" include stock, securities convertible or exchangeable into stock, warrants, options, rights to purchase stock, and other types of equity related securities. *See* Rule 405 under the Securities Act.
15 *See* proposed Rule 902(h) under the Proposed Amendments.

currently reporting non-US issuers would be covered by the Proposed Amendments and also that the potential would be great for many non-US issuers entering the US markets in the future to become subject to the Proposed Amendments. Given the disadvantages of being subject to the Proposed Amendments, also discussed below, it is possible that the Commission's proposed changes to Regulation S would have had the effect of discouraging non-US issuers from accessing the US markets.

Commentators addressing the proposed definition of "principal market in the United States" also generally agreed that non-US issuers should not be covered by the Proposed Amendments, but that, if they were to be covered, the proposed definition should be narrowed. The commentators' suggested amendments to the definition varied, but in most cases were directed at ensuring that non-US issuers would only be covered by the Proposed Amendments if the US market is the non-US issuer's sole or only significant market for its equity securities.

Adopted Amendments
In February 1998, the Commission adopted amendments to Regulation S (Adopted Amendments) that reflected, in a large part, the provisions of the Proposed Amendments. Importantly, however, the Commission decided not to restrict the application of Regulation S to offers and sales of equity securities of non-US issuers. The following are the most important requirements and restrictions contained in the Adopted Amendments.

Application only to US issuers
The Commission decided that the Adopted Amendments should not increase the restrictions under Regulation S applicable to offers and sales of equity securities of non-US issuers. The Commission acknowledged that the lack of evidence of abuse of Regulation S in such offers and sales did not warrant restricting such offers and sales in the same manner as for US issuers.

Longer restricted periods
The distribution compliance period (formerly the restricted period) for equity securities of these issuers was lengthened from 40 days to one year (for US issuers previously included in Category 2) or

maintained at one year (for US issuers previously included in Category 3). The Proposed Amendments would have increased the distribution compliance period to two years, but the Commission decided to adopt a one-year period in order to conform the Category 2 distribution compliance period to the restricted periods under Rule 144.

Designation as restricted securities
In addition to lengthening the distribution compliance period applicable to US issuers, distributors and their affiliates involved in the offer and sale of equity securities of US issuers, the Adopted Amendments designate the equity securities of these issuers offered and sold in reliance upon Rule 901 or 903 under Regulation S as restricted securities.[16] This is significant in that for the first time the Commission imposed restrictions not just upon issuers, distributors and their affiliates, but upon every holder of the securities, regardless of whether a holder acquired the securities in connection with a distribution or a normal secondary market transaction. This provision is perhaps more significant because it represents a movement away from the territorial approach to regulation that was the regulatory underpinning for Regulation S.

Under the Proposed Amendments, non-US reporting issuers with more than 50% of the trading volume for their equity securities in the United States would have been required to apply essentially US private placement procedures to offers in their home and other non-US markets unless the offers were registered under the Securities Act. This would have resulted from the fact that under the Proposed Amendments any equity securities sold by such a non-US issuer would have been considered restricted securities regardless of whether such securities were sold solely in the non-US issuer's home jurisdiction in accordance with its home jurisdictional practices or in an offer into the United States. An odd and unfortunate result of a provision such as this would have been that non-US issuers either might have avoided the US markets entirely or, in conducting offers outside the United States, relied not on Regulation S but attempted to structure an offer in a manner

---

16 Unrestricted equity securities for non-US issuers with their principal market in the United States sold by affiliates under Rule 904 will not be restricted securities.

which would allow them to claim the lack of application of Section 5 of the Securities Act.

Purchaser certifications
Purchasers of equity securities of US issuers offered and sold in reliance on Regulation S are required to certify that they are not US persons and are not acquiring the securities for the account or benefit of a US person, or that they are US persons who purchased securities in a transaction that did not require registration under the Securities Act.

Purchaser and distributor agreements
All purchasers of equity securities of US issuers offered and sold in reliance on Regulation S are required to agree to resell the securities only in transactions registered or exempt from registration under the Securities Act or in accordance with Regulation S. In a footnote to the Proposed Amendments Release, the Commission stated that some level of investigation would be required by the issuer and any distributor in order to confirm the reasonableness of relying on the certification delivered to it by a purchaser.

This approach presents significant practical problems as it is impossible in many markets to require the delivery of certificates and in some markets, even if certificates are permitted, it is unclear what mechanism could reasonably be implemented to ensure compliance.

Prohibition on hedging activities
Purchasers of covered equity securities of US issuers are required to agree not to engage in hedging transactions unless they are registered or exempt from registration under the Securities Act. Distributors are required to agree to a similar restriction until the expiration of the distribution compliance period. All offer materials used in connection with offers and sales of the covered equity securities during the distribution compliance period are required to contain a statement regarding this restriction on hedging activities

Legended certificates
Issuers of covered equity securities are required to place a legend on all covered securities sold outside the United States, which states

that the transfer of such securities is prohibited other than in accordance with the Securities Act. The legend must mention the applicable restrictions on hedging activities. If the equity securities are in an uncertificated form, an issuer may satisfy the legend requirement by any means reasonably designed to put holders and subsequent purchasers on notice of the applicable resale restrictions.

Stop transfer instructions
The issuer, by contract or a provision in its bylaws, articles, charter or comparable document, must refuse to register any transfer of equity securities unless the transfer is registered or exempt from Securities Act registration, or made in compliance with Regulation S.

Prohibition on payment for equity securities using promissory notes
Promissory notes or similar obligations or contracts can be used to buy equity securities of US issuers, but the holding period under Rule 144 will begin to run only if: (a) the promissory note obligation or contract provides for full recourse against the issuer and is secured by collateral having a fair market value at least equal to the purchase price of the equity securities; and (b) (after the holding period requirement has been met) the promissory note obligation or contract is paid in full before the resale of the security under Rule 144.

Under the Proposed Amendments, Regulation S would have been unavailable for sales of equity securities of issuers where the purchaser delivers a promissory note as payment for some or all of the purchase price, or enters into an instalment purchase contract relating to the sale. The Commission noted that this condition was proposed due to the fact that, in many of the Regulation S abuse cases, purchases had been made using promissory notes in arrangements that contemplated US resales of the securities after the end of the restricted period and use of the proceeds to pay the purchase price. The Commission stated that under such an arrangement the issuer is raising funds from the US market and that such practice is inconsistent with an offshore distribution.

Effects of Regulation S amendments
Given the Commission's decision not to cover equity securities of non-US issuers under the Adopted Amendments, the greatest

impact of the Adopted Amendments has been on US issuers. The effect of the Adopted Amendments for US issuers offering and selling equity securities in reliance on Regulation S is essentially to create a private placement exemption for sales outside the United States, which in some respects is more liberal than the procedures required in a US private placement under Section 4(2) of the Securities Act or Regulation D, but in other respects is more restrictive and difficult to implement. Like a private placement into the United States, an offer and sale of equity securities of a US issuer require certifications from purchasers and the imposition of restrictions designed to prohibit inappropriate resales of securities. In addition, such securities are "restricted" under Rule 144. Experience appears to indicate that the effect of the amendments has been to discourage US issuers from relying on Regulation S, resulting in a greater reliance on registered offerings to avoid the practical difficulties of complying with the adopted amendments requirements, discussed below.

Required certifications
Several of the requirements under the Adopted Amendments applicable to offers and sales of equity securities of US issuers have been difficult to implement in practice. For example, purchasers of securities are required to certify that: (a) they are not US persons and are not purchasing for the account of a US person or that they purchased in a transaction not requiring registration under the Securities Act; (b) they will resell only in accordance with the resale restrictions; and (c) they will not engage in impermissible hedging activities. Requiring such certifications from investors in markets outside the US is a substantial change from general market practice outside the United States, and may cause US issuers not to rely on Regulation S. The SEC has acknowledged the difficulty this certification requirement presents to US issuers and, through the no-action letter process, and subject to various conditions, has allowed offerings by non-US issuers on certain non-US exchanges without compliance with this certification requirement.

Resales of restricted securities
Rule 905 provides that equity securities of domestic issuers sold in reliance on the Issuer Safe Harbour or the Rule 901 general statement

are restricted securities under Rule 144, and that subsequent resales of these securities under the Resale Safe Harbour or Rule 901 do not change the restricted nature of these securities. This position taken by the Commission under the Adopted Amendments represents a change in the previous situation under Regulation S whereby equity securities of US issuers initially sold in a *bona fide* Regulation S transaction would not be restricted and, therefore, would be eligible for resale into the US public market. In practice, it is extremely difficult for US issuers to monitor trading in such restricted securities in markets outside the United States.

Legending and stop transfer instructions
Under the Adopted Amendments, US issuers selling equity securities are required to legend the securities and refuse to register transfers of the securities unless the transfer is registered or exempt from registration under the Securities Act. These procedures, which are not uncommon in the US private placement market, are difficult for US issuers to implement outside the United States without greatly impeding the trading efficiency, and therefore the liquidity, of those securities. In the Adopted Amendments Release, the Commission acknowledged the difficulty these procedures may present for US issuers, but noted that the potential for abuse is so great that US issuers either would have to deal with the difficulty or not rely on Regulation S in making offshore offers.

The Adopted Amendments have limited Regulation S as a practical alternative for many US issuers offering and selling equity securities outside the United States. It is essential in cross-border offers of securities of such issuers that after the initial distribution investors hold securities that are fungible with securities of the same class trading in the issuer's primary public market or, if the securities are restricted, a large pool of restricted securities. Apart from the practical problems with compliance for issuers and underwriters noted above, another effect of the amendments is to adversely impact the potential market liquidity and investor demand, as non-US investors in publicly traded equity securities of US issuers reporting under the Exchange Act are hesitant to take securities which cannot be sold in the US public markets for one or more years. As a result, Exchange Act reporting US issuers undertaking a global offer of equity securities are more likely to register all such securities under the Securities Act.

Another impact of the Adopted Amendments has been the virtual elimination of the euro-convertible market for US issuers that had developed during the few years before the adoption of the amendments. Under the amendments, these convertible securities are "equity" securities subject to the new Regulation S restrictions (regardless of the conversion or exercise premium or other characteristics of the convertible security), thus presenting US issuers with many of the problems noted above.

US issuers contemplating unregistered offers and sales of their equity securities are likely to weigh carefully the advantages and disadvantages of Regulation S and other exemptions from Securities Act registration which might be used in offer and selling equity securities outside the United States. The Commission noted in the Adopted Amendments Release that it believed there were certain advantages in using Regulation S compared with relying upon Section 4(2) of the Securities Act or Regulation D. For example, sales can be made in reliance upon Regulation S without taking into account the nature or number of the purchasers and without having to provide specified information. On the other hand, however, Regulation S requires certification and procedures that would not be required in a Section 4(2) or Regulation D private placement, particularly where offers and sales are only made to QIBs. Given the different procedures that would be implemented in respect of Regulation S and Section 4(2) or Regulation D restricted securities, a US issuer contemplating an unregistered offer of its equity securities would choose to offer all securities in a Section 4(2) or Regulation D private placement. In any event, it is clear that Regulation S no longer provides any significant advantages over Section 4(2) or Regulation D for unregistered offers and sales of equity securities of US issuers outside the US.

Conclusion

Regulation S and related rules have had the effect of more clearly defining a realm in which issuers can conduct offers and sales of securities without having to comply with the registration requirements of Section 5 of the Securities Act. The effect of this has been, on balance, positive for US and non-US markets, institutions and investors alike. The SEC's imposition of new restrictions on the application of the regulation to offers and sales of equity securities of US issuers, however, greatly diminishes its usefulness to US issuers legitimately applying Regulation S. Any change in the SEC's position regarding the application of Regulation S to offers and sales of equity securities of non-US issuers, as well as its fundamental approach to regulating cross-border securities offers and market activities, may have a marked effect on the evolution of international securities markets in the years to come.

RULE 144A
Overview of Rule 144A
Rule 144A, adopted in April 1990, is a non-exclusive safe harbour under the Securities Act for resales of restricted securities to certain sophisticated institutional investors, QIBs, following the idea that this category of investors do not need to be protected by the Securities Act registration and disclosure requirements. Resales by any person (other than the issuer or any affiliate or a dealer) of restricted securities to QIBs in compliance with Rule 144A are not subject to the registration requirements of the Securities Act because such person is deemed not to be engaged in a "distribution" (and therefore not a statutory "underwriter") within the meaning of Section 2(10) of the Securities Act. Under Section 4(1) of the Securities Act "[t]ransactions by any person other than an issuer, underwriter or dealer" are exempt from registration. Resales by dealers of restricted securities to QIBs in compliance with Rule 144A are exempt from registration because: (i) such securities will be deemed not to have been "offered to the public"; and (ii) the dealer will neither be deemed a participant in a "distribution" nor an "underwriter".

Conditions to be met
To qualify for the exemption afforded by Rule 144A, an offer or sale of securities must meet the following four conditions:

1. the securities must be offered or sold only to a QIB or to an offeree or purchaser that the seller reasonably believes is a QIB;
2. the seller must take reasonable steps to ensure that the purchaser is aware that the seller may be relying on Rule 144A;

3. the securities being offered or sold, when issued, must not be of the same class as securities listed on a national securities exchange in the US or in a US automated inter-dealer quotation system; and
4. subject to certain exceptions, issuers must be required to provide to any holder of Rule 144A securities and any prospective purchaser designated by a holder, upon request, certain current information regarding the issuer.

QIBs status
QIBs include: (i) institutions specified in the rule, acting for their own account or the account of other QIBs, that in aggregate own and invest on a discretionary basis at least US$100 million in securities of non-affiliated issuers; (ii) banks and savings and loans institutions that (a) own and invest at least US$100 million in the securities of non-affiliated issuers and (b) have an audited net worth of at least US$25 million; (iii) registered broker–dealers that own and invest on a discretionary basis at least US$10 million in securities of non-affiliated issuers; and (iv) registered broker–dealers acting in a riskless principal transaction on behalf of a QIB.

In order to rely on the rule, the seller and any person acting on its behalf must offer and sell the securities only to QIBs or to persons whom they reasonably believe to be QIBs. The rule specifies several non-exclusive means of satisfying this requirement. Information concerning the amount of securities owned or under investment management may be determined from the most recently publicly available financial statements of the prospective purchaser or the most recent information appearing in documents filed by the prospective purchaser with the SEC or other governmental agencies or in a recognised securities manual. The seller may also rely on a certification by an executive officer of the prospective purchaser.

Notice of possible reliance on Rule 144A
Rule 144A(d)(2) provides that a seller must also take "reasonable steps" to ensure that the purchaser is aware the seller may rely on Rule 144A in its transaction with the purchaser. Such notice should be given to the prospective purchaser at the time of the offer and

not be delayed until the confirmation of sale is forwarded to the purchaser.

Non-fungible securities
Rule 144A is not available for transactions relating to securities that, when issued, were of the same class as securities listed on a national securities exchange or quoted in an automated inter-dealer quotation system, such as NASDAQ. This requirement was designed to prevent the development of side-by-side private and public trading markets for securities of the same class. Securities quoted in the pink sheets or in the NASD's PORTAL system are not excluded. Securities that are convertible into securities that are listed on a national securities exchange in the United States or quoted in a US automated inter-dealer quotation system are treated as securities of the same class as those into which they are convertible unless at the time of issuance the effective conversion premium is at least 10%. Securities of the same class as those underlying ADRs that are listed on a national securities exchange in the United States or quoted in a US automated inter-dealer quotation system are not eligible for resale under the rule.

Information delivery
If the issuer of the securities is not (i) a reporting company under the Exchange Act, (ii) a foreign issuer exempt from reporting pursuant to Rule 12g3–2(b), or (iii) a foreign government eligible to register securities under Schedule B of the Securities Act, the availability of Rule 144A is conditioned upon the holder of the securities and a prospective purchaser having the right to obtain specified information from the issuer, upon request, and the prospective purchaser having received that information, if requested, prior to the sale. The information that is required to be furnished is a brief description of the issuer's business, products and services, the most recent balance sheet and profit and loss and retained earnings statements and similar information for the two preceding fiscal years.

PORTAL
One of the stated goals of Rule 144A is to provide liquidity in the private placement market by creating a secondary market in which

restricted securities can be freely traded by QIBs. In order to facilitate the development of this secondary market, the NASD established the PORTAL (the acronym for "Private Offerings, Resales and Trading through Automated Linkages") system, a screen-based trading system for the trading, clearing and settlement of Rule 144A securities. PORTAL provides trading facilities for secondary trading as well as primary placements of Rule 144A securities.

The PORTAL system was originally designed as a "closed" trading system requiring pre-qualification of PORTAL participants as QIBs and imposing restrictions on a participant's ability to trade securities out of the system. PORTAL rules were subsequently amended in 1993 and 2001 to cover all transactions effected by NASD members relating to PORTAL securities. The amended rules also eliminated certain restrictions on exiting the trading system. Under current PORTAL rules, Rule 144A securities and Regulation S securities may be designated as PORTAL securities. Current PORTAL rules mandate NASD members which deal in Rule 144A securities to sell such securities to QIBs only and to keep a record demonstrating that all such transactions were effected in compliance with Rule 144A.

PORTAL eligibility of Rule 144A securities has been important not because of the trading facilities PORTAL provides, but rather because such eligibility also makes the securities eligible for deposit into the DTC settlement and clearance system.

RESTRICTED SECURITIES AND RULE 144

It is not often easy to resell restricted securities that have been received in transactions exempt from registration under the Securities Act.

Under Rule 144, restricted securities are securities that are: (a) acquired directly or indirectly from the issuer or an affiliate in a transaction not involving a public offer; (b) acquired from the issuer and are subject to the resale limitations of Regulation D or Rule 701(c) under the Securities Act; (c) acquired in a transaction or chain of transactions meeting the requirements of Rule 144A; (d) acquired from the issuer and are subject to the resale limitations of Regulation E; or (e) equity securities of domestic issuers acquired in a transaction or chain of transactions subject to the conditions of Rule 901 or 903 under Regulation S.

Under Rule 144, a holder of restricted securities may sell these securities in brokers' transactions (rather than by means of a private placement or registered offer) in an amount up to the greater of one% of the outstanding amount of securities of that class or the average weekly trading volume in such securities in the preceding four weeks. In addition, the holder is required to have held the securities for at least one year from the time of their purchase from the issuer to the date of their resale by the holder or subsequent holder. In the alternative, a holder that is not an affiliate of the issuer may in most cases sell the restricted securities of that issuer free of any Rule 144 requirements if two years elapse between the purchase of the shares from the issuer and their resale into the public markets.

Restricted securities held by persons that are deemed to be affiliates of the issuing company must comply with the requirements of Rule 144 in selling their shares. They must also ensure that they do not complete a purchase and sale of their equity shares within six months and make a profit, in order to avoid having to disgorge their profits under the short-swing profit liability provisions of Section 16 of the Exchange Act.

In certain instances, it is possible to hedge or write exchange-traded call options against restricted securities.

Many fledgling companies (US incorporated and otherwise) offer securities outside the US in private placements with a view to raising seed money to fund start-up operations. These securities are usually restricted, so purchasers of these instruments may find themselves having to comply with a holding period or other requirements before they are able to sell their shares. Placing an order to sell restricted securities with a non-US broker or dealer may have consequences for the selling firm in that it may, depending on how and with whom it places the sell order, have to comply with the requirements of Rule 15a-6 under the Exchange Act (*see* Chapter 7).

PUBLIC ANNOUNCEMENTS DURING PENDING PRIVATE PLACEMENTS

It is important to note that while certain activities, such as announcements in the United States required to be published under US or foreign law, are not considered "directed selling efforts" under Regulation S, they may pose a general solicitation issue in connection with a simultaneous private placement of securities eligible for resale pursuant to Rule 144A. Reporting issuers offering equity securities or debt securities convertible into or exchangeable for equity securities, in simultaneous Regulation S and Rule 144A offerings, are faced with an additional dilemma when the amount of equity securities offered or receivable upon conversion or exchange is significant relative to the issuer's outstanding equity securities. Due to the potential impact of such an offer upon the market price of US publicly traded securities, the issuer may conclude that it is required to disclose the proposed offer to the market in the United States prior to the completion of the US private placement, but at the risk of destroying its private placement exemption. While the Commission contemplated that Regulation S and Rule 144A offers could take place simultaneously, they did not intend to provide an exception to the prohibition on general solicitations for private placements of Rule 144A-eligible securities that occur simultaneously with a Regulation S offer. In order to address this difficulty, in 1994 the Commission adopted Rule 135c,[17] which provides a safe harbour for notices of certain proposed unregistered offers.

Rule 135c provides that a notice given by an issuer that is required to file reports under the Exchange Act, or a foreign issuer that is exempt from Exchange Act registration pursuant to Rule 12g3–2(b) under that Act, that proposes to make, is making or has made an offer of securities not registered or required to be registered under the Securities Act shall not be deemed to offer any securities for sale, if such notice:

❏ is not used for the purpose of conditioning the market in the United States for any of the securities offered;
❏ states that the securities offered will not be or have not been registered under the Securities Act and may not be offered or sold in the US absent registration or an applicable exemption from registration requirements; and
❏ contains no more than the following: (a) the name of the issuer; (b) the title, amount and basic terms of the securities offered, the amount of the offer, if any, made by selling security holders, the time of the offer and a brief statement of the manner and

---

[17] Securities Act Release 7053 (19 April 1994).

purpose of the offer without naming the underwriters;[18] and (c) any statement or legend required by state or foreign law or administrative authority.

Notices may be in the form of a news release or a written communication directed to security holders or employees or other published statements. Subject to certain conditions, information as to the interest rate, conversion ratio and subscription price of securities to be listed on a national securities exchange or quoted on NASDAQ may be disseminated through the facilities of the exchange, the consolidated transaction reported system, NASDAQ or the Dow Jones broad tape, provided such information is already disclosed in a Form 8-K on file with the Commission, in a Form 6-K furnished to the Commission or, in the case of an issuer relying on Rule 12g3–2(b), in a submission made pursuant to that exemption to the SEC. In addition, notices must be filed with the Commission under cover of Form 8-K or furnished under Form 6-K as applicable and, if the issuer is relying on Rule 12g3–2(b), furnished to the Commission in accordance with that exemption.

Rule 135c is interesting in several respects. In part, it was directed at addressing a difficulty that developed as a result of the important decision by the SEC in 1990 to allow for the inclusion of equity and equity-related securities of reporting US and non-US issuers in Category 2 of Regulation S. During the course of drafting Regulation S, the Commission considered whether equity and equity-related securities of reporting US and non-US issuers should be included in Category 2 or 3 and, after discussion with market participants, the Commission was persuaded to include these securities in Category 2. As a result of this decision, due to the less restrictive requirements set forth in Category 2, it became more likely that securities sold by reporting issuers in substantial non-US equity offers would be resold into the US in legitimate secondary market transactions within a relatively short period of time after a Regulation S offer. This meant that these non-US transactions were more likely to have a depressing effect upon the price of the issuer's equity securities in the US public market than if the transactions

---

[18] Rule 135c(a)(3) sets forth specific limited information regarding rights offers, exchange offers and offers to employees which may be included in notices relating to those offers.

were subject to Category 3 restrictions, which would likely lead to the equity securities remaining outside the United States for a longer period of time.

Rule 135c is also interesting because it indicated a willingness of the Commission to assist market participants in resolving difficulties arising in connection with the use of Regulation S by adopting a regulation to permit necessary market activity rather than eliminating the availability of the regulation for the activity presenting the regulatory concern. This response is quite different from that of the Commission demonstrated in connection with recent amendments to Regulation S.

OFFSHORE PRESS CONFERENCES, MEETINGS AND PRESS-RELATED MATERIALS

With the world's securities markets being globalised and the increasing speed and efficiency with which information is transmitted around the globe, issuers and underwriters undertaking offers of securities that include investors in the US markets have faced certain difficulties in conducting those offers in a manner which is consistent with the practices in the non-US markets in which the securities are being offered, as well as with the US federal securities laws. For instance, in many cases it is difficult for non-US issuers conducting global offers of securities or undertaking customary activities in non-US markets, and not intended to condition the market for those securities in the United States, to confirm with certainty compliance with the prohibition on directed selling efforts under Regulation S and the "general solicitation" prohibition under Regulation D under the Securities Act.

A particular difficulty for issuers, underwriters and their advisers, as well as for US journalists and press and news services, which has arisen since the adoption of Regulation S and the growth in global offers involving offers and sales to US investors, has been how to deal with press conferences and meetings with company representatives, as well as the delivery of press-related materials, outside the United States during the course of a distribution of securities. In many non-US markets, the practices with respect to these matters are quite different compared with the United States, and this has presented challenges to issuers, underwriters and their advisers to find methods to reconcile these conflicting practices. In many cases, the US federal securities law requirements and the uncertainty of their application have interfered with legitimate selling and press activities in markets outside the United States. The difficulty has become even more of a challenge due to the speed with which information delivered outside the United States is communicated by news and information services in the United States.

In addition, the approaches by US legal counsel to addressing the challenge have varied greatly depending on the degree of experience and conservatism of counsel as well as the facts and circumstances relating to the particular offer but, not uncommonly, they have either prohibited offshore activities, unless conducted in accordance with US standards, or permitted offshore activities subject to varied restrictions including the exclusion of US journalists, publications and news services. This has resulted in confusion and frustration on the part of non-US issuers and their advisers and other participants in non-US offers, as they have great difficulty in discerning a clear method of dealing with the difficulty that can be applied on a consistent and predictable basis to activities undertaken during the course of the offer. This frustration has been felt not only by issuers and participants in their distributions of securities, but also internal compliance personnel who monitor advertising and marketing activities on an on-going basis, as well as newspapers and periodicals that attempt to put in place procedures to ensure that their policies and procedures comply with US federal securities law requirements. Finally, these issues and the manner in which they have been addressed by issuers, underwriters and their legal counsel have presented difficulties for US journalists and news and information services who frequently have been excluded from offshore press conferences and other press-related activities and, in their view, placed at a competitive disadvantage compared with their non-US counterparts.

In October 1997, the SEC adopted two safe harbours intended to address certain problems presented by these offshore press-related activities.[19] The first clarifies under what circumstances US journalists can be allowed access to non-US press conferences and meetings attended by the issuer or selling security-holder and their representatives, as well as press-related materials released outside

---

19 Securities Act Release 7470 (10 October 1997).

the United States, in each case at or in which present or proposed offers of securities are discussed. Subject to compliance with the requirements of the safe harbour, allowing such access would not be deemed an "offer" for the purpose of Section 5, "directed selling efforts" under Regulation S or a "general solicitation" under Regulation D. Under the second safe harbour, providing such access would not result in the bidder for the securities of a foreign private issuer, the subject company, their representatives, or any other person specified in Rule 14d-9(d) under the Exchange Act being subject to the filing and procedural requirements of Regulations 14D and 14E under that same act.

The following is a summary of the two safe harbours relating to offshore press conferences, meetings and deliveries of press-related materials. It is interesting to note that the Commission did not make these new safe harbours available to US issuers. In the adopting release relating to that safe harbour, the Commission stated that it did so in the belief that non-US issuers adopting these practices are unlikely to be doing so for the purposes of circumventing US restrictions on publicity, but that extending the safe harbour to US issuers that have not traditionally made use of such practices would invite the potential for abuse. The Commission stated that it would consider the case for US issuers in what it terms a "comprehensive fashion" with respect to offshore and US press activities. It also should be noted that the Securities Act safe harbour only applies to the registration requirements of Section 5, and does not affect the application of the anti-fraud or other provisions of the US federal securities laws.

Securities Act Safe Harbour – Rule 135e
Parties eligible for safe harbour
Rule 135e is available to any foreign private issuer or foreign government issuer, any selling security holder of the securities of such issuers or their representatives. The release adopting Rule 135e makes clear that the Rule is not available to any party that does not have a relationship with the issuer or selling security holder.

Offshore press activity
Under the Rule, press conferences, meetings and releases of press-related information must occur outside the United States. Specifically excluded from the coverage of the safe harbour are

conference calls in which at least one of the parties is located in the US. In addition, follow-up communications by a journalist who is located in the United States at the time of the follow-up would not qualify for the safe harbour. The Commission believed that an offshore press conference or meeting to which US and non-US journalists are invited is less likely to be undertaken solely for the purpose of conditioning the US market.

Offshore offer requirement
Rule 135e is not available for any present or proposed offer made or to be made solely in the United States. In Rule 135e, an offer qualifies for the safe harbour if there is "an intent to make a *bona fide* offer offshore". It is important to note that the Commission did not require any specific amount of securities to be offered or sold outside the United States in order to qualify for the safe harbour. However, the Commission did state that the offer of a token amount would not be sufficient to bring a transaction within the safe harbour. In a warning to the market, the Commission stated that if it detects abuses of the offshore offer requirement of Rule 135e it would consider imposing a stricter, more objective standard.

The Commission believed that an offer made solely in the United States was not the type of offer that needed the protection of the safe harbour. The Commission noted that US-only offers would not be included in the safe harbour even if the nature of the offer may require disclosure in the foreign jurisdiction. The Commission's reasoning was that such offshore releases of information might have the protection of Rules 134, 135 or 135c or, if those Rules are not available, the facts and circumstances might lead to the conclusion that such release of information would not violate Section 5. The position an issuer or selling security holder would find itself in under these circumstances would not be different from that which it would have found itself in before the availability of the Rule 135e safe harbour.

Access is not provided solely to US journalists
Rule 135e is not available for an offer that otherwise would meet the offshore offer requirement of the Rule, but which does not allow for access to or participation by non-US journalists. Interestingly, the SEC stated that, while equal access by non-US journalists is required under the Rule, there would be no requirement that such

journalists actually attend conferences or meetings, for example. The SEC took this position because actual attendance or participation is beyond an issuer's control and also because it believed a monitoring requirement would be too burdensome.

An issue that the Commission considered is whether an exclusive one-on-one meeting with a US publication could qualify for the protection of the safe harbour if no other one-on-one interviews are given to non-US publications. The Commission adopted the position that, if a press conference open to US and non-US journalists is conducted either before or after the exclusive meeting with the US publication, exclusive meetings would qualify for the safe harbour. While some commentators objected to the need for a qualifying press conference to take place in order for the one-on-one meeting to be eligible for the safe harbour, the Commission indicated it was simply attempting to require some evidence that the one-on-one meeting was not an attempt to condition the US markets.

Written materials requirements
In order to qualify for the safe harbour, all press materials which discuss an offer of securities by any non-US private issuer or foreign government where part of the offer is or will be conducted in the United States (regardless of whether the US portion of the offer will be registered, or exempt from registration, under the Securities Act) must meet the requirements outlined below.

All press materials must be in writing
In the adopting release, the Commission noted that paid advertisements are not covered by the safe harbour. In the proposing release relating to Rule 135e, the Commission excluded analysts' research reports on the protection of the safe harbour. In the adopting release, the Commission noted that several commentators had opposed the exclusion of these research reports from the safe harbour due to the common practice in many jurisdictions outside the United States of using such reports as part of the selling effort. In adopting Rule 135e, the Commission stated that analysts' research reports would be covered to the same extent as other materials included in a package of press materials covered by the Rule. This would be the case even if Rules 138 and 139 as now in force and as amended, which are rules governing the publication of research reports by analysts, were not

available. However, the publication of analysts' research reports by analysts themselves, as opposed to publication by an issuer in accordance with Rule 135e, would continue to be subject to Rules 138 and 139 (see above). The Commission noted that it was never intended to cause other materials in the package to lose the protection of the safe harbour due to the inclusion of analysts' research reports.

The press materials must state the following: (a) the written press-related materials are not an offer of securities in the United States; (b) the securities may not be offered or sold in the United States under Securities Act registration or an exemption therefrom; (c) any public offer of securities to be made in the United States will be made by means of a prospectus that may be obtained from the issuer or the selling security holder; (d) the prospectus will contain detailed information regarding the company and management as well a financial statements; and (e) whether the issuer or selling security holder intends to register any part of the present or proposed offer in the United States, if that is the case.

The press materials may not include, or have attached to them, any purchase order or return coupon indicating interest in the offer.

These requirements do not apply to materials released by a foreign private issuer or foreign government that relate to offers and sales of securities made wholly outside the United States. The Commission adopted this position in the belief that these types of offers are of less significant interest to US investors than offers of securities that include offers and sales to US investors.

Tender Offer Safe Harbour

As discussed in more detail in Chapter 5, the Tender Offer Safe Harbour, which was added by amending Rule 14d-1 under the Exchange Act, is intended to accommodate non-US offer practices in cases where the target company is not a US company. As a result, this safe harbour is only available where the target company is a foreign private issuer[20] and regardless of whether the bidder is a

---

20 Commentators noted the difficulty that bidders might face in determining whether a foreign issuer is a "foreign private issuer" as defined in Rule 3b-4 under the Exchange Act. In response, the SEC has stated that a bidder may presume that a target company qualifies as a "foreign private issuer" if the target company files registration statements with the SEC or reports on the disclosure forms designated for use by foreign private issuers, claims an exemption pursuant to Rule 12g3–2(b) under the Exchange Act, or is not a reporting company in the United States.

US or non-US company. Under amended Rule 14d-1, a bidder, the foreign target company, the representatives of either and any person who may have a filing obligation under the Williams Act[21] will not trigger the filing and procedural requirements of the Williams Act by allowing US and non-US journalists access to offshore press conferences and meetings or written press materials delivered outside the US that contain a discussion of a present or proposed tender offer of securities.

Like the Securities Act Safe Harbour, the Tender Offer Safe Harbour does not affect the scope or applicability of the anti-fraud provisions of the US federal securities laws. In addition, since the Tender Offer Safe Harbour is intended only to prevent the application of the US tender offer rules before a bidder is prepared to proceed with an offer, the safe harbour is unavailable after offer documents have been filed with the commission under Regulation D.

Research and Regulation S/Rule 144A offers
Aircraft Carrier Release Guidance
In the Aircraft Carrier Release, the SEC proposed amending Rules 138 and 139[22] to provide guidelines for the dissemination of research reports used in connection with Rule 144A and Regulation S offers. The Commission proposed that research that may be published or distributed under proposed Rules 138 and 139 would not be considered direct selling efforts or offers to persons other than QIBs if it is set forth in a publication published with reasonable regularity and as long as the issuer:

❏ has been a reporting company for three years;
❏ has been a reporting company for one year and has a public float of US$75 million;
❏ is a foreign private issuer that has a public float of US$75 million and a one-year trading history on a designated offshore securities market; or

---

21 The requirements are those set forth in Section 14(d)(1) through (d)(7) of the Exchange Act, Regulation 14D and Rules 14e-1 and 14e-2 thereunder.
22 These rules permit the dissemination of certain information and publications by broker–dealers in circumstances where issuers meeting specified criteria propose to file or have filed a registration statement under the Securities Act.

❏ is a foreign government issuing at least US$250 million of securities in a firm commitment offer.

It should be noted that the SEC stated in the Aircraft Carrier Release that its position on research in Regulation S and Rule 144A offers is their "view today" and thus can be relied upon effective as of November 1998, despite the fact that the Aircraft Carrier Release has been abandoned.

Securities Offering Reform
In Release, the Commission adopted amendments to Rules 138 and 139 to provide that the dissemination of research reports[23] in accordance with these rules will not (i) be considered offers or general solicitation or general advertising in connection with offerings relying on Rule 144A or (ii) constitute directed selling efforts or be inconsistent with the offshore transaction requirement of Regulation S.

Rule 138. This rule permits a broker–dealer participating in a distribution of an issuer's common stock, or debt or preferred stock convertible into common stock, to publish research reports regarding the issuer's non-convertible debt and preferred securities, and if the offering relates to the issuer's non-convertible securities to publish research regarding the issuer's common stock or convertible securities. Under the amended rule, the safe harbour would be available if the broker–dealer publishes or distributes the research reports in the regular course of its business and:

❏ the issuer is required to file and has filed all of its required periodic reports on Forms 10-K, 10-KSB, 10Q, 10-QSB and 20-F; or
❏ is a foreign private issuer that:
  ❏ meets the registrant requirements of Form F-3 (other than reporting history);

---

23 In Release, the Commission amended Rule 137 to add a definition of "research report," which means a "written communication . . . that includes an analysis of a security or an issuer and provides information reasonably sufficient upon which to base an investment decision."

- satisfies the US$75 million public float test or is issuing non-convertible investment grade securities; and
- has had its equity securities trading on a designated offshore securities market for at least 12 months; and
- the issuer is not and any predecessor during the past three years was not a blank check company, a shell company or an issuer offering penny stock.

Rule 139. This rule permits a broker–dealer participating in a distribution of securities of seasoned and large publicly traded foreign private issuers to publish research regarding the issuer and any class of its securities in a publication distributed in the regular course of its business. Under the amended rule, a safe harbour for issuer specific research reports would be available if:

- the broker–dealer publishes or distributes research reports in the regular course of its business and is at the time of release publishing and distributing research reports about the issuer or its securities; and
- the issuer satisfies the requirements of Form S-3 or F-3 and the US$75 million public float or investment grade securities provisions of these forms; or
- is a foreign private issuer that:
  - meets the registrant requirements of Form F-3 (other than reporting history);
  - satisfies the US$75 million public float test or is issuing non-convertible investment grade securities; and
  - has had its equity securities trading on a designated offshore securities market for at least 12 months; and
- the issuer is not and any predecessor during the past three years was not a blank check company, a shell company or an issuer offering penny stock.

Under amended Rule 139, a safe harbour for industry reports is available if:

- the issuer is required to file periodic reports or satisfies the foreign private issuer requirements set forth immediately above;
- the issuer is not and any predecessor during the past three years was not a blank check company, a shell company or an issuer offering penny stock;

- ❏ the research report includes similar information on a substantial number of issuers in the issuer's industry or contains a comprehensive list of securities currently recommended by the broker or dealer;
- ❏ the analysis on the issuer or its securities is given no materially greater space or prominence than that given to other issuers or securities; and
- ❏ the broker–dealer publishes or distributes research reports in the regular course of its business and, at the time of release of the subject report, includes similar information about the issuer or its securities in similar reports.

INTEGRATION
Integration of abandoned offerings
As part of the Aircraft Carrier Release, the SEC proposed rules to assist issuers in determining whether two offers would be considered the same offer (i.e. integrated) for purposes of the Securities Act. If two offers are integrated, the combined offer either would need to be registered under the Securities Act or qualify for an exemption. Late in 1999, the Division of Corporation Finance announced that it was putting this release on hold indefinitely. In January 2001, however, the SEC adopted new Rule 155 under the Securities Act that provides safe harbours allowing issuers to change an offering from private to registered, and *vice versa*, without integrating the two offerings. This new Rule reflects many aspects of the original integration proposal from the Aircraft Carrier Release, modified to reflect public comments.

Abandoned private offering followed by a registered offering
Because an issuer may not offer securities prior to filing a registration statement, there is a risk that the marketing in respect of an abandoned prior private offer could be viewed as an impermissible offer, or gun-jumping, with respect to a subsequent public offer. Under Rule 155(b), an issuer may abandon a private offering and commence a registered offering, without raising integration issues, if the following conditions are met:

- ❏ no securities were sold in the private offering;
- ❏ all offering activity in the private offering is terminated before the registration statement is filed;

- ❑ the prospectus filed as part of the registration statement discloses information regarding the abandoned private offering, including: (a) the size and nature of the private offering; (b) the date on which all offering activity relating to the private offering was terminated; (c) that any offers to buy or indications of interest in the private offering were rejected or otherwise not accepted; and (d) that the prospectus delivered in the registered offering supersedes any selling material used in the private offering; and
- ❑ the registration statement is not filed until at least 30 calendar days after termination of all offering activity in the private offering, unless securities were offered in the private offering only to persons who were, or were reasonably believed to be, accredited investors or sophisticated (each as defined by reference to Regulation D).

In all cases, the initial private offering must comply with the conditions of Section 4(2) or 4(6) of the Securities Act or Rule 506.

In the adopting the release relating to Rule 155, the Commission noted that the Staff of the Division of Corporation Finance has been directed to monitor use of the new Rule and, in particular, it is expected that the Staff may request supplemental information regarding the termination of all private offering activity.

Abandoned registered offering followed by a private offering

Under current regulations, offers of securities on a private placement basis after a registered offer has been initiated but not completed could jeopardise the private placement exemption because the marketing of the public offer may have resulted in offers being made to ineligible offerees, or such marketing may be deemed to constitute a general solicitation. Historically, the SEC advised issuers to wait six months to be certain that the private placement exemption would not be jeopardised.

Under Rule 155(c), the risk of integration for an issuer that files a registration statement and subsequently undertakes a private offer would be removed if the following conditions were met:

- ❑ no securities were sold in the registered offering;
- ❑ the registration statement has been withdrawn;

- the private offering is not commenced earlier than 30 calendar days after the effective date of withdrawal of the registration statement;
- each offeree in the private offering is notified that: (a) the offering is not registered under the Securities Act; (b) the securities will be "restricted securities" as defined in Rule 144 and cannot be resold without registration unless an exemption is available; (c) purchasers do not have the protection of Section 11 of the Securities Act; and (d) a registration statement for the abandoned offering was filed and withdrawn, specifying the effective date of the withdrawal; and
- any disclosure document used in the private offering discloses any changes in the issuer's business or financial condition that occurred after the issuer filed the registration statement that are material to the investment decision in the private offering.

PIPE TRANSACTIONS

As an alternative to the public offering markets, many companies are turning to alternative financing techniques, such as PIPE (private investment in public equity) transactions to support growth. In a PIPE transaction, a private investor purchases securities directly from a publicly traded company, typically at a discount to the market price of the company's stock, in reliance upon a registration exemption (such as the private placement and Regulation S exemptions). The purchased securities are restricted and cannot be immediately resold by the investors in the public markets. Often, the terms of the transaction require the company to promptly register the restricted securities with the SEC on consummation of the deal. PIPE transactions, once viewed as uncommon or unfavourable in the marketplace, are now accepted as rapid and legitimate financing vehicles.

Valid exemption required

The initial sale of securities in a PIPE transaction must be validly structured to comply with the registration exemption pursuant to the securities laws. Issuers may rely, for example, on exemptions provided by Section 4(2) of the Securities Act and/or Regulation D.

Integration issues

As stated above, the terms of a PIPE transaction often involve a private offering to the PIPE investors, followed by the filing of a registration statement for the resale public offering by the PIPE investors. The SEC's "integration doctrine", however, prevents companies from avoiding registration requirements by splitting a single offering into multiple offerings. If the private offering in a PIPE transaction is integrated with the subsequent resale registration, the two will be regarded as one general solicitation requiring registration and the issuer will not be entitled to rely on the private placement exemptions. This is referred to as a "burst PIPE" and the violation is commonly known as gun jumping.

Rule 152 of the Securities Act provides a safe harbour for PIPE issuers to avoid integration. The private placement of PIPE securities will not be integrated with the subsequent resale registration of those securities if the private placement was completed before the issuer filed its registration statement. The private placement is "completed" if the investors' obligations (i.e. the purchase price and the number of securities to be purchased) are firmly in place and such obligations are subject only to conditions outside of the investors' control, and no further renegotiation of the transaction is possible.

Liability issues

Issuers involved in PIPE transactions are subject to liability under Rule 10b-5 of the Exchange Act, but not liability under Section 11 of the Securities Act (which does not apply to the contents of an offering memorandum used in a private placement) as that section only deals with public offerings.[24]

Shareholder approval

Both the NYSE and NASDAQ require shareholder approval prior to the issuance of PIPE securities at a price less than the market value if the amount of common stock issued (or ultimately

---

[24] However, see Section 12 of the Securities Act; *Gustafson v. Alloyd Co.*, 115 S.Ct. 1061, 1056–71 (1995) (implying that Section 12(2) does not apply to private placement offering brochures or documents other than prospectuses contained in registration statements filed with the SEC). See also the discussion on liability in Chapters 2 and 9.

issuable) exceeds 20% of the company's outstanding common stock. In addition, shareholder approval is required when, after the completion of the PIPE transaction, a shareholder beneficially owns 20% or more of the outstanding securities of the issuer. Companies must be sensitive to these shareholder approval requirements when considering whether to complete a PIPE transaction.

Certifications

An issue arises with respect to PIPE transactions that incorporate past filings made pursuant to the securities laws into the PIPE offering materials. SOX requires certain certifications by the principal executive officer and principal financial officer of any issuer that files quarterly and annual reports with the SEC under either Section 13(a) or 15(d) of the Exchange Act. Where the issuer incorporates such reports into the offering materials in an extraterritorial PIPE transaction, a question exists as to whether the certifications contained in such reports may subject the certifying officer to criminal or civil liability in the jurisdiction in which the securities are offered for sale. The answer to this question depends on the local law of the jurisdiction in which the securities are offered.

Regulation FD

Although not applicable to foreign private issuers, Regulation FD prohibits the selective disclosure of material non-public information by public companies.[25] Regulation FD excludes communications made in connection with most registered securities offerings. However, statements made in connection with private placements, including PIPE transactions, are not excluded. Issuers engaging in PIPE transactions, to the extent they are subject to Regulation FD, should obtain non-disclosure commitments from, or refrain from providing any material, non-public information to, prospective investors. Alternatively, issuers could publish a Rule 135c press release. A disadvantage of this approach, however, is that it would result in disclosure of the transaction prior to the execution of a definitive agreement.

---

25 Regulation FD is comprised of three rules, Rules 101–103.

4

Financial Information: Accounting and Disclosure

Abigail Arms

Shearman & Sterling LLP

In this chapter, we discuss matters relating to accounting and financial information disclosures under the US federal securities laws. Particular focus will be made on MD&A disclosures and recent SEC initiatives relating to the disclosure of financial information.

The US financial markets in 2001 and 2002 saw several high-profile accounting and financial scandals, corporate governance breakdowns and business failures. These scandals provided the impetus for the adoption of SOX. Since then, additional financial scandals and corporate governance failures have occurred and public companies have filed restated financial statements with the SEC.

SOX represents sweeping US federal government reform enacted by Congress intended to protect investors by increasing the accuracy, reliability, transparency and timeliness of corporate disclosures made under the US federal securities laws. Among other requirements, SOX provides for increased audit committee oversight, responsibility for financial and general corporate disclosures, enhanced audit committee qualification and independence requirements, and added civil and criminal penalties, including disgorgement, fines and prison terms for violations of SOX and the rules and regulations adopted thereunder. SOX also provides for the establishment of the independent Public Company Accounting Oversight Board (PCAOB), which is given the statutory authority, under SEC oversight, to oversee and regulate all accounting firms that provide audit services to public companies.

SOX generally applies to foreign private issuers who either have securities listed for trading in the United States, principally on NASDAQ and the NYSE, or have conducted Securities Act registered public offerings and are filing reports with the SEC. In the absence of a reporting obligation under either Section 12 or 15(d) of the Exchange Act, merely having securities traded in the United States, such as through an over-the-counter ADR programme, will not cause a foreign private issuer to become subject to the provisions of SOX and the rules and regulations thereunder.

THE PCAOB

Section 101 of SOX required the establishment of the PCAOB to oversee the audit of public companies, domestic and foreign, that are subject to the US federal securities laws.[1] The PCAOB's responsibilities include registration and inspection of audit firms, setting standards relating to audits, quality control and independence, and investigations and disciplinary proceedings.

The PCAOB, a non-profit corporation, is not an agency or establishment of the US Government. The SEC has oversight authority over the PCAOB and generally must approve the rules and standards adopted by the PCAOB. While the SEC rules implement different disclosure and regulatory schemes for foreign private issuers, there are no blanket statutory or regulatory exemptions for foreign private issuers with respect to the PCAOB. Although the PCAOB's activities are directed at audit firms, its activities are relevant to public companies in several ways. First, the PCAOB is funded through fees levied on public companies based on their market capitalisation. Second, the PCAOB is permitted to collect public company client information in the course of an audit firm investigation. Since the PCAOB is authorised to establish rules that would require the testimony of, and production of any document in the possession of, any audit firm client, and to seek issuance by the SEC of a subpoena to require the testimony of or production of any document in the possession of an audit firm client that the PCAOB considers relevant and material, public companies should be aware of how their confidential and proprietary information

---

1 SOX, H.R. 3763, Section 101(a).

will be protected in the course of an audit firm investigation. In general, such information will be treated as confidential and privileged as an evidentiary matter (and will not be subject to civil discovery) in any proceeding in any federal or state court or administrative agency. It will also be exempt from disclosure. The PCAOB, however, may make such information available to the SEC and, in the PCAOB's discretion, to one or more of the US Attorney General, state attorneys general (in connection with any criminal investigation) or state regulatory authorities, each of which will be required to maintain the information as confidential and privileged. A public company should consider including a notice provision in their audit engagement letter that would require the company's audit firm to advise the company when the PCAOB has requested copies of the audit firm's work papers regarding the company, and preferably before such disclosure is actually made.

Consistent with the SEC's long-standing position that a foreign accounting firm that issues an audit report for a foreign reporting issuer is subject to SEC regulation, SOX requires that all public accounting firms, including foreign public accounting firms that prepare or furnish audit reports with respect to Exchange Act reporting issuers, register with the PCAOB or be banned from participating in public company audits. SOX also gives the PCAOB the latitude to determine (by rulemaking) "that a foreign public accounting firm that does not issue audit reports [but] nonetheless plays such a substantial role in the preparation and furnishing of such reports" be subject to PCAOB registration and oversight.

Concerned that excluding foreign accountants from US oversight could put US accounting firms at a disadvantage, prompt accountants to move outside the US or compromise investor protection, the PCAOB endorsed the concept of universal registration and adopted rules to that effect in May 2003.[2] Under the PCAOB's rules, any US public accounting firm and non-US public accounting firm that wants to prepare or issue any audit report with respect to a public reporting company must register with PCAOB. In addition, any US public accounting firm and non-US public accounting firm that will have a "substantial role" in the preparation or issuance of an audit report for a public reporting company

---

2 *See* PCAOB Release 2003–007 (6th May 2003).

must register with the PCAOB. As of 26th April 2005, 1,493 accounting firms were registered with the PCAOB.[3]

In accordance with Section 107 of SOX, the SEC must approve the rules of the PCAOB before those rules become effective. Rules adopted by the PCAOB and submitted to the SEC for approval, PCAOB's final rules as approved by the SEC and other information (including staff questions and answers on accounting standards) are available on the PCAOB's website, which is accessible directly or through the SEC's website.

OVERVIEW OF FINANCIAL STATEMENT REQUIREMENTS

The primary financial statements that US reporting issuers file with the SEC are prepared in accordance with in US GAAP whereas the statements that foreign private reporting issuers file with the SEC may be prepared in accordance with either (1) US GAAP or (2) another comprehensive body of GAAP and reconciled to US GAAP. In addition, issuers must comply with Regulation S-X in connection with filings made under the Securities Act and the Exchange Act. Regulation S-X sets out the form and content requirements for the financial statements required to be included in registration statements filed under the Securities Act and the Exchange Act, and in the periodic reports (annual and quarterly reports), current reports, proxy and information statements, tender offer documents and other reports filed under the Exchange Act.

If a foreign private issuer does not prepare its financial statements in accordance with US GAAP, the issuer must provide a reconciliation of its financial statements to US GAAP. The two different levels of reconciliation to US GAAP are set out in Items 17 and 18 of Form 20-F. Item 17 requires:

- ❏ a discussion of the material variances in accounting principles, practices and methods used in preparing the primary financial statements and US GAAP;
- ❏ a reconciliation of net income from the foreign GAAP to US GAAP that quantifies and describes each significant difference;
- ❏ a quantitative description of the balance sheet differences under foreign GAAP as compared with US GAAP;

---

3   Numerical data appeared on the PCAOB website as of 3rd May 2005.

FINANCIAL INFORMATION: ACCOUNTING AND DISCLOSURE

- a cashflow statement prepared under US GAAP or IAS 7, or a reconciliation of a cashflow statement, or statement of changes in financial position to US GAAP; and
- disclosure of earnings per share calculated in accordance with US GAAP, if materially different from foreign GAAP.

Item 18 requires the same information as Item 17 plus all of the disclosures required by US GAAP and Regulation S-X. The following information is required under Item 18, but not Item 17:

- segment information (FAS 14);
- fair value information (FAS 107);
- concentration of credit risk (FAS 105);
- information about investment securities (FAS 115);
- information about off-balance-sheet financial instruments (FAS 119);
- components of pension and benefits (FAS 87, FAS 106); and
- components of tax expense and deferred tax liability and deferred tax asset (FAS 109).

Item 18 is required for securities offerings with certain exceptions such as dividend reinvestment plans, conversions of securities and investment-grade debt offerings. An Item 17 reconciliation is permitted for the exceptions to Item 18 and for purposes of the annual report.

Selected financial data should also be reconciled to US GAAP in registration statements filed under the Securities Act and the Exchange Act and annual reports filed under the Exchange Act, but only for the periods for which the primary financial statements and any interim financial statements included in those registration statements and annual reports must be reconciled to US GAAP.

Rule 3–20 of Regulation S-X sets out special rules that govern the currency in which a foreign private issuer's financial statements must be presented. The rule permits a foreign private issuer to state its primary financial statements in the currency that it deems appropriate. The front page of financial statements must contain prominent disclosure of the currency used. The rule requires disclosures in the financial statements if the issuer expects to declare dividends on its publicly traded equity securities in a currency different from the reporting currency. Disclosures are also required if there are material exchange restrictions or controls that affect the reporting currency, the currency of the company's domicile or the currency in which dividends are paid.

The rule gives a foreign private issuer free selection of the currency it should use for measurement purposes. Under the rule, a foreign private issuer must separately measure its own transactions and those of each of its material operations (such as branches, divisions, subsidiaries, joint ventures and similar entities) that are included in the consolidated financial statements and not operating in a hyperinflationary environment, using the currency of the primary economic environment in which the issuer or a material operation conducts is business. For the purposes of Rule 3–20, that currency is usually the currency in which cash is primarily generated and spent.

If the financial statements are not presented in US dollars, there must be disclosure of the exchange rate between the financial reporting currency and the US dollar as of the latest practicable date, the high and low for each of the last six months and for the five most recent financial years and any subsequent interim period for which financial statements are presented. A foreign private issuer may include "convenience" translations of the issuer's home currency to US dollars for the most recent financial year and any subsequent interim period.

In addition to the consolidated financial statements of the issuer (whether United States or foreign), financial statements of other persons also may be required. These financial statements include the following.

Audited financial statements of businesses acquired or about to be acquired. An issuer may conduct a registered public offering without the financial statements of an acquired business or probable acquisition within 75 days after consummation of the acquisition unless the acquisition or probable acquisition exceeds the 50% level of significance. The significance of an acquired business or probable acquisition is determined according to: (1) the amount of the foreign private issuer's investment in (stated as the total GAAP purchase price that will be allocated to assets and liabilities acquired, which includes consideration paid and acquisition costs) the acquired business compared with the consolidated assets of the foreign private issuer; (2) a comparison of the acquired entity's total assets to the foreign private issuer's consolidated assets; and (3) a comparison of the acquired entity's pre-tax income from continuing operations to that of the foreign private issuer's. After the 75-day period, the issuer must include one or two years of audited financial statements for an acquired business at the 20 or 40% significance levels, respectively. At the 50% level of significance, three years of audited financial statements are required. Under the rule, the acquisition of related businesses (those under common ownership or management or whose acquisitions are conditional on each other or on a single common condition) are treated as a single business acquisition. In addition, if a registrant has, since the date of its last audited balance sheet, acquired unrelated businesses that individually are not significant but in the aggregate exceed the 50% significance level, audited financial statements for the most recent financial year and any subsequent interim periods that cover at least the substantial majority of such businesses must be included in the registration statement.

In addition to audited financial statements of the acquired business, pro forma financial statements may be required under Article 11 of Regulation S-X.

If a US reporting company or any of its majority-owned subsidiaries acquires or disposes of a significant amount of assets not in the ordinary course of business, the company should file an Item 2 Form 8-K within a specified number of days (currently 15 days) after completion of the transaction. In determining whether a Form 8-K filing is required, a 10% significance test is used. The acquiring company may also need to file audited financial statements for an acquired business required to be described in an Item 2, Form 8-K. The financial statement requirements, historical and pro forma, are set out in Item 7 of Form 8-K and Regulation S-X.

Financial statements of guarantors. A Securities Act registration statement covering an offering of guaranteed securities generally must include audited financial statements for both the issuer of the securities and the guarantor of the securities. Similarly, the annual report of the issuer of the guaranteed securities also must include audited financial statements of the guarantor of the issuer's securities. Specific exceptions to this general requirement are set out in

Rule 3–10 of Regulation S-X that the SEC adopted in August 2000 to replace SAB 53. Rule 3–10 largely codifies SEC Staff practices and no-action letters under SAB 53. [4]

The exceptions apply where a parent company is issuing securities that will be fully and unconditionally guaranteed by one or more wholly-owned subsidiaries or where a wholly-owned subsidiary is issuing securities that will be fully and unconditionally guaranteed by its parent company and one or more other wholly-owned subsidiaries. If an exception under the Rule is applicable, the Rule permits the inclusion of condensed consolidating financial information in place of separate audited annual and unaudited interim financial statements of a subsidiary issuer or a subsidiary guarantor. When the parent company's financial statements are prepared on a basis other than US GAAP, the Rule requires that the information in each column of the condensed consolidating financial information be reconciled to US GAAP to the extent necessary to permit investors to evaluate the sufficiency of the guarantees. The reconciling information may be based on Item 17 of Form 20-F.

The Rule provides that condensed consolidating financial information generally will not be required where either: the parent has no independent operations or assets and any other subsidiaries are minor; or the subsidiary is a finance subsidiary and does not have any independent operations.

There are two threshold requirements of the Rule. First, 100% of all outstanding voting shares of the subsidiary issuer or guarantor must be owned directly or indirectly by its parent company. The SEC Staff, however, has granted no-action relief to the 100% ownership requirement when the non-parent company ownership is at the minimum level required to comply with the laws under which the entity is incorporated.[5] Second, each guarantee must be full and unconditional so that if the issuer of the guaranteed security fails to pay, the holder of the guaranteed security may immediately, without the need to comply with any conditions precedent, demand payment from the guarantor.

---

4   Securities Act Release 7878 (4th August 2000).
5   *See Maxcom Telecommunicaciones, S.A. de C.V.* (31st October 2001); *Travelex plc* (1st February 2001); and the Rule 3–10 Adopting Release, Securities Act Release 7878, in which the SEC concurred with the Staff's no-action response to *Crown Cork & Seal Company, Inc* (10th March 1997).

Third-party financial statements deemed material to an investment decision. In general, the SEC Staff will require audited financial statements of a third-party to be included in an issuer's registration statement and annual report when the financial statements of that third-party are deemed material to the investor's investment decision. Examples of these situations include financing structures that provide for some form of credit enhancement, such as financial insurance or warranty, or are significantly linked to the performance of a third party, such as often exists in equity linked debt securities, collateralised bond or loan obligations or other asset-backed securities, principal protected securities and indexed securities. In evaluating whether separate financial information is required, the SEC Staff applies the general materiality test set out in Rule 3–13 of Regulation S-X and, by analogy to other rules and interpretations, a significance test of 10 and 20%.[6] A significance of less than 10% generally requires no separate financial information, a significance of between 10 and 20% usually requires condensed consolidating financial information and a significance of more than 20% usually requires full audited financial statements.

The SEC Staff has required that full financial statements of foreign parent banks prepared in accordance with or reconciled to US GAAP be included in the Securities Act registration statement and subsequent periodic reports of special limited purpose bank finance subsidiaries when the securities sold to the public are intended to be treated as risk-based capital by the parent bank, the source of funds for the subsidiary to meet its payment obligations on its securities is dependent on the income generated by the assets of the subsidiary, and the assets must, under applicable bank regulations, be returned to the parent bank upon the occurrence of a financial regulatory event.

The SEC Staff, through the review and comment process of registration statements for offerings of principal protected financial products, is requiring full audited financial statements of the

---

[6] *See*, for example: the definition of the term "significant subsidiary" contained in Rule 1–02(w) of Regulation S-X; SAB 71, "Financial statement or properties securing mortgage loans", and SAB 71A, "Determining adequacy of borrower's equity in underlying property"; Division of Corporation Finance, *Current Issues and Rulemaking Projects*, "Structured Financings" (14th November 2000); and Securities Act Release 8518 (22nd December 2004) at section III.B.7 *Significant Obligors*.

third-party credit provider. The financial statements must either be prepared in accordance with US GAAP or, if prepared in accordance with home-country GAAP, be reconciled to US GAAP.

The SEC Staff addressed certain disclosure issues applicable to third-party derivative securities in a 1996 no-action letter to *Morgan Stanley & Co, Inc*. In general, where there is sufficient market interest and publicly available information about the third party, abbreviated disclosure may be satisfactory. The abbreviated information consists of a brief description of the third-party's business, disclosure about the availability of information about the third party and information about the market price of the underlying securities. For example, if the third party is a seasoned issuer eligible to use the short-form registration statement, Form F-3 for foreign private issuers or Form S-3 for US issuers, the issuer of the security need only include a short description of the third party and may refer investors to that third-party's filings with the SEC. Otherwise, the issuer of the security must include full audited financial statements and financial information, including MD&A, in its filings and assume liability on that information.

The SEC Staff also has applied the Morgan Stanley no-action letter disclosure framework in contexts other than third-party derivative securities, such as corporate debt securitisations.

FINANCIAL STATEMENTS PREPARED UNDER INTERNATIONAL FINANCIAL REPORTING STANDARDS

In April 2005, the SEC amended Form 20-F to allow a foreign private issuer that for the first time prepares its financial statements in accordance with IFRS to file two years rather than three years of statements of income, changes in shareholders' equity and cashflows, with appropriate related disclosures.[7] If an issuer has published audited IFRS financial statements for all three years it must include all three years of IFRS financial statements in its filings with the SEC. The SEC accommodation retains the existing US GAAP reconciliation requirements.

The amendments, which become effective on 19th May 2005, operate as a one-time accommodation to foreign private issuers

---

7   Securities Act Release 8567 (12th April 2005).

who adopt IFRS (voluntarily or by mandate)[8] for the first time prior to or for the first financial year[9] starting on or after 1st January 2007.

Eligibility

A foreign private issuer may use the accommodation if each of the following conditions is satisfied.

❑ the issuer is a "first-time adopter" and adopts IFRS prior to or for its first financial year starting on or after 1st January 2007. For example, an issuer with a 30th September 2007 financial-year-end that adopts IFRS for its financial year beginning 1st October 2007 would be eligible to apply the SEC's accommodation when filing with the SEC its Annual Report on Form 20-F by March 2009.

❑ the issuer "unreservedly and explicitly" states that its financial statements comply with IFRS and are not qualified in any way as to the application of IFRS as issued by the IASB. Some countries may adopt, and in certain cases such as Australia, have adopted, IFRS by incorporating IFRS into their home country standard in which case this condition is modified to require that companies assert compliance with both IFRS and home-country GAAP.

❑ the issuer's independent auditor opines, without qualification, on compliance with IFRS.

Annual reports and registration statements

The SEC's first-time IFRS adopter accommodation applies to annual reports filed on Form 20-F and to registration statements filed under the Exchange Act and the Securities Act. The accommodation is also available for financial statements of:

❑ businesses acquired or to be acquired;

---

8 For instance, in June 2002, the EU adopted a regulation that requires companies incorporated under the laws of an EU member state and whose securities are publicly traded within the EU to prepare their consolidated financial statements for each financial year starting on or after 1st January 2005 using accounting standards issued by the International Accounting Standards Board (IASB). Regulation (EC) No 1606/2002 of the European Parliament and of the Council of 19th July 2002 on the application of international accounting standards, Official Journal L. 243, (11th September 2002) P.0001–0004 (EU). Except for certain companies who meet specified criteria, listed EU companies that are not now using IFRS must convert to IFRS, as endorsed by the EU, no later than 2005. Other countries, including Australia, also have adopted requirements that incorporate IFRS as their own standards for periods beginning after 1st January 2005.

9 Consistent with usage outside the United States, the term financial year refers to a fiscal year.

❏ non-consolidated subsidiaries and 50% or less owned persons; and
❏ guarantors and issuers of guaranteed securities registered or being registered and affiliates whose securities collateralise a class of securities registered or being registered.

US GAAP reconciliation requirements and condensed US GAAP financial information

The current requirement to provide US GAAP reconciliation will continue to apply to the two years of financial statements prepared in accordance with IFRS. The reconciliation must be audited and included as a note to the audited financial statements. Foreign private issuers relying on the accommodation, however, will not be required to present condensed US GAAP financial information.

Previous GAAP financial statements

A foreign private issuer that uses the accommodation may (ie, purely voluntary) include financial statements, a narrative discussion or other financial information based on its previous financial statements prepared in accordance with home-country GAAP (Previous GAAP) prior to the issuer's adoption of IFRS.

If a foreign private issuer elects to include, incorporate by reference or refer to Previous GAAP financial information, the issuer must include or incorporate by reference its Form 20-F Item 5 narrative disclosure of its operating and financial review and prospects for the reporting periods covered by the Previous GAAP financial information. If the issuer includes, incorporates by reference or refers to Previous GAAP selected financial data or financial information in a SEC filing, it also must include appropriate cautionary disclosures at an appropriately prominent location, that the filing contains financial information based on Previous GAAP, and that such information is not comparable with financial information based on IFRS. The SEC did not adopt specific legends or language, concluding that the language may vary depending on how an issuer uses its Previous GAAP information.

Selected financial data
IFRS
Item 3.A of Form 20-F generally requires a foreign private issuer to provide selected financial data for each of its past five financial

years. A first-time adopter must present financial data for its two most recent financial years based on IFRS.

US GAAP

A foreign private issuer, including a first-time adopter, must continue to provide selected financial data based on US GAAP for the five most recent financial years unless the issuer can rely on the instructions to Item 3.A to provide US GAAP financial information for a shorter time period.

The SEC advises issuers not to have a side-by-side columnar presentation that combines financial data based on two or more sets of accounting principals. The SEC further advises that a format presenting the same information on a single page would be permitted, assuming that the presentation includes appropriate legends and explanations about the non-comparability of the information.

Operating and financial review and prospects

General Instruction G to Form 20-F explains how issuers should present their discussion about their financial condition and the quality and potential variability of their earnings and cashflow. The SEC advises management to focus on the IFRS financial statements for the two most recent financial years, as well as the reconciliation to US GAAP for the same two years. Among other matters, the discussion should explain the differences between IFRS and US GAAP that are not otherwise discussed in the reconciliation, to the extent necessary for an understanding of the financial statements as a whole. The SEC warns management not to include any discussion relating to Previous GAAP financial statements in this section.

Interim periods for the transition year

The SEC provides specific guidance to assist first-time adopters in complying with Item 8.A.5 of Form 20-F, which sets out the requirements for filing interim financial statements.

❏ *Form 6-K.* The SEC did not impose any changes to Form 6-K for issuers that are switching from Previous GAAP to IFRS.
❏ *Securities Act registration statements and prospectuses and initial Exchange Act registration statements used less than nine months after the financial-year-end.* Under certain circumstances, a foreign private issuer that switches to IFRS during a financial year may

publish interim financial information prepared either fully or partly in accordance with IFRS before it has filed audited year-end IFRS financial statements in its most recent annual report on form 20-F. To avoid the burdens that would result from a strict application of the US GAAP reconciliation requirements of Item 8.A.5 that would require a US GAAP reconciliation relating to the IFRS interim financial information, a new Instruction G to Form 20-F was added. This new Instruction G permits an issuer to include IFRS financial information pursuant to Item 8.A.5 without also providing either descriptive or quantified US GAAP reconciliation information. The relief also extends to annual year-end financial information that does not fully comply with IFRS and that an issuer may publish during its transition year, as long as the published information is accompanied by a statement that the information is not in compliance with IFRS and other appropriate cautionary language.

- *Securities Act registration statements and prospectuses and initial Exchange Act registration statements used more than nine months after the financial-year-end.* A foreign private issuer must include, in a SEC filed document that is dated more than nine months after the end of the last audited financial year, consolidated interim financial statements, which may be unaudited, covering the first six months of the current financial year. Issuers must prepare these unaudited interim financial statements using the same accounting standards as their audited financial statements and provide US GAAP reconciliation. A first-time adopter required to include interim period financial statements in documents dated more than nine months after the end of the last audited financial year may choose one among four alternatives.
  - the *Previous GAAP Option* (which is consistent with current rules) allows a foreign private issuer to present three years of audited Previous GAAP financial statements as well as Previous GAAP interim financial statements for the current and prior year comparable interim periods, all reconciled to US GAAP.
  - the *IFRS Option* allows a foreign private issuer to present two years of audited financial statements as well as interim financial statements for the current and comparable prior year interim periods, all prepared in accordance with IFRS and

reconciled to US GAAP. An issuer that applies EU GAAP may either use the reconciliation to IFRS as published by the IASB as the basis for its reconciliation to US GAAP or use its EU GAAP financial statements as the basis for its US GAAP reconciliation.

❑ the *US GAAP Condensed Information Option* allows foreign private issuers to present: (i) audited Previous GAAP financial statements for the prior three years, reconciled to US GAAP; (ii) unaudited IFRS financial statements for the current and prior year comparable interim periods, reconciled to US GAAP; and (iii) unaudited condensed US GAAP balance sheet and income statements for the most recent prior financial year and the current and prior year comparable interim periods. This option allows issuers to use condensed US GAAP information to bridge the gap in interim financial information between Previous GAAP and IFRS.

❑ the *Case-by-Case Option* allows issuers that cannot comply fully with any of the other options, but do have available comparable financial information based on a combination of Previous GAAP, IFRS and US GAAP to contact the SEC's Office of International Corporate Finance in writing for guidance.

Required disclosures about first-time adoption of IFRS
Exceptions to IFRS
First-time adopters, regardless of the year in which they change their accounting standards must provide disclosures about:

❑ their reliance on any of either the elective[10] or mandatory[11] exceptions to the general restatement and measurement principles allowed under IFRS; and

❑ the reconciliation of Previous GAAP financial statements to IFRS.

---

[10] The elective exceptions relate to: (i) business combinations, fair value or re-evaluation deemed as cost; (ii) employee benefits; (iii) cumulative translation differences; (iv) compound financial instruments; and (v) assets and liabilities of subsidiaries, associates and joint ventures.

[11] The mandatory exceptions prohibit retroactive application of IFRS to: (i) derecognition of financial instruments and financial liabilities; (ii) hedge accounting; and (iii) information to be used in preparing IFRS estimates.

Issuers must discuss in detail their reliance on any of the exceptions to IFRS in the operating and financial review and prospectus disclosures.

Reconciliation from Previous GAAP

IFRS requires first-time adopters to include in the notes to their audited financial statements a reconciliation from Previous GAAP to IFRS that gives "sufficient data to users to understand the material adjustments to the balance sheet and income statement," and if presented under Previous GAAP, the cashflow statement. The SEC added an instruction to Item 8 of Form 20-F that calls for a similar level of information in the Form 20-F.

MD&A: OPERATING AND FINANCIAL REVIEW AND PROSPECTS
Introduction

The Operating and Financial Review and Prospects standard of Form 20-F, the disclosure item comparable with the MD&A disclosure requirement set out in Regulation S-K applicable to US issuers, is intended to provide investors with a stand-alone, comprehensive textual discussion of a company's financial statements and accompanying footnotes so as to allow investors and other users to assess the quality of a company's financial condition and results of operations, with particular focus on the company's future prospects. The Operating and Financial Review and Prospects standard along with the financial statements and accompanying footnotes disclosures are generally viewed as providing the most important and critical disclosures about a company to investors and the financial markets. While the line item names are different, the disclosure requirements of the Operating and Financial Review and Prospects standard and MD&A are largely the same in fact, the standard expressly refers to the guidance set out in the SEC's 1989 MD&A Interpretive Release. A foreign private issuer, when preparing its Operating and Financial Review and Prospects disclosures, must fully consider the MD&A disclosure requirements and related guidance, including SEC releases, SEC enforcement actions, judicial decisions, SEC Commissioner statements and SEC Staff statements. A list of source materials that may assist companies in preparing the Operating and

Financial Review and Prospectus discussion may be found at the end of this chapter.

According to the SEC, MD&A has three related purposes:[12]

❑ provide a narrative explanation of a company's financial statements that allow investors and other users to see the company through the eyes of management;
❑ provide investors and other users with a framework within which to analyse a company's financial statements; and
❑ provide information about the quality of, and potential variability of, a company's earnings and cashflow, so that investors and other users can ascertain the likelihood that past performance is indicative of future performance.

Preparation of MD&A
Guiding principle
The SEC has stated that a company, when preparing its MD&A, must remember that the basic purpose of the MD&A disclosure requirements is

> *"to give investors an opportunity to look at the company through the eyes of management by providing historical and prospective analyses of the company's financial condition and results of operations, with particular emphasis on the company's prospects for the future."*

The SEC in its 2003 Interpretative Release encouraged issuers and their management to step back and take a fresh look at the disclosures with a view towards improving its quality. In particular, the SEC emphasised the following points regarding the overall presentation.

❑ Focus on and prominently disclose the most important information and not bury it in the discussion and analysis.
❑ Use a "layered approach" to highlight the most important information and eliminate immaterial information that does not promote an understanding of the issuer's financial condition, liquidity and capital resources, changes in financial condition and results of operations.

---
12 *See* Securities Act Release 8350 (19th December 2003) (2003 Interpretive Release); and Securities Act Release 8098 (10th May 2002) (Critical Accounting Policies Proposing Release); *quoting* Securities Act Release 6711 (23rd April 1987), Section II.

- Avoid unnecessary duplicative information.
- Identify and disclose known trends, events, uncertainties, commitments and demands that are reasonably likely to materially affect the issuer's financial condition and operating performance.
- Identify and discuss key financial and non-financial performance indicators that management uses to manage the business and that investors would find material.
- Include an analysis of the information that provides investors with an understanding of management's views about the implication and significance of, for example, any disclosed known trends, events, uncertainties and commitments. For instance, if an issuer's financial statements show a material increase in revenues, its MD&A should analyse the reasons for the increase such as increased volume and the reasons for the increase when the reasons are material and determinable.
- Start the MD&A with an executive-level overview that includes the most important matters that management focuses on in evaluating financial condition and operating results and provides readers with a context for the remainder of the discussion and analysis. The SEC indicated that a good overview would:
  - Include economic or industry-wide factors pertinent to the issuer;
  - Explain how the issuer earns revenue and income and generates cash;
  - Discuss the issuer's business lines, location of operations and principal products and services in a manner that does not merely duplicate the business description section; and
  - Provide investors with an insight into material opportunities, challenges and risks for both the short and long terms and the actions that management is taking to address the opportunities and manage challenges and risks.
- Consider all relevant information, even if that information is not required to be filed with the SEC, in evaluating the information required to be disclosed. Examples include information contained in earnings releases, publicly accessible analysts' calls, website postings, letters to shareholders and analyst reports.

Requirements

The Operating and Financial Review and Prospects standard (in Item 5 of Form 20-F), like the MD&A requirements (in Item 303 of Regulation S-K), requires a discussion of a company's liquidity, capital resources and results of operations. In addition to the express requirements, the discussion must also address "such other information that the company believes to be necessary to an understanding of its financial condition, changes in financial condition and results of operations".[13] The discussion should provide investors with a look behind the consolidated financial results when a discussion of the consolidated basis would present an incomplete or misleading picture of the company or where different segments contribute in materially disproportionate ways to revenues, profitability or financing demands.[14] Consequently, the discussion should cover each relevant, reportable segment, other service or product line or other operating subdivision of a company's business where such discussion is necessary to an understanding of the company's historical and future business as a whole. The discussion should identify the important elements of the company's business model as well the dynamics of the business and the key variables of the business model and business dynamics. In this regard, the discussion should answer basic questions such as the following.

❑ What businesses does the company have, how did such businesses perform during the periods reported and what were the significant driving factors (positive and negative) that caused the businesses to perform as they did?
❑ What are the company's obligations (including contingent) within the next year, three years, five years and beyond?
❑ What were the company's short- and long-term sources of capital (eg, cashflow from operations or financing activities) during the reporting period? How strong were and are those sources? Did the company use any off-balance-sheet financing? If yes, what were the reasons for doing so and what are the material

---

13 Item 5 of Form 20-F, Item 303 of Regulation S-K.
14 Securities Act Release 6835 (MD&A Interpretative Release) (18th May 1989) at section III.F.1.

short- and long- term exposure risks (actual or contingent) to the company?
❑ Has the company evidenced any short- or long-term liquidity problems? If yes, how is the company addressing them?
❑ What were the company's significant uses of cash (eg, working capital, property plant and equipment, product or business acquisitions)? What were the company's capital expenditures? What are the company's short- and long-term sources of capital? Are those sources of liquidity adequate to finance the company's operations over the short term (the next 12 months) and long term? If not, how does the company intend to address the inadequacy?
❑ What factors and activities were significant drivers of the company's revenues and earnings during the reporting periods? How strong were the company's revenues and earnings during the reporting period?
❑ How quickly can the company respond to material external change due to, for example, economic, business, regulatory or political events or the loss of a significant customer or supplier? How quickly can the company respond to material internal change due to, for example, sudden management changes, property loss or labour issues?
❑ What were the significant risks to a company's revenues, earnings, cashflow from operations and cashflow from financing activities?
❑ Is the reported financial information indicative of future operating results or financial condition and, if not, why not?
❑ Does management believe that existing disclosures may be materially deficient due to misstatements or omissions of material information?
❑ Did the company incur any material restructuring or impairment charges, or a decline in the profitability of a plant or other business activity?
❑ Is there a reasonable likelihood that the historical reported financial information is not indicative of future operating performance and financial condition due to, for example, changes in the estimates used to prepare the financial statements, asset or business acquisitions, lost customers or suppliers, new products, asset impairments, litigation claims, settlements or judgments, or changes in the law?

Operating results

The standard requires a company to explain the reasons for any material change from one year to another in net sales or revenues, including the extent to which the changes are due to changes in price, or amount of products or services sold, or to the introduction of new products or services. Where multiple factors contribute to a change, the discussion should attempt to identify, and quantify the contribution of, each factor. However, if the reasons for changes are common among line items, the reasons need not be repeated in a line-by-line analysis. Companies should discuss those significant "factors, including any unusual or infrequent events or new developments materially affecting the company's income from operations, indicating the extent to which income was so affected". A company also should "[d]escribe any other significant components of revenue or expense necessary to understand the company's results of operations".

Although the line item disclosures do not require that companies provide the amount of any change that is readily computable from the financial statements, as a matter of practice, companies often do so to facilitate the investors reading and understanding of the discussion.

The standard, in addition to the material change discussion, calls for disclosures about the impact of inflation, foreign currency fluctuations and hedging instruments on the company's operating results. A company should also discuss any governmental, economic, fiscal, monetary or political policies or factors that have had a material effect on the company's operations or investments or could have such an effect in the future.

Liquidity and capital resources

Item 5.B to Form 20-F sets out the liquidity and capital resources disclosure requirements. The SEC's most recent views about the detail necessary to meet the liquidity and capital resource disclosure requirements are extensively set out in the 2003 Interpretive Release and the 2002 MD&A Release. Broad general disclosures stating that "the company has sufficient short-term funding to meet its liquidity requirements for the next year ..." are inadequate – this might invite regulatory scrutiny. A discussion of the reasons for material period-to-period changes is applicable to liquidity and capital resources. One starting point for this discussion and analysis of the issuer's cash requirements is the contractual obligations table supplemented with other additional material information necessary to allow investors to fully understand the issuer's cash requirements.

The discussion should address liquidity in the broadest sense, evaluating the amounts and certainty of cashflows from internal operations and from outside sources, current and future commitments, known trends, changes in circumstances and uncertainties. The discussion should explain both the short- and long-term liquidity requirements of the company. In general, short-term liquidity and capital resources cover a company's cash requirements over the next 12 months. A company should use its statement of cashflows in analysing its liquidity and present a balanced discussion about cashflows from investing and financing activities as well as from operations. For example, the discussion should:

❏ Address material changes in any of the underlying drivers of an issuer's cashflows;
❏ Discuss the issuer's short- and long-term cash requirements;
❏ Describe the company's internal and external sources of liquidity and any unused sources of liquidity and include the company's views as to the adequacy of its working capital;
❏ Evaluate the sources and amounts of the company's cashflows, including the nature and extent of any legal or economic restrictions that prevent the company's subsidiaries from transferring funds to the company in the form of cash dividends, loans or advances, and the historical and future effects of such restrictions on the company's ability to satisfy its obligations;
❏ Provide information about the amount, the seasonality, maturity profile of its borrowings and committed borrowing facilities with a description of any restrictions on the uses to which any borrowing may be put;
❏ Provide information about the types of financial instruments used, the maturity profile, currency and interest rate structure of the company's debt;
❏ Describe the company's funding and treasury policies and objectives, the currencies of its cash and cash-equivalent assets and the use of financial instruments for hedging purposes;

FINANCIAL INFORMATION: ACCOUNTING AND DISCLOSURE

- Provide information about the company's material capital expenditure commitments as of the end of the latest financial year and any subsequent interim period, the general purpose of such commitments and the anticipated sources of funds to meet those commitments;
- Identify and discuss any known trends, demands, commitments, events, uncertainties or contingencies that will result in or that are reasonably likely to result in the company's liquidity increasing or decreasing in any material way;
- Describe any expected material changes in the mix and relative cost of a company's capital resources;
- Explain which balance-sheet conditions or income or cashflow items an investor should consider in assessing the company's liquidity; and
- Disclose any identified material deficiency in either short- or long-term liquidity and any proposed remedy to address the deficiency or, if no remedy has been determined, that it currently is unable to address the deficiency.

Required forward-looking event, trend and contingency disclosures

In its 2002 MD&A Release, the SEC reminded companies that forward-looking disclosure is *mandatory* where a known trend or uncertainty is reasonably likely to have a material effect on a company's financial condition, results of operations, liquidity or capital resources. The disclosure should facilitate an investor's analysis of a company's future performance in light of its historical performance. The SEC further reminded companies that the "reasonably likely" to occur disclosure standard is lower than a "more likely than not" standard.

A MD&A disclosure obligation exists where a trend, event, demand, commitment or uncertainty is both presently known to management and reasonably likely to have a material effect on a company's financial condition or operation results. Management must make two assessments to determine whether a known trend or contingency triggers a disclosure obligation.

- Is the known trend, demand, commitment, event or uncertainty likely to come to fruition? If management determines that it is *not* reasonably likely to occur, no disclosure is required.

❑ If management cannot make that determination, it must evaluate objectively the consequences of the known trend, demand, commitment, event or uncertainty, on the assumption that it will come to fruition. Disclosure is required unless management determines that a material effect on the company's financial condition or results of operations is *not* reasonably likely to occur.[15]

This MD&A disclosure analysis is distinct from the "probability/magnitude" materiality analysis articulated by the US Supreme Court in *Levinson* and adopted for the purposes of determining disclosure duties under the Exchange Act's general anti-fraud provision, Section 10(b) and Rule 10b-5 thereunder. The SEC has stated that the probability/magnitude test is "inapposite to" MD&A disclosures. However, disclosure comments issued by the SEC Staff suggest that the Staff may require disclosure of a known trend, event commitment or uncertainty if either disclosure standard is met.

The 2002 MD&A Release advises companies to consider the following non-exclusive factors to identify trends, demands, commitments, events and uncertainties that will result in or that are reasonably likely to result in material increases or decreases in a company's liquidity:

❑ Provisions in financial guarantees or commitments, debt or lease agreements or other arrangements that could trigger a requirement for an early payment, additional collateral support, changes in terms, acceleration of maturity, or the creation of an additional financial obligation, such as adverse changes in the company's credit rating, financial ratios, earnings, cashflows or stock price, or changes in the value of underlying, linked or indexed assets;

❑ Circumstances that could impair the company's ability to continue to engage in transactions that have been integral to historical operations or are financially or operationally essential, or that could render that activity commercially impracticable, such as the inability to maintain a specified investment-grade credit rating, level of earnings, earnings per share, financial ratios or collateral;

---

[15] Securities Act Release 8056 (22nd January 2002) *citing* Securities Act Release 6835 (18th May 1989).

FINANCIAL INFORMATION: ACCOUNTING AND DISCLOSURE

- Factors specific to the company and its markets that the company expects to be given significant weight in the determination of the company's credit rating or will otherwise affect the company's ability to raise short-term and long-term financing;
- Guarantees of debt or other commitments to third parties; and
- Written options on non-financial assets (for example, real estate puts).

A company should consider the effect known events, trends, commitments or uncertainties that may have on future operating results. Examples of such factors include:

- expiration of a material contract;
- adoption of new legislation;
- changes in supply or labour costs;
- change in business lines;
- introduction of new products or services; and
- receipt of government approval to sell products or services and curtailment of segments or business lines.

Off-balance-sheet arrangements

In January 2003, the SEC adopted amendments to the MD&A disclosure requirements to implement the disclosure mandate of Section 401(a) of SOX.[16] New Section 13(j) to the Exchange Act, which was added by SOX Section 401(a), directed the SEC to adopt rules to require each annual and quarterly financial report required to be filed with the SEC to disclose "all material off-balance sheet transactions, arrangements, obligations (including contingent obligations), and other relationships of the issuer with unconsolidated entities or other persons, that may have a material current or future effect on financial condition, changes in financial conditions, results of operations, liquidity, capital expenditures, capital resources, or significant components of revenues or expenses".

In the adopting the release, the SEC stated that the then-existing MD&A already requires disclosure about off-balance-sheet arrangements and other contingencies that may not otherwise be required to be disclosed under US GAAP. The SEC further stated that the

---

[16] Securities Act Release 8182 (28th January 2003).

January 2003 amendments "clarify disclosures that company's must make with regard to off-balance-sheet arrangements".

The amendments are intended to provide investors with a clear understanding of a company's off-balance-sheet arrangements and the material effects of such arrangements on the company's financial condition, changes in financial condition, revenues and expenses, results of operations, liquidity and capital resources. In a separately captioned section of its MD&A, a company should disclose the nature and business purpose of the off-balance-sheet arrangements and explain to investors why each arrangement is used: to finance inventory, transportation or research and development costs without recognising a liability; to reduce the borrowing costs of unconsolidated entities by extending payment guarantees to their creditors; to enable the company to obtain cash through sales of receivables to a special purpose entity such as a trust; or to engage in leasing, hedging, research and development services with the company.

Off-balance-sheet arrangements typically enable a company to structure transactions so as not to appear on its balance sheet as a liability or to obscure the risks of loss to the company. A company should inform investors of the importance of off-balance-sheet financing arrangements to it as a financial matter. For instance, if a company materially relies on a program of securitisations of financial assets for its liquidity and capital resources, the company should provide sufficient information for investors to understand the extent of the risks that have been transferred or retained as a result of the arrangements.

Definition of "Off-balance-sheet arrangement". An off-balance-sheet arrangement includes any contractual arrangement between a company and an unconsolidated entity, under which the company has:[17]

❑ any obligation under a guarantee contract that requires initial recognition and measurement under US GAAP (specifically FASB Interpretation 45 (*Guarantor's Accounting and Disclosure Requirements for Guarantees, Including Indirect Guarantees of Indebtedness of Others*); FIN 45);

---

17 *See* Item 303(a)(4) of Regulation S-K.

FINANCIAL INFORMATION: ACCOUNTING AND DISCLOSURE

- a retained or contingent interest in assets transferred to an unconsolidated entity or similar type of arrangement that serves as a credit, liquidity or market-risk support to that entity;
- any obligation under certain derivative instruments; or
- any obligation under a "material variable interest" held by the company in an unconsolidated entity that provides financing liquidity, market-risk or credit-risk support to the company, or engages in leasing, hedging or research and development services with the company.

Guarantees. The definition of off-balance-sheet arrangements covers guarantees that may be a source of potential risk to a company's future financial performance, regardless of whether or not they are recorded as liabilities by the company.[18]

In general, the definition of guarantee uses concepts from US GAAP to identify those types of guarantee contracts for which disclosure is required. A company's application of FIN 45 provides the basis for determining those guarantee contracts that are subject to the required disclosures set out in the Off-Balance-Sheet Arrangements release. The references to US GAAP apply equally to foreign private issuers who do not present their primary financial statements according to US GAAP. Such issuers are expected to look at the US GAAP definitions to determine what information should be disclosed. Some examples of guarantees covered by the disclosure requirements generally would include any contract that contains one or more of the following characteristics:

- contracts in which a company may be required to make contingent payments to the guaranteed party based on changes in an underlying price, rate or index reference that is related to an asset, liability or equity security of the guaranteed party (ie, a guarantee of the market price of the common stock of the guaranteed party);
- contracts in which a company may be required to contingently make payments to the guaranteed party based on another entity's failure to perform under an obligating agreement (ie, a performance guarantee);
- indemnification agreements that require a company to contingently make indemnification payments to the indemnified/

---

[18] Specific guidance on the type of guarantees covered by the definition is provided in FIN 45.

guaranteed party based on changes in an underlying price, rate or index reference that is related to an asset, liability or equity security of the indemnified/guaranteed party (ie, adverse judgment in a lawsuit or the imposition of additional taxes due, for example, to changes in the tax law or adverse interpretations of the tax law); or

❏ indirect guarantees of the indebtedness of others that obligate the company to transfer funds to another entity upon the occurrence of a specified events and specified conditions identified in FIN 45, such as keepwell agreements.

Another form of off-balance-sheet arrangement likely would include an agreement to make future cash payments to a special purpose vehicle (SPV) to cover the SPV's expenses, to directly pay the SPV's expenses or to be liable for any collection shortfalls on the SPV's assets.

Retained or contingent interests. A company should disclose those arrangements that are not guarantees but under which the company retains a subordinated interest in the assets it has transferred to an unconsolidated SPV, such as may occur in a securitisation transaction. For example, a company may maintain a subordinated retained interest in a pool of receivables it has transferred to an unconsolidated entity. The holders of senior interests will benefit from such support because the company's retained interests provide credit support. In the event that a portion of the receivables becomes uncollectable, senior holders can look to the company for payment. This type of senior/subordinated structure may have a material effect on the company's cashflow and therefore should be disclosed. Other examples may include retained loan servicing rights coupled with an obligation to advance funds to cover temporary collection shortfalls, buy-back obligations for breaches of certain representations and warranties regarding the quality or performance of the transferred assets.

Certain derivative instruments. Derivatives that fall within the definition include, for US issuers, derivative instruments that are indexed to a company's stock and classified as stockholders' equity under US GAAP. For non-US issuers who do not prepare their financial statements in accordance with US GAAP, a derivative that must be disclosed is one that is indexed to its own stock and classified in stockholders' equity, or not reflected in its statement of financial position. The SEC Staff stated that these types of derivatives fall within the definition because a change in value may not be readily apparent to the investor because the derivative is classified as equity and subsequent changes in fair value may not be periodically recognized in the financial statements.

Variable interests. In general, a variable interest is an interest held in another entity that can vary based on changes in the entity's net asset value.[19] Variable interests are investments that absorb a portion of an entity's expected losses if they occur or receive portions of the entity's expected residual returns if they occur. The rule requires companies to assess the variable interests they hold in an unconsolidated entity and to disclose the arrangements that are material to the company, in entities that provide financing, liquidity, market-risk or credit-risk support to the company, or engage in leasing, hedging or research and development services with the company.

Disclosure threshold. The rule tracks the general threshold disclosure requirements of MD&A in that it specifies that companies must disclose off-balance-sheet arrangements that either have or are reasonably likely to have, a current or future effect on the company's financial condition, changes in financial condition, revenues or expenses, results of operations, liquidity, capital expenditure or capital resources that is material to investors. The disclosure is required in registration statements, quarterly and annual reports and proxy or information statements that are required to include financial statements.

The rule calls for management to first identify and critically analyse the company's off-balance-sheet arrangements. Second, management must assess the likelihood of the occurrence of any known trend, demand, commitment, event or uncertainty that could affect an off-balance-sheet arrangement (ie, trigger a performance under a guarantee obligation). No disclosure is required if management concludes that any such event is not reasonably likely to occur. If management cannot make this determination, it must objectively assess the consequences if the known trend, demand, commitment,

---

[19] *See*, generally, FASB Interpretation No 46.

event or uncertainty came to fruition. Disclosure is required unless management determines that a material effect on the company's overall financial condition is not reasonably likely to occur.

Required disclosure. The rule requires companies to disclose any material facts and circumstances so as to provide investors with a clear understanding of a company's off-balance-sheet arrangements and their material effects on financial condition, changes in financial condition, revenues and expenses, results of operations, liquidity, capital expenditures and capital resources. In addition, the discussion should address such other information that a company believes is necessary for an understanding of its off-balance-sheet arrangements and specified material effects. The disclosure should generally cover the most recent financial year and changes from the prior year, if necessary to an understanding of the disclosures covering the most recent financial year. Companies should disclose:

❏ the nature and purpose of the off-balance-sheet arrangements, such as the arrangement permits the lease, instead of purchase, of the asset, provides working capital financing or provides lower borrowing costs; and

❏ the importance of its off-balance-sheet arrangements to its liquidity, capital resources, market-risk support, credit-risk support or other benefits.

Given the contractual nature of the off-balance-sheet arrangements covered by the rule, the SEC stated that no disclosure of an off-balance-sheet arrangement is necessary until an unconditionally binding definitive agreement, subject only to customary closing conditions exists, or if no such agreement exists, when settlement of the transaction occurs.[20]

The overarching purpose of disclosure regarding off-balance-sheet arrangements should be to increase an investor's understanding of:

❏ the amounts of revenues, expenses and cashflows arising from such arrangements;

❏ the nature and amount of any interest retained, securities issued or other indebtedness incurred with such arrangements;

---

20 *See*, eg, Instruction 1 to Item 5.E of Form 20-F and Instruction 1 to Item 303(a)(4) of Regulation S-K.

- the nature and amount of any other obligations arising from the arrangements that are or are reasonably likely to come to fruition and be material; the company should disclose any triggering events that could lead to payment obligations on the part of the company;
- any known event, demand, commitment, trend or uncertainty that would or is reasonably likely to result in the termination or material reduction in availability to the company of off-balance-sheet arrangements that provide the company with material benefits, such as, for example, credit-rating downgrades or contractual provisions such as those relating to early termination of a securitisation arrangement; and
- the course of action the company has taken or proposes to take in response to a termination or a material reduction in the availability of an off-balance-sheet arrangement that provides material benefits.

A company is also encouraged to disclose any other information it believes is necessary for a complete understanding of the company's off-balance-sheet arrangements and their material affects.

Overall, the rule emphasises the SEC's view that disclosure should follow a principles-based approach and, as such, any information that would provide investors with an understanding of material off-balance-sheet arrangements and the impact and proximity of material risks that are reasonably likely to occur should be disclosed.

Presentation of disclosure. The SEC instructs companies to disclose off-balance-sheet arrangements in a separately captioned section of its MD&A. Disclosure of off-balance-sheet arrangements should be aggregated in groups or categories that provide information to investors in a concise manner and that facilitate their understanding of circumstances that would have common effects with respect to a number of off-balance-sheet arrangements. Disclosure that can only be deciphered by an expert will not suffice. The SEC warns that boilerplate disclosures that do not specifically address the company's particular circumstances and operations, or disclosure that is simply transferred from year to year or from company to company with no change, will not satisfy the MD&A requirements, will not inform

Disclosure of off-balance-sheet arrangements

Contractual obligations	Payments due by period				
	Total	Less than 1 year	1–3 years	3–5 years	More than 5 years
Long-term debt					
Capital lease obligations					
Operating leases					
Purchase obligations					
Other long-term liabilities reflected on the company's balance sheet under GAAP					

investors and will not reflect the independent thinking that management must precede any provision of disclosure in the MD&A.

Disclosure of contractual obligations. The rule requires that companies include in their annual reports tabular disclosure about contractual obligations, encompassing both on- and off-balance-sheet arrangements, as of the latest financial-year-end balance sheet date. The SEC noted that by aggregating information on various types of contractual obligations, investors are aided in their ability to identify and assess the impact of such contractual obligations in a comprehensive manner. In addition, investors will be able to compare the obligations of different companies.

The rule requires companies to provide disclosure in tabular format as of the latest financial-year-end balance sheet date, substantially in the following form.

A company may use other categories of obligations specific to its business but all must include the obligations that fall within the specified categories above. The table should be accompanied by any necessary explanatory footnotes describing material contractual provisions in order to aid investors in understanding the timing and amount of the contractual obligations. Non-US issuers that prepare financial statements in accordance with non-US GAAP should include contractual obligations that are consistent with the classifications used in the GAAP under which the non-US issuer's primary financial statements are prepared.

Companies should consult the applicable US GAAP definitions for the first three categories of obligations: long-term debt (FASB SFAS 47); capital lease obligations (FASB SFAS 13); and operating leases (FASB SFAS 13). With respect to purchase obligations, the rule defines "purchase obligation" as an agreement to purchase goods or services that is enforceable and legally binding on the company and that specifies all significant terms. If the purchase obligations are subject to variable price provisions, then the company must provide estimates of the payments due. In this case, the table should include footnotes that inform investors of the payments that are subject to market risk, if such information is material to investors. In addition, the footnotes should discuss any material termination or renewal provisions to the extent necessary for an understanding of the timing and amount of the company's payments under its purchase obligations. The SEC acknowledged that some purchase obligations would not be recognised as liabilities under GAAP (ie, executory contracts), but because purchase obligations could have a significant effect on a company's liquidity, it is necessary to delineate them in the table and assess the categories in the table.

Companies (except for small business issuers) are expected to include the table in registration statements, annual reports and proxy or information statements that are required to include financial statements for financial years ending on or after 15th December 2003. Companies may voluntarily comply with the new disclosure requirements before the compliance date.

Non-US issuers also must comply with the rule's requirements when they file their annual reports on Forms 20-F or 40-F. The rules, however, does not apply to reports furnished on Form 6-K provided that the issuer provides copies of the materials required to be made public in its home jurisdiction.

Non-US issuers' disclosure pertaining to off-balance-sheet arrangements and the table of contractual obligations must focus on the primary financial statements presented in the document and also include a discussion on the reconciliation to US GAAP. The definition of off-balance-sheet arrangements covers the same types of arrangements regardless of whether a company is a foreign private issuer or a domestic issuer. As such, foreign issuers should consult the US GAAP definitions and assess its arrangements in accordance with such definitions in order to ensure they are providing adequate disclosure. Consequently, although the rules are not mandating the adoption of US GAAP by foreign private issuers, the rule does intend for foreign private issuers to consult such definitions and provide the same type of disclosure in MD&A as domestic companies.

Guarantor's accounting and disclosure requirements for guarantees

In November 2002, the FASB issued FIN 45. It is important to note that FIN 45 is intended to clarify the requirements of FASB Statement No 5 (*Accounting for Contingencies*) with respect to both the accounting for and disclosures about enumerated guarantee obligations. Because of the tie between MD&A disclosures and FIN 45, it is important to know the FIN 45 requirements as they affect both the MD&A disclosures and the financial statements. FIN 45 provides guidance as to the disclosures a guarantor should make in its interim and annual financial statements about its guarantee obligations.

Consolidation of variable interest entities

In January 2003, the FASB issued Interpretation No 46 (*Consolidation of Variable Interest Entities, an Interpretation of Accounting Research Bulletin (ARB) No 51*) (FIN 46). FIN 46 significantly changed whether SPVs and other entities within its scope are, for accounting purposes, consolidated with their sponsors. Consolidation or non-consolidation likely will affect disclosure about financial information, including MD&A. What follows is a summary of the interpretation.

The interpretation provides a new consolidation model, the variable interests model. Factors one should consider in determining whether an entity is or is not a variable interest entity are:

❑ whether the equity investment at risk is sufficient to finance the entity's activities without additional subordinated financial support from other parties;
❑ whether the holders of the equity investment at risk as a group have the ability to make decisions about the entity's activities;

- whether the holders of the equity investment at risk have assumed the obligation to absorb any losses incurred by the entity;
- whether the holders of the equity investment at risk have the legal right to receive any residual returns of the entity.

FIN 46 is broad in reach in that almost any legal structure used to hold assets or conduct activities may be subject to the interpretation, including corporations, partnerships, limited liability companies, grantor trusts, business trusts and majority owned subsidiaries. The principal elements of a variable interest entity are that it: (i) has insufficient equity to absorb the entity's expected losses, (ii) the equity owners as a group cannot make decisions about the entity's activities; or (iii) has a class of equity that does not absorb the entity's losses or receive the entity's residual return.

Staff review issues

Based on remarks that various SEC Staff members continue to make, and in anticipation of easing the burdens of a possible SEC Staff Review, a company should consider the following matters when preparing its MD&A.

- Losses of, or reductions in business with, significant customers or suppliers (especially in industries where there are insolvencies).
- The cost or availability of insurance coverage.
- Reasons for and effects of related party transactions (SAS 57 financial footnote disclosure is not sufficient).
- The liquidity section should be given a "fresh look" each year. Among the items that may need to be discussed are:
  - The effects of debt covenants, including violations, waivers or amendments;
  - The need to reclassify long-term debt as current debt;
  - Securitisations and the effect of a shrinking market;
  - Difficulties in raising capital or obtaining funding (eg, in the commercial paper market), including the effects of changes in credit ratings; and
  - Funding sources.
- The effects of credit risk on operating results, including a discussion of:
  - Industry or geographical concentrations;

- ❏ Receivables and loans;
- ❏ Changes in customers; and
- ❏ Changes in credit-risk policies.
- ❏ The effects of asset impairments (eg, inventory, intangibles and fixed assets) on operating results and financial condition, including a discussion of the effect on compliance with financial covenants.
- ❏ The effect of business restructurings on liquidity and results of operations.
- ❏ The value of pension plans (including a relook at the underlying actuarial and investment return assumptions) and related funding obligations.

Critical accounting policies

In December 2001,[21] and again in its 2003 Interpretative Release, the SEC issued guidance regarding disclosures of a company's critical accounting policies. In May 2002 the SEC published rule proposals that expand upon and codify its earlier December guidance.[22] The guidance and rule proposals are intended to improve the quality and transparency of financial information disclosures. The guidance and proposed disclosures build on the acknowledgements in GAAP and generally accepted auditing standards of the exercise of judgment and use of estimates in the preparation of financial statements by companies.[23] The SEC Staff has warned companies that merely copying from their accounting policies footnote to the financial statements will not satisfy the required disclosures. Rather, companies should explain why the selected policies are critical and the effect changes in the estimates would have on financial results.

2001 and 2003 guidance

The SEC advised issuers that the selection and application of a company's accounting policies must be "appropriately reasoned". The SEC alerted companies of the need for greater transparency regarding the sensitivity of financial statements to the methods, assumptions and estimates underlying the preparation of such

---

21 Securities Act Release 8040 (12th December 2001).
22 Critical Accounting Policies Proposing Release.
23 *See* the discussion in the Proposing Release.

statements. Accordingly, the SEC encourages companies to include full, plain-English discussions of their three, four or five most "critical accounting policies", the judgments and uncertainties inherent in the application of those policies and the likelihood that materially different amounts would have been reported under different conditions or assumptions. The SEC set out a four-point disclosure scheme to assist companies in meeting the disclosure objectives.

- ❏ Management and the auditor should evaluate the critical accounting policies used in the preparation of the company's financial statements. A company's auditors must obtain an understanding of the judgments employed by management in selecting and applying accounting principals and methods. This process should focus especially on the most critical accounting policies. Auditors must be thoroughly satisfied with the selection, application and disclosure of such policies by management.
- ❏ The MD&A disclosure must be balanced and responsive. Accordingly, the SEC encourages a company to explain in its MD&A the effects of the critical accounting policies used, the judgments made by management in the application of such policies and the likelihood of materially different reported results if different assumptions or conditions were to exist.
- ❏ A company's audit committee should actively review the selection, application and disclosure of critical accounting policies with senior management and the auditors. The SEC encourages a company to consult with the SEC accounting staff when a company, management, audit committee or auditors are uncertain about the application of specific GAAP principles.

Robert K Herdman, former Chief Accountant of the SEC, provided guidance regarding critical accounting policies disclosures in a January 2002 speech to the Financial Executives International, San Diego Chapter.[24] Herdman explained that "a critical accounting policy is one that is both very important to the portrayal of

---

[24] 24th January 2002 Speech by Robert K Herdman, former Chief Accountant of the SEC, to the Financial Executives International – San Diego Chapter, Annual SEC Update (Critical Accounting and Critical Disclosures). The speech, available on the SEC's website, provides examples of disclosures in three areas: energy trading; loan loss allowances; and product warranty.

the company's financial condition and results, and requires management's most difficult, subjective or complex judgments". This typically arises when management must "make estimates about the effect of matters that are inherently uncertain". Herdman advised that when preparing the MD&A, management should ask itself whether the disclosures give investors sufficient "insight into the level of precision inherent in the financial statements and the sensitivity of reported amounts to the methods, assumptions and estimates underlying their preparation". Management should provide investors with its views about future events that provide the basis for management's assumptions that underlie estimates used in preparing the company's financial statements. The SEC's disclosure objective is greater transparency with respect to how management forms its judgments about future events and the sensitivity of those judgments to different assumptions should provide investors with information so as to better analyse the strength of the company's historical financial condition and operating results.

The SEC expects that few companies will have no critical accounting policies with the vast majority of companies having between three to five. A critical accounting policy is one that is both very important to the portrayal of the company's financial condition and operating results and requires management to make very difficult, subjective or complex judgments.

Rule proposal
The primary objectives of the critical accounting policies rule proposal is to:

❏ improve the investor's understanding of the existence of and necessity for estimations in preparing a company's financial statements;
❏ focus the investor on those accounting estimates that require significant management judgment;
❏ give the investor an understanding of the impact the critical accounting estimates have on the presentation of a company's financial condition, changes in financial condition or operating results;
❏ give the investor an understanding of the sensitivity of the critical accounting estimates; and

❏ give the investor an understanding of any new material accounting policy when adopted by a company and the effect of that policy on the company's financial condition, changes in financial condition or operating results.

The proposals would require disclosure in two areas: accounting estimates made by a company in applying its critical accounting policies and the initial adoption by a company of an accounting policy that has a material impact on the company's financial statements. The SEC received substantial comments on the proposal, especially with respect to certain definitions and quantitative sensitivity disclosures. While the rule proposal remains outstanding, much of it has been implemented through SEC interpretive releases.

Under the rule proposals, an accounting estimate would be critical and disclosure would be required if both:

❏ the accounting estimate requires that the company make assumptions about matters that involve a high degree of uncertainty at the time the accounting estimate was made; and
❏ different accounting estimates that the company reasonably could have used in the current period, or changes in the accounting estimates that are reasonably likely to occur from period to period and would have a material impact on the presentation of the company's financial condition, changes in financial condition or results of operations.

The disclosure about each critical accounting estimate would involve three elements:

❏ basic information necessary to understand the accounting estimate, including a description of where and how the estimate affects the company's reported financial results, financial condition and changes in financial condition, as well as the impact of the estimate on the company's financial statements and segments;
❏ a sensitivity analysis of changes to the estimate or underlying assumptions by (i) discussing the reasonably possible, near-term changes in the most material assumptions underlying the estimate or (ii) replacing the recorded estimate with the

ends of the range of reasonably possible amounts that the company likely determined when deciding to use the recorded estimate; and
- a statement as to whether senior management discussed the development, selection and disclosure of the estimate with the company's audit committee.

In addition, the proposals would require MD&A disclosure about the initial adoption of an accounting policy that had a material impact on the company's financial condition and operating results, unless the policy was adopted solely from new accounting literature issued by a recognised accounting standard setter. The proposed disclosure, which is intended to elicit more qualitative information, would include a description of:

- the events or transactions that gave rise to the initial adoption;
- the accounting principal adopted and the application of that principal; and
- the qualitative impact of the principal on the company's financial condition and operating results.

If a company had a choice between acceptable accounting principals under GAAP, the company would be required to disclose the fact that a choice was made among allowable alternatives, explain the other alternatives and state why the particular choice was made. In addition, if no accounting literature governed the accounting upon initial adoption, the company would be required to explain how it reached its decision regarding the selection of the accounting principal and method of applying such principal.

Foreign private issuers
The proposed rules would apply equally to foreign private issuers. However, the rules could be potentially more burdensome for those foreign private issuers who prepare their financial statements in accordance with non-US GAAP. In that circumstance, the foreign private issuer would have to consider critical accounting estimates with respect to both its primary financial statements and its reconciliation to US GAAP.

Application of existing safe harbour for forward-looking information

The Proposing Release notes that the proposed MD&A disclosures would require a company to make a forward-looking statement and discusses the availability of various existing safe harbours. The SEC did not propose to expand the statutory safe harbour under the Private Litigation Reform Act of 1995. Consequently, the statutory safe harbour would not apply to forward-looking statements made in a MD&A in connection with initial public offerings and exchange offer-tender offers.

Quantitative and qualitative market risk disclosures

The disclosure requirements, set out in Item 11 of Form 20-K and Item 305 of Regulation S-K, are intended to provide greater transparency and clarity with respect to a company's use of derivatives and its exposure to the market risks inherent in derivatives and other financial instruments. Derivative financial instruments, as defined in FASB Statement No 119, include futures, forwards, swaps and options. Derivative commodity instruments, as defined in Securities Act Release 7386, are commodity contracts that by contract or business practice settle in cash or another financial instrument such as commodity futures, commodity forwards, commodity swaps or commodity options. Other financial instruments, as defined in FASB Statement No 107, include structured notes, loan receivables, debt obligations and deposit liabilities. In general, a company should:

- clearly describe its accounting policies for derivatives in the footnotes to its financial statements; and
- provide clear quantitative and qualitative disclosures about the market risk(s) inherent in derivatives and other financial instruments, the company's use of derivatives and other financial instruments and the risk exposure or mitigation from its use of derivatives and other financial instruments to its operating results and financial condition.

A company should use a tabular presentation to disclose quantitative information about all of the significant terms of related market-sensitive instruments, the method and assumptions used to determine estimated fair value, cashflows and future variable rates. Instruments should be segregated by common characteristics and by risk classification.

At least as important as the quantitative tabular information is the company's qualitative disclosures about how it manages its risk exposure, including the objectives, general strategies and instruments, if any, used to manage that exposure. The discussion should explain any known or expected changes to either its risk exposure or its policies to manage that exposure.

Segment disclosure
A US company typically must provide disclosure at the operating segment level. If the operating results of a component of an enterprise are regularly reviewed by the chief operating decision maker(s) when evaluating the component's performance and deciding about the amount of resources to be allocated to that component, that component likely would be a segment for the purposes of SFAS 131. The Staff will challenge a company's decisions about its reported segments. The Staff looks at management statements about the company's performance, analyst reports, press releases, letters to shareholders and other public information in evaluating the consistency of that information with the disclosures in the financial statements and MD&A. Where the information reveals different or additional segments, the company most likely will have to amend its filings.

For foreign private issuers, Form 20-F provides two alternative disclosure approaches. As set out in Item 17 of Form 20-F, the financial statements need not include segment information required by SFAS 131 if the foreign private issuer provides the disclosures required by Item 4.B.1 and 4.B.2 of Form 20-F, which among other information require a "breakdown of total revenues by category of activity and geographic market for each of the last three financial years". Alternatively, if the financial statements are prepared in accordance with US GAAP, the issuer pursuant to Item 18 of Form 20-F must include the SFAS 131 information.

Conditions for the use of non-GAAP financial measures
In January 2003, the SEC adopted a new disclosure framework, Regulation G and paragraph (e) to Item 10 of Regulation S-K, to address public companies' disclosure or release of financial

information that is calculated and presented on the basis of methodologies other than in accordance with GAAP.[25] The SEC Staff published frequently asked questions (FAQs) and answers about the use of non-GAAP financial measures in June 2003.

The adopted rules are different based on whether the information disclosed is contained in a press release or similar public announcement or is contained in a SEC filing. The SEC also adopted rules amending various forms and item requirements in order to further specify the slightly more stringent disclosure requirements pertaining to non-GAAP financial measures included in filings made with the SEC.

Regulation G requires public companies that disclose or release non-GAAP financial measures to include in that disclosure or release, a presentation of the most directly comparable GAAP financial measure and a reconciliation of the disclosed non-GAAP financial measure to the most directly comparable GAAP measure.

Applicability

Any entity, domestic or foreign, that is required to file reports with the SEC pursuant to Section 13(a) or 15(d) of the Exchange Act, is covered by Regulation G. Foreign private issuers are allowed a specified exemption from the rule, described more fully below. Only registered investment companies are exempted from Regulation G.

Definition

Regulation G applies whenever a company publicly discloses or releases any material information that includes a non-GAAP financial measure. The "non-GAAP financial measure" is defined as a numerical measure of an issuer's historical or future financial performance, financial position or cashflows that:

❑ excludes amounts, or is subject to adjustments that have the effect of excluding amounts, that are included in the comparable measure calculated and presented in accordance with GAAP in the statement of income, balance sheet or statement of cashflows (or equivalent statements) of the issuer; or

---

[25] Securities Act Release 8176 (22nd January 2003).

❑ includes amounts, or is subject to adjustments that have the effect of including amounts that are excluded from the comparable measure so calculated and presented.

"GAAP" generally refers to US GAAP, but the rule clarifies that with respect to non-US issuers whose primary financial statements are prepared in accordance with non-US GAAP, "GAAP" refers to the principles under which the foreign private issuer prepared its financial statements and the required reconciliation would be to the comparable home-country GAAP measure.

The SEC intends for the definition to capture all measures that depict either:

❑ a measure of performance that is different from that presented in the financial statements, such as income or loss before taxes or net income or loss, as calculated in accordance with GAAP; or
❑ a measure of liquidity that is different from cashflow or cashflow from operations computed in accordance with GAAP.

An example of a non-GAAP financial measure is earnings before interest, taxes, depreciation and amortisation (EBITDA), because it can be presented using elements derived from GAAP, but is not presented in accordance with GAAP. Another example is operating income that excludes one or more expense or revenue items because they are identified as "non-recurring". Non-GAAP financial measures do not include:

❑ operating and other statistical measures (such as unit sales, numbers or employees, numbers of subscribers and similar numerical measures); or
❑ ratios or measures that are calculated using exclusively one or both of (i) financial measures calculated in accordance with GAAP and (ii) operating measures or other statistical measures that are not non-GAAP financial measures.

Disclosure
Regulation G has two requirements: a general disclosure requirement; and a specific reconciliation requirement of the non-GAAP financial measure to the most directly comparable GAAP financial measure. The disclosure requirement prohibits the publication of any non-GAAP financial measure that, taken together with the

information accompanying that measure, contains an untrue statement of material fact or omits to state a material fact necessary in order to make the presentation of the non-GAAP financial measure, in light of the circumstances under which it is presented, not misleading. The reconciliation requirement requires a company that publicises a non-GAAP financial measure to provide both of the following:

❑ a presentation of the most directly comparable financial measure calculated and presented in accordance with GAAP; and
❑ a reconciliation (by schedule or other clearly understandable method) of the differences between the non-GAAP financial measure presented and the most directly comparable financial measure or measure calculated and presented in accordance with GAAP. Forward-looking prospective non-GAAP financial measures should be compared with the appropriate forward-looking GAAP financial measures by means of a schedule or other presentation that outlines the differences between the two. In the event the GAAP financial measure is not accessible on a forward-looking basis, the company must disclose this fact, explain why it is not accessible on a forward-looking basis and provide any reconciling information that is available without an "unreasonable effort". The company is also required to identify any unavailable information and disclose its probable significance.

If a non-GAAP financial measure is released orally, telephonically, in a webcast or broadcast or by similar means, the company is allowed to provide the required accompanying information on its website and disclose, during its presentation, the location of the accompanying reconciling information.

Requirements for non-US issuers and the limited exemption
Regulation G applies to non-US issuers, but is subject to a limited exception. In general, the exception focuses on whether the information presented relates to US GAAP and whether persons located in the US are the targeted audience. As such, Regulation G will not apply to public disclosure of a non-GAAP financial measure by a non-US issuer if the following conditions are met:

❑ the securities of the non-US issuer are listed or quoted on a securities exchange or inter-dealer quotation system outside the United States;

- the financial measure is based on non-US GAAP financial data; and
- the disclosure is made by or on behalf of the non-US issuer outside the United States, or is included in a written communication that is released by or on behalf of the company outside the United States.

The exception applies even if:

- a written communication is released in the United States as well as abroad, provided that the communication is released in the United States contemporaneously with or after the release abroad and is not targeted at persons located in the United States;
- foreign or US journalists or other third parties have access to the information;
- the information appears on one or more websites maintained by the non-US issuer, provided that the websites, when taken together, are not available exclusively to, or targeted at, persons located in the United States; and/or
- following the disclosure or release of the information outside the United States, the information is included in a submission to the SEC made under cover of a Form 6-K.

However, if the SEC determines that US persons were the targets of a non-US issuer's publication of non-GAAP financials, the limited exception is not available and Regulation G would apply.

Business combinations
Excepted from Regulation G are non-GAAP financial measures included in disclosures relating to a business combination transaction, an entity resulting from a business combination transaction or an entity that is a party to the business combination transaction provided that the disclosure is contained in a communication that is subject to the SEC's communications rules applicable to business combinations.

Regulation G and Regulation FD
Regulation FD mandates the public disclosure of material non-public information that an enumerated official of a US issuer provides to persons specified in the regulation including shareholders and analysts. Regulation FD does not apply to non-US issuers. If the information disclosed pursuant to Regulation FD contains a

non-GAAP financial measure, Regulation G will be implicated. Consequently, the SEC expects Regulation FD and Regulation G to work in tandem.

Non-compliance with Regulation G
If a public reporting company fails to comply with Regulation G, the company could be subject to a SEC enforcement action alleging violations of Regulation G. Also, and depending on the circumstances, the SEC could bring an enforcement action under both Regulation G and Rule 10b-5 Exchange Act.

Non-GAAP financial measures in SEC filings
The final rules amend line item disclosure requirements set out in Regulation S-K and Regulation S-B, and in the form requirements for Forms 10-K, 20-F, 40-K and 8-K such that they mandate the inclusion of statements regarding the use of non-GAAP financial measures. The rules apply to filings of any annual or quarterly report with a fiscal period ending after 28th March 2003.

Requirements
Disclosure in filings of non-GAAP financial measures with the SEC must follow more extensive and detailed requirements than those specified in Regulation G. The disclosure in filings must include:

- a presentation, with equal or greater prominence, of the most directly comparable financial measure calculated and presented in accordance with GAAP;
- a reconciliation (by schedule or other clearly understandable method) of the differences between the non-GAAP financial measure presented and the most directly comparable financial measure or measure calculated and presented in accordance with GAAP;
- a statement disclosing the reasons why management views the presentation of the non-GAAP financial measures as useful information to the investor; and
- if material, and not otherwise disclosed, a statement disclosing the additional purposes, if any, for which the company's management uses the non-GAAP financial measure presented.

In its statement as to the utility of inclusion of the non-GAAP financial measure, management must provide a clear and understandable explanation to investors. The statement cannot be boilerplate. The rule requires specific statements as to the non-GAAP measure used, the nature of the company's business and industry, and the manner in which management assesses the non-GAAP financial measure and applies it to management decisions. If a company includes the statements in its most recent annual report filed with the SEC and updates such statements as necessary, the rule states that management does not need to include the statements in each SEC filing containing a non-GAAP financial measure.

As in Regulation G, if a GAAP financial measure is not available on a forward-looking basis, the company must disclose that fact and provide any reconciling information that is available without "unreasonable effort". Information that remains unavailable must be identified and the company must disclose its probable significance.

Prohibitions in filings

The SEC prohibits the filing of non-GAAP financial measures that:

❑ exclude charges or liabilities that required, or will require, cash settlement, or would have required cash settlement absent an ability to settle in another manner, from non-GAAP liquidity measures, *other than earnings before interest and taxes (EBIT) and EBITDA;*
❑ adjust a non-GAAP performance measure to eliminate or smooth items identified as non-recurring, infrequent or unusual, when the nature of the charge or gain is such that it is reasonably likely to recur within two years or there was a similar charge or gain within the past two years;
❑ present non-GAAP financial measures on the face of the company's financial statements prepared in accordance with GAAP or in the accompanying notes;
❑ present non-GAAP financial measures on the face of any pro forma financial information required to be disclosed by Article 11 of Regulation S-X;

FINANCIAL INFORMATION: ACCOUNTING AND DISCLOSURE

- use titles or descriptions of non-GAAP financial measures that are the same as, or confusingly similar to, titles or descriptions used for GAAP financial measures; and
- present a non-GAAP per-share measure.

Exemptions

The rules specifically exempt EBIT and EBITDA from the prohibitions. If a company includes EBIT or EBITDA, it must reconcile the measure to its most directly comparable GAAP financial measure and discuss why investors would find the EBIT or EBITDA measure useful in the context presented. Depending on the entity, EBITDA may be viewed as a liquidity measure, an income measure or both. Consequently, some issuers are reconciling the measure to its most directly comparable cashflow and income measurements. An adjusted EBITDA financial measure that excludes cash charges or liabilities is no longer permitted.

Non-US issuers

Foreign private issuers who file on Form 20-F are subject to the same rules as domestic issuers with respect to filing requirements of non-GAAP financial measures. Only filers on Form 40-F are exempt from the rule's filing requirements under the US/Canadian multi-jurisdictional disclosure system (MSDS). Unlike Regulation G, there is no exception for non-US issuers with respect to filings. The requirements do not apply to interim earnings releases submitted on Form 6-K since those releases are already covered by Regulation G.

A non-US issuer may, however, include a non-GAAP financial measure that would otherwise be prohibited in the filings of a US issuer, if:

- the non-US issuer can prove that the measure is required or expressly permitted by the foreign issuer's local standard-setter that establishes GAAP; and
- such measure was used in the issuer's annual report or financial statements used in its home-country market (the SEC noted that it would allow the measure only in situations where the local standard-setter affirmatively acted to approve the measure and not merely where the measure is not prohibited).

The SEC Staff has advised that the term "expressly permitted" means that a particular non-GAAP financial measure is "clearly and specifically identified as an acceptable measure" by the home-county regulator of the GAAP used in preparing the issuer's primary financial statements included in its SEC filings.

Business combinations

Similar to the exception provided in Regulation G, there is an exception for non-GAAP measures included in disclosure relating to business combination transactions provided that such communication is subject to the SEC rules applicable to business combination transactions.

Requirement to furnish earnings releases on Form 8-K

Item 2.02, "Results of Operations and Financial Condition", of Form 8-K[26] requires issuers to *furnish* as opposed to file, any public announcement or release disclosing material non-public information regarding a company's results of operations or financial condition for an annual or quarterly fiscal period that has ended. The SEC clarified that it is material information released regarding a *completed* fiscal period that triggers Item 2.02. As such, Item 2.02 does not apply to public disclosure of earnings estimates for future or ongoing fiscal periods, unless those estimates are included in the public announcement or release of material non-public information regarding an annual or quarterly fiscal period that has ended.

The requirements of Item 2.20 will apply regardless of whether or not the release or announcement contains a non-GAAP financial measure. Companies are required to identify briefly the announcement or release and include the announcement or release as an exhibit to their Form 8-K.

Item 2.02 includes an exception from its requirements where non-public information is disclosed orally, telephonically or by webcast or broadcast or similar means in a presentation that is complementary to and occurs within 48 hours *after* a related written release or announcement that triggers the requirements of Item 2.02. As such, the company would not need to furnish an additional Form 8-K with regard to information disclosed orally, telephonically, by webcast, by broadcast or similar means if:

---

[26] The SEC amended Form 8-K to add 10 new disclosure items (including transferring two items to Form 8-K from periodic reports) and shorten the filing period from 15 calendar days to four business days in most instances. *See* Securities Act Release 8400 (16th March 2004) and Securities Act Release 8400A (4th August 2004).

FINANCIAL INFORMATION: ACCOUNTING AND DISCLOSURE

- ❑ the related, written release or announcement has been furnished to the SEC on Form 8-K pursuant to Item 7.01 before the presentation;
- ❑ the presentation is broadly accessible to the public by dial-in conference call, webcast or similar technology;
- ❑ the financial and statistical information contained in the presentation is provided on the company's website, together with any information that would be required under Regulation G; and
- ❑ the presentation was announced by a widely disseminated press release that included instructions as to when and how to access the presentation and the location on the company's website where the information would be available.

Item 2.02 requirement to "furnish" versus "file"
earnings information

Item 2.02 of Form 8-K requires companies to "furnish" not "file" earnings releases and similar disclosures. The SEC clarified the main distinctions between furnishing *versus* filing Form 8-K:

- ❑ information that is furnished to the SEC is not subject to Section 18 of the Exchange Act, which allows civil actions for damages for false or misleading statements; and
- ❑ information that is furnished to the SEC is not incorporated by reference into a registration statement, proxy statement or other report unless the company specifically incorporates that information into those documents by reference.

Earnings releases only need be "furnished" and not "filed" with the SEC.[27] The rule does not affirmatively require a company to issue an earnings release, but if it does issue an earnings release or an announcement that contains a non-GAAP financial measure, Regulation G would apply to the release or announcement.

Use of a non-GAAP financial measure in the earnings release

Item 2.02 of Form 8-K requires that the company also disclose:

- ❑ the reasons why the company's management believes that presentation of the non-GAAP financial measure provides useful information to investors; and

---

27 Securities Act Release 8176 (22nd January 2003) (Non-GAAP Adopting Release).

❏ if material, a statement disclosing any additional purposes for which the company's management uses the non-GAAP financial measure presented.

Regulation FD and Item 7.01

Earnings releases and similar "written" disclosures that trigger Item 2.02 are also subject to Regulation FD. Regulation FD and Item 2.02 differ in that the requirements of Item 2.02 *always* require disclosure on Form 8-K once Item 2.02 is triggered, whereas Regulation FD provides that a Form 8-K disclosure is an alternative means of satisfying the FD requirements. Under Regulation FD, public disclosure satisfying the requirements of Regulation FD need not be limited to only filing a Form 8-K.

In addition, if an issuer chooses to furnish information pursuant to Regulation FD under Item 7.01 of Form 8-K, it must do so within the time periods specified by Regulation FD, which is shorter than the four-day requirement of Item 2.02. A Form 8-K furnished within the time frame required by Regulation FD and otherwise satisfying the requirements of both Item 2.02 and Item 7.02, could be furnished to the SEC once, indicating that it is being furnished under both Item 2.02 and Item 7.01, and satisfy both requirements.

Staff Accounting Bulletin No 99: "Materiality Guidance"

A company and its advisors, in preparing the company's MD&A, should consider the materiality guidance set out in the SEC's Staff Accounting Bulletin No 99 (SAB 99).[28] SAB 99 cautions companies against relying exclusively on quantitative thresholds in making materiality judgments with respect to factors associated with the preparation of financial statements.

The Staff clarifies that use of a numerical threshold, such as a five per cent test, is only the start of any materiality analysis, an analysis that requires full consideration of all quantitative and qualitative factors. The Staff advises companies to apply the governing principles in making a materiality assessment. Under this, the company in question must evaluate the facts in the context of the "surrounding circumstances" (accounting literature) or the "total mix" of information (dicta of the US Supreme Court), both

---

28 Release No. 99 (12th August 1999).

FINANCIAL INFORMATION: ACCOUNTING AND DISCLOSURE

of which require consideration of qualitative and quantitative factors.

SAB 99 sets out a non-exclusive list of qualitative factors that could render material a quantitatively small misstatement of a financial statement item. These factors include whether the misstatement:

- arises from an item capable of precise measurement or whether it arises from an estimate and, if so, the degree of imprecision inherent in the estimate;
- hides a change in earnings or other trends;
- hides a failure to meet analysts' consensus expectations for the enterprise;
- changes a loss into income or vice versa;
- concerns a segment or other portion of the company's business that has been identified as playing a significant role in the company's operations or profitability;
- affects the company's compliance with regulatory requirements;
- affects the company's compliance with loan covenants or other contractual requirements;
- has the effect of increasing management's compensation – for example, by satisfying requirements for the award of bonuses or other forms of incentive compensation; or
- involves concealment of an unlawful transaction.

Among other factors that the Staff suggests be taken into account are the volatility of a company's stock price in response to certain types of disclosures as a possible indicator of the importance of small misstatements to investors and consideration of potential reaction to disclosure of a misstatement. While the Staff indicates that consideration of market reaction alone is "too blunt an instrument to be depended on", it should be taken into account in a materiality analysis.

Management's intent may also be evidence of materiality, particularly when misstatements have been made to "manage" reported earnings. With respect to earnings management, the Staff stated:

> "[I]nvestors generally would regard as significant a management practice to over- or under-state earnings up to an amount just short of a percentage threshold in order to "manage" earnings. Investors presumably also would

regard as significant an accounting practice that, in essence, rendered all earnings figures subject to a management-directed margin of misstatement".

Materiality also may turn on where a misstatement appears in the financial statements. As an example, if a misstatement involves a segment, the company should consider the significance of the segment information to the consolidated financial statements.

The Staff also gives guidance on aggregating and netting misstatements. In assessing materiality, companies should:

❏ consider each misstatement separately and the aggregate effect of all;
❏ determine whether a misstatement of an individual amount causes the financial statements as a whole to be materially misstated; if so, the effect cannot be reduced by relying on other misstatements;
❏ exercise care in deciding whether to offset (or the appropriateness of offsetting) "a misstatement of an estimated amount with a misstatement of an item capable of precise measurement"; and
❏ consider the effect of misstatements from prior periods; the cumulative effect may become material in a given year.

SAB 99 addresses immaterial, intentional misstatements that "[i]n certain circumstances … are unlawful and may violate the requirement under the Exchange Act to keep books and records that are accurate in reasonable detail".[29] Since an intentional misstatement of an immaterial item may violate Section 13(b)(2) of the Exchange Act and, thus, be an illegal act, it may trigger an obligation on the part of the company's auditors under Section 10A(b) of the Exchange Act to take steps to see that the company's audit committee is adequately informed about the misstatement irrespective of whether it has a material effect on the company's financial statements.[30]

Revenue recognition

The SEC Staff views revenue recognition as a primary area of accounting abuses. The key question is whether the substance of a transaction is a sale for which revenue recognition or a consignment,

---

29 *See* Exchange Act, section 13(b)(2)–(7).
30 *See SEC v. Arthur Andersen LLP* (19th June 2001), discussed in Appendix B.

financing or other arrangement for which revenue recognition should be delayed to a later reporting period.

The governing principle, set out in Statements of Financial Accounting Concepts No 5 (SFAC No 5) is that revenue should not be recognised until it is both realised or realisable and earned. In December 1999, the SEC Staff published Staff Accounting Bulletin 101 (SAB 101)[31] to provide guidance on revenue recognition principles promulgated by the FASB and AICPA, including the application of those principles in various hypothetical examples. In October 2000, the SEC Staff issued "Frequently Asked Questions about Staff Accounting Bulletin No 101" that provides further guidance on revenue recognition matters.

SAB 101 sets out criteria that must be in order for revenue to be recognised.

- *The existence of persuasive evidence to support an arrangement.*
  - Customary documentation practices and processes likely will vary among companies, industries and even among business units within a single company. A company must have appropriate policies, procedures and internal controls that are appropriately documented so as to provide reasonable assurances that sales transactions, including those affected by side agreements are properly accounted for in accordance with GAAP.
  - If a company's customary practice is to obtain a sales contract or purchase order signed by the buyer, evidence of an oral purchase agreement entered into prior to the close of the accounting period generally would not be persuasive evidence so that recognition of revenue from the sale during that accounting period would be precluded.
  - If an arrangement is subject to approval by a management committee or execution of another agreement, revenue recognition would be precluded until that later approval or agreement is complete.
  - If a product is delivered for sale under a consignment arrangement, revenue recognition is not appropriate until the sale occurs since the seller retains the risks and benefits of product ownership and title to the product usually does not

---

[31] Release No. 101 (3rd December 1999).

pass to the consignee. Even if title has passed to the buyer, characteristics of the transaction relating to such matters as rights to return the product and payment terms may preclude revenue recognition.

- *Delivery has taken place or services have been rendered.*
    - Revenue should not be recognised until the seller has substantially fulfilled its obligations to the buyer.
    - Delivery usually has not occurred until the buyer has taken title and assumed the risks and benefits of product ownership that usually occurs when a product is delivered to the buyer's delivery site and no uncertainty exists about the buyer's acceptance of the product. Receipt of payment from the buyer may not evidence delivery or performance by the seller.
    - If the arrangement calls for delivery of multiple elements or deliverables, delivery of one element will not have occurred if undelivered elements are essential to the functionality of the delivered element.
- *The seller's price to the buyer is fixed or determinable.* If the buyer has the unilateral right to cancel an arrangement, then the price is not fixed or determinable until the cancellation right lapses. Typically, short-term rights to return products such as 30-day money back guarantees are not viewed as cancellation privileges that would cause a sales price not to be fixed or determinable.
- *Collectability of payment is reasonably assured.* A seller should not recognise revenue where the buyer is an entity with no significant assets or operations or financially troubled such that the seller has no reasonable assurance of being paid.

Loss contingencies

Staff Accounting Bulletin 92, "Accounting and Disclosures Relating to Loss Contingencies" (SAB 92)[32] provides SEC Staff interpretative guidance about contingent liabilities (also referred to as loss contingencies) under US GAAP and under SEC disclosure requirements. SAB 92 is intended to both promote timely

---

[32] Release No 92 (8th June 1993).

financial statement recognition of contingent losses and elicit more meaningful and transparent disclosure that will allow investors to evaluate the nature and scope of contingencies. SAB 92 addresses the disclosure of contingencies within and outside the financial statements, including the adequacy of accruals and MD&A disclosure.

An estimated loss from a loss contingency must be accrued by a charge to income if it is probable that the liability has been incurred and the loss amount can be reasonably estimated. Ordinarily the Staff believes it inappropriate to offset in the balance sheet a claim for recovery that is probable of realisation against a probable contingent liability. The risks and uncertainties associated with the contingent liability are, in the Staff's view, distinct and separate from those associated with any recovery claim against a third party. Further, the Staff warns that recognition of a contingent liability cannot be delayed until only a single amount can be reasonably estimated. If management expects that the liability amount will come within a range and no amount within that range is a better estimate, a loss equal to the minimum amount of the range must be recognised even if the upper limit of the range is uncertain.

In addition to technical accounting guidance, SAB 92 also provides disclosure guidance. A company should consider the disclosure requirements relating to its business, legal proceedings and MD&A. The SAB further advises a company to consider the availability of insurance, indemnification or contribution in evaluating whether the criteria for disclosure have been met with respect to a loss contingency. A company's assessment of a contingency should include consideration of various facts "such as the periods in which claims for recovery may be realized, the likelihood that the claims may be contested, and the financial condition of third parties from which recovery is expected". If disclosure is required, the disclosures should be reasonably specific so that a reader understands the potential exposure, nature, scope and magnitude of the contingency to the company.[33] General boilerplate disclosures will not suffice.

---

[33] Speech by Christine Q Davine, former Associate Chief Accountant, SEC Division of Corporation Finance, to the AICPA's 23rd Annual National Conference (1996).

Restructuring charges

Staff Accounting Bulletin 100, "Restructuring Charges" (SAB 100)[34] sets out SEC Staff guidance about accounting for and disclosure of restructuring charges. The term "restructuring charge" is not defined in the authoritative literature. These charges may be incurred in connection with a variety of transactions, such as a business combination, change in a company's strategic plan or a managerial response to changes in consumer demand, competitive pressure or other environmental factors.

SAB 100 addresses disclosures about a restructuring within the financial statements and MD&A. The disclosures should be company specific and presented in all periods, including interim periods, until the restructuring plan is completed. These disclosures should provide the reader with an understanding of the plan itself. If the activities to be discontinued are qualitatively or quantitatively significant to the company's revenues or operating results, or if the charges are material, the company should describe the effects that the discontinuation of the activities will have on the company's operating results and financial condition, and an explanation of the amounts recognised as liabilities and their income statement classification. SAB 100 reminds a company that the disclosures must be updated in subsequent reports to reflect material changes. The SEC Staff advises that material exit or involuntary termination costs, whether or not currently recognisable in the financial statements, may constitute a known trend, demand, commitment, event or uncertainty that should be disclosed in MD&A. The SEC Staff further advises that the MD&A should discuss the events and decisions that gave rise to the exit plan and associated costs and the likely quantitative and qualitative effects of the plan on the company's financial condition, future operating results (including earnings) and cashflows, and liquidity, unless management determines that a material effect is not reasonably likely to occur. The liquidity discussion should describe expected future cash outlays, including the anticipated periods in which they will arise and the expected sources of capital to fund those cash outlays. Due to the discretionary nature of exit plans and the components thereof, the SEC Staff finds that a tabular presentation of each category of charges

---

[34] Release No 100 (24th November 1999).

from balance sheet date to balance sheet date is necessary to explain fully the components and effects of significant charges.

Other accounting and disclosure issues

Other areas in which the SEC Staff has focused and provided guidance include cashflow statement classification of cash receipts from inventory sales, cashflow statement classifications of payments related to settlement of pension liabilities assumed by the Pension Benefit Guaranty Corporation, accounting practices in the oil and gas industry (including reserve valuations), lease accounting, accounting for buy/sell arrangements, accounting for service agreements, off-balance-sheet disclosures, accounting for advertising revenues and related party transactions. The Current Accounting and Disclosure Issues Outline prepared by the Division of Corporation Finance and available on the SEC's website provides specific information about these issues and other areas of interest.

CERTIFICATIONS – SECTIONS 906 AND 302

SOX contains significant provisions intended to improve financial reporting by public reporting companies. These provisions relate to among other matters, disclosure certifications and heightened audit committee responsibilities (discussed in part in the following). Congress, in providing for the CEO and CFO certifications, wanted to ensure that high-level corporate officials not only reviewed reports issued by the company, but also that corporate executives took an active role in establishing and evaluating the reporting procedures within the company.

SOX Section 906 certification

The Section 906 Certification provides for criminal penalties and, unlike Section 302 Certification does not require any further rulemaking by the SEC. Section 906 provides that every periodic report that contains financial statements filed by an issuer with the SEC under Sections 13(a) and 15(d) of the Exchange Act must be supplemented with a certification by the CEO and the CFO of the company or, if the company does not have a CEO or CFO, the individual whose position is equivalent to a CEO or CFO. The CEO and CFO must state that the periodic report fulfils the requirements of Sections

13(a) and 15(d) of the Exchange Act and that the information "fairly presents, in all material respects," the company's "financial condition and results of operations".

Section 906 applies to all periodic reports containing financial statements filed by issuers with the SEC after 30th July 2002. Periodic reports include annual and quarterly reports, but have not been considered by the SEC and its Staff to include "current reports", like the reports submitted on Form 8-K, which are used for, among other purposes, to announce that a specific event has happened or reports furnished on Form 6-K by foreign private issuers.

There has been no official supplementing interpretation of Section 906. Practice questions about the Section 906 certification requirements have to do with whether or not the officer's certification may contain some form of qualification as to his or her knowledge of the report's contents. While the Act does not provide for a qualifier in the text of the certification, the Act provides that the officer would have to know that the company's report was inadequate before being held criminally liable for giving a false certification.

On 5th June 2003, the SEC amended its rules so that the Section 906 certifications accompany periodic reports that contain financial statements as exhibits. Prior to the effective date of the amendments, a company could submit the Section 906 certifications as correspondence. As companies will "furnish" not "file" the Section 906 certifications, the Section 906 certifications will not be subject to liability under Section 18 of the Exchange Act. Failure to furnish a Section 906 certification will cause the periodic report to which it relates to be incomplete, thereby causing a violation of Section 13(a) of the Exchange Act.

There are two separate categories of penalties for a CEO's or CFO's false Section 906 certification. First, if the CEO or CFO certifies the company's periodic report *knowing* that the report does not comply with Sections 13(a) and 15(d) of the Exchange Act or that the report does not fairly present the company's financial condition or results of operations, that CEO or CFO will be fined up to US$1 million or imprisoned for up to 10 years, or both. Second, if the CEO or CFO *willfully* certifies a periodic report that does not meet the requirements of Sections 13(a) and 15(d) of the Exchange Act or that does not fairly present the financial conditions or results of operations of the company, then that CEO or CFO will be fined up to US$5 million or imprisoned for up to 20 years.[35] Based on the language used in the statute, it appears that a CEO or CFO would not be criminally liable for certifying a false statement with regards to the company's period report unless the officer knew that the certification was false.

Congress expects that the Section 906 certifications will cause CEOs and CFOs to read their company's periodic reports, to establish and review the company's internal procedures with regard to documenting and reporting financial information, and to meet with the other various company officers, including financial and legal officers, so as to ensure that the proper disclosures are being made in the company's report.

SOX Section 302 certification

Congress mandated that the SEC adopt rules pertaining to CEO and CFO certification of periodic reports filed by companies pursuant to Sections 13(a) and 15(d) of the Exchange Act. The SEC adopted Exchange Act Rules 13a-14 and 15d-14 in August 2002,[36] to apply to all types of companies that file reports pursuant to Sections 13(a) and 15(d) of the Exchange Act. This list includes banks and savings associations, registered investment companies, issuers of asset-backed securities, small businesses, foreign private issuers and companies that file reports under the Exchange Act voluntarily. Therefore, annual reports on Forms 10-K, 20-F and 40-F must be certified, as do quarterly reports on Forms 10-Q. CEOs and CFOs do not need to certify current reports on Form 8-K; however, they must certify any amendments and any transition reports to the annual and quarterly reports listed above. The rules became effective 29th August 2002 and require that the certification be included with all periodic reports filed or submitted to the SEC after 29th August 2002. The SEC amended the rules on 5th June 2003.[37] The SEC is applying an extended compliance period to the section of the introductory language in paragraph 4 of the Section 302 certification relating to the CEO's and CFO's responsibility for establishing

---

[35] SOX Section 906(a) (emphasis added).
[36] Release 46427 (29th August 2002).
[37] Securities Act Release 8238 (5th June 2003).

and maintaining internal control over financial reporting as well as paragraph 4(b) of the certifications that must be included in the first annual report required to contain management's internal control report and thereafter.

Based on SOX and the subsequent SEC rule, as amended, CEOs and CFOs, or if the company does not have a CEO or CFO an individual in an equivalent position, are required to certify as to the following:

- as CEO and CFO, they have reviewed the annual report;
- based, as applicable, on the CEO's or CFO's knowledge, the report does not control any misstatements or omission of material information;
- based, as applicable, on the CEO's or CFO's knowledge, the financial statements and other financial information included in the report fairly present in all material respects, the company's financial condition, operating results and cashflows as of and for the periods presented in the report;
- that, as CEO and CFO, they are responsible for establishing and maintaining disclosure controls and procedures and internal control over financial reporting;[38]
- that they have disclosed: (i) based on their most recent evaluation, all significant deficiencies and material weaknesses in the design or operation of the company's internal control over financial condition that are reasonably likely to adversely affect the company's ability to record, process, summarise and report financial information; and (ii) any fraud, whether or not material, involving management or other employees who have a significant rile in the company's internal control over financial reporting to the company's auditors and to the company's audit committee; and
- that they have included the results of their evaluation of the company's internal controls and any changes that have or may occur and have disclosed other significant factors that may affect the internal controls, even if after their evaluation, in the company's periodic report.

---

[38] The SEC revised its rules to make clear that a company's disclosure controls and procedures may be designed under the supervision of the CEO and CFO.

In particular, this means that the CEO and CFO of a company filing periodic reports pursuant to Sections 13(a) and 15(d) of the Exchange Act must first certify that they have reviewed the company's report. Second, the CEO and CFO must state that "based on his or her knowledge", the report does not make any false statements or omit material facts that would make a statement misleading. The CEO and CFO must certify, also based on their knowledge, that the financial statements contained in the report "fairly represent in all material respects the financial condition, results of operations and cashflows" of the company for the period to which the report pertains. According to the SEC's final rule release, the company's financial disclosure includes financial statements, the footnotes to the financial statements, selected financial data, the MD&A and any other financial information contained in a company's quarterly report. It was not the intent of the SEC that the CEO or CFO merely state that the financial statements provided in their company's report conforms to GAAP. It is the SEC's view that even though a company's report may follow GAAP, that does not mean that GAAP figures give the public or the SEC a fair or complete view of the company. Therefore, the CEO and CFO must look at the company's reported financial information in its entirety and state whether or not those disclosures give a clear picture of the company.

In addition to supervising the establishment and maintenance of disclosure controls and procedures, the CEO and CFO must certify that they have evaluated the effectiveness of those controls and procedures and presented their conclusions in the company's periodic report. They also must certify that they have disclosed the results of their evaluation to the company's auditors and to the audit committee of the company's board of directors or, if the company does not have an audit committee, those persons performing equivalent functions. Specifically, the CEO and CFO must disclose to the auditors and audit committee whether there were any "significant deficiencies" in the company's reporting or disclosure of its financial information or whether there was any fraud involving the company's management or employees having to do with the company's reporting procedures for its financial information.

Finally, the CEO and CFO must certify that the company's report includes any significant changes or factors that would affect the company's internal control over financial reporting, including changes that the company might undertake in order to correct problems that they might have had during the previous reporting period, even if these changes might occur after the CEO and CFO conducted their evaluation.

The SEC requires that the certification be included in the periodic report and exactly follow the certification language included in the SEC's final rule.

However, non-accelerated filers and foreign private issuers, because they are not subject to the internal control over financial reporting provisions of Section 404 of SOX and the SEC's rules thereunder until their first annual reports for financial years ending on after 15th July 2006, may modify the CEO and CFO Section 302 certifications with respect to matters relating to internal control over financial reporting.

The SEC expects that, by having the CEO and CFO provide the required certifications, CEOs and CFOs will take the responsibility to ensure that information as to the company's internal controls and procedures are properly documented and reported to the SEC in the time period specified in the SEC's rules. The SEC does not directly mandate that companies develop any specific procedures;[39] rather, the SEC states that each company should implement the procedures needed to make the CEO and CFO certification possible, taking into account the practices of their own business and management practices. For example, the SEC rules do not specify what measures should be taken by the CEO and CFO when they evaluate the company's disclosure controls and procedures, but the SEC assumes that companies will establish methods that permit the required certifications to be made. For example, CEOs and CFOs should consider reading the company reports, meeting with the independent auditors and audit committee to discuss, among other matters, topics and changes having to do with the company's accounting procedures. Furthermore, the company may want to establish a disclosure committee so as to ensure that disclosure controls and procedures are established and implemented.

The certification requirement mandated by SOX Section 302 and Exchange Act Rules 13a-15 and 15d-15 does not necessarily change

---

[39] The SEC does, however, recommend that companies create a committee to consider company disclosures for the purpose of determining whether disclosure items are material and to ensure that the disclosures are made in a timely manner.

the legal responsibility of a company's CEO or CFO. Such officers already face liability under the Exchange Act, including the anti-fraud provisions. However, if a CEO or CFO falsely certifies their company's periodic report, that CEO or CFO could be exposed to SEC action for violating Sections 13(a) and 15(d) of the Exchange Act and Rule 106-5 thereunder, and could be subject to both SEC and private actions pursuant to Section 10(b) and Rule 10b-5 of the Exchange Act, and a CEO or CFO could be liable under Sections 11 and 12 of the Securities Act of 1933, as amended if the certified reports are incorporated by reference into a registration statement or prospectus.

The SEC and its Staff have recognised the difficulties that issuers of asset-backed securities have in meeting the Section 302 certifications and therefore have provided compliance guidance to such issuers. Issuers of asset-backed securities are, at least for a period of time, subject to the periodic reporting requirements of either Section 13(a) or 15(d) of the Exchange Act. Due to the nature of asset-backed issuers, the SEC Staff traditionally has allowed such issuers to file reports under Form 8-K that are tied to the payment dates of the securities and contain specific information about the performance of the underlying assets that service the payment obligations of the asset-backed securities. Recognising the significant differences in the information provided by asset-backed issuers, the Commission adopted Exchange Act Rules 13a-14 and 15d-14 that require asset-backed issuers (as defined therein) to provide a modified certification signed by the trustee of the trust (if the trustee signed the periodic report) or the senior officer in charge of the depositor's securitisation programme (if the depositor signed the periodic report).[40] The SEC Staff has subsequently issued interpretive letters to address specific compliance issues.[41]

CONTROLS AND PROCEDURES
Disclosure controls and procedures

Exchange Act Rules 13a-15 and 15d-15 require companies with securities registered with the SEC to maintain disclosure controls

---

[40] *See* Revised Statement: Compliance by Asset-Backed Issuers with Exchange Act Rules 13a-14 and 15d-14 (21st February 2003).

[41] *Merrill Lynch Depositor, Inc* (28th March 2003), *Mitsubishi Motors Credit of America, Inc* (27th March 2003) and *Bank of America, N.A.* (13th November 2002).

and procedures designed to ensure that the information required to be disclosed in reports filed with the SEC is recorded, processed, summarised and reported within the time periods specified in the SEC's rules.

Each reporting company must disclose the CEO and CFO conclusions about the effectiveness of the company's disclosure controls and procedures based on their evaluation "as of the end of the period" covered by the annual or quarterly report.

For a US public reporting company, the disclosures are required in the quarterly reports filed on Form 10-Q and the annual report filed on Form 10-K, and for a foreign private issuer, in the annual report filed on Form 20-F. The term "disclosure controls and procedures" is defined to mean those disclosure controls and procedures designed to ensure that the information required to be disclosed in reports filed with the SEC is recorded, processed, summarised and reported within the time periods specified in the SEC's rules. As defined, disclosure controls and procedures include but are not limited to controls and procedures designed to ensure that information required to be disclosed by the issuer in its reports filed or submitted with the SEC is accumulated and communicated so as to permit management to make timely and informed decisions regarding the issuer's disclosures.[42]

Disclosure controls and procedures are broader than a reporting company's internal financial controls, which companies have been required to maintain pursuant to Section 13(b)(2) of the Exchange Act and Regulation 13B-2 thereunder. Each reporting company should have and maintain disclosure controls and procedures that are consistent with its business, internal management and supervisory practices: "one size" does not fit all issuers. As part of this process, the SEC suggests (but does not require) that companies establish a disclosure committee to consider the materiality of the information provided from the operating businesses and oversee the companies' compliance with its disclosure obligations, both required disclosures with its regulators and voluntary disclosures through, for example, press releases.

---

[42] *See* Rule 13a-14(c), 17 C.F.R. 240.13a-14(c) and Rule 15d-14(c), 17 C.F.R. 240.15d-14(c).

Internal control over financial reporting

On 5th June 2003, the SEC adopted rules[43] to require each reporting company to include in its annual report (Form 20-F for a foreign private issuer, Form 40-F for a multi-jurisdictional issuer and Form 10-K for a US issuer) a report of management about the company's internal control over financial reporting. The new rules, among other purposes, implement Section 404 of SOX.[44] The SEC revised the compliance dates in February 2004 and again on 2nd March 2005.[45] As a result of Release 8392, accelerated filers whose financial year ends on or after 15th November 2004 started complying with the internal control over financial reporting rules. As a result of Securities Act Release 8545, non-accelerated filers and foreign private issuers must start complying with the requirements for the issuer's first financial year ending on or after 15th July 2006 (originally 15th April 2005). On 30th November 2004, the SEC issued an exemptive order that granted an accelerated filer that had a public float of less than US$700 million at the end of its second financial quarter in 2004 an additional 45 days to include in their annual reports their management's report on internal control over financial reporting and the related auditor's report.

A company must file both management's report and the registered public accountant's attestation report as part of its annual report. Although the final rules do not specify where management's report about internal control over financial reporting, the SEC expects that most companies will decide to place both management's report and the attestation report either near the MD&A disclosure or immediately before the financial statements.

PCAOB Auditing Standard No 2, "An Audit of Internal Control Over Financial Reporting Performed in Conjunction with An Audit of Financial Statements" (AS 2), which became effective in June 2004, sets out the requirements for an auditor engaged to audit both management's assessment of the effectiveness of an issuer's internal control over financial reporting and its financial

---

43 *See* Securities Act Release 8238 (5th June 2003).
44 The SEC proposed that a company file the accounting firm's attestation report as part of its annual report.
45 Securities Act Release 8392 (24th February 2004) and Securities Act Release 8545 (2nd March 2005).

statements. It is important that lawyers and their company clients be familiar with AS 2.

Definition of "internal control over financial reporting"
Except for the PCAOB's use of the term "company" instead of "registrant," the SEC and the PCAOB have defined the term "internal control over financial reporting" as

> *"A process designed by, or under the supervision of, the registrant's principal executive and financial officers, or persons performing similar functions, and effected by the registrant's board of directors, management and other personnel, to provide reasonable assurance regarding the reliability of financial reporting and the preparation of financial statements for external purposes in accordance with generally accepted accounting principles and includes those policies and procedures that:*
> *(1) pertain to the maintenance of records that in reasonable detail accurately and fairly reflect the transactions and dispositions of the assets of the registrant;*
> *(2) provide reasonable assurance that transactions are recorded as necessary to permit preparation of financial statements in accordance with generally accepted accounting principles, and that receipts and expenditures of the registrant are being made only in accordance with authorizations of management and directors of the registrant; and*
> *(3) provide reasonable assurance regarding prevention or timely detection of unauthorised acquisition, use or disposition of the registrant's assets that could have a material effect on the financial statements"*.[46]

Definitions of significant deficiency and material weakness
A *control deficiency* exists when the design or operation of a control does not permit management or employees, in the normal course of performing their assigned tasks, to prevent or detect a misstatement on a timely basis. There can be design deficiencies (such as

---

[46] *See* the discussion in Securities Act Release 8238 and amended Exchange Act Rules 13a-14(d) and 15(d)-14(d). Clauses (1) and (2) of the definition include the internal controls matters set out in Section 103 of SOX that the registered public accounting firm is required to evaluate as part of its audit or attestation report. The PCAOB is responsible for establishing the Section 103 standards. The explicit reference in Clause (3) to assurances about the use and disposition of company assets is intended by the SEC to make clear that the safeguarding of assets is one element of internal controls over financial reporting and to provide consistency with the 1994 Addendum to the 1992 Report published by Committee of Sponsoring Organizations of the Treadway Commission (COSO). COSO, *Internal Control – Integrated Framework* (1992) (COSO Report). The AU section 319 in the Codification of Statements on Auditing Standards also incorporates the COSO definition.

FINANCIAL INFORMATION: ACCOUNTING AND DISCLOSURE

when a control is missing or the control objective is not always met because of a design problem) and operational deficiencies (such as when a person performing the control does not have the necessary authority or qualifications to perform the control effectively).

A *significant deficiency* is one or more control deficiencies that adversely affect an issuer's ability to initiate, authorise, record, process or report external financial reliably in accordance with GAAP such that there is *more than a remote likelihood* that a misstatement in the issuer's annual or interim financial statements that *is more than inconsequential will not be prevented or detected*. The term "remote" has the same meaning as the term is used in FASB Statement No 5, *Accounting for Contingencies*, which is that the chance that a future event will occur is "slight". Therefore, AS 2 states that when the likelihood of an event occurring is reasonably possible or probable, the event is "more than remote". AS 2 also advises that a misstatement is inconsequential if a reasonable person would conclude that the misstatement individually or when aggregated with other misstatements would clearly be immaterial to the financial statements.

A *material weakness* is a significant deficiency or combination of significant deficiencies that results in more than a remote likelihood that a material misstatement in the issuer's annual or interim financial statements will not be prevented or detected. AS 2 indicates that a restatement of financial statements is a significant deficiency and strong evidence of a material weakness.

Management's assessment of and report on a company's internal control over financial reporting

Management's internal control report (there is no SEC prescribed form) to be included as in a company's annual report must include:

❑ a statement of management's responsibilities for establishing and maintaining adequate internal control over financial reporting for the company;
❑ management's assessment of the effectiveness of the company's internal control over financial reporting as of the end of the company's most recent financial year, including a statement as to whether or not such control is effective. The assessment must

disclose a "material weaknesses" in the company's internal control over financial reporting identified by management; and
❑ a statement that the company's registered public accounting firm that audited the financial statements included in its annual report has issued an attestation report on management's assessment of the company's internal control over financial reporting.

Management's assessment is expressed at the level of reasonable assurance, which AS 2 advises includes an understanding that there is a remote likelihood that one or more material misstatements will not be prevented or detected on a timely basis. While not an absolute assurance, the PCAOB states that it is a high level of assurance.

Assessment of internal control over financial reporting
The SEC decided not to mandate use of a particular framework to evaluate internal control. Rather, the management must base its evaluation on a recognised control framework that is established by a body or group that followed due-process procedures with respect to the adoption of the framework. The SEC states that the COSO Framework meets the rules' criteria.[47]

The SEC and PCAOB provide guidance as to the elements of a suitable framework. It must:

❑ be unbiased;
❑ permit reasonably consistent qualitative and quantitative measurements of a company's internal control over financial reporting;
❑ be sufficiently complete so that those relevant factors that would alter a conclusion as to the effectiveness of a company's internal control are not omitted; and
❑ be relevant to an evaluation of a company's internal control over financial reporting.

Auditor independence issues
The SEC and PCAOB have reminded a company and its auditors that auditor independence rules prohibit an auditor from

---

47 *See* footnote 67 to Securities Act Release 8238.

providing designated non-audit services. In this regard, while auditors may help management document a company's internal controls, management must be actively involved in the process.[48] Management cannot delegate its obligation to assess the effectiveness of a company's internal control over financial reporting to the company's auditor. Further, management acceptance of responsibility for the documentation and testing conducted by the company's auditor will not meet the auditor independence requirements.

Evaluation methods
The SEC advises that the methods used by management to evaluate a company's internal control over financial reporting "will, and should, vary from company to company". However, each company must maintain evidence, including documentation relating to the design of internal control and testing processes, to provide reasonable support for management's assessment of the effectiveness of the internal control. A company's independent auditors also will require management to develop and maintain evidentiary matter supportive of management's assessment.

Procedures used by management to evaluate a company's internal control over financial reporting should be based on procedures adequate to evaluate both the design and operating effectiveness of such internal control. The final release provides a non-exclusive list of controls that would be subject to management's assessment, including controls over initiating, recording, processing and reconciling account balances, classes of transactions and disclosure and related matters in the financial statements; controls related to the selection and application of appropriate accounting policies; and controls related to the prevention, detection and identification of fraud. Management must do more than inquire.

Report on previously identified material weakness
The PCAOB on 31st March 2005[49] proposed a new auditing standard that would allow issuers, who reported one or more material

---
[48] See "5.17 Auditor Independence".
[49] See "Proposed Auditing Standard–Reporting on the Elimination of a Material Weakness", PCAOB Release 2005–002 (31st March 2005) available at www.pcaobus.org/Rules_of_the_Board/rulemaking_docket.asp.

weaknesses as of their annual assessment of the effectiveness of the internal control over financial reporting, the option at any time during a financial year to engage their independent auditor to assess and report on whether such material weaknesses have been remediated. The proposed stand-alone engagement would be voluntary and performed only at the request of the issuer.

Disclosure controls and procedures compared with internal control over financial reporting

The SEC acknowledges that there will be substantial overlap between the components or elements of a company's disclosure controls and procedures and its internal control over financial reporting.

The internal control over financial reporting compliance dates are:

❏ *management report on internal control over financial reporting and attestation report of the independent auditor.* For a company who is an accelerated filer as defined in Exchange Act Rule 12b-2, the initial compliance date is for its first financial year ending on or after 15th November 2004. Other companies, including foreign private issuers, must start complying for their first financial year ending on or after 15th July 2006 (previously 15th July 2005);

❏ *evaluation of any material change if a company's internal control over financial reporting.* First periodic report, that is, Q1 quarterly report for domestic issuers and next annual report for foreign private issuers) due after the first annual report required to include a management report on internal control over financial reporting.

The SEC advises that early voluntary compliance is permitted.

The SEC has excluded asset-backed issuers from the disclosure requirements adopted under Section 404.

SEC and PCAOB internal control guidance

The Staffs of the SEC and PCAOB have each published sets of FAQs regarding rules under SOX Section 404 and AS 2. These FAQs are available through the SEC's and PCAOB's websites. Most significantly, the SEC provided favourable guidance with respect to a material business acquisition by a public company. FAQ 3 provides that management may exclude an acquired business from its assessment of internal control over financial reporting if it is not possible to assess the acquired business's internal control in the time available. Management's report must contain a cross reference to a discussion that explains the scope limitation, identifies the acquired business and indicates the significance of the acquired business to the issuer's consolidated financial statements. The acquired business may only be omitted from one annual management report and only within one year from the acquisition date.

SEC roundtable on internal control reporting

On 13th April 2005, the SEC held a roundtable discussion regarding the implementation of the SOX Section 404 internal control provisions. There were over 50 panellists representing the interests of issuers, auditors, securities analysts and investors. SEC Chairman Donaldson noted that of the 2,500 public reporting companies that timely filed management's internal control report, approximately 8% reported material weaknesses. Several key themes emerged through out the discussions such as: (1) compliance costs were far greater than anticipated; (2) whether the definition of material weakness picks up items that should not raise investor concerns; (3) uncertainty about how to apply AS 2 and the need for guidance on audit objectives, preferably principles-based, so as to give auditors greater flexibility in designing their internal controls audit; and (4) the working relationship between issuers and their auditors. At the end of the discussions the PCAOB described the steps it intends to take including:

- ❑ issuance of staff guidance on AS 2 by 16th May 2005;
- ❑ review at its June 2005 meeting what additional guidance, if any, should be provided; and
- ❑ work with auditors in the PCAOB inspection process regarding the processes used by auditors to support their decisions.

Webcast archives of the roundtable discussion, as well as written statements of certain panellists and other related materials are available through the SEC's website at www.sec.gov/spotlight/soxcomp.htm.

THE AUDIT COMMITTEE
Overview
SOX and the SEC's rules thereunder have created a new relationship among management, a company's independent auditors and the audit committee.[50] A company's audit committee has been placed in a significantly stronger gatekeeper role with respect to, among other matters, the accuracy, integrity and completeness of a company's financial statements and financial disclosures (including MD&A).

Requirements for a listed company audit committee
On 9th April 2003, the SEC adopted final rules that the US direct national securities exchanges and national securities associations, which are SROs, to prohibit the listing of securities of issuers who are not in compliance with the audit committee requirements of SOX.[51] Listed domestic issuers had to comply with the new requirements by the date of their first annual shareholders meeting after 15th January 2004, but no later than 31st October 2004. Foreign private issuers must comply by 31st July 2005. On 4th November 2003, the SEC approved the corporate governance listing standards of the NYSE and NASDAQ. On 3rd November 2004, the NYSE Listing Standards were amended to clarify application of the bright line independence test relating to a listed company's audit firm.

Audit committee requirements
Rule 10A-3 under the Exchange Act requires issuers listed or quoted on a SRO to comply with the following requirements:

❑ each member of the audit committee of the issuer must be independent according to specified criteria;
❑ the audit committee must be directly responsible for the appointment, compensation, retention and oversight of the work of the issuers outside auditors;
❑ the audit committee must establish procedures for the receipt, retention and treatment of complaints regarding accounting,

---
50 *See* the discussion in Securities Act Release 8220 (9th April 2003).
51 *See* Securities Act Release 8220.

internal accounting controls or auditing matters, including procedures for the confidential, anonymous submission by employees of concerns regarding questionable accounting or auditing matters;
❑ the audit committee must have the authority to engage independent counsel and other advisers, as it determines necessary to carry out its duties; and
❑ the issuer must provide appropriate funding for the audit committee.

An issuer is not required to have a separately designated audit committee. In such event, the entire board will constitute the audit committee so that the SRO rules adopted under Rule 10A-3, including the independence requirements, will apply to the board as a whole.

Independence requirement
In addition to the independence requirements applicable to all board members under the SRO listing standards, an audit committee member, to be considered independent, may not, other than in the member's capacity as a member of the board or board committee member:

❑ accept any consulting, advisory or other compensatory fee from the issuer or any subsidiary of the issuer; or
❑ be an affiliated person of the issuer or any subsidiary of the issuer.

The SEC clarified that the "no compensation" prohibition does not cover non-advisory financial services such as lending relationships, maintaining customer accounts or brokerage services. The SEC also clarified that the prohibition would not include the payment of fixed compensation to an audit committee member under a retirement plan that is not contingent upon continued service. Principally due to the express language of the SOX, the SEC determined not to adopt a "de minimis" payment exception.

With respect to the "affiliated person" prohibition, the SEC adopted a safe harbour so that a person will not be deemed to be an affiliated person if the person is not an executive officer or beneficial owner of more than 10% of any class of voting equity securities of the issuer. The SEC clarified that the independence of a shareholder owning more than 10% of any class of an issuer's equity voting securities will depend on the facts and circumstances analysis of control.

Foreign private issuers
The SEC made several refinements in the final rule to address commenters' concerns regarding specific areas in which foreign corporate governance arrangements differ significantly from US practices.

- an employee of a foreign private issuer who is not an executive officer is exempt from the independence requirements if the employee is elected to the board or audit committee pursuant to the issuer's governing law or documents, an employee collective bargaining or similar agreement or other home-country legal or listing requirements. This exemption is intended to accommodate issuers from countries that require employee representatives to serve on an issuer's board.
- recognising that controlling shareholders are more common among foreign private issuers than among US issuers, the final rule provides that an audit committee member is exempt from the "affiliated person" prohibition if:
  - the member is an affiliate of the issuer or a representative of the affiliate;
  - the member only has observer status on, and is not the chair of, the audit committee; and
  - neither the member nor the affiliate is an executive officer of the issuer.
- an audit committee member is exempt from the "affiliated person" prohibition if the member is a representative of a foreign government or foreign governmental entity that is an affiliate of the issuer. The SEC made clear that more than one member of the audit committee can qualify under this exemption.

The audit committee member under the latter two exemptions relating to controlling shareholders and foreign government representatives remain subject to the "no compensation" prohibition. Certain countries, such as Brazil and Japan, require or provide for auditor oversight through a board of auditors or similar body or statutory auditors. The final rule provides that a foreign private issuer generally will not be subject to the audit committee requirements if the following conditions are met:

- the issuer has a board of auditors (as defined in the rule) established and selected pursuant to home-country legal or listing provisions expressly requiring or permitting such a board or similar body;
- the board of auditors is required to be either separate from the board of directors or composed of one or more members of the board of directors and one or more members that are not also members of the board of directors;
- the board of auditors is not elected by management and no executive officer of the issuer is a member of the board of auditors;
- home-country legal or listing provisions set out independence standards of the board of auditors from the issuer or its management;
- the board of auditors, pursuant to home-country legal or listing requirements or the issuer's governing documents, is responsible to the extent permitted by law, for the appointment, retention and oversight of the work of the issuer's outside auditors;
- the remaining requirements of the rule relating to such matters as the complaints procedures, the authority to engage advisors and related funding, apply to the board of auditors to the extent permitted by law; and
- the board of auditors is subject to the "audit committee financial expert" disclosure requirements.

Disclosure requirements
The final rule specifies certain required disclosures in proxy statements and annual reports with respect to the use of any exemption to the rule. Disclosure is also required as to the identification of the audit committee in proxy statements and annual reports and for issuers that have not separately designated an audit committee disclosure that its entire board is acting as the audit committee.

Audit committee financial expert
On 23rd January 2003, the SEC adopted final rules implementing SOX Section 407. The final rules require a company to disclose in its annual reports on Form 10-K, Form 20-F or Form 40-F that its board of directors has determined that the company either:

❏ has at least one audit committee financial expert serving on its audit committee; or
❏ does not have a financial expert serving on its audit committee and the reasons why not.

If a company discloses that it has an audit committee financial expert, it must disclose the person's name. The SEC encourages, but does not require, a company to disclose the names of additional experts. A company also must state whether that person is independent of management and, if not, why not.

The SEC advised in the final rules release that a company will not meet its new disclosure requirements by stating that its board had not made the necessary determination, only disclosing the qualifications of all its audit committee member or disclosing that it does not have an audit committee financial expert if the board has determined otherwise.

US issuers who elect to include the disclosure in its proxy or information may incorporate that information by reference into their annual reports on Form 10-K provided that they file the proxy or information statement with the SEC no later than 120 days after the end of the financial year covered by the Form 10-K.

Definition of the "audit committee financial expert"
The final rules[52] provide that a person will qualify as an audit committee financial expert if that person has each of the following five attributes:

❏ an understanding of GAAP and financial statements;
❏ the ability to assess the general application of such principles in connection with the accounting for estimate, accruals and reserves;
❏ experience in preparing, auditing, analysing or evaluating financial statements that present a breadth and level of complexity of accounting issues that are generally comparable with the breadth and complexity of issues that can reasonably be expected to be raised by the issuer's financial statements or experience in actively supervising one or more persons engaged in such activities;

---

[52] Securities Act Release 8177 (23rd January 2003).

- an understanding of internal controls and procedures for financial reporting; and
- an understanding of audit committee functions.[53]

A person must have acquired the required necessary attributes through any one of the following means:

- education and experience as a principal financial officer, principal accounting officer, controller, public accountant or auditor or experience in one or more positions that involve the performance of similar functions;
- experience actively supervising a principal financial officer, principal accounting officer, controller, public accountant, auditor or person performing similar functions;
- experience overseeing or assessing the performance of companies or public accountants with respect to the preparation, auditing or evaluation of financial statements; or
- other relevant experience.

Active supervision means more than seniority in a traditional reporting hierarchy and should involve active participation in preparing, auditing, analysing or evaluating financial statements at a supervisory level. Further, the supervisor's experience should be at least comparable with the general expertise of the persons being supervised. Consequently, the SEC advises that a CEO with significant involvement in operational matters, but little involvement in financial or accounting matters likely would not qualify as a financial expert.

If a person qualifies as a financial expert by means of other relevant experience, the issuer should include in its disclosure a brief list of the person's relevant experience.

The pool of eligible candidates under the rule includes investment bankers, venture capitalists, professional analysts, lawyers, fund managers, academics and others whose positions require them to scrutinise financial statements and diligently question management and auditors.

---

53 *See* Securities Act Release 8177.

Foreign private issuers
The full board of directors, or in the case of a foreign private issuer having a two-tiered board of directors the supervisory or non-management board, must make the determination that an audit committee member qualifies as an audit committee financial expert. In assessing candidates, a board should consider "all available facts and circumstances" and not be limited by a mechanical checklist. The SEC also advises boards to make sure that the financial expert "embodies the highest standards of personal and professional integrity".

The audit committee financial expert of a foreign private issuer must possess expertise relating to the accounting principals used by the issuer in preparing its primary financial statements. While the SEC states that an understanding of reconciliation to US GAAP would be "helpful", the primary focus should be on the accounting principals used by the issuer. Accordingly, a foreign private issuer that uses home-country GAAP or international accounting standards to prepare its primary financial statements would not be required to have an audit committee financial expert familiar with US GAAP.

Safe harbour from liability for audit committee financial experts
The SEC set out its views that the requirements of Section 407 of SOX are solely disclosure based and are not intended to change the duties, obligations or liability of any audit committee member, including the audit committee financial expert. To codify its position, the SEC adopted a safe harbour intended to address concerns that the mere designation of an audit committee financial expert might be viewed as imposing a higher degree of individual responsibility on that person or decreasing the duties and obligations of other audit committee members. Under the safe harbour:

❑ a person who is an audit committee financial expert will not be deemed an expert for any purpose, including Section 11 of the Securities Act;
❑ the designation of a person as an audit committee financial expert pursuant to the new disclosure requirement does not

impose on that person any duties, obligations or liabilities greater than those imposed on an audit committee member in the absence of such designation; and
- the designation of a person as an audit committee financial expert pursuant to the new disclosure requirement does not affect the duties, obligations or liability of any other audit committee or board member.

Auditor independence
The federal securities laws mandate that every Securities Act registration statement and Exchange Act registration statement and annual report filed with the SEC contain annual financial statements that are examined and reported upon by a public or certified public accountant who meets the SEC's standards of auditor independence – a requirement that dates to 1933. The SEC views this requirement as reflecting the importance of independent audits in protecting investors. Accordingly, public reporting companies and their auditors must diligently comply with all independence requirements.

Under SOX, observance of the independence rules is the responsibility of both the auditor and a company's audit committee. Audit committees must request, receive and evaluate assurances received from the company's outside auditor to assess whether the auditor meets the statutory and SEC independence standards. As part of this diligence and oversight, the audit committee must pre-approve the provision of audit and non-audit services that are not prohibited under either SOX or the SEC's auditor independence rules. Moreover, an audit committee must take seriously any independence issues that come to their attention. If a company's auditor is not independent, the company's filing will not comply with the SEC's financial statement requirements that are set out in Regulation S-X.

The SEC's auditor independence requirements are set out in Rule 2–01 of Regulation S-X, in the interpretations, guidelines and examples that are contained in Section 600 the Codification of Financial Reporting Policies entitled "Matters Relating to Independent Accountants" and in publicly available SEC Staff written responses to informal requests for advice on the SEC's auditor independence requirements. In addition, the SEC's website at www.sec.gov/hot/auditor.htm lists useful reference material on the subject.

The auditor independence rules have been subject to significant controversy and revisions during the past few years. The SEC strengthened its auditor independence rules in November 2000 and again in January 2003.[54] The January 2003 amendments implement Section 208(a) of SOX. The amended rules create a more rigorous regulatory framework for auditors, public companies and audit committees. The effective date of the amended rules was 6th May 2003, with transition periods as summarised in the following for certain of the rules.

The amended rules focus on matters that Congress and the SEC view as key attributes of auditor independence: (1) the provision of non-audit services by an auditor to its registrant audit client; (2) the ability and responsibility of a registrant's audit committee to insulate the auditor from pressures that may be exerted by management; (3) employment relationships between a registrant and its auditor; (4) maintenance of effective channels of communications between the audit committee and the auditor; and (5) audit partner compensation packages tied directly to selling services, other than audit, review and attest services, to the audit client.

Auditor engagement duties

A company's audit committee must pre-approve all audit and non-audit services to be rendered by the company's independent auditors. The audit committee may satisfy its duty to pre-approve audit and non-audit services by either giving general pre-approval of categories of services based on established polices and procedures or individual pre-approval on an engagement-by-engagement basis. As an initial matter, the audit committee should understand each audit and non-audit service that the company's auditors have provided in the recent past, currently are providing and are expected to provide. That list of services should be compared with the list of prohibited and permitted services set out in the SEC's rules. The audit committee and auditor should established communication channels and processes to permit timely, effective and

---

54 Securities Act Release 7919 (21st November 2000); Securities Act Release 8183 (28th January 2003). *See* reference materials posted on the SEC website at www.sec.gov/hot/auditor.htm and at www.sec.gov/info/accountants/independentref.shtml. See also PCAOB Rules – Professional Standards, Rule 3600T. Interim Independence Standards, Exchange Act Release 49624, PCAOB-2003–11 (28th April 2004).

efficient compliance by both parties with the new pre-approval requirements.

Non-audit services
The provision of non-audit services impairs independence under the SEC's existing auditor independence rules except in specified limited situations. With the adoption of SOX, Section 10A(g) of the Exchange Act and the SEC's recent amendments to its rules prohibit a public accounting firm registered with the PCAOB that audits a registrant's financial statements from providing, contemporaneously with an audit or other engagement requiring independence, any non-audit services to its audit client, including the nine categories of non-audit services set out in the Exchange Act. The prohibition covers any person associated with the accounting firm. Any non-audit service that is not a prohibited service will impair an auditor's independence unless the service is *pre-approved* by the registrant's audit committee. The nine prohibited non-audit services are as follows:

- book-keeping or other services related to the client's accounting records or financial statements, including the preparation and maintenance of source data underlying financial statements;
- financial information systems design and implementation;
- appraisal or valuation services, fairness opinions or contribution-in-kind reports;
- actuarial services;
- internal audit outsourcing services;
- management functions or human resources;
- broker or dealer, investment-adviser or investment-banking services;
- legal services and expert services unrelated to the audit; and
- any other service that PCAOB determines, by regulation, is impermissible.

The rules provided for a transition period for the provision of prohibited non-audit services. Until 6th May 2004, the provision of the above services did not impair an auditor's independence as long as they were permitted under the existing rules and provided under contracts in existence on 6th May 2004.

The SEC sets out four guiding principles to determine whether a non-audit service would impair an auditor's independence. Specifically, an auditor must not:

❑ perform management functions as would result if it provided human resources services such as recruiting, hiring and designing compensation plans for officers, directors and managers of an audit client;
❑ audit its own work as would result if it provides internal audit outsourcing services, financial information systems design or appraisal, valuation, actuarial or book-keeping services that would later be subject to it own audit procedures to an audit client;
❑ act as an advocate for its audit client as it would if it provided legal and expert services to an audit client in a judicial or regulatory proceedings; or
❑ promote the audit client's stock or other financial interests as it would if it served as a broker, dealer, investment adviser or investment banker for the audit client.

Under these principles, auditors generally will no longer be able to provide book-keeping services, financial information systems design and implementation services, appraisal, valuation, fairness opinions or contribution-in-kind reports, actuarial services and internal outsourcing services, unless it is reasonable to conclude that the results of such services will not be subject to audit procedures during an audit of the client's financial statements. These restrictions will be a significant change for some audit firms.

Expert services
The provision of expert services, while not prohibited under the SEC's existing independence rules, are a prohibited service under the amended rules because the provision of such services violates the basic principle that an auditor should not act as an advocate for its audit client. Specifically, the amended rules prohibit an auditor from providing expert witness or other services, including accounting advice, opinions or forensic accounting services in connection with the client's participation in a legal, administrative or regulatory proceeding. Consequently, the amended rules prohibit an auditor from providing forensic accounting services to the audit

client's counsel in connection with an enforcement action by the SEC or other securities regulator. The amended rules also will prohibit an auditor from serving as an expert witness in a regulatory rate setting proceeding in support of the audit client's request for fee increases. The amended rules will not, however, prohibit an auditor from assisting a client's audit committee in its own investigation of a potential accounting impropriety or complying with the auditor's obligations under Section 10A of the Exchange Act to search for fraud material to the client's financial statements and keep the audit committee informed of its findings, as long as the auditor does not take on the role as an advocate. For example, an auditor may render forensic accounting services to the audit committee and share its work product with the audit committee's outside counsel as long as the auditors remain in control of their work and do not become subject to the direction or control of the client's counsel. An auditor also may testify as a fact witness to its audit work.

Tax services
While the existing rules permit auditors to provide tax services to their audit clients, the amended rules limit such services and permit auditors to continue to provide tax services such as tax compliance, tax planning and tax advice provided that (1) the client's audit committee has pre-approved the services and (2) the services would not constitute a prohibited legal or expert service. For example, representation of an audit client before a tax court, which would involve an auditor serving as an advocate for its client, and formulating tax shelters, which may require the auditor to audit its own work, assume a management function or become an advocate for a client in seeking to minimise tax obligations or defend novel tax structures.

Contingency fees
The receipt by an audit firm of contingent fees[55] for tax services provided to an issuer likely will impair the audit firm's indepen-

---

55 *See* 21st May 2004 Letter from Donald T Nicolaisen, Chief Accountant, to Bruce P Webb, Chair of the AICPA (American Institute of Certified Public Accountants) Professional Ethics Executive Committee available at www.sec.gov/info/accountants/staffletters/webb052104.htm.

dence with respect to its client. "Contingent fee" is defined under the SEC rules to mean:

> *"except as stated in the next sentence, any fee established for the sale of a project or the performance of any service pursuant to an arrangement in which no fee will be charged unless a specified finding or result is attained, or in which the amount of the fee is otherwise dependent upon the finding or result of such product or service. Solely for the purposes of this section, a fee is not a 'contingent fee' if it is fixed by courts or other public authorities, or, in tax matters, if determined based on the results of judicial proceedings or the findings of governmental agencies. Fees may vary depending, for example, on the complexity of services rendered".*[56]

In approving any audit or non-audit service, an audit committee should be aware that any arrangement – from a direct contract provision to "a wink and a nod" – that provides for the possible additional payment of a "value added" fee based on the results of an audit firm's performance of a tax or other service would be viewed by the SEC as impairing the firm's independence. In addition, an audit committee should consider carefully the impact on an accounting firm's independence of the possibility of even a completely voluntary payment of a "value added" fee by an audit client to the firm.

Audit partner rotation

The requirement of audit partner rotation is not new in the United States. The underlying principle of the audit partner rotation requirement is to provide a "fresh set of eyes" in a client's audit while ensuring that the audit team is appropriately qualified and knowledgeable about the client and its industry. Existing professional accounting rules in the United States currently contain audit partner rotation requirements. Section 203 of SOX strengthens the existing rules by requiring the lead audit partner and reviewing partners directly involved in an audit, review or attest engagement to rotate off the engagement after five consecutive financial years.

The SEC's amended rules implement this provision by requiring that the lead and concurring partners rotate after five consecutive financial years as the lead or concurring partner on an engagement and require a five-year "time-out" period after that. The rotation rules also apply to a group of partners defined as "audit partners", other than the lead and concurring partners, who must rotate off the

---

[56] 17 CFR 210.2–01(f)(10).

engagement after seven consecutive years for a two-year "time-out" period. The rules define "audit partners" as those partners who have responsibility for decision-making that affects the audit or who maintain regulator contact with the client's management and audit committee. In addition to the lead and concurring partners, "audit partners" would include all partners who serve the client at the parent or issuer level, other than "specialty" partners. Further, the lead partner on significant subsidiaries (those constituting 20% or more of consolidated revenues or assets of the client) is included within the definition of "audit partners". A partner could, in compliance with the rotation requirements, serve as either a lead partner of a significant subsidiary or as an "audit partner" at the parent or issuer level for two years prior to becoming the lead or concurring partner on the engagement and still serve in that capacity for five years.

The rotation and time-out requirements apply to "tax" partners who perform significant tax services related to the audit and necessary to its completion, but not to partners who provide tax compliance or tax planning services pursuant to audit committee pre-approval.

"National office" partners who serve as technical resources for the audit team and may be regularly consulted on issues related to a specific client would not be considered members of the audit engagement team and, thus, not subject to the rotation and time-out requirements.

For all partners with foreign accounting firms who are subject to the rotation requirements, including lead and concurring partners, the rotation and time-out rules are effective as of the beginning of a client's first financial year after 6th May 2003. In determining time served for these partners, that first financial year will constitute the first year of service for such partners. The SEC adopted staggered effective and varying treatments of years of service so as to allow for the orderly transition of audit engagement teams, including the provision of longer transition periods for partners that had not previously been subject to the rotation requirements.

Conflicts arising from employment and compensation
Employment relationships
The existing rule does not specify any "cooling-off" period before an audit client may hire a former partner, shareholder, principal or

professional employee of an audit firm. Rather, the existing rule considers three conditions: whether the person was in a position to influence the audit firm's operations or financial policies; whether the person has a capital balance at the audit firm; and whether the person has a continuing financial arrangement with the audit firm and, if so, the type of arrangement.

The amended rules do contain a one-year "cooling-off" period, during which certain members of an audit engagement team may not take a position and serve in a financial reporting oversight role at an "issuer". The term "financial reporting oversight role" means a role in which a person is in a position to, or does, influence (1) the financial statements and related financial information, such as MD&A, to be included in a SEC filing or (2) any person who prepares the financial statements and related financial information including directors, president, chief executive officer, chief financial officer, chief operating officer, general counsel, chief accounting officer, controller, director of internal audit or financial reporting or treasurer.

The cooling-off period must be for one full audit year and is based on the dates an issuer files its annual report with the SEC. The one-year period begins the day after the prior year's annual report (eg, Form 20-F, Form 40-F or Form 10-K) is filed with the SEC and ends the day the current year's annual report is filed with the SEC. Any person who performed audit, review or attest services at any time during an audit year could not begin employment with an issuer until one full audit year had passed subsequent to when such person what a member of the audit engagement team. For example, if an issuer client files its Form 20-F annual report for 2002 on 30th June 2003 and its Form 20-F annual report for 2003 on 15th June 2004, the issuer client's audit firm will lose its independence if an audit firm employee was a member of the audit engagement team that provide any audit, review or attest services to that client any time between 1st July 2003 and 15th June 2004 and is hired before 16th June 2004.

All partners, principals, shareholders and professional employees participating in an audit, review or attestation engagement and all persons who consult with others on the audit engagement team regarding technical or industry specific issues, transactions or events who provided more than 10 hours of services are subject to the cooling-off period. The lead and concurring partner would be subject to the cooling-off period regardless of the number of hours of services provided. The rules provide a narrow exception to the cooling-off period for persons who become employed by the issuer as a result of a business combination provided that the employment was not in contemplation of the business combination and the audit committee of the successor is aware of the prior employment relationship. There also is a limited exception for audit firm personnel who are employed by the client due to an emergency or other unusual situation provided that the audit committee determines that the relationship is in the investor's interest.

The rules are effective for employment relationships with an issuer that commence after 6th May 2003.

Compensation

An audit partner would not be independent if at any time during the audit and professional engagement period they earn or receive compensation based on performing or procuring an engagement to provide a service other than an audit, review or attestation. The term "audit partner" is a new term that the SEC defines as including the lead and concurring partners and other partners on an audit engagement who have significant decision-making responsibilities in connection with the audit or who maintain regular contacts with management or the audit committee. Compensation concerns affecting auditor independence exist only where the audit partner's compensation is based on the act of procuring engagements to provide non-audit services to his or her own clients. The rules do not preclude an audit partner from receiving as compensation a proportionate share of an accounting firm's overall profits, including fees for non-audit services earned by other partners. A specialty partner, such as a tax partner, may be compensated for selling non-audit services within his or her discipline without threatening his or her independence.

While the rule applies only to audit partners, the SEC indicated that an audit committee when pre-approving non-audit services, may wish to consider whether compensating a senior Staff member of the audit engagement team based on his or her success in selling such non-audit services to the client, compromises that person's or the audit firm's independence.

Improper influence on the conduct of audits

As directed by Section 303 of SOX, the SEC adopted new rules that prohibit an issuer's officers and directors (and persons acting under their direction) from improperly influencing the conduct of the issuer's audit.[57] The new rules in conjunction with existing Rule 13B-2 of the Exchange Act are designed to ensure that officers and directors make open and full disclosure to and have honest discussions with the auditor of the company's financial statements.

New Rule 13b2–2(b)(1) prohibits officers and directors (and persons acting under their direction) from coercing, manipulating, misleading or fraudulently influencing any independent public or certified public accountant engaged in the performance of an audit or review of a company's financial statements if that person knew or should have known that such action, if successful, could result in rendering the company's financial statements required to be filed with the SEC materially misleading.

Persons covered by the new rule

Rule 13b2–2(b)(1) covers activities by an officer or director of an issuer, or any other person acting under the direction of an officer or director. The SEC has defined the term officer to include an issuer's "president, vice president, secretary, treasurer or principal financial officer, comptroller or principal accounting officer, and any person routinely performing corresponding functions …".[58]

This Rule also covers the activities of any other person acting under the direction of an officer or director. A person may be acting under the direction of an officer or director even if they are not supervised or controlled by the officer or directors. The SEC states that such persons could include, in addition to employees, customers, vendors or creditors who, at the direction of the officer or director, provide false or misleading information to the auditors or who enter into "side agreements" that allow the issuer to mislead the auditor. The SEC also advises that such persons could include other partners or employees of the accounting firm, attorneys, securities professionals or other advisers who pressure an auditor to

---

57 Exchange Act Release No 34-47890 (20th May 2003).
58 Exchange Act Rule 3b-2.

limit the scope of the audit, issue an unqualified audit report when such a report is not supportable, to not object to inappropriate accounting treatment or not withdraw an issued audit report.

Prohibited conduct based on negligence standard
The SEC uses the phrase "knew, or should have known", which the SEC views as indicative of a negligence standard. The SEC also makes clear that word "fraudulently" modifies only the word "influence". Consequently, conduct to coerce, manipulate or mislead need not be fraudulent to be actionable under the new Rule.

Prohibited conduct
The SEC lists types of conduct that it believes could constitute improper influence if the person engaged in the conduct knows or should have known that the conduct, if successful, could render the issuer's financial statements materially misleading. Some of the prohibited activities referred to in the non-inclusive list include:

- offering or paying bribes or other financial incentives, including offers of future employment or contracts for non-audit services;
- providing an auditor with inaccurate or misleading legal analysis;
- threatening to cancel or cancelling existing non-audit or audit engagements if the auditor objects to the issuer's accounting;
- seeking to have a partner removed from the audit engagement because the partner objects to the issuer's accounting;
- blackmailing; and
- making physical threats.

When the Rule's prohibitions apply
The prohibitions apply during the professional engagement period and any other time the issuer's auditor is called upon to make decisions or judgments regarding the issuer's financial statements, including during negotiations for the auditor's retention and after the engagement periods when the auditor is considering whether to consent to the use of, reissue or withdraw the prior years' audit reports or conducting a SAS 100 review of the issuer's interim financial statements.

SEC REGULATION OUTSIDE THE UNITED STATES

Potentially reportable violations

The SEC notes its views in the adopting release that violations of the new Rule would constitute illegal acts within Section 10A and thus might require the auditor to report a violation to management and ensure that the issuer's audit committee is made aware of the violation.[59]

Disclosure of fees paid to auditors

A company subject to the SEC's proxy statement disclosure rules must disclose the professional fees paid in the most recent financial year to its principal independent accountant for both audit and non-audit services.

On 28th January 2003, the SEC amended its disclosure rules to breakout the disclosure of fees paid into four categories: audit fees, audit-related fees, tax fees and all other fees. The amendments were effective as of 6th May 2003.

The SEC expanded the types of fees that a company should include in audit services to include fees for services that auditors typically would provide in connection with statutory and regulatory filings or engagements, such as comfort letters, statutory audits, attest services, consents and assistance with and review of materials filed with the SEC. The SEC advised that audit-related fees are assurance and related services, such as employee benefit plan audits, due diligence related to mergers and acquisitions, internal control reviews, attest services that are not required by statue or regulation and consultations with respect to financial accounting and reporting standards. Tax fees would include all

---

59 Section 10A(a) of the Exchange Act requires an auditor to conduct procedures designed to provide, among other things, reasonable assurance of the detection of illegal acts that would have a direct and material effect on the determination of financial statement amounts. If the auditor becomes aware of information that indicates an illegal act has or may have occurred, the auditor must perform additional procedures to determine whether it is likely that an illegal act has occurred and, if so, its possible effects on the financial statements, and report the act to management and assure that the issuer's audit committee is informed of the act. If the auditor concludes that the illegal act has a material effect on the financial statements, appropriate remedial actions are not taken and the failure to take such actions is reasonably expected to warrant a modified audit report or resignation for the audit engagement, then the auditor must report his or her conclusions to the issuer's board of directors. If the board does not notify the SEC that it has received such a report, then the auditor must furnish a copy of its report to the SEC.

services performed by the professional staff of an independent accountant's tax division, other than those services related to the audit.

A company should include the new disclosures in its annual report. If a company is required to file a proxy statement, the disclosures should be in the proxy statement. A US issuer will satisfy the annual report disclosure requirements as long as the proxy statement or information statement containing the disclosures is filed within 120 days of the end of the company's financial year, since the statement will automatically be incorporated into the company's annual report on Form 10-K. A company, such as a foreign private issuer, that is not required to file proxy statements should provide the required disclosures in its annual report.

REFERENCE LIST

In the following we give a list of reference materials that were used in preparing this chapter.

SEC Releases

Proposing and adopting releases are important reference tools. The listed below are certain releases that include citations to other sources not necessarily listed below.

Securities Act Release 6711 (23rd April 1987)

Securities Act Release 6791 (1st August 1988) (Commission Statement Regarding Disclosure Obligations of Companies Affect by the Government's Defense Contract Procurement Inquiry and Related Issues)

Securities Act Release 6835 (18th May 1989) (MD&A Interpretive Release)

Securities Act Release 8040 (12th December 2001) (Cautionary Advice Regarding Disclosure About Critical Accounting Policies)

Securities Act Release 8098 (10th May 2002) (Proposing Release: Critical Accounting Policies)

Securities Act Release 8176 (22nd January 2003) (Final Release: Use of Non-GAAP Financial Measures)

Securities Act Release 8182 (28th January 2003) (Final Release: Off –Balance Sheet Financing)

Securities Act Release 8350 (19th December 2003) (Interpretation: Commission Guidance Regarding Management's Discussion and Analysis of Financial Condition and Results of Operations)

SEC enforcement actions

In the Matter of Caterpillar, Inc, Administrative Proceeding File No 3–7692 (31st March 1992)

In the Matter of Bank of Boston Corp, Administrative Proceeding File No 3–8270 (22nd December 1995)

In the Matter of Gibson Greetings, Inc, Administrative Proceeding File No 3–8866 (11th October 1995)

SEC v. Sony Corporation, Litigation Release 15832 (5th August 1998)

Other

Other information (including Commissioner speeches, Staff speeches, archives of certain SEC open meetings, accounting and non-accounting outlines prepared by the Division of Corporation Finance) is available on the SEC website at www.sec.gov. Materials are also available on the Public Company Accounting Oversight Board website at www.pcaob.org.

APPENDIX A
Sample of Section 302 certification

The text in **bold** may be omitted until the new rule on internal control over financial reporting is effective (ie, for companies that are "accelerated filers" as of the end of the of their first fiscal year ending on or after 15th November 2004, beginning with their annual reports for that fiscal year and for non-US companies and companies that are not accelerated filers, beginning with their annual reports for fiscal years ending on or after 15th July 2006).

Certification

I, [identify the certifying individual], certify that:

1. I have reviewed this annual report on Form 20-F of [identify registrant];
2. Based on my knowledge, this report does not contain any untrue statement of a material fact or omit to state a material fact necessary to make the statements made, in light of the circumstances

under which such statements were made, not misleading with respect to the period covered by this report;
3. Based on my knowledge, the financial statements, and other financial information included in this report, fairly present in all material respects the financial condition, results of operations and cashflows of the registrant as of, and for, the periods presented in this report;
4. The registrant's other certifying officer(s) and I are responsible for establishing and maintaining disclosure controls and procedures (as defined in Exchange Act Rules 13a-15-(e) and 15d-15(e)) **and internal control over financial reporting (as defined in Exchange Act Rule 13a-15(f) and 15d-15(f))** for the registrant and have:

   (a) designed such disclosure controls and procedures, or caused such disclosure controls and procedures to be designed under our supervision, to ensure that material information relating to the registrant, including its consolidated subsidiaries, is made known to us by others within those entities, particularly during the period in which this report is being prepared;
   (b) **designed such internal control over financial reporting, or caused such internal control over financial reporting to be designed under our supervision, to provide reasonable assurance regarding the reliability of financial reporting and the preparation of financial statements for external purposes in accordance with generally accepted accounting principles;**
   (c) evaluated the effectiveness of the registrant's disclosure controls and procedures and presented in this report our conclusions about the effectiveness of the disclosure controls and procedures, as of the end of the period covered by this report based on such evaluation; and
   (d) disclosed in this report any change in the registrant's internal control over financial reporting that occurred during the registrant's most recent fiscal quarter (the registrant's fourth fiscal quarter in the case of an annual report) that has materially affected, or is reasonably likely to materially affect, the registrant's internal control over financial reporting; and

5. The registrant's other certifying officer(s) and I have disclosed, based on our most recent evaluation of internal control over financial reporting, to the registrant's auditors and the audit

committee of the registrant's board of directors (or persons performing the equivalent functions):

(a) all significant deficiencies and material weaknesses in the design or operation of internal control over financial reporting which are reasonably likely to adversely affect the registrant's ability to record, process, summarise and report financial information; and

(b) any fraud, whether or not material, that involves management or other employees who have a significant role in the registrant's internal control over financial reporting.

Date: _____

[Signature]
[Title]

APPENDIX B

Here we give three examples of management's Section 404 annual report on internal control over financial reporting. The associated auditor's report has not been included in the examples.

Example 1

The management of ABC Company is responsible for establishing and maintaining adequate internal control over financial reporting. ABC Company's internal control system is designed to provide reasonable assurance to the Company's management and board of directors regarding the preparation and fair presentation of published financial statements.

All internal control systems, no matter how well designed, have inherent limitations. Therefore, even those systems determined to be effective can provide only reasonable assurance with respect to financial statement preparation and presentation.

ABC Company's management assessed the effectiveness of the Company's internal control over financial reporting as of 31st December 2004. In making this assessment, management used the criteria set forth by the COSO Report. Based on its assessment management believes that, as of 31st December 2004, the Company's internal control over financial reporting is effective based on those criteria.

ABC Company's independent auditors, XYZ LLP, have issued an attestation report on management's assessment of the Company's internal control over financial reporting. Their report follows.

Example 2

The management of ABC Company is responsible for establishing and maintaining adequate internal control over financial reporting for the company. With the participation of the CEO and the CFO, our management conducted an evaluation of the effectiveness of our internal control over financial reporting based on the framework and criteria established in the COSO Report. Based on this evaluation, our management has concluded that our internal control over financial reporting was effective as of 31st December 2004.

ABC Company's independent auditor, XYZ LLP, a registered public accounting firm, has issued an audit report on our management's assessment of our internal control over financial reporting. This audit report follows.

Example 3

The management of ABC Company is responsible for establishing and maintaining adequate internal control over financial reporting. Internal control over financial reporting is a process designed under the supervision of ABC's CEO and CFO to provide reasonable assurance regarding the reliability of financial reporting and the preparation of the Company's financial statements for external purposes in accordance with GAAP.

ABC Company's internal control over financial reporting includes those policies and procedures that: (1) pertain to the maintenance of records that, in reasonable detail, accurately and fairly reflect the transactions and dispositions of the assets of the Company; (2) provide reasonable assurance that transactions are recorded as necessary to permit preparation of financial statements in accordance with GAAP, and that receipts and expenditures of the Company are being made only in accordance with authorisations of management and directors of the Company; and (3) provide reasonable assurance regarding prevention or timely detection of unauthorised acquisition, use or disposition of the Company's assets that could have a material effect on the financial statements.

Due to its inherent limitations, internal control over financial reporting may not prevent or detect misstatements. Projections of any evaluation of effectiveness to future periods are subject to the risk that controls may become inadequate because of changes in conditions, or that the degree of compliance with the policies or procedures may deteriorate.

With the participation of the Company's CEO and CFO, ABC Company's management assessed the effectiveness of the Company's internal control over financial reporting as of 31st December 2004. In making this assessment, the Company's management used the criteria set forth by the COSO Report. Based on its assessment, management has concluded that, as of 31st December 2004, the Company's internal control over financial reporting is effective based on those criteria.

ABC Company's independent registered public accounting firm, XYZ LLP, has audited management's assessment of the effectiveness of the Company's internal control over financial reporting as of 31st December 2004, as stated in their report shown in the following, which expresses unqualified opinions on management's assessment and on the effectiveness of the Company's internal control over financial reporting as of 31st December 2004.

5

US/European Cross-Border M&A: Regulatory Framework and Recent Developments

Scott Simpson
Skadden Arps LLP

This chapter addresses material US and European Union (EU) regulations applicable to cross-border transactions and reviews regulatory developments in the United States and Europe that are on deal makers' radars when structuring cross-border mergers and acquisitions.

The first part of this chapter provides an overview of certain US securities law issues that commonly arise in the context of structuring cross-border transactions involving non-US public targets that have a US shareholder base or are publicly traded in the United States. Bidders and their advisers must carefully assess whether and to what extent the Exchange Act's tender offer rules and exemptions and the Securities Act's registration requirements and exemptions apply to a contemplated public bid. This first part also examines some of the concerns raised in connection with the application of the Tier I and Rule 802 exemptions of the SEC's cross-border tender offer rules which came into effect at the beginning of 2000. These rules were intended to eliminate or at least mitigate the regulatory reasons for exclusion of US shareholders from cross-border tender offers by providing specific relief from many of the disclosure and procedural requirements of the Exchange Act and the Securities Act that may otherwise apply to such offers. Five years later, although these cross-border tender offer rules have represented a significant step forward, they have turned out to be not entirely user-friendly and require careful consideration.

The second part of this chapter reviews some of the major issues raised by foreign companies and regulators in connection with SOX and the steps that the SEC has taken and may take in the future to resolve some of these issues. SOX came into effect in July 2002 as a legislative response to a series of significant corporate accounting and disclosure crises that arose from the Enron, WorldCom, Global Crossing, Adelphia, Tyco and other corporate scandals.[1] SOX requirements address fundamental and comprehensive re-evaluation of corporate governance arrangements, accounting and disclosure policies, and internal controls by all companies that are currently listed or reporting in the United States, without distinguishing between foreign and domestic issuers, as well as by all companies that are considering accessing the US capital markets for the first time. Companies looking to make cross-border acquisitions must understand and take into account the gradual implementation of SOX. While it was initially thought that the requirements mandated by SOX would not directly influence the conduct of cross-border merger activity, deal makers are beginning to rethink this particularly in relation to exchange offers.

The third part of this chapter examines why the judicial disagreement and lack of SEC guidance surrounding the interpretation of Rule 14d-10 of the Exchange Act, the "all holders/best price" rule, influences cross-border transactions. In recent years the use of tender offers as the preferred acquisition vehicle has declined despite its many attractions. Many believe that this is the result of the confusion generated by US courts over the interpretation of Rule 14d-10 EU and the related increased risk of litigation in the tender offer context.

The fourth part of this chapter focuses on the regulatory landscape in Europe, reviewing the likely effect of provisions limiting takeover defences introduced by the EU's 13th Takeover Directive (Takeover Directive).[2] While continental Europe has been the venue of

---

[1] US companies are not alone when it comes to scandals. Over the past two years, many non-US companies, including Parmalat, Vivendi, Holllinger, Ahold, Adecco, Royal Dutch Shell and others have been accused of accounting irregularities, managerial fraud and other corporate governance abuses.

[2] Directive 2004/25/EC of the European Parliament and of the Council of 21st April 2004 on Takeover Bids (Takeover Directive).

prominent cross-border hostile takeover battles in the last few years,[3] often the cultural and political aversion of continental EU member states to these takeovers has manifested itself strongly, in some cases heavily influencing their outcome. The debates on and the compromises reached to adopt the Takeover Directive, after 15 years of failed attempts, stand as clear evidence of this continuing cultural and political sentiment in continental Europe. Initially, the objective of the Takeover Directive was to harmonise EU takeover law through the adoption of a pan-European takeover code (along the lines of the UK Takeover Code) that would foster consolidation in Europe by creating a level playing field for companies across the EU. While regulators and companies anxiously await the implementation of the Takeover Directive by individual member states (by 20th May 2006), there are already strong indications that the Takeover Directive will not align takeover rules throughout Europe as originally expected.

Finally, the fifth part of this chapter reviews several of the continually evolving regulations affecting cross-border restructurings. One of the consequences of the downturn in global economic conditions that has persisted in the last few years is that an increasing number of cross-border transactions now involve "distressed companies", or companies that are in financial difficulty and require significant balance sheet and/or operational restructurings. To appeal to companies carrying out cross-border restructurings, legislative reforms have recently been introduced or adopted in the United States and Europe to make international insolvency systems more coherent and efficient.

THE US REGULATORY FRAMEWORK FOR CROSS-BORDER TENDER OFFERS

In structuring a cross-border offer for a non-US target, a bidder faces the threshold issue of whether the US securities rules will apply to the bid. If the target has shareholders in the United States, the anti-fraud rules under Section 14(e) and Regulation 14E of the Exchange Act may apply and, if the target's shares are listed in the United States or if the target is otherwise a reporting company under US securities laws, the more expansive disclosure and

---

[3] For example, LVMH's attempt to acquire Gucci, Vodafone's takeover of Mannesmann and Sanofi-Synthélabo's acquisition of Aventis.

procedural rules for tender offers under Section 14(d) and Regulation 14D (or Rule 13e-4 for issuer tender offers) of the Exchange Act may apply. Moreover, if the bidder is issuing securities as consideration in the bid, then the registration requirements of the Securities Act may also apply to the offer.

A common desire among non-US bidders who are not listed or reporting in the United States is to minimise or avoid entirely the extensive requirements of the US securities laws. This may be because US requirements conflict with local rules (for example, with respect to minimum offer periods, withdrawal rights and disclosure requirements),[4] or because extending the offer into the United States is perceived as increasing the transaction's exposure to potential shareholder or other litigation in the United States (again, this may not be the case in local law and practice), or simply because compliance may add significant time and cost to the deal (particularly given the potential for intensive review by the SEC of the offer documentation). Depending on the situation, there are generally two basic options available to bidders to reduce the potential burden of compliance with US rules: (i) exclude the United States from the offer; or take advantage of the Tier I, Tier II and Rule 802 exemptions from the cross-border tender offer rules.

Excluding the United States

One strategy to avoid US requirements is to not extend the offer into the United States. This strategy is only viable, of course, if the participation of US shareholders of the target is not essential to the success of the offer and if there is no duty under the applicable home jurisdiction to extend the offer to all holders wherever they may be.[5]

Bidders should be mindful of the risks involved in attempting to avoid US jurisdiction in conducting an offer, particularly in view of the significant restrictions on communication that should be implemented to pursue this option. US court decisions and SEC policy

---

4 Many European jurisdictions do not provide for withdrawal rights and the requirements for offer documentation are not as extensive as under US rules.

5 For example, in certain jurisdictions bidders may force minority shareholders to sell their shares if the bidder reaches a percentage of ownership (90% of the class of shares subject to the bid in the UK, 95% of the share capital in Germany, 95% of the voting rights in France, 98% of all shares with voting rights in Italy), which may be impossible if US shareholders are excluded.

statements from the SEC make clear that the scope of jurisdiction of the anti-fraud and anti-manipulation rules under US securities laws is broader than the scope of jurisdiction relating to the registration provisions of US securities laws.[6] While excluding the United States from an offer minimises the risk that a bidder will expose itself to anti-fraud jurisdiction, this distinction between the scope of jurisdiction for purposes of the registration and anti-fraud provisions of the US securities laws should be kept in mind, particularly when drafting disclosure for offering materials. In addition, as a policy matter, the SEC is opposed to transactions that exclude US shareholders. The SEC adopted the Tier I, Tier II and Rule 802 exemptions in part to bring an end to this practice and to eliminate the disadvantageous treatment of US investors. Accordingly, the SEC is vigilantly monitoring offers that exclude the United States to see if they trigger US jurisdiction.

Given the above, the following is a summary of certain key measures that should be implemented by a bidder excluding the United States from its offer in order to minimise the risks of triggering US jurisdiction.[7]

No solicitation in the United States

The bidder and its advisors should not arrange or attend personal meetings in the United States to discuss the offer, nor should they place phone calls to the United States to discuss the offer or discuss the offer on any phone calls originating in the United States. To deal with potential difficulties in phone conversations, the bidder and its advisors should consider drafting a script that could be used by all individuals responding to shareholder inquiries and that could also function as a log of all such inquiries. Such a script should include a statement to the effect that the bidder's offer is not being made in the United States and cannot be discussed with any person in the United States.

No offering materials or any other documents relating to the offer, including press releases, should be sent to the United States.

---

6 *See Consolidated Gold Fields plc v. Minorco S.A.*, 871 F.2d 252 (2d Cir. 1989) and related amicus curiae brief of the SEC. See also Securities Act Release 6866 (6th June 1990).

7 This overview is derived, in part, from US court decisions that have ruled that the bidder in question did not avail itself of US jurisdiction in the conduct of a public offer. *See Plessey Co. plc v. General Electric Co. plc*, 628 F. Supp. 477 (D. Del. 1986).

The bidder and its advisors should consider establishing a control system to filter requests for offer materials to avoid distribution in the United States and to obtain confirmation of the non-US status of recipients of offer materials. Offer materials should not be distributed to persons or entities that the bidder knows or has reason to know have an obligation to pass such materials along to persons in the United States. In addition, the bidder should not accept any offer materials or requests for offer materials that are postmarked from the United States.

Disclosure in offer documents
All offer materials should contain disclosure that includes the following points.

- ❏ The offer is not being made in the United States or by US jurisdictional means, or in any jurisdiction, including the United States, in which the making of the offer or acceptance thereof would not be in compliance with the laws of such jurisdiction.
- ❏ Acceptances with US postmarks or other indicia of US origin will be invalid.
- ❏ The offer documents are not being mailed to the United States and recipients should not send offer documents to the United States.

In addition, acceptance forms should include appropriate representations from tendering shareholders regarding their participation in the offer from outside the United States. All offer materials should bear the following legend:

> *"The offer is not being made in the United States or to US persons and is intended only to be available to persons to whom the offer may lawfully be made."*

Press/media policy
Press conferences and interviews may only be held outside the United States. US journalists may only be invited if foreign journalists are also invited.[8] However, "one-on-ones" with US journalists may be allowed immediately following press conferences at which international journalists are present (and given similar opportunities for one-on-one interviews). Representatives of the bidder

---

8 *See* definition of "directed selling efforts" under Rule 902(c) and the provisions of Rule 135(e) under the Securities Act.

should explain clearly in all meetings with the press that the bidder's offer is not being extended to the United States.

Advertisements may not be placed in the US media regarding the offer. This requirement may be difficult to achieve where notice requirements in particular jurisdictions mandate global press announcements including the substantive terms and conditions of the offer. All written press materials should contain the heading "not for distribution or publication in or into the United States." In addition, written press materials should also contain the following legend:

> *"These materials are not an offer to purchase securities in the United States. Bidder does not intend to conduct the offer in the United States."*

Acceptance forms or coupons that could be returned indicating interest in the offer should not be attached or otherwise be part of any written press materials.

Arrangements with dealer-managers, advisors, brokers, etc

The bidder should consider preparing a global instruction letter for dealer-managers, advisors, brokers, clearing house participants, any information agent and other professionals participating in the offer, stating that no offer materials are to be distributed, and no solicitations of acceptances are to be made, in or towards the United States. To the extent practicable given timing and other considerations, contractual arrangements with offer participants (eg, dealer-manager agreement, soliciting broker agreement, etc) and other transaction contracts should include provisions to the effect that: (a) all offer materials are not to be sent to the United States, nor are any solicitation efforts to be made in the United States; and, potentially, (b) no commissions will be granted for tenders originating in or accepted from the United States.

A written instruction should be given to analysts at all meetings in which analysts participate that research reports or other materials prepared in whole or in part as a follow up to such meetings and that include a discussion of the proposed offer should not be distributed in the United States. As a more stringent alternative, analysts who attend such meetings could be required to sign an agreement to the same effect.

As regards trading in target company securities during an offer, even if such purchases are permitted under local rules, the bidder and its advisors and representatives (as well as, in a negotiated transaction, the target and its advisors) should not engage in market transactions in target shares in the United States.

Internet policy
The Internet has evolved into a highly effective medium for shareholder relations. Many jurisdictions permit (or require) offer materials to be posted on the bidder's website. The global access of the Internet presents particular issues in the context of a bid that is not intended to be extended to the United States. As a general rule, the fact that offering materials of a non-US entity are posted on a website in English, even though the entity is based in a non-English speaking country, will not, by itself, demonstrate that an offer is targeted at the United States. However, in the event the offer materials are to be posted on a website, certain procedures should be implemented that are designed to avoid targeting the United States.[9]

Prior to accessing offering materials on a website, a viewer should first see the legends set forth above and the viewer should be required to provide information regarding their location and US residency status as a condition to accessing the offer materials. If any offering materials are requested from website, controls should be in place to prevent any offering materials from being sent to the United States. Viewers could also be required to represent their non-US status either on-line or in a follow-up written request as a condition to receiving any offer materials.

The bidder should also ensure, through relevant contractual provisions, that websites of any parties assisting the bidder with the offer also comply with the procedures set forth above with respect to any offer information on their website. An example would be the website of the bidder's dealer-manager. If a third-party website is frequented by US investors, or is oriented generally towards investment activity, additional precautions should be implemented, such as preventing access to visitors who cannot make the representations set forth above regarding non-US status.

Many bidders will find these necessary restrictions cumbersome or perhaps impracticable to implement. Even if these measures can be established and effectively implemented, bidders may still be reluctant to accept the exposure to the risk that third parties or the

---

9 *See* generally Securities Act Release 7516.

SEC would nevertheless assert US jurisdiction in order to force compliance with US securities laws and SEC rules. Accordingly, if the target has few US shareholders, bidders may be able to take advantage of the Tier I, Tier II and Rule 802 exemptions implemented by the SEC in 2000 and discussed in detail below.

The Tier I/Tier II/Rule 802 exemptions

One of the SEC's major accommodations to foreign issuers in the cross-border M&A context was the implementation in 2000 of the cross-border tender offer rules.[10] These rules recognise that in certain circumstances the interests in applying a US regulatory scheme are limited and the benefits of the opportunity for US holders to participate in cross-border tender and exchange offers, mergers and similar transactions and rights offerings outweigh the detriments of not receiving the full protection of the US securities laws.

The cross-border rules introduced a basic regulatory distinction between offers for non-US targets (whether or not they are reporting companies under the Exchange Act) that have 10% or fewer US shareholders,[11] or the Tier I and Rule 802 exemptions, and offers for non-US targets (again whether or not they are reporting companies under the Exchange Act) with between 10 and 40% US shareholders, or the Tier II exemption. Bidders making an offer for a non-US target with more than 40% US shareholders must either fully comply with the SEC's tender offer and registration rules or exclude the United States from the offer. The following summarises the key elements of these exemptions.

---

10 In response to the globalisation of the US capital markets, the SEC has worked to accommodate foreign issuers and to facilitate their access to US markets. Some of the principal accommodations that have been adopted by the SEC under the Exchange Act and Securities Act include exempting foreign private issuers from: (i) having to file Form 10-K annual reports, Form 10-Q quarterly reports and Form 8-K current reports (although filing Form 20-F annual reports and furnishing Form 6-K current reports to the SEC is required); (ii) being required to apply US generally accepted accounting principles (US GAAP) to the issuer's primary financial statements (although reconciliation to US GAAP is required); (iii) Section 14 and Regulation 14A proxy rules; (iv) their officers, directors and 10% shareholders being required to file Forms 3, 4 and 5 reports of beneficial ownership under Section 16 of the Exchange Act; (v) the "short-swing" profit rules imposed on insiders who purchase and sell securities within a six-month period; and (vi) Regulation FD, which prohibits selective disclosure of material information.

11 The term "US holders" is defined under the Exchange Act and the Securities Act as any beneficial security owner resident in the United States.

Tier I and Rule 802 exemptions (10% US shareholders)
(a) *Tier I exemption*

Under the Tier I exemption, a bidder is not subject to the Exchange Act rules dealing with disclosure, filing, dissemination, minimum offering period, withdrawal rights and proration requirements (Rules 13e-3 and 13e-4, Regulation 14D and Rules 14e-1 and 14e-2 of the Exchange Act). In effect, except for certain limited procedural requirements summarised below, the offer can be extended to the United States without significant amendment from local requirements. Instead of complying with US tender offer rules, the bidder may comply solely with applicable rules of the target company's home jurisdiction.[12]

The bidder, however, will be subject to the US anti-fraud and anti-manipulation rules. In practice, this means that tender offer documents must not contain any material misstatements or omissions and that bidders must not engage in any fraudulent, deceptive or manipulative activities during the offer. For example, sufficient notice must be provided to shareholders regarding extensions of the offer, changes in consideration, any anticipated delays in payment for tendered shares or other material changes in the offer.[13]

Eligibility conditions. US and non-US bidders may take advantage of the Tier I exemption under the following circumstances.

- ❏ the target corporation must be a "foreign private issuer", meaning any non-US issuer *except* for a non-US issuer that has greater than 50% of its voting securities held of record directly or indirectly by residents of the United States *and either*: (a) the majority of its executive officers and directors are US citizens or residents; (b) more than 50% of its assets are located in the United States; *or* (c) its business is administered principally in the United States.
- ❏ the number of US resident beneficial owners of the target's securities must be equal to or less than 10% of the total number of target shares outstanding.

---

[12] The Tier I exemption, however, is not available for offers for securities of a registered investment company, other than a registered, closed-end investment company.

[13] The fact that these US requirements continue to apply (despite their similarity when compared with UK rules) has caused the UK Takeover Panel to continue its policy of not requiring offers to be extended to the US despite the relaxations.

It is worth noting that, for purposes of calculating US ownership, the total number of shares outstanding is to be calculated by *including* the shares represented by the target's ADRs, but *excluding* other types of securities that are convertible into or exchangeable for the target's securities (such as warrants, options and convertible securities). Furthermore, shares held by all holders of more than 10% of the target's shares, as well as shares held by the bidder and its affiliates, are *excluded* from the calculation (ie, from both the numerator and the denominator).

Equal treatment. Bidders are required to allow US security holders to participate in the offer on terms at least as favourable as those offered to any other holders, including price, duration, proration and withdrawal rights (additional procedural requirements imposed by ADR depositaries do not violate this principle).

The rules provide for a limited number of exceptions to this principle. For example, bidders may make a cash only offer available in the United States and include securities as consideration in the offer terms available outside the United States without violating the equal treatment requirement. In order to be free to do so, however, a bidder must have a reasonable basis to believe that the cash-only consideration is substantially equivalent to the value of the securities and any cash or other consideration being offered outside the United States, and the bidder must adjust the US cash consideration during the offer if it no longer has such reasonable belief.[14]

Bidders may also exclude target company security holders in any US state that does not exempt the offered securities from state registration or refuses to register or qualify the offer and sale of the offered securities in that state after a good faith effort by the bidder to seek registration. If a cash-only alternative is available under the terms of the offer, it must be extended to US holders in such states.

---

[14] If the security is not a "margin security" within the meaning of Regulation T (which is issued by the Board of Governors of the Federal Reserve System), the bidder must provide upon the request of any US holder or the SEC an opinion from an independent expert stating that the cash-only consideration is substantially equivalent to the securities and any cash offered outside the US. If the security offered is a "margin security" the bidder must undertake to provide any US holder or the SEC staff upon request information on recent trading prices of the bidder's securities. If cash is to come from a "vendor placement", or an offshore sale of the securities that would otherwise have been available to the US holder, SEC no-action relief may be required. *See* Securities Act Release 33–7759, "Cross-Border Tender and Exchange Offers, Business Combinations and Rights Offerings."

A bidder may offer a "loan note" alternative to UK security holders and not to US security holders, provided the loan notes are not listed on an exchange, are not registered under the Securities Act and are offered solely to enable shareholders to benefit from UK tax planning advantages not available in the United States.

Filings and other procedural requirements. From a procedural standpoint, bidders relying on the Tier I exemption are required to furnish (rather than file) a copy of the offering materials (or an English language translation of the offering materials if they are in another language) to the SEC under cover of Form CB, and non-US bidders must file a consent to service of process in the United States on Form FX no later than the next business day after the publication or dissemination of the offer documentation being filed.[15] Financial statements included in offering materials that comply with home country requirements do not need to be reconciled to US GAAP. Bidders must provide US security holders with an English translation of the tender offer circular or other offering documents on a comparable basis as such documents are provided to non-US security holders (eg, dissemination by newspaper publication alone is allowed if such practice is followed in the home jurisdiction). The offering document must bear a specific legend provided by Rule 802 of the Securities Act in a prominent portion of the document.

Target company management may also rely on the exemption when distributing recommendations regarding the offer (that is, no requirement to file a Schedule 14D-9).

Purchases outside the tender offer. Under Exchange Act rules, bidders are prohibited from purchasing or arranging to purchase, directly or indirectly, the target's shares other than pursuant to the offer.[16] Offers eligible for the Tier I exemption are exempt from this

---

15 If the tender offer is for a non-reporting non-US company, the offering document and any recommendation do not need to be submitted to the SEC because the regulations do not require a filing in connection with those offers. Nonetheless, the offer must comply with certain provisions of Section 14(e) and Regulation 14E of the Exchange Act.

16 Rule 14e-5 of the Exchange Act. The rule applies to the offeror and its affiliates, the offeror's dealer-manager and its affiliates, any advisor to the offeror, dealer-manager or their affiliates, whose compensation is dependent on the completion of the offer, and any person acting, directly or indirectly, in concert with any of these persons in connection with any purchase or arrangement to purchase any subject securities or related securities. Significantly, the SEC has taken the position that the target company in a negotiated transaction is "acting in concert" with the bidder for purposes of applying the rule.

prohibition. Accordingly, bidders are permitted to purchase securities outside the offer in the United States and outside the United States as long as these purchases are compliant with applicable laws and regulations of the home jurisdiction. This exemption is subject to the following limitations.

- the offering document furnished to US holders must disclose prominently the possibility of any purchases other than pursuant to the terms of the offer.
- the offering document must disclose the manner in which any information about any such purchases will be disclosed.
- the bidder must disclose information in the United States regarding such purchases in a manner comparable to disclosure made in the home jurisdiction.

This exemption is not available to offers eligible for the Tier II exemption. However, parties may seek specific SEC no-action relief on a case-by-case basis for transactions that fall outside Tier I.

Rule 13e-3. Tier I exempts an issuer or third-party tender offer from the going private disclosure requirements under Rule 13e-3. Under Rule 13e-3, a Schedule 13E-3 is required to be filed, containing disclosure about the fairness to unaffiliated security holders of the transaction that may cause an equity security to lose its public trading market. The SEC decided to exempt Tier I offers from Rule 13e-3 because it concluded that it may not be practical to impose the procedural, disclosure and other filing requirements under Rule 13e-3 in connection with an offer when the dissemination and disclosure requirements under US tender offer rules do not apply. Rule 13e-3 does continue to apply, however, to offers that qualify for the Tier II exemption.

Beneficial ownership reporting. Tier I does not exempt entities that acquire beneficial ownership of more than five percent of a class of securities which are registered under the Exchange Act from filing required beneficial ownership reports under the cover of Schedule 13G or 13D. This applies whether or not the target is a US entity and is triggered by the fact that the target securities are registered under the Exchange Act.

Subsequent bidders. A subsequent bidder may rely on the exemption being used by the original bidder as long as the new bid meets

293

all the criteria for Tier I treatment other than the number of US beneficial shareholders of target. As such, a subsequent bidder will not be disadvantaged by any movement of securities into the United States following the announcement of the initial offer.

(b) *Rule 802 exemption*
Under Rule 802 of the Securities Act, US and non-US bidders issuing securities to US security holders of a foreign private issuer in a business combination or exchange offer are exempt from the registration requirements of the Securities Act under circumstances similar to those applying to the Tier I exemption.[17] As with the Tier I exemption, US resident beneficial owners must hold 10% or less of the target company's securities and the terms and conditions of the offer must be the same for US and non-US security holders, subject to the same exceptions provided under the Tier I exemption. The requirements on disclosure and dissemination of informational documents are also similar to those applicable to the Tier I exemption.

Rule 802 restricts the transferability of the securities acquired in an exempt transaction. If the securities of the target are "restricted securities" as defined under Rule 144 of the Securities Act, the bidder's securities exchanged for such securities would likewise be restricted securities. Conversely, if the target's securities are unrestricted, the bidder's securities offered or exchanged for such securities would likewise be unrestricted and freely tradable by non-affiliates of the bidder.

An offering that complies with Rule 802 will not be integrated with any other exempt offering by the bidders, even if both transactions occur at the same time. Information furnished to the SEC pursuant to the requirements of Rule 802, or disseminated to investors in compliance with the rule does not constitute a "general solicitation" within the meaning of Regulation D or "directed selling efforts" within the meaning of Regulation S.

An exempt offering under Rule 802 will not trigger reporting obligations under Section 15(d) of the Exchange Act and will not

---

17 In practice this means that equity or debt securities may be issued in an eligible exchange offer without registration under the Securities Act. In addition, debt securities are not required to be registered under or comply with the TIA. As with the Tier I exemption, the exemption under Rule 802 is not available for offers for securities of a registered investment company, other than a registered, closed-end investment company.

disqualify a foreign private issuer from using the existing Rule 12g3–2(b) exemption from the periodic reporting requirements *unless* the acquired company is an Exchange Act reporting company.

As with the Tier I exemption, in order to provide a level playing field in the case of competing offers, a subsequent bidder may rely on the Rule 802 registration exemption as long as the new bidder meets all of the criteria for the Rule 802 exemption other than the number of US beneficial shareholders of the target and the original bidder relied on Rule 802 or the new bidder meets all of the criteria for the Rule 802 exemption (including the number of US beneficial shareholders of the target).

Tier II exemption (40% US shareholders)
Under the Tier II exemption, bidders who make an offer for a foreign private issuer are granted limited relief from the US tender offer rules to minimise certain conflicts with non-US regulatory schemes. Under the Tier II exemption, the bidder remains subject to the Exchange Act rules (ie, the bidder must file required documentation and must structure the offer terms to conform to Exchange Act requirements), subject to adjustments that have been developed in a series of no-action letters granted by the SEC in relation to cross-border tender offers over recent years. These adjustments have been designed to minimise certain conflicts between the Exchange Act and home country rules and are codified in the Tier II exemption. Both US and non-US bidders may take advantage of the Tier II exemption if the target corporation is a foreign private issuer (as with the Tier I exemption) and US resident beneficial security holders hold 40% or less of the target company's securities.

Certain exemptions that had initially been proposed by the SEC in the preparatory phases of the revised cross-border rules were pre-empted by the enactment in 2000 of Regulation M-A. Regulation M-A, for example, provides that an offer is deemed to commence once the bidder disseminates transmittal forms or discloses instructions on how to tender into the offer, bringing the timing of the US offer process in line with the timing for production of the offer document and removing a problem in satisfying the US filing requirement previously faced in many European transactions. Furthermore, under Regulation M-A a bidder may provide for a "subsequent offering period" after the expiration of the initial offer, without extending withdrawal rights. In essence, this brings the United States process substantially into line with the UK process under which an offer is kept open after it has become wholly unconditional and withdrawal rights cease to be exercisable in the post-unconditional period. However, it is still not possible to terminate withdrawal rights at the point at which an offer is declared unconditional as to acceptances (as permitted under eg, the UK City Code) when making an offer in reliance on the Tier II exemption.

Under the Tier II exemption, a bidder may divide its offer into two separate offers: a US offer that would comply with US regulatory requirements and a non-US offer that would comply with the home jurisdiction's regulatory requirements, so long as the offer to US security holders is made on terms at least as favourable as those offered to any other holder of target securities. A bidder may also offer a loan note alternative to non-US security holders and not to US security holders if such notes are, among other things, not listed on any organised securities market or registered under the Securities Act.

Tier II exemptions include the bidder's ability to rely on the settlement procedures of the home jurisdiction's law and practice instead of complying with the Exchange Act prompt payment rules. A bidder may announce extensions of the offer in accordance with the home jurisdiction's practice (rather than comply with the Exchange Act requirement to announce extensions before the beginning of trading on the next business day).

Furthermore, a bidder may reduce or waive the minimum acceptance condition (for example, in a UK context reducing an acceptance condition from 90 to 50%) without extending withdrawal rights during the remainder of the offer (as Exchange Act rules would otherwise require) subject to the following conditions:

- ❏ the bidder must announce that it may reduce the minimum condition five business days prior to such reduction – a statement at the commencement of the offer that the bidder may subsequently reduce the minimum is insufficient;
- ❏ the bidder must disseminate this announcement through a press release and other methods reasonably designed to inform US security holders;

- the press release must state the exact percentage to which the acceptance condition may be reduced and that the reduction is possible – the bidder must state its actual intention to waive or reduce the minimum condition once it is required to do so under the regulations of the home jurisdiction;
- security holders who have tendered their shares continue to have withdrawal rights during the five-day period following the announcement;
- the announcement must contain language advising security holders to withdraw their tendered securities immediately if their willingness to tender into the offer would be affected by a reduction in the minimum condition;
- the offer document must contain a description of the procedure for reducing the minimum condition; and
- the bidder must hold the offer open for acceptances for at least five business days after the revision or waiver of the minimum condition.

As with the Tier I exemption, a subsequent bidder may rely on the exemption being used by the original bidder as long as the new bidder meets all of the criteria for Tier II treatment other than the number of US beneficial shareholders of the target.

Offers that qualify for the Tier II exemption would still be subject to any disclosure, timing, dissemination, filing, and other procedural and equal treatment requirements of the US tender offer rules.

Issues with the application of the Tier I and Rule 802 exemptions

While the Tier I, Tier II and Rule 802 exemptions have been recognised as facilitating cross-border M&A transactions into the United States, the Tier I and Rule 802 exemptions are considered the cornerstones of the cross-border rules adopted in 2000 as they allow non-US bidders who are not listed or reporting in the United States to minimise or avoid entirely the extensive requirements of the US securities laws. Bidders who in the past may have thought twice before including US holders in a bid for a foreign company that has a minimal US shareholder base will today not hesitate to launch a Tier I bid or Rule 802 exchange offer.

Despite the Tier I and Rule 802 exemptions' unequivocal success, however, bidders have expressed concern over the rules governing the US ownership threshold calculation.

As explained above, bidders may take advantage of the Tier I and Rule 802 exemptions as long as the target corporation is a foreign private issuer and the number of US resident beneficial owners of the target's securities is less than or equal to 10% of the total number of target shares outstanding. While the test for a foreign private issuer is relatively straightforward, the test for determining US percentage ownership has some shortcomings.[18]

First, the type of inquiry required depends on whether the offer is made "pursuant to an agreement with the issuer of the subject securities"[19] or not, that is, whether the offer is "friendly" or "hostile". If friendly, bidders are expected to work with the target advisers to conduct a US holders "look through" inquiry by distributing beneficial ownership questionnaires to record owners. Bidders must also take into account any information accumulated by the target in relation to beneficial ownership, at least if relatively contemporaneous. Hostile bidders, on the other hand, may assume US holders' thresholds are not exceeded if a trading volume test described below is met and public filings of the target do not indicate otherwise.

In a friendly deal, when determining the number of US holders of the target, bidders and their advisers must "look through" the record ownership of brokers, dealers, banks or nominees appearing on the issuer's books or those of transfer agents, depositaries or others acting on the issuer's behalf in the United States, the target's home jurisdiction, and the primary trading market for the target's securities. If such record holders hold securities for the accounts of customers, the bidder is required to determine the residency of those customers. The "look through" inquiry must be reasonable

---

[18] The test is set out in Rule 14d-1 of the Exchange Act for the Tier I exemption and Rule 802 of the Securities Act for the Rule 802 exemption.

[19] Rule 14d-1 of the Exchange Act, instructions to paragraphs (c) and (d). This characterisation of the type of transactions requiring the "look through" analysis is important, as in certain countries such as the UK oftentimes the parties do not agree a deal although the target board recommends the bid to its shareholders. Bidders in such transactions would not be required to do a "look through" analysis and may avail themselves of the presumptions available to "hostile" bidders.

and must include a review of beneficial ownership reports filed in the United States and the target's home jurisdiction or otherwise provided to the target and sending, or requesting that the target send, inquiry letters to all nominee holders. The number of US holders must be calculated as of 30 days before the commencement of the offer (for tender offer purposes, "commencement" means the first date on which target security holders are given the materials to accepts the offer, or are instructed as to how to obtain such materials). For UK and Irish deals, the date of announcement of a firm intention (whether or not pre-conditional) to make an offer is treated as commencement. Shares held by all holders of more than 10% of the subject class, as well as shares held by the bidder and its affiliates, are excluded from the calculation.

In the case of hostile offers, a third-party bidder is entitled to a presumption that the percentage threshold requirements of the Tier I and Rule 802 exemptions are not exceeded unless: (i) the aggregate trading volume on all national securities exchanges in the United States, on the NASDAQ or on the Over-the-Counter market, exceeds 10% of the worldwide aggregate trading volume of the subject class of securities over the 12 calendar month period ending 30 days prior to commencement of the offer; (ii) the most recent annual report or annual information filed or submitted by the target company or security holders with securities regulators in its home jurisdiction or with the SEC indicates that US security holders hold more than the applicable threshold; or (iii) the bidder knows, or has reason to know, that the level of US ownership exceeds the applicable threshold (for example, by reviewing any beneficial ownership reports on Schedule 13G and Schedule 13D).

One of the frustrations expressed by non-US bidders with the cross-border rules is with respect to the 30-day "look back" rule used to determine the level of US ownership in a friendly transaction. These bidders support removal of the 30-day "look back" rule and, instead, requiring US ownership to be determined based on the test required to be observed by bidders that have not reached an agreement with the target. Further, in assessing the state of the bidder's knowledge, bidders have objected to the presumption that the bidder has access to information known to the target. In the context of a friendly, public tender offer, a bid approach may lead to an open exchange of information, but each bid is different and the extent and nature of information released varies from one bid to another. For example, it is commonplace for a UK target to resist providing information to any bidder, whether friendly or hostile, that is not in the public domain, even when the target board is prepared to recommend that shareholders tender their shares into the offer. This reflects to a degree the fiduciary obligation of a UK board to conduct itself in a manner that provides a level playing field for all potential bidders, including with respect to the provision of information. Removing the "look back" rule would address a number of additional objections, including: (i) the practical difficulty of conducting an inquiry once a transaction has been announced, in sufficient time to enable US holders to participate in the initial offer period;[20] (ii) lack of incentive to undertake an inquiry, particularly when trading and anecdotal evidence suggest a low level of US ownership and corresponding limited benefit in terms of any meaningful US audience to which to address the offer; and (iii) the poor and sometimes inconclusive responses from record holders.

Foreign issuers would also like to see the categories of shareholders excluded from the US ownership calculation extended to QIBs and accredited investors and directors and officers of the bidder and target, irrespective of the size of their particular holding. These exclusions from the US ownership calculation can be justified on the basis that the relevant shareholder is sophisticated and able to understand the implications of considering an offer prepared in compliance with non-US requirements. Furthermore, given the overall objective that the Tier I and Rule 802 exemptions should operate when US ownership (excluding major holders) is *de minimis*, excluding substantial non-US shareholders has an artificial, inflationary impact on the assessment of the relevant US shareholder base. For example, if US shareholders hold approximately 5% of the outstanding share capital and a non-US shareholder that holds 50% of the outstanding share capital is excluded from the 10% calculation, the Tier I and Rule 802 exemptions would not be available in the bid, even though US shareholders account for a small minority of the target's shareholders. Bidders

---

20 Foreign bidders are concerned over launching such inquiry before a deal is announced, fearing there would be inevitable speculation in the target's stock.

would also welcome a general increase in the 10% percentage threshold for transactions to qualify for the Tier I and Rule 802 exemptions, which would inevitably enhance interest in extending offers into the United States.

Brian Breheny, the Chief of the SEC's Office of Mergers and Acquisitions, remarked in an October 2004 American Bar Association International Securities and Capital Markets Committee presentation (Breheny Speech), that the SEC is reviewing the cross-border rules to see whether any adjustments need to be made. He noted that one element under consideration is whether certain presumptions for hostile transactions should apply to all deals. Bidders are encouraged by the fact that the SEC is prepared to consider marginal cases that would otherwise not be excluded, such as a significant holder falling marginally below a 10% holding. Such flexibility is likely to foster dialogue with the SEC in marginal cases. Additional guidance from the SEC as to circumstances in which discretion might be exercised, in particular where the outcome is expected to be consistent with the underlying purpose of the cross-border tender offer rules, would be welcomed and would likely lead to more bidders extending their offers into the United States.

THE IMPACT OF SOX ON CROSS-BORDER M&A

SOX is the most significant securities legislation affecting public companies to be enacted in the United States since the adoption of the Securities Act and the Exchange Act in the 1930s. Congress passed SOX in an effort to restore investor confidence following the aftermath of the financial corporate scandals in the United States, which resulted in enormous losses to shareholders and other constituents of the affected companies.

Currently, non-US companies that are not listed or reporting in the United States or who benefit from the Rule 12g-3(2)(b) exemption are not subject to SOX.[21] However, one result of a cross-border bid that must include US shareholder and is not eligible for the Tier I exemption is that a non-US bidder may "back into" SOX

---

21 Rule 12g-3(2)(b) under the Exchange Act exempts certain non-US listed foreign private issuers from the registration requirement established by Section 12(g) of the Exchange Act under certain conditions.

requirements due to the fact that it may end up having a significant US shareholder base or because securities offered in the bid would be required to be registered under the Securities Act. In addition, foreign companies that elect to list on a US exchange or NASDAQ in order to use their US-listed securities as currency in exchange offers are subject to SOX.[22] While all of these non-US participants in cross-border transactions are mindful of the many potential US securities law issues relating to a particular transaction today, chief on their list of concerns is SOX.

SOX marks a general change in the SEC's attitude towards foreign issuers. The Act creates a uniform application of corporate governance and disclosure requirements that are equally applied across the board to domestic and foreign issuers and deviates from the traditional mutual recognition approach that has been followed by the SEC. Whereas, historically, the SEC did not attempt to regulate the corporate governance of foreign corporations, even when issuers entered the SEC reporting and disclosure system and afforded a great deal of deference to standards of home country jurisdictions, SOX does not make such accommodations. Under SOX, foreign issuers must comply with US corporate governance rules with a few exceptions for non-US reporting companies. Congress and the SEC have taken a unilateralist approach to regulation under SOX, retreating to the view that, if foreign issuers wish to tap the US capital markets, they need to play by US rules.[23]

As a result of this new approach to the treatment of foreign issuers under SOX, the Act has generated frustrated and angry reactions

---

[22] Listing on a US stock exchange has been perceived for many years as crucial for a company to compete effectively in international markets. Large corporations are unlikely to be deterred from listing on US exchanges because of SOX, but may chose to do private offerings in place of public offerings or deal with institutional investors to the exclusion of small, individual investors. (Sohne, Estelle M., 2003, "The Impact of Post-Enron Information Disclosure Requirements Imposed under US Law on Foreign Investors", *Columbia Journal of Transnational Law*, **42**, p 217.)

[23] The growing number of foreign issuer registrants and international competition for investments and capital make it more difficult for the SEC to impose stringent rules on US companies and not on foreign issuers. Senator Paul Sarbanes, co-sponsor of SOX, resisted calls for SOX to include some exemptions for foreign issuers on the grounds that such exemptions would encourage US companies to move offshore. (*See* Tracey, Patrick, "Europe Braced for SEC Rules Implementing Sarbanes–Oxley Act", *34 Sec. Reg. & L. Rep. (BNA) 1750*, 28th October 2002.)

from foreign companies and appears to have caused a decline in the number of foreign listings in the United States.[24] Foreign issuers view US financial corporate scandals as the context for SOX and argue that the SEC should not impose corporate governance standards on corporations that function in different corporate finance systems and with different structures than US corporations. They object to this new approach that they believe would result in US oversight of foreign companies, which, for example in Europe, are already subject to EU and national laws and regulations. A consequence of SOX is that non-US bidders face additional corporate governance and reporting obligations as a result of an acquisition of a company that is listed and reporting in the United States. Foreign issuers also feel that certain requirements under SOX are either inconsistent with or are duplicative of substantially similar corporate governance protections in their home countries, which impose more costs on foreign issuers than on domestic issuers.

While there have been no de-listings so far, the available evidence suggest that SOX may have placed a dampener on foreign issuers' enthusiasm for US listings.[25] German automaker Porsche, for example, announced that it would postpone its plans to seek a US stock listing, citing confusion over the regulatory environment and the impracticable requirements of SOX with respect to certifications, forming an independent audit committee of the Board and auditor independence issues generally.[26] The UK pharmaceutical company Provalis announced that it is planning to terminate its ADR program and delist from NASDAQ for similar reasons.[27]

Given the reaction of the international community to SOX, the SEC has softened some of the Act's more controversial provisions

---

[24] Economic factors are also believed to have contributed to this decline, including the worldwide recession in the year following the passage of SOX and generally poor stock-market performance worldwide. The corporate scandals that prompted SOX may have also taken some of the lustre off a US listing.

[25] Chairman Donaldson explained in his January 2005 speech, that since nearly half of all the world equity shares, by market capitalisation, trade in the US and non-US investors have approximately US$4.5 trillion invested in US stock markets, the risk of the backlash from SOX having a long-term effect on US markets is minimal and indications are that most foreign issuers who have already listed on US exchanges will agree to satisfy all the requirements of SOX.

[26] Michaels, Adrian, "SEC Bows to Foreign Pressure on Company Laws", *Financial Times*, 9th January 2003, at. 2.

[27] *The Lawyer*, 11th April 2005, at. 13.

by providing limited exemptions to foreign issuers. One example of such accommodation is SOX Section 301, which generally requires all members of audit committees of listed issuers to be independent directors. The goal of Section 301 is to prevent misstatements of financials and encourage communication with auditors. However, Section 301, in its original form, was in conflict with corporate governance laws of several European countries, including Germany, that mandate two-tier boards (a management board and a supervisory board) on which both labour and management representatives must be represented. These boards were created to address local corporate governance and social structures concerns. SOX does not, however, consider employees of an issuer "independent" for fear that employees with close ties to a company's management may be appointed as board members. Following a dialogue with the EU and other regulators and companies, the SEC became more comfortable with the idea that in those jurisdictions with dual boards, the mandatory employee representatives were independent of the company's management and, in fact, part of their role as board members is to provide a check on management. The final rule under SOX relating to audit committees contains an exception allowing employees who are not officers of a company to be members of the audit committee where the foreign jurisdiction requires a dual board structure. The rule allows non-executive employees to serve on the audit committee, or one of the two-tier boards, which is independent from the second board of directors. While not exempting foreign issuers outright, this accommodation enables affected companies to comply with both sets of laws and preserves the intent of SOX.

A further example of the SEC seeking to accommodate foreign issuers is Section 401(b) of SOX, which relates to the conditions for use of non-US GAAP financial measures. Section 401(b) was created to address Congress' concerns that companies were abusing *pro forma* figures in their filings. Under the rules promulgated under Section 401(b), all public disclosure by reporting companies, whether made in SEC filings or otherwise, must be evaluated to determine whether the financial information is calculated and presented on a basis that is not in accordance with US GAAP. If a non-US GAAP measure is used in a SEC filing, the company must, among other things, disclose the most directly comparable US GAAP measure and include a reconciliation of the non-GAAP financial measure to the GAAP financial measure. While not exempting foreign issuers all together from Section 401(b), the SEC adopted Regulation G, which provides a safe harbour for the use of non-GAAP financial performance measures in public communications made outside the United States. As discussed in Chapter 4, Regulation G provides limited exemptions where: (i) the securities of the issuer are listed on a non-US exchange; (ii) the issuer does not use US GAAP; and (iii) the non-GAAP communications are made outside the United States, even where those communications reach the United States. The SEC took this action because it did not want to interfere with the practices governing how foreign companies communicated with investors outside the United States.[28]

Finally, the SEC is currently re-evaluating the deregistration process for foreign private issuers that would like to deregister from the SEC to avoid the compliance burdens and costs associated with SOX.[29] Currently, the Exchange Act generally requires registration with the SEC of equity securities of foreign issuers, even if the securities are not listed on a national securities exchange, as long as 300 or more persons that hold such securities are resident in the United States at the end of the company's fiscal year.[30] These rules effectively involuntarily subject foreign issuers to US reporting requirements. A foreign issuer that has made a US public offering or that has engaged in a business combination with a reporting person (including an acquisition of a reporting foreign company in a completely foreign transaction) can find itself inadvertently subject to US reporting requirements.

Despite the above efforts and other limited accommodations to foreign issuers under SOX, disagreement over the proper regulation of foreign issuers under SOX remains. In particular, foreign issuers have identified Section 404 of SOX (internal control over financial reporting) as being the most burdensome and costly

---

[28] Speech by SEC Chairman William H. Donaldson, "US Capital Markets in the Post-Sarbanes–Oxley World: Why Our Markets Should Matter to Foreign Issuers" given on 25th January 2005 in London, England (Donaldson Speech).

[29] Donaldson Speech and speech by SEC Commissioner Cynthia A. Glassman titled "EU-US Dialogue on Financial Market Regulation – A US Perspective" (14th March 2005).

[30] Section 12(g) and Rule 12g of the Exchange Act. For companies with assets valued at less than US$10 million, the threshold is 500 US residents.

compliance obligation of the Act, Section 404, which does not currently contain an exemption for foreign issuers. Section 404 requires that foreign issuers include in their annual reports on Form 20-F a report on the company's internal control over financial reporting, including a management's evaluation of the effectiveness of those controls and an attestation report of the company's auditors on management's evaluation. Section 404 also requires that the company's auditors provide opinions on the management's assessment and effectiveness of the internal controls. Of all the reforms contained in SOX, completing the processes necessary to report on internal controls is likely to have the greatest long-term impact on enhancing the reliability of financial reports, but is also the most time-consuming and costly new rule to implement.

Section 404 has led some foreign private issuers to declare that they may wish to leave the US markets altogether rather than have their internal controls certified. Section 404 was initially to apply to Forms 20-F covering fiscal years ending after 15th April 2005, however, given the strong negative response to Section 404, in February 2004, the SEC pushed back the effective date of the rule that will now first apply to Forms 20-F covering the fiscal years ending after 15th July 2005. The SEC is also considering whether to delay the effective date of Section 404 even further for non-US companies.

Responding to protests of foreign issuers with respect to Section 404, former SEC Chairman Donaldson, stated that the SEC was sensitive to the need to accommodate unique foreign structures and requirements.[31] Donaldson acknowledged that companies outside the United States faced additional challenges that go above and beyond those faced by companies in the United States, in particular European companies who will have to adopt international financial reporting standards for the first time in 2005. Donaldson stated that the SEC was committed to a level playing field for all its issuers, but recognised that cross-border listings frequently entail issuers having to navigate duplicate or even contradictory regulations in different jurisdictions.[32]

The SEC should consider taking a pro-active approach and not simply implement Section 404 with rigid uniformity. It should

---

31 "Donaldson Speech".
32 "Donaldson Speech".

articulate the goals of Section 404 and enter into a dialogue with the foreign regulators and companies to establish whether there are local equivalent structures intended to implement internal control and other processes. How the SEC decides to enforce Section 404 of SOX with respect to foreign issuers may determine whether foreign issuers accept SOX as a whole or elect to exclude or pull out of the US capital markets.

CONFUSION REGARDING THE "ALL HOLDERS/BEST PRICE RULE"

In recent years, the use of tender offers as the preferred acquisition vehicle has declined despite its many attractions: in particular, the ability to complete transactions quickly. Many believe that this is the result of the confusion generated by US courts over the interpretation of Rule 14d-10 of the Exchange Act, the "all holders/best price" rule. The Rule states that a bidder may not make a tender offer unless "the consideration paid to any security holder pursuant to the tender offer is the highest consideration paid to any other security holder during such tender offer."

Neither the Congress nor the SEC has provided much guidance on how to interpret the phrase "paid . . . pursuant to the tender offer," leaving it to the US federal courts to adopt different, conflicting tests to determine whether a bidder is in breach of Rule 14d-10. US federal courts are split as to how a bidder should determine whether privately negotiated compensatory agreements, such as employment, bonus or severance agreements with target management, who are also security holders, in connection with a friendly tender offer violate the Rule. Courts have argued that certain such agreements represent a hidden premium paid to a select group of shareholders, that is, senior management, in exchange for their support for the transaction. Courts have allowed other shareholders that do not receive this additional benefit to bring a claim against the bidder and have it pay the additional consideration paid to the employee shareholders to all public shareholders of the target.

Three leading tests have emerged from the various federal cases that deal with Rule 14d-10: the "Integral Part/Functionalist Test", the "Bright Line/Formalist Test" and the relatively recent "Hybrid Test". The "Integral Part/Functionalist Test" examines whether the employee arrangements are an "integral part" of the tender offer, irrespective of whether such arrangements were entered into prior to commencement of the tender offer and are to be completed following the closing of the offer. According to the "Bright Line/Formalist Test", transactions entered into before or after a tender offer are outside the tender offer and not covered by Rule 14d-10. Finally, the "Hybrid Test", which was invoked in the *In Re Digital Island Securities Litigation* case[33] in the US Third Circuit, rejects the rigid interpretation of the other two tests and looks at whether the tender offer "has fraudulently devised a scheme to circumvent the Rule."

The illicit threat of litigation, partially caused by the differing judicial interpretations of the Rule and lack of SEC guidance, is believed to be the primary reason why acquisitions through a single step merger in the United States have risen in numbers, while more and more bidders shy away from tender offers. The increased litigation in this area is of particular interest to bidders in cross-border M&A transactions. Tender offers are the primary means by which foreign companies may acquire US corporations since mergers are not accessible to European companies that do not have US subsidiaries as European companies cannot be merged with US corporations.

The SEC has been lobbied for many years to clarify how Rule 14d-10 should be interpreted in an effort to level the playing field among tender offers or two-step mergers (especially exchange offers) and one-step mergers. At the end of 2004, the SEC hinted that fixing the confusion over the Rule is among its top priorities. In the Breheny Speech, Breheny stated that the SEC intends to recommend changes to Rule 14d-10 to clarify that certain employee compensation arrangements do not run afoul of the rule. Breheny further stated that the SEC understands that being able to retain management is vital to the success of many acquisitions and bone fide compensation arrangements should not be counted as part of the consideration offered in a tender offer. While it is unlikely that the SEC will set a bright line test, any clarity on this issue is expected to encourage bidders to use tender offers as their preferred acquisition mechanism.

---

[33] *In Re Digital Island*, 357 F.3d 322 (3d Cir. 2004).

THE CHANGING EUROPEAN TAKEOVER LANDSCAPE

Cross-border and national takeover legislation in the EU is likely to change dramatically in the coming years as a result of the adoption of the Takeover Directive, which is due to be implemented by all Member States by 20th May 2006. Initially, the objective of the Takeover Directive was to harmonise EU takeover law through the adoption of a pan-European takeover code (along the lines of the UK Takeover Code) that would foster consolidation in the EU market by creating a level playing field for companies across the EU. While regulators and companies anxiously await the implementation of the Takeover Directive by individual member states, there are already strong indications that the Takeover Directive will not align takeover rules throughout Europe as originally expected. The Takeover Directive's harmonising effect has been substantially curtailed by political concessions known as the Portuguese compromise. As a result of this compromise, regulatory arbitrage will continue to be a characteristic of cross-border European M&A in the post-Takeover Directive environment.

Overview

The Takeover Directive will apply only to takeover bids for securities of a company governed by the law of a Member State, where all or some of those securities are admitted to trading on a EU market, but not to bids for securities issued by central banks nor securities issued by funds repurchasing or redeeming shares.[34] The Takeover Directive defines a "takeover bid" as a public offer to the security holders of a target for the purpose of achieving control over the target.[35] Therefore, bids for unlisted targets, offers by a company for its own securities and offers for less than a controlling position will not be covered by the Takeover Directive. By implication, the Takeover Directive will not apply to companies that are incorporated outside the EU, even if all or part of their shares are listed in the EU-and this would include US companies. That said, it is worth noting that each Member State will be free to extend the applicability of the Takeover Directive's rules to companies that do not fall within the original scope of the Takeover Directive (unless this is

---

34 *See* Article 1(1) and 1(2) of the Takeover Directive.
35 *See* Article 2(1)(a) of the Takeover Directive.

expressly prohibited by the Takeover Directive, as is the case with respect to central banks).

The Takeover Directive will ensure that certain key rules apply to takeovers throughout the EU:

- ❏ a requirement to launch a mandatory offer to acquire all of the shares of a target company at an equitable price upon reaching a specified percentage ownership threshold;
- ❏ basic standards relating to the conduct of bids, including minimum and maximum tender offer acceptance periods, minimum content and dissemination requirements for tender offer documents and the target board's duty to respond by publishing its views on the offer;
- ❏ enhanced disclosure requirements, including the duty to publish in annual reports, details relating to a company's capital structure and defensive mechanisms;
- ❏ squeeze-out rights for bidders reaching a 90–95% ownership threshold; and
- ❏ sell-out rights for minority shareholders when a bidder has reached a 90–95% ownership threshold.

In addition, the Takeover Directive gives Member States the option of introducing certain rules limiting the use of defensive measures.

General principles

The Takeover Directive requires that Member States implement rules to reflect the general principles set out in the Takeover Directive.

The first general principle is that all holders of target company securities of the same class be treated equally. This principle is similar to the "all holders" rule in the United States. Each shareholder is entitled to receive the same price, the same consideration and participate in the offer under the same terms and conditions as any other shareholder.

The second principle is that shareholders in a target company be guaranteed sufficient time and information to enable them to reach a properly informed decision on the bid. In addition, where the target board advises the shareholders in connection with the bid, it must also give its views on the effects of the implementation of the bid on employment, conditions of employment and the locations of the company's places of business. In keeping with this approach, the third principle is that the board of a target company must act in the interests of the company *as a whole* and must not deny shareholders the opportunity to decide on the merits of the offer.[36]

The Takeover Directive also prohibits the creation of false markets in shares of the target company. This is to be achieved through increased transparency in the information process, the introduction of rules on the national level governing the conduct of the bid and imposing minimum time periods for an offer to remain open.

The next principle prohibits a bidder from announcing a bid for a target company until it has taken reasonable measures to ensure that it can pay for the target shares. This principle would eliminate offers with a financing condition or offers made based on a "highly confident" letter from an investment bank, a form of support popular in the US takeover practice in the 1980s.

Finally, the Takeover Directive provides that takeover bids should not unreasonably hinder the operations of the target company.

Mandatory bids

One of the most important provisions of the Takeover Directive is the mandatory bid requirement, which requires bidders to make an offer for all target company shares at an "equitable price" upon reaching a specified ownership threshold. The Takeover Directive does not specify this threshold, which is to be determined by each Member State. The purpose of this provision is to prevent a person from acquiring creeping control of a target by accumulating shares without making an offer to all shareholders at a fair price.

Mandatory offer control thresholds

The European Economic and Social Committee, an EU advisory body called to opine on certain legislative proposals by the Council, had recommended that, in order to ensure a more level

---

[36] The scope of the Directive was progressively expanded during its history to encompass the general principle that, in addition to minority shareholders, employees should also be protected in a takeover scenario and should be enabled to express their views on the effects of the implementation of the bid. While the more radical proposals on employee rights, such as the proposal that the target board's actions must be taken with a view to safeguarding jobs, were abandoned at different stages in the process, the scope of certain principles was expanded to cover the interests of other target company constituencies, including the interests of employees.

playing field, the Takeover Directive incorporate a relatively narrow range of percentage voting thresholds (30–40%) as the control threshold triggering mandatory bids.[37] However, neither the EU Commission proposal nor the final version of the Takeover Directive specified this threshold, leaving it up to each Member State to independently determine it. Many commentators fear that the difference in ownership control thresholds will encourage forum shopping by companies, which will incorporate in countries providing the lowest ownership control thresholds to enhance their takeover defence options.

Arguably, a specific threshold or a range would have provided some degree of harmonisation in Europe as to the level of control that would trigger mandatory offers. Nonetheless, the mandatory offer provision will cause at least some harmonisation among EU jurisdictions, as all Member States, including the 10 countries who joined in May 2004,[38] will be required to introduce in their respective takeover codes the notion of a mandatory offer requirement and link the notion of control to the ownership of a specified percentage of voting rights.[39]

The Takeover Directive exempts bidders that had achieved control through a voluntary bid directed to all target shareholders for all of their shares from the requirement to launch a mandatory offer after the close of the bid, a concept that is already enshrined in several EU jurisdictions.[40]

Equitable price
The Takeover Directive defines "equitable price" as the highest price paid by the bidder over a period of between six and 12 months

---

37 Opinion of the European Economic and Social Committee on the "Proposal for a Directive of the European Parliament and of the Council on Takeover Bids" (14th May 2003); OJ C208 (3rd September 2003), p 55 (COM(2002) 534 final – 2002/0240 (COD)).
38 The countries that joined the EU in May 2004 are the Czech Republic, Estonia, Hungary, Latvia, Lithuania, Poland, the Slovak Republic, Slovenia, Cyprus and Malta.
39 While in most EU jurisdictions mandatory offers are the current practice (the UK (30%), France (33%), Germany (30%) and Italy (30%)), the takeover directive will introduce the mandatory offer requirement in the Netherlands, which historically stood out for its lack of this requirement. It will also cause Belgium, which does have a mandatory offer requirement but where the definition of control is not linked to a specific percentage ownership threshold, to introduce this threshold, clarifying the applicability of the mandatory offer rule.
40 This concept, however, is not yet recognised in Denmark.

prior to the bid, to be adjusted upwards or downwards by national supervisory authorities according to certain pre-determined criteria. For example, the Takeover Directive allows the adjustment of the price where the highest price was set by agreement between the purchaser and the seller, where prices have been manipulated or where market prices have been affected by exceptional occurrences, or in order to enable a firm in difficulty to be rescued.

The Takeover Directive also requires a bidder to offer a cash alternative when the consideration offered in connection with a mandatory bid does not consist of "liquid securities", which are defined as securities listed on a European market.[41] This definition of liquid securities may prove to be a hindrance to takeovers of EU targets by, for instance, US and EU bidders who do not have shares listed on an EU exchange, as listings on NYSE or NASDAQ are insufficient to satisfy this requirement.[42]

Conduct of bids
Tender offer period
The Takeover Directive requires a bidder to keep its bid open for a period of acceptance not less than two and not longer than 10 weeks from the date of publication of the offer document. Member States may provide that the maximum period be extended on condition that the bidder give at least two weeks' notice of its intention to close the bid. However, any such rule adopted by Member States cannot be in contrast with the general principle that takeover bids should not unreasonably hinder the operations of the target company, which, at least in theory, should eliminate the possibility that acceptance periods will be extended indefinitely in EU jurisdictions.

---

[41] "Regulated market" is defined in Article 1 of the proposed directive as "regulated market within the meaning of Council Directive 93/22/EEC in one or more Member States". Council Directive 93/22/EEC provides that Member States are required to provide each year an updated list of the markets that should be considered regulated markets within their territory, for publication by the Commission.

[42] Furthermore, the principle that EU listed securities should be automatically considered liquid seems unreasonable. The liquidity of a security is a function of the amount of free-floating securities and of their trading volume, not solely the market where the securities are listed. In addition, as mentioned above, this definition excludes the most liquid markets for equity securities worldwide, the NYSE and NASDAQ. In so doing, this definition of liquid securities runs contrary to the best interests of shareholders as it could potentially limit the range of bidders willing to launch competing offers for target companies, potentially limiting the value shareholders could extract from their investment.

Member States may promulgate rules modifying the acceptance period in specific cases, although these cases are not set out in the Takeover Directive. In addition, Member States may authorise national supervisory authorities to grant derogations from the ordinary acceptance periods in order to allow target companies to call general meetings to consider a bid.

Conduct of bids

A general principle of the Takeover Directive proposed by the Council is that shareholders have sufficient time and information to enable them to reach a properly informed decision on the bid. The Takeover Directive requires that Member States enact rules requiring a bidder to promptly make its bid public and keep the national supervisory authority informed of the bid. Member States may also require that the national supervisory authority be informed before the decision to make a bid is made public.

As soon as the bid is made public, both the bidder and the target boards are required to inform their respective employees. The bidder would not be required to inform employees prior to the announcement of the bid because of the risk of insider trading. There is no exception to this rule for non-EU bidders.

Each Member State will be required to enact rules governing the conduct of the offer with respect to at least the following matters:

❑ lapse of the offer;
❑ amendments to the offer;
❑ competing bids;
❑ disclosure of the results of an offer; and
❑ irrevocability of the offer and the permitted conditions.

Offer document

The bidder would be required to prepare an offer document with sufficient information to enable shareholders to make an informed decision on the bid. The bidder is required to submit the offer document to the competent national supervisory authority before it is made public. As soon as the offer document is made public, the bidder and the target are required to communicate it to their respective employees. While the Takeover Directive requires that bidders submit the offer document to the national supervisory authority, it does not require that national supervisory authorities formally approve the offer document, leaving it up to each Member State.

Where, however, the offer document is subject to the prior approval of a supervisory authority and has been approved, the Takeover Directive provides that this offer document has to be recognised (subject to translation) in any other Member State on whose market the securities of the target company are admitted to trading, without it being necessary to obtain the approval of the supervisory authority of that Member State. Such Member States may only require additional information to be included in the offer document if: (a) it is specific to the market of the Member State or Member States where the securities of the target company are admitted to trading; and (b) it relates to the formalities to be complied with for accepting the bid and for receiving the consideration due at the close of the bid as well as to the tax arrangements to which the consideration offered to the holders of securities will be subject. The Takeover Directive, however, does not require that offer documents be recognised in Member States where the securities of the target company are *not* admitted to trading, but where the target company has a significant shareholder base. Therefore, bidders will continue to be subject to potential restrictions on the distribution of offer documents in jurisdictions where the target company's shares are not listed.

The offer document must include the following information:

- the terms of the bid;
- the identity and jurisdiction of the bidder;
- the securities for which the bid is made;
- the consideration offered;
- the minimum and maximum percentage of shares that the bidder undertakes to acquire;
- details of the bidder's existing holdings in the target;
- the conditions to which the bid is subject;
- the bidder's intentions with respect to the future business and undertakings of the target company, its employees and its management, including any material change in the conditions of employment and specifying the bidder's strategic plans for the two companies and the likely repercussions on employment and the locations of the companies' places of business;

- the period for accepting the offer;
- if the consideration is non-cash, information about the securities offered;
- information on financing of the bid;
- the identity of any persons acting in concert with the bidder; and
- information as to the governing law and competent courts chosen for contracts between the bidder and any target shareholder in relation to the bid.

Target response
The target board is required to publish its response to the offer, including its recommendation to target shareholders and its views on the effects of the bid on the target and on employment, and its evaluation of the bidder's strategic plans for the target company. In accordance with the general principles of the Takeover Directive, this response must be communicated to employees. In addition, where the target board receives an opinion of the employee representatives prior to publication of its response to the bid, such opinion must be appended to the response.

Enhanced periodic reporting disclosure rules

The Takeover Directive includes provisions aimed at enhancing disclosure requirements, particularly with respect to a company's capital structure and defensive mechanisms. This provision, which was first introduced by the Commission in its October 2002 proposal, is aimed at creating a level playing field. The rule mandates disclosure of the following information in the annual report of any company listed on a market in the EU:

- the capital structure;
- restrictions on transfers of securities;
- significant direct and indirect shareholdings (including shareholdings through pyramid structures and cross-shareholdings);
- special voting or control rights, restrictions on voting rights;
- system of control of any employee share scheme;
- rules on the appointment and replacement of board members and amendments to the articles of association, powers of board members;

- agreements between shareholders, which are known to the company and may result in restrictions on the transfer of securities and/or voting rights;
- significant agreements, which include change of control clauses (except where disclosure would be seriously prejudicial to the company); and
- golden parachute type arrangements.

Furthermore, the Takeover Directive provides that the Board of the company will be required to present an explanatory report to the annual general shareholders meeting on these matters.

This provision could arguably prove to be one of the most effective innovations to EU takeover law enacted by the Takeover Directive. Broad disclosure requirements of the type contemplated by this provision are not the norm in the EU where annual reports usually only set out a company's financial results and a brief commentary on the company's business. This disclosure-based approach will force boards to confront shareholders (including institutional investors) and justify the adoption of any defensive mechanism. Increased transparency will enable shareholders to take more informed investment decisions. Also, the disclosure of unreasonable defensive measures and perhaps the quality of the disclosure itself could influence the level of investment by sophisticated institutional investors.

Restrictions on defensive measures: breakthrough rules

The most controversial provisions of the Takeover Directive were those intended to limit a target's ability to raise takeover defences (Articles 9 and 11).

Rule against frustrating actions

Article 9 provides that from the time the target board is informed of a bid until the end of the offer period, the target board may not take any "frustrating action" that might cause the offer to fail, other than seeking alternative bids, without obtaining prior shareholder approval (Article 9(2)). As regards decisions taken before the beginning of the offer period and not yet fully implemented, the Takeover Directive provides that a general shareholders' meeting must approve any decision during an offer period that does not form part of the normal course of the target's business and the implementation of which may result in the frustration of a bid (Article 9(3)). These rules, for example, limit a target's ability to adopt or implement a shareholder rights plan (that is, a poison pill) or otherwise issue shares to dilute a bidder's stake in the target, without prior shareholder approval. One rule prevents boards from adopting takeover defences without first obtaining shareholder approval (Article 9).

Breakthrough rules
Article 11 of the Takeover Directive contains breakthrough provisions designed to render unenforceable clauses in the articles of association of target companies and agreements between the target and target shareholders or among target shareholders that could have the effect of limiting the ability of target shareholders to tender into a bid. The breakthrough rules provide that:

❏ share transfer restrictions in the target's articles of association, and in agreements between the target and target shareholders or among target shareholders (such as irrevocable undertakings, assuming the bidder is a shareholder, and shareholders' agreements contemplating lock-ups or rights of first refusal), are unenforceable *vis-à-vis* a bidder during the tender offer acceptance period;
❏ restrictions on voting rights (except where they are compensated by specific pecuniary advantages, as with, for example, preference shares), in the target's articles of association or in agreements between the target and target shareholders or among target shareholders, lapse at a general meeting called to decide upon the adoption of defensive measures during the period when a bid has been made public;
❏ multiple voting securities carry one vote only at any general meeting called to decide on the adoption of defensive measures during the period when a bid has been made public; and
❏ following a bid, if the bidder has acquired at least 75% of the capital carrying voting rights, any restrictions on transfer of securities or the exercise of voting rights (except where voting right restrictions are compensated by specific pecuniary advantages) or any special rights of shareholders regarding the

appointment or removal of board members will cease to have an effect and multiple voting securities will carry one vote only, at the first shareholders' meeting after the bid called by the bidder in order to amend the articles of association or to remove or appoint board members.

The breakthrough provisions will be applicable only to agreements between shareholders entered into after the adoption of the Takeover Directive. Where rights are being removed, equitable compensation must be provided for any loss incurred by the holders of these rights. The rules for determining this compensation are to be determined by member states, and the terms of this compensation are required to be disclosed in the bidder's offer document. Commentators and practitioners have questioned the practical ability of member states to implement rules that will set the parameters for valuing special rights. It is likely that for those member states that decide to adopt the Takeover Directive's breakthrough rules, the determination of what is equitable compensation will become a serious contentious issue, with potential effects on the use or substance of irrevocable undertakings and shareholders' agreements.

The breakthrough provisions would nullify contractual provisions providing for joint voting agreements, lock-up and exit arrangements, irrespective of the law governing the agreement, the place of incorporation of the contracting parties and the size of their combined share ownership. As such, these rules may conflict with constitutional, property and contractual principles both in EU and non-EU countries. The jurisdictional basis for neutralising clauses of an agreement governed by New York law, for example, and entered into by two non-EU shareholders – even when the agreement relates to an EU company – is an issue that is likely to be contentious and will need to be addressed.

Opt out provision
As part of a compromise (the Portuguese compromise) intended to garner support for the adoption of the Takeover Directive notwithstanding opposition to Articles 9 and 11, Article 12 of the Takeover Directive allows member states to opt out of the rules restricting defensive measures (Article 9(2) and (3)) and/or the breakthrough provisions (Article 11). Member states may, in fact, reserve the right

not to require companies to apply these provisions. However, in such a case, member states have to give companies the right to opt in by voluntarily adopting Article 9 and/or Article 11. The rule is drafted loosely and leaves many questions unanswered as to its practical application. For example, are member states authorised to opt out selectively, only with respect to certain industries, or adopt the rules only in part, by incorporating a list of exceptions to the rules? By way of further example, with respect to Article 11, it is unclear how a company could voluntarily opt in to rules providing for the neutralisation of agreements it is not a party to, such as shareholders' agreements.

Reciprocity
A further element of the Portuguese compromise is the reciprocity rule, set forth in Article 12(3). It provides that where targets apply Articles 9(2) and (3) and/or Article 11, member states may exempt targets (under conditions determined by national law) from the application of those articles in situations where the bidder (or the entity controlling the bidder) has not adopted the same rules. This provision of Article 12 is especially unsophisticated. It does not state what regime would apply in the event of competing offers: would a member state be permitted to exempt targets from applying Article 9 and/or 11 *vis-à-vis* all bidders, or only those that do not apply Article 9 and/or 11? Furthermore, if, for example, a target applied only Article 9 and of two bidders one only applied Article 9 while the other only applied Article 11, would the target be permitted to raise takeover defences against both bidders? The reciprocity rule also provides that member state legislation may exempt targets from applying Articles 9 and 11, even if the bidder applies those rules, if the bidder is controlled by an entity that does not apply Articles 9 and 11 (such as a US or a private parent). The purpose of this is to prevent bidders from circumventing the rule by incorporating special takeover vehicles. However, in practice this could mean that any European public company controlled by a private person or by a non-EU entity could be at a disadvantage in a takeover battle. Much will depend on how loosely the term control is defined by each member state, and which definition of control will apply – that adopted by the bidder's jurisdiction or that adopted by the target's jurisdiction.

Developments in the UK, France, Germany, Italy and the Netherlands in relation to rules limiting takeover defences

Member states are required by the Takeover Directive to implement its provisions by 20th May 2006. What follows is a brief look at the direction that takeover law is likely to take in four of the principal takeover jurisdictions in Europe (the UK, France, Germany, Italy and the Netherlands), focusing on the future availability of defensive mechanisms.

1 Developments in the UK[43]

The UK is, from a cultural and a regulatory standpoint, more open to cross-border takeovers than any other jurisdiction in Europe. As such, the impact of the Takeover Directive on rules governing takeover defences will be minimal, given that the ideas and concepts for the Takeover Directive – in particular Article 9 – were largely drawn from the UK model and rules. Indeed, as a minimum standards directive, the Takeover Directive provides a relatively compatible underlay for the UK takeover regime.

The UK Takeover Panel (Panel) confirmed that the UK would adopt Article 9, which broadly reflects the concept already contained in General Principle 7 and Rule 21 of the UK Takeover Code prohibiting frustrating action being taken by a target during a bid or when a bid is imminent, without approval by shareholders in a general meeting. To align the provisions of the UK Takeover Code to those of the Takeover Directive, the Panel intends to broaden the definition of frustrating action in the Takeover Code (although this will probably have a minor impact on how the rule is applied in practice). The Panel also intends to eliminate the added flexibility under Rule 21, which allowed the Panel to permit pre-existing contractual arrangements (the completion of which would otherwise be frustrating) to be completed.

Given the disparity of conceptual approach between Article 11 and UK general market practice, it appears likely that the UK will

---

[43] In January 2005, the UK Government's Department of Trade and Industry (DTI) issued a consultation document, and the UK Takeover Panel (Panel) published an explanatory paper on the implementation of the Takeover Directive. The DTI and the Panel largely confirmed that it would be business as usual in the UK once the Takeover Directive has been implemented. However, fine-tuning will be required.

opt out of Article 11. Otherwise, and ostensibly unintentionally, the ordinary market practice in the UK of gathering irrevocable undertakings from offeree shareholders (not to accept a rival offer and not to transfer their shares) would be rendered ineffective. Furthermore, Article 11 potentially prevents offeree shareholders coming together to form a consortium to make a joint bid for an offeree company by cutting across the share transfer restrictions that would typically be contained in their consortium agreement. Moreover, dual-listed company transactions involving voting structures (where the votes of one company are replicated at meetings of the corresponding entity in that structure) could not, on the face of it, be sustained.

2 Developments in France

While French securities laws and regulations, including takeover laws and regulations, have been amended considerably over the past three years, French takeover law will have to be further amended in connection with the implementation of the Takeover Directive. At this stage, it is generally assumed that France will implement Article 9(2) and (3) of the Takeover Directive.

If Article 9 of the Takeover Directive was adopted, the target board's obligations with respect to the use of defensive measures during offer periods would be more stringent than those currently applicable under French takeover law. In general, neither French corporate law nor securities regulations expressly prohibit target companies from adopting measures designed to fend off hostile takeovers. However, this general principle is tempered by several rules that tend to reduce the scope of a target board's discretion in responding to hostile takeover threats:

❏ although not expressly set forth in applicable laws and regulations, absolute defences (*défenses absolues*) – that is, defences precluding the success of any tender offer – are prohibited (this prohibition being qualified as a general principle of French securities laws by numerous scholars);
❏ any defence must comply with the requirements set forth by the somewhat fuzzy notion of social interest (*intérêt social*); and
❏ in contested takeover situations, defences that confer an advantage to a bidder, determining the success of that bidder's offer, are prohibited.

Based on these restrictions, so far French corporations have not used many US-type defence mechanisms, most notably shareholder rights plans (ie, poison pills). There are instances, however, in which takeover defences could be implemented during an offer period by a target board without the approval of a shareholders meeting (for example, crown-jewel lock-ups or strategic acquisitions).[44] These takeover defences would no longer be available if Article 9(2) of the Takeover Directive were implemented.

It is not clear whether France will adopt Article 11, but the consequences would be dramatic from the perspective of target companies if France were to do so. Given that French companies may not easily adopt takeover defences during the offer period (without shareholder approval), preventive takeover defence mechanisms, including share transfer restrictions and restrictions on voting rights in particular, play a key role in the French context. According to a study we recently performed, more than half of the French CAC 40 companies have adopted these types of defences or shareholder arrangements. For example, these defence mechanisms include voting right limitations set forth in a company's articles of association that prevent shareholders from voting shares in excess of a certain threshold. Neutralising such restrictions in connection with takeover bids would render French companies vulnerable to hostile takeover attempts.

3 Developments in Germany

Hostile takeover attempts have been rare in Germany so far.[45] The low number of hostile takeover attempts is due to the German economy being characterised by a strong base of owner-managed (often family owned) businesses, cultural and political aversion to confrontational resolution of conflicts and the lesser importance of the capital markets in Germany as a source of financing compared with

---

[44] Pechiney considered carrying out a defensive acquisition of the aluminium business of Corus in the summer of 2003 to fend off Alcan's hostile bid. However, Pechiney finally decided not to proceed with this defensive strategy and was eventually taken over by Alcan. The bidder is entitled, subject to the approval of the relevant regulatory authority (the AMF), to withdraw its offer if the target adopts concrete and immediate actions modifying the target's consistency (*mesures d'application certaines et immédiates modifiant sa consistance*).

[45] Vodafone's takeover of Mannesmann in 2000 was one of the few exceptions and it provided some momentum for the enactment of German takeover legislation in 2002.

other countries. The German Takeover Act, *Wertpapierwerbs-und Übernahmegesetz*, adopted in January 2002, did not contemplate measures designed to open Germany to hostile takeovers. On the contrary, the German Takeover Act provides management with considerable flexibility (compared, for example, with the UK) to take frustrating actions against unsolicited takeovers.

It appears that the Takeover Directive will not do much to change this state of affairs in Germany, as it intends to avail itself of all the flexibility resulting from the Portuguese compromise.[46] It is likely that, consistent with its historical stance against flat prohibitions of defence mechanisms, Germany will opt out of the requirement to implement the provisions of Article 9 and retain the *status quo*.

As many other jurisdictions in Europe, Germany is likely to opt-out of Article 11. On the other hand, the relevance of this rule with respect to provisions of German statutory law is not extensive. German law does not permit shares with multiple voting rights (which is more common in Scandinavian jurisdictions), and restrictions on share transfers in public companies are generally restricted to a limited number of industries. The breakthrough rules, however, would be more relevant with regards to contractual arrangements among shareholders, which commonly include provisions for pooling voting rights and provide for rights of first refusal and lock-ups.

4 Developments in Italy

While Italy has not yet taken an official position on the adoption of Article 9 or 11, the impact of the Takeover Directive on rules governing takeover defences in Italy will likely be minimal. Italy's takeover code already prohibits any frustrating action being taken by a target during a bid, other than seeking alternative bidders, without approval by shareholders in a general meeting. The law goes further, requiring a special quorum at the shareholders meeting where a frustrating action is approved.

---

[46] Historically, Germany has been the principal opposition of the Takeover Directive, and voted in favour of its rejection by the European parliament in 2001. When the Commission proposed a new draft of the Takeover Directive in 2002, Germany continued to oppose it on the same or similar grounds until member states reached the Portuguese compromise.

Similarly, most of the principles of Article 11 are already contemplated by Italy's takeover code. Italian public companies are not permitted to provide for restrictions to share transfers and multiple voting right shares are expressly prohibited under Italian law. Furthermore, while shareholders may enter into shareholders agreements providing for share transfer and voting right restrictions, such restrictions are neutralised by law during an offer period in order to allow shareholders to tender their shares and vote in favour of a tender offer.

While the principles of Article 9 and 11 are embodied in the law, Italian companies have been able to rely on other protections (including regulatory barriers) to shield themselves from cross-border takeover activity. A recent example for which Italy has been heavily criticised is the rules protecting Italian banks and other financial institutions from non-Italian ownership. Until these alternative takeover barriers are addressed by EU or national legislation, Italian public companies will remain difficult takeover targets for non-Italian bidders.

5 Developments in the Netherlands[47]

Dutch takeover law has so far been characterised by the absence of a takeover code similar to that in force in the UK, France, Germany and Italy. While Dutch takeover practice will be deeply affected by the implementation of the Takeover Directive (particularly by virtue of the mandatory offer rule provisions), it appears at this stage that the Dutch government intends to opt out of Article 9 and adopt Article 11 only in part, which should soften the impact of the Takeover Directive with respect to the availability of takeover defences in the Netherlands.

In the Netherlands there is no set rule for or against takeover defences. Rather than following the takeover code approach, Dutch law relies on essential principles of good business judgment, *elementaire beginselen van behoorlijk ondernemerschap*, as

---

[47] On 7th September 2004, the Dutch Minister of Justice issued a policy document on the modernisation of Dutch company law, where reference was made to the general aspects of the implementation of the Takeover Directive. The Dutch government's Department of Justice (the DoJ) is currently preparing a proposal of law, intending to follow as much as possible the guidelines laid down in the policy document.

interpreted by the Dutch courts. Historically, Dutch courts have been relatively inclined to accept the use of anti-takeover devices by target companies if such companies could make a good faith argument that the takeover threat was against the best interest of the target and all its constituents (which not only includes its shareholders, but also its employees, creditors and other relevant parties). While the use of anti-takeover devices has in recent years become the subject of increased criticism in the Dutch market and scrutiny by the courts (particularly the use of devices that were put in place by target companies before an actual threat materialised), they have been consistently upheld in the Dutch courts.

The Takeover Directive is likely to have a limited impact on the range of anti-takeover devices currently available under Dutch law. The Dutch government intends to opt out of Article 9. In particular, the DoJ believes that target companies should have the option to trigger a pre-existing anti-takeover device (previously approved by the general meeting) or to leave in place such a device for a limited amount of time, for instance following a successful offer. According to the DoJ, this would allow the target's board time to negotiate with the bidder, which could result in an increased takeover premium or continued employment commitments for the benefit of the target's employees. The DoJ also points out that the (temporary) use of an anti-takeover device could allow the target company time to enter into discussions with a white knight, with the aim of obtaining a competing offer.

The Netherlands is considering a partial adoption of Article 11. Although share transfer restrictions and restrictions on voting rights would not be neutralised by law during the offer period, the Netherlands is considering the adoption of the post-bid 75% rules contemplated by Article 11. The DoJ has indicated that it believes that, notwithstanding companies' freedom to determine the level of anti-takeover devices they desire to adopt, it would be undesirable for target companies' to ignore (new) realities within their shareholder base indefinitely. Consistent with intentions voiced by the Dutch government in recent years, the DoJ states that it is desirable that a successful bidder can break through the target company's anti-takeover defences following a reasonable period of time.

Squeeze-out and sell-out rights

The Takeover Directive enables successful bidders to launch a compulsory acquisition for all remaining shares of a target (following an offer to all holders for 100% of the securities) upon reaching 90–95% of the capital carrying voting rights of the target or 90% of the voting rights (leaving it up to each Member State to determine the exact threshold). The form of consideration must be the same as in the bid, with a presumption of fairness of the consideration if the compulsory acquisition is launched within three months of the end of the offer period and the price is the same as in the bid. Sell-out rights of remaining shareholders are designed to mirror squeeze-out rights of successful bidders. Remaining target shareholders may force the bidder to acquire their securities (following an offer to all holders for 100% of the securities) if the bidder reaches 90–95% of the capital of the target (once again leaving the determination of the exact threshold to each Member State). However, the Takeover Directive provides that sell-out rights may not be exercised where the threshold is reached temporarily. The consideration is determined in the same manner as with squeeze-out rights.

National supervisory authority and determination of applicable law

The Takeover Directive requires each Member State to establish a supervisory authority to regulate takeovers. In cross-border takeovers the supervisory authority of the country where the target company has its registered office would have jurisdiction over a bid, provided that the target's securities are traded in that country. However, if the target company has its registered office in one country and its securities are traded exclusively in another country, jurisdiction would be with the country of the primary trading market. While the supervisory authority of the country where the securities are traded would have jurisdiction over the takeover process, matters relating to employees and company law would continue to be subject to the rules and supervisory authority of the Member State where the target company has its registered office. This shared jurisdiction regime has been heavily criticised due to the potential confusion, uncertainty and delays to takeovers it may cause.

DEVELOPMENTS IN CROSS-BORDER RESTRUCTURINGS

Recent developments in cross-border restructurings include (i) in the United States, the continued use of bankruptcy proceedings under Chapter 11 of the US Bankruptcy Code (Chapter 11), the reliance on exemptions from registration under US securities laws to effect restructurings and the enactment of the Bankruptcy Reform Bill, and (ii) in Europe, efforts by many European countries to promote the renewal rather than immediate liquidation of financially troubled companies and the adoption of the EU Regulation on Insolvency Proceedings (Insolvency Regulation).

Developments in the United States

Parties involved in cross-border US/European restructurings have to determine what laws and regulations apply. Many cross-border restructurings have in recent years included proceedings under Chapter 11, either as a result of the parent or subsidiary being located, or having sufficient contacts in the United States, or have included Chapter 11 proceedings in conjunction with other insolvency proceedings or restructuring transactions in Europe.

There are several advantages to implementing a cross-border restructuring under Chapter 11. In a Chapter 11 proceeding, securities issued by a debtor, or an affiliate of (or successor to) the debtor under a Chapter 11 plan in exchange for a claim against (or an interest in) the debtor are exempt from registration under the Securities Act. In addition, when the Chapter 11 proceeding is done in conjunction with European proceedings, it may be used as the vehicle for ratification of such proceedings if necessary under US law. Further, the use of Chapter 11 in conjunction with a European proceeding provides an established process and an additional measure of procedural certainty that may otherwise be missing. Importantly, Chapter 11 is a debtor-friendly process and provides an extraterritorial automatic stay that is often vital in restructuring scenarios.

If a US/European cross-border restructuring plan does not include a proceeding under Chapter 11 – because it is unavailable, a European jurisdictional scheme provides appropriate relief or otherwise – and securities are being issued to shareholders, bondholders or other US creditors, the securities and the offer thereof, are required to be registered with the SEC absent an applicable exemption. One such exemption from registration is provided under Section 3(a)(9) of the Securities Act. Section 3(a)(9) is available when securities are exchanged by an issuer (it must be the "same" issuer) with its existing security holders and no commission or other remuneration is paid directly or indirectly for soliciting the exchange. Section 3(a)(10) of the Securities Act is another exemption from registration that applies to securities, property or other claims of a company, the terms and conditions for issuance of which have been approved by a governmental authority after a hearing on the fairness of the transaction at which interested parties may participate. The SEC has confirmed that the UK "scheme of arrangement" is eligible for 3(a)(10) treatment, but has not issued formal guidance on the analogous reorganisation proceedings of other European jurisdictions. Finally, depending on the number and/or character of the US investors involved in a restructuring proceeding, private placement exemptions from registration under the Securities Act may be available. This is particularly true if the investor group is composed entirely of hedge funds, private equity funds, arbitrageurs or other sophisticated investors and there has been no "general solicitation efforts."

In 2005, the US Congress passed the Bankruptcy Reform Bill, which, among other matters, contains the United Nations Commission on International Trade Law's (UNCITRAL) Model Law on Cross-Border Insolvency. The UNCITRAL Model Law aims to help with three issues, namely access to foreign courts, recognition of insolvency practitioners appointed in one jurisdiction by another and the degree of relief available to protect the assets in foreign jurisdictions. Other countries such as Japan, South Africa and Mexico have already enacted the Model Law, but now that the United States has passed it, there is the hope that countries such as Australia, New Zealand, Canada and the UK will quickly follow suit. The Bankruptcy Reform Bill will help make the US bankruptcy system more coherent and efficient with insolvency systems worldwide.

Developments in Europe

Many European countries have begun to promote the renewal rather than immediate liquidation of financially troubled companies. These states recognise that a vigorous entrepreneurial society is vital to sustaining economic growth and development. Although a certain number of businesses will always fail in competitive economic conditions, it is now generally accepted that viable business entities should not be allowed to terminate unnecessarily. For example, England, France, Italy and Spain have been promoting more debtor-friendly insolvency procedures and processes, in some cases largely influenced by the Chapter 11 model in the United States, to help companies survive restructuring. It has been widely accepted that encouraging the long-term rescue of the corporate entity often results in a much fairer balance between the interests of the company and its shareholders and those of its secured creditors. This movement towards the renewal of corporate entities in Europe may lead to fewer US bankruptcy filings by European companies going forward.

A further recent legislative development in the restructuring area in Europe is the coming into force of the Insolvency Regulation in May 2002. The Insolvency Regulation aims to introduce uniform conflicts of law rules for insolvency proceedings and connected judgments in the EU.[48] With the exception of Denmark, the Insolvency Regulation is directly applicable in all member states. The objective of the Insolvency Regulation is to establish common rules on cross-border insolvency proceedings, based on principles of mutual recognition and cooperation. It replaces various conventions between member states insofar as they relate to insolvency proceedings. In particular, the Insolvency Regulation aims to make pan-European insolvencies and restructurings more efficient and effective. As both the UNCITRAL Model Law and the Insolvency Regulation emphasise recognition of foreign proceedings and mutual co-operation between states, going forward these regulations are expected to reduce the need for parties to seek the protection of Chapter 11 in the United States and its automatic world wide stay.

CONCLUSION

As US/European cross-border M&A activity increases, deal makers and practitioners alike are closely following trends in takeover regulations on both sides of the Atlantic. Companies that operate and/or compete globally have realised that when engaging in cross-border M&A activity they are likely to be affected by both US and European issues, even in the context of off-shore transactions.

---

[48] The Insolvency Regulation does not, however, seek to harmonise substantive law or policy between different EU countries.

Corporate scandals in recent years in the US and Europe have resulted in expanded regulation of public companies by the SEC that is not likely to dissipate. Although many foreign issuers have objected strenuously to SOX becoming applicable to them, SOX is important because it has already produced and will continue to produce improvements that help to restore and reinforce confidence in the US markets and lower the cost of capital to both foreign and domestic issuers in the long run. The continuing globalisation of the world economy has made it virtually impossible for the SEC to adopt and enforce securities regulation without considering its impact on both domestic and foreign issuers. Foreign issuers' reaction to SOX will likely lead to a give and take by both foreign issuers and the SEC, with appropriate accommodations to foreign issuers continuing to be an irreversible feature of US securities regulation.

On the EU front, based on the range of positions taken by Member State governments on the key provisions of the Takeover Directive, it would appear that the attempt to harmonise the approach to takeover defences in the EU has failed. As a general matter and with the exception of the Netherlands, to date, courts have not factored in any significant way in many cross-border European takeover situations. Given the differences that are likely to develop between European jurisdictions as a result of the Takeover Directive, European courts may have a much more prominent role going forward.

Finally, "distressed company" regulations in the United States and Europe are continually evolving. When faced with restructurings, investors are always looking to those jurisdictions that offer certainty and mature financial markets and legal systems. This has given weight to the movement towards more debtor-friendly regimes, bankruptcy processes that aim to preserve the corporate entity and regulations that aim to harmonise international procedures in the United States and Europe.

6

Fund Managers, Investment Advisers and Funds

Barry P Barbash; Simon F T Cox

Shearman & Sterling LLP; Norton Rose

London, Tokyo, Hong Kong, Boston and other world financial centres have developed highly sophisticated fund management houses with a wealth of investment expertise. Fund managers and their clients frequently look to the US securities markets for investment opportunities. At the same time, US investors look to European fund managers to provide international investment advice. Dealing with US securities or clients can, however, subject fund managers to the requirements of the US securities laws.[1]

This chapter examines in broad terms the regulatory consequences of dealing in US securities and of providing advice to US clients. This chapter begins with a review of some of the regulatory consequences of investing in US securities. It then examines the US regulation of investment advisers and the application of that regulatory regime to non-US advisers. The regulation of non-US investment funds is then discussed, including action to avoid

---

1   It is worth noting at the outset that the terms "fund manager" and "investment adviser" are often used interchangeably in the United States and, accordingly, this chapter for most purposes does not distinguish between them. A possible distinction could be made between an investment adviser as an entity and a fund manager as an individual employed by the entity to make investment decisions. Employees who make investment decisions are also sometimes referred to as "portfolio managers". Under the US regulatory scheme, only the entity must register with the SEC as an investment adviser in general, although some states impose registration requirements on employees of the adviser who act as the adviser's "advisory representatives". In some cases individuals may register with the SEC as investment advisers, but such persons tend to be financial planners or other similar professionals serving non-institutional clients.

registration obligations under the 1940 Act. Next, the ancillary US regulations such as certain special US federal income tax rules and ERISA, which addresses the management of US pension funds, are summarised. Finally, the application of SOX to the investment management industry is described.

TRADING US SECURITIES
Trading on a non-US exchange

As suggested above, many non-US fund management houses employ staff that are experts on the US markets and wish to trade in US securities on behalf of their clients. The ability of a non-US fund manager to trade directly in US securities will depend in part on where such trading takes place. For example, trading US securities "offshore" is treated differently from dealing in such securities in the United States.

In London, for example dealings in international securities can be effected on the London Stock Exchange (LSE) through the "International Order Book" (IOB), and the "International Bulletin Board" (ITBB). The IOB and ITBB are administered by the LSE. The IOB enables trading of depositary receipts, and the ITBB facilitates trading in overseas equity securities. As of June 2005 there were some 224 overseas securities traded on the IOB and 243 securities traded on the ITBB.

The IOB and ITBB enable trading in these securities – this is not the same as a listing. If a security is not listed in London, to be eligible for the IOB and ITBB, a security must be listed on at least one exchange that is a member or corresponding member of the World Federation of Exchanges. The IOB is an order driven system, whereby orders are submitted by a member firm, usually on behalf of a client, and are executed electronically. While the ITBB offers the same advantages of electronic execution as that of the IOB, this mechanism also offers the opportunity for participants to register as Market Makers to support trading liquidity. The core trading hours for the IOB and the ITBB are 09.00 to 15.30 with an auction which both precedes and follows these times.

Where a security is traded on IOB or ITBB, the relevant trading rules will be those of the LSE and any other body regulating the individual participants, not the SEC. These rules can afford London and other European fund management houses greater flexibility in buying and selling US securities than if they were to seek to deal in such securities in the United States.[2] Non-US fund managers are not permitted to trade on a US exchange without SEC registration as a broker–dealer and therefore must trade through a US-registered broker–dealer. (For a discussion of Exchange Act Rule 15a-6, see Chapter 7.) Provided that it deals solely through a registered broker–dealer registered with the SEC, a non-US fund manager will not be required to register for that activity.

Potential disclosure requirements

Simply by purchasing the equity shares of a US corporation, an investor (including non-US investors), whether acting as principal or on behalf of clients, may become subject to certain SEC reporting requirements.

5% beneficial owners

As discussed in Chapter 2 and elsewhere in this book, Section 13 of the Exchange Act requires that any person who acquires beneficial ownership of more than 5% of a class of equity securities that are registered with the SEC under the Exchange Act must file a report on Schedule 13D with the SEC, the issuer and the exchange where the securities trade within 10 days of crossing the threshold.[3] Certain institutional investors, however, may be eligible to file a short form Schedule 13G if they satisfy a number of specific criteria, including, among other requirements, that the institutional investor:

(a) has acquired more than 5% of an issuer's equity securities in the ordinary course of business;
(b) has not acquired the securities for the purpose of changing or influencing control of the issuer; and
(c) is an investment adviser registered with the SEC pursuant to the Advisers Act or an investment company registered with the SEC under the 1940 Act.

Schedules 13D and 13G require the disclosure of information such as a description of the purchaser and the purchaser's business, a

---

2 However, as described below, there may be SEC implications in relation to the amount of holdings.
3 As defined in Section 13(d)(3) of the Exchange Act, the term "person" includes two or more people acting as a partnership, limited partnership, syndicate or other group for the purpose of acquiring, holding or disposing of securities of an issuer.

description of the securities purchased and the amount of securities owned by the purchaser. In addition, Schedule 13D requires the disclosure of such additional information as the purpose for acquiring the securities, including any intended acquisition or merger.

10% beneficial owners
The US federal securities laws presume that "statutory insiders" – namely, officers, directors and certain persons who acquire beneficial ownership of more than 10% of a class of equity securities registered under the Exchange Act – can use their position of influence to obtain and trade on the basis of confidential information. To prevent this potential abuse, Section 16 of the Exchange Act requires statutory insiders to refrain from making "short-swing" profits (i.e. gains made or losses avoided from the purchase and sale of the issuer's securities or certain security-based swap agreements involving these securities in any six-month period). Under Section 16, statutory insiders must also submit to the SEC the following forms, which the agency uses to monitor compliance with the short-swing profit prohibition:

(a) an initial report, on a Form 3, to be filed generally within 10 days of the person becoming a statutory insider;
(b) a Form 4, to be filed before the end of the second business day following the day on which the insider's securities holdings changed, or the purchase or sale of a security-based swap agreement, save for specified cases where the person cannot control the trade date;[4] and
(c) a Form 5, to be filed within 45 days of the close of the issuer's calendar year on which the insider should report exempt and previously unreported transactions.

In determining whether an investment adviser is subject to Section 16 based on the 10% test, two levels of analysis are required. First, an investment adviser must possess beneficial ownership of the relevant securities. The term beneficial ownership generally includes situations where an adviser maintains voting or investment power. Most

---

4 The SEC extended the two-business-day filing requirement in the following instances: (1) discretionary transactions under an employee benefit plan (e.g. intra-plan transfers) and (2) transactions pursuant to a contract, instruction or plan that satisfies the requirements of Rule 10b5-1 under the Exchange Act. Exchange Act Release 46421 (27th August 2002).

investment advisers fall under this broad definition of beneficial owner. Secondly, however, an investment adviser may be excluded from the definition of beneficial owner for the purposes of Section 16 if it holds shares as a fiduciary for clients in the ordinary course of business, not for the purpose of changing or influencing control of the issuer, and is properly registered under the Advisers Act.[5]

Finally, if an investment adviser becomes subject to Section 16, only transactions in which it holds a "pecuniary interest" must be reported and only those transactions are subject to the short-swing profit prohibition. In general, a pecuniary interest only arises for an investment adviser where it charges a performance-based fee, but not where the fee is based on net capital gains or appreciation generated from the portfolio or the fiduciary's overall performance over a period of at least one year and the equity securities of the issuer do not account for more than 10% of the portfolio.

Institutional investment managers

US securities laws also require that certain fund managers who invest in large amounts of US equity securities must submit quarterly reports to the SEC. The SEC uses this information to maintain a database on the activities of investment managers. Section 13(f) of the Exchange Act and Rule 13f-1 thereunder require quarterly reports from "institutional investment managers" who exercise investment discretion[6] over US$100 million in US equity securities that trade on a US exchange or on NASDAQ. "Institutional investment managers" include non-natural persons who invest in or buy securities for their own account, or who exercise investment discretion over the account of any other person. These regulations also apply to both US and non-US fund managers who otherwise meet the stated requirements.

An institutional investment manager must file a Form 13F report within 45 days of the end of the calendar quarter during which it crossed the US$100 million threshold. It must continue to file this form for each quarter that its applicable holdings exceed the

---

5 A similar analysis must be undertaken to determine whether an investment company is subject to the requirements of Exchange Act Section 16.
6 Investment discretion generally occurs when a person has the authority to determine which securities to buy and sell for an account, exercises influence over which securities to buy or sell, or actually makes such decisions.

threshold amount. The Form 13F requires the disclosure of four basic types of information:

(a) details regarding the identity of the manager;
(b) a description of the securities over which it exercises investment discretion;
(c) the degree of voting authority it exercises; and
(d) the names of any other institutional investment managers with whom it exercises any shared investment discretion. In recognition of the fact that the information on a Form 13F may be sensitive, the SEC will consider requests to keep the information confidential.[7]

Implications of Regulation S and Rule 144A

As discussed in Chapter 2, Section 5 of the Securities Act requires that any securities publicly sold in the United States must be registered with the SEC. In 1990, the SEC introduced Regulation S under the Securities Act to provide market participants with some assurance as to when securities offered and sold outside the United States do not need to be registered with the SEC. As discussed in Chapter 3, Regulation S contains two safe harbours – that is, detailed sets of procedures that if followed will ensure that registration is not required. The first safe harbour addresses offers and sales of securities issued outside the United States by issuers, distributors and respective affiliates. The second safe harbour addresses resales of securities outside the United States. In this chapter, we focus on the responsibilities of fund managers in relation to participation as investors in primary offers and in relation to trades in existing securities in the secondary market.

In relation to an offer of new securities, the primary responsibility for ensuring compliance with US securities laws falls on the issuer and those effecting or promoting the issue on their behalf. As such, mere receipt of a US information memorandum that should not have been sent to the recipient will not cause the recipient to breach US securities laws. However, assuming that the issue is being properly effected, a non-US person may be required to

---

[7] The SEC has issued a comprehensive Q&A regarding Form 13F filings called "Frequently Asked Questions about Form 13F", posted on the SEC's website at www.sec.gov/offices/invmgt/13ffaq.htm.

execute a representation letter on which the Regulation S issuer and its advisers will rely in determining whether or not the relevant securities may be sold to such person. In a Regulation S offer, the key representation will typically be that the applicant is not a US person as defined thereunder. If a potential buyer makes a false representation in connection with a Regulation S offer, the issuer could bring a private cause of action against applicants who misrepresent their status. The laws governing the private action would typically be determined by reference to choice of law provisions contained in the purchase agreement.

In relation to the secondary market, a fund manager involved in the disposal of Regulation S securities should seek to ensure that resales are made in conformity with the requirements of Regulation S. This may or may not require the fund manager to establish whether the purchaser is a US person, depending on the category of the Regulation S security. In any event, securities acquired in a Regulation S offer may not be resold in the United States unless they are registered under the Securities Act or are otherwise exempt. If a fund manager sells the securities outside the Regulation S safe harbour, it could, under certain circumstances, be deemed a "statutory underwriter" (under Section 2(11) of the Securities Act) and in violation of Section 5 of the Securities Act.

Similarly, fund manager may wish to purchase tranches of securities that have been offered to them by QIBs. Rule 144A, discussed in Chapter 3, is a safe harbour from the registration requirements of Section 5 of the Securities Act and permits QIBs to buy and sell tranches of securities that have been initially sold in an offer that is exempt from registration under Section 5 of the Securities Act (commonly, Regulation S or Regulation D) and then resold to QIBs. Broker–dealers that place Rule 144A securities, which are "restricted securities", require that the purchasers of such securities certify that they are QIBs. Rule 144A securities, if they are purchased by a fund manager for the portfolio of a client – whether or not a US person – must ensure that they obtain assurances from the buyer of their client's securities that the buyer is, in fact, a QIB.

NASD 2790

In December 2003, the NASD issued Rule 2790 regarding the distribution of new issues, which are equity securities as defined in

Section 3(a)(11) of the Securities Act sold through an SEC registered initial public offering. NASD Rule 2790 replaced the Free-Riding and Withholding Interpretation that established the rules for distributing hot issues.

NASD Rule 2790 made several important changes regarding the distribution of equity securities in initial public offerings. For example, while the Free-Riding and Withholding Interpretation applied to hot issues,[8] Rule 2790 applies to new issues of equity securities that are distributed in IPOs registered with the SEC. Rule 2790 also eliminated the category of "conditionally restricted persons" – under the Rule someone is either a "restricted person" or they are not.

Rule 2790 generally prohibits NASD members from selling new issues to accounts in which a restricted person has a beneficial interest. For purposes of the Rule, restricted persons include, among others:

- NASD members or other broker-dealers;
- broker–dealer personnel;
- portfolio managers; and
- immediate family members of the above.

The general prohibition is subject to a *de minimis* exemption for accounts in which the beneficial interests of restricted person in the aggregate do not exceed 10%.

An account can qualify for the *de minimis* exemption even if restricted persons have, in the aggregate, greater than 10% beneficial interests if the account allocates not more than 10% of any new issues allocation it receives to such restricted persons. This carve-down provision provides flexibility to pooled investment accounts that have restricted persons with greater than 10% beneficial interests in the pooled account. Such an account can remain eligible to receive new issues by allocating not more than 10% of any new issues allocation it receives to restricted persons in the account. A pooled investment account will need to provide a certification to NASD members that either it has no restricted persons with beneficial interests in the account, or it meets the *de minimis* exemption.

---

8   Hot issues are equity securities distributed in an initial public offering that trade in the open market at prices greater than their offering price.

THE REGULATION OF INVESTMENT ADVISERS – SOLICITING AND SERVICING US CLIENTS

Just as non-US clients may wish to contract with a US fund manager or adviser in respect of, typically, the US component in their portfolio, so may US investors wish to contract with overseas fund managers for specialist advice on non-US securities. The US securities laws generally apply to non-US fund managers providing advice to US clients. This section begins with an overview of US regulation of investment advisers. Some of the more significant provisions of the Advisers Act are then highlighted, and the reach of the Advisers Act to non-US advisers and the requirement to register with the SEC are examined. Finally, some of the US regulatory implications for US advisers servicing non-US clients are briefly reviewed.

Overview of US regulation of investment advisers

The Advisers Act, enacted by Congress, and the rules thereunder, adopted by the SEC, regulate the activities of investment advisers. In general, the Advisers Act and its rules require any investment adviser that uses the US mail or any other means of US interstate commerce in connection with its business as an investment adviser to register with the SEC. Consequently, domestic US investment advisers and non-US investment advisers with more than a specified number of US clients are generally required to register under the Advisers Act and are subject to a host of regulations.

The Advisers Act has been interpreted by the SEC as reflecting two basic principles aimed at protecting the interests of clients: (a) an investment adviser is a fiduciary with respect to its clients and customers; and (b) as fiduciary, the adviser is required to disclose to its clients and customers any actual or apparent conflicts of interest to which the adviser is subject. The Advisers Act also restricts performance fees, advertising and cross-selling, and contains disclosure, record-keeping and other obligations. The Advisers Act and its related rules are relatively succinct, but have been supplemented by SEC enforcement actions and Staff interpretations and guidance.

The term "investment adviser" is defined in Section 202(a)(11) of the Advisers Act, and generally includes any person or firm that:

1. for compensation;
2. is engaged in the business of;

3. providing advice, making recommendations, issuing reports or furnishing analyses on securities, either directly or through publications. A person or firm must satisfy all three elements to be regulated under the Advisers Act. However, the SEC Staff has construed the elements quite broadly and, for example performing any of the following activities would generally satisfy the "providing advice" element: advice about market trends; advice in the form of statistical or historical data (unless the data is no more than an objective report of facts on a non-selective basis); advice about the selection of an investment adviser; advice concerning the advantages of investing in securities instead of other types of investments; and publishing a list of securities from which a client can choose, even if the adviser does not make specific recommendations from the list.[9]

Persons meeting the definition of an "investment adviser" generally must register with the SEC, unless they are eligible for any one of a number of exemptions from the registration requirement in Section 203(b) of the Advisers Act. Although these exemptions do not apply to the typical fund manager, in some cases these exemptions may be relevant.[10] In particular, the Advisers Act exempts advisers who:

(a) during the previous 12 months have had a total of fewer than 15 clients;
(b) do not hold themselves out generally to the public as an investment adviser; and
(c) do not act as an investment adviser to a registered investment company or "business development company" (which is, in essence and as defined in the Advisers Act, a pooled entity engaged in the venture capital business). The SEC has interpreted this exemption as requiring US advisers to include all non-US clients when counting its total number of clients. However, non-US advisers need only count their US clients.[11]

---

[9] See Investment Advisers Act Release 2376 (12th April 2005), which contains a general discussion of the regulatory scheme contained in the Advisers Act; and Investment Advisers Act Release 1092 (8th October 1987).
[10] See Section 203(b) of the Advisers Act for a complete list of exemptions.
[11] See *Murray Johnstone Holdings Limited* (17th April 1987); *Alexander, Holburn, Beaudin & Lang* (13th April 1984).

Any adviser not exempt from the registration requirements must complete and submit to the SEC a Form ADV, which contains two parts. Part I of the Form requires advisers to provide information concerning, among other matters, the adviser's name and address, its form of organisation and background information regarding legal and disciplinary matters. Part I of the Form was amended in 2000 by the SEC to increase the level of disclosure regarding disciplinary information relevant to the adviser and certain members of its advisory personnel. At the same time, other changes were made to Part I of the Form to enable it to be filed electronically.[12] Part II, which must be provided to clients, requires the provision of additional information such as a description of business operations, fees charged, types of clients serviced, types of securities about which the adviser provides advice and methods of securities analysis. Part II also requires disclosure of actual and potential conflicts of interest, including whether an adviser engages in principal trades with clients, effects cross trades between clients or uses itself or an affiliate to effect client trades for a fee. Part II of the Form is currently not required to be filed electronically, pending amendments to the Form by the SEC. Every Form ADV must be kept up-to-date by filing prompt and periodic amendments, including an annual amendment to Schedule I of the Form. Advisers seeking SEC registration must submit a completed Form ADV to the SEC, with Part I to be filed electronically through the Investment Advisers Registration Depository (IARD) and Part II to be filed on paper.[13] Within 45 days of receipt, the SEC will issue an order granting the registration or, in some instances, institute a proceeding to determine whether such registration should be granted.

Advisers who do not have a principal place of business in a location subject to US jurisdiction must undertake additional steps at US time of registration. These "non-resident" advisers need to complete an appropriate form granting the SEC a power of attorney and consent for the SEC to act as agent for service of process in civil matters.[14] In addition, a non-resident investment adviser

---

12 *See* Advisers Act Release 1897; available at www.sec.gov/rules/final/ia-1897.htm
13 *See* www.iard.com for more information on the Form ADV electronic filing process.
14 The SEC forms to meet this requirement are: Form 4-R for individual non-resident investment advisers; Form 5-R for corporate non-resident investment advisers; Form 6-R for

may need to attach a notice to its Form ADV that identifies the address where the adviser will maintain books and records required by the Advisers Act.[15]

There are specific obligations that arise in the context of particular types of clients. These include ERISA plans, to which we refer in the following.

Significant provisions of the Advisers Act

The following is a summary of some of the key provisions of the Advisers Act and rules under the Advisers Act that apply to those subject to regulation under the Act.

The brochure rule – delivery of Form ADV

Rule 204–3 under the Advisers Act places an obligation on advisers to make initial and periodic deliveries of its Form ADV to clients or prospective clients. The Advisers Act requires an adviser to furnish an initial copy of Part II of its Form ADV (or a brochure containing all of the information required under Part II) to a prospective client at least 48 hours before entering into an advisory agreement, or at the time of the agreement if the client has five days thereafter to terminate the agreement without penalty. Thereafter, an adviser must deliver, or offer in writing to deliver, a copy of its brochure annually, as long as clients meet certain *de minimis* requirements.

Record-keeping requirements

Registered investment advisers must keep and preserve certain books and records and make them available for inspection by the SEC. The books and records that Rule 204–2 under the Advisers Act requires to be kept generally include business organisation records, accounting records, client records (including contracts and correspondence), securities trading records, advertising records and certain e-mail correspondence and records. Advisers who maintain custody of client assets must keep and preserve additional books and records. Non-resident investment advisers must maintain copies of the required books and records at a place in the United States designated

---

partnership non-resident investment advisers; and Form 7-R for non-resident general partners of investment advisers.
15 The requirements for maintaining books and records are set out in Rule 204 under the Advisers Act. Rule 204-2(j) addresses the requirements for non-resident investment advisers.

by it in a notice to the SEC or, alternatively, must file an undertaking with the SEC to provide accurate copies of the required books and records on demand by the SEC.

Fees

The Advisers Act limits the types of fees that advisers may charge their clients. Section 205(a)(1) of the Advisers Act states as a general proposition that advisers may not perform advisory services where compensation is based "on a share of capital gains upon or capital appreciation of the funds or any portion of the funds of the client". Notwithstanding this clause, an adviser may charge a "fulcrum fee", a form of a performance fee, to 1940 Act registered investment companies or to a client who invests more than US$1 million with the adviser. An adviser may also charge a performance fee to any person who is not a resident of the United States. The SEC has granted additional relief from the performance-fee prohibition in Rule 205–3 of the Advisers Act. This Rule provides that an adviser may charge a performance fee to certain types of financially sophisticated clients, including:

(a) any client with at least US$750,000 under management by the adviser or whom the adviser reasonably believes has a net worth of more than US$1.5 million;
(b) qualified purchasers as defined in the 1940 Act; and
(c) certain members of the adviser's "knowledgeable" employees, as defined in Rule 3c-5 under the 1940 Act.

In the case of *inter alia* a private investment company[16] and an investment company registered under the 1940 Act, each equity owner of any such company (except for the investment adviser entering into the contract and any other equity owners not charged a fee on the basis of a share of capital gains or capital appreciation) will be considered a client for the purposes of this Section. As such, where a registered investment adviser is entitled to a performance fee from a fund, US investors must fall within one of these exemptions, in addition to any other exemptions required under other provisions of applicable laws.

---

16 Being a company that would be defined as an investment company under Section 3(a) of the 1940 Act but for the exception provided from that definition by Section 3(c)(1) of such Act.

Advertising restrictions

The Advisers Act bars specific types of advertising by registered advisers. Rule 206(4)-1 prohibits or restricts: the use of testimonials; references to past specific recommendations without also disclosing extensive information about a variety of past recommendations; representations that graphs, charts or formulas can be used to determine which securities to buy or sell; any suggestion that services will be rendered free of charge unless such services are actually free of charge; and any untrue or misleading statements.

Although Rule 206(4)-1 generally restricts the use of past specific recommendations in advertisements by advisers, the Staff granted a no-action request in March 2004 regarding an investment adviser's use of past specific recommendations in written materials provided to clients, prospective clients or consultants. The Staff stated that the use of past specific recommendations in written materials under certain circumstances would not be considered an advertisement within the meaning of Rule 206(4)-1. The Staff's position in *Investment Counsel Association of America, Inc.* was based on the client, prospective client or consultant making an unsolicited request of the adviser to provide written information about the adviser's past specific recommendations. In addition to being unsolicited, the request from the client, prospective client or consultant needs to specifically request information about the adviser's past specific recommendations.

Insider trading – required policies and procedures

Under Section 204A of the Advisers Act, an adviser must "establish, maintain and enforce written policies and procedures reasonably designed, taking into consideration the nature of such investment adviser's business, to prevent the misuse of material non-public information by such investment adviser or any person associated with such investment adviser". To meet the requirements of this Section, the policies and procedures must be customised to the adviser's particular operations and activities and generally:

(a) place reasonable restrictions on employees' personal securities trades;

(b) establish monitoring and reviewing of employee trades;

(c) limit access to internal, non-public information; and (d) provide continuing education for their employees.[17]

Proxy voting procedures

Rule 206(4)-6 under the Advisers Act prohibits a registered adviser from exercising voting authority with respect to client securities unless:

- ❏ the adviser establishes written policies and procedures that are reasonably designed to ensure that the adviser votes client securities in the best interest of its clients;
- ❏ the policies and procedures include a description of how the adviser addresses material conflicts of interest that may arise between the interests of the adviser and the interests of its clients;
- ❏ the adviser discloses to its clients how they may obtain information about how the adviser voted with respect to their securities; and
- ❏ the adviser describes its proxy voting policies and procedures to its clients, and furnishes a copy of the policies to clients, upon request.

Custody rule

Rule 206(4)-2 under the Advisers Act generally prohibits a registered investment adviser from maintaining custody of client funds or securities unless a qualified custodian maintains the funds or securities. For purposes of Rule 206(4)-2, an adviser is deemed to have custody of client funds or securities if:

- ❏ it has possession of client funds or securities (but not of cheques drawn by clients and made payable to third parties);
- ❏ any arrangement under which the adviser is authorised or permitted to withdraw client funds or securities maintained with a custodian upon instruction to the custodian; and
- ❏ any capacity (such as general partner of a limited partnership or managing member of a limited liability company) that gives the adviser legal ownership of or access to client funds or securities. A qualified custodian includes banks, registered broker–dealers,

---

17 *See In re Gabelli & Co., Inc.*, Exchange Act Release 35057 (8th December 1994); *In re Fox-Pitt, Kelton, Inc.*, Exchange Act Release 37940 (12th November 1996); and *In re Guy P Wyser-Pratte*, Advisers Act Release 1943 (9th May 2001).

registered futures commission merchants and non-US financial institutions that customarily hold financial assets for customers, provided that the institution keeps the client's funds and securities in accounts segregated from the institution's proprietary assets.

In maintaining a client's funds and securities, the qualified custodian may maintain either separate accounts in the name of the clients, or an account in the name of the adviser, if that account contains only the clients' funds and securities. An adviser must notify its clients of the qualified custodian's name and contact information. The client must also receive a quarterly statement either from the custodian or from the adviser. If the adviser elects to send the quarterly statements itself, the adviser must have an independent auditor examine and verify the client funds and securities at least once per year. The examination is required to be done without notice to the adviser and on an irregular schedule from year to year. The auditor is required to notify the SEC of any material discrepancies discovered during the examination.

Rule 206(4)-2 contains an exception from its provisions for certain privately offered securities. An adviser does not have to comply with the Rule with respect to securities that are:

- acquired from the issuer in a transaction that does not involve a public offering;
- uncertificated; and
- transferable only with the prior consent of the issuer or the holders of the outstanding securities of the issuer. Securities that are held for the account of a pooled investment vehicle may rely on this exception only if the pooled vehicle is audited annually in accordance with GAAP and the audited statements are sent to holders of the pooled vehicle's securities within 120 days of the end of the fiscal year of the pooled vehicle. A fund-of-funds that has at least 10% of its assets invested in other pooled investment vehicles must send audited financial statements within 180 days of the end of its fiscal year.

Compliance procedures
Rule 206(4)-7 under the Advisers Act requires that registered investment advisers implement written policies and procedures reasonably

FUND MANAGERS, INVESTMENT ADVISERS AND FUNDS

designed to prevent violation of the Advisers Act and the rules issued under the Advisers Act, by the adviser or by "associated persons of the adviser" as defined. The adviser is required to review, on at least an annual basis, the adequacy of the policies and procedures, as well as the effectiveness of their implementation. The adviser must also appoint an individual that is a supervised person of the adviser as the chief compliance officer. The chief compliance officer (COO) is responsible for administering the policies and procedures adopted pursuant to Rule 206(4)-7. The CCO can be someone other than an employee of the adviser, which is to say that the position can be outsourced, although the Staff has suggested that doing so needs to be undertaken carefully.[18]

Transactions with clients

The Advisers Act limits the ability of advisers to engage in principal transactions as well as agency cross transactions with or on behalf of clients. Section 206(3) requires that, prior to completing each such transaction, an adviser must disclose in writing to the client the capacity in which it is acting and the terms of the proposed transaction, as well as obtain the consent of the client prior to the completion, or settlement, of the transaction. Rule 206(3)-2, however, grants advisers some flexibility in executing agency cross transactions. If such transactions conform to a strict five-part test that includes prior written disclosure and the receipt of prospective authorisation from the client, the adviser does not need to comply with the separate disclosure and consent requirement for each transaction.

In addition, the SEC has also established restrictions on an adviser's ability to use itself or an affiliate to act as broker for executing client transactions. If an adviser uses itself or an affiliate, the adviser must disclose this practice on its Form ADV and, as with any client transaction, continue to ensure that these transactions receive best price and execution.

Anti-fraud provisions

Section 206 of the Advisers Act prohibits an adviser from engaging in acts or practices that would constitute a fraud on clients. This prohibition extends to practices such as trading ahead of buy or sell

---

[18] Speech by Lori A. Richards, Director, Office of Compliance and Examinations, SEC, 28th June 2004.

recommendations, unfairly favouring certain clients in the allocation of securities and accepting prohibited or undisclosed soft-commission benefits.

US regulation of non-US investment advisers

With the growing internationalisation of securities markets and increasing investments by non-US persons in the United States and by US citizens abroad, the SEC has been confronted with issues concerning the application of the Advisers Act to various situations involving non-US advisers or non-US clients. Recognising that the requirements of the Advisers Act can be cumbersome for companies that have most of their dealings outside the United States and detrimental to the interests of US investors who might not receive the benefit of the most expert advice on certain foreign investments, the SEC and its Staff have, over time, tried to interpret the Advisers Act to balance its concerns of protecting investors with its desire to promote efficiency in the global markets. Meeting this challenge is critical. For instance, as of May 1997, there were some 400 non-US advisers registered with the SEC, with an aggregate of over US$2.3 trillion under management.[19] As discussed in more detail below, a non-US adviser may be required to register with the SEC either based on the "conduct and effects" test, or based on recently amended Rule 203(b)(3)-2, which applies new guidelines on counting clients for advisers of "private funds".

Historical background

Before 1992, the Division of Investment Management took an extremely broad view of the extraterritorial application of the Advisers Act – namely, that non-US investment advisers with US clients who are required to register with the SEC must comply with all of the Advisers Act's provisions, even with respect to their non-US clients. Since 1981, many non-US advisers entered the US market through registered, separately established advisory affiliates under the guidelines of the Staff's Richard Ellis, Inc no-action letter (hereafter referred to as *"Richard Ellis"*),[20] because these non-US firms were generally unwilling to subject their entire operations to

---

[19] Speech by SEC Commissioner Isaac C. Hunt, Jr, 5th May 1997.
[20] Richard Ellis, Inc. (17th September 1981).

US regulation.[21] Complying with *Richard Ellis* was less than an ideal solution – establishing a separate registered affiliate was both cumbersome and expensive, and compliance with its requirements resulted in an unsatisfactory delivery of advisory services. For example, portfolio managers were not permitted to work for both the principal company and the registered affiliate. As a result, US clients were disadvantaged as they were being denied access to a non-US adviser's most-talented managers.

Current SEC position
The Staff acknowledged the shortcomings of *Richard Ellis* in its 1992 study, Protecting Investors: A Half Century of Investment Company Regulations (1992 Study). The 1992 Study recommended a new "conduct and effects" test whereby the Advisers Act would be applied to activities where a sizeable amount of advisory services takes place in, or where the advisory services have substantial effects in, the United States. In essence, the 1992 Study suggested that a non-US adviser registered under the Advisers Act would no longer be required to adhere to the substantive requirements of the Advisers Act with respect to its non-US clients. This position would eliminate the need for non-US advisers to establish and register a separate affiliate to service only their US clients. Additionally, if a non-US fund management house already had such an affiliate, the principal company would no longer be required to maintain strict separation between it and the subsidiary as was required under *Richard Ellis*.

The Staff acted upon its 1992 Study and took a more liberal position with respect to requirements imposed on US-registered advisers based outside the US and their affiliates. The Staff's initial effort at reform occurred in July 1992 in a no-action letter, Uniao de Bancos de Brasileiros S.A.[22] In this letter, the Staff took the position that the substantive provisions of the Advisers Act *generally do not apply* to dealings between a non-US adviser registered under the Advisers Act and its clients. The Staff also indicated that a parent company sharing personnel with a registered non-US adviser did not need to register under the Advisers Act.

---

21 Among the requirements set out in *Richard Ellis* was that the affiliate have employees who were separate from those of the principal company.
22 Uniao de Bancos de Brasileiros S.A (28th July 1992).

The Staff's next significant position on the issue of non-registered, non-US affiliates occurred in April 1993 in the no-action letter *Mercury Asset Management plc*.[23] In this letter, the Staff took the position that employees of non-registered, non-US affiliates of a US-registered adviser – that is, participating affiliates – may advise US clients of the registered adviser through the registered adviser if certain conditions (described in the following) were met. The Staff's position in the Mercury Asset Management letter was reinforced in the subsequent letters *Kleinwort Benson Investment Management Limited et al.*[24] and *Murray Johnstone Holdings Limited et al.*[25]

These letters appear to recognise the benefits of non-US affiliates of registered advisers providing advice to US investors and/or sharing their research with their registered US affiliates without having to register under, and comply with, the substantive requirements of the Advisers Act. These non-US affiliates often have greater expertise in dealings with specific markets, industries or securities. The Staff recognises that depriving US investors of the benefit of these non-US affiliates' expertise can be detrimental to the investors and leads to an inefficient allocation of investment resources.

Limited application of the Advisers Act

Under the "conduct and effects" approach, non-US advisers can register under the Advisers Act, yet abide by its substantive requirements only with respect to US clients. The Staff has applied this principle when an adviser has indicated that it will:

- comply with all requirements of the Advisers Act with respect to its US clients;
- comply with the record-keeping requirements of the Advisers Act and Rule 204–2 with respect to all its clients;
- promptly provide to the SEC books and records that Rule 204–2 requires the adviser to keep at any time when the adviser receives an administrative subpoena, demand or request for voluntary co-operation made during an inspection;

---

23 *Mercury Asset Management plc* (16th April 1993).
24 *Kleinwort Benson Investment Management Limited et al.* (15th December 1993), which took the position that a registered foreign adviser could employ personnel simultaneously with a participating affiliate without the participating affiliate having to register under the Advisers Act.
25 *Murray Johnstone Holdings Limited et al.* (7 October 1994).

- make available to the SEC any personnel for testimony at any time when the adviser receives an administrative subpoena, demand or request for voluntary co-operation made during a Staff inspection;
- list on its Form ADV all directors of the adviser and each investment manager who provides advice to US clients; and
- not hold itself out to non-US clients as being registered under the Advisers Act – more specifically, if an adviser sends correspondence to both US and non-US clients, it must send separate communications, delete references to the adviser's registration under the Advisers Act in communications sent to non-US clients and explain in the correspondence to non-US clients that the adviser adheres to the requirements of the Advisers Act only with respect to US clients.

Requirements for use of participating affiliates

The Staff has taken the position that when a participating affiliate of a registered adviser provides investment advice to the clients of the registered adviser, both the registered adviser and the participating affiliate should satisfy the following criteria aimed at safeguarding the interests of the registered adviser's clients.

Obligations of the registered adviser. A registered adviser whose US clients receive advice from its participating affiliates should follow certain practices in addition to ordinary compliance with the record-keeping and disclosure requirements under the Advisers Act and the related rules. These include the following:

- the registered adviser must be a legal entity separate and distinct from its participating affiliate;
- each participating affiliate and each employee of the participating affiliate, including research analysts who provide advice to the registered adviser's US clients or have access to any information concerning securities being recommended to the registered adviser's US clients must be considered an "associated person"[26] of the registered adviser;

---

26 The registered adviser is obligated to monitor the activities of "associated persons" as defined in Section 202(a)(17) of the Advisers Act. Under the Section, such a person includes, among others, partners, officers, directors and employees of an adviser. The Advisers Act and its rules have numerous requirements applicable to such persons. *See* Section 203(e)(5) of the Advisers Act (adviser registration can be revoked if associated persons have wilfully

- ❏ if the registered adviser and a participating affiliate jointly employ personnel, a situation often referred to as resulting in "dual employees", the registered adviser must ensure that, in any communications between dual employees and the registered adviser's clients, it is clear that the communications are from the registered adviser and not from the employees of the participating affiliate;
- ❏ similarly, dual employees must make clear when dealing with clients or potential clients of the registered adviser that they are acting in their capacity as representatives of the registered adviser and not of the participating affiliate; and
- ❏ the registered adviser must disclose in its Form ADV that participating affiliates may recommend to, or invest on behalf of, their own clients the securities that they recommend to, or trade on behalf of, the registered adviser's clients.

Obligations of the participating affiliate. The participating affiliate that advises clients of the US registered adviser should:

- ❏ ensure that advice given to US persons is provided only through the registered adviser;
- ❏ provide to the registered adviser the names and other required information for all associated persons that the registered adviser is required to disclose on its Form ADV;
- ❏ maintain certain personal trading records[27] under the Advisers Act for all "advisory representatives"[28] of the participating affiliate who provide advice to the US clients of the registered adviser;

---

violated securities laws before or after their association with adviser) and Section 204A of the Advisers Act described above (adviser must enforce procedures to prevent violation of securities laws by associated persons).

27 Rule 204-2(a)(12) under the Advisers Act requires an investment adviser to maintain a record of every transaction in a security in which the investment adviser or any of its advisory representatives has any direct or indirect beneficial ownership. The Staff's position with respect to advisory representatives of participating affiliates is designed to ensure that US clients are treated the same as non-US clients.

28 An "advisory representative" is defined in Rule 204-2(a)(12)(iii)(A) to include: (a) any partner, director or officer of the investment adviser; (b) any employee who makes or participates in the determination of any recommendation; (c) any employee who, in connection with his duties, obtains any information concerning the securities to be recommended prior to such recommendation; and (d) any person in a control relationship with the adviser, any affiliated person of such controlling person or any affiliated person of such affiliated person who obtains information of the recommendations to be made prior to such recommendations.

- keep certain books and records specified in Rule 204–2(a)(1), (2) and (4)–(6)[29] and Rule 204–2(c)[30] under the Advisers Act for all transactions; it should also keep books and records required in Rule 204–2(a)(3) and (7)[31] under the Advisers Act for transactions involving the registered adviser's US clients and all related transactions; the participating affiliate should keep books and records for five years from the end of the fiscal year during which the last entry was made;
- translate, if necessary, the required books and records into English;
- provide to the SEC or to the registered adviser all required books and records during an inspection or upon receipt of an administrative subpoena from the SEC; the participating affiliate should make available for testimony, in a locale specified by the SEC, all personnel identified as having been involved in providing advice to the registered adviser's US clients; it should authorise all personnel to testify about all advice given to the registered adviser's US clients; in addition, it should agree not to contest the validity of administrative subpoenas;
- submit to the jurisdiction of the US courts for actions arising under securities laws arising out of, or relating to, any investment

---

[29] These books and records include: (a) journals, including cash receipts and disbursement records, and any other records of original entry forming the basis of entries in any ledger; (b) general and auxiliary ledgers (or other comparable records) reflecting asset, liability, reserve, capital, income and expense accounts; (c) all cheque books, bank statements, cancelled cheques and cash reconciliations of the investment adviser; (d) all bills and statements (or copies of them), paid or unpaid, relating to the business of the investment adviser; and (e) all trial balances, financial statements and internal audit working papers relating to the business of the investment adviser.

[30] This rule requires that, with respect to each portfolio being supervised or managed, the investment adviser keep the following records: (a) records showing separately for each client the securities purchased and sold, and the date, amount and price of each purchase and sale; and (b) for each security in which any client has a current position, information from which the investment adviser can promptly furnish the name of each client and the current amount or interest of such client.

[31] These books and records include: (a) memoranda of each order given by the investment adviser for the purchase or sale of any security, of any instruction received by the investment adviser from the client concerning the purchase, sale, receipt or delivery of any security, and of any modification or cancellation of any such order or instruction; and (b) originals of any written communication received and copies of all written communication sent by the investment adviser relating to: (i) any recommendation or advice given or proposed to be given; (ii) any receipt, disbursement or delivery of funds or securities; and (iii) the placing or execution of any order to purchase or sell any security.

advisory services provided to US clients of the registered adviser; it should also appoint an agent for service of process;
❑ report to the SEC any changes in laws of its jurisdiction that would prevent it from performing its undertakings.

Staff's evolving approach to the conduct and effects test
The goal of the arrangements described above is to enable non-US advisers to undertake non-US operations outside of the scope of SEC regulation while still protecting the interests and expectations of US clients of those advisers. This aim has been approached in two ways. First, the SEC has stated that where a fund management house has established an affiliated adviser that is registered with the SEC, the principal company may allow its experts to provide advice to US clients through its registered affiliate without subjecting the principal company to registration requirements. Secondly, the Staff has confirmed that a non-US based investment adviser may register with the SEC and only comply with the requirements of the Advisers Act with respect to its US clients. These advisers need not comply with the substantive provisions of the Advisers Act with respect to their non-US clients as described above.

The evolution of these provisions and the principal options currently open to non-US firms wishing to provide investment advisory services to US clients are discussed below.

Initially, the options open to a non-US firm wishing to provide investment advisory services to US clients comprised the following:

❑ register the principal firm under the Advisers Act and submit the worldwide operation to SEC supervision;
❑ establish and register an affiliate and operate under the strict separation approach under *Richard Ellis*; or
❑ qualify for an exception from the definition of "investment adviser" under the Advisers Act, so as to avoid the need for registration.

Until the development of the conduct and effects approach outlined above, the most likely exception for a non-US firm wishing to serve US clients without subjecting itself to the full panoply of Advisers Act rules was to restrict its client base to fewer than 15 US clients, not hold itself out as an investment adviser to prospective US clients and comply with certain other restrictions.

With the establishment of the conduct and effects approach, the options that are available are as follows:

- register the principal firm under the Advisers Act – in which event it need now only conform to the substantive requirements of the Advisers Act with respect to its US clients;
- establish and register an affiliate and comply with the less imposing Staff positions summarised above; a non-US firm that has a US-registered affiliate may now provide advisory services through the affiliate, provided that the criteria described above are complied with; or
- restrict the US client base to fewer than 15 clients within a 12-month period, not hold itself out as an investment adviser to prospective US clients and comply with certain other restrictions, in which event the firm is excepted from the definition of an investment adviser and may avoid registration and the requirements applicable to registered advisers[32] – it does, however, remains subject to the anti-fraud provisions of the Advisers Act.[33]

It should be noted that, although the SEC has discretion to reject applications in certain circumstances, the process of registration principally involves providing all of the required information and agreeing to be subject to the conduct of business and disclosure rules applicable to registered advisers. It is not necessary to establish compliance with particular capital adequacy requirements, staff qualifications or any physical presence in the US.

In seeking to take advantage of the third option, a non-US firm must be careful to take into account the SEC's broad interpretation of activities that can be deemed "holding out" of providing advisory services. The SEC views a variety of representations and actions, including most solicitation efforts, as "holding out" as an adviser within the US. However, servicing those clients utilising the US postal and equivalent services would not in itself require an adviser's registration. US firms can obtain the benefit of this exception as

---

[32] In addition, an investment adviser can operate outside the scope of the Advisers Act if it limits its types of activities in certain respects. Some of the activities that do not trigger the requirements of the Advisers Act include, but are not limited to, (a) using the means and instrumentalities of US commerce to acquire information about securities of US issuers and effect transactions through US broker–dealers in those securities on behalf of clients and (b) engaging solely in certain publishing activities.

[33] *See* above for a discussion of the anti-fraud provisions of the Advisers Act.

well, but must include worldwide (and not just US) clients in determining whether they fall within the fewer than 15 limit.

New Rule 203(b)(3)-2 – "private funds" and counting clients

The ability of a non-US adviser to follow the third option became further complicated when the SEC adopted a rule designed to result in the managers of most hedge funds having to register as investment advisers under the Advisers Act. New Rule 203(b)(3)-2 under the Advisers Act[34] is in effect an SEC interpretation of the exemption from registration set out in Rule 203(b)(3). As explained above, under the exemption, a person meeting the Advisers Act definition of an "investment adviser" will nonetheless be exempt from registration under the Act if, among other things, it has had fewer than 15 clients over the previous 12 months. New Rule 203(b)(3)-2, described in detail in the following, reverses a long-standing SEC position[35] and requires a manager of certain types of pooled investment vehicles to count not the vehicle but investors in the vehicle in determining whether the manager has fewer than 15 clients.

By its terms, new Rule 203(b)(3)-2, which became effective on 10th February 2005, requires an investment adviser to count *each* owner – that is, each shareholder, limited partner, member or beneficiary – of interests in a "private fund" in determining whether it has fewer than 15 clients for the purposes of the exemption contained in Section 203(b)(3) of the Advisers Act. The Rule further requires a non-US fund manager desiring to rely on the exemption to look through each such fund that it advises, regardless of whether the fund is formed under the laws of a non-US jurisdiction, and count towards the fewer than 15 threshold each investor in the fund that is a US resident[36] at the time the investor initially

---

34 The new rules are discussed in detail in Investment Advisers Act Release 2333 (2nd December 2004).
35 Prior to the adoption of the new rule, Rule 203(b)(3)-1(a)(2)(i) deemed "A corporation, general partnership, limited partnership, limited liability company, trust (other than a trust referred to in paragraph (a)(1)(iv) of this section), or other legal organization (any of which are referred to hereinafter as a 'legal organization') that receives investment advice based on its investment objectives rather than the individual investment objectives of its shareholders, partners, limited partners, members, or beneficiaries (any of which are referred to hereinafter as an 'owner')" as a single client for purposes of Section 203(b)(3).
36 In determining whether a client is a US resident, the SEC has stated an adviser may look to: (i) in the case of individuals to their residence; (ii) in the case of corporations and other business entities to their principal office and place of business; (iii) in the case of personal trusts and estates to the rules set out in Regulation S; and (iv) in the case of discretionary or

invested in the fund. As a consequence of Rule 203(b)(3)-2, a private fund adviser whose principal office and place of business is outside the United States must register with the SEC if it has more than 14 clients resident in the United States regardless of the amount of assets the adviser has under management. Advisers that are required to register as a result of new Rule 203(b)(3)-2 will have to be registered with the SEC, at the latest, by 1st February 2006.

A "private fund" for the purposes of new Rule 203(b)(3)-2 is defined by Rule 203(b)(3)-1(d) by reference to three characteristics. A fund is not a private fund:

1. unless it is a company that would be subject to regulation under the 1940 Act but for the exclusions from the definition set out in either Section 3(c)(1) or Section 3(c)(7) of the 1940 Act – both of which are discussed in the following;
2. if it does not permit an investor in the fund to redeem the investor's interest in the fund, or amount of capital the investor contributed to the fund, within two years of the purchase of the interest or the contribution; and
3. if interests in the fund are not offered on the basis of the investment advisory skills, ability or expertise of the fund's investment adviser.

Under Rule 203(b)(3)-2, a manager of a non-US mutual fund or closed-end fund whose interests are offered publicly outside the United States is not required to register under the Advisers Act notwithstanding that more than 14 of the investors in such fund are US residents.

A non-US fund manager employing a master – feeder structure needs to be aware of an interpretation of Rule 203(b)(3)-2 relating to that structure.[37] To the extent that the manager uses such a structure and a feeder is organised as a limited partnership or corporation in a non-US jurisdiction offering its shares exclusively to more than 14 US investors, then the feeder is itself a private fund for purposes of

---

non-discretionary accounts managed by another investment adviser to the location of the person for whose benefit the account is held. *See* Investment Advisers Act Release 2333 (2nd December 2004), at footnote 201.

37 A master–feeder structure most commonly involves a non-US master fund established as a partnership or corporation in a tax-efficient jurisdiction. The master fund has multiple feeders, including US and non-US funds. The feeder funds seek to achieve their investment objectives by investing all of their assets in the master fund.

Rule 203(b)(3)-1(d). In such a case, the manager of the master fund must look through the master fund as well as the feeder in counting US investors in determining the manager's ability to rely on the Section 203(b)(3) exclusion. The practical effect of the manager's having to count US clients in a master–feeder structure in this manner is to increase the likelihood of the manager's having to register as an investment adviser under the Advisers Act.

Under Rule 203(b)(3)-2, a non-US fund manager whose clients include a fund of funds that is itself a private fund within the meaning of the Rule, must look through the top tier private fund and count the top tier's investors as clients for purposes of the Section 203(b)(3) exception. If a fund of hedge funds is itself registered as an investment company under the 1940 Act, then Rule 203(b)(3)-2(b) under the Advisers act requires the non-US fund manager to the underlying private fund to look through the registered investment company and to count the registered investment company's investors as clients for purposes of the Section 203(b)(3) exception.

Rule 203(b)(3)-2 limits the extraterritorial reach of the Advisers Act on a non-US manager of a private fund formed under non-US law by permitting such a manager to treat the fund and not the investors in the fund as the manager's client for most purposes of the Advisers Act. Such a manager if required to be registered under the Advisers Act, would need to keep books and records as required under the Act's rules and would be subject to SEC examination. However, the Adviser Act's compliance rule, custody rule and proxy voting rule would not apply to the manager, as long as it has no US clients other than those counted for the purposes of the Section 203(b)(3) exception.

Regulation of US investment advisers servicing non-US clients

The Staff has long taken a position that a registered US investment adviser located within the United States must abide by the substantive and procedural requirements of the Advisers Act with respect to both its US and non-US clients. The Staff bases this position on the assumption that when a non-US client conducts business with a US investment adviser, the client expects that US regulations will govern its business dealings with the adviser. A more difficult question arises when a registered investment adviser conducts advisory operations with or provides advice to a non-US office, and conducts business with non-US clients using personnel from the overseas office to service the accounts of those clients and generate investment decisions. In its 1992 Study, the Staff suggested that the Advisers Act would not generally apply in such cases. The Staff indicated that it would consider the application of the Advisers Act to overseas offices and multinational investment advisers on a case-by-case basis. To date, however, the Staff has not provided significant, formal guidance in this area.

UK regulatory implications

The FSMA provides that no person may carry on regulated activities in the UK or purport to do so unless that person is authorised by the FSA or is exempted from requiring authorisation. Contravention of this provision is a criminal offence. Agreements made in the course of carrying on an activity in contravention of the general prohibition may also be unenforceable in English courts. The body responsible for supervision of the investment fund business, and other regulated activities, in the UK is the FSA.

Regulated activities for which authorisation is required (and applicable exclusions) are set out in secondary legislation.[38] Such activities include, but are not limited to, dealing in investments (for example buying and selling shares/securities trading activities), arranging deals in investments (for example some investment banking activities), advising on investments and managing investments (asset management activities).

Financial promotions in or from the UK are potentially subject to regulation under the FSMA. Section 21 of the FSMA states that a person must not in the course of business, communicate an invitation or inducement to engage in investment activity unless they are authorised or the content of the communication is approved by an authorised person or the activity or the communication is exempt from the application of this provision. Unapproved communications constituting financial promotions that are made by unauthorised persons are accordingly normally restricted to such specified categories of recipients as will cause them to fall outside Section 21.

---

[38] The Financial Services and Markets Act 2000 (Regulated Activities) Order 2001 (as amended).

There are additional restrictions under FSMA on the promotion by authorised persons of collective investment schemes that are not authorised unit trusts or open-ended investment companies (OEICs) or recognised schemes. Great care has to be taken to ensure that the correct language is included in relevant documentation and that the relevant provisions are complied with.

The FSA, in its assessment of an applicant for authorisation, will take into account all relevant matters, including the extent (if any) to which a non-UK applicant is regulated in its home state. In such cases the FSA may liase with any home state regulator and would take into account information provided by that regulator, for instance, in relation to the adequacy of the applicant's resources and the applicant's suitability, having regard to the need to ensure that the applicant's affairs are conducted soundly and prudently. Information with respect to the conduct of the applicant's affairs would extend, in particular, to the adequacy of the applicant's internal control systems.

Similar matters will be considered if a change of control of an authorised person is proposed. Any direct or indirect change of control, which in most cases includes acquiring an interest of as little as 10% or more, will require the prior approval of the FSA. This approval can take up to three months to obtain.

The FSA's regulatory requirements will apply to a firm in full and worldwide, unless otherwise stated. In some cases the single market "passport" for investment services may enable relevant, duly authorised EU nationals to conduct certain types of investment business throughout the EU without the need for separate authorisation in each relevant state. Varying degrees of host state regulation will nonetheless apply to their activities.

NON-US FUNDS
Introduction

While there are a number of possible exemptions from regulation under the 1940 Act available to non-US issuers deemed not to be an "investment company" within the meaning of the 1940 Act (including exemptions for non-US banks, non-US insurance companies and finance subsidiaries of non-US issuers[39]), there are four principal

---

39 *See*, in general, Section 3(c) of the 1940 Act.

exemptions from regulation typically relevant for entities that meet that definition. Sections 3(b) and 3(c) of the 1940 Act contain many of these exemptions. These exemptions include:

- Rule 3a-1 under the 1940 Act;
- Rule 3a-2 under the Act, which provides temporary relief only;
- Section 3(c)(7) of the Act; and
- Section 3(c)(1) of the Act, the so-called "100-person limitation" exemption.

The last two are most likely to be relevant to the marketing of non-US funds in the US and are discussed below. It is important to note, that a fund that relies on either the Section 3(c)(7) or Section 3(c)(1) exclusion could come within the definition of "private fund" within the meaning of new Rule 203(b)(3)-2.

"Qualified purchasers" exemption

Section 3(c)(7) of the 1940 Act provides an exemption from the definition of investment company for any issuer: (i) all of the outstanding securities of which are exclusively owned by only persons who, at the time of the acquisition of such securities, are "qualified purchasers" within the meaning of the Act; and (ii) which is not making and does not at that time propose to make a public offering of such securities. Pursuant to this provision and Staff interpretations of Section 7(d) of the 1940 Act, an issuer that would otherwise be deemed to be an investment company within the meaning of the 1940 Act may privately offer and sell its securities to an unlimited number of US investors that are "qualified purchasers" (as defined in the following), as well as offer and sell its securities to an unlimited number of non-US investors, as long as all of its outstanding securities placed in the United States are originally placed with qualified purchasers and are not resold to US persons that are not qualified purchasers. Accordingly, if an issuer intends to conduct a Rule 144A offering of securities in the United States in reliance on the unlimited qualified purchasers exemption, it should establish procedures to ensure that, at any given time, all of the US purchasers of its securities are qualified purchasers. The procedures should provide the issuer with a means of limiting original US purchasers, and their transferees, to qualified purchasers and a mechanism by which the issuer can void any transfer that causes a violation of the requirements of the unlimited qualified purchasers exemption. Offerings of securities by such issuers frequently are structured so that:

- initial sales in the United States are limited to persons that are qualified purchasers, each of whom has executed a letter representing its status as a qualified purchaser and its agreement to comply with the transfer restrictions described in the following;
- US purchasers are permitted to resell their securities only outside the US in reliance on Regulation S under the Securities Act or within the United States to other qualified purchasers who have executed a letter to the same effect as that of the initial US purchaser;
- legends are placed on the securities (to the extent permitted by applicable laws, rules and regulations) describing the restrictions on transfer of the securities;
- procedures are adopted to enable depositories and/or transfer agents to stop or void any transfer of securities if such transfer would result in a violation of the 1940 Act;
- provisions are added to the issuer's articles of association that permit the issuer or its agents to void any transfer of securities made in violation of the 1940 Act;
- high minimum denominations on purchases are imposed to help ensure that only qualified purchasers will purchase in the US; and
- non-US purchasers are restricted from reselling their securities in the United States until 40 days after the offering of the securities is complete; alternatively, it is also possible for certain issuers relying on Section 3(c)(7), under certain circumstances, to arrange for the deposit of their securities into the Depository Trust Company (DTC) clearance system in the United States; market participants working with DTC have established detailed procedures intended to enable the issuer to satisfy the unlimited qualified purchaser exemption on an ongoing basis without the need for investment letters from purchasers. Note, however, that the Staff has not formally considered whether these particular procedures meet all applicable requirements of the US securities laws and has indicated an unwillingness, at least at this time, to consider the legal appropriateness on any particular set of procedures.

In general terms, a "qualified purchaser" is defined in Section 2(a)(51) of the 1940 Act as:

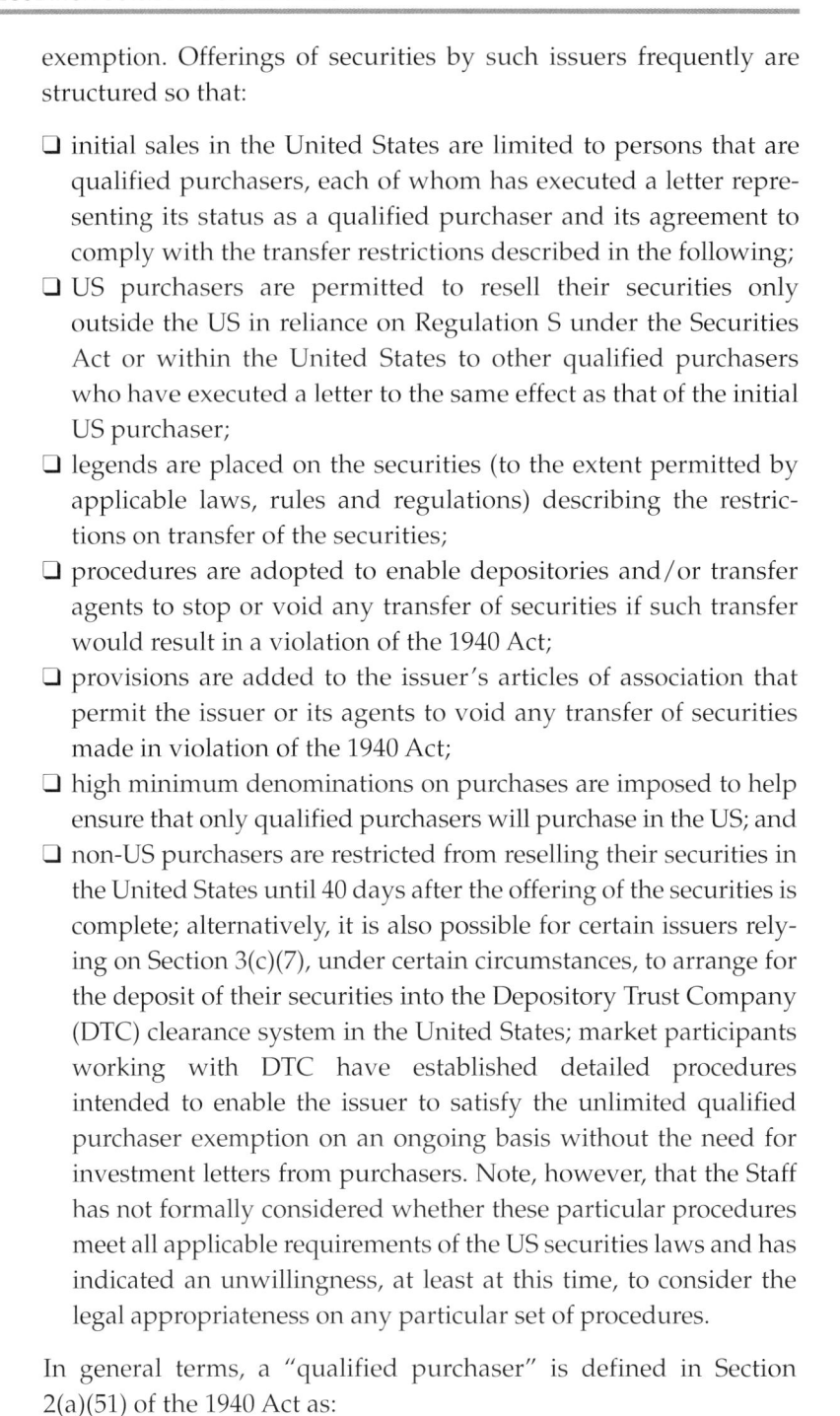

- any natural person that owns at least US$5 million in investments (as defined in the following);
- any family-owned entity that owns at least US$5 million in investments (however, if the entity is formed specifically for the purpose of acquiring the securities offered, then each beneficial owner of the entity's securities must be a qualified purchaser);
- any trust established and funded and for which investment decisions are made by qualified purchasers, as long as the trust was not established specifically for the purpose of acquiring the securities offered;
- any business entity, acting for its own account or for the accounts of other qualified purchasers, that in aggregate owns and invests on a discretionary basis at least US$25 million in investments; and
- any business entity if each owner of the entity's securities is a qualified purchaser.

To satisfy this exemption, every investor must be a qualified purchaser – but there must not be more than 499 US qualified purchasers to avoid the Exchange Act Section 12(g) registration threshold.[40]

The SEC has defined "investments" in Rule 2a51–1 for the purposes of the qualified purchaser definition as including a wide range of securities (except securities issued by a non-public company with shareholders' equity of less than US$50 million or by a company controlling, controlled by or under common control with the prospective qualified purchaser), investment real estate and cash or cash equivalents held for investment purposes. In each case, all outstanding debt incurred to acquire the investments must be deducted from the amount of the investments.

"100-person limitation" exemption

Section 3(c)(1) of the 1940 Act provides an exemption from the definition of investment company for any issuer: (1) all of the outstanding securities of which are beneficially owned by not more than 100 persons; and (2) which is not making and does not presently propose to make any public offering of its securities. Pursuant to Section 3(c)(1) and Staff interpretations of Section 7(d)

---

[40] Securities of registered investment companies are exempt from Section 12(g) by Section 12(g)(2)(B), so they may have more than 499 beneficial owners. This would not apply to non-registered funds.

of the 1940 Act,[41] an issuer that would otherwise be deemed to be an investment company within the meaning of the 1940 Act may privately offer and sell its securities to 100 or fewer beneficial owners resident in the United States, as well as offer and sell its securities to an unlimited number of non-US investors, as long as none of the issuer's outstanding securities that are originally placed in the United States are resold in the United States in such a manner as to leave the issuer with more than 100 US-resident beneficial owners of its securities.

The calculation of the number of US resident beneficial owners to whom an issuer's securities can be sold includes all US resident beneficial holders of each class of the issuer's securities (including all debt and equity securities of the issuer, other than short-term debt securities) that have purchased or will purchase such securities from the issuer in private offerings in the United States, together with any subsequent US resident transferees of such securities (US Purchasers). In addition, the Staff has determined that the 100-person limitation applies at the time of the issuer's first offering in the United States and on a going-forward basis, as a maintenance test ie, an issuer is required to maintain its 100-person limitation on US Purchasers on a continuing basis. As a result, an issuer may violate the 1940 Act if subsequent resales of any of its securities by US Purchasers result in an increase in the number of US Purchasers of all its securities above the 100-person threshold. This could occur, for example upon the sale by one US Purchaser to several US investors who would then become US Purchasers. Non-US persons that purchase an issuer's securities from US Purchasers selling the issuer's securities outside the United States in reliance on Regulation S under the Securities Act would not be considered US Purchasers and would therefore not be counted towards the issuer's 100-person limitation. In addition, purchases of an issuer's securities by investors (whether or not US residents) who acquired such securities outside the United States in a secondary market transaction without the involvement of the issuer, its affiliates or agents would not be considered to be US

---

41 *See Goodwin, Proctor & Hoar LLP* (24th October 1996); *Touche Remnant & Co.* (27th July 1984).

Purchasers and would not be counted towards the 100-person limitation.[42]

In light of the various interpretations set out above, an issuer that intends to make a private placement of securities in the United States in reliance on the 100-person limitation exemption should establish procedures to ensure that, at any given time, no more than 100 beneficial owners of its securities are US Purchasers. The procedures should provide the issuer with a means of controlling or limiting the number of US Purchasers who own its securities and a mechanism by which it can void any transfer that causes a violation of the 100-person limitation. Offerings of securities by such issuers frequently are structured so that:

- ❏ initial sales of the securities are limited to 100 or fewer persons in the United States (more typically to 75 or fewer persons in the United States in order to be cautious), each of whom has executed a letter agreeing to comply with the transfer restrictions described below;
- ❏ initial US purchasers are permitted to resell their securities only outside the United States in reliance on Regulation S under the Securities Act (or another exemption);
- ❏ legends are placed on the securities (to the extent permitted by applicable laws, rules and regulations) describing the restrictions on transfer of the securities;
- ❏ procedures are adopted to enable depositories and/or transfer agents to stop or void any transfer of securities if such transfer would result in a violation of the 1940 Act;
- ❏ provisions are added to the issuer's articles of association that permit the issuer or its agents to void or refuse to recognise a transfer of securities made in violation of the 1940 Act; and
- ❏ high minimum denominations on purchases are imposed to help reduce the overall numbers of investors in the United States.

Market participants have not developed procedures intended to enable issuers relying on the 100-person limitation to make their securities eligible for deposit into the DTC clearance system in the United States.

---

[42] See *Investment Funds Institute of Canada* (4th March 1996).

US PERSONS

A seminal issue under the 1940 Act and also the Advisers Act – and other key provisions of the US securities laws – is how to define "US Person".

1940 Act

Individuals. The definition of US Person for purposes of the 1940 Act traditionally included US citizens, regardless of where they resided. Including US citizens in the definition of US Person reflected SEC no-action letters and interpretations under Section 3(c)(1), most recently, the *Goodwin* letter. Prior to the *Goodwin* letter, non-US funds nearly always included US citizens in the US Person definition, as well as persons residing in the United States (deciding "residency" was left to the non-US fund and its counsel). In *Goodwin*, the SEC Staff said that the Regulation S definition of US Person (which is based on *residence*, not citizenship) could be used.[43] But the Staff also said that, for purposes of 1940 Act Section 7(d), a distinction should be made between US citizens and others that reside permanently outside the United States, and others that are "temporarily overseas". Under this reading of *Goodwin*, certain non-US funds do not use the Regulation S definition of US Person and instead include US citizens in their definition of US Person. Accordingly, and until the SEC or the Staff re-address this issue, do away with the link between Section 3(a)(1) and Section 7(d) and articulate a clear position, non-US funds must consider which definition of US Person they wish to use and, once a decision is taken, use a single defined term in all materials and for all purposes and at all times in the life of the fund – and they must also coordinate what definition they use with their adviser for the reasons discussed below.

Entities. In the case of corporations and partnerships, Regulation S includes within the definition of US Person any partnership or corporation organised or incorporated under the laws of the United States or resident in the United States. A trust or estate is a US Person under Regulation S if any trustee, executor or administrator is a US Person. Regulation S also includes within the definition of

---

[43] *See ABN AMRO Bank N.V.; ABN AMRO Asset Management (USA) Inc.; ABN AMRO Asset Management (Far East) Limited*, SEC No-Action Letter (1st July 1997); *Goodwin, Procter & Hoar* (5th October 1998).

US person any non-discretionary account or similar account (other than an estate or trust) held by a dealer or other fiduciary for the benefit of a US Person. US Person also includes any discretionary account (other than an estate or trust) that is held by a dealer or other fiduciary organised, incorporated or resident in the United States. In the case of employee benefit plans, an employee benefit plan established and administered in accordance with the law of the United States is deemed to be a US Person.[44]

Advisers Act

The term "US Person" is not defined in the Advisers Act. Prior to the new rules governing the registration of certain hedge fund investment advisers,[45] many non-US investment managers (advisers) used the same definition of US Person that was used under the 1940 Act. When the SEC published Release 2333, it stated that, until it reconsidered the question, it would not object if to help define US Person for purposes of the Advisers Act advisers looked:

- in the case of individuals, to their residence;
- in the case of corporations and other business entities, to their principal office and place of business;
- in the case of personal trusts and estates, to the rules set out in Regulation S; and
- in the case of discretionary or non-discretionary accounts managed by another investment adviser, to the location of the person for whose benefit the account is held.

Restricted marketing and monitoring

As noted above, non-US funds must limit their US marketing efforts to private sales involving only restricted groups of investors. Thus, any general promotion in the United States is effectively prohibited and any promotion of the fund will seek to limit US participants by requiring non-US certification from prospective investors. This certification will typically provide that if an applicant cannot make a non-US person declaration, its application for investment will only be accepted if specifically approved by the fund or its adviser. This

---

44 *See Goodwin, Procter & Hoar* (28th February 1997).
45 Investment Advisers Act Release 2333, *Registration Under the Advisers Act of Certain Hedge Fund Advisers* (2nd December 2004).

procedure is not only required for monitoring applications by US persons to ensure that they fall within the private placement or other safe harbour provisions that avoid the need for registration under the Securities Act, but also to ensure that the number of US beneficial investors remains at 100 or below or that each US investor is a "qualified purchaser" as defined previously. For the reasons stated previously, it will be necessary to ascertain the status of investors other than natural persons to ensure that the "beneficial ownership" rules do not cause the limit to be breached even though there are 100 or fewer US holders of record.

Any US marketing of a non-US fund must consider the following as well as taking necessary actions:

- ❏ restrict the initial offer for general US securities laws purposes and keep within the 1940 Act limit;
- ❏ resales of any securities in the secondary market will have to take account of the 1940 Act limit and the resale opportunities and restrictions under US securities laws, particularly Regulation S and Rule 144A under the Securities Act;
- ❏ any concurrent non-US marketing will have to be conducted in a manner so as to avoid any problems under US securities laws;
- ❏ persons involved in the issue will be subject to the US anti-fraud laws and other areas of potential exposure;
- ❏ persons involved in the marketing in the United States will have to be authorised under, and act in accordance with, the US securities laws and the regulations thereunder;
- ❏ compliance with ERISA and other requirements (including tax regulations) must be satisfied;
- ❏ if the fund holds futures or certain other derivative products, it may also be regulated by the CFTC as a commodity pool.

The approach to trading in the secondary market will depend on whether the fund is open-ended (i.e. where shares can be subscribed and redeemed at specified times at prices based on the underlying net asset value) or closed-ended. In most cases, the secondary market trading in open-ended funds is extremely limited or non-existent and accordingly supervision of applications should enable the number or type of US investors to be controlled, with applications being rejected if the fund's limit (100) on US beneficial owners would be exceeded by accepting them or (if the qualified purchasers exemption is being utilised) that no US purchaser is not a qualified purchaser. Notwithstanding this, there will frequently be provisions enabling compulsory redemption (and/or transfer) of security holdings by US or other persons if their ownership could imperil the relevant fund, for regulatory, tax, ERISA or other reasons. Applying such provisions is typically unnecessary as a practical matter, but it is prudent to ensure that they are present in a non-US fund's Articles of Association and its prospectus or private offering memorandum. Having them in place for extenuating circumstances and exercising them is easier than having to amend Articles that may require an extraordinary general meeting (and the passing of a shareholder vote), exercises that are time-consuming and expensive and may be put in place later than actually required.

Closed-ended funds will frequently have rights to refuse transfers that could have the same adverse consequences, or to require or implement subsequent transfers where the beneficial owner has already acquired fund securities. Clearly, these limits on transfers are not in line with the concept of free-transferability, which is a normal pre-requisite for obtaining a listing on (for example) the Official Listing of the UK Listing Authority (UKLA). However, the UKLA may permit funds' articles of incorporation or equivalent documents to contain transfer restrictions for these purposes, but the restrictive provisions may need to be pointed out to, and cleared with, the LSE.

Where securities are held through Euroclear Bank or Clearstream International, it will not normally be possible for the issuer to monitor who the holders are at any one time, although certifications may have been obtained at the time of the initial subscription. However, Euroclear has a disclosure policy for non-US funds (which requires the participant's prior authorisation where the relevant securities are in bearer form, but not for those in registered form). Under this policy, Euroclear will be prepared to provide to fund management companies (or their agents) at their request, at most on a monthly basis in respect of their funds, certain details (the participant's name and holdings) of each Euroclear participant who is holding securities in their funds through Euroclear. This will not provide any details of beneficial ownership or other information about any clients holding through the participants. The relevant participants will be notified that this disclosure has been made, via a Deadlines and Corporate Events (DACE) notice. In addition, it may be possible to arrange for Euroclear to collect non-US beneficial ownership certification from participants prior to payment of dividends, as for other securities. These arrangements now include accelerated procedures for electronic disclosure. To date, beneficial ownership non-residency certification has only been undertaken for a small number of funds.

Euroclear has developed an integrated (order routing, settlement and asset servicing) electronic platform solely for open-ended funds called "FundSettle". This service aims to automate and standardise the dealing and settlement process of funds, linking transfer agents, fund distributors and fund management companies from around the world. Euroclear participants who also register for the FundSettle service can send orders electronically for funds registered on the FundSettle system. There are currently some 185 registered participants using this service and some 25,000 funds, from 19 jurisdictions. These funds are both "offshore" and "onshore". Funds from other jurisdictions may be eligible for inclusion in the system.

If a fund is traded on Euroclear but not on FundSettle its administrators may need to obtain separate confirmation of non-US status, Euroclear may not provide for this. However on FundSettle, subscriptions, redemptions and transfers are fed through the FundSettle platform to the fund's transfer agent or administrator and the transaction will show up on the participant's electronic cash and securities account. The involvement of the transfer agent or administrator provides the opportunity for assessment of compliance with jurisdictional requirements and restrictions. If, for example a fund has restrictions on investors with US residency, then a field can automatically show up on the electronic order form and there can be an obligation for evidence of identification and/or residency to be sent to the transfer agent or administrator, who will review such documentation in considering the application. The FundSettle settlement process provides for different settlement periods to meet the requirements of the relevant fund and caters (where applicable) for the possibility that the administrator may reject an applicant and that liquidation of the holding, if the shares have been issued, might be required. As transfers are also processed through the transfer agent or administrator (there is no secondary market as such through FundSettle) and require separate instructions both parties, certification of non-US residency can, if required, be obtained when the transfer-in instruction is input into the system by the transferee.

Other US regulatory considerations for non-US funds
Anti-money laundering
On 18th September 2002, the US Treasury Department's Financial Crimes Enforcement Network (FinCEN), by authority granted under the Patriot Act, proposed new anti-money laundering regulations that would require investment companies that are not registered under the 1940 Act to disclose their identities to FinCEN.[46] The proposed rule would, if adopted, apply to non-US funds that:

(1) permit investors to redeem their ownership interests within two years of purchasing their interests;
(2) have total assets of US$1 million or more; and
(3) have US clients or are owned or operated by a US person.[47] The proposed rule would, if adopted, also require non-US funds to develop anti-money laundering programs, appoint internal compliance officers, adopt employee training programs to identify and prevent criminal activity, and commission independent audits of their anti-money laundering programs. To date, FinCEN has not finalised this rule, nor has it given a clear indication of when this rule will be finalised.

Safeguards Rule
On 17th May 2002, the US Federal Trade Commission issued a Safeguards Rule to establish standards under which financial institutions must develop and maintain administrative, technical and physical safeguards to protect the security and confidentiality of their customer information.[48] The extent to which the Rule applies to non-US funds is presently unclear, but if deemed applicable to non-US funds it would obligate them to:

❑ develop a written information security program;
❑ designate employees to coordinate the program;
❑ identify reasonably foreseeable risks to the security of customer information; and

---
46 Department of Treasury, 31 C.F.R. Part 103 (proposed 18th September 2002).
47 Department of Treasury, 31 C.F.R. Part 103 (proposed 18th September 2002).
48 Federal Trade Commission, 16 C.F.R. Part 314 (17th May 2002).

❏ design, implement and maintain specific information safeguards, systems and procedures.

PASSIVE FOREIGN INVESTMENT COMPANY – QUALIFYING ELECTING FUND TREATMENT IMPLICATIONS
Overview

Two principal US tax benefits traditionally associated with investments in non-US funds are the deferral of US taxation of income and the conversion of earnings from ordinary income to capital gains that are eligible for preferential tax treatment upon the sale or exchange of interests in the fund. The "passive foreign investment company" rules (PFIC rules) were originally enacted in 1986 to close these perceived loopholes. The rules encourage US shareholders of certain non-US funds to pay current US federal income tax on their share of the funds' undistributed earnings. Alternatively, the economic equivalent of current tax is achieved through the imposition of an interest charge when the US shareholder actually realises a cash return on his investment.

Passive foreign investment companies – the PFIC definition

In general, any non-US pool that has substantially "passive income" or holds principally "passive assets" will be classified as a PFIC under the PFIC rules, and the pool's US investors will be subject to the PFIC rules. Note that the PFIC rules only apply to non-US pools that are treated as corporations for US federal income tax purposes. In some cases, a non-US pool may be structured to qualify as a partnership under US federal income tax law. US investors in such a pool would be currently taxable on their share of the earnings of the pool under the normal tax accounting rules applicable to partnerships.

A non-US fund will be classified as a PFIC for US federal income tax purposes in any tax year in which: (a) 75% or more of its gross income constitutes "passive income" (Income Test); or (b) 50% or more of its assets produces passive income or is held for the production of passive income (Asset Test). With certain exceptions, "passive income" is foreign personal holding company (FPHC) income. As defined in the US Internal Revenue Code of 1986, as amended (Code), FPHC income includes virtually all income an investment fund would earn, such as dividends, interest, certain rents and royalties, net gains from the sale or exchange of assets that produce passive income, net gains from commodities transactions and foreign currency gains.

Determination of PFIC status

The PFIC status of a non-US investment fund must be determined annually. Once a fund is determined to be a PFIC for any taxable year during the US shareholder's holding period, the fund retains the PFIC designation for all future years. Consequently, any US shareholder at the time the PFIC status attaches to the fund will be subject to the PFIC rules for as long as the shareholder holds an interest in the fund, unless the US shareholder elects to "purge" the PFIC taint or had a "qualified electing fund" election in effect as discussed in the following. For the purposes of the PFIC rules, a shareholder is any US person that directly, or indirectly, owns PFIC stock. Under the Code, a US person is an individual citizen or resident of the US, a corporation or partnership organised under the laws of the US or any political subdivision of the US, an estate where the income of which is subject to US federal income tax (regardless of source) and a trust, if one or more US persons has the authority to control all substantial decisions of the trust and a US court is able to exercise primary supervision over the administration of the trust.

For purposes of the PFIC rules, certain entities are not treated as PFICs. Among those entities are the following.

❑ *Controlled non-US company.* In general, if a non-US corporation is a "controlled foreign corporation" (CFC), certain US shareholders owning 10% or more of the voting stock of the corporation will not be subject to the PFIC rules even though the corporation meets the definition of a PFIC. Instead, these 10% shareholders are subject to other special rules under the Code designed to prevent tax deferral. Any non-US corporation can qualify as a CFC if more than 50% of the total combined voting power or the total value of stock of the corporation is owned by US shareholders, each of whom owns at least 10% of the corporation's voting power.
❑ *Company subject to purging election.* If a non-US fund was, but is no longer, a PFIC, a US shareholder can purge the PFIC taint from stock in the entity by electing to mark the stock to the market and pay tax on any gain in value, subject to certain interest charge rules. Gain is calculated as if the stock had been sold as of the last

day of the tax year that PFIC status existed. A shareholder who elects to purge the PFIC taint increases the basis of the stock by the amount of the gain recognised and starts a new holding period for purposes of the PFIC rules.

Tax effect of PFIC rules on US shareholders
Interest charge rules
A US shareholder who makes no elections under the PFIC rules will pay an interest charge on the gains from the sale or exchange of PFIC stock and certain "excess distributions" made by the PFIC. "Excess distributions" include the portion of distributions received during a tax year that exceed 125% of the average distributions received for the prior three tax years. Any gains recognised upon disposition of the PFIC stock are treated as excess distributions. In addition, dividends received on PFIC stock are generally not eligible for the 15% maximum capital gains rate applicable to qualified dividend income.

Excess distributions are allocated rateably to each day in the US shareholder's holding period. Any amounts allocated for the current year are taxed, under US law, as ordinary income. Amounts allocated for prior years are taxed at the highest ordinary income rate for those years, subject to an interest charge computed from the due date for the US shareholder's tax return for the tax year to which the amount is allocated to the due date for such return for the tax year of disposition or distribution.

Qualified electing fund treatment
Due to the significant US federal income tax consequences relating to investment by US persons in PFICs, potential US investors in non-US funds should generally consider the PFIC rules when making an investment decision. Consequently, competitive pressures may exist to offer US investors the opportunity, to make a "qualifying electing fund" (QEF) election and a non-US fund may be asked to comply with certain QEF election reporting requirements.

A QEF election is made at the shareholder level by the due date for filing the shareholder's US federal income tax return for any tax year. As QEF treatment is an option at the shareholder level, a PFIC may be a QEF as to one shareholder, but not as to another. Once made, however, the QEF election applies to all subsequent tax years of the shareholder, unless revoked by the shareholder with consent of the US Internal Revenue Service (IRS).

FUND MANAGERS, INVESTMENT ADVISERS AND FUNDS

To be eligible for the QEF election, the PFIC must agree to comply with IRS requirements for reporting its ordinary earnings and net capital gains annually. Many non-US funds today follow a "fund of funds" investment approach under which they invest in other non-US pooled investment vehicles rather than investing directly in securities issued by operating companies. A PFIC fund of funds would typically invest in entities that are PFICs. Complying with the IRS requirements in such a case could prove difficult; as a practical matter, the underlying PFICs may not be willing to supply the information needed for a US investor in the top-tier entity to make a QEF election.

If a US shareholder's QEF election is in effect for the duration of the PFIC stock holding period, the shareholder's pro rata share of the QEF's earnings are classified into ordinary income or capital gains, depending on the character of the underlying income of the PFIC, and are passed through to the shareholder. Any amounts included in the income of the US shareholder will increase the basis of the stock. In return for current income inclusion of QEF earnings, the shareholder will retain capital gains treatment upon any disposition of the PFIC stock and will not be subject to the interest charge rules.

Under US Treasury regulations, in order for an investor in a non-US fund to make an effective QEF election, the fund is required to make an annual information statement available to the investor, containing the following information:

❏ the first and last days of the taxable year of the fund that is the PFIC to which the information statement applies;
❏ the investor's pro rata share of the ordinary earnings and net capital gains of the PFIC for the taxable year of the PFIC, or sufficient information to enable the shareholder to calculate these items;
❏ the amount of cash and other property distributed or deemed distributed to the shareholder during the taxable year of the PFIC; and
❏ a statement that the PFIC will permit the investor to inspect and copy the PFIC's permanent books of accounts, records and such other documents necessary to verify that the PFIC's ordinary earnings and net capital gain required to be reported above are computed in accordance with US income tax principles.

The following is the text of a typical PFIC annual information statement.

[NAME OF COMPANY]

PFIC ANNUAL INFORMATION STATEMENT

This information statement is furnished to holders of the Company's [Common Stock] (the "Stock"), and provides certain information with respect to the Company's taxable year beginning [date], 20__ and ending [date], 20__ (the "20__ tax year"). US Holders of the Stock, who elect to have the Company treated as a qualified electing fund pursuant to Section 1295 of the United States Internal Revenue Code ("Code") (a "QEF election") must include in gross income for US tax purposes their pro rata shares of the Company's ordinary earning and net capital gain for the 20__ tax years as provided in Section 1293 of the Code.

The daily amounts of ordinary earnings and net capital gain per share of Stock for the 20__ tax year are set forth below. A holder's pro rata share of ordinary earnings and net capital gain is determined by multiplying the daily, per share amount of ordinary earnings and net capital gain by the number of shares of Stock held by the holder during the 20__ tax year and the number of days held.

Ordinary Earnings: US$
(Daily dollar amount per share of Stock)
Net Capital Gain: US$
(Daily dollar amount per share of Stock)

Per Share Distributions: The Company distributed $[amount] in cash per share of Stock during the 20__ tax year. No other property was distributed or deemed distributed with respect to the Stock during the 20__ tax year.

Upon the written request of any holder making a QEF election, the Company will make available to such holder, for inspection and copying, the Company's permanent books of account and records and such other documents as are necessary to establish that the ordinary earnings and net capital gain, as provided in Section 1293(e) of the Code, are computed in accordance with US income tax principles.

An important point to note is that the earnings and gains must be computed in accordance with US accounting rules. This may cause difficulties and the fund's accountants will have to be involved in determining whether the fund can commit to supplying the relevant information. If this is at all possible, any additional cost or administrative requirements will need to be assessed in the light of the level of US demand.

USE OF THE INTERNET

The Internet has grown in popularity as a means for offering securities to potential investors. The SEC has provided guidance in this area and suggested that a non-US fund must consider adopting special procedures to avoid being deemed as offering securities in the United States.[49] The SEC has stated that, as a general rule, Internet offers must not target US persons. To avoid targeting US persons through the Internet, a non-US fund should, according to the SEC: (a) include a "prominent disclaimer" on its website notifying viewers that the offer is "directed only to countries other than the United States"; and (b) maintain procedures to avoid sales to US persons, such as requiring a home address or telephone number prior to any sales. Other steps may be necessary if a non-US fund becomes aware that a US person is attempting to evade the fund's procedures. For instance, if a non-US fund receives a cheque drawn on a US bank or correspondence containing a US social security number, the fund may need to request proof of residency such as a passport, drivers licence or some other type of identification. A non-US fund's website should also monitor hyperlinked information on the site to ensure that the information is not presented in a manner that could be construed to be an extension of the non-US fund's own website or an offering of the fund's interests to US persons.[50] Finally, a non-US fund should not advertise the existence of its website in a US publication.

ERISA

US laws and regulations relating to the management of employee benefit plans sponsored by private US employers are of relevance both in the context of the activities of non-US based investment advisers and of non-US funds with US investors. The relevant regulations are promulgated by the US Department of Labor (DOL), which is responsible for implementing certain provisions of ERISA. The regulations govern both the plans and the managers of the plans. US plans resemble, in structure, other types of pooled investment entities, such as mutual funds and other investment companies. As a practical

---

[49] Securities Act Release 7516 (23rd March 1998).
[50] *See* Securities Act Release 7856 (28th April 2000).

matter, a plan manager must be a US bank, a US insurance company or a US-registered investment adviser.

Classification of fund assets as ERISA "plan assets"

Under DOL regulations, assets of a pooled investment fund in which a plan subject to ERISA (ERISA plan) has invested are considered to be "plan assets" if either the investment fund is not registered with the SEC or interests in the fund are publicly traded in the US and 25% or more of any class of the equity interests in the investment fund is held by "benefit plan investors". DOL regulations indicate that all employee benefit plans, whether or not they are plans of US employers and whether or not such plans are covered by ERISA, are considered to be "benefit plan investors", and are therefore counted in determining whether the 25% threshold has been met. This rule can lead to the result, for example that a fund whose investors include over 25% of non-US plan investors and one ERISA plan investor, who would be subject to ERISA even though the ERISA plan holds less than 25% of the fund.

A further potential result under the DOL regulations is that even a fund with no ERISA plan investors, but more than 25% non-US plan investors, would itself be considered a "benefit plan investor". While the fund would not be subject to ERISA as long as it did not have an ERISA plan investor, when making its own investments, the fund would typically be required (particularly in the fund of funds context) to represent whether or not it is itself a benefit plan investor. The potential pitfalls for such a fund can be illustrated by considering the case of a non-US fund that has no ERISA plan investors and that does not monitor investment in the fund by non-US plan investors. Such a fund could inadvertently breach a representation to another fund in which it has invested, and in some cases could even then, in turn, cause that underlying fund itself to be considered as investing plan assets and become subject to ERISA. Several non-US funds have recently requested relief from the DOL that a fund in which only non-US plans have invested should not itself be considered a benefit plan investor. As of April 2005, the DOL has not ruled on this issue.

In calculating whether the 25% threshold described above has been met, any non-plan interests held by a person who has discretionary authority or control over the assets of the fund, or who provides investment advice for a fee with respect to those assets, or any of their affiliates, are not counted. For example, "seed money" invested in a fund by its sponsor or affiliate will not be counted in the denominator.

Manager subject to ERISA fiduciary responsibility provisions

If the assets of a fund are characterised as "plan assets" for the purposes of ERISA, then the fund manager is subject to the stringent fiduciary responsibility provisions of ERISA in managing the fund.[51] In meeting these rules, the fund manager must, in general, invest the fund's assets:

❏ solely in the interest of, and for the exclusive purpose of providing benefits to, plan participants;
❏ with the care, skill, prudence and diligence of a prudent man acting in like circumstances;
❏ by diversifying the investments so as to minimise the risk of large losses, unless it is clearly not prudent to do so;
❏ unless otherwise permitted by DOL regulations, so as to maintain the indicia of ownership of the plan assets within the jurisdiction of the US district courts; and
❏ without using the assets for his own benefit, interest or account.

A non-US fund manager must, under ERISA, meet ERISA's fiduciary responsibility provisions if investment in the fund by benefit plan investors and ERISA plans exceeds the 25% threshold. It is uncertain, however, whether the DOL, an ERISA plan participant or any other party would be able to obtain a judgement against a non-US fund manager with no US presence for an ERISA violation, or to enforce a judgement obtained.

A typical investment adviser, whether located within or outside the US, that manages the monies of an ERISA plan is a "fiduciary" within the meaning of ERISA with respect to the plan assets the adviser manages. Under ERISA, a fiduciary is prevented from entering into two general types of "prohibited transactions": "party in interest transactions" and "conflict of interest transactions". An investment adviser to a plan is always a party in interest with respect to the entire plan by

---

51 This discussion assumes that the Manager has discretion over the investment of fund assets. The term "Manager" as used here includes any person with such discretion.

virtue of it providing services to the plan. It is deemed a fiduciary, however, only to that portion of the plan's assets that it controls or with respect to which it provides investment advice for a fee.

Party in interest transactions are those undertaken between an ERISA plan and/or certain parties related to the plan. These related persons, termed "parties in interest" in ERISA, include: any fiduciary of the ERISA plan; an employer of plan participants; any person providing a service to the plan; and an employee, officer, director, or 10% or more shareholder or partner of a person providing such a service. Prohibited transactions that may not be undertaken between an ERISA plan and a party in interest of the plan include: sale or exchange or leasing of property; lending of money or extension of credit; furnishing of goods, services or facilities; and transfer to, or use of, any asset of the plan. A number of "class exemptions", however, have been issued by the DOL exempting particular types of party in interest transactions from ERISA's prohibitions.

A fiduciary of an ERISA plan is prohibited from engaging in conflict of interest transactions, which are designed to ensure that the fiduciary is not faced with significant conflicts of interest in managing the monies of the plan. In particular, the fiduciary cannot:

- deal with plan assets in his own interest or for his own account;
- act in any transaction involving the plan on behalf of a party whose interests are adverse to the interests of the plan's participants or beneficiaries; or
- receive consideration for his own personal account from any party dealing with such a plan in connection with a transaction involving the assets of the plan.

The consequences for violating the fiduciary responsibilities imposed by ERISA can be considerable. Under ERISA, a fiduciary of an ERISA plan is personally liable to cover any losses to the plan resulting from a breach of responsibility and to restore to the plan the loss of any profits arising from the breach. In addition, a fiduciary of an ERISA plan may be removed and subject to penalties of up to 20% of the amount recovered from the fiduciary. A party in interest transaction also subjects the relevant party in interest to an automatic excise tax of at least 15% of the amount of the transaction.

To protect against losses due to fraud or dishonesty, investment advisers with discretionary authority over ERISA funds generally must obtain a bond. ERISA requires that the bond covering a fiduciary equal not less than 10% of the funds handled, and in any case not less than US$1,000 or more than US$500,000. The amount of funds handled by a fiduciary is generally calculated on the amount of funds managed by the adviser in the previous year. The coverage amount is required for each ERISA plan for which the fiduciary handles funds, though one bond may be purchased that covers multiple plans.

Possible strategies for avoiding plan assets

Due to the significant consequences outlined above, most pooled investment funds seek to avoid "plan assets" classification. An unregistered non-US fund is generally left with two possible strategies, in addition to excluding ERISA plans as investors, for dealing with the characterisation of its assets as "plan assets" and the consequences flowing from such characterisation.

Limit participation by employee benefit plans to less than 25%

Imposing such a limit will allow the fund to avoid having its assets characterised as "plan assets". This strategy has two elements. First, the fund must be able to monitor and control both the initial and secondary market sales of shares in the fund to ensure that the 25% limit is not reached. Secondly, the fund must have adequate provisions in the governing documents – typically, a Private Placement Memorandum and Investment Letter and the Articles of Association – to ensure that compliance with the 25% limit can be maintained. The Private Placement Memorandum and Investment Letter should disclose that the fund may limit employee benefit plan participation and has the right to reject the attempted acquisition of an interest in the fund by any employee benefit plan or compulsorily redeem shares in order to comply with or remain below the 25%.

In addition to the above, although the fund will actively attempt to limit employee benefit plan participation to less than 25%, the possibility exists that, due to error or time lag in discovering that shares in the fund are owned by a plan or redemption by a large non-plan investor, employee benefit plan ownership will nevertheless reach or exceed the 25% limit. Therefore, the fund should consider making a disclosure advising potential ERISA plan investors of the risk that, even though the fund will undertake to limit employee benefit plan ownership to less than 25%, a possibility exists that this threshold could be reached or exceeded and the fund could be deemed to hold plan assets as to any investing ERISA plans. In this event, the fund may reserve the right (which should also be disclosed) to cause the mandatory redemption of shares held by ERISA plans.

Venture capital operating company
As discussed above, the manager of a non-US fund will be deemed to be managing plan assets, and will thus be subject to ERISA's various rules, if interests in the fund are not securities that are either publicly traded or registered in the US and if ERISA plans and other employee benefits plans, in the aggregate, have a significant (25% or more) equity interest in the fund. Nonetheless, such a fund may not need to be operated in accordance with ERISA's rules if the fund can qualify as an "operating company", in particular a "venture capital operating company" (VCOC).

For an entity to qualify as a VCOC it must satisfy a number of conditions. The entity must have at least 50% of its assets invested in "operating companies" with respect to which the entity has direct contractual "management rights" to substantially participate in, or substantially influence, the conduct of the management of the operating company. For the purposes of this asset test, short-term investments are disregarded. An "operating company" for these purposes is an entity that is primarily engaged in the production or sale of a product or service other than the investment of capital and therefore would not include investment funds. Whether the entity has management rights with respect to an operating company will be a matter of fact. Among the issues to be taken into account are the right to appoint directors or officers of the company, the right to be present at and observe board meetings of the company, the right to examine the books, records and properties of the company, the right to consult with the company's management, the right to receive certain financial information regarding the company, and the proportion of the company's equity held. Qualification as a VCOC is determined on "valuation dates" and if the asset test is met, the entity will qualify as a VCOC for the ensuing approximately 12-month period, as long as it actually exercises its management rights with respect to at least one of its venture capital investments.

A fund that seeks to qualify as a VCOC will need to ensure that in satisfying the above tests it does not breach the requirements of its law of incorporation or domestic regulations, or the requirements of any stock exchange on which the fund's securities are to be listed. For example, the LSE will not normally permit a listed investment company to take legal or management control of investments in its portfolio.

IMPLICATIONS FOR INVESTING IN US COMPANIES AND US FUNDS FOR FUND INVESTORS

A number of limitations set out in the US securities laws regarding the investment activities of investment funds are generally directed at the activities of the funds and their advisers and promoters, rather than passive investors in the funds.

Section 12(d)(1) of the 1940 Act, for instance, generally restricts ownership of shares of registered US funds by any company that is an "investment company" within the meaning of the 1940 Act, which definition can include a non-US fund. The investment limits are generally that such an investment company can hold no more than 3% of the voting stock of a registered US fund and no more than 5% of the investment company's assets can be invested in any one other fund or 10% in all other funds. Certain exceptions are available if the acquiring fund invests solely in one registered investment company or has sales charges not exceeding 1.5%. Other US regulatory schemes restrict foreign ownership of US companies in areas such as banking, public utilities and industries that are deemed sensitive to national security. These limitations are directed towards the fund, rather than its investors.

Compliance with the restriction imposed on one fund investing in the securities of a US registered fund is the responsibility of the investing fund. The investing fund is liable for any breaches of the investment limitations. Liability may take the form of, among other things, a SEC enforcement action for violation of Section 12 of the 1940 Act. The passive investors in the transgressing fund would not be liable in general (but presumably they could suffer losses due to any decline in a fund's net asset value).

Can a non-US fund invest directly in US securities?

Funds generally are not restricted in their ability to invest directly in US securities, except that the purchase or sale of securities in the United States must be made through an SEC-registered broker–dealer or in compliance with Rule 15a-6 and may not exceed the limits discussed above.

Can a US feeder fund–master fund be established?
As discussed above, a master–feeder structure most commonly involves a non-US master fund established as a partnership or corporation in a tax-efficient jurisdiction. The master fund has multiple feeders, including US and non-US funds. The feeder funds seek to achieve their investment objectives by investing all of their assets in the master fund. A properly structured master–feeder structure allows tax-exempt and non-US investors to avoid the tax disadvantages that would otherwise result from a direct investment in the master fund without impairing the tax treatment of investors subject to US taxation that invest in the same master fund.

A US-registered master fund could sell to a non-US feeder fund that invests exclusively in that master fund, as long as other applicable conditions are met. A US feeder fund probably could not be established for a non-US fund unless it was privately offered and, aggregated with other sales, complied with either 1940 Act Section 3(c)(1) or 3(c)(7) (i.e. the 100 US beneficial owner and qualified purchaser exemptions).

SARBANES–OXLEY AND THE INVESTMENT MANAGEMENT INDUSTRY
SOX contains a number of provisions that affect the investment-management business. Although mutual funds and other investment companies were not the primary targets of SOX, the SEC has adopted a number of rules providing specific application of SOX's provisions to investment companies. SOX's key measures involving investment-management activities are described below.

SOX investment-management-related provisions
SOX applies to "issuers" as defined in Section 2(a)(7) of SOX. This definition includes any "issuer" (as defined under the Exchange Act) that has securities registered under Section 12 of the Exchange Act or is required to file reports under Section 15(d) of that act, and any issuer that files, or has filed, a registration statement under the Securities Act that has not yet become effective. The breadth of the definition covers most investment companies registered under

the 1940 Act and business-development companies as well. Key provisions as applied to investment companies take the form of certifications of reports filed with the SEC, governance, reporting and disclosure requirements, disclosure controls and procedures, increased criminal and civil liabilities for corporate misconduct and standards of conduct for attorneys that represent these companies. These measures were designed to increase corporate responsibility for financial disclosures and to provide investors with additional protections.

Section 302 Certification requirement

In seeking to enhance responsibility, the SOX provisions, as implemented by the SEC, impose a requirement relating to certifications by the principal executive officers and principal financial officers of registered investment companies. Section 302 directs the SEC to issue rules requiring each company filing periodic reports under Section 13(a) or 15(d) of the Exchange Act to include certifications by the company's principal executive officers and principal financial officers certifying the adequacy and accuracy of the company's financial statements and the adequacy of the company's disclosure controls in "each annual or quarterly report filed or submitted under each such section". Virtually all registered investment companies that have reporting obligations under either Section 13(a) (eg, exchange-traded funds with a class of securities registered under Section 12) or Section 15(d) (eg, open-end funds, unit investment trusts (UITs) and publicly held closed-end funds not listed on an exchange) file their annual and periodic reports with the SEC under Section 30 of the 1940 Act and the rules under that section. The SEC concluded that investment companies fall under Section 302 of SOX and immediately adopted rules applying the section to registered investment companies.[52]

Form N-SAR

In order to implement the certification requirement specified in Section 302 of SOX (Section 302 Certification) for investment companies, the SEC amended the investment company reporting rules and Form N-SAR. Unlike Forms 10-K and 10-Q filed by public

---

[52] Investment Company Act Release 25722 (28th August 2002).

operating companies, Form N-SAR does not require the filing of financial statements. Form N-SAR, however, requires management-investment companies to provide certain financial information based on the financial statements as of the same date contained in the investment company's annual and semi-annual reports to shareholders. As a result, the SEC modified the certification to require the signing officers of a registered management-investment company to certify that the financial information included in the report and the financial statements on which the financial information is based fairly present, in all material respects, the financial condition, results of operations and changes in net assets and cashflows (if the financial statements are required to include a statement of cashflows) of the investment company.

Each certifying officer is required to state that:

❏ the officer has reviewed the report being certified and filed;
❏ based on the officer's knowledge, the report does not contain any untrue statement of a material fact or omit to state a material fact necessary to make the statements made, in light of the - circumstances under which such statements were made, not misleading with respect to the period covered by the report; and
❏ based on the officer's knowledge, the financial information included in the report, and the financial statements on which the financial information is based, fairly present in all material respects the financial condition, results of operations and changes in net assets and cashflows (if the financial statements are required to include a statement of cashflows) of the investment company as of, and for, the periods presented in the report.

The rules require additional certifications concerning the establishment, maintenance and efficacy of the investment company's disclosure controls and procedures. These certifications also effectively require the certifying officers to disclose their conclusions about the investment company's internal controls to its audit committee, including any material defects or fraudulent activities affecting the controls.

The certifications are structured so that the persons certifying cannot rely on GAAP; that is, it will not be sufficient to state that the financial statements have been prepared in accordance with GAAP. The language "fairly present" is intended to go beyond

GAAP to cover the selection and application of accounting methods, disclosure of financial information that is informative and reasonably reflects the underlying transactions and events and any other facts necessary to provide a materially accurate and complete financial picture of an investment company's financial condition, results of operations and cashflows.

When SOX was passed, many investment company principals were uncertain as to who should certify the funds' financial information. This problem was particularly significant for registered investment companies that outsourced their administration, management and custodial roles to third-party service providers. Initially, a question arose whether the third-party service providers could provide the requisite certifications. The applicable rule of the SEC, however, expressly requires that "the principal executive officer or officers and the principal financial officer or officers of the investment company, or persons performing similar functions" sign the certifications. If an investment company has more than one principal executive officer or principal financial officer, or their equivalents, each must sign a separate Section 302 Certification.

Special cases and exceptions
In the case of a master–feeder fund, the report of the master fund would include a certification on Form N-SAR based on the financial statements of the master fund included in the report to shareholders of the feeder fund.

UITs and small business investment companies (SBICs) were initially required to provide the Section 302 Certification with respect to the items of Form N-SAR specific to them. However, because these issuers are not required to transmit reports to their shareholders containing their financial statements and Form N-SAR does not require them to report financial information based on their financial statements, the SEC has exempted them from the Section 302 Certification requirement.[53]

Since originally requiring Section 302 Certifications in Form N-SAR, the SEC has adopted Form N-CSR and amended its reporting rules so that the Section 302 Certifications are required in Form N-CSR rather than in Form N-SAR. Form N-SAR has been

---

[53] Investment Company Act Release 25914 (27th January 2003).

re-designated so that it is no longer a report filed under Section 13(a) or 15(d) of the Exchange Act and no longer includes a certification requirement.

Form N-CSR is a certified shareholder report that is designated as a report filed with the SEC under Sections 13(a) and 15(d) of the Exchange Act. Form N-CSR is a report that encloses (for filing with the SEC) and certifies an investment company's required annual and semi-annual reports to shareholders. The SEC required that these reports be certified because the shareholder reports that would be included in Form N-CSR, rather than Form N-SAR, are the primary vehicles for providing financial statements to investors. The certified shareholder reports consist of a copy of any required shareholder report, information regarding the issuer's disclosure controls and procedures and the certifications required by Section 302. Form N-CSR also requires disclosure relating to the company's audit committee financial expert required by Section 407 of SOX and the code of ethics required by Section 406, both of which are discussed separately below.

Section 906 – criminal liability for false certifications

Section 906 of SOX requires that every periodic report containing financial statements filed with the SEC pursuant to Section 13(a) or 15(d) of the Exchange Act be accompanied by a written statement from both the principal executive officer and the principal financial officer certifying that the report fully complies with the requirements of Section 13(a) or 15(d) and that the information in the report fairly presents, in all material respects, the financial condition and results of operations of the issuer (Section 906 Certification). To date, the SEC has made no public statements interpreting Section 906, other than to say that the certification requirement of Section 906 was "separate" and "independent" of the requirement of Section 302, and that separate certifications are required by the two sections.

Section 906 imposes strict criminal penalties on any officer who "knowingly" or "knowingly and wilfully" provides a false certification. Penalties include fines up to US$1 million or imprisonment for up to 10 years for "knowing" violations and fines up to US$5 million or imprisonment for up to 20 years for "knowing and wilful" violations. Unlike the Section 302 Certification, the Section

FUND MANAGERS, INVESTMENT ADVISERS AND FUNDS

906 Certification is not expressly qualified by the certifying officer's knowledge, although no violation can be found unless the certifying officer "knowingly" submits a false certification.

Application to SEC-registered investment companies
Although other public companies filing on Forms 10-Q and 10-K have typically included Section 906 Certifications with their filings of periodic reports since SOX's enactment, registered investment companies filing on Form N-SAR generally have not. Although, consistent with the SEC's rulemaking under Section 302, investment companies may be considered to file reports on Form N-SAR under either Section 13(a) or 15(d) of the Exchange Act, Form N-SAR does not contain financial statements and therefore one of the elements that would trigger the requirement to file the Section 906 Certification is missing. Form N-CSR, however, contains financial statements and has been designated by the SEC as an Exchange Act report. Therefore, Form N-CSR should be considered subject to the Section 906 Certification requirement and, when it is filed, needs to be accompanied by Section 906 Certifications.

Operating companies' compliance with Section 906 – the "knowledge" qualification

Although Section 906's language is not expressly qualified by the certifying officer's knowledge, many Section 906 Certifications for investment companies have included some form of qualification limiting the certification to the "knowledge" or "best knowledge" of the certifying officer. The basis for inserting these qualifications appears to be the recognition that criminal liability does not arise under Section 906 unless the officer, at a minimum, knowingly submits a false certification.

Requirements for disclosure controls
Although registered investment companies are exempt from Section 404 of SOX, which directs the SEC to issue rules requiring other issuers to include internal control reports in their annual filings, the SEC has imposed a similar requirement for investment companies under Section 302. In particular, rules require each investment company filing reports under Section 13(a) or Section 15(d) of the Exchange Act to adopt and maintain "controls and procedures" to make sure their disclosure in their Exchange Act reports

is complete and accurate. A rule under the 1940 Act requires all registered management investment companies filing reports on Form N-CSR to adopt and maintain disclosure controls and procedures to ensure that the disclosure in those reports is complete and accurate. The effect of the latter rule is to make the disclosure control requirement applicable to privately offered registered investment companies that do not have Exchange Act reporting obligations.

These disclosure controls are intended to be more encompassing than the "internal controls" that pertain to an issuer's financial reporting and control of its assets. The rules also require investment companies to evaluate their disclosure controls and procedures within 90 days prior to filing a report that includes a certification relating to those controls (Form N-SAR or N-CSR).

Section 2(a)(3) – audit committees
Establishment of an audit committee
An investment company that is not listed on an exchange is not currently required to have an audit committee. Although SOX does not require registered investment companies to establish audit committees, funds may find (and have found) it useful to establish audit committees because several provisions of SOX require the participation or approval of the issuer's audit committee. Section 2(a)(3)(A) of SOX defines "audit committee" as "a committee (or equivalent body) established by and amongst the board of directors of an issuer for the purpose of overseeing the accounting and financial reporting process of the issuer and audits of financial statements of the issuer". If a company does not establish an audit committee, Section 2(a)(3)(B) provides that the entire board of directors is to be considered the audit committee. In light of SOX's definition of audit committee, investment companies that are not listed on an exchange will be considered to have an audit committee, either by designation or by default.

Sections 202, 301, 302 and 407 – requirements for audit committees
As noted above, SOX imposes certain responsibilities on an issuer's audit committee. Section 202 generally requires that audit and non-audit services performed by auditors be approved in advance by the issuer's audit committee. Certifying officers of an investment company are required to disclose their evaluation of the invest-

ment company's disclosure controls and procedures to the investment company's board of director's audit committee. Under Section 407 of SOX, the SEC has adopted rules that require every issuer to disclose in its periodic reports whether its audit committee has at least one member who is an audit committee financial expert and whether that person is independent of management. If the audit committee has no such member, the company must disclose why it does not. The SEC has defined "audit committee financial expert", for the purposes of these rules, as a person who has:

(1) an understanding of generally accepted accounting principles and financial statements;
(2) the ability to assess the general application of such principles in the accounting for estimates, accruals and reserves;
(3) experience preparing, auditing, or evaluating financial statements of comparable companies;
(4) an understanding of internal accounting controls; and
(5) an understanding of audit committee functions. The rule also requires the investment company to use the 1940 Act's "interested person"[54] standard in place of SOX's "affiliated person" standard in determining audit committee member independence.

Section 301 of SOX establishes several requirements for audit committees of listed companies, including that the audit committee: is directly responsible for the appointment, compensation and oversight of the company's auditors; must consist solely of independent directors (i.e. the director may not accept any consulting, advisory or other compensation from the issuer or be an affiliated person of the issuer or any subsidiary, other than in the director's capacity as a board or committee member); must establish procedures for receiving and reviewing accounting-related complaints and concerns regarding questionable accounting or auditing practices; and must have authority to engage independent counsel and advisors as it deems necessary. The Section also requires each issuer to provide funding to compensate auditors and advisers retained by the audit committee. Section 301 further directs the

---

[54] *See* Section 2(a)(19) of the 1940 Act for the definition of "interested person". The definition includes, among others, any affiliated person of the investment company, the immediate family of a natural person who is an affiliated person of the investment company and any interested person of the adviser of or principal underwriter for an investment company.

SEC to adopt rules that direct national securities exchanges and national securities associations to prohibit the listing of any security of an issuer that is not in compliance with these requirements.

The SEC has adopted rules implementing these provisions of Section 301, stating that the rules, and the corresponding provisions of SOX, apply only to listed companies. Thus, only investment companies whose shares are listed on an exchange are affected by these provisions. The SEC exempted UITs, as they do not have a board of directors.

Under the SEC's audit committee rules, investment companies that are subject to the rules (listed closed-end funds and non-UIT exchange-traded funds) are required to appoint the issuer's auditors. Investment companies are also required to use the 1940 Act standard for "interested person" in determining the independence of the members of the audit committee. The SEC has taken the position that any company subject to these provisions that did not have a designated audit committee must have a board constituted entirely of independent directors.[55]

Enhancement of auditor independence

In the wake of the passage of SOX, the SEC adopted amendments to its requirements regarding auditor independence to enhance the independence of accountants that audit and review financial statements and prepare attestation reports filed with the Commission.[56] The rules cover several aspects of the registrant–auditor relationship, and the principal provisions applicable to registered investment companies are described below.

Pre-approval of audit and non-audit services

A registered investment company's audit committee must pre-approve all audit and non-audit services provided by the auditor of the investment company's financial statements to the investment company or any entity in the investment company complex where the nature of the services provided have a direct effect on the operations or financial reporting of the investment company. SEC rules specify, however, that services can be performed under pre-established policies and procedures, as long as the services to

---

55 *See* Investment Company Act Release 26001 (9th April 2003).
56 *See* Investment Company Act Release 25915 (28th January 2003).

be performed are specifically contemplated by the policies and procedures, the audit committee is informed of each service and the policies and procedures do not include delegation of the audit committee's responsibilities to management.

Audit partner rotation and "time-out"
Partners on the audit engagement team are prohibited from working on the audit engagement of a registered investment company (and any other registered investment company in the same investment company complex) for more than five consecutive years (lead and concurring partners) or seven consecutive years (all other partners). These partners will not be able to return to the engagement until after the expiration of a "time-out" period of either five years (lead and concurring partners) or two years (all other partners). The rules provide an exemption for certain small accounting firms.

Certain employee relationships
An accounting firm is prohibited from auditing a registered investment company's financial statements if a former audit engagement team member is employed in a financial reporting oversight role with the registered investment company (or with any entity in the same investment company complex that is responsible for the financial reporting or operations of the registered investment company or any other registered investment company in the same investment company complex) within a one-year period preceding the commencement of audit procedures.

Communications with the audit committee
The auditor of a registered investment company is required to report certain matters to the audit committee, including critical accounting policies, alternative accounting methodologies and other material information. Such communications are required at least annually and possibly as frequently as quarterly.

Disclosures to investors
A registered investment company is required to disclose in its annual proxy statement (or in Form N-CSR, if it does not file a proxy statement) information related to audit and non-audit services provided by, and fees paid to, the auditor of the investment company's financial statements. Information also needs to be provided for

certain non-audit services and fees relating to other entities in the investment company complex.

Privately offered funds

Investment companies that have not made a public offering of their shares and that do not have a class of shares registered under Section 12 of the Exchange Act are not obligated to file reports under either Section 13(a) or 15(d) of the Exchange Act or under Section 30 of the 1940 Act. The SEC has confirmed that its rules implementing Sections 302 and 906 of SOX do not apply to registered investment companies that do not file periodic reports under Section 13(a) or 15(d). The SEC, however, has adopted rules requiring all registered investment companies, not just those subject to Section 13(a) or 15(d) of the Exchange Act, to File From N-CSR, to include Section 302 Certifications in Form N-CSR and to adopt related disclosure controls and procedures. This requirement applies to privately offered investment companies that are registered under the 1940 Act, but have not made, and are not proposing to make, a public offering of their shares.

Code of ethics

Under SEC rules implementing Section 406 of SOX, an investment company registered under the 1940 Act must disclose annually whether it has adopted a code of ethics that applies to its senior executive and financial officers.[57] For the purposes of SOX, a code of ethics should consist of written procedures designed to deter wrongdoing and to promote:

(a) honest and ethical conduct, including the ethical handling of actual or apparent conflicts of interest between personal and professional relationships;
(b) full, fair, accurate, timely and understandable disclosure in reports and documents filed with or submitted to the SEC and in other public communications made by the investment company;
(c) compliance with applicable governmental laws, rules and regulations;

---

57 The rules require coverage of the investment company's principal executive officer, principal financial officer, principal accounting officer or controller or persons performing similar functions, regardless of whether these individuals are employed by the investment company or a third party. This requirement is broader than the language of SOX, which refers only to coverage of "senior financial officers".

(d) prompt internal reporting of violations of the code to identified persons; and
(e) accountability for adherence to the code.

If the investment company has not adopted such a code, it must explain why it has not done so. If a company has adopted a code, the company must file a copy of the code as an exhibit to Form N-CSR or post the code on its website. As an alternative, the investment company must provide an undertaking in its Form N-CSR to provide a copy of the code upon request without charge. An investment company must also disclose amendments to the code or waivers of its provisions on Form N-CSR or, if certain conditions are met, on the investment company's website.

Other provisions of SOX

Section 405 – exemptions for registered investment companies
Section 405 exempts registered investment companies from Sections 401, 402 and 404 of SOX. These provisions require public companies to disclose all material correcting adjustments identified by auditors and all material off-balance sheet transactions with special purpose entities in certain reports, prohibit personal loans to executive officers and directors of the issuer and require the addition of internal control reports in annual reports. Registered investment companies are exempted from these disclosure requirements because their objectives are adequately addressed by existing federal securities laws and rules issued under these laws (e.g. Section 17(a) of the 1940 Act and Rule 17j-1).

Section 403 – accelerated reporting of insider trading
SOX amends Section 16(a) of the Exchange Act to require that insiders (i.e. executive officers, directors and beneficial owners of more than 10% of a class of an issuer's registered equity securities) file reports of changes in beneficial ownership (i.e. Form 4) with the SEC. Such transactions must be reported to the SEC by the end of the second business day after the trade date, except for specified cases in which the reporting person might not be aware of the trade until after it is made.

Exchange Act Rule 16a-3 requires certain other transactions to be reported on a current basis on Form 4. For example, transactions between issuers and their officers or directors exempted by

Exchange Act Rule 16b-3 (e.g. grants, awards and acquisitions from the issuer, dispositions to the issuer, exempted discretionary transactions) must be reported on Form 4 within the two-business-day deadline. Pursuant to Section 30(h) of the 1940 Act, insiders of a registered closed-end investment company are subject to the requirements for accelerated reporting of transactions in securities of the fund.

Section 403 of SOX requires that:

(1) insiders file their transaction reports on Form 4 electronically;
(2) the SEC place such reports on its website by the end of the business day following the filing; and
(3) issuers that maintain corporate websites place their insiders' Form 4 reports on their websites by the end of the business day following the filing.

In 2003, the SEC amended its applicable rules to require electronic filing of its forms contemplated by Section 16(a) of the Exchange Act. The rule also requires an issuer that maintains a corporate website to post such forms filed with respect to its equity securities on its website by the end of the day after filing.[58]

Section 408 – regular SEC review

Under Section 408 of SOX, the SEC must review the reports and disclosures, including financial statements, of issuers that have securities listed on an exchange or traded on NASDAQ, at least once every three years. By its terms, the Section only applies to investment companies that are listed on an exchange, such as exchange-traded closed-end funds and other exchange-traded funds (ETFs).

Section 307 – new rules of professional conduct for attorneys

In January 2003, the SEC issued rules governing the conduct of a lawyer practicing before the SEC, requiring any such lawyer representing a public company to report evidence of a material securities law violation, breach of fiduciary duty or similar violation to the company's chief legal officer or chief executive officer. The rules also provide that, if that officer does not appropriately respond (i.e. by adopting, as necessary, remedial measures or sanctions with respect

---

58 Investment Company Act Release 16044 (7th May 2003).

to the violation), the lawyer must report the evidence to officials at successively higher levels, including the company's audit committee, another committee composed of the company's independent directors and, if necessary, the company's board of directors.

The rules under SOX can be enforced under a recently added provision to the Exchange Act, Section 4C, which permits the SEC to censure, suspend or bar persons, including lawyers, who appear or practice before the SEC when it determines that the person has engaged in "improper professional conduct". In adding Section 4C, Section 602 of SOX codified Rule 102(e) of the SEC's Rules of Practice. The SEC may impose a sanction under Section 4C upon a lawyer when it finds, after notice and an opportunity for hearing, that the lawyer:

(1) does not possess the requisite qualifications to represent others;
(2) is lacking in character or integrity or has engaged in unethical or improper professional conduct; or
(3) has wilfully violated, or wilfully aided and abetted the violation of, any provisions of the federal securities laws or the rules and regulations under those laws.

CONCLUSION

For UK and other non-US fund managers and advisers, the United States provides a potentially large market for their specialist skills. In the case of fund managers and advisers, the ability to access that market without submitting to registration is relatively limited and can only be undertaken with care. Recent years have seen some relaxation in the US regime and greater ease for such skills to be made available in the United States. However, the greater cooperation between the US and UK regulators has not yet introduced the kind of reciprocity of regulation and authorisation that exists within the EU and the European Economic Area.

7

Broker–Dealer Regulation

Mark Berman; Steven F Gatti

Threadneedle Asset Management Limited;
Clifford Chance US LLP

Participation by non-US brokers, dealers and banks in the US securities markets has increased substantially in recent years. At the same time, the desire and ability of US persons, particularly institutional investors, to access non-US markets has increased dramatically. Non-US broker–dealers seeking to conduct business, directly or indirectly, with US investors or to participate in multi-national offers involving a distribution of securities in the United States must comply with applicable US laws and regulations governing the conduct of such activities.

The provisions of the Exchange Act and the rules and regulations thereunder and also the SRO rules govern or provide for, among other things, broker–dealer registration, capital adequacy and customer protection, books and record-keeping requirements, anti-fraud and civil liability standards, trading practices, continuing disclosure obligations and other requirements. These requirements are exacting and are administered and enforced so as to ensure orderly markets and investor protection. Non-US firms proposing to do business with their US counterparts or directly with US clients will naturally wish to avoid US broker–dealer registration and also to avoid, where appropriate, the broad, non-US reach of US regulation.

In response to the September 2001 terrorist attacks, governmental agencies and regulators have embarked on a robust, comprehensive approach to ensure that regulated firms, investors and the markets themselves are free from the taint of money laundering and terrorist financing. The USA Patriot Act of 2001 and the rules adopted thereunder by the US Treasury, FinCEN and the SEC will have a marked effect not just on US institutions, but also on their non-US branches, affiliates and agencies, and other institutions with links to the United States. In addition, recent accounting scandals and market upheaval on Wall Street has resulted in significant structural changes in the intra-firm relationships between investment bankers and research analysts and the relationship of firms to their customers.

The most significant broker–dealer requirements impacting non-US firms are discussed in this chapter. These include anti-money laundering considerations and the Patriot Act, the regulation of analysts and research/investment banking conflicts, Rule 15a-6, Regulation M and "information barrier" requirements.

BROKER–DEALER REGISTRATION

Because of the fundamental role of the broker–dealer as the intermediary through which US investors access the securities markets, broker–dealer registration is a cornerstone in the structure of the Exchange Act and federal and state securities regulation.

Section 15(a) of the Exchange Act requires any person that effects transactions in securities by means of interstate commerce for his own account or for the account of others to register with the SEC as a broker–dealer. Section 3(a)(17) of the Exchange Act defines "interstate commerce" as "trade [or] commerce ... between any foreign country and any state". Under Section 3(a)(4) of the Exchange Act, a "broker" is any person that is engaged in the business of effecting transactions in securities for the account of others. "Dealer" is defined in Section 3(a)(5) of the Exchange Act as any person engaged in the business of buying or selling securities for his own account. Neither broker nor dealer is defined in terms of jurisdictional limits.

Persons acting as brokers or dealers register with the SEC if they are physically present in the United States or if, regardless of their location, they effect, induce, or attempt to induce securities transactions with investors in the United States. Thus, any entity or person engaged in the business of effecting securities transactions using "US jurisdictional means" or "interstate commerce" (eg, US mail, telephone, physical visits, Internet, etc.), may be required to register as a broker–dealer with the SEC, absent an exemption. Failure to follow a safe harbour – such as Rule 15a-6 – or obtain an exemption or register as a broker–dealer could result in transactions being effected by an unregistered entity or person. As a consequence, any transactions effected by an unregistered entity or person could be subject to a rescission right by a US investor, and could ultimately subject the unregistered entity or person to legal or disciplinary action by a US regulator. In addition, US registered broker–dealers must also join either a registered national securities association or a registered national securities exchange, such as the NASD or the NYSE. Through membership in these SROs, US registered broker–dealers become subject to standards of professional competence, disciplinary standards, and rules governing their sales practices.

The definition of "broker" was amended by this GLB to carve out banks from this definition, to the extent that they satisfied the requirements of one or more exceptions – thus permitting banks to engage in certain securities activities without becoming brokers and having to register with the SEC. The SEC proposed Regulation B to add further exemptions for banks from the definition of broker. When it did this, the SEC also proposed a conforming amendment to Rule 15a-6 (discussed below) to clarify that the exemptions in Rule 15a-6 would apply to transactions with US banks that are themselves acting under an exception to the definitions of "broker" and "dealer".

Once registered, a broker–dealer is subject to regulatory and supervisory oversight to ensure basic competency, to provide the public with information regarding its business, to promote financial solvency, to safeguard the interests of public investors, and to ensure the integrity of the US securities markets. A broker–dealer must also register with an SRO, typically the NASD, and join SIPC. Every registered broker–dealer must comply with the SEC's net capital[1] and customer protection rules, maintain adequate

---

[1] As discussed below, the SEC adopted rule amendments under the Exchange Act that establish a voluntary, alternative method of computing deductions to net capital for certain broker–dealers that qualify as CSEs. This alternative method permits a broker–dealer to use mathematical models to calculate net capital requirements for market and derivatives-related credit risk. A broker–dealer using the alternative method of computing net capital is subject to, among other things, enhanced net capital, early warning, recordkeeping, reporting, and certain other requirements, and must implement and document an internal risk management system. This rule is now in force.

competency levels by satisfying NASD and other SRO requirements, satisfy record-keeping and reporting obligations, and not run foul of the anti-fraud and civil liability provisions of the Exchange Act and the rules thereunder. Its employees must be properly registered and qualified, and adequately supervised within a system of controls reasonably designed to achieve compliance with applicable requirements.

The SEC takes a territorial approach in applying the broker–dealer registration requirements of Section 15(a). A broker–dealer that effects or attempts to induce securities transactions with US or non-US investors while physically operating within the United States would normally be required to register. A non-US firm that conducts its activities totally outside the United States would typically not be required to register. However, any communication from outside into the United States – fax, telephone call, letter or email – would constitute the use of jurisdictional means under Section 15(a). Consequently, any non-US firm that solicits or effects a securities transaction with any person in the United States is potentially subject to the registration requirements[2].

Recently, the SEC adopted new rules for Consolidated Supervised Entities (CSEs) and Supervised Investment Bank Holding Companies (IBHCs). The new rules are applicable to large US broker–dealer holding companies. They are voluntary requirements, involving increased recordkeeping and reporting, increased supervision outside the broker–dealer entity, and a reporting of holding company capital based on Basel standards.

The requirements for CSEs are as follows.

- The entity in question must have a minimum US$1 billion in tentative net capital at broker–dealer;
- The substantive provisions are patterned after the "BD Lite" requirements;
- The rules would permit broker–dealers to calculate capital requirements based on internal risk models; and
- The requirements harmonise net capital charges with their internal risk management systems and capital allocations.

---

[2] For more guidance on US broker–dealer registration requirements *see* the Guide to Broker–dealer Registration, on the SEC's web site (updated 11th March 2005) at www.sec.gov/divisions/marketreg/bdguide.htm.

The CSEs rules are available to broker–dealers that are affiliated with banks, including non-US banks.

IBHCs are required to comply with the following:

- they cannot affiliate with general-purpose insured US banks (but can do this with certain limited purpose US banks);
- they must maintain at least US$100m in tentative net capital at the broker–dealer or otherwise; and
- they must demonstrate a substantial presence in the securities market.

These provisions at first blush may not appear relevant to non-US entities, but their provisions are far-reaching. As regards entities engaged in financial services in the EU, the Financial Conglomerates Directive (FCD) requires that investment firms engaged in an activity that is caught by the FCD and by the Investment Services Directive would be subject to prudential standards that was equivalent" to EU standards – and to ensure a co-ordinated approach to regulation. SEC registered US broker–dealers that operate in the EU would be required to be regulated by a "global supervisor" – the same would hold true for a non-US EU-based investment firm with an SEC-registered US affiliate. Thus, these entities would be required to identify a single regulator to be its global supervisor as regards prudential regulation – and depending on how the SEC applied the CSE and the IBHC rules and the FSA or another EU regulator interpreted the FCD, it may mean that a regulator foreign to the institution in hand would be its global supervisor. Certain regulators, including the US Office of Thrift Supervision (OTS) and the SEC, have started to issue findings about institutions caught by these provisions – for example, in December 2004, and after consultation with the Commission Bancaire and the BaFin, the OTS was named the EU coordinating supervisor for GE Capital Services Limited, the financing arm of General Electric.[3]

SEC Rule 15a-6

The SEC adopted Rule 15a-6 under the Exchange Act in order to facilitate access by US institutional investors through non-US

---

[3] See OTS Press Release OTS 04–54, "OTS Named EU Coordinating Supervisor of GE" (22nd December 2004), available at www.ots.treas.gov/docs/7/77454.html.

broker–dealers to foreign securities markets and research on foreign issuers. The Rule provides a non-exclusive safe-harbour exemption from broker–dealer registration requirements for non-US firms[4] that engage in certain securities activities with US investors in compliance with the provisions of the exemption. In summary, under Rule 15a-6 non-US broker–dealers can, without registration:

- ❑ effect unsolicited transactions in securities with US persons;
- ❑ subject to certain conditions described below, solicit US persons who are "major US institutional investors" by furnishing them directly with research reports;
- ❑ solicit transactions in securities from, and execute transactions with or for, "US institutional investors," subject to certain conditions; and
- ❑ solicit and execute transactions in securities directly with: SEC registered broker–dealers (whether acting as principal or as agent for others); banks acting in a broker–dealer capacity; international organisations; non-US persons temporarily present in the United States with which the non-US broker–dealer has a pre-existing relationship; non-US agencies or branches of US persons permanently located outside the United States (provided the transactions occur outside the United States); and US citizens resident outside the United States (provided the non-US broker–dealer does not direct its selling efforts toward identifiable groups of US citizens resident abroad).

Central to understanding and complying with Rule 15a-6 are two key terms:

- ❑ **Major US institutional investor** means any entity, including a corporation or any investment adviser, whether or not registered under the 1940 Act, that owns or controls, or in the case of an investment adviser has under management, more than US$100 million in aggregate financial assets. Under this definition, unregistered investment advisers (such as hedge funds), as well as US business corporations and partnerships, may qualify as major US institutional investors, provided they meet the aggregate financial assets test.

---

4 Rule 15a-6(b)(3) requires that the non-US broker or dealer is not a US resident or an office or branch of an SEC-registered broker–dealer.

❑ **US institutional investor** means a person that is an investment company registered with the SEC under the 1940 Act; a bank, savings and loan association, insurance company, business development company, small business investment company or employee benefit plan defined in Rule 501(a)(1) of Regulation D under the Securities Act; a private business development company defined in Rule 501(a)(2) of Regulation D; an organisation described in Section 501(c)(3) of the US Internal Revenue Code of 1985 as amended; or a trust defined in Rule 501(a)(7) of Regulation D.

Unsolicited transactions
If a transaction is not "solicited" by a non-US broker–dealer, the transaction may be effected directly with the US person without the non-US firm being required to register with the SEC. This exemption would appear to be quite broad. However, its usefulness is limited by the SEC Staff's view of the activities that constitute solicitation. In adopting Rule 15a-6, the SEC broadly defined "solicitation" as including:

> *"any affirmative effort by a broker or dealer intended to induce transactional business for the broker–dealer or its affiliates. Solicitation includes efforts to induce a single transaction or to develop an ongoing securities business relationship. Conduct deemed to be solicitation includes telephone calls from a broker–dealer to a customer encouraging use of the broker–dealer to effect transactions, as well as advertising one's function as a broker or a market maker in newspapers or periodicals of general circulation in the United Sates or on any radio or television station whose broadcasting is directed into the United States... . A broker–dealer also would solicit customers by, inter alia, recommending the purchase or sale of particular securities, with the anticipation that the customer will execute the recommended trade through the broker–dealer."*[5]

Thus, solicitation in the Rule 15a-6 context is so expansive as to make it unlikely that this exemption would be available other than in extremely limited circumstances.

---

5   Exchange Act Release 27017 (11th July 1989).

Research exemption

Rule 15a-6(a)(2) makes clear that certain types of solicitation of US persons are allowable without the need for registration under the Exchange Act. In particular, non-US broker–dealers may provide major US institutional investors and US institutional investors with research reports subject to the following conditions, without triggering broker–dealer registration requirements.

Under certain circumstances, non-US firms may send research reports (whether electronically or in written form) directly to major US institutional investors. However:

- the research reports must not recommend the use of the non-US broker–dealer which prepared the report to effect transactions in securities. The reports must state that interested persons should contact a US-registered broker–dealer to effect transactions in securities;
- the non-US broker–dealer must not initiate contact with the major US institutional investor to follow-up on the research reports or otherwise attempt to induce securities transactions with such investors (except as permitted by Rule 15a-6 (a)(3), as described in the next section);
- any transactions resulting from the provision of the research reports must, in fact, be effected only through a US-registered broker–dealer; and
- no separate fee should be charged for the research report.

If a customer does not qualify as a major US institutional investor, the non-US broker–dealer may distribute research to it, but only through an SEC-registered broker–dealer.[6] Such reports must refer the customer to the registered broker–dealer to execute transactions in any securities covered in the report, and all such transactions must, in fact, be executed through the registered broker–dealer. In addition, the research report must clearly identify who prepared the report and state, prominently, that the registered US-broker–dealer accepts responsibility for the content of the report.

6 Typically, the US-registered broker–dealer is the non-US broker–dealer's affiliate, though recent years have seen an increase in the number of arrangements whereby registered broker–dealers "purchase" the research products of unaffiliated, non-US broker–dealers and redistribute that research to their clients in the United States, or otherwise agree to distribute the research in connection with a "15a-6 agreement."

In accepting responsibility, the US-registered broker–dealer should take reasonable steps to satisfy itself regarding the key statements in the report. In practice, this normally means that a qualified supervisory analyst at the registered broker–dealer approves the report after carefully reviewing it and comparing its content with public information that is readily available about the subject issuer and securities.

Transactions with institutional investors
Non-registered broker–dealers may also solicit transactional business with US institutional investors provided that:

- any resulting transactions are effected through an SEC-registered broker–dealer;
- information or documents relating to transactions carried out under Rule 15a-6 are provided to the SEC upon request; and
- the US-registered broker–dealer through which transactions are effected takes supervisory responsibility for the transactions and for the non-US entity's related activities (eg, research furnished to customers as described above), and maintains adequate books and records relating to the transaction in accordance with the Exchange Act.

The transactions may be effected by the registered broker–dealer acting in either a principal or an agency capacity but, in each event, the registered broker–dealer must maintain proper books and records and adequate regulatory capital, and unless the terms of an April 1997 Staff no-action letter are satisfied (*see* below), it must perform the required clearing and settlement function or utilise another US broker–dealer to do so. Though required to retain responsibility for clearance and settlement, in certain circumstances the registered broker–dealer may arrange for the performance of some of the mechanical functions of clearance and settlement by an affiliated entity outside the United States or, perhaps, by a third party settlement or clearing agent. Thus, by way of example, it may be appropriate for the non-US broker–dealer to generate, in accordance with US regulatory requirements, trade confirmations in accordance with Exchange Act Rule 10b-10 on behalf of, and in the name of, the registered broker–dealer and to physically send them to customers in the name of and as agent for the registered broker–dealer.

In addition, Rule 15a-6(a)(3) requires the US registered broker–dealer to be responsible for maintaining required regulatory capital; and again, unless the terms of the April 1997 no-action letter are satisfied, receiving, delivering and safeguarding funds and securities on behalf of major US institutional investors or US institutional investors; obtaining consent to service or process from the non-US broker–dealer and each non-US associated person; and gathering and maintaining information regarding non-US associated persons akin to the information required on NASD forms for registered persons.

Direct execution of transactions
Rule 15a-6(a)(4) provides a separate exemption that permits non-US broker–dealers to execute transactions directly with registered broker–dealers, banks acting in the capacity of broker–dealers and certain other limited categories of investors. The wording of the exemption seems to allow transactions to be effected directly with broker–dealers whether they act as principal (for their own account) or as agent (for the account of others). This wording has been taken by some practitioners to indicate that non-US broker–dealers may deal with US customers without the need to comply with the extensive requirements of paragraph (a)(3) of the Rule so long as a registered broker–dealer acts as agent or principal in the subject transaction. The Staff, however, interprets the exemption to mean that non-US broker–dealers seeking to avail themselves of this provision may not, at the same time, maintain contacts with the US investors with which or on whose behalf the registered broker–dealer is dealing. If the non-US broker–dealer is to maintain such contacts, it must do so by complying with the other exemptive provisions of the Rule. Consequently, non-US broker–dealers seeking to deal with US institutional investors will, in most instances, need to enlist the intermediation of a US registered broker–dealer in accordance with the provisions of paragraph (a)(3).

SEC no-action positions

For more than six years after the Rule's adoption there was little formal interpretation published by the Staff. However in 1996 and 1997, the Staff issued three no-action letters which, taken together, expanded the Rule's application and usefulness.

BROKER–DEALER REGULATION

The 1996 "fiduciaries" letter

In January 1996, the Division of Market Regulation issued a no-action letter in response to a request by several US broker–dealers.[7] This letter clarified the Staff's views with respect to several issues that concerned the securities industry since the introduction of the Rule. In summary, the letter makes clear that non-US broker–dealers may effect transactions in foreign securities[8] with US resident fiduciaries (which includes, for example, a US registered investment adviser) for offshore clients[9] without the non-US broker–dealer having to register as a broker–dealer or comply with Rule 15a-6. This relief is conditional upon the non-US broker–dealer obtaining a written assurance from the US resident fiduciary that the relevant account is managed for an offshore client, and that the non-US broker–dealer's transactions, other than in non-US securities with offshore clients, will be effected in compliance with Section 15(a) or an exemption provided by Rule 15a-6.

The Morgan Stanley letter

In a no-action letter issued to Morgan Stanley & Co. Inc. (Morgan Stanley),[10] the Division of Market Regulation confirmed that it would not recommend enforcement action under Section 15(a) of

---

7 *Cleary, Gottlieb, Steen & Hamilton* (22nd November 1995, revised 30th January 1996).
8 A "foreign security" is a: (a) security issued by a company that is not incorporated in or otherwise domiciled in the United States, when the transaction is not effected on a US exchange or on NASDAQ; or (b) a debt security (including a convertible instrument) issued by a US incorporated company and offered in a non-US distribution. Whether an over-the-counter (OTC) derivative constitutes a foreign security is determined by reference to the underlying instrument. A depositary receipt issued by a US bank is not a foreign security unless it is initially offered and sold outside the United States under Regulation S under the Securities Act. Generally, securities that are offered and sold outside the United States in accordance with Regulation S would not lose their status as foreign securities as a result of offers and sales of such securities to US investors pursuant to Securities Act Section 4(2), Rule 144A or another resale transaction exemption under the Securities Act.
9 An "offshore client" is defined as: (a) any entity not organised or incorporated under the laws of the United States and not engaged in a trade or business in the United States for US federal income tax purposes; (b) any natural person who is not a US resident; or (c) any entity not organised or incorporated under the laws of the US with substantially all of the outstanding voting securities beneficially owned by the persons described in (a) and (b) above. A US citizen residing outside the United States is considered a resident of the US unless the citizen: (a) has US$500,000 or more under the management of the US resident fiduciary with which the non-US broker–dealer transacts business; or (b) has, together with his spouse, a net worth in excess of US$1,000,000.
10 *Morgan Stanley India Securities Pvt. Ltd* (20th December 1996).

the Exchange Act if Morgan Stanley India Securities Pvt Ltd. (MSISL) effected transactions in Indian securities in India for Morgan Stanley's US institutional customers without having to register as a broker–dealer. The Staff also confirmed that it would not recommend enforcement action under Exchange Act Rules 15c3-3, 17a-3, 17a-4, 17a-5 and 17a-13[11] if transactions in Indian securities effected in India by MSISL for Morgan Stanley's US institutional customers were: (a) not separately entered onto the books of Morgan Stanley; (b) not taken into account for the purpose of filing Morgan Stanley's "FOCUS Report;" (c) conducted without a physical examination and counting of the subject securities, or otherwise accounted for by Morgan Stanley as securities subject to its control or direction; and (d) settled without Morgan Stanley promptly obtaining and subsequently maintaining physical possession of the subject securities.

This relief was subject to a number of conditions and was predicated on specific undertakings given by Morgan Stanley regarding the procedures that it undertook to follow in effecting, settling and recording the securities transactions in question. These include the following:

- ❏ the firm will provide its US customers with a trade confirmation satisfying applicable requirements of Exchange Act Rule 10b-10 (the contract note rule);
- ❏ information regarding each transaction on MSISL's books and records will be available to Morgan Stanley employees;
- ❏ Morgan Stanley employees will be responsible for verifying that all trade entries on MSISL's books accurately reflect the trade tickets prepared by Morgan Stanley;

---

11 Exchange Act Rule 15c3-3 requires, in part, that registered broker–dealers promptly obtain and maintain the physical possession or control of all fully paid securities and excess margin securities carried for the account of customers. Exchange Act Rule 17a-3 requires the maintenance by registered broker–dealers of certain books and records, including, inter alia, trading blotters and account ledgers. Rule 17a-4 requires broker–dealers subject to Rule 17a-3 to retain these records for prescribed periods of time. Rule 17a-5 requires registered broker–dealers to file with the SEC Form X-17A-5, the Financial and Operational Combined Uniform Single Report (FOCUS Report). The FOCUS Report is the basic financial and operating report required from broker–dealers that are subject to the minimum net capital requirements of Exchange Act Rule 15c3-1. Exchange Rule 17a-13 requires a registered broker–dealer physically to examine and count securities held by it and to account for all securities that, though not in its physical possession, are subject to that broker–dealer's control or direction.

- ❏ the firm will make available to the SEC all MSISL records relating to the transactions;
- ❏ the firm will be responsible for fails in accordance with Rule 15c3–1 and will account for transactions in accordance with Rule 15c3–3; and
- ❏ the firm will develop procedures for reconciling the trades so as to perform its net capital and reserve formula calculations, and to prepare customer statements.

The restrictions under Indian law preventing Morgan Stanley from holding funds and securities in India on behalf of its US customers, and requiring that settlement occur through each customer's custodian in India, appear to have been important considerations underpinning the relief granted. These considerations may be particularly significant as an indicator of the Staff's inclination to grant similar relief in the future – in particular, without some intervening rule making by the SEC. The relief granted in this letter was quite broad and, while well received by the industry, the Staff may require the existence of similarly prohibitive local regulation, or some other set of constraining facts, before it would be inclined to grant further requests for such extensive relief.

The April 1997 relief

In an April 1997 letter, the Staff granted further no-action relief under Rule 15a-6.[12] The effect of this relief was to: expand the definition of major US institutional investor; relax the chaperoning requirements; permit the direct clearance and settlement (transfer of securities and funds) between non-US broker–dealers and US institutional investors; and ease the restrictions on the dissemination of quotations in the United States by foreign broker–dealers.

Revised definition of major US institutional investor. The Staff expanded the definition of major US institutional investor to include any entity, including any investment adviser, whether or not registered under the 1940 Act, that owns or controls or, in the case of an investment adviser, has under management more than US$100 million in aggregate financial assets.

---

12 *Giovani Prezioso* (9th April 1997).

Expanded clearance and settlement. The letter permits clearance and settlement of transactions in foreign securities effected pursuant to Rule 15a-6(a)(3) through the direct transfer of funds and securities between a major US institutional investor or a US institutional investor and a non-US broker–dealer in situations where the non-US broker–dealer is not acting as custodian of the funds and securities of the US investor. Notwithstanding this relief, the letter recognises that Rule 15a-6 will still require the non-US firm to involve a US broker–dealer in these transactions, to issue confirmations and maintain books and records.

Relaxation of the chaperoning requirements. Rule 15a-6 requires that communications between foreign broker–dealers and US institutional investors be "chaperoned" by a representative of a US broker–dealer. After the April 1997 letter, certain communications between foreign broker–dealers and major US institutional investors do not need to be chaperoned. Prior to the April 1997 letter, all visits by representatives of foreign broker–dealers to US institutional investors and US major institutional investors in the United States were required to be chaperoned (ie, a US-registered person needed to present). Responding to industry concerns, the SEC relaxed these requirements. Under the letter, employees of a non-US broker–dealer may, without the participation of an associated person of an affiliated registered broker–dealer: (a) speak from outside the United States with US institutional investors where such communications take place outside NYSE trading hours (between 09.30 and 16.00 New York time); and (b) have in-person contacts in the United States with major US institutional investors, so long as such contacts do not exceed 30 days per year. When speaking with US institutional investors from outside the United States, the non-US broker–dealer employee may accept orders to effect transactions only in foreign securities. Further, such persons involved in in-person contacts may not accept any orders while in the United States.

Electronic quotation dissemination. The April 1997 letter extended the ability of non-US broker–dealers to distribute quotations in the United States via electronic quotation systems by confirming: (a) that such quotations may be distributed through third-party

BROKER–DEALER REGULATION

systems which distribute quotations both in the United States and in other countries; and (b) that furnishing US investors with access to proprietary screen-based systems that supply quotations, prices and other trade reporting information input directly by the non-US broker–dealer will be a permissible contact between the US investor and the foreign broker–dealer, provided that resulting transactions are intermediated by a US registered broker–dealer in accordance with Rule 15a-6(a)(3).

The Web Site Release and the Rule 15a-6 Internet letter

In the Web Site Release, the SEC clarified its views on the treatment of materials posted on a website that may be accessible to US investors. Generally, under the SEC's interpretation, the use of a website by a non-US broker–dealer would not subject the broker–dealer to registration, even though the website may be viewed by persons located in the United States, if:

❏ the website contains a "prominent disclaimer" either affirmatively stating the countries in which the broker–dealer's services are offered (which obviously would not include the United States) or stating that its services are "not available to US persons;" and

❏ the non-US broker–dealer refuses to provide brokerage services to any US person or to a potential customer that gives reason (eg, "residence, mailing, payment method or other grounds) to suspect that it is a US person.

In addition, any non-US broker–dealer doing business with a US customer based on the (rarely used) Rule 15a-6 "unsolicited" exemption should obtain an "affirmative representation" from the US customer that the US customer has "not previously accessed" the firm's website, or maintain records that are sufficiently detailed and verifiable to reliably determine that US customers had not obtained access to its website.

Footnote 56 in the Web Site Release further explained that "because a securities firm's website itself typically is a solicitation, orders routed through the website would not be considered 'unsolicited'." Some commentators noted that this footnote may be construed as applying beyond Rule 15a-6 to imply that all orders routed through the website are "solicited" by the foreign broker–dealer. To clarify the issue, the SEC issued a letter to Merrill Lynch, stating that the language contained in footnote 56 relates only to Rule 15a-6's "unsolicited" transaction exemption, and was not intended to address the question of whether a registered broker–dealer's website constitutes a "solicitation" for other purposes.[13]

Interplay with Regulation S and Rule 144A

As discussed in Chapter 3, Regulation S under the Securities Act is a non-exclusive safe harbour for specified offers and sales of securities that take place outside the United States. If made in accordance with Regulation S, the offer need not be registered with the SEC under Section 5 of the Securities Act. Rule 144A is a safe harbour from the registration provisions of the Securities Act for resales of restricted securities to QIBs.

The Issuer Safe Harbour of Regulation S states that directed selling efforts in the United States may not be made during the period in which the issuer, distributors, their respective affiliates or persons acting on their behalf offer and sell the securities. When it adopted Regulation S, the SEC stated that the scope of directed selling efforts was not coextensive with activities constituting "solicitation," as that term is used in considering the need for broker–dealer registration. The SEC also stated that "while limited activities directed at a single customer or prospective investor may be offers for purposes of Regulation S or solicitation for purposes of Rule 15a-6, they generally will not constitute directed selling efforts for purposes of Regulation S because of their confined effect".[14] As such, the direct dissemination of a non-US market maker's quote to a US person in the United States through a private quotation medium controlled by such a foreign broker–dealer might be viewed as both an offer and a directed selling effort under Regulation S.

The Rule 144A adopting release noted that, in adopting the Rule, the SEC was not altering the registration requirements under Section 15(a) of the Exchange Act for a person that functions as either a broker or a dealer in transactions pursuant to this Rule.

---

[13] *Merrill Lynch & Co.* (13th January 1999).
[14] Securities Act Release 6863 (24th April 1990).

The term dealer includes any institution that, in addition to investing in Rule 144A securities, also holds itself out to other institutions as willing to buy and sell such securities on a regular and continuous basis – that is, through two-sided quotations. Thus, a foreign broker–dealer that engages in resales under Rule 144A might bring itself within the broker–dealer registration requirements of the Exchange Act.

In a Regulation S-Rule 144A offer, non-US firms may wish to place securities with US investors. Caution must be exercised. A careful reading of Rule 144A and Rule 15a-6 will reveal that, due to differences in their definitions, not all QIBs are major US institutional investors.[15] Thus, if a non-US firm contacts an investor in the United States that is a QIB but fails the test to be treated as a major US institutional investor, the investor will be a US institutional investor and the firm must comply with the chaperoning and other restrictions on contacting that institution enumerated in the April 1997 no-action letter, or risk violating Rule 15a-6.

When would an investment adviser become a broker–dealer?

Non-US investment managers may engage in marketing shares of funds that they advise to US prospects. The SEC has issued very few no-action letters addressing the application of the Exchange Act's broker–dealer registration provisions to such entities, but it would be prudent, in the absence of clear pronouncements, to follow the provisions of Rule 15a-6 or to work with SEC-registered broker–dealers or investment advisers when engaging in this practice. Prior to any contact, a potential investor should be screened and a certification obtained from it to confirm whether it is a QIB and a major US institutional investor, and also either an accredited investor (for the 1940 Act Section 3(1)(1) exemption) or a qualified purchaser (for the 1940 Act Section 3(1)(7) exemption).

---

15 The term QIB is defined in Rule 144A(a)(1) as a designated entity, acting for its own account or for the account of other QIBs that, in the aggregate, owns and invests on a discretionary basis at least US$100 million in securities of issuers with which it is not affiliated. The entities designated in Rule 144A include registered broker–dealers and investment companies, banks, investment advisers, certain employee benefit plans and other entities. The US$100 million test for major US institutional investors focuses on aggregate financial assets, whereas the threshold for QIBs excludes certain items that would otherwise be included in aggregate financial assets.

When is a broker–dealer not an investment adviser?

The SEC adopted temporary Rule 202(a)(11)T under the Advisers Act. This rule, which was in force until 15 April 2005, provided that a broker–dealer that provided *non*-discretionary advice solely incidental to its brokerage services is excepted from the definition of investment adviser, regardless of whether it charges an asset-based or fixed fee. The temporary rule also exempted from the Advisers Act those broker–dealers that offered full service brokerage and discount brokerage services, and execution only brokerage, for reduced rates. The conditions of the rule are that the broker–dealer not exercise investment discretion over accounts from which it receives special compensation; and that any advice provided is solely incidental to its brokerage services. The SEC re-proposed to adopt Rule 202(a)(11)-1 under the Advisers Act, which largely tracks the provisions of Rule 202(a)(11)T.[16]

SEC Broker–dealer Regulation and the Internet

While the Internet offers opportunities and advantages for consumers, investors, broker–dealers, and other financial services companies around the world, it also creates substantial legal challenges for regulators entrusted with the responsibility of investor protection and market regulation. For the past several years, the SEC and the US SROs, like their counterparts abroad, have been grappling with how to apply existing laws and regulatory frameworks to the Internet, without unduly restricting the Internet's breadth, scope, and potential as a medium for the delivery of financial services.

Because the Internet enables market participants to disseminate, via proprietary or third party websites, advertising and sales literature, research, and other information about securities and investment services across national boundaries, Internet activities of non-US issuers and/or broker–dealers will most likely trigger the application of US federal and state securities laws. By its very nature, the Internet has no jurisdictional parameters. Accordingly, non-US issuers and/or broker–dealers must not only ensure that their activities comply with their domestic regulatory frameworks, but also that their activities do not run afoul of US federal and state securities laws.

---

[16] Advisers Act Release 2340 (6th January 2005).

The Internet activities of non-US issuers and/or broker–dealers may implicate US federal and state securities laws in a variety of ways, most importantly, in relation to: (a) broker–dealer registration requirements; (b) offers and sales of securities over the Internet; (c) national securities exchange (or alternative trading systems) registration requirements; (d) investment company registration and regulatory requirements; and (e) investment adviser registration and regulatory requirements.

Broker–dealer registration requirements
Entities or individuals that post on proprietary or third-party websites, securities or investment related information that could be construed as involving an offer or sale of securities, or the offering of securities brokerage services, should be mindful of US federal and state registration requirements. Since the Internet allows material that is posted on a website to be accessed from anywhere in the world, securities or investment related material of non-US issuers and broker–dealers must be analysed to ensure that it does not constitute inappropriate activity in the United States for broker–dealer regulatory purposes. Given the developed regulatory structure governing securities and investment related activities in the United States, it is particularly important for a non-US firm that utilises the Internet, even for solely informational purposes, to understand US regulatory interpretations and requirements.

As noted above, the Exchange Act definitions of "broker" and "dealer" specifically exclude persons who buy and sell securities for their own accounts, either individually or in some fiduciary capacity, but not as part of a regular business. The test used by the SEC to determine whether a person is a broker is generally three-pronged: (a) is the person "in the business?;" (b) does the activity constitute "effecting a transaction in securities?;" and (c) is the activity "for the account of others?"

The SEC has traditionally analysed a number of factors to determine whether a person is acting as a broker. For example, brokers typically: (a) engage in holding themselves out to be in the business of buying and selling securities for the account of others (which does not necessarily have to be conducted on a full time basis); (b) receive transaction-based compensation; or (c) have access to, or custody of, customer funds and/or securities. None of these factors, however, is determinative and the analysis is fact sensitive.

In light of the jurisdictional reach of the broker–dealer registration requirements imposed by the SEC, non-US broker–dealers that have websites that reach or may reach the United States should, in order to protect themselves from potential exposure under US securities laws, exercise caution in accepting orders or accounts from US persons, especially non-institutional investors. As a precautionary measure, broker–dealers relying on the "non-solicitation" exemption should obtain from potential US customers, affirmative representations that those customers have not previously accessed their websites, in addition to ensuring compliance with all other requirements under the Rule. In practice, conducting securities activities in conformity with Rule 15a-6 is extremely burdensome for non-US broker–dealers.

Non-US broker–dealers acting as access providers
Given the improvements in communications brought on by the Internet and the increasing appetite on the part of US persons for non-US securities, in a May 1997 concept release[17] the SEC appeared to be ready to address issues related to the provision of access to US persons to non-US markets by non-US broker–dealers. In that release, the SEC asked "whether [it] should require non-US broker–dealers to register as US broker–dealers if they act as access providers to non-US markets on behalf of US persons." After reviewing the full array of regulatory requirements for US broker–dealers, such as the maintenance of minimal net capital and SIPC and SRO membership, the SEC suggested that a less stringent regulatory framework tailored to access provider activities might be more appropriate. To date, however, the SEC has not provided further guidance on the issue.

Steps to avoid triggering US registration for activities over the Internet
In the Web Site Release, the SEC gave its views on the application of US federal securities law to the use of electronic media by issuers, broker–dealers, exchanges, investment companies, and

---

[17] Exchange Act Release 38672 (23rd May 1997).

investment advisors who offer securities, solicit securities transactions or advertise investment services outside the United States. The Web Site Release focuses on the situations in which the posting or offering of solicitation materials on Internet websites would be considered activity taking place "in the United States," requiring the securities, broker–dealer, exchange, investment adviser, or investment fund to be registered in the United States.[18] Placing an unrestricted prospectus on a website would generally be deemed an offer of securities (and an offer made in the United States, if accessible from the United States unless precautions are taken). The Web Site Release provides constructive guidance to US and non-US broker–dealers on utilising the Internet to communicate with the worldwide investing public without triggering US registration requirements.

The mere posting of offering or solicitation materials on websites in and of themselves are not considered activities taking place in the United States that would trigger a US registration requirement. Registration is required, however, where Internet offers, solicitations or other communications are targeted to the United States or US persons. The SEC has stated that issuers and broker–dealers must implement precautionary measures "reasonably designed" to guard against targeting the United States. Where reasonable measures are employed to avoid targeting US investors, an Internet offering would not trigger a registration obligation under US securities laws.

Among other issues, the SEC explained that a non-US broker–dealer that advertises on its website will not be deemed to be soliciting securities transactions with US investors if the non-US broker–dealer takes affirmative steps, reasonably designed to ensure that it does not effect securities transactions with US investors as a result of its Internet activities. Accordingly, a non-US broker–dealer should: (a) post a prominent disclaimer on its website either expressly identifying the countries in which the broker–dealer's services are available or stating that the services are not available to US investors; and (b) refuse to provide brokerage

---

[18] The Web Site Release applies only to broadly disseminated website materials and does not apply to targeted methods of communication such as email, which is considered comparable to paper mail because the sender directs the information to a particular person.

services to any potential investor that the broker–dealer has reason to believe is a US investor, based on residence, mailing address, payment method, or other indicia.

In order to support a position that the non-US broker–dealer's procedures are so "reasonably designed," to ensure that it does not effect securities transactions with US investors due to its Internet presence, the broker–dealer should require potential customers to provide sufficient background information. The SEC has stated, however, that no one set of procedures is exclusive. Adoption of other equally, or more effective measures, can also suffice to show that the broker–dealer is not effecting securities transactions with US investors as a result of its Internet activities. An exemption from US broker–dealer registration requirements, however, does not impact or eliminate the non-US broker–dealer being subject to the antifraud or anti-manipulative provisions of the securities laws, which continue to reach all Internet activity that satisfies the relevant jurisdictional test. Finally, the SEC also made it clear that as technology and practice develop, it may revisit the interaction between the United States securities laws and the Internet and related issues.

State Blue Sky Laws

In 1997, the North American Securities Administrators Association (NASAA)[19] adopted a model interpretative order on the issue of how a broker–dealer or investment adviser could maintain a presence on the Internet without being viewed as "transacting" business in a particular state.[20]

Under the NASAA model, broker–dealers, investment advisers or their agents who use the Internet to distribute information on products or services will not be deemed to be transacting business in that state if they satisfy several conditions. First, the communication must contain a legend clearly stating that the individual or individuals may only transact business in those states in which

---

[19] NASAA is an organisation comprised of regulators from the various state securities commissions.

[20] See NASAA Interpretive Order Concerning Broker–dealers, Investment Advisers, Broker–dealer Agents and Investment Adviser Representatives Using the Internet for General Dissemination of Information on Products and Services (27th April 1997), at www.nasaa.org/NASAA.

they are registered, excluded, or exempted from registration. Second, the communication must contain a mechanism, such as technical "firewalls" or other policies and procedures designed to reasonably ensure that, prior to any subsequent direct communication with prospective customers or clients residing in states where the firm or the agent is not registered, the broker–dealer, investment adviser or representative is registered or qualifies for an exemption. Third, the communication must be limited to the dissemination of information on products and services and must not involve effecting securities transactions or rendering investment advice for compensation.

Finally, broker–dealer agents or investment adviser agents or representatives must: (a) prominently disclose the agents' or representatives' affiliation with a broker–dealer or investment adviser in the communication; (b) have their communications reviewed and approved by the associated broker–dealer or investment adviser who retains responsibility for the communication; and (c) obtain authorisation from the associated broker–dealer or investment adviser for the agents' distribution of product or service information. Although states are not obligated to adopt their own regulations to conform to the NASAA model regulation, the NASAA strongly encourages states to do so. Accordingly, offerors of securities over the Internet are advised to check with each state regulatory authority to ensure that the offer is exempt from registration in that state.

INFORMATION BARRIERS, INSIDER TRADING AND RULE 10B-5
Information Barriers

Under US securities laws, a broker–dealer is subject to sanctions for failure to institute supervisory measures designed to prevent the improper use of material non-public information (inside information). As a practical matter, the primary means of policing the use of inside information is through use of information barriers, or Chinese Wall procedures employed, typically, on a firm-wide (ie, global) basis.

The Exchange Act in effect requires the implementation of information walls. Section 15(f) of the Exchange Act requires that registered broker–dealers "establish, maintain and enforce written policies and procedures, reasonably designed, taking into consideration the nature of such broker's or dealer's business, to prevent the misuse in violation of ... [the federal securities laws], or the rules or regulations thereunder, of material non-public information by such broker or dealer or any person associated with such broker or dealer". Pursuant to Section 21A(b) of the Exchange Act, treble damages can be imposed on a broker–dealer if the SEC proves that the broker–dealer "knowingly or recklessly failed to establish, maintain, or enforce any policy or procedure required under Section 15(f) ... and such failure substantially contributed to or permitted the occurrence of the ... violation". In order to establish a broker–dealer's liability under Section 21A(b), the SEC is not required to demonstrate that the broker–dealer's failure to establish insider trading procedures was essential to the violation, only that the failure "provided some assistance to the ... violations".

Section 15(f) authorises the SEC to promulgate specific information wall procedures, but the SEC has not to date specified a set of required procedures. After the adoption of Section 15(f), the Staff conducted a study of broker–dealer insider trading prevention procedures with the aims of identifying adequate procedures and determining whether specific rulemaking was required. It ultimately released a report noting certain elements of information wall procedures that, although not technically mandated, would be regarded by the SEC as essential. Following the publication of the SEC's Information Wall Survey, the NASD and NYSE each issued to their members a joint notice as to their view of minimum information wall requirements identifying the following:

- a firm's information wall procedures must be formalised, organised and compiled within a firm's procedural/policy manuals;
- employees should be educated as to laws and regulations and the firm's own policies and procedures relating to the use of material non-public information, including, at a minimum, providing information about firm information wall requirements to all employees, obtaining a signed attestation of receipt of such materials (in sensitive areas, annually), and instituting a process for updating employees on new or revised requirements;

❏ any broker–dealer that may receive inside information should: (a) maintain a list of "restricted" securities, as to which the firm and its employees are prohibited from trading; and (b) maintain a "watch list" for use by the compliance department (and perhaps a limited number of other officers) in reviewing proprietary and employee trades for signs of impropriety. In addition, trading in securities issued by the broker–dealer or any of its affiliates should be subject to ongoing review;

❏ to avoid even the appearance of improper trading, broker–dealers may limit certain types of trading by their employees, for example, the acquisition of securities in an initial public offer or excessive or short-term trading. Many broker–dealers require that their employees trade only with the employing firm or with another approved firm.

❏ firm employees that have access to inside information concerning an issuer should not have authority to make sales or trading decisions regarding the securities of such issuer and should be "walled off" from communicating any inside information to those that make such decisions. While the investment-banking department is the most likely to have inside information, it may be necessary to wall off other departments as well;

❏ the broker–dealer should have procedures in place that allow the investment banking department to request information from the research or sales departments without disclosing the purpose for the request. In some circumstances, it may be necessary to bring a research or sales employee "over the wall" before making the request. Proper documentation of any "wall-crossing" would be required;

❏ the broker–dealer should conduct regular, periodic reviews of proprietary and employee trading, for specified time periods. The broker–dealer should establish an exception report to record the pertinent details of any transaction by an employee or proprietary account in a restricted list or watch list security;

❏ a broker–dealer must reasonably inquire into or investigate for possible misuse of inside information any transactions by an employee or by a broker–dealer's proprietary accounts that involve restricted or watch list securities. Any investigation of insider trading must be documented.

Section 10(b) and Rule 10b-5

Exchange Act Section 10(b) prohibits the use of any manipulative or deceptive device in connection with the purchase or the sale of the security. Under Rule 10b-5, it is unlawful in connection with the purchase or sale of the security to employ a device or scheme to defraud, make a materially false statement or misleading omission or engage in any act or business practice that operates as a fraud or deceit. In a Rule 10b-5 case, a plaintiff must prove:

- fraud in connection with the purchase or sale of a security (direct participation);
- materiality;
- misrepresentation or disclosure;
- scienter;
- reliance and causation; and
- damages.

Under the Private Securities Litigation Reform Act of 1995, circumstantial evidence may be used to satisfy the scienter requirement. In certain cases, recklessness or even severe recklessness may suffice to show scienter.[21]

Some plaintiffs cannot meet the reliance element. They may instead use the "fraud on the market" theory, which in certain instances, excuses a plaintiff asserting a 10b-5 claim from proving reliance. Here, a plaintiff proves (i) the defendant made misrepresentations, (ii) that were material, (iii) the stock traded on an efficient market, (iv) the misrepresentations induced a reasonable investor to misjudge the value of the security and (v) plaintiff traded between the time the misrepresentations were made and the time the truth was revealed. *Nathensen* held that investors could not rely on a presumption of reliance under the fraud on the market theory because the markets (in question in that case) did not respond to the alleged misstatements. In 1988, the US Supreme Court held in *Basic, Inc. v Levinson*[22] that a plaintiff in a fraud on the market case is not required to show direct reliance but is presumed to have relied on the security's market price that should reflect all publicly available market information.

---

[21] *See Nathensen v Zonagen, Inc.* 267 F.3d 400, 425 (5th Cir. 2001) (*Nathensen*).
[22] 485 U.S. 224 (1988).

Does the fraud on the market theory apply to analyst reports? This is an issue in a case pending in the SDNY, *DeMarco v. Robertson Stephens*,[23] a class action suit, where an analyst maintained a "buy rating" on the common stock of an equity security while privately selling his own shares. To ascertain whether the fraud on the market theory could be applied the court did not adopt a high standard (for purposes of class certification) but found that by pleading an overall mix of information the plaintiffs made "some showing" of their ability to set forth arguments on the reliance element.

Insider trading
the law of insider trading

Generally, trading on material nonpublic information (inside information) occurs when a person in possession of inside information uses such information to buy or sell securities. Information is considered "material" when there is a substantial likelihood that an investor would consider it important in deciding whether to buy or sell securities. The US Supreme Court held in *TSC Industries, Inc. v Northway, Inc*[24] that inside information alters the total mix of information available to the market. This is a facts and circumstances test. If it is proved that the information is not material, it is not likely that a case or enforcement action would be brought.

In the United States, and other than in the context of a tender offer (*see* Chapter 5), insider trading (and tipping) cases are brought under Section 10(b) of the Exchange Act and Rule 10b-5 thereunder. Section 10(b) prohibits the use of any manipulative or deceptive device or contrivance in connection with the purchase or sale of securities. Rule 10b-5 makes it unlawful in connection with the purchase or sale of securities to employ a device or scheme to defraud, make a materially false statement or misleading omission or engage in any act or business practice that operates as a fraud or deceit. Insider trading cases may be brought as a civil matter and/or a criminal offence.

The US Supreme Court has held that Section 10(b) reaches "any deceptive device used 'in connection with the purchase or sale of

---

[23] 318 F.Supp 110 (S.D.N.Y. 2004).
[24] 426 U.S. 438 (1976).

any Security'"[25] in contravention of rules adopted by the SEC, but also held that Rule 10b-5 "does not extend beyond conduct encompassed by [Section] 10(b)'s prohibitions".[26] The language of Section 10(b) and Rule 10b-5 does not expressly speak to insider trading, but the US courts have relied on the "in connection with" language and the anti-fraud purpose behind these provisions to make insider trading and tipping – and in certain cases, tippee trading (*see* below) – actionable under these provisions.

There are two theories of insider trading liability:

- the **classical theory** – a corporate insider (**insider**) trades on the basis of material nonpublic information (inside information); and
- **misappropriation** – a person other than a corporate insider (**outsider**) trades on the basis of material inside information obtained by reason of that individual's relationship with the person possessing the information.

The law of insider trading has developed and is even now being shaped by case law, prosecutions and SEC administrative proceedings. Some of the key cases are noted below.

- *Cady, Roberts* (SEC 1961): in this SEC administrative action, the concept of "disclose or abstain" was articulated.
- *SEC v Texas Gulf Sulphur Co*. (2nd Cir. 1968): the court held that any person with material non-public information must either disclose the information or abstain from using it until the information is made public.
- *Chiarella v United States* (US 1980): in this case, an employee of a financial printing company "deduced" the names of targets from confidential offering documents that his employer was printing and trading on that information. It held that only insiders may be guilty or trading on inside information. There must be a breach of fiduciary duty or another relationship of trust/confidence before a duty arises to disclose or abstain. It was in the dissent of this case that the misappropriation theory – discussed below – was first articulated, in an *amicus* brief filed by the SEC.

---

25 *United States v O'Hagan*, 521 U.S. 642 (1997) (*O'Hagan*) at 651, citing *United States v Newman*, 664 F.2d 12, 17 (2nd Cir. 1981).
26 *O'Hagan*, 521 U.S. at 651, citing *Ernst & Ernst v Hochfelder*, 425 U.S. 185, 214 (1976).

- *Dirks v. SEC* (US 1983): here, a former employee of a company "tipped" an analyst with information that the assets of the company that was engaged in selling life insurance and other products, were overrated. The analyst investigated the matter and informed others about his findings – and was investigated for his actions. This case held that a "tippee" assumes a fiduciary duty to company's shareholders to not trade on basis of material non-public information when the insider "tipper", with "an improper purpose", breaches his fiduciary duty by disclosing the information to the tippee and the tippee knows or should know that there has been such a breach. Absent a pre-existing fiduciary duty and where the tipper did not have an improper purpose and individual involved is not an insider, no duty on tippee to disclose or abstain.
- *SEC v. Switzer* (W.D. Okla. 1984): In this case, Switzer inadvertently overheard inside information, knew the information was from an insider tipper and traded. However, because the insider-tipper was unaware of Switzer overhearing the tip, there was no unlawful tipping, the insider-tipper did not breach a fiduciary duty and the tippee was allowed to retain benefits of trade.
- *US v. Chestman* (2nd Cir. 1991): In this case, the defendant was held not liable under Section 10(b) and Rule 10b-5 because, it was found, the tipper did not breach a fiduciary duty in tipping. However, the Court upheld the defendant's conviction under Rule 14e-3 because he traded while in possession of inside information relating to a tender offer that came from a corporate source. It was held that marriage alone would not establish fiduciary duty: must be a relationship of trust and confidence (statement to keep information confidential, pre-existing basis of keeping information confidential, etc.).

The misappropriation theory

Under the **misappropriation theory**, an alternative to the fiduciary duty theory (derived from the dissent in *Dirks*), a person is liable under Section 10(b) and Rule 10b-5 if he acquires from another and makes use of non-public information to purchase or sell securities, in breach of a duty of trust or confidence.

- ❏ The misappropriation theory was upheld in *United States v O'Hagan* (US 1998) – attorney-client relationship established the duty of confidence.
- ❏ In *United States v Larrabee* (1st Cir. 2001), the defendant obtained material non-public information in breach of duty owed to source of the information and passed the information to a broker who traded before merger was announced). The court held that "opportunity in combination with circumstantial evidence of a well-timed and well-orchestrated sequence of events, culminating with successful stock trades, creates a compelling inference of possession by the tipper".
- ❏ In *United States v Falcone* (2nd Cir. 2001), the defendant argued that the misappropriation must be linked to the unlawful securities trade. The court rejected this: it held that what was required was a breach by the tipper of a duty owed to the owner of the misappropriated information and the knowledge that defendant knew that the tipper had breached the duty. In this case, the court found that there was a duty present because the publisher of *Business Week* told distributors not to release a magazine before a specified time and date. Before distribution, the employee faxed copies of a column to a broker known to the defendant, and the broker used the information to trade and passed same to the defendant who did likewise.

SEC rule making
"Awareness" and Rule 10b5–1
Does insider trading liability under Section 10(b) and Rule 10b-5 require the *use* of material inside information, or will holding such information when one trades suffice?

To address this issue, the SEC adopted Rule 10b5–1. Rule 10b5–1 works on a standard of knowing possession (or awareness) and provides a defence where a person established that he *did not actually use* the information in question. Under Rule 10b5–1, a person cannot trade on the basis of material non-public information in violation of a duty of trust or confidence owed to a company, its shareholders or any person who was the source of the information. Trading "on the basis of" material non-public information means trading by a person who is *aware of* that information when he buys or sells. There is no "use" test. Thus, insiders and companies may design a trading plan with dates, amounts and prices – and be able to buy at a time when he actually had material non-public information. However, the federal circuit courts have taken different views on whether "use" or "possession" is an appropriate standard and there will in all probability be further litigation on this point.

Misappropriation and Rule 10b5–2

Rule 10b5–2 is a codification of case law. It provides a non-exclusive definition of circumstances in which a person has a duty of trust or confidence for the misappropriation theory of insider trading under Section 10(b) and Rule 10b-5. Under Rule 10b5–2, a duty arises where:

- a person agrees to maintain information confidentially;
- there is a history, pattern or practice of sharing confidential information or confidences so that the person communicating the information knew or reasonably should have known that the recipient would keep the information confidential; or
- the recipient trader receives or gets the material non-public information from his or her spouse, parent, child or sibling, but the recipient trader has a defence of he can prove that no duty of trust or confidence existed in that he neither knew or could reasonably have known that the family member in question expected the recipient trader to keep the information confidential.

Tipping, tippers and tippees

Insiders and outsiders (as defined above) are prohibited not only from trading on the basis of material inside information, but cannot pass that information to another person, a "**tippee**".[27]

Tippee liability is based on three elements:

1. the person who passed the tippee the material inside information (**tipper**) did so in breach of a fiduciary duty (also called a breach of the duty of loyalty and confidentiality) and the tippee knew or had reason to know this;
2. the tippee assumed/took on a fiduciary duty or the fiduciary duty of the tipper;

---

[27] *See* Complaint in *SEC v Hertz* CV 05–2848 (JA) (E.D.N.Y.) (company chairman and CEO tipped in violation of duties and corporate directive); *SEC v Davi Thomas*, 03-CIV-4087 (ADS) (E.D.N.Y.), Litigation Release 19212 (2nd May 2005). *See also SEC v Sam D Waksal and Jack Waksal*, 02 Civ. 4407 (NRB) (second amended complaint (10th October 2003).

3. the tipper intended, expected to or did receive a benefit from the disclosure of the material inside information.[28]

A tippee who received material inside information and traded on the basis of that information or passed it onto others would be liable under Section 10(b) and Rule 10b-5. According to *Yun*, it makes no difference whether a tippee received material inside information from an insider or an outsider – the elements to establish tippee liability under both theories of insider trading (above) are the same. Liability may extend through several layers of tipping, as was the case in *SEC v Eric Patton* and others[29] – a case the SEC described in its complaint as "a one-day frenzy of illegal insider trading" involving more than four layers of tipping and trading.

Generally, a tippee would not be liable under Section 10(b) or Rule 10b-5 if:

❏ the misappropriator tipper did not expect to benefit from the tip;
❏ when the tip was made, the tipper was not in breach of a fiduciary duty and the tippee had not assumed any duty of confidentiality toward the tipper; or
❏ a third party inadvertently overheard a tip of material inside information and traded on it, the third party was not under a fiduciary duty and the tipper and the tippee were unaware of the third party overhearing their conversation.[30]

The fiduciary duty test was developed by case law and is codified in Rule 10b5–2, discussed above.

Apart from Rule 10b5–2 and under case law, a fiduciary duty arises where:

❏ there is a business relationship, such as an attorney-client (*see O'Hagan*) or an employer-employee relationship;[31]

---

28 *See* eg, *SEC v Yun*, Slip Op (11th Cir. 2003) (*Yun*) (holding, in part, that "[t]he benefit requirement is inextricably linked to the tippee's duty); citing *Dirks v SEC*, 463 US 646 (1983) (*Dirks*). Convictions were obtained against Donna Yun, the tipper, and Jerry Burch, the tippee, as announced in *SEC v Donna Yun and Jerry Burch*, Case No. 6:99-CV-117-ORL-22KRS (Middle district Fla. 22nd July 2004), Litigation Release 18805, 28th July 2004.
29 02 Civ. 2564 (RR) E.D.N.Y. 30th April 2002 (Patton). *See also SEC v Dimitrios Kostopolous*, Administrative Proceeding File 3–11784 (3rd February 2005).
30 *SEC v Switzer* (W.D. Okla 1984) (*Switzer*).
31 *United States v Carpenter*, 791 F.2d 1024, 1028 (2nd Cir. 1986).

❑ other than in Rule 10b5–2, non-business relationships such as husband and wife where, under *Yun*, the tipper spouse gave the information in reasonable reliance on a promise that the information would be safeguarded or held a reasonable and legitimate expectation of confidentiality in the tippee spouse.[32]

The fiduciary duty may be present on an actual basis. An example of this would be if a tippee, after having been told by the tipper that the information that was passed to him was material inside information, told the tipper that he would remain silent or signed a document to that effect. Examples of this are *Yun*, where the husband tipped his wife who agreed to keep the information confidential, and *Galucci*, where the wife misappropriated material inside information from the law firm that employed her and tipped her husband who had "expressly assured" her that he would not disclose the information.

The fiduciary duty may also arise by knowledge or conduct.

In *Galucci*, the husband-tippee tipped one Ronald Manzo, a friend, who not only traded but also tipped others. It was alleged in the Complaint that when Galucci tipped Manzo, Galucci told Manzo that the tips were based on information obtained from his wife, "with the **knowledge** and intent that Manzo would use it for trading purposes" (emphasis added)[33] and "in order to increase his status with a more successful friend with whom he had historically relied upon for financial and other assistance".[34] Manzo, in turn, tipped others, including Gary Taffet, Manzo's business associate and friend. The Complaint alleged that Manzo "**knew or was reckless in not knowing** that Manzo's information was material, non-public information and provided in violation of duties of trust and confidence" (emphasis added)[35] and that when Taffet realised trading profits, he asked Manzo to reveal the source of the information, which Manzo did.

---

32 The view prior to Yun was set down in *United States v Chestman*, 947 F.2d 551 (2nd Cir. 1991) (*Chestman*), which held that there must be either an express agreement of confidentiality or the "functional equivalent" of a fiduciary relationship between the spouses. Until the US Supreme Court hears this issue Court, there will be a "split among the circuits" between the narrow position in *Chestman* and the broad position in *Yun*. See *SEC v Fiore J Gallucci, Ronald A Manzo and Gary B Taffet*, SEC Complaint, Civ. Ac. No 04- Civ 04993 (SAS), S.D.N.Y. (16th June 2004) (*Galucci*) (serial breaches of spousal duties of trust and confidence).
33 Complaint in *Galucci*, ¶ 20.
34 *Id*. at ¶ 26.
35 *Id*. at ¶ 28.

In *Patton*, which involved multiple layers of tipping, the SEC alleged that the insider tipper, Eric Patton, who tipped his brother, Steven Patton, "**knew, or was reckless in not knowing**" (emphasis added), that his brother would trade on the information or "disclose the information to others who were likely to effect such transactions".[36] Similar charges were levied against Steven Patton for his tipping others.

A benefit is present if there is a personal gain to the tipper. Such a gain could as noted in *Dirks* be broadly defined as pecuniary, a kickback, an expectation of a reciprocal tip in the future or be reputational (future earnings, a quid pro quo, conferred as a gift) or as in *Yun*, where persons are friendly, worked together and split commissions.

RESEARCH DISTRIBUTION

In 2002 and 2003, significant changes were made to SEC and SRO (NYSE and NASD) rules governing research analysts. In Spring 2002, the NASD and NYSE adopted new rules designed to address the potential conflicts of interest between member firms' research and investment banking departments. In early 2003, the SEC finalised Regulation AC that applies to all registered broker–dealers, and governs the interaction of research departments and investment banking departments. This section outlines the basic principles of these new rules and the application to non-US research distributed in the United States. With respect to the SRO rules, this Section focuses on the NASD rules, but the NYSE also has instituted a similar regulatory regime governing research.

Existing SRO rules

Prior to approval of NASD Rule 2711 and revisions to NYSE Rule 472, few NYSE and NASD rules specifically impacted the production and distribution of research reports. In addition to general rules of fair dealing and practice under NASD Rule 2210 and NYSE Rule 472, research is required to be reviewed and approved by a General Securities Principal (Series 24 Principal). In addition, copies of research reports distributed to the public must be retained for at least three years, the first two in a readily accessible place.[37]

---

[36] Complaint in *Patton* at ¶ 47.
[37] NASD Rule 2210(b)(2). Copies of approved research reports should be kept in the office where they are approved or in a location where they can be produced within 24 hours.

The research report must also contain the name of the entity that prepared the report.[38]

NASD Rule 2711 requirements

In early 2002, the SEC approved NASD Rule 2711[39] which requires broker–dealers that are NASD member firms to effect certain measures to separate the firm's research function from the investment banking/corporate finance function and to make disclosures concerning its (and its affiliates) relationships with companies that are the subject of the research report.[40] NASD Rule 2711(b) prohibits investment banking departments from supervising or controlling research analysts and prohibits research analysts from receiving compensation based on work done on a specific investment banking transaction. In addition, certain disclosures with respect to the relationship between an analyst's compensation and the investment banking department business for the company being discussed, in writing or orally by the analyst, must appear in the analyst's written reports and must be disclosed during the analyst's public appearances.[41] Neither investment banking department personnel nor issuers may review research reports prior to issuance other than to verify the factual accuracy of the report.[42] Any amendments to the reports made after the issuer's review must be cleared by the member firm's legal or compliance department.[43]

Rule 2711(e) also prohibits NASD member firms from offering or promising favourable research reports, ratings, or price targets as an inducement for receiving investment banking business from an issuer. Moreover, the rule requires firms to disclose, on the face of

---

[38] NASD Rule 2210(d)(2)(A).
[39] Exchange Act Release No. 45908 (10th May 2002).
[40] NASD Rule 2711 relates solely to research reports analysing the equity securities of an issuer. Debt securities research reports currently are not covered by this rule.
[41] NASD Rule 2711(h). For example, member firms must disclose the member's and the analyst's financial interests in the subject company's securities, beneficial ownership of the member or its affiliates in the subject securities, analyst's compensation which is based on the member's investment banking revenues, and involvement in the issuer's securities offerings.
[42] NASD Rule 2711(b) and (c).
[43] NASD Rule 2711(c). Although prudent to do so, it is not necessary to obtain the approval of the legal or compliance department of amendments made to the research report after the investment banking department's review.

the research report, a substantial amount of information, including whether investment banking compensation has been received from the issuer,[44] the firm's research ratings distributions (eg, ratio of buy to sell recommendations), a uniform rating system, and the financial interests in the issuer held by the firm, its affiliates, and the analyst's household.[45] Finally, personal trading by analysts is restricted by Rule 2711(g). As discussed below, however, only certain aspects of the NASD research rules apply to research distributed by US broker–dealers in the United States that is prepared by a non-US affiliate.

In July 2002, the NASD provided additional interpretations of Rule 2711 in several areas including the application of Rule 2711 to research distributed by an NASD member firm pursuant to Rule 15a-6 or otherwise, but prepared by an affiliated or unaffiliated third party.[46] Under the NASD interpretation, an NASD member firm is required to disclose the member firm's and its affiliate's ownership interests (assuming the ownership threshold is met) in the securities of the issuer that is the subject of the research report. Ownership interests are calculated in accordance with the standards under Exchange Act Section 13(d), specifically, SEC Rule 13d-3.[47]

The NASD interpreted Rule 2711 in the context of research reports prepared by non-US affiliates of a US broker–dealer, but distributed in the United States under Rule 15a-6. In these cases,

---

44 Under NASD Rule 2711(h)(2), the member must disclose on its research reports if the member or its affiliates: (a) managed or co-managed a public offering of securities for the subject company in the past 12 months; (b) received compensation for investment banking services from the subject company in the past 12 months; or (c) expects to receive or intends to seek compensation for investment banking services in the next 3 months. Investment banking services include, without limitation, "acting as an underwriter in an offering for the issuer; acting as a financial adviser in a merger or acquisition; providing venture capital, equity lines of credit, PIPEs or similar investments; or serving as placement agent for the issuer." Rule 2711(a)(2).
45 NASD Rule 2711(h).
46 NASD Notice to Members 02–39 (July 2002).
47 Under Rule 13d-3, a beneficial owner is defined as anyone who, through any contract, arrangement, understanding, relationship, or otherwise has or shares (1) voting power (power to vote or direct the voting), and/or (2) investment power (power to dispose, or direct the disposition of the security). The rule also states that the calculation should include rights to acquire beneficial ownership within 60 days, such as through the exercise of options or warrants, or through the conversion of a security. Please note that the definition of beneficial ownership under the US securities laws has been subject to numerous interpretations, and the foregoing is intended merely as a summary.

the following disclosures must be made on such research reports prepared by non-US affiliates of US broker–dealers, if applicable:

❑ the member's and its affiliates' ownership of the subject company's securities "if as of the end of the month immediately preceding the date of publication of the research report or the public appearance (or the end of the second most recent month if the publication date is less than 10 calendar days after the end of the most recent month), the member firm or its affiliates beneficially own 1% or more of any class of common equity securities of the subject company" (computation of beneficial ownership of securities must be based upon the same standards used to compute ownership for purposes of the reporting requirements under Section 13(d) of the Exchange Act);
❑ that the member or its affiliates managed or co-managed a public offering of the subject company's securities in the past 12 months, received compensation for investment banking services from the subject company in the past 12 months, or expects to receive or intends to seek compensation for investment banking services from the subject company in the next 3 months;
❑ that the member was making a market in the subject company's securities at the time the research report was published; and
❑ any other actual, material conflict of interest of the member known at the time of distribution of the research report.

The foregoing disclosures required by the NASD Rules must appear on the front page of the research report or the front page must refer to the page on which disclosures are found. Disclosures and references to disclosures must be clear, conspicuous, and prominent.[48] In addition, NASD Rule 2711 requires NASD member firms to attest annually that the member firm has adopted and implemented written supervisory procedures reasonably designed to ensure compliance with the provisions of the NASD research rules.

Approval of SRO Rule Amendments
On 29th July 2003, the SEC approved SRO rule changes addressing research analyst conflicts of interest.[49] Among other things, these

---
48 NASD Notice to Members 02–39 (July 2002).
49 Exchange Act Release No. 34–48252.

rule changes fulfilled the mandates of SOX Section 501. Approval of the SRO rule amendments represented yet another initiative by the SEC to address potential conflicts of interest relating to research analysts. The approved rule amendments were proposed as two different sets of SRO rule approvals; one set conceived as improvements to the May 2002 SRO rule changes and another set to comply with the mandate in SOX Section 501. The amendments include the following provisions, among others:

- requiring member firms to form a committee to review and approve research analysts' compensation; such committee may not have representation from the firm's investment banking department;
- prohibiting analysts from issuing positive research reports or reiterating a "buy" recommendation around the expiration of a lock-up agreement;
- extending current quiet periods for the issuance of written research reports to public appearances by managers and co-managers of initial and secondary offerings.
- prohibiting the committee from considering an analyst's contribution to the firm's investment banking business for the purposes of determining his or her compensation;
- requiring member firms to annually document and certify to the NASD the basis for analysts' compensation;
- requiring member firms to notify customers when research coverage of a company is terminated;
- prohibiting research analysts from participating in "pitches" to prospects; and
- imposing additional registration, qualification, and continuing education requirements on research analysts to establish a new registration category and require a qualification examination for research analysts.

Effective 15th March 2005, the NASD adopted two new sanction guidelines for violations of Rule 2711. One guideline recommends sanctions for violations regarding the limitations on the relationships between the research departments and investment banking departments, the relationships between research analysts and subject companies, and the manner of compensation for research analysts. The second guideline addresses violations in two categories.

In the first category, the guideline provides recommended sanctions for failing to comply with restrictions on personal trading by research analysts. In the second category, the guideline provides recommended sanctions for failing to comply with restrictions on publishing research reports; restrictions on the public appearances of research analysts; and disclosure requirements for research reports and public appearances.[50]

On 21st April 2005, the SEC approved changes to NYSE/NASD Rules to prohibit research analysts from participating in road shows relating to an investment banking services transactions and from engaging in any communication with a current or prospective customer in the presence of investment banking personnel or company management about an investment banking services transaction. The rule amendments also require a research analyst's business communications about an investment banking services transaction to be fair, balanced, and not misleading; however, investment banking department personnel are prohibited from directing a research analyst to engage in sales and marketing efforts and other communications with a customer about an investment banking services transaction. This is yet another example of the SEC's initiative to address research analyst conflicts of interests concerns in the industry. In the NASD's words, these new amendments, "further fortify the wall between investment banking and research by prohibiting research analysts from participating in a road show related to an investment banking services transaction."[51] The new rules become effective 6 June 2005.

Regulation AC

Regulation Analyst Certification, "Regulation AC", requires US broker–dealers or any person associated with a broker or dealer that publishes, circulates or provides a research report prepared by a research analyst to a US person in the United States, to include in that research report, a clear and prominent certification by the research analyst that: (a) the research report accurately reflects the analyst's personal views on the subject securities and the issuer;

---

50 *See* NASD NTM 05–17 (Effective 15th March 2005).
51 *See* Broker/Dealer Compliance Report, "SEC Approves Changes to NYSE, NASD Rules Barring Research Analysts from Road Shows," Vol. 07, No. 17, 27th April 2005.

(b)(i) that no part of the analyst's compensation was, is, or will be directly or indirectly related to the specific recommendation or views contained in the research report, or (ii) that part or all of the analyst's compensation[52] was, is, or will be, directly or indirectly, related to the specific recommendation or views contained in the research report (if the analyst did receive such compensation, the statement must include the source and amount of such compensation, the purpose of the compensation, and that such compensation may influence the recommendation in the research report).[53] Unlike the NASD and NYSE rules, Regulation AC applies to both debt and equity securities. Analysts also are now required to submit quarterly certifications to their firms that statements made during their public appearances accurately reflect their personal views and whether or not the analyst received related compensation for their views or recommendations.

Under Regulation AC, a research report is defined as "a written communication (including an electronic communication) that includes an analysis of a security or an issuer and provides information reasonably sufficient upon which to base an investment decision." Unlike the current NASD and NYSE rules, the definition of research report does not require that the report contain a recommendation to be deemed a research report under Regulation AC.

Exemption for foreign research reports

Regulation AC includes a narrow exemption for research on foreign securities produced outside the United States and distributed to Major Institutional Investors in the United States under Rule 15a-6(a)(2).[54] Non-US research otherwise distributed in the United States pursuant to other sections of SEC Rule 15a-6 is not exempt from Regulation AC. A "foreign security" for the purposes of Regulation AC, is "a security issued by a foreign issuer for which a US market is not the principle trading market."[55] Research analysts employed outside the United States by a foreign person are not

---

52 "Compensation," for the purposes of proposed Regulation AC, would also include payments received from sources other that the analyst's employer, including issuers, underwriters, dealers, and other related persons.
53 Exchange Act Release 47384 (20th February 2003).
54 17 C.F.R. 242.503.
55 17 C.F.R. 242.500.

required to make certifications for public appearances outside the United States, but are required to make certifications for appearances while present in the United States.

In a recent release, the SEC's Division of Market Regulation provided answers to frequently asked questions concerning Regulation AC[56]. One question was whether a password-protected conference call or webcast in which a research analyst participates with clients should be considered a public appearance. The SEC responded that such activities by a research analyst, whether or not the conference call or webcast was password protected, would be considered a public appearance under Regulation AC. However, the SEC would not consider such participation by a research analyst to be a public appearance if the conference call or webcast is limited to a group of fewer than 15 persons.

Exemption for third party research
Regulation AC exempts research distributed by US broker–dealers but prepared by third party research analysts. Regulation AC does not apply to "third party" research analysts if the research analysts' employers do not have officers or employees in common with the broker–dealer or covered person distributing the research; and (2) the broker–dealer has written policies and procedures designed to prevent the broker–dealer, its controlling person, officers, and employees from influencing the activities of the third party research analysts and the content of their reports.[57] In addition, broker–dealers are not required to obtain certifications for public appearances of third party analysts.

Other recent regulatory initiatives affecting research production and distribution
Although the primary focus of SOX is corporate governance reform, this act also includes a provision requiring the SEC to promulgate regulations governing the issuance of research. The regulations promulgated under SOX are intended to fulfil many of the same objectives as the NASD rules (discussed above) and the rules

---

[56] *See* Division of Market Regulation Responses to Frequently Asked Questions Concerning Regulation Analyst Certification, Revised 26th April 2005.
[57] 17 C.F.R. 242.500.

under Regulation AC (discussed above). Under the regulations to be promulgated under SOX, Congress has directed the SEC to adopt rules to protect the objectivity and independence of securities analysts, including several specified rules delineating the spheres of influence of the firm's investment banking and research departments.

Specifically, SOX forbids broker–dealer firms from retaliating against any securities analyst who gives a negative or adverse rating or research report that may adversely affect "the present or prospective investment banking relationship of the broker–dealer with the issuer that is the subject of the research report." Again, the rules to be promulgated under SOX are currently slated to only apply to equity securities research, although it is likely that the eventual SEC rule-making in this area will also apply to debt securities.

On 30 July 2003, the SEC approved the SRO proposals to implement the SOX requirements. The SROs extended the anti-retaliation provisions to cover public appearances and have clarified that the rule would not preclude termination of a research analyst for causes unrelated to issuing or distributing adverse research or for making an unfavourable public appearance regarding a current or potential investment-banking relationship. The SEC confirmed that the SRO proposals are designed to protect the objectivity and independence of research analysts, and meet the requirements of Section 15D of the Exchange Act, which requires that a rule be adopted that prohibits broker–dealers engaged in investment banking activities from, directly or indirectly retaliating or threatening to retaliate, against a research analyst who publishes a negative, adverse, or otherwise unfavourable research report that may adversely affect the broker–dealer's present or prospective investment banking relationship with an issuer.

Wall Street research analyst conflicts settlement
On 28th April 2003, the SEC, NASD, NYSE, the New York State Attorney General and NASAA announced a settlement requiring ten top investment banks to pay approximately US$1.4 billion in penalties and other payments and mandating sweeping reforms.[58]

---

[58] The US$1.4 billion was divided into the following parts: US$487.5 million in penalties, US$387.5 million for disgorgement, payments of US$432.5 million to fund independent

The settlement was the result of joint investigations by the securities regulators into the alleged conflicts of interest between investment banking interests and securities research.[59]

The enforcement actions brought by the securities regulators allege that all of the firms "engaged in acts and practices that created or maintained inappropriate influence by investment banking over research analysts, thereby imposing conflicts of interest on research analysts that the firms failed to manage in an adequate or appropriate manner."[60] Additional charges were also brought against the individual firms for among things, fraud, issuing research that was not based on principles of good faith and fair dealing, that contained exaggerated or unwarranted claims, contained opinions for which there was no reasonable basis in violation of NASD and NYSE rules, and for failing to disclose payments received for research in violation of the Section 17(b) of the Securities Act of 1933 and NASD and NYSE rules.

As a result of the settlement, impacted firms are also required to abide by reforms intended to bolster the integrity of equity research, including:

❏ Research analysts cannot receive compensation for investment banking activities;
❏ Research analysts are prohibited from being involved in investment banking pitches;
❏ Research analysts are prohibited from participating in investment banking "road shows" or other marketing efforts during the offering period of an investment banking transaction;
❏ Firms must physically separate the investment banking and research departments to prevent the flow of information between the departments;

---

research, and US$80 million to fund investor education. *See* Joint Press Release (28th April 2003) (available at www.sec.gov/news/press/2003–54.htm).

59 Furthermore, on 26th August 2004, the SEC, the NASAA, NASD, NYSE and state securities regulators announced enforcement actions against Deutsche Bank Securities Inc. and Thomas Weisel Partners LLC. These settlements, which related back to the April 2003 settlement with the ten other investment banks reiterate the comprehensive regulatory effort to reform the relationship between investment banking and research. Deutsche Bank Securities was fined US$87.5 Million while Thomas Weisel Partners was fined US$12.5 Million.

60 *See* fn. 39 *above*.

- ❏ Research department budgets must be determined without input from investment banking and without taking into consideration investment banking revenue;
- ❏ Research analysts' compensation must not be based, directly or indirectly, on investment banking revenues and investment bankers will neither evaluate nor provide input on research analysts' compensation;
- ❏ Investment bankers will not make decisions on company-specific research coverage;
- ❏ Research departments will make all decisions regarding terminating research coverage of a company; and
- ❏ Brokerage firms will create and enforce "firewalls" (a/k/a "Chinese Walls") to restrict interaction between the investment banking and research departments.

In addition to the above requirements, firms are required to furnish independent research to customers for a five-year period by contracting with at least three independent research firms. Firms must engage an independent consultant who will have final authority to procure independent research. Firms are also required to publicly disclose research analysts' historical ratings and price targets to assist investors in elaborating and comparing the performance of research analysts over a period of time.

As a part of the settlement, twelve separate funds for investors who purchased specified stocks through a "Settling Firm" during specified time frames. A fairness hearing was held on 11th April 2005, and an order setting forth the official plans of distribution for each of the distribution funds is to be issued.[61]

NATIONAL SECURITIES EXCHANGES

Non-US persons or entities conducting securities and investment related activities over the Internet should also be mindful of the SEC's position on the scope of exchange and alternative trading systems (ATSs) regulations, where electronic systems function like markets.

---

61 The website www.sec.gov/spotlight/globalsettlement.htm contains links to all of the Final Judgments and Orders entered in the SEC's actions and related information grading the settlement.

New interpretation of the meaning of exchange

The SEC has recently addressed the issue of exchange regulation. Section 3(a)(1) of the Exchange Act defines an exchange as:

> "any organisation, association, or group of persons, whether incorporated or unincorporated, which constitutes, maintains, or provides a market place or facilities[62] for bringing together purchasers and sellers of securities or for otherwise performing with respect to securities the functions commonly performed by a stock exchange as that term is generally understood and includes the market place and the market facilities maintained by such exchange."

Section 5 of the Exchange Act makes it unlawful for any exchange to use US jurisdictional means to effect any transaction in a security unless it is registered as a national securities exchange under Section 6 or is exempted by the SEC from registration upon application to the SEC. Such an exemption is granted if the SEC deems it not practicable and not necessary or appropriate in the public interest, or for the protection of the investors, to require registration.

In adopting Regulation ATS, the SEC broadened its interpretation of the statutory definition of "exchange" to mean:

> "any organisation, association, or group of persons that: (1) brings together the orders of multiple buyers and sellers; and (2) uses established, non-discretionary methods (whether by providing a trading facility or by setting rules) under which such orders interact with each other, and the buyers and sellers entering such orders agree to the terms of trade."[63]

The new definition of exchange was intended to modify the regulatory scheme to more adequately recognise or regulate electronic trading systems, or ATSs, that function as markets.[64] The revised interpretation explicitly excludes systems that the SEC believes perform, electronically, traditional broker–dealer activities, such as

---

[62] When used with respect to an exchange, the term "facilities" is defined in Exchange Act Section 3(a)(2) to include the exchange's "premises, tangible or intangible property whether on the premises or not, any right to the use of such premises or property or any service thereof for the purpose of effecting or reporting a transaction on an exchange (including, among other things, any system of communication to or from the exchange, by ticker or otherwise, maintained by or with the consent of the exchange), and any right of the exchange to the use of any property or service".

[63] Rule 3b-16(a); *see* also Exchange Act Release 40760 (8th December 1998)(Regulation ATS Release).

[64] *See* Regulation ATS Release.

order routing to markets, or the display and execution of orders within a single market maker or dealer.[65]

Regulation ATS

ATSs must submit to regulation as exchanges under Section 6 of the Exchange Act, register as a broker–dealer and submit to the requirements of Regulation ATS, or obtain an exemption therefrom.[66] Adopted in December 1998, the purpose of Regulation ATS was to accommodate technological developments, incorporate ATS more fully into the national market system through increased transparency and access and to provide more effective market regulation of the exchange like qualities of the ATS. An ATS is defined as:

> "Any organisation, association, person, group of persons, or system: (1) that constitutes, maintains, or provides a market place or facilities for bringing together purchasers and sellers of securities or for otherwise performing with respect to securities the functions commonly performed by a stock exchange within the meaning of Rule 3b-16 under the Exchange Act; and (2) that does not: (i) set rules governing the conduct of subscribers other than the conduct of such subscribers' trading on such organisation, association or group of persons, or system; or (ii) disciplines subscribers other than by exclusion from trading."[67]

The SEC's exemptive authority[68] provides ATSs with an option between regulation as an exchange or as a broker–dealer that complies with Regulation ATS. Thus, systems that satisfy the meaning of "ATS" are exempt from exchange regulation, provided such systems comply with Regulation ATS.

Trading systems that meet the definition of "exchange" and choose to submit to Regulation ATS must notify the SEC of this intention to operate under Regulation ATS at least 20 days prior to

---

65 *See* Exchange Act Rule 3b-16(b).
66 In addition to requiring registration as an exchange, Section 5 of the Exchange Act also authorises the SEC to grant an exemption from exchange registration if the exchange would transact only a limited volume of transactions. The SEC has exempted two such trading systems on the basis of limited volume, that is, the Arizona Stock Exchange and Tradepoint. *See* Exchange Act Release 28899 (20th February 1991) (exempting the AZX); Exchange Act Release 41199 (22nd March 1999) (exempting Tradepoint).
67 *See* Rule 300(a).
68 In 1996, US Congress provided the SEC with greater regulatory flexibility by giving it exemptive authority under the Exchange Act. *See* National Securities Markets Improvement Act of 1996, Pub. L. 104–290.

operation, informing the SEC as to how the trading system will operate, who the intended subscribers are and other information about the operations, security and capacity of the system. Trading systems that generate increasing levels of volume as a percentage of the annual trading volume in the security may have additional disclosure and reporting obligations with respect to the security. In addition, trading systems with significant market share may be subject to access requirements to ensure that market participants have an opportunity to access the trading system. Trading systems regulated pursuant to Regulation ATS are subject to detailed record-keeping, reporting and margin examination requirements.

Access to non-US exchanges by US persons

Technology exists that allows investors, regardless of physical location, to obtain real-time market information about securities trading on non-US Exchanges and to allow US persons to enter orders from remote locations to purchase or sell non-US securities. Although such functionality exists, non-US exchanges may, by providing their services, trigger US jurisdiction.

In the Web Site Release, the SEC provided guidance to non-US exchanges on the question of under what circumstances a non-US exchange that provides direct access must register as a US exchange. The SEC stated that exchange registration would not apply to a non-US exchange that sponsors a website advertising the exchange, disseminating quotes and directing those quotes to the United States, so long as the non-US exchange takes steps reasonably designed to prevent US persons from directing orders to the exchange. The SEC suggested that such steps would include: (a) posting a disclaimer stating that the non-US exchange is not available to US persons; (b) requiring potential participants to state their residences and mailing addresses; (c) refusing trading privileges to US persons; and (d) refraining from arranging for US persons to gain access through non-US exchange member firms.

Issuer bulletin board systems

To facilitate secondary trading of their securities, a number of issuers (and other entities) are using electronic forums, including the Internet, to operate electronic bulletin boards for investors to advertise interest in buying or selling the issuer's securities. Issuers operating electronic bulletin board trading systems play a passive role in facilitating the trading of shares. The standard functions offered by these systems include only the ability for buyers or sellers to post their names, addresses, phone numbers, the number of shares offered for sale or desired to be purchased, the price at which the shares are offered for sale or desired to be purchased, and the date the information was entered into they system. The information may be submitted by prospective buyers and sellers via telephone, facsimile, mail, or electronic mail directed to the issuer, who would, in turn, enter the information onto the bulletin board. In all cases, the issuer does not play a role in effecting the transaction between shareholders; rather all transactions are effected only by direct contact between the shareholders.

The Staff has issued a series of no-action letters outlining the circumstances under which issuers may facilitate "off the grid" trading systems without registering as national exchanges, broker–dealers, or investment advisors.[69] Issuers are not required to register if their activities are limited in such a way that they do not act as markets, broker–dealers or investment advisers.

In each of the SEC's no-action letters regarding issuer bulletin board systems, each issuer agreed to, among other things, the following conditions: (a) to maintain its status as a registrant under Section 12 of the Exchange Act, or otherwise make available on its website the financial information required of issuers of registered securities; (b) to provide notices regarding operation of and participation on the system that will be set forth or contained on the screens and/or hard copy; (c) to keep records of all quotes entered on the systems and make those records available to the SEC and NASD (or any other regulated market on which the issuer's securities are listed); (d) to provide no information regarding the advisability of buying or selling any securities; (e) to advertise in a manner limited by the no-action letters; (f) not to use the system (by either the issuer or any affiliate) to offer to buy or sell securities, except in compliance with securities laws; (g) not to receive any compensation for creating or maintaining the website, receive any

---

69 Real Goods Trading Corp., (24th June 1996); PerfectData Corp., (5th August 1996); The Flamemaster Corp., (29th October 1996); Portland Brewing Co., (14th December 1999); Spring Street Brewing Company, (22nd March 1996).

compensation for use of the system, or receive any transaction-based compensation; (h) not to be involved in the purchase or sale negotiations arising from the system; and (i) not to receive, transfer, or hold funds or securities.

INVESTMENT ADVISER REGISTRATION AND REGULATORY REQUIREMENTS

Investment advisers receive compensation for providing tailored advisory services to a specific person on investing in securities and investment-products. Section 202(a)(11) of the Advisers Act defines investment advisers to include: "any person who, for compensation, engages in the business of advising others, either directly or through publications or writings, as to the value of securities or as to the advisability of investing in, purchasing, or selling securities, or who, for compensation and as part of a regular business, issues or promulgates analyses or reports concerning securities…". Thus, if a financial advisor satisfies each of the elements of the definition of investment adviser, that is, if it provides investment advice for compensation and is "in the business" of providing investment advice, it typically will be an investment adviser unless it is eligible to rely on one of the exclusions from the definition of investment adviser in the Advisers Act. Investment advisers subject to US jurisdiction are required to register in the United States and are subject to substantive regulation including examination, record-keeping requirements, and anti-fraud rules.

A non-US investment adviser that uses a website to provide its advisory services must register with the SEC unless the adviser implements specific measures reasonably designed to guard against directing website information about its advisory services to US investors. The SEC suggests that possible measures non-US investment advisers could take would be to provide disclaimers on their websites stating that the services are not available to US investors and to limit access to the advisory services by requiring specific information about the customer's location.

A recent SEC rule that became effective 15 April 2005 provides guidance on when activities would subject a broker–dealer to registration under the Advisers Act[70]. The Advisers Act and the

---

[70] Exchange Act Release 51523 (12th April 2005).

Exchange Act are not exclusive in their application to advisers and broker–dealers, respectively. Many broker–dealers are also registered with the SEC as advisers because of the nature of the services they provide or the form of compensation they receive. Until recently, the division between broker–dealers and investment advisers was fairly clear, and the regulatory obligations of each fairly distinct. Recently, however, the distinctions have begun to blur, raising difficult questions regarding the application of statutory provisions written by Congress more than half a century ago.

The SEC acknowledges that the lines between full-service broker–dealers and investment advisers continue to blur. The SEC did not agree, however, that requiring most or all full service broker–dealers to treat most or all of their customer accounts as advisory accounts was an appropriate response to this convergence, nor that Congress' intentions were to apply the Advises Act to all brokerage accounts receiving investment advice, even where that adverse was substantial. Instead, Congress required only that such advice be "solely incidental to" a person's "business as a broker or dealer" and not for "special compensation."

Under the final rule, a broker–dealer providing non-discretionary advice that is solely incidental to its brokerage services is excepted from the Advisers Act regardless of whether it charges an asset-based or fixed fee (rather than commissions, mark-ups, or mark downs) for its services, provided it makes certain disclosures about the nature of its services. According to the rule, however, exercising investment discretion is not "solely incidental to" the business of a broker or dealer within the meaning of the Advisers Act nor is a broker–dealer charging a separate fee or creating separate contracts for advisory services. These activities would, absent the availability of a separation exemption, trigger Advisory Action registration.

In addition, the rule states that when a broker–dealer provides advice as part of a financial plan or in connection with providing planning services, such advice is not solely incidental if the broker–dealer: (a) holds itself out to the public as a financial planner or as providing financial planning services; (b) delivers to its customer a financial plan; or (c) represents to the customer that the advice is provided as part of a financial plan or financial planning services. Broker–dealers, however, are not subject to the Advisers Act under the rule solely because they offer full-service brokerage and discount brokerage services (including electronic brokerage) for reduced commission services.

REGULATION M

Apart from their activities that directly involve purchases or sales of securities into the United States or contacts with US clients, non-US broker–dealers also become subject to regulation under the US federal securities laws when they participate in a global offer that involves a "distribution" of securities in the United States.

The Exchange Act proscribes fraudulent, manipulative and deceptive acts and conduct. It strives to provide a marketplace that is fair, efficient and accessible, and to protect investors and help maintain a free and open market where prices are established naturally through the free interplay of supply and demand. Many of these provisions are present in the laws and regulations of other markets and nations. However, laws, rules and market practices do differ. Activities that are restricted or not permissible in the United States might be required or accepted practice in other markets to offer securities and maintain fair and orderly markets. For example:

- in Germany, underwriters (major commercial banks) will trade in offered shares, manage the risks associated with maintaining an orderly market and completing the issue by hedging through the listed options market and the OTC derivatives market, and provide investment advice to investors;
- on the LSE in the pre-Stock Exchange Trading System (SETS) environment (and now for non-SETS securities), market makers that are affiliated with or have subsidiaries that underwrite or distribute relevant offers would wish to continue to make markets on the LSE in the offered securities.

These activities are not permissible under Sections 9(a) and 10(b) of the Exchange Act and rules and regulations thereunder.

How Regulation M operates

Absent an exception or an exemption, Regulation M[71] (Rules 101 to 105) generally prohibits issuers, selling shareholders, underwriters and others participating in a distribution of securities, together with their affiliated purchasers, from bidding for, purchasing or

---

71 Exchange Act Release 38067 (20th December 1996).

attempting to induce any person to bid for or purchase the securities subject to the distribution (and certain other securities) during a specified period prior to the start of the US distribution until the completion of the distribution. The Regulation M prohibitions are to prevent the issuer, underwriters and others that have a financial interest in a distribution from engaging in activity intended to manipulate the price of a security, or boost its trading volume, and so mislead investors as to the true state of the public market for the security. The SEC takes the view that, in connection with the conduct of a distribution into the United States, the non-US securities activities of non-US distribution participants are subject to Regulation M.

Regulation M does *not* apply to redeemable securities issued by an open-end investment company. The SEC gave exemptive relief to a Puerto Rico-based non-diversified open-end investment company to redeem its shares periodically from fund shareholders during a continuous offering of shares.[72]

Meaning of "distribution"

Regulation M applies when there is a "distribution" of securities in the United States. The term "distribution" is defined in Rule 101 under Regulation M as an offer of securities that is distinguished from ordinary trading activity by the magnitude of the offer and the presence of special selling efforts. This includes SEC-registered offers.

Persons subject to Regulation M

The anti-manipulation provisions of Regulation M are contained in two separate rules that apply to two categories of entities. Rule 101 covers underwriters, prospective underwriters, or other persons who have agreed to participate, or are participating, in a distribution (distribution participants) and their affiliated purchasers. Rule 102 covers issuers and selling shareholders, and their affiliated purchasers.

Regulation M defines "affiliated purchaser" to include:

❑ a person acting, directly or indirectly, in concert with a distribution participant, issuer or selling security holder in connection with the distribution;

❑ an "affiliate" (which need not be a separate legal entity from the distribution participant, so long as it is a separately identifiable

---

[72] *Popular Total Return Fund, Inc.* (January 2001). *Accord*, *UBS/PaineWebber Inc. of Puerto Rico* (March 2001).

department or division of the distribution participant, issuer or selling security holder) that directly or indirectly controls the purchases of any securities by a distribution participant, issuer or selling security holder, whose purchases are controlled by any such person or whose purchases are under common control with any such person; or
- an "affiliate" (as defined above) that regularly purchases securities for its own account or for the account of others, or that recommends or exercises investment discretion with respect to the purchase or sale of securities.

The third branch of the definition, which generally applies to financial services affiliates, contains a proviso excluding from the definition of "affiliated purchaser" those affiliates that satisfy the following conditions:

- the distribution participant, issuer or selling shareholder must have information wall procedures that satisfy the Rule;
- the securities affiliate has no common officers who "direct, effect, or recommend" securities transactions (effectively permitting such common officers provided they are so senior that they only manage one of the two entities); and
- the securities affiliate does not engage in market making, solicited transactions or proprietary trading in the securities that are subject to the offer.

The information barrier is supposed to restrict the passage of "market sensitive" information between an underwriter and its trading affiliate: presumably, the information intended to be restricted would be the size of the book, intentions regarding exercise of the over-allotment option, and similar matters. The information barrier must be established by the underwriter (not the affiliate) and must prevent the flow of information from the underwriter to the affiliate, and vice versa. The procedures setting up the information barrier must be given an annual, independent assessment, which can be performed by an internal audit group.

The actively traded security exception
Regulation M's trading restrictions apply only to "covered securities". These are the securities being distributed (subject securities) and any "reference security". A "reference security" is defined to

include any security into which a subject security may be converted, exchanged or exercised, or which under the terms of the subject security may "in whole or significant part" determine its price.

Regulation M therefore covers equity-linked securities. The effect is that Regulation M can restrict trading in the underlying ordinary shares when an underwriter or issuer is distributing a convertible security, but does not restrict a convertible security when there is a distribution of the shares themselves.

Through an exception, Regulation M does not apply to offers of equity securities with an average daily trading volume (ADTV) of at least US$1 million and a public float of at least US$150 million or more (actively traded securities). The Staff requires both limbs of the test to be met, and that exceeding the requirements of one, even by a significant amount, cannot make up for failure on the second. ADTV is defined as the average daily trading volume for two months prior to filing a registration statement or, for shelf transactions or non-registered ones, a 60-day period ending within 10 days before pricing. "Public float value" is defined as the aggregate market value of common equity securities held by non-affiliates of the issuer. The "actively traded security" exception applies to underwriters and their affiliates, but not to the issuer and its affiliates, except under limited circumstances (as discussed below). This means that issuers will have to "get out of the market" in their own stock when they are involved in distributions, even though the underwriters are free to continue trading. In certain countries where affiliates of issuers are often involved in trading issuer stock (eg, Spain), this distinction could cause difficulty.

On 9 December 2004, the SEC proposed to amend Regulation M.[73] In the Regulation M Amending Release, the SEC proposed to change the actively traded exception ADTV thresholds to US$1.2m and the public float value to US$180m. Other proposed amendments to Regulation M are noted below.

Regulation M restricted period
Equity securities with an ADTV of US$1m and a public float of at least US$150m are exempt from Regulation M (*as noted above, the SEC*

---

[73] Exchange Act Release 50381 (9th December 2004) (Regulation M Amending Release).

is proposing to change these figures). For other distributions, Regulation M restrictions apply during a "restricted period", which starts:

- *one day* before pricing, for securities with an ADTV of at least US$100,000 and where the issuer has a public float of at least US$25m and ends when the distribution ends – *the SEC is proposing to change this to US$120,000 and US$30m for the public float value;*
- *five days* before pricing and ending on the completion of distribution for all other securities; and
- for mergers, acquisitions or tender offers, from *the day when proxy or offer materials are first disseminated* and ends at the time of the shareholder vote or the expiry of the offer, and also is in effect from one or five days before (depending on the size and public float) any valuation period for the offered security until the end of the valuation period.

Rule 101

Rule 101 applies to distribution participants (eg, underwriters, dealers and their affiliates) and, like former Rule 10b-6, prohibits bidding for, purchasing or inducing others to purchase covered securities during a distribution. As with Rule 10b-6, the substance of Rule 101 is in the exceptions. The most important exception is for actively traded securities. Also, Rule 101 does not apply to investment grade debt and preferred stock (so long as they are not convertible), or – in a change from Rule 10b-6 – investment grade asset-backed securities. Also excepted are "exempted securities" under Section 3(a)(12) of the Exchange Act (ie, governments, municipals, bank trust funds, etc.) and certain types of mutual funds and unit and investment trusts (UITs).

Rule 101 contains 10 exceptions, as follows.

Research. In a codification of previous practice, underwriters are permitted to continue circulating research during the entire course of an offer, so long as the research satisfies the conditions applicable to the distribution of research during the pendency of a registered public offer. In practice most underwriters impose upon themselves some sort of "quiet" period before a deal prices to mitigate the possibility that the research might become the subject of later lawsuits on the theory that the research was part of the prospectus (but not subject to the indemnity from the issuer).

NASDAQ passive market making. Passive market making activities conducted on NASDAQ with respect to eligible securities (as discussed below) will be exempt from Regulation M and Rule 101.

Stabilisation. As discussed below, stabilising transactions effected in reliance on Rule 104 are exempt from Rule 101.

Odd lots. Odd lot transactions or transactions to offset an odd-lot tender offer are excepted.

Exercises and conversions. The exercise of any option, warrant, right or any conversion privilege set forth in the instrument governing a security is excepted.

Unsolicited transactions. As long as a trade is unsolicited, it need not be in "block" size as required under the Trading Practices Rules. The trade must be executed off-exchange, and cannot be effected through NASDAQ or an "electric communications network" such as Instinet.

Baskets. Regulation M excepts baskets with more than 20 stocks, so long as a covered security does not comprise more than five per cent of the value of the basket. Adjustment transactions for changes in "standardised indices" affecting baskets are also excepted.

De minimis. If during the restricted period an underwriter makes a bid that is not hit, or makes purchases of less than an aggregate of two per cent of the ADTV of the covered security, Regulation M will not apply. However, the offending underwriter must qualify for this treatment by having in place written procedures reasonably designed to prevent violations of Regulation M – even though these procedures must, in this particular circumstance, have failed to do so.

The securities being distributed. This exception permits underwriters to sell the securities that are actually being distributed. However, this exception does not permit a distribution participant or the issuer to buy those securities. Likewise, the exception does not permit the solicitation of people to buy the securities being distributed outside of the distribution itself (such as by assembling a group of buyers together to take up distributed securities that come on the market during an exchange offer).

Inter-syndicate transactions. Transactions among the syndicate members, or with selling security holders, are excepted.

Rule 144A. The Rule 10b-6 exception for Rule 144A transactions by non-US issuers has been expanded to cover all Rule 144A transactions, whether by US or non-US issuers. It should be noted, however, that the SEC did not adopt a suggestion in the comments that asked that they except the so-called "side-by-side" – where a Rule 144A offer to QIBs is combined with a private placement under Securities Act Section 4(2) to institutional accredited investors.

In February 2000, the SEC Staff issued a letter granting relief under Rule 101 to managers and affiliates of issuer of debt securities to purchase and make bids during the distribution.[74]

Readers should consider the effects of the January 2005 enforcement actions brought against Morgan Stanley and Goldman Sachs. Both of these firms were subject to civil injunctive actions and a monetary penalty in federal court for violations of Rule 101 by attempting to induce certain customers who received allocations of shares in IPOs sold by the firms to place orders to but additional shares after the distribution closed and, in one instance, by soliciting an aftermarket order for additional shares before all of the IPOs shares were distributed. These activities took place in the restricted period.

Rule 102

Rule 102 imposes the same restrictions on issuers and selling shareholders as Rule 101 imposes on distribution participants. As originally proposed, Rule 102 would have contained few exceptions, but the SEC thought better of this and a number have been added to the final Rule. Rule 102 includes the Rule 101 exceptions for odd-lot purchases, exercises and conversions, unsolicited purchases and Rule 144A transactions, as well as two special exceptions for closed-end investment company self-tenders, commodity pool

---

[74] *Federal Republic of Brazil* (25th February 2000).

redemptions and transactions involving employee stock plans. The "de minimis" exception does not apply to the issuer. Rule 102 also contains the same exclusions for investment grade non-convertible debt and preferred securities, and excepted securities under Securities Act Section 3(a)(12) and securities of mutual funds and UITs, all found in Rule 101.

Although the Rule 101 exception for actively traded securities does not apply to transactions by issuers or selling shareholders, Rule 102 does contain an exception for actively traded "reference securities" that are not issued by the issuer of the security in distribution or its affiliate; this exception is intended to permit customary hedging activities by issuers of equity-linked securities. Of course, this hedging – purchases of the underlying stock by the issuer of an equity linked security, for example – would only be permitted if the underlying stock qualified for the actively traded exception.

Rule 102 provides that any distribution participant that is also an affiliated purchaser of the issuer or selling shareholder – so long as it is not itself the issuer – may comply with Rule 101, rather than Rule 102. This means that an affiliate of the issuer in the securities business could elect Rule 101 treatment, but not such an affiliate that was not in the securities business, since the later entity would not be a "distribution participant" within the definition.

In a March 2001 no-action letter to Liberty Floating Rate Advantage Fund, the SEC Staff granted an exemption under Rule 102 to permit a fund to conduct a rescission offer under Rule 13e-4 (to a limited number of investors with no publicity) while simultaneously offering shares to the public.

In the September 2000 no-action letter *TotalFinaElf S.A.*, the staff issued exemptive relief under Rule 102 to permit a French company conducting an exchange offer in Belgium to extend it into the United States, while at the same time engaging in a buy-back of its shares.

Rights issues
The SEC rescinded former Rule 10b-8 – the legal underpinning of "Shields Plan" rights offer activities. This follows logically the removal of "rights to acquire" as a test for a covered security. But it does not mean rights offers are completely deregulated.

Underwriters cannot freely purchase the underlying stock unless it qualifies for another exception, such as the actively traded one. And if Rule 101 is applicable (eg, because the security does not have a large enough ADTV), the underwriters are still only permitted to solicit buyers for the stock being distributed in the rights offer, not to buy outstanding stock outside of the distribution.

Stabilisation

Rule 104, which replaced Rule 10b-7, was adopted largely as proposed and codifies the position consistently applied by the SEC since the 1991 "Stabilisation Release".[75]

Under Rule 104, stabilising bids may be established with reference to prices in the principal market for the security in question wherever located, and (as under Part 10 of the FSA Rules) bids may be raised to follow bids in the independent market, so long as no bid is higher than the public offer price. There is required a brief stabilising legend directing investors to a discussion of stabilising activities in the "plan of distribution" section of the prospectus; the "plan of distribution" section will be required to include a brief description of the existence and potential market effect of any prospective stabilising or after-market activities, such as syndicate covering transactions or the imposition of penalty bids. (note the proposed revisions to Regulation M to ban penalty bids). The managing underwriter must keep records of all syndicate covering transactions, in addition to stabilising information. Under the proposed amendments to Regulation M, every syndicate covering bid must be identified or designated as such, wherever it is communicated (and to prohibit penalty bids).

In the course of proposing Regulation M, the SEC requested comment on these particular syndicate practices and it was believed by some practitioners that regulatory consequences might ensue, such as, perhaps, the establishment of price levels. In the end, Rule 104 as adopted only requires a brief discussion in the "plan of distribution", and that the underwriters provide prior notice to the NYSE or NASD of intent to initiate short covering or penalty bids, which will produce one more piece of paper for these SROs to file.

---

[75] Exchange Act Release 38732 (3rd January 1991).

NASDAQ passive market making

Passive market making on NASDAQ, which was the subject of former Rule 10b-6A, is more loosely regulated under new Rule 103. There is no longer any eligibility criteria, so all NASDAQ stocks now qualify for "passive" treatment. Moreover, a NASDAQ market maker who is caught by Rule 101 can stay passive in the market throughout the covered period, provided no stabilisation activities are in evidence.

Otherwise, the mechanics of being passive have not been changed. As before, there are limits on the levels of bids and purchases and amounts of a subject security that can be purchased, a disclosure requirement for the prospectus, a requirement that advance notice to be given to the NASD, and that passive bids are identified as such in the NASDAQ quote system.

Rule 10b-6 "class" exemptions

Under former Rule 10b-6, the Staff issued class exemptions for distributions of securities in certain countries that met eligibility criteria. The exemptions ended when Regulation M was adopted. Hence, non-US issuers proposing to offer securities with a US tranche that would qualify as a distribution under Regulation M should, in the absence of an applicable exception under Rule 101 or 102, seek relief from the Division of Market Regulation.

U.K. passive market making

The SEC granted a new exemption from Regulation M Rule 101 for passive market making on the LSE during distributions of qualifying SEAQ and SEAQ International securities with a US tranche.[76] The exemption supersedes the 1995 passive market making exemption. Under the new exemption, distribution participants and certain affiliated purchasers may bid for, purchase, or solicit the purchase of a security that is the subject of a distribution in the United States or a reference security (Covered Securities) when the "Covered Security" is listed for quotation on SEAQ or a firm quote security on SEAQ International, and is not otherwise excepted by Rule 101.

---

[76] Letter Regarding Distributions of Certain SEAQ and SEAQ International Securities (5th August 1997).

Certain LSE-traded SEAQ or SEAQ International securities will satisfy the exception for "actively traded securities". Underwriters will not have to restrict trading prior to the offer of an equity security that has an average daily trading volume of at least US$1 million and a public float of at least US$150 million. Nearly all NYSE, AMEX and NASDAQ National Market System equities will satisfy this test, together with most FTSE 100 securities and a significant number of FTSE 250 securities. However, for SEAQ and SEAQ International securities that do not satisfy this test, the new exemption will allow LSE affiliated purchasers or LSE distribution participants to enter bids and engage in certain market making activities in a SEAQ or SEAQ International security, if such efforts follow the bids or purchases of non-affiliated market makers and are not designed to lead the market.

The exemption is applicable for periods commencing:

- one business day before the determination of the offer price and ending upon the completion of participation in a distribution in the United States for a Covered Security with an ADTV of US$100,000 or more that is issued by a company whose equity securities have a public float value of US$25 million or more; or
- five business days before the determination of the offer price and ending upon the completion of participation in a distribution in the United States for all other Covered Securities.

All other LSE-traded securities (non-SEAQ securities, non-SEAQ International "firm quote" securities, SEATS securities and Alternative Investment Market securities) will not have an exemption or exception from Rule 101, and will require a specific grant of relief from the SEC. Transactions effected in the United States and in other "significant markets" during an offer of securities that are conducted in reliance on the new exemption will continue to be subject to restrictions under Regulation M, unless the SEC grants an exemption.

Nearly all SETS securities will qualify for the new exemption. Those SETS securities that did not do so may otherwise qualify for the new exemption or would be the subject of an application for exceptive relief.

Participants in distributions of securities offered under the new exemption must comply fully with conditions that relate to the disclosure of trading activities, record keeping and reporting, effecting transactions other than in the United Kingdom, and the disclosure of such transactions, as well as certain general conditions. LSE member firms using the exemption should submit the required notice to the Exchange during the mandatory quote period of the business day immediately prior to the mandatory quote period when passive market making activity will first begin, and before engaging in any passive market making activity. The LSE will provide the SEC with copies of all passive market makers' notifications received under the new exemption.

Shorting into a public offer

Rule 105 replaced former Rule 10b-21 on the regulation of persons who sell stock short before an offer, intending to drive the price down and then cover the short with stock obtained in the offer itself. Since the practice was detrimental to an offer even if the short was not covered directly in the offer, Rule 10b-21 was a bit of an anomaly. The loosening-up given in Rule 105 makes it even less useful. The NASD asked the SEC to include a "directly or indirectly" phrase to the prohibited short covering language, but the SEC refused to do so.

Amendments to Regulation M

In light of the recent IPO cases (discussed in Chapter 9), the SEC issued the Regulation M Amending Release. In addition to the points noted above, Regulation M would be amended to:

❑ change the restricted periods – the proposal would mean that,
❑ for IPOs, the restricted period would begin from the earlier of (a) the time when the issuer and a broker–dealer reached agreement that the broker–dealer would act as underwriter or when such person became a distribution participant or (b) if there was no broker–dealer (a self-underwriting), when the issuer filed a registration statement or an offering document was first circulated to potential investors, which period would end when the distribution was completed;
❑ for mergers, acquisitions and exchange offers, the restricted period would include valuation and election periods, as applicable, and to include definitions of them in Regulation M Rule 100(b);

- change the Rule 101 *de minimis* exception to require under proposed new Exchange Act Rule 17a-4(b)(13) record-keeping of each bid or purchase made in reliance on this exception;
- amend the Rules 100, 101 and 102 ADTVs, as noted above;
- require the disclosure of syndicate covering bids;
- prohibit penalty bids (where the managing underwriter reclaims a selling concession from a syndicate member in connection with an offering when the securities originally sold by the syndicate member in question are purchased in syndicate covering transactions); and
- adopt a new Rule 106 under Regulation M, which would prohibit the demand, solicitation, attempt, inducement or acceptance from a customer of any consideration in addition to the stated offering price of the security being distributed.

ANTI-MONEY LAUNDERING

On 26th October 2001, President Bush signed into law the "Uniting and Strengthening America by Providing Appropriate Tools Required to Intercept and Obstruct Terrorism Act of 2001" (Patriot Act). The Patriot Act, among other things, was designed to prevent terrorists and other criminals from using the US financial system for illicit purposes through the imposition of new and heightened due diligence, monitoring, reporting and recordkeeping requirements for covered financial institutions, including securities broker–dealers. Since the passage of the Patriot Act, the Treasury has proposed and finalised many new regulations implementing the Patriot Act requirements applicable to broker–dealers.

To date, those requirements include: (1) the implementation of anti-money laundering (AML) programmes; (2) the implementation of customer identification programmes; (3) prohibition on opening or maintaining correspondent accounts for foreign "shell banks;" (4) the filing of suspicious activity reports (SARs); (5) special due diligence for private banking accounts; and (6) information sharing between financial institutions and government agencies.

Anti-money laundering programmes

Section 352 of the Patriot Act requires broker–dealers to implement an AML programme designed to achieve compliance with the BSA and rules thereunder. Treasury has implemented Section 352 with respect to broker–dealers through the SEC and applicable SRO rules regarding the establishment and maintenance of AML programmes.[77] In this regard, both the NASD and the NYSE have adopted rules requiring their respective member firms to implement, with the approval of senior management, a written AML programme. At a minimum, the AML programme must:

- Establish and implement policies and procedures that can be reasonably expected to detect and cause the reporting of suspicious transactions;
- Provide for independent testing of the AML programme either by firm personnel or qualified third parties;
- Designate and identify an individual or individuals responsible for implementing and monitoring the daily operations and internal controls of the AML programme and provide prompt notification to the applicable SRO regarding any changes in such designation; and
- Provide ongoing training for appropriate personnel.[78]

AML programmes should cover all aspects of the broker–dealer's business and be tailored to the firm's specific business, customers, and risks of potential money laundering. Appropriate AML procedures will vary based on, for example, the type of account, the type of customer, the type of trading engaged in by the customer base, and other risk-based factors including the jurisdiction from which the customer originates. The AML programme also should include a system of internal controls and checks designed to monitor and to ensure compliance with the AML procedures.

Customer Identification Programs

As a part of the AML programme described above, Section 326 of the Patriot Act and the regulations thereunder require broker–dealers to develop a Customer Identification Program (CIP) that implements reasonable procedures to: (i) collect identifying information about customers opening an account; (ii) verify that the customers are who they say are they are; (iii) maintain records of the information used to verify their identity; and (iv) determine whether the

---

77 Financial Crimes Enforcement Network; Anti-Money Laundering Programs for Financial Institutions, 67 Fed. Reg. 21,110 (29th April 2002); NASD Rule 3011; NYSE Rule 445 ; NASD Anti-Money Laundering Frequently Asked Questions (updated 10th May 2005).
78 NASD Rule 3011; NYSE Rule 445.

customer appears on any list of suspected terrorists or terrorist organisations.[79] All broker–dealers are required to develop and implement a CIP as part of their AML programme.

Under the rules, a "customer" is generally a person who opens a new account. The rule specifically excludes from the definition of "customer" financial institutions regulated by a US federal functional regulator or a state-regulated bank. The rule also excludes persons with existing accounts with the broker–dealer provided that the broker–dealer has a reasonable belief that it knows the true identity of the person. It is important to note that broker–dealers are not required to look through a trust, or similar account, to its beneficiaries. With respect to omnibus accounts, a broker–dealer is not required to look through the beneficiary to the underlying beneficial account owners. Only the identity of the named account holder must be verified.

Under the Treasury's rules, a broker–dealer is required to develop procedures to collect relevant identifying information from customers opening a new account. For individuals, such information includes a name, address, date of birth, and a taxpayer identification number such as a social security number (for US taxpayers) or a similar government-issued identification number such as a passport (for non-US persons). For entities (eg, corporations, partnerships, etc.) the broker–dealer should obtain the name, address of the principal place of business, local office, or other physical location, and a taxpayer identification number (such as a Federal Employer Identification Number or, for non-US entities, a similar government issued identification number).

Broker–dealers must also have procedures in place to verify the identity of customers opening accounts through documents or other methods. For individuals, such additional documents that will be used to verify the identity of the customer may include an unexpired driver's license or passport. For entities, a broker–dealer may use documents evidence the existence of the entity, including certified articles of incorporation, government-issued business licenses, partnership agreements, or a trust instrument. The rule, however, provides flexibility to permit the broker–dealer to utilise

---

[79] Securities and Exchange Commission and Department of the Treasury; Customer Identification Programs for Broker–dealers, 68 Fed. Reg. 25,113 (9th May 2003) (codified at 31 CFR 103.122).

alternate methods to verify the identity of customers, including non-documentary methods.

The broker–dealer must also implement procedures that describe: (i) when the broker–dealer should not open the account, (ii) the terms under which a customer can utilise the account while the broker–dealer is verifying the customer's identity; (iii) when the broker–dealer should file a suspicious activity report (SAR) in accordance with applicable law (see below); and (iv) when the broker–dealer should close an account after attempts to verify the customer's identity have failed.

The CIP should also include procedures for maintaining records relating to verifying the identities of customers. The rule requires the broker–dealer to make a record of the information obtained about each customer, including a description of any document used to verify the identity of the customer (ie, type of document, identification number on the document, place of issuance, and expiration date, if any). If non-documentary methods were used to verify the identity of the customer, a description of such methods must be included in the record. The broker–dealer is not required to retain copies of the documents used to verify the identity of the customer.

Broker–dealers are required to retain basic information (eg, name, address, tax identification number) regarding a customer for five years after the account is closed. Any other information obtained pursuant to this rule need only be retained for five years after the record was made.

The CIP must also include procedures for determining whether a customer appears on any list of known or suspected terrorist or terrorist organisations issued by a US federal government agency and designated as such by Treasury. Such lists must be checked within a reasonable time after the account is opened, or earlier if required by another federal law or regulation.

Correspondent account rules – foreign shell banks

Section 313(a) of the Patriot Act requires broker–dealers to: (i) terminate any "correspondent account" that is established, maintained, administered, or managed on behalf of a "foreign shell bank;" and (ii) take "reasonable steps" to ensure that any correspondent account established, maintained, or administered on behalf of a foreign bank is not being used directly or indirectly to provide banking services to a foreign shell bank. Section 319(b) of the Patriot Act requires covered financial institutions to maintain records with respect to any foreign bank correspondent account that identifies the owners of the foreign bank and the name and address of an agent for the foreign bank in the United States who has been designated to accept service of legal process from US governmental agencies for foreign bank records regarding the account. Section 319(b) further obligates covered financial institutions to terminate any correspondent account maintained on behalf of a foreign bank that fails to provide the information requested.

In September 2002, Treasury published final rules that implement Sections 313(a) and 319(b) of the Patriot Act with respect to broker–dealers and certain other financial institutions.[80]

Prohibition on correspondent accounts for foreign shell banks
The rules under Section 313(a) prohibit US broker–dealers from establishing, maintaining, administrating or managing a correspondent account in the United States for, or on behalf of, a foreign "shell bank." These rules further require broker–dealers to "take reasonable steps to ensure" that any foreign bank correspondent account is not used by that foreign bank to indirectly provide banking services to a foreign shell bank. The prohibition applies only to accounts established, maintained, administered or managed in the United States. The prohibition does not extend to correspondent accounts maintained at non-US affiliates of the US bank or broker–dealer.

"Foreign shell bank" is defined as a bank without a physical presence in any country, but expressly excludes a shell bank that is both (i) an affiliate of a depository institution, credit union, or foreign bank that has a physical presence, and (ii) subject to regulation by the affiliate's home country banking authority. Under the rules, a foreign bank is deemed to have a "physical presence" if it: (i) maintains a place of business at a fixed address (other than solely an electronic address or a post-office box) in a country in which it is

---

[80] Counter Money Laundering Requirements – Correspondent Banks; Recordkeeping and Termination of Correspondent Accounts for Foreign Banks, 57 Fed. Reg. 60,562 (published 26th September 2002).

authorised to conduct banking activities; (ii) has at least one full-time employee; (iii) maintains operating records; and (iv) is subject to inspection by the banking authority which licensed the foreign bank.[81] A correspondent account is broadly defined as "an account established by a covered financial institution for a foreign bank to receive deposits from, to make payments or other disbursements on behalf of, or to handle other financial transactions related to the foreign bank."[82] As applied to broker–dealers, this definition would include: (i) accounts used to purchase, sell, lend or otherwise hold securities; (ii) prime brokerage accounts; (iii) custody accounts; (iv) foreign exchange accounts; (v) over-the-counter derivatives accounts; and (vi) futures or commodity options trading accounts maintained by broker–dealers dually registered as futures commission merchants.[83]

A foreign bank is a bank organised under foreign law, or an agency, branch or office of a bank located outside the United States.[84] The term foreign bank does not include an agent, agency, branch or office of a bank organised under foreign law that is located within the United States. The term "bank" is defined as a depository institution, including a commercial bank, a trust company, a private bank, a savings and loan association, a savings bank, an industrial bank, a thrift institution, or a credit union.[85]

Recordkeeping requirements regarding owners and agents
Broker–dealers also are required to obtain and to maintain information regarding the foreign bank's owners and the name and address of the designated agent for service of process with respect to foreign bank correspondent accounts. Broker–dealers are required to terminate any foreign bank correspondent account for which it has not received the required information.

❑ Owners of the Foreign Bank. Under Treasury's rules, the term "owner" means any person who, directly or indirectly, owns, controls, or has the power to vote 25% or more of any class of

---

81 67 Fed. Reg. at 60,570 (codified at 31 C.F.R. 103.175).
82 67 Fed. Reg. at 60,570 (codified at 31 C.F.R. 103.175(d)).
83 67 Fed. Reg. at 60,565.
84 31 C.F.R. 103.11(o).
85 31 C.F.R. 103.11(c).

voting securities of the foreign bank or controls the election of a majority of its directors.[86]

❏ Agent for Service of Process. Broker–dealers are required to obtain from, and retain for, each foreign bank with a correspondent account, the name and address for a US resident person authorised to accept service of process for records regarding such account. Broker–dealers are required to terminate any foreign bank correspondent account for which they have not timely received proper information on a designated agent for service of process.[87]

Certification safe harbour

The rules promulgated by Treasury provide broker–dealers with a "safe harbour" for establishing compliance with both the foreign shell bank prohibitions and recordkeeping requirements if, at least once every three years, the broker–dealer obtains a completed certification or re-certification from the foreign bank.[88] The model certification (and re-certification) requires the foreign bank to certify, among other things, that it: (i) is not a foreign shell bank; (ii) does not use any correspondent account with the broker–dealer to indirectly provide banking services to a foreign shell bank; (iii) has no "owners" other than those disclosed in the certification; and (iv) has a registered agent located at a physical address in the United States that is authorised to receive service of process from Treasury or the US Attorney General, as identified in the certification.

Production of records to the US Government

Either Treasury or the DOJ may issue a subpoena to any foreign bank through service on its designated agent for records relating to correspondent accounts, including records maintained outside the United States, "that relate to the deposit of funds into the foreign bank." The foreign bank has seven days after receipt to respond to the subpoena. Broker–dealers must terminate any foreign bank correspondent account within ten business days of receiving a written

---

86 67 Fed. Reg. at 60,571 (codified at 31 C.F.R. 103.175(l)). Ownership information need not be maintained for foreign banks whose shares are publicly traded or for foreign banks that are required to file an annual report (FRY-7) with the Federal Reserve Board (Fed).
87 67 Fed. Reg. at 60,571 (codified at 31 C.F.R. 103.177(a)(2)).
88 67 Fed. Reg. at 60,571 (codified at 31 C.F.R. 103.177(a)(1)).

notice from either Treasury or DOJ that the foreign bank failed to comply with the subpoena.[89]

Limitation on liability

Treasury's rules expressly provide that broker–dealers and other covered financial institutions "shall not be liable to any person in any court or arbitration proceeding for terminating a correspondent relationship" as a result of a foreign bank's failure to timely respond to a request for required information regarding foreign shell banks, owners, or designated service agent, as described above.[90] Broker–dealers also cannot be held liable for terminating a correspondent account in response to a proper notice received from Treasury or DOJ of a foreign bank's failure to comply with a subpoena.[91]

Suspicious activity reports

On 1st July 2002, Treasury published final rules requiring broker–dealers to file Suspicious Activity Reports (SARs) with FinCEN.[92] The SAR rules apply to US-registered broker–dealers that are located in the United States. Broker–dealers that are subsidiaries of bank holding companies previously were required to file SARs under federal banking laws. The new rules apply to all US-registered broker–dealers, including those that, as subsidiaries of bank holding companies, already were required to file SARs.[93] Each broker–dealer involved in a transaction has an independent obligation to monitor for, identify and report suspicious transactions.[94]

Broker–dealers are required to report to FinCEN on form SAR-SF any suspicious transactions that meet certain criteria. Specifically, broker–dealers are required to report any transaction[95]

---

89 67 Fed. Reg. at 60,572 (codified at 31 C.F.R. 103.185).
90 67 Fed. Reg. at 60,572 (codified at 31 C.F.R. 103.177(d)(5)).
91 67 Fed. Reg. at 60,572 (codified at 31 C.F.R. 103.185(e)).
92 Financial Crimes Enforcement Network; Amendment to the Bank Secrecy Act Regulations – Requirement that the Brokers or Dealers in Securities Report Suspicious Transactions, 67 Fed. Reg. 44,048 (1st July 2002). The SAR Rules become effective on 30th December 2002, and apply to transactions that occur after that date.
93 12 C.F.R. §225.4(f). The new rules have different threshold and reporting requirements than those rules previously in effect.
94 NASD Frequently Asked Anti-Money Laundering Questions (10th May 2005).
95 The term "transaction" is defined broadly to include any "deposit, withdrawal, transfer between accounts, exchange of currency, loan, extension of credit, purchase or sale of any stock, bond, certificate of deposit, or other monetary instrument or security, purchase or redemption of any money order, payment or order for any money remittance or transfer, or any other payment, transfer, delivery by, through or to a financial institution, by whatever means effected."

conducted or attempted through a broker–dealer involving aggregate funds of at least US$5,000 and which the broker knows, suspects, or has reason to suspect:

- involves funds derived from illegal activity or is intended or conducted in order to hide or disguise funds or assets derived from illegal activity as part of a plan to violate or evade any federal law or regulation or to avoid any transaction reporting requirement under federal law or regulation;
- is designed, whether through structuring or other means, to evade any requirements under the BSA;
- has no business or apparent lawful purpose or is not the sort in which the customer normally would be expected to engage, and the broker–dealer knows there is no reasonable explanation for the transaction after examining the available facts, including the background and possible purpose of the transaction; and
- involves the use of the broker–dealer to facilitate criminal activity.[96]

Exceptions to reporting requirements
The rules provide for three exemptions to the SAR obligations of broker–dealers. First, a broker–dealer is not required to file a SAR-SF to report a robbery or burglary that is properly reported to an appropriate law enforcement authority. Second, a broker–dealer is not required to file a SAR-SF to report lost, missing, counterfeit, or stolen securities with respect to which it files a report pursuant to the requirements of Exchange Act Rule 17f-1. Finally, a broker–dealer need not file a SAR-SF to report violations of federal securities laws or rules (other than a violation of Exchange Act Rule 17a-8 or 17 C.F.R. 405.4[97]) by an officer, director, employee, or other registered representative of the broker–dealer to the extent the broker–dealer has reported the matter, under existing industry procedures, to the SEC or applicable SRO. Broker–dealers relying on this third

---

96 67 Fed. Reg. at 44,056 (to be codified at 31 C.F.R. 103.19).
97 Exchange Act Rule 17a-8 states, in part: "[e]very registered broker or dealer who is subject to the requirements of the Currency and Foreign Transactions Reporting Act of 1970 shall comply with the reporting, recordkeeping and record retention requirements of part 103 of title 31 of the Code of Federal Regulations." Section 405.4 requires financial recordkeeping and reporting of certain currency and foreign transactions by registered government securities brokers and dealers to Treasury.

exception are required to retain records of their "determinations to do so," which may be satisfied by retaining a copy of a properly filed NYSE Form RE-3, Form U-4 or Form U-5.[98]

FinCEN also issued interpretative guidance on 23rd December 2004 regarding the requirement to file a SAR if a US financial institution, including a broker–dealer, has already filed a blocking reporting in compliance with the OFAC. In this guidance, FinCEN clarified that filing a blocking report with OFAC will be deemed by FinCEN to satisfy the financial institution's requirements to file a SAR. However, FinCEN cautioned that a financial institution must still file a SAR to the extent that the financial institution is in possession of information not included in the blocking report filed with OFAC.[99]

Filing deadline and record retention

Broker–dealers must file an SAR-SF within 30 calendar days after initially detecting facts that may constitute a basis for filing a SAR-SF. If no "suspect" is identified on the date of initial detection of the suspicious transaction, the broker–dealer may delay the filing to identify a suspect for an additional 30 days. Broker–dealers are required to keep copies of the reports and supporting documentation for a period of five years.[100] In situations that involve an ongoing violation that requires immediate attention, Treasury advises broker–dealers immediately to notify the appropriate law enforcement authority and the SEC by telephone, in addition to filing the SAR-SF.

Confidentiality requirements

Broker–dealers are prohibited from notifying a customer or any other person involved in the subject transaction of their intent to file or that they have filed a SAR-SF. If a broker–dealer is subpoenaed or otherwise requested to disclose a SAR-SF or the information contained therein, except where the disclosure is requested by certain governmental entities, the broker–dealer must decline to produce the information and notify FinCEN of the request for information

---

98 67 Fed. Reg. at 44,056 (codified at 31 C.F.R. 103.19(c)).
99 Financial Crimes Enforcement Network: Interpretative Release No. 2004–02 – Unitary Filing of Suspicious Activity and Blocking Reports, 69 Fed. Reg. 246,76847.
100 67 Fed. Reg. at 44,056 (codified at 31 C.F.R. 103.19(d)).

and the broker–dealer's response.[101] Treasury's rules provide a safe harbour from civil liability (including in an arbitration proceeding) for reporting suspicious transactions and for complying with the confidentiality restrictions with respect to SAR-SF filings.[102]

Special due diligence for private banking accounts

Section 312 of the Patriot Act requires US financial institutions to establish due diligence policies, procedures, and controls reasonably designed to detect and report money laundering through "correspondent accounts" and "private banking accounts" that US financial institutions establish or maintain for "non-US persons."[103] By its terms, Section 312 took effect in July 2002. On 19th July 2002, Treasury issued an interim final rule providing guidance to financial institutions, including broker–dealers, on their compliance obligations after the statutory effective date of 23rd July 2002, while Treasury continues to consider the terms of its final rules.

The interim rules require all SEC-registered dealers, including broker–dealers located outside the United States, to implement a due diligence programme reasonably designed to detect and report money laundering and the existence of the proceeds of "foreign corruption." In this regard, broker–dealers must take "reasonable steps" to identify the nominal and beneficial owners of, and the source of funds deposited into, any private banking account maintained on behalf of a non-US person. "Private banking account" is broadly defined in the Patriot Act as an account (or any combination of accounts) that: (i) require a minimum aggregate deposit of funds or other assets of not less than US$1,000,000; (ii) is established on behalf of one or more individuals who have a direct or beneficial ownership interest in the account; and (iii) is assigned to, or administered or managed by, in whole or in part, an officer, employee, or agent of a financial institution acting as a liaison between the financial institution and the direct or beneficial owner of the account. A "non-US person" includes anyone who is neither a US citizen nor a lawful permanent resident.[104]

---

[101] 67 Fed. Reg. at 44,056 (codified at 31 C.F.R 103.19(e)).
[102] 67 Fed. Reg. at 44,056 (codified at 31 C.F.R 103.19(f)).
[103] Patriot Act §312(a) (codified at 31 USC. 5318).
[104] Id.

With respect to private banking accounts that have nominal or beneficial owners, broker–dealers are required to: (i) ascertain the identity of the nominal and beneficial owners of the accounts; (ii) ascertain the source of the funds deposited into the accounts; and (iii) report suspicious transactions. If the private banking account is requested or maintained on behalf of "a senior foreign political figure, an immediate family member or close associate," the broker–dealer must conduct "enhanced scrutiny" of any such account that is reasonably designed to detect and report transactions that involve the proceeds of "foreign corruption."[105]

Pending implementation of the final rule, Treasury advises that a "reasonable" due diligence programme for private banking accounts would focus on "those private banking accounts that present a high risk of money laundering." In this regard, Treasury directed broker–dealers to the guidance on sound practices for private banking issued by the Fed[106] and the guidance for enhanced scrutiny for transactions that may involve the proceeds of foreign corruption jointly issued in January 2001 by Treasury and the US State Department. Treasury further advises that broker–dealers should prioritise the application of enhanced due diligence to covered accounts opened on and after 23rd July 2002.[107]

Section 312 of the Patriot Act also imposes due diligence and enhanced scrutiny requirements on covered financial institutions, including broker–dealers, for all "correspondent accounts" maintained or requested by a foreign bank that is operating: (i) under an offshore banking license; (ii) under the banking license of a foreign country that is designated as noncooperative with international anti-money laundering principles by an intergovernmental group of which the United States is a member or with which it concurs; or (iii) under the banking license of a foreign country that Treasury determines warrants special measures, as described below, due to money laundering concerns. The interim rules defer the application to broker–dealers of the Section 312 special due diligence requirements for correspondent accounts until further notice.

---

[105] Id.
[106] SR 97–19 (SUP) "Private Banking Activities" (30th June 1997).
[107] 67 Fed. Reg. at 48,351.

Special measures for jurisdictions, financial institutions or international transactions of primary money laundering concern

Section 311 of the Patriot Act allows the Secretary of the Treasury to require domestic financial institutions and agencies to take one or more special measures if the Secretary has reasonable grounds to conclude that a jurisdiction, financial institution, class of transactions, or type of account outside of the United States is of primary money laundering concern. Among the special measures that the Secretary can take are to require institutions to keep certain records, to obtain beneficial ownership information, or to prohibit or impose conditions upon the opening or maintaining of a correspondent or payable through account by any domestic financial institution or agency.

FinCEN has proposed rules to designate several jurisdictions and institutions as being of primary money laundering concern under this rule.[108] In general, these proposed rules would prohibit any domestic financial institution or agency, including broker–dealers who are required to be registered with the SEC, from opening or maintaining a correspondent account. For broker–dealers, these accounts would include any account that permits the foreign bank to engage in (1) trading in securities and commodity futures or options, (2) funds transfers, or (3) other types of financial transactions.[109]

---

[108] On 26th April 2005, FinCEN proposed rules to designate and impose special measures against VEF Banka and Multibanka. Financial Crimes Enforcement Network; Amendment to Bank Secrecy Act Regulations – Imposition of Special Measures Against VEF Banka (70 Fed. Reg. 79,21369); Financial Crimes Enforcement Network; Amendment to Bank Secrecy Act Regulations – Imposition of Special Measures Against Multibanka (70 Fed. Reg. 79,21362). In 2004, FinCEN proposed rules to designate Infobank, First Merchant Bank and its subsidiaries, and the Commercial Bank of Syria and its subsidiaries as financial institutions of primary money laundering concern. Financial Crimes Enforcement Network; Amendment to Bank Secrecy Act Regulations – Imposition of Special Measures against Infobank as a Financial Institution of Primary Money Laundering Concern (69 Fed. Reg. 163,51973); Financial Crimes Enforcement Network; Amendment to Bank Secrecy Act Regulations – Imposition of Special Measures Against First Merchant Bank OSH Ltd, including its Subsidiaries, FMB Finance Ltd, and First Merchant Trust Ltd., as a Financial Institution of Primary Money Laundering Concern (69 Fed. Reg. 163,519789); Financial Crimes Enforcement Network; Amendment to Bank Secrecy Act Regulations – Imposition of Special Measures Against Commercial Bank of Syria, including its Subsidiary, Syria Lebanese Commercial Bank, as a Financial Institution of Primary Money Laundering Concern (69 Fed. Reg. 96,28098).

[109] 69 Fed. Reg. 163, 51976–77.

Information sharing rules

Section 314 of the Patriot Act directs Treasury to adopt rules providing for the sharing of information between and among the government and financial institutions in order to facilitate law enforcement efforts against money laundering and terrorism. Specifically, Section 314(a) of the Act requires regulations that encourage cooperation between financial institutions and the federal government through an information exchange regarding individuals, entities and organisations engaged in or reasonably suspected of being engaged in terrorist acts or money laundering activities. Section 314(b) allows financial institutions, upon proper notice to the Treasury, to share information amongst themselves to help them better identify and report to the federal government activities that may involve money laundering or terrorist activities. The final rule implementing Section 314(a) became effective on 26 September 2002 and established a process through which law enforcement agencies may communicate with financial institutions in order to solicit information on named subjects so that the accounts and transactions involving these individuals or entities may be promptly located.

Information sharing between financial institutions
Treasury's rules regarding information sharing also provide a safe harbour that permits certain financial institutions to share information for the purpose of detecting, identifying, or reporting activities involving possible money-laundering or terrorist activities.[110] To receive the safe harbour protection, a broker–dealer must file a notice with FinCEN, in the form attached to the rules, advising FinCEN of its intent to share information with other financial institutions covered by the rules. The broker–dealer also must take reasonable steps before sharing the information to verify that the receiving financial institution also has filed a notice with FinCEN. The broker–dealer must submit a new notice on an annual basis if it intends to continue sharing information.

Law enforcement information requests
The rules also provide for federal law enforcement agencies to submit requests for information regarding suspected terrorists and

---

[110] 67 Fed. Reg. at 60,587 (codified at 103.110(a)(2)).

money laundering to FinCEN, which will then issue requests for information to financial institutions, including registered broker–dealers (314(a) requests).[111] After a brief moratorium on 314(a) requests, on 18th February 2003, FinCEN reinstated such requests to financial institutions, and issued guidance and new procedures governing such requests.[112]

Under the procedures, information requests from FinCEN are batched and issued every two weeks in electronic form via facsimile transmission, unless circumstances require more expeditious action. Upon receiving an information request, broker–dealers are required to conduct the search and respond with any positive identification within two weeks (14 calendar days) of receipt (Named Subject). Broker–dealers only need to respond to a request if they have found a positive match and should direct any questions concerning a possible positive identification to the requesting federal law enforcement agency.

Broker–dealers are required to search their records for current accounts and accounts maintained by a named subject during the preceding twelve months and transactions not linked to an account conducted by a Named Subject during the prior six months. Records not maintained in electronic form need be searched only if they are required to be kept under federal law or regulation, except safe deposit records, which are required to be searched only if they can be searched electronically. Unless otherwise noted, an information request is not continuing in nature and is satisfied by a "one-time" search of the records covered by the request.

Unless specifically directed by a request, broker–dealers should not search the records of their foreign branch offices and should not send the request to their foreign branch offices. Similarly, US offices of non-US broker–dealers should not search the records of any office located outside the United States, including its head office, and should not send the request to any such office unless otherwise provided for in the request.

Once a single positive match of a named subject has been identified, the broker–dealer can halt their search, submit their

---

111 31 USC. §5312 (a)(2).
112 FinCEN reinstates USA Patriot Act Section 314(a) Information Requests, Treasury Press Release (6th February 2003).

response and need not continue to search for additional matches. Broker–dealers, however, should continue their search with respect to any other Named Subject set forth in the information request.

The broker–dealer generally should not disclose to any other person that FinCEN has requested or been provided information unless such disclosure is necessary to comply with the information request. A third-party service provider or vendor may assist a broker–dealer in responding to an information request provided that the broker–dealer takes appropriate measures to ensure that the third-party protects the confidentiality of the information.

Broker–dealers are not required to close any account by virtue of a match to a Named Subject. While they are free to close an account if they so choose, they are encouraged to consult in advance with the appropriate law enforcement agency to determine whether closing the account would interfere with an active investigation.

Penalties for violation of the Patriot Act

The Patriot Act imposes significant civil and criminal penalties for violation of its provisions. For example, under Section 319(b), broker–dealers that fail to terminate correspondent accounts within ten days after receiving written notice from Treasury or DOJ that the foreign bank account holder has failed to respond to a subpoena are subject to a US$10,000 per day penalty for each day the account remains open. In addition, broker–dealers that fail to take "reasonable steps" to prevent the direct or indirect usage of correspondent accounts by foreign shell banks under Section 313 may be held liable for up to two times the amount of any transaction through such accounts, up to US$1,000,000. Failure to implement an AML programme under Section 352, or to file a SAR-SF as specified in the rules under Section 356, similarly carry penalties of up to US$1,000,000.

8

Developments in International Regulation and Enforcement

Michael D Mann, William P Barry

Richards Spears Kibbe and Orbe LLP

In today's global marketplace cross-border securities transactions have become routine: firms and investors frequently undertake activities in one jurisdiction that impact the laws and regulations of other jurisdictions. In response, efforts to formalise cooperation among regulators have redoubled. Whereas in the past authorities paid polite lip service to cooperation, today it is real. Indeed, the scope of cooperation has developed and expanded over time, from requests under the Hague Convention and pursuant to Letters Rogatory, to the implementation of Mutual Legal Assistance Treaties (MLATs) among governments and less formal bilateral and multilateral Memoranda of Understanding (MOUs) among securities regulators. With each new development international regulatory authorities have enhanced their ability to investigate and prosecute activities that cross into another regulator's jurisdiction.[1]

The need for information about cross-border activities has defined recent developments in international cooperation among securities regulators. In many instances, no single regulator will have access to all of the information necessary to protect the interests of investors and the integrity of domestic securities

---

1 This chapter is a follow up to *International Agreements and Understandings for the Production of Information and Other Mutual Assistance*, Michael D Mann *et al*, 29 International Law 780 (Winter 1995). Please *see* that article for a detailed discussion of developments in international enforcement occurring prior to this chapter.

markets.[2] In addition, the globalisation of the securities markets and the growing interdependence of the world's economies has fostered a need for the international community to be able to respond to prevent potential cross-market disruption. Regulators are looking for cooperative means for promoting improved internal controls and better risk management by securities market participants.[3] Such improved controls will result in more complete documentation of securities transactions and will potentially open a new front for exposure of securities firms to liability for failure to maintain the appropriate records.

On a worldwide basis, securities regulators have developed a successful, multi-faceted approach to the challenges posed by the internationalisation of the world's securities markets. This approach includes unilateral undertakings as well as bilateral and multilateral initiatives with foreign authorities. At the same time, firms that engage in multi-national securities activities have begun to recognise the importance of developing proactive and effective regulatory relationships with regulators in several nations.

Underscoring these recent efforts is the recognition by regulators that information represents power. The goal of regulators is to enhance their ability to oversee conduct and events occurring elsewhere in the world that could affect their particular markets. The relationships, agreements, declarations and rule changes described herein demonstrate that the SEC has gone a long way toward achieving this goal. Regulators have established a nexus between regulation and enforcement, enabling them to take action before problems arise and, at the same time, to respond better to the needs of the marketplace. The level of innovation and sophistication of initiatives reflects the responsiveness of the SEC and other regulators to dramatic changes brought about by globalisation.

The impact of SOX in expanding the extraterritorial reach of the SEC has profoundly changed the global regulation and enforcement environment. The United States is continuing to aggressively

---

2 *See, eg,* the SEC/IMRO Declaration (recognising the "dramatic increase in cross-border investment management activity" and the need to formalise mechanisms for sharing in formation and jointly conducting inspections) and the section on FIA MOU (promoting "collective market integrity").

3 *See, eg,* the Bank of England MOU and the Joint Statement Regarding OTC Derivatives Oversight.

assert jurisdiction under SOX, which has caused other national regulators to react by establishing more aggressive regulatory initiatives of their own. While perceived overreaching by the United States has caused tension in the international enforcement community, the reaction to SOX has been to raise standards across jurisdictions. These heightened standards, combined with the existing information sharing infrastructure, have raised the risk of regulatory exposure for international firms.

The exercise by the SEC of its potency under SOX and with other laws and rules has once again raised the question of the reasonable limits to the scope of United States jurisdiction. Foreign companies registered in the United States are clearly subject to this jurisdiction, as are their auditors and officers. Does such jurisdiction similarly apply to their foreign employees? Can the SEC affect the governance of the foreign corporation, which is already governed by foreign law? Should the percentage of US ownership of a foreign company affect these judgments?

All of the above questions need to be viewed in the context that, at the same time as the United States is expanding its extraterritorial reach, investors are continuing to seek investment opportunities in companies in ways that bypass US regulation. Regulation S/Rule 144A offerings or direct purchases on foreign markets are increasingly easy to access directly. As a result, the jurisdictional means that the SEC uses as the basis of its cases is being eroded. This begs the question of where US regulators should draw their "line in the sand" and whether US investors should have any say in where the line is drawn. The struggle to find the balance between the exercise of jurisdiction and the fundamental goal of protecting investors is exemplified in *SEC v. TV Azteca SA de CV*,[4] discussed below.

With the enhancement of enforcement initiatives and tools has come a resurgence in focus on the FCPA. This resurgence, coupled with an increased willingness on the part of the SEC to assert jurisdiction in global matters involving broker–dealers, has led to a fascinating balancing act on the part of US courts in which US interests in the protection of American investors and the integrity

---

4 *Securities and Exchange Commission v. TV Azteca SA de CV, Azteca Holdings, SA de CV, Ricardo Salinas Pliego, Pedro Padilla Longoria and Luis Echarte Fernandez*, Civil Action No. 1:05-CV-00004 (DDC) (4th January 2004).

of the global securities market are weighed against the interest in global cooperation and fairness to targets. It has also resulted in an increased focus by multi-national corporations on the maintenance of accurate, transparent books and records both at corporate headquarters and at international divisions or subsidiaries.

The explosion of instant communication and access to information via the Internet has had a significant impact on enforcement – particularly on the SEC's willingness to assert jurisdiction in matters involving foreign nationals operating on foreign soil.

Globalisation of securities markets has also resulted in courts in the United States and elsewhere having to address novel and complex issues. For example, does a regulator have the power under local law to provide assistance to a foreign authority under a MOU? Under what circumstances does a US court have the authority to assert jurisdiction over securities transactions that are international in character? The results of recent cases are both interesting and varied. However, as discussed herein, courts generally have recognised both the global nature of the securities markets and the importance of international cooperation in enforcement.

INTERNATIONAL COOPERATION
SEC approach to information sharing

The SEC entered into its first information-sharing arrangement to obtain evidence located abroad in 1982. Since then, the SEC has made international evidence gathering a priority and has entered into more than 30 cooperative arrangements. Securities regulators around the world now use cooperative arrangements modelled on those pioneered by the SEC as a significant means of enforcing domestic securities laws. Indeed, the negotiation of cooperative agreements has become an important hallmark for newly established securities commissions as well as standard operating procedure for regulators in developed markets. Regulatory authorities around the world are increasingly willing to use compulsory powers on behalf of a foreign authority without requiring an underlying or parallel domestic violation.

MOUs form the basis of the SEC's ability to take enforcement action when the evidence is located overseas. The SEC may negotiate a MOU with its counterpart in a country where there is a great deal of cross-border business or where there is a broader US government interest in establishing closer ties. In each case, the MOU must be crafted to fit the circumstances of the foreign market and the powers of the foreign authorities. Indeed, the actual texts of the documents reflect these differences in legal and regulatory authorities. Thus, before entering into a MOU with a foreign authority, the SEC and the foreign securities authority exchange information about their respective regulatory systems and thereby learn about each other's specific interests, needs and capabilities.

In addition to MOUs, the SEC actively seeks to identify and use other formal and informal information gathering mechanisms, most notably US MLATs with foreign criminal authorities. In particular, the MLAT between the United States and Switzerland has provided a useful mechanism for the SEC, working with the US Justice Department, to obtain information located in Switzerland, including detailed banking information.[5] In addition, the Swiss authorities have been willing in specific cases to freeze profits traceable to illegal securities activities, thereby preserving the status quo pending further SEC action.

The SEC's bilateral understandings with foreign regulators and other formal and informal information-sharing arrangements provide a framework in which the SEC can seek and provide assistance for the purpose of enforcing the securities laws of the US and foreign jurisdictions. Each year the SEC makes an increasing number of requests for assistance to foreign jurisdictions and, not unexpectedly, receives a larger volume of requests in return.

Legislative basis for providing assistance

When the SEC began to use international cooperation as a primary vehicle for gaining access to foreign-based information, it became clear that the success of such an approach would depend on legislative changes. Indeed, at that time, the SEC and most of its foreign counterparts lacked the authority to use compulsory investigative powers unless there was an independent basis for suspecting a violation of domestic securities law. The SEC sought specific

---

[5] However, a case recently decided by the Swiss Supreme Court has indicated that there remain significant issues still to be addressed regarding the reconciliation of US regulatory interests and Swiss privacy laws. *See* the discussion of *In the Matter of W, X, Y and Z v. Swiss Banking Commission*.

legislation authorising it to assist its counterparts and urged its counterparts to seek similar legislation in their countries.

In 1988, as part of its efforts to assist foreign authorities, the SEC proposed, and Congress enacted, legislation authorising the SEC to conduct investigations on behalf of foreign securities authorities, using subpoena authority if necessary. Section 21(a)(2) of the Exchange Act, added by ITSFEA, empowers the SEC to conduct a formal investigation upon the request of a foreign securities authority[6] without regard to whether the facts stated in a request would constitute a violation of the laws of the United States. In June 1988, a measure similar to the Commission's proposal was introduced in the Senate (S.2544) and, that month, the Commission's proposal was introduced in the House (H.R.4945). Hearings on the bill were held in both the House and the Senate, and the Senate Banking Committee favourably reported out the bill. The House Energy and Commerce Committee reported out the investigatory assistance section of the bill (discussed below) and that legislation (Act) was enacted on 22nd October 1988 as Section 6 of ITSFEA.

It is important to note that, unlike corresponding statutes in other countries, the Exchange Act does not require that a matter under investigation on behalf of a foreign securities authority also constitutes a violation of US law. Because the US securities laws are broader than the securities laws of most other countries, a "dual criminality" requirement, if applied on a reciprocal basis by other nations, would tend to limit the applicability of bilateral agreements to a narrow range of cases and hence limit the Commission's ability to obtain assistance from other nations.

The Act requires that the SEC, in deciding whether to provide the requested assistance, consider whether the foreign authority has agreed to provide reciprocal assistance. It allows the SEC to refuse to process any request on the grounds that the request violates the public interest. Furthermore, it provides witnesses with all the protection and remedies afforded to witnesses in SEC proceedings. Accordingly, witnesses could obtain access to a formal order identifying the basis and subject matter of an investigation. In addition,

---

6 Section 3(a)(50) of the Exchange Act broadly defines the term "foreign securities authority" to include "any foreign government, or any governmental body or regulatory organisation empowered by a foreign government to administer or enforce its laws as they relate to securities matters".

they would be able to resist enforcement of an unnecessarily burdensome subpoena. In accordance with SEC practice, any challenge to a SEC subpoena would be reviewed by the SEC as part of the authorisation process for a subpoena enforcement action.

The memorandum submitted by the SEC in support of the proposed legislation states that the SEC anticipates that any person resisting the subpoena would make his reasons known at the time he/she initially resists the subpoena. This information would be available to the SEC for its consideration before a decision was made to institute a subpoena enforcement action. Accordingly, the SEC would have an opportunity to review the matter, and the facts as argued by the subject of the subpoena, before seeking a court determination. The memorandum further notes that the SEC believes that, by providing a witness with the same rights and protections provided to witnesses in SEC investigations, the proposed legislation resolves any constitutional due process and Fourth Amendment concerns that could be raised. Because testimony would be taken pursuant to existing investigative procedures, a witness would be entitled to assert all relevant rights and privileges under US law. In addition, a witness would be entitled to assert privileges available in the country seeking the evidence, even in cases where the United States does not recognise the privileges. Issues of privilege would be preserved on the record for later consideration by a court of the requesting authority. The SEC also stated that it anticipated that foreign countries providing reciprocal assistance will follow a similar procedure.

The Act provides the SEC with flexibility, as it is not required to enter into a MOU before granting assistance to a foreign securities authority. In the absence of a MOU, the SEC may, if it receives all necessary confidentiality and use assurances, assist a foreign regulator and thereby demonstrate the value of international cooperation. This allows the SEC to use its powers to encourage the development of reciprocal assistance powers in countries that may not yet be able to enter into broad MOUs.

The SEC's 1988 recommendation also contained three provisions that were approved in substantially similar form by the House and the Senate in 1990. Those provisions, along with two new provisions, were introduced in the House (H.R.1396) and in the Senate (S.646) in March 1989. In December 1990, Congress enacted the

International Securities Enforcement Cooperation Act (ISECA) that, *inter alia*, amended Section 24 of the Exchange Act. ISECA has improved substantially the SEC's ability to cooperate with the securities regulators of other countries.

Sub-section 24(d) of the Exchange Act provides a basis for withholding disclosure under the FOIA of certain records obtained from a foreign securities authority. This exemption complements existing exemptions from disclosure under FOIA. Information obtained from a foreign securities authority, therefore, which does not satisfy the specific requirements of Sub-section 24(d), may also be withheld if it is entitled to any other FOIA exemption. The exemption provided for in Sub-section 24(d) could be claimed where the information requested was provided by a foreign securities authority, and the foreign securities authority has in good faith determined and represented to the SEC that disclosure of such information would violate the laws applicable to the foreign securities authority.

ISECA also clarified the Commission's authority to provide foreign and domestic securities authorities with non-public information, and authorised the SEC to obtain reimbursement from a foreign authority for expenses incurred in providing assistance to that authority. Finally, the SEC and US SROs were authorised to impose sanctions on a securities professional found by a foreign court or securities authority to have engaged in illegal or improper conduct.

IOSCO resolution on principles for record keeping, collection of information, enforcement powers and mutual cooperation to improve the enforcement of securities and futures laws

Securities regulators around the world have also entered into MOUs or similar understandings with one another,[7] thereby enhancing securities enforcement globally.[8] In addition, regulators have joined such

---

7   For a listing of MOUs among the members of the International Organisation of Securities Commissions (IOSCO), *see* IOSCO's website www.iosco.org.
8   For example, the Forum of European Securities Commissions, now CESR, has implemented a multilateral MOU among its members to improve the efficiency of enforcement actions relating to cross-border transactions. Currently, there are many bilateral MOUs in place among CESR members; however, reliance on such bilateral arrangements requires regulators to adhere to varying terms and standards relating to the provision of assistance. The adoption of a single, multilateral MOU will provide a single set of procedures for European regulators to follow. *See* World Securities Law Report, February 1999, at 9; *FESCO to Ink Europea MOU to Speed Up Cross-Border Enforcement*, Global Compliance Rep., 5th October 1998, at 1.

organisations as the International Organisation of Securities Commissions (IOSCO) to establish principles that form the basis for further cooperation in securities enforcement.[9] The increased need for information on a cross-border basis has been a central theme in recent initiatives relating to enforcement of securities laws and regulations.

On 1st October 1998, IOSCO adopted a Resolution on Principles for Record Keeping, Collection of Information, Enforcement Powers and Mutual Cooperation to Improve the Enforcement of Securities and Futures Laws.[10] The Resolution was adopted in response to self-evaluations by IOSCO members, which revealed that information and record keeping are not always adequate, due in part to the absence of mandatory provisions for record keeping in certain jurisdictions and in part to the limited resources of regulators. The members recognised that "comprehensive record keeping, improved collection of information, strong enforcement powers and the removal of impediments to cooperation are fundamental to effective enforcement of securities and futures laws, market transparency and more generally the development of sound securities and futures markets".

The IOSCO Resolution first sets forth the principles that the participants agree are important for record keeping and enforcement and second, focuses on the importance of information sharing among IOSCO members. The Resolution suggests the creation of contemporaneous records of all securities and futures transactions, including information as to funds and assets transferred, beneficial ownership and details such as price, quantity of securities and identity of brokers. Record keeping as prescribed by the Resolution will provide a more complete document trail for transactions, which will assist in monitoring and enforcement.

---

9 The Rio Declaration, which first established the basis for such cooperation and the goals of IOSCO, recognised "the need to enhance investor protection through both oversight of the internationalised markets and securities related businesses as well as through enforcement of national securities laws with respect to international transactions". *A Resolution Concerning Mutual Assistance*, Executive Committee, International Organisation of Securities Commissions, November 1986, at 1. The Asian Regional Committee of the International Organisation of Securities Commissions (Asian IOSCO) has been established, comprised of representatives from Australia, Japan, Hong Kong and Malaysia.

10 The resolution derives from the 1994 IOSCO Resolution in which the members renewed their commitment to the principles of mutual assistance and cooperation and agreed to undertake self-evaluations. Resolution on Commitment to Basic IOSCO Principles of High Regulatory Standards and Mutual Cooperation and Assistance, President's Committee, International Organisation of Securities Commissions, October 1994.

IOSCO members also agreed in the Resolution that a competent authority in each member's jurisdiction should have the power to identify persons who own or control public companies, bank accounts and brokerage accounts, emphasising that domestic secrecy laws should not prevent or restrict the collection of such information. As a result of the self-evaluations, IOSCO members recognised that the ability of members to implement the desired measures may vary significantly depending on many factors, including domestic legislation. Due to the importance of access to information, each IOSCO member agreed under the Resolution to "strive to ensure that it or another authority in its jurisdiction has the necessary authority…" to obtain the relevant information. This provision suggests that, while the regulator itself may not have the power to provide assistance in some cases, another government authority in the jurisdiction – eg, the criminal prosecutor – may have such power to share information with foreign regulators. Because of the different legal structures among IOSCO members, this is an important alternative.

Equally important to effective enforcement, however, is the sharing of such information with other IOSCO members. The Resolution therefore provides that members will take appropriate efforts to ensure that such information may be shared among them. Finally, members agreed generally to take efforts to remove such other impediments to cooperation as may exist under their domestic legislative and regulatory schemes. The IOSCO MOU, promulgated in 2002, is a product of the recognition among securities regulators of the underlying need for cross-border cooperation. The IOSCO MOU is discussed *infra* in the next section.

SEC COOPERATION UNDERSTANDINGS, AGREEMENTS AND DECLARATIONS[11]
Memoranda of understanding and statements of intent
In recent years, the SEC has entered into MOUs with regulators in Germany, Portugal, India, Singapore, Japan and Jersey. In addition, as noted above, in 2002, the first broad-based multilateral MOU was

---

11 The SEC has established cooperative agreements with regulators world-wide, including regulators in Argentina, Australia, Brazil, Canada, Chile, Costa Rica, Egypt, the European Community, France, Germany, Hong Kong, India, Indonesia, Israel, Italy, Japan, Jersey, Mexico, Netherlands, Norway, Portugal, Russia, Singapore, South Africa, Spain, Sweden, Switzerland, the UK and the members of IOSCO.

endorsed by members of IOSCO. Each of these Understandings establishes another important relationship of cooperation in securities enforcement.

German MOU

The SEC and the German Bundesaufsichtsamt für den Wertpapierhandel (BAWe) entered into a Memorandum of Understanding[12] on 17th October 1997.[13] The German MOU provides for broad assistance, although its scope is circumscribed by the somewhat limited extent of the BAWe's authority.[14] The German MOU addresses cooperation in connection with the enforcement of securities laws and regulations, including, among others, insider trading, misrepresentation or manipulative practices in connection with the offer, purchase or sale of any security or in the conduct of an investment business, the making of a false or misleading statement or material omission in any application or report to either of the authorities, and disclosure duties. Like most of the SEC's MOUs, the German MOU provides that the parties will consult periodically regarding matters relevant to the securities markets, in order to promote stability, efficiency and integrity.

The grounds on which assistance may be denied are articulated in greater detail in the German MOU than in many of the SEC's other MOUs. For example, the MOU makes clear that assistance can be denied when prosecution in the requesting country could result in an individual being subjected to multiple prosecutions for the same offence.[15] Presumably, this section was added at the request of the

---

12 *Memorandum of Understanding Concerning Consultation and Cooperation in the Administration and Enforcement of Securities Laws*, SEC International Series Release No. IS-1129 (14th April 1998).

13 The CFTC and the German BAWe have also entered into a Memorandum of Understanding Concerning Consultation and Cooperation in the Administration and Enforcement of Futures and Options Laws, pursuant to which a framework was established for assistance in regulating the futures markets, including providing access to files, taking statements from witnesses, obtaining information and conducting compliance inspections and investigations of futures transactions and futures businesses.

14 The BAWe does not have regulatory authority over securities exchanges in Germany, nor does it have regulatory power over issues relating to capital or to the safety and soundness of the securities markets.

15 The MOU is unclear as to whether assistance will be denied if the individual can be prosecuted multiple times in the United States by different US Attorneys or local district attorneys.

German authorities, since prosecution in more than one country does not raise double jeopardy concerns under US law[16] and the SEC has not ordinarily included such a clause in its other MOUs.[17]

The German MOU establishes a strong basis for cooperation in obtaining information to assist in enforcement against securities violations. The SEC and the BAWe each agree to provide assistance in interviewing persons, conducting inspections and obtaining information in order to determine whether violations of securities laws have been committed or to prove such violations. However, unlike the Portuguese MOU discussed below, the German MOU does not provide for participation by the requesting authority in any such inspections or investigations. Nevertheless, the cooperation of the German authority in obtaining information that is located in its territory is a critical element in the SEC's ability to investigate potential securities violations and to take action against appropriate parties.

Portuguese MOU

The MOU between the SEC and the Comissao do Mercado de Valores Mobiliàrios of Portugal[18] (CMVM), provides for broad-based cooperation and contains a high level of detail regarding the scope of assistance and the procedures to be used in implementing the MOU. Perhaps the most important element of the Portuguese MOU is the broad scope of its provisions for cooperation in obtaining information. Like the German MOU, the Portuguese

---

16 Cf *US v. Balsys*, 524 US 666, 118 S.Ct. 2218 (1998), discussed (holding that fear of foreign prosecution is not a "criminal case" for purposes of the US Constitution Fifth Amendment right against self-incrimination).

17 But *see Understanding Regarding the Establishment of a Framework for Consultations and Administrative Agreement, between the SEC and the Commission des Operations de Bourse of France*, SEC International Series Release IS-116 (12th January 1990), which includes a similar provision. The German MOU also states expressly that assistance may be denied in cases of insider trading if a criminal proceeding has already been initiated in the State of the requested authority based on the same facts and against the same persons, or if the same persons have been sanctioned on the same charges by the competent authorities of the State of the requested authority; provided that, if the requesting authority can demonstrate that the relief or sanctions imposed would not be duplicative, the parties agree to consult regarding assistance.

18 *Memorandum of Understanding Concerning Consultation and Cooperation in the Administration and Enforcement of Securities Laws*, International Series Release 1104 (7th October 1997).

MOU provides for assistance in interviewing persons, conducting inspections and obtaining information. However, the Portuguese MOU goes further in allowing the active participation by one authority in inspections and investigations conducted in the jurisdiction of the other authority.

For example, under the MOU, a representative of the requesting authority may be present for the taking of testimony and may present questions to be asked of any witness by the representative of the requested authority. In addition, a representative of the requesting authority may attend any inspection and, subject to approval by the requested authority, may participate in such an inspection. Finally, the requesting authority may seek to have examinations and inspections conducted by a person designated by it, provided that the discretion to grant or deny such requests rests solely with the requested authority.

While the Portuguese MOU expressly permits the SEC and the CMVM to use whatever unilateral means are available to obtain information,[19] the detailed framework set forth in the MOU increases the likelihood that the parties would first seek to use the MOU. Although the SEC and the CMVM have acknowledged in the MOU that they may not have the authority to implement all of the MOU's provisions, they have agreed to use all reasonable means to obtain such authority and to obtain the aid of other governmental agencies where appropriate.

India MOU

The MOU[20] between the SEC and the Securities and Exchange Board of India (SEBI) is significant primarily because it establishes a basis for mutual cooperation in securities enforcement. In light of the size of the Indian market, this general commitment to cooperation is a critical step.

Unlike the German MOU and the Portuguese MOU, the India MOU is fairly narrow in scope and contains few details or

---

19 The Canadian MOU, International Series Release 6 (7 January 1988), which is perhaps the broadest MOU the SEC has entered into, expressly provides that the parties will use the procedures set forth in the MOU before resorting to any unilateral measures.

20 *Memorandum of Understanding Regarding Cooperation, Consultation and the Provision of Technical Assistance*, International Series Release 1124 (18th March 1998).

procedures.[21] Rather, the parties state their "intent to provide each other assistance in obtaining information and evidence to facilitate the enforcement of their respective laws relating to securities matters", in particular in the offer, purchase or sale of securities. The SEC and the SEBI also agree to use all reasonable efforts to obtain the cooperation of other domestic governmental agencies in providing assistance, as well as to consult periodically in order to develop a framework for cooperation.

The India MOU also addresses the provision of technical assistance by the SEC, which has agreed that, upon the request of the SEBI, it will consult with a view to establishing a technical assistance program. Such a program would include, among other things, the establishment of laws and regulations to protect investors, establishment of standards for offering securities, including disclosure standards, and market oversight and enforcement mechanisms.

Singapore MOU

The MOU[22] between the SEC and the Monetary Authority of Singapore (MAS) followed closely upon the passage in March 2000 of legislation in Singapore allowing the MAS to cooperate with foreign securities and futures authorities by conducting investigations on behalf of those entities. The MOU is broad in scope, providing for the "fullest mutual assistance" permitted by law. It contemplates mutual assistance through the provision of information in the files of the authority from which assistance is

---

21 The SEC has entered into other MOUs which, like the India MOU, express a general intention of the parties to cooperate without setting forth any detailed procedures for implementation. As a general matter, these MOUs have been entered into with emerging market countries, such as China, Egypt and Costa Rica. *See Memorandum of Understanding between the US Securities and Exchange Commission and the Egyptian Capital Market Authority Regarding Exchange of Information, Consultation and Technical Assistance*, International Series Release 932 (11th February 1996); *Memorandum of Understanding between the US Securities and Exchange Commission and the China Securities Regulatory Commission Regarding Cooperation, Consultation and the Provision of Technical Assistance*, International Series 662 (29th April 1994); and *Communique between the US Securities and Exchange Commission and the Costa Rican Comsion de Valores on the Provision of Technical Assistance for the Development of the Costa Rican Securities Markets, Exchange of Information and the Establishment of a Framework for Cooperation*, International Series Release 331 (16th October 1991).

22 *Memorandum of Understanding Concerning Cooperation, Consultation and the Exchange of Information*, International Series Release (16th May 2000).

requested, the taking of statements and the obtaining of information and documents. The MOU states that information provided pursuant to the agreement may be used in civil and administrative enforcement matters, as well as for investigation and prosecution of criminal matters.

In addition to providing for assistance upon request, the MOU acknowledges the importance of proactive, global enforcement by way of unsolicited assistance. The agreement notes the understanding that should one authority come into possession of information that gives rise to a suspicion of a breach or anticipated breach of the laws or regulations of the other, the authority will use reasonable efforts to alert the other of this fact and to provide the information.

The Japanese Statement of Intent Concerning Cooperation, Consultation and the Exchange of Information

In May 2002, the SEC, the CFTC and the Japanese Financial Services Agency (Japan FSA) jointly announced the signing of a Statement of Intent Concerning Cooperation, Consultation and the Exchange of Information.[23] The Statement of Intent (SOI) is intended to facilitate cooperation in connection with both supervisory and enforcement matters and supersedes the more general memorandum of understanding signed by the SEC and the Ministry of Finance of Japan in 1986. The diplomatic *Notes Verbale* (Notes) supporting the SOI discuss the shared view of the US and Japanese governments regarding the use of information obtained pursuant to the SOI by the criminal authorities of the respective countries.

The SOI contemplates the desirability of harmonisation of regulatory efforts. It states that the authorities will consult periodically in an effort to improve cooperation and to "avoid the conflicts that may arise from the application of differing regulatory laws, regulations and practices".

---

[23] Also in June 2002, the Tokyo Stock Exchange and the NYSE signed an agreement for exchanging market surveillance information. The agreement expands the 2000 agreement between the SROs and enables the exchanges to request information or documents related to financial instruments traded on their respective exchanges, as well as to members and trading participants on the exchange.

The SOI states that the authorities will provide each other with the fullest assistance permissible under the laws of the United States and Japan. This assistance includes the provision of information held in the requested authority's files, as well as assistance in obtaining information and documents from persons.

Similar to other information-sharing arrangements, the SOI provides for unsolicited assistance in the event that one authority comes into possession of information giving rise to the suspicion of a breach or anticipated breach of the laws or regulation of the other authority.

The IOSCO MOU

The recently established IOSCO MOU provides another powerful tool for international information gathering. The MOU establishes a complex framework for cooperation to which IOSCO members can subscribe. The framework was agreed upon unanimously at IOSCO's 2002 Annual Meeting. To date, 23 regulators have become signatories.[24] While it is too soon to tell the extent of the understandings' impact on international cooperation, it clearly constitutes a redoubling of efforts to facilitate the access to and collection of information from foreign jurisdictions. The MOU is broad-based, authorising regulators to obtain information and evidence from a variety of sources, including the following:

❑ information and documents in the files of the requested authority;
❑ information and documents regarding the matters set forth in the request for assistance. Upon request, the requested authority can require production from any person designated in the

---

24 The following regulators are signatories to the IOSCO MOU: Australia, Australian Securities and Investments Commission; British Columbia, British Columbia Securities Commission; France, Commission des operations de bourse; Germany, Bundesanstalt fur Finanzdienstleistungsaufsicht; Greece, Capital Market Commission; Hong Kong, Securities and Futures Commission; Hungary, Hungarian Financial Supervisory Authority; India, Securities and Exchange Board of India; Italy, Commissione Nazionale per le Societa e la Borsa; Jersey, Jersey Financial Services Commission; Lithuania, Lithuanian Securities Commission; Mexico, Comision Nacional Bancaria y de Valores; New Zealand, New Zealand Securities Commission; Ontario, Ontario Securities Commission; Poland, Polish Securities and Exchange Commission; Portugal, Comissao do Mercado de Valores Mobiliarios; Quebec, Commission des valeurs mobilieres du Quebec; Spain, Comision Nacional del Mercado de Valores; South Africa, Financial Services Board; Turkey, Capital Markets Board; UK, Financial Services Authority; US, US Securities and Exchange Commission and Commodity Futures Trading Commission.

request or any person who may possess the requested information or documents. The types of information and documents subject to required production include:
- ❏ contemporaneous records sufficient to reconstruct all securities and derivatives transactions, including records of all funds and assets transferred into and out of bank and brokerage accounts relating to these transactions;
- ❏ records that identify the beneficial owner and controller, and for each transaction, the account holder, the amount purchased or sold, the time of the transaction, the price of the transaction, and the individual and the bank or broker and brokerage house that handled the transaction; and
- ❏ information identifying persons who beneficially own or control non-natural persons organised in the jurisdiction of the requested authority.
- ❏ compelled, sworn testimony (where permissible) or the statement of a person regarding the matters set forth in the request for assistance. Where permissible under the laws of the jurisdiction of the requested authority, a representative of the requesting authority may be present at the taking of statements and may provide specific questions to be asked of any witness.

The MOU also provides that each authority will make all reasonable efforts to provide unsolicited assistance to the other authorities in the form of information that it considers likely to be helpful to the other authorities in securing compliance with the laws and regulations applicable in their jurisdictions.

The Jersey MOU

In May 2002, the SEC, CFTC and the Jersey Financial Services Commission (FSC) entered into a MOU establishing a framework for information sharing and cooperation in cross-border investigations. The MOU is likely to enhance the cooperative nature of the relationship that already exists between US regulatory authorities and the Jersey FSC. Jersey has assisted the United States in connection with investigations and requests to freeze assets. Jersey's status as an offshore financial centre makes this MOU particularly significant in the development of global enforcement mechanisms.

Oversight of cross-border investment business

Among the challenges to effective regulation in a global marketplace, it is particularly difficult for a regulator in one territory to accurately assess a firm's capital risk exposure unless that regulator has access to information relating to such a firm's operations in other jurisdictions. The following is a discussion of recent initiatives that seek to formalise mechanisms for the regular exchange of information and to enhance cooperation in oversight of market participants.

The SEC's bilateral MOUs discussed above generally establish procedures for cooperation in obtaining information necessary for enforcement. In addition to such MOUs, the SEC and other regulators have undertaken certain initiatives relating to the improvement of management controls and oversight. An important element of such measures is the prompt notification of significant concerns and remedial actions. The purpose of information sharing in this context is improved oversight, early warning and the prevention of adverse effects on the markets, rather than enforcement against individual securities law violators.

SEC/IMRO Declaration on Cross-Border Investment Management Activity

The SEC and IMRO[25] issued a Declaration on Cooperation and Supervision of Cross-Border Investment Management Activity,[26] within the framework of the 1991 MOU among the SEC, the CFTC, the UK Department of Trade and Industry and the UK Securities and Investments Board (SIB).[27] The stated goal of the declaration was to promote investor protection and formalise existing mechanisms for sharing information and jointly conducting supervisory inspections of firms engaged in securities businesses in both the United States and the UK. The declaration was the first formal arrangement for the supervision of cross-border fund management activity. It created a new mechanism whereby both the SEC and

---

25 IMRO was a self-regulatory organisation recognised under the Financial Services Act of 1986.
26 *See* International Series Release 806 (3rd May 1995).
27 *Memorandum of Understanding on Mutual Assistance and the Exchange of Information*, International Series Release 323 (30th September 1991).

IMRO were able to obtain information regarding registered investment advisers located in the other authority's jurisdiction. It related to investment advisers, investment fund managers, fund administrators, fund trustees, investment companies and investment funds subject to the respective laws and regulatory requirements of the United States and the UK.

The two key elements of the declaration were the regular flow of information and arrangements for joint inspections and surveillance. The declaration provided for periodic sharing of information and prompt notification of significant information learned by either authority regarding dual registrants. Each party to the declaration agreed to notify the other, to the extent permitted by law, upon obtaining information "clearly giving rise to a suspicion of a breach of any legal rule or requirement of the other Authority, as defined in the MOU". Finally, the declaration provided for joint inspections to be conducted by the SEC and IMRO, thereby allowing more effective surveillance of firms doing business in both territories.

SEC/Hong Kong Declaration on Cross-Border Investment Management Activity

A declaration nearly identical to the SEC/IMRO declaration was signed in October 1995 by the SEC and the Hong Kong Securities and Futures Commission (SFC). It establishes a framework for cooperation and assistance between the SEC and the SFC in supervising cross-border investment management activity.

Financial Regulation MOU

In August 1988, the SEC, the NYSE, the NASD, the Chicago Board of Options Exchange, Inc and the AMEX entered into a MOU with the SIB, the Association of Futures Brokers and Dealers, the Financial Intermediaries Managers and Brokers Regulatory Association, IMRO, the Securities Association Limited and the Bank of England. The Financial Regulation MOU provides that, upon request, certain information concerning the capital position of broker–dealers will be made available by the US authorities to the UK authorities. By making this information available, the Financial Regulation MOU allows the UK regulators to exempt their capital adequacy rules in relation to US-regulated broker–dealers that conduct business in the UK.

Cooperation to address potential market disruption

Joint statement regarding OTC derivatives oversight

On 15th March 1994, the SEC, the CFTC and the SIB issued a joint statement setting forth an agenda for oversight of the OTC derivatives market. Once again, the primary focus of the joint statement was the promotion of controls, risk management and disclosure and the sharing of information. The joint statement identified ways in which the SEC, the CFTC and the SIB could cooperate in their regulatory approaches to the OTC derivatives market and set forth common goals to be achieved by the three authorities.[28]

The seven-point program set out in the joint statement included: improving international oversight of OTC derivatives trading through enhanced information sharing; improving risk management by promoting the use of legally enforceable netting arrangements; addressing concerns about excess leverage by promoting the establishment of prudent risk-based capital charges and increased use by firms of stress simulations of severe market conditions; promoting the development and use of sound management controls as part of an effort to monitor and control firms' activities and risk; encouraging strengthened standards for customer protection examining the regulatory framework for multilateral clearing arrangements; and promoting improved standards for accounting recognition, to work actively with other domestic and international securities, futures and financial regulators to promote wider regulatory cooperation.

This first international understanding among securities and futures regulators for developing and coordinating an approach to the OTC derivatives market demonstrated the need for, and the ability of, regulators to work in a coordinated fashion to address some of the most complex issues arising in the markets today.

Windsor Declaration

Representatives of regulatory authorities from 16 countries[29] came together in May 1995 and issued the Windsor Declaration in an

---

28 The Joint Statement recognises the work of IOSCO in the area of cross-border activity in the OTC derivatives markets.

29 Australian Securities Commission, Comissao de Valores Mobiliarios (Brazil), Commission de Valeurs Mobiliers du Quebec and Ontario Securities Commission (Canada), Commission des Operations de Bourse (France), Bundesaufsichtsamt fur den Wertpapierhandel (Germany), Hong Kong Securities and Futures Commission, Commissione Nazionale per le Society e la Bolsa (Italy), Securities Bureau of the Ministry of Finance of Japan, Securities Board of the

effort to "prevent or contain adverse effects of financial disruptions in light of increased volume of cross-border [futures] transactions". Like the Bank of England MOU and the SEC/IMRO Declaration, the Windsor Declaration focuses on the regular flow of information and on the development of procedures to address emergency situations in the futures markets. The four main elements of the Windsor Declaration are:

(i) cooperation between exchanges;
(ii) protection of customer positions, funds and assets;
(iii) default procedures; and
(iv) regulatory cooperation in emergencies. The declaration is a statement by the parties recommending areas to be addressed, and changes to be implemented, through the Technical Committee of IOSCO.

With respect to cooperation between market authorities, the Windsor Declaration prescribes a survey of current procedures used to identify large exposures and specifies the type of information necessary to evaluate such exposures, as well as certain triggers and thresholds, the occurrence of which would entitle the authorities to request assistance from one another. It also establishes mechanisms for information sharing within the framework of the declaration.

Customer positions, funds and assets are to be protected through the development of best practices with a view to maximising the safety of such funds and risk management for protection of the intermediary. The Windsor Declaration also proposes the development of best practices with respect to the treatment of positions and funds in the event of a default or disruption at a member firm and recommends the establishment of standards for providing information to market participants in the event of a default. Finally, the Windsor Declaration affirms the parties' commitment to regulatory cooperation in the event of an emergency situation in the futures markets or with respect to a market participant.

Netherlands, The Monetary Authority of Singapore, Financial Services Board (South Africa), Commission Nacional del Mercado de Valores (Spain), Swedish Financial Supervisory Authority, The Federal Banking Commission (Switzerland), CFTC, SEC and SIB.

Joint initiative to improve oversight of global securities firms

In July 1995, the SEC and the SIB announced the first joint initiative to assess the global activities of major international securities firms by conducting in-depth studies of the financial, operational and management controls used by selected securities firms that conduct significant cross-border derivatives and securities activities. The initiative was significant in that it brought together two major securities regulators in a practical exercise leading to a better understanding of each regulator's approaches as well as contributing to a better information exchange between the regulatory authorities in the United States and the UK.

Pursuant to this initiative, the SEC and the SIB worked to review and evaluate internal controls used by firms with significant international securities activities, including controls relating to market, credit, liquidity and funding risks. Because the selected firms were likely to have significant operations in third countries, the SEC and SIB expected to work jointly with representatives of other relevant regulators.

Futures Industry Association MOU

In March 1996, 49 market authorities and self-regulatory organisations entered into an International Information Sharing Memorandum of Understanding and Agreement (FIA MOU). The central focus of the FIA MOU is information sharing and, in particular, notification of certain significant events and disciplinary actions. This initiative is a complex two-tier approach involving both the exchanges and their corresponding regulators.

The exchanges that are parties to the FIA MOU recognised the need for cooperation with respect to certain significant events and the MOU therefore sets out criteria and procedures for notification and information sharing with respect to such events. Information to be provided under the FIA MOU is limited to that which is relevant to the event that actually gives rise to a request for assistance. The parties also agree to use best efforts to keep one another informed of conclusions made on the basis of information provided and of any action taken, including disciplinary action.

In order to assist in the implementation of the FIA MOU, a Declaration on Cooperation and Supervision of International

Futures Markets and Clearing Organisations was also issued in March 1996 by futures exchanges and clearing organisations in the territories of the parties to the FIA MOU. The regulators who are parties to the declaration endorsed the FIA MOU, acknowledged that the exchanges that have signed the MOU may need the assistance of their regulators in making information available to exchanges in other jurisdictions and stated their intent to assist by all legal means.

In furtherance of the principles set out in the FIA MOU, 15 regulatory authorities issued a Joint Communiqué in October 1997 in which they encouraged the development of best practices in contract design and review and in approaches to market surveillance and information sharing. The authorities agreed upon the first international benchmarks for supervision of the futures market and stressed, in particular, cooperation in respect of large exposures. The authorities also stated their intent to amend the Declaration on Cooperation and Supervision adopted in March 1995 in order to increase the scope of participation.

Bank of England MOU
In October 1997, the SEC, the CFTC and The Bank of England[30] entered into an MOU[31] relating to oversight of management controls, assistance in obtaining information and cooperation in emergency oversight. The scope of the Bank of England MOU extends to firms that operate in both the United States and the UK. The parties to the Bank of England MOU expressly recognised that "the growth of cross-border financial activity, including the globalisation of securities and futures firms and banks, has made the sharing of supervisory and financial information critical to the ability of the Authorities to carry on their respective oversight responsibilities". The MOU was intended to formalise mechanisms between the authorities in order to enhance the effectiveness of regulatory oversight.

Management controls. The Bank of England MOU articulated certain specific areas with respect to which the authorities

---

[30] The FSA also signed the MOU to confirm that its provisions would continue in effect upon the transfer of banking supervision from The Bank of England to the FSA in 1998. Therefore, the MOU should now be thought of as an agreement between the US authorities and the FSA.

[31] *Memorandum of Understanding*, 1997 WL 685306 (4th November 1997).

believed Relevant Firms[32] must have management controls. These included:

(i) market risk management;
(ii) credit risk management;
(iii) balance sheet and liquidity management;
(iv) operations and systems;
(v) counterparty and legal risk controls; and
(vi) compliance and audit. Under the Bank of England MOU, the parties agreed to notify one another promptly of any significant concerns in respect of such management controls and also to inform one another of any remedial action taken against a firm. The authorities also agreed to consult prior to taking remedial action where appropriate.

Assistance in obtaining information. The Bank of England MOU provided a mechanism by which each authority might obtain information from firms located in the other authority's territory. The MOU also contained an undertaking that the authorities would endeavour to communicate information relating to firms facing "serious financial difficulties" in the United States or the UK that "could have a material adverse effect on the operations of the firm in the other country", thereby establishing an early warning system.

Cooperation in emergency oversight. Finally, the authorities also recognised that cooperation in emergency situations can be critical to ensuring that on a worldwide basis problems are addressed in a timely manner. In that regard, the Bank of England MOU created a basis for "mutual consultation in the prompt and productive exchange of information in such emergency situations" and provided for assistance in monitoring as well as the provision of information, including "current financial position (balance sheet and off-balance sheet) and income statement; portfolio and credit information, including details of major long and short positions; and counter party exposures". It also provided that the authorities

---

32 A "Relevant Firm" is defined by the Bank of England MOU as a broker–dealer, futures commission merchant or bank, if that entity, its parent or holding company is incorporated or has headquarters in the US or the UK and any holding companies, subsidiaries and affiliates of such entity if that entity, alone or together with one or more of its related entities, conducts securities, futures and/or banking transactions (including derivatives transactions) in both the United States and the UK.

would make information available on a timely basis, advise each other of actions they intend to take and consult concerning those actions as appropriate. The Bank of England MOU reinforced the already close relationship between US and UK securities regulators by formalising arrangements between them to enhance their ability to monitor securities transactions and serve as a model for addressing potential cross-border contagions. The necessity of cross-border real time cooperation has become more evident and critical following the September 11 terrorist attacks. The international cooperation in the area of source of funds identification and money laundering that has arisen since the attack is likely a harbinger of similar efforts in the global financial services industry.

Limited purpose broker–dealer
In October 1998, the SEC adopted amendments[33] to certain rules under the Exchange Act to create a new class of broker–dealer with tailored capital, margin and other regulatory requirements for over-the-counter (OTC) derivatives dealers, provided such dealers engage only in limited activities. The amendments were unilaterally adopted by the SEC without the involvement of any foreign regulator. However, they are included in this discussion because, like the Bank of England MOU, the SEC's new rules reflect an increased focus on controls, risk management and the regular flow of information.

Historically, many US firms located their OTC derivatives businesses offshore in order to avoid the restrictions – particularly with respect to capital requirements – of US securities regulation, as well as the expense related to such regulation. The broker–dealer "lite" rules reflect an effort by the SEC to bring this business back onshore in order to regulate it directly, but in a manner appropriate to the OTC derivatives market. This new alternative to registration as a fully regulated broker–dealer should allow US firms to compete more effectively with foreign dealers who are not subject to regulation by the SEC.[34] However, the alternative regulatory

---

33 The new rules, commonly referred to as the broker–dealer "lite" rules, came into force on 4th January 1999.
34 *See* Kyra K. Bergin *et al, Regulatory Developments and Current Issues in Regulation of Trading Markets and International Dealers*, International Securities Markets 1998.

scheme is available only for dealers whose activities are limited to privately negotiated OTC derivatives transactions.

The books and records provisions of the new rules are particularly relevant to this discussion. Under such provisions, OTC derivatives dealers have an obligation to maintain certain records and to report periodically to the SEC. OTC derivatives dealers are required to register with the SEC and thereby become subject to, among other things, the books and records requirements of the Exchange Act, which have been amended to include records relevant to the OTC derivatives business. In addition, such dealers are required to report capital and other operational problems to the SEC within specified time periods and to fulfil regular reporting requirements including quarterly and annual financial statements and risk evaluation.

In addition to reporting requirements, the broker–dealer "lite" rules require OTC derivatives dealers to establish internal controls for managing the risks associated with an OTC derivatives business. The rules also articulate the basic elements for review of OTC derivatives risk management systems by the SEC. Together with regular reporting and notification of important developments, these provisions enhance the SEC's ability to understand OTC derivatives transactions and to obtain the information necessary for effective enforcement. In its focus on internal controls and risk management, the regulatory scheme under the broker–dealer "lite" rules is in some respects a departure from the SEC's typical regulatory approach and is instead more easily analogised to traditional banking regulation.

SEC initiatives relating to oversight of the trading of foreign securities listed in the United States – the foreign issuer notification system

Due to the securities of many companies being traded in multiple jurisdictions, regulators deem it critical that they be made aware of disciplinary actions taken against such companies in jurisdictions other than their own. Improper behaviour in one securities market may be indicative of similar behaviour elsewhere and certain actions, such as suspensions, against a company may affect its ability to continue operating in other markets. In recognition of the importance it attaches to information relating to disciplinary actions taken by regulators, the SEC entered into information sharing agreements with regulators from a number of foreign nations, including Brazil, Japan, Korea, Luxembourg, Mexico, New Zealand, Peru, Singapore, Spain and the UK, to improve the oversight of companies that trade in the United States and in foreign securities markets.[35]

Since March 1996, the SEC has entered into arrangements with securities authorities in a wide range of other nations to improve oversight of companies whose securities trade both in the US and foreign securities markets. Under the arrangements, the SEC and the foreign regulator will advise each other whenever certain announced enforcement-related regulatory actions are taken against issuers whose securities trade in the markets of both countries. These actions generally include:

- suspension from trading on a regulated exchange or market for more than one day;
- de-listing from a regulated exchange or market; and
- a regulator's initiation of proceedings against an issuer, such as an administrative action or enforcement lawsuit by the SEC.

The new system is expected to provide the SEC with a prompt, systematic "early warning" of sanctions involving foreign companies taken in their home countries that may be of concern to regulators and investors in the United States. The SEC also will provide notice to foreign regulators about actions taken in the United States regarding the securities of dually traded issuers.

The notification arrangements are intended to complement a number of existing direct market-to-market agreements under which United States exchanges and markets already share information directly with certain foreign counterparts regarding issuers with securities trading in the United States and abroad. The arrangements will complement existing MOUs and other arrangements the SEC has to obtain assistance in investigations and enforcement actions, and to provide for the exchange of non-public information.

---

35 Like the SEC's MOUs previously discussed, these information-sharing agreements reflect the importance of bilateral arrangements between the SEC and foreign regulators in achieving effective enforcement.

INTERNATIONAL ASSISTANCE

Courts in a number of different countries have decided cases regarding the validity of actions taken domestically to assist foreign regulators. Even in situations where bilateral or multilateral understandings exist among regulatory authorities, the ability to implement such agreements relies on domestic authority to do so. Indeed, many MOUs and other initiatives expressly recognise that there may be limitations on the domestic authority of the parties. A clear example of such limitations occurred in connection with the SEC's MOU with Canada, where neither the SEC nor its Canadian counterparts had the necessary powers to implement the MOU when executed, but where each subsequently sought and received such authority. The cases discussed below evidence a range of different results. Significantly, the holdings turn on the issue of the basis for the domestic legal authority to provide assistance and not the legitimacy of cooperation. Indeed, in each case the courts have generally recognised the need for international cooperation in securities law enforcement.

Evidence gathering

British Columbia – Global Securities Corporation

In April 2000, the Supreme Court of Canada lay to rest any question about the validity of regulatory understandings for international securities cooperation that were implemented by Provincial law. In *Global Securities Corporation v. British Columbia (Securities Commission)*,[36] a case challenging a request for assistance under the 1988 MOU between the SEC and the British Columbia Securities Commission (BCSC), the *Global* Court ruled that domestic legislation to implement the MOU provided a valid means for compelling evidence from a Canadian person and that such evidence could thereafter be given to the foreign regulator for use in its own proceedings. In so holding, the *Global* Court affirmed the principle that international cooperation among securities regulators was critical for the protection of domestic investors and markets.[37]

---

[36] 2000 SCC 21, File No: 26887 (13th April 2000) ("*Global*").
[37] *See* KPMG *Klynvold Accountants v. Stitching Toezicht Effectenverkeer (Securities Trade Supervision Foundation)*, No. 92/1954/113/226, Amsterdam (17th December 1992) (subject of inquiry unsuccessfully challenged underlying Dutch legislation under which Dutch regulator had ordered provision of information requested by SEC).

Prior to the enactment of the challenged statute, the BCSC and the SEC had entered into a MOU in which the parties agreed to provide assistance to one another, including taking evidence and obtaining information from persons within their jurisdiction. Section 141(b)(1) of the British Columbia Securities Act was enacted by the British Columbia legislature to facilitate the implementation of the MOU. In particular, Section 141(b)(1) permits the executive director of the BCSC to make an order "to assist in the administration of the securities laws of another jurisdiction".[38] Therefore, the executive director was authorised under the statute to require certain persons to provide information in response to a request for assistance by the SEC under the MOU.

Global Securities Corporation was a securities firm registered in British Columbia but not registered in the United States with the SEC under the Exchange Act. In furtherance of its investigation of the activities of an employee of this company, the SEC requested assistance from the BCSC under the MOU. In response, the BCSC issued orders to the company to deliver account listings and certain other information.[39] The company's challenge to the order was two-fold. First, it alleged that Section 141(b)(1) was *ultra vires* and therefore constitutionally invalid. Second, it alleged institutional bias on the part of the BCSC as a result of the execution of the MOU and the BCSC's interest in obtaining the mutual cooperation of the SEC thereunder.[40] In defence of Section 141(b)(1), the BCSC argued that the purpose of the statute was to facilitate inter-jurisdictional cooperation, which aids the BCSC in doing its job under the Securities Act.[41] The lower court agreed and dismissed the *ultra vires* claim on the basis that Section 141(b)(1) was incidental to the primary function of the Exchange Act.[42] Moreover, the lower court had been satisfied that "without cross-border and interjurisdictional cooperation in the investigative process, the primary function of the [BCSC] would be seriously hampered".[43] The Court of Appeal found no institutional bias, but did hold that Section 141(b)(1) was *ultra vires* the province.

---

[38] *Id* at 3.
[39] *Id* at 5.
[40] *Id* at 5–6.
[41] *Id*.
[42] *See Id* at 7.
[43] *Id* at 7.

In reversing the lower court's decision, the Court of Appeal acknowledged that the BCSC routinely exchanged information with foreign securities regulators.[44] The Court of Appeal also noted that provincial legislation may in some cases be valid notwithstanding an extra-territorial effect provided its "pith and substance" lies within the province.[45] In this case, however, the Court of Appeal found that the information was requested by the BCSC from Global Securities Corporation for the sole purpose of being delivered to the SEC and not in connection with any enforcement of rights within the province.[46] The Court of Appeal found that an administrative tribunal such as the SEC does not fall within the principle at this time and stated that "[e]ventually, these considerations may militate as well in favour of a recognition of the desirability of cooperation between jurisdictions outside the Canadian federation".[47]

The Supreme Court of Canada disagreed, stating that while the dominant purpose of Section 141 was the enforcement of the province's securities law, to regulate effectively it needed to be able to cooperate on a reciprocal basis with other foreign regulatory authorities, both within and outside of Canada.[48] Such cooperation had the additional beneficial effect of assisting the local regulatory in identifying fraud in its own jurisdiction.[49] As a result, the Supreme Court of Canada held that the authority of the BCSC to provide assistance to the SEC under the MOU was constitutional.[50]

Singapore – the APL case

In another case in which the SEC requested assistance in obtaining information relevant to potential violations of US securities laws, the High Court of Singapore found that assistance was permissible under domestic law. The case, *In Re Evidence (Civil Proceedings in Other Jurisdictions) Act*,[51] arose out of litigation brought by the SEC relating to suspected violations of Section 10(b) and Rule 10b-5 of the Exchange Act by certain Singapore residents. The SEC charged

---

44 *Id* at 4.
45 *Id* at 13.
46 *Id* at 20.
47 *Id* at 22.
48 *Global Securities Corporation v. British Columbia (Securities Commission)*, [2000] S.C.R. 494, ¶32.
49 *Id*.
50 *Id* at ¶36.
51 No. 162/1998 (High Court of Singapore 27th July 1998) (APL).

that such persons had engaged in insider trading of the stock of APL Ltd while in possession of non-public information regarding the potential acquisition of the company by Neptune Orient Line Ltd. The SEC made an application for the appointment of an examiner in Singapore to take evidence to be used in a civil proceeding in the United States in which the SEC was seeking an order:

(i) enjoining the defendants from future violations of securities laws;
(ii) ordering disgorgement of profits; and
(iii) imposing civil penalties.[52] Two people named as witnesses disputed the SEC's right to obtain evidence under the Evidence (Civil Proceedings in Other Jurisdictions) Act of Singapore (E(CPOJ)A).

Under the E(CPOJ)A, assistance may be provided to foreign authorities only if the High Court of Singapore is satisfied that the evidence sought is to be "obtained for the purpose of *civil* proceedings which either have been instituted before the requesting court or whose institution before that court is contemplated".[53] Moreover, the proceeding must be considered civil in nature under the laws of both the requesting jurisdiction and those of the court addressed in the request.[54] The witnesses argued that the US proceeding instituted by the SEC would in fact be characterised as criminal in nature under Singapore law and therefore assistance should not be granted under the E(CPOJ)A.

The Singapore court, however, ruled that assistance under the E(CPOJ)A could be provided to the SEC.[55] The "civil" penalties sought by the SEC were found by the court to be penal in nature because the money collected would go to the Treasury rather than to injured persons.[56] However, a proceeding seeking injunctive relief is considered a civil proceeding under both US and Singapore law and therefore the requested assistance was held to be permissible.[57] The court determined that the significant issue was the nature

---

52 *See* APL, supra note 59, at 2.
53 *Id* at 3 (emphasis added).
54 *Id* at 5.
55 *Id* at 10.
56 *Id* at 7.
57 *Id* at 8.

of the proceeding – a civil action in the US courts – and not the nature of the potential relief.[58]

Swiss securities law and recent case law

The Swiss have been one of the leading authorities in international cooperation. Assistance between the SEC and Swiss regulators was historically governed by the Swiss Treaty, and was traditionally handled as a criminal matter thereunder. In 1995, however, the Swiss enacted the Federal Law on Stock Exchanges and Trading in Securities (Swiss Act). The stated purpose of the law is to provide a framework for the functioning of the securities markets and to enhance transparency in securities transactions. Its importance lies in the procedures contained within the law itself, which permit Swiss regulators to grant assistance to, as well as request assistance from, foreign regulators. However, as described below, interpretation of the Act has been restrictive and it has served recently to frustrate the very cooperation for which it was designed.

Under the Swiss Act, the Swiss Federal Banking Commission (Supervisory Authority) is granted supervisory authority over the enforcement of the Swiss Act and the implementation of its provisions. This authority includes the power to issue orders requiring persons subject to supervision under the Swiss Act to provide information and documents to the Supervisory Authority, and the power to enforce certain penalties for failure to comply with such orders.

Chapter 7 of the Swiss Act further empowers the Supervisory Authority to request information from foreign supervisory authorities concerning stock exchanges and security dealers and to submit certain information to foreign supervisory authorities upon request. Article 38, clause 2 of the Swiss Act provides:

> "[The Supervisory Authority] may only submit to foreign supervisory authorities for stock exchanges and security dealers, information which is not publicly available and documents related to the matter under examination, in so far as these authorities:

---

58 In a 1975 case entitled *Schemmer v. Property Resources Ltd*, 1973 No. 6773, Eng., an English trial court held that the Securities Exchange Act is a penal statute and therefore unenforceable in the UK notwithstanding that private citizens may get civil relief thereunder. In *Schemmer*, a receiver that was appointed in a US insider trading action brought by the SEC had sought appointment as receiver over certain assets located in the UK, as well as injunctive relief through UK courts. The court's judgment in *Schemmer* was never challenged in a higher court and has not generally been followed.

- ❏ use such information exclusively for the direct supervision of stock exchanges and trading in securities;
- ❏ are bound by official or professional secrecy; and
- ❏ do not transmit this information to competent authorities and bodies which are entrusted with supervisory tasks which are in the public interest, without the prior approval of the Swiss supervisory authorities or on the basis of a blanket approval contained in a state treaty. The transmittal of information to the penal prosecuting authorities is not permitted if administrative assistance in penal matters would be excluded. The Supervisory Authority shall decide after consulting with the Federal Office of the Police".

In addition to the Swiss Act, Swiss banking laws also provide a basis for international cooperation.[59]

A recently decided example of the restrictive interpretation given by Swiss authorities to the Swiss Act is *In the Matter of W, X, Y and Z v. Swiss Banking Commission (In the Matter of W, X, Y and Z)*. This case relates to a US federal court action entitled *SEC V. Euro Security Fund*.[60] The decision of the Swiss Supreme Court is significant in that it held that the assurances given by the SEC were not sufficient to protect the interest of customers in the privacy of relevant customer information. The case underscores the growing recognition of the ease with which information flows when confidentiality provisions are relaxed. The Swiss Supreme Court expressed its concern that if otherwise confidential information were provided to the SEC, it might, through the course of SEC or other proceedings, make its way into the domain of the general public, local and national tax authorities, or other entities which would otherwise not have had access.

The concerns in the case were that if relevant customer information were provided to the SEC by Swiss authorities pursuant to cooperative agreements, there was a danger that such information might inappropriately be forwarded to authorities and third parties within the United States to which dissemination was not authorised under Swiss law. The request at issue in this matter was associated with price developments immediately preceding the

---

[59] See *International Regulatory Talk*, Compliance Reporter, 1st February 1999, at 10 (director of Swiss Banking Commission discussing cooperation under securities and banking laws). See also the Swiss agreements discussed *infra*.

[60] See *below* for a discussion of *SEC v. Euro Security Fund* as it relates to international asset freezes.

takeover of Elsag Bailey Process Automation NV by ABB. The price developments raised suspicion of insider trading and the SEC requested the aid of the Swiss regulatory authorities, the Banking Commission, in obtaining information to assist in its investigation.

Respondents W, X, Y and Z objected to provision of the requested information, arguing that while the information and documents to be provided would be subject to confidentiality provisions, those provisions were insufficient as a matter of Swiss law in light of the open nature of SEC hearings. The Swiss Supreme Court held that the Banking Commission's contention, that provision of the information to the SEC was predicated upon an agreement that it would be used only for investigative purposes and potentially for inclusion in an amended Complaint to be filed in US District Court, was unavailing in light of an SEC letter that was ambiguous as to whether the information would be provided to other authorities. The Court held that unless there is an advance agreement between the Banking Commission and a foreign authority to permit onward disclosure, the Commission must refrain from providing the information in a situation where such onward disclosure appears possible. During 2001, the SEC and the Banking Commission worked to respond to the concerns raised by the Swiss Supreme Court and, in late December 2001, the Swiss Supreme Court rejected these efforts and denied assistance.

Challenges to confidentiality of information obtained under MOUs
In the matter of Global Minerals & Metals Corp., R David Campbell, and Carl Alm, CFTC Docket 99-11, 3rd October 2001
(Global Minerals)

A decision by the CFTC underscores the importance attached to maintaining the confidentiality of information provided pursuant to cooperative agreements. *Global Minerals* demonstrates the potential impact on cross-border information sharing of less restrictive interpretations of confidentiality agreements. In this instance, the FSA made clear that disclosure of confidential information provided to the SEC pursuant to the UK MOU would make further disclosure unlikely. The recognition of the importance of strict confidentiality constraints was taken a step further by the Swiss Supreme Court in *In the Matter of W, X, Y and Z*, discussed above. In that case, the Swiss Supreme Court prohibited dissemination of information altogether, absent a pre-existing specificity clause addressing onward disclosure of confidential information. While *Global Minerals* addresses concerns related to disclosure to counsel for a defendant of confidential material, *In the Matter of W, X, Y and Z* expresses significant reservations related to disclosure of confidential information to a government enforcement entity that could in turn disclose to another enforcement entity within the same government.

In *Global Minerals,* the CFTC reversed the order of the Administrative Law Judge (ALJ) compelling the CFTC's Division of Enforcement to provide to respondents Global Minerals & Metals Corp. (Global), R. David Campbell and Carl Alm copies of documents it obtained from regulators in the UK pursuant to the terms of the UK MOU. The CFTC determined that the ALJ's interpretation of the MOU undermined expectations of confidentiality that are vital to the continuing success of the cooperative efforts of international regulators.

The matter stemmed from the CFTC Division of Enforcement's (Division) investigation into unusual price movements in the world copper market. During the investigation, the Division obtained documents from UK financial regulators pursuant to the UK MOU. Eventually, the investigation led to a Complaint filed by the CFTC against the respondents, alleging that between October and December 1995 respondents attempted to manipulate the price of copper and copper futures contracts and actually succeeded in manipulating the price. The Division made some of these documents available to the respondents for inspection, but withheld others on the ground that the information was obtained from a foreign futures authority on the condition that the information not be disclosed, within the meaning of CFTC Rule 10.42(b)(2)(v). The ALJ granted an order compelling production of these documents, holding that the UK authorities waived confidentiality when they shared these documents with the Division. The Division moved to delay production and for certification of the issue for interlocutory appeal. When the ALJ denied this request, the Division filed an application for interlocutory review.

Granting of interlocutory review. The CFTC granted the application, finding "extraordinary circumstances that justify immediate consideration of the ruling at issue". In this respect, the CFTC noted that the Division, the SEC and the FSA all agreed that the ALJ's interpretation was so contrary to the regulator parties' intent to the MOU that future cooperative efforts would be threatened as long as the validity of the ALJ's interpretation remained unresolved. The CFTC also agreed with the Division's argument that a post-disclosure decision that the documents should have remained confidential would not be effective or consistent with the MOU.

The CFTC cited the letter submitted to the ALJ by the FSA's Director of Enforcement, Daniel F Waters, in which he described the potential effect of the forced disclosure of consultative documents shared by the FSA with the CFTC. Director Walters explicitly affirmed that "where confidential information is disclosed pursuant to the MOU, the FSA considers that there is a clear understanding . . . that no disclosure would occur save to the extent and in the manner provided for under the MOU". Director Waters continued, noting the potentially deleterious effects of this type of disclosure:

> "The FSA's policy has been, and continues to be, one of promoting cooperation with overseas regulators in the regulation of increasingly globalised markets. If appropriate and effective regulatory policy is to be maintained in respect of ensuring continued efficient mutual assistance and cooperation between overseas regulators such as the CFTC and the FSA, it is essential that the FSA should be able to communicate with the CFTC in the knowledge that confidential documentation will not be disclosed save to the extent and in the manner provided for in the MOU. Such confidential information would not be so readily provided by the FSA if the FSA could not be sure that its confidence would be respected".[61]

Interpretation of the MOU. The CFTC was guided in its interpretation of the MOU by the same principles that guide the interpretation of treaties and viewed its role as "limited to giving effect to the intent of the parties to the MOU". When the parties to a MOU agree as to the meaning of its provisions, and that interpretation follows from its clear language, "we must, absent extraordinarily strong evidence, defer to that interpretation" (*In the Matter of Global Minerals & Metals Corp., R. David Campbell, and Carl Alm*, CFTC Docket 99-11, 3rd October 2001, citing *Sumitomo Shoji America, Inc v. Avagliano*, 457 U.S. 176, 180 (1982)). To the extent that the MOU's

---

[61] Letter of Director Waters, 6th March 2000.

terms are not clear, the US Supreme Court stated that it "must give great weight to the meaning attributed to them 'by the Government agencies charged with their negotiation and enforcement'." (*In the Matter of Global Minerals & Metals Corp., R. David Campbell, and Carl Alm*, CFTC Docket 99-11, 3rd October 2001, quoting *Iceland Steamship Co v. US Department of the Army*, 201 F.3d 451, 458 (DC Cir. 2000).)

The CFTC interpreted Paragraphs 16, 17 and 19 of the MOU as creating a presumption "that shared information retains its confidentiality unless disclosed to a third party in the course of an investigation or proceeding". If information is not used for one of the purposes identified in paragraph 16, it is supposed to be kept confidential. Paragraph 16 provides that information will be provided "solely for the purpose of . . . conducting civil or administrative enforcement proceedings . . . or conducting any investigation related thereto for any general charge applicable to the violation of the legal rule or requirement identified in the request [for information]". The MOU also states that communications between regulators regarding the sharing of documents or their content are to remain strictly confidential, unless disclosure is "absolutely necessary". In reaching its decision to vacate the order compelling production, the CFTC noted that "the mere act of supplying information pursuant to the MOU demonstrates an intent to keep the information confidential" and that if the ALJ's view were correct, that sharing information pursuant to the MOU constituted a waiver of confidentiality, there would be not reason for the negotiated confidentiality provisions contained within the MOU itself.

International assistance in asset freezes

Securities and Exchange Commission v. Dunne Finance Limited[62]

While the SEC has successfully frozen allegedly ill-gotten gains in a variety of circumstances pursuant to formal agreements, repatriation has usually been accomplished through the ultimate cooperation of the defendant.[63]

---

62 LR-15300; IS-1065 (Royal Court of Guernsey 28th February 1997).
63 *See* Michael D Mann *et al*, *The Establishment of International Mechanisms for Enforcing Provisional Orders and Final Judgments Arising from Securities Law Violations*, 55 Law and Contemporary Problems 303 (Autumn 1992).

In *Securities and Exchange Commission v. Dunne Finance Limited*, however, the SEC sought the repatriation of US$195,305. These funds had been previously frozen by an order of the Guernsey courts in the first action ever filed by the SEC in Guernsey. Dunne Finance Limited was a relief defendant – not itself accused of substantive wrongdoing – in an action filed by the SEC in the federal court in Nevada, in which the SEC alleged that the stock of Pacific Waste Management, Inc was sold in the United States through fraudulent misrepresentations. The proceeds of such sales were located in an account in Guernsey in Dunne Finance's name. The significance of the *Dunne Finance* case is that the Guernsey court froze and repatriated the assets of Dunne Finance as a routine matter, without questioning or challenging the SEC in any way. *Dunne Finance* is but one example of the increased willingness of courts to use their authority to assist foreign regulators in matters of securities enforcement.[64]

Securities and Exchange Commission v. Roys Poyiadjis, Lycourgos Kyprianou and AremisSoft Corp., et al, Civil Action 01-DV-8903 (CSH) (SDNY)[65]

The AremisSoft case is a recent example of the development of cooperation. On 22nd November 2002, the High Court of the Isle of Man entered a judgment holding that the SEC was entitled to participate directly in pending asset freeze proceedings commenced by the Isle of Man Attorney General at the request of the US Attorney General.

In response to a request from the United States, the Isle of Man High Court issued restraint orders freezing approximately US$175 million deposited in two Isle of Man banks.[66] The funds were held in the accounts of Olympus Capital Investment, Inc, and Oracle Capital, Inc, two relief defendants named in the SEC enforcement action. The United States alleged that the money constituted the proceeds of insider trading involving the stock of AremisSoft.

---

64 *See* also *SEC v. Felix, Inc* (Royal Court of Jersey 7th July 1997) (freezing certain assets of an off-shore corporation administered in Jersey, Channel Islands).
65 SEC Litigation Release 17862 (25th November 2002). See also SEC Litigation Releases 17172 (4th October 2001) and 17641 (31st July 2002).
66 The Commission also obtained an asset freeze in the US through an 19th October 2001 injunction entered by the US District Court for the Southern District of New York.

According to the SEC, Poyiadjis and Kyprianou, two former officers with AremisSoft Corporation, engaged in massive insider trading during 1999 and 2000. The SEC alleged that during that period the company, the two officers and others overstated the company's revenues and inflated the value of acquisitions. The US Attorney for the Southern District of New York obtained indictments against Poyiadjis, Kyprianou, both of who resided in the Republic of Cyprus, and against M C Mathews, who resides in India, on counts of conspiracy to commit securities fraud, mail fraud and wire fraud, substantive counts of securities fraud, conspiracy to commit money laundering and substantive counts of money laundering.

In reversing the lower court decision and permitting the SEC to participate in the asset freeze proceedings, the High Court held that the SEC was a "person affected" by the proceedings and held that "the overall circumstances in this case justify our exercising discretion in favour of the SEC becoming a Noticed Party". The Isle of Man Attorney General worked with the SEC and the US Attorney for the Southern District of New York in seeking repatriation of the funds.

Efforts to increase international cooperation in the freezing and repatriation of assets constituting the proceeds of criminal conduct
In an October 2003 address delivered at the IOSCO meeting in Seoul, Korea, Ethiopis Tafara, the Director of the SEC's Office of International Affairs, noted the need for increased international cooperation with respect to the freezing and repatriation of assets constituting the proceeds of criminal conduct.[67] Tafara described this area as "one remaining hole in our international cooperative efforts". He noted that, despite options currently available to freeze and repatriate assets, it remained "considerably more difficult" to "get money out of the hands of those who commit fraud and back into the hands of fraud victims", once the money leaves the country.

Tafara advocated a "multilateral approach to enforcement cooperation that allows for asset freezes and asset repatriation". He suggested an "informal, albeit widespread, expanded understanding of

---

[67] The text of the address is available at www.sec.gov/news/speech/spch 101703iosco.htm.

what powers securities regulators should have and should be able to exercise on behalf of their foreign counterparts". He noted that in Canada certain provinces have granted their securities regulators authority to freeze assets on behalf of their foreign counterparts.

US COURT ACTION
US court assertion of jurisdiction over assets
Securities and Exchange Commission v. Heden
In *Securities and Exchange Commission v. Heden*,[68] the US District Court for the Southern District of New York held that there was no doubt that the assets of a relief defendant in an insider trading case could be frozen, but only to the extent that such assets represented profits from the alleged insider trading. The *Heden* court held that, unlike a preliminary injunction enjoining violations of securities laws, an asset freeze requires the SEC to show only that it is likely to succeed on the merits or that "there is a basis to infer that the appellants traded on inside information".[69] The SEC is not required to show risk of irreparable injury, as a private litigant would be.[70] However, the court also held that it is inappropriate to freeze the assets of a relief defendant, as opposed to a defendant, to the extent that such assets represent the principal amount invested, rather than profits, finding that in such a case the relief defendant has a legitimate claim to the assets.[71]

Grupo Mexicano de Desarrollo, SA v. Alliance Bond Fund, Inc
Whether an asset freeze in advance of judgment would withstand challenge under the laws of various nations or when considered by the European Council of Human Rights is an open question. Moreover, whether US courts will issue broad asset freeze orders in advance of judgment is perhaps less certain than it once was in light of the US Supreme Court's recent decision in *Grupo Mexicano de Desarrollo, SA. v. Alliance Bond Fund, Inc*[72] In *Grupo Mexicano*, certain holders of unsecured notes issued by Grupo Mexicano de

---

68 51 F. Supp.2d 296 (SDNY 1999).
69 *Id* at 296 (quoting *SEC v. Cavanagh*, 155 F.3d 129, 132 (2d cir. 1998)).
70 *Id*.
71 *Id* at 301.
72 527 U.S. 308, 119 S.Ct. 1961 (1999) *("Grupo Mexicano")*.

Desarrollo, SA brought an action against the company based on its failure to make scheduled payments on the notes. The holders sought a preliminary injunction restraining the company from transferring its assets pending resolution of their claims. The district court issued the preliminary injunction and the US Court of Appeals for the Second Circuit affirmed. However, the US Supreme Court reversed the lower courts' decisions, focusing on the history of equitable relief and the nature of the relief requested.

Specifically, the US Supreme Court noted that the equity powers of US courts were generally fixed at the time of the US Judiciary Act of 1789 and that, at that time, the "well-established general rule was that a judgment fixing the debt was necessary before a court in equity would interfere with the debtor's use of his property".[73] In the absence of the enactment by Congress of a modification to that rule, the US Supreme Court found no authority for granting the requested relief. However, *Grupo Mexicano* may be distinguishable from asset freeze cases brought by the SEC on a number of grounds. In particular, *Grupo Mexicano* involved an action by private litigants for money damages, rather than by an agency serving a public purpose.[74] Moreover, the *Grupo Mexicano* litigants were general unsecured creditors of the debtor, and the US Supreme Court expressly noted that the bankruptcy and fraudulent conveyance laws were developed to protect such parties.[75] Such laws are not applicable – and therefore provide no protection – in cases where the SEC seeks the preliminary relief of an asset freeze in, eg, an insider trading case.

SEC v. Euro Security Fund, SDNY Civil Action 98 Civ. 7347, DLC (18th June 2001)

In this case, a Swiss Broker trading through a Luxembourg account was charged with insider trading in the United States. His assets were frozen by a federal court judge in New York. *SEC v. Euro Security Fund* is related to *In the Matter of W, X, Y and Z*, discussed above for its information-sharing ramifications. In the context of

---

[73] *Id* at 1963.
[74] *See Id* at 1971 (quoting *United States v. First National City Bank*, 379 U.S. 378 (1965) in noting that "courts of equity will 'go much farther both to give and withhold relief in furtherance of the public interest than they are accustomed to go when only private interests are involved' ").
[75] *Id* at 1970.

asset freezes, the case is significant for the immediacy of the reaction from US authorities and the willingness of the US courts to freeze the assets of foreign nationals trading through foreign accounts.

Giovanni Piacitelli, a former stockbroker at the Swiss office of a New York brokerage, agreed on 18th June 2001 to settle a civil action brought by the SEC alleging insider trading violations and pay over US$350,000 in settlement. This was in addition to over US$11 million in disgorgement and penalties obtained previously from co-defendants in the case and in related litigation. The SEC's Complaint alleged that Piacitelli purchased 10,000 shares of Elsag Bailey Process Automatiou NV while in possession of inside information concerning Asea Brown Boveri Ltd's 14th October 1998 tender offer for Elsag Bailey. The alleged purchase took place through an account at Banco Del Gottardo in Luxembourg, one day before the tender offer was announced. While the SEC alleged that Piacitelli's potential profits were US$164,375 on this purchase, he never accessed the money because the SEC filed an emergency action on 19th October 1998 and US federal court Judge Denise Cote entered an order freezing assets that same day. As part of the settlement, Piacitelli agreed to be barred from future securities law violations. He also agreed to disgorge US$164,375 in profits and US$1,740 in commissions from the Elsag trades, to pay prejudgment interest and to pay a civil penalty of US$164,375.

Cognisability of foreign money judgments

In addition to using the power to freeze the assets of foreign nationals on the basis of alleged extra-territorial conduct, US courts have demonstrated a willingness to assist foreign regulatory authorities in their efforts to collect foreign money judgments based on securities enforcement actions.

Alberta Securities Commission v. Ryckman, Ariz.
Ct. App., No. 1 CA-CV 00-0440 (7th August 2001)
The Arizona Court of Appeals affirmed a lower court decision that a money judgment entered in a Canadian court in favour of the Alberta Securities Commission (ASC) against a Canadian businessman now living in Arizona was properly domesticated in Arizona.

The money judgment issued stemmed from the ruling of an ASC hearing panel that Lawrence Ryckman had engaged in market manipulation by purchasing and selling shares of Wesgroup Corp. in order to artificially boost the share price. Following the ruling, the ASC filed with the Alberta court a certified order assessing investigative costs of US$492,640.14 against Ryckman. One week later, the parties reached a settlement under which the ASC would accept US$250,000 as full payment for investigative costs, provided that Ryckman paid that sum no later than 16th May 1996. Ultimately, Ryckman paid only US$7,500 in 1996. In March 1999, the ASC filed in Maricopa County Superior Court seeking a judgment against Ryckman and his wife based on the judgment of the Court of the Queen's Bench of Alberta.

The Court of Appeals noted that "Canadian judgments have long been viewed as cognisable in courts of the United States", and that "[n]either Ryckman's allegations concerning the ASC administrative proceedings nor anything else he presents tends to establish that the judicial system of Alberta is one that 'does not provide impartial tribunals or procedures compatible with due process of law'".

Production of evidence; conflict with foreign laws

The US courts have held that a defendant generally may not refuse to comply with discovery requirements in a US action on the basis that compliance would violate foreign laws. The rationale behind this general rule is that a party who does business internationally, thereby subjecting himself to conflicting laws, must bear the burden of such conflict. Where a party can show that production of evidence would violate a foreign law, US courts have sometimes undertaken a comity analysis, in which the courts have balanced the hardships to the relevant jurisdictions depending on whether the evidence is produced.

A recent case in the US District Court for the Southern District of New York (SDNY) illustrates this principle. In *Securities and Exchange Commission v. Euro Security Fund* (*Euro Security Fund*) the SEC had brought an insider trading action against certain institutions and individuals, some of whom were foreign nationals. The defendants failed to respond to numerous discovery requests and ultimately failed to comply with discovery orders entered by the court, arguing in part that the production of the requested materials could violate Swiss laws. The SDNY held that it is "well established that a court has the power to impose discovery under the US Federal Rules of Civil Procedure when it has personal jurisdiction over the foreign party".[76] The Court in *Euro Security Fund* further held that, contrary to the defendants' arguments, the Hague Convention is not the only means of obtaining evidence from a foreign party.[77] As for the defendants' argument that compliance with the discovery orders could violate Swiss law, the *Euro Security Fund* Court found that it was up to the defendants to produce evidence that a specific Swiss law would be violated and that they had failed to make such a showing. With the absence of such evidence, this court refused to undertake a comity analysis.[78] Finally, this court noted that even if it were to apply a comity analysis, the United States has a "keen interest in its securities markets" and the defendants had not acted in good faith.[79] Although the interest of US courts in enforcing securities laws will not always trump the interests of other jurisdictions, courts have generally acknowledged that the protection of the securities markets is of great importance to the United States.

The SEC has recognised the need for discretion in exercising its power to obtain information pursuant to broad cooperation arrangements with foreign regulators. In some cases, regulators may not need to obtain certain evidence, even though it is within their power to do so. For example, in *SEC v. Certain Purchasers of the Call Options of Duracell International*,[80] in order to prevent removal of funds from the jurisdiction, the SDNY imposed a freeze on the proceeds of the sale of call options without requiring certain unknown purchasers of a Bahamian account to be identified. By stopping at the level of the managers of the account, the SEC was able to achieve its objectives without requiring disclosure of the account's beneficial owners. Similarly, in *SEC v. One or More Unknown Purchasers of Call Options and Common Stock of USCS International*,[81] the SDNY entered a preliminary injunction freezing

---

76 *Id* (quoting *Societe Nationale Industrielle Aerospatiale v. US District Court*, 482 U.S. 522, 553 n. 4 (1987)).
77 *Id*.
78 *Id*.
79 *Id* at 4.
80 1996 WL 559938 (SDNY 2nd October 1996).
81 No. 98-Civ-6327 (SDNY 26th January 1999).

approximately US$2 million of the defendants' assets without requiring them to be identified. The defendants ultimately identified themselves only after the injunction was entered.[82] As noted, whether US District Courts will issue such broad freeze orders in the future in light of *Grupo Mexicano* remains to be seen.

Subject matter jurisdiction

The SEC's jurisdiction in cases where conduct occurs in the United States has in the past been virtually unlimited. In several recent cases, however, US courts have considered whether assertion of subject matter jurisdiction is appropriate in actions alleging violations of US federal securities laws under certain circumstances. The courts in these cases recognised that the United States has a strong interest in regulating its securities markets and that US courts have historically taken a broad view of jurisdictional issues in securities cases. However, each of the courts ultimately concluded that in some cases there is no US interest significant enough to justify an assertion of jurisdiction. As a result, important limitations have been established on the extension of jurisdiction under US securities laws. As the US Court of Appeals for the Tenth Circuit stated in one of the *Lloyd's* cases, discussed in further detail below, "[w]e cannot have trade and commerce in world markets and international waters exclusively on our terms, governed by our laws, and resolved in our courts".[83]

Banque Paribas case

In June 1998, the Court of Appeals for the Second Circuit (Second Circuit) decided the most recent in a series of cases[84] addressing the assertion of subject matter jurisdiction under US federal securities laws. In *Europe and Overseas Commodity Traders, SA (EOC) v. Banque Paribas London*,[85] the Second Circuit found that the provisions of the

---

[82] See also *SEC v. One or More Unknown Purchasers of Call Options and Common Stock of USCS International*, No. 98-Civ-6327 (SDNY 26th January 1999), in which the SEC had commenced an action against certain unknown defendants who ultimately identified themselves and settled the case.
[83] *Riley v. Kingsley Underwriting Agencies, Ltd*, 969 F.2d 953, 957 (10th Cir.), *cert. denied*, 506 U.S. 1021 (1992).
[84] *See Leasco Data Processing Equip. Corp. v. Maxwell*, 468 F.2d 1326 (2d Cir. 1972); *Schoenbaum v. Firstbrook*, 405 F.2d 200, 206 (2d Cir. 1968), *cert. denied*, 395 U.S. 906 (1969), and *Itoba Ltd v. Lep Group PLC*, 54 F.3d 118 (2d Cir. 1995), *cert. denied*, 516 U.S. 1044 (1996).
[85] 147 F.3d 118 (2d. Cir. 1998), *cert. denied*, 525 U.S. 1139 (1999).

Securities Act did not reach the transactions at issue because, although the buyer was in the United States when he made certain of his purchases, none of the buyer, the seller or the issuer was a US person and the presence of one of the parties in the United States was "personal and fortuitous". There was therefore no material interest for the US courts to protect.[86] The Second Circuit's conclusion makes clear that, although the United States will not permit itself to serve as a base for fraud, neither will it serve as a jurisdictional haven for all securities transactions.

Alan Carr, a Canadian citizen, was the sole owner of Europe and Overseas Commodity Traders, SA (EOC), a Panamanian corporation. EOC maintained a non-discretionary investment account at Banque Paribas (Paribas) in London. In 1993, John Arida, an account manager at Paribas' London office, informed Carr that EOC had accumulated a large amount of cash in its account and offered to recommend an investment opportunity. At that time, Carr was planning to leave for a vacation in Florida. Arida ultimately went on to recommend that EOC invest in Paribas Global Bond Futures Fund, SA, a Luxembourg corporation (Fund). Although the parties disputed whether the first discussions regarding the Fund and the first buy order took place before or after Carr arrived in Florida, it is undisputed that certain correspondence took place by telephone and by facsimile once Carr was in Florida and that at least six buy orders originated from Carr's vacation home there.[87] EOC alleged that:

(i) the defendants made fraudulent misrepresentations about the Fund and such misrepresentations were repeated on each occasion that EOC purchased shares; and
(ii) the Fund sold unregistered securities in the United States in violation of Section 5 of the Securities Act.

The issue addressed by the Second Circuit was whether telephone calls and facsimiles to a person in the United States provide enough of a connection to the United States to implicate both the registration and fraud provisions of US securities laws and to give subject matter jurisdiction over such matters to US courts. The lower court had granted the defendants' motion to dismiss for lack of subject

---

[86] Id.
[87] Id at 122.

matter jurisdiction, reasoning that the contact was initiated offshore, the purchaser's agent was in the United States solely for personal reasons and the parties involved were non-US entities.[88] In affirming the lower court's dismissal, the Second Circuit reviewed the registration issue and the fraud claim separately.

Initially, the Second Circuit noted that the extra-territorial reach of the federal securities laws, in particular the anti-fraud provisions, is well established. Numerous courts have recognised that "Congress would not want the United States to become a base for fraudulent activity harming foreign investors, or 'conduct' ... and Congress would want to redress harms perpetrated abroad which have a substantial impact on investors or markets within the United States, or 'effects' ".[89]

With respect to the fraud claim, the Second Circuit found that the "conduct and effects" tests clearly applied to the issue, stating that telephone calls and facsimiles conveying offers to sell securities and investment information could be characterised as either conduct or effects in the United States.[90] However, the Second Circuit found that no US interest was affected by the transaction and there was no US entity to protect.[91] In other words, there was no effect in the United States. Under the conduct test, the Second Circuit said, the case was more difficult. Activity in the United States did directly cause harm to EOC.[92] However, the Second Circuit held that "a series of calls to a transient foreign national in the United States is not enough to establish jurisdiction under the conduct test without some additional factor".[93] Therefore, the Second Circuit concluded that it was not appropriate to extend jurisdiction to EOC's fraud claims.

The Second Circuit determined that the conduct and effects tests also applied to the registration issue, but that the applicable standard would be different than that applied in cases of fraud. Specifically, the extent of the conduct or effects in the United States necessary to invoke US jurisdiction over alleged violations of the

---

88 *See Europe and Overseas Commodity Traders, SA v. Banque Paribas London*, 940 F.Supp. 528, 535 (SDNY 1996), *aff'd*, 147 F.2d 118 (2d Cir. 1998), *cert. denied* 525 US 1139, 119 S.Ct. 1029 (1999).
89 *Europe and Overseas Commodity Traders*, 147 F. 3d at 125 (citing *Psimenos v. E.F. Hutton & Co*, 722 F.2d 1041, 1045 (2d Cir. 1983) and *Schoenbaum*, 405 F.2d at 206).
90 *Id* at 128.
91 *Id*.
92 *Id* at 129.
93 *Id*.

Securities Act's registration provisions is greater than that required for fraud.[94] The Second Circuit held that registration under US securities laws should not be required for an offering with only "incidental jurisdictional contacts". In this case, the actual purchaser was an offshore corporation with no place of business in the United States. Moreover, the presence of Carr in Florida was "personal and fortuitous" and not business-related. Under those circumstances, the court concluded that the "nearly de minimus" US interest in the transactions prevented assertion of jurisdiction under the more limited conduct and effect standard applicable to the registration issue.[95]

It is worth noting that the Second Circuit also recognised that the transactions at issue in this case were clearly subject to the regulatory jurisdiction of the UK.[96] The applicability of foreign laws and regulations, and the availability of adequate remedies thereunder, would also be important to the courts deciding the Lloyd's of London cases, discussed below.

Lloyd's of London cases

The Lloyd's of London cases[97] are a series of US federal circuit court cases deciding the enforceability of forum selection and choice of law provisions in subscription documents which chose England and English law, respectively. The issue in the Lloyd's of London cases was quite simple: could Society & Council of Lloyd's (d/b/a Lloyd's of London) (Lloyd's) avoid the application of US securities laws by requiring a US person to subscribe in London to an offering and to execute documentation which provided that English law would

---

[94] Id at 125–26.
[95] Id at 126.
[96] Id at 129.
[97] See, eg, Lipcon v. Underwriters of Lloyd's London, 148 F.3d 1285 (11th Cir. 1998), cert. denied 118 S.Ct. 851 (1999); Richards, et al, v. Lloyd's of London, 107 F.3d 1422 (9th Cir. 1997), rev'd en banc, 135 F.3d 1289 (9th Cir. 1997), cert. denied 119 S.Ct. 365 (1998); Haynsworth v. The Corporation, 121 F.3d 956 (5th Cir. 1997), cert. denied, 118 S.Ct. 1513 (1998); Richards v. Lloyd's of London, 121 F.3d 565 (9th Cir. 1997), cert. denied, 119 S.Ct. 365 (1998); Allen v. Lloyd's of London, 94 F.3d 923 (4th Cir. 1996), mandamus denied sub nom. In re Allen, 521 U.S. 1102 (1997); Shell v. Sturge, Ltd, 55 F.3d 1227 (6th Cir. 1995); Roby, et al, v. Corporation of Lloyd's, 996 F.2d 1353 (2d Cir. 1993), cert. denied, 510 U.S. 945 (1994); Bonny v. The Society of Lloyd's, 3 F.3d 156 (7th Cir. 1993), cert. denied, 510 U.S. 1113 (1994); and Riley v. Kingsley Underwriting Agencies, Ltd, 969 F.2d 953 (10th Cir. 1992), cert. denied, 506 U.S. 1021 (1992).

govern the transaction? In the Lloyd's cases, the US plaintiffs contended that US courts had jurisdiction over Lloyd's for its promotion in the United States of its insurance syndicates, despite the fact that:

(i) the US plaintiffs travelled to London to execute the operative agreements; and
(ii) the operative agreements provided that the governing law would be English law and that English courts would be the forum for disputes. The plaintiffs argued that, because the US securities laws contained anti-waiver provisions,[98] they could seek the protections of such laws, notwithstanding the forum selection and choice of law provisions. Moreover, the plaintiffs argued that the transactions at issue in the Lloyd's cases had a substantial effect in the United States. The importance of the Lloyd's cases is that, like the *Banque Paribas* case, they establish limitations on the applicability of US securities laws to transactions that are primarily extraterritorial.

The alleged facts of the various Lloyd's cases are substantially the same. Between 1970 and 1993, seeking to increase its underwriting capacity, Lloyd's initiated a program in the United States to recruit "Names" or members of its insurance underwriting syndicates. As part of its recruitment program, Lloyd's representatives travelled to the United States in order to offer investment contracts by which US residents could become Names of Lloyd's.[99] Lloyd's employed the US mails to provide printed information on its history and operations and to send questionnaires, applications and agreements to potential Names resident in the United States. The information provided by Lloyd's to potential Names did not comply with the standards required of prospectuses by the SEC under the Securities Act.[100] Essentially, the investment contracts offered by Lloyd's were

---

[98] The anti-waiver provisions of the US securities laws render unenforceable any agreement that effectively eliminates compliance with such laws. The 1993 Act provides that "[a]ny condition, stipulation, or provision binding any person acquiring any security to waive compliance with any provision of this title or of the rules and regulations of the [Securities and Exchange] Commission shall be void" (15 US Code Section 77n (1997)). The Exchange Act contains a substantially identical provision. *See* 15 US Code Section 78cc(a) (1997).

[99] *Richards v. Lloyd's of London*, 107 F.3d 1422, 1424 (9th Cir. 1996), *rev'd en banc* 135 F.3d 1289 (9th Cir. 1997), *cert. denied,* 119 S.Ct. 365 (1998).

[100] *Id.*

securities but were not registered under either federal or state securities laws.[101]

In addition to meeting certain financial requirements,[102] a potential Name was also required to execute one or more contracts with Lloyd's:

(1) the "General Undertaking", which contained a choice of forum (England) clause[103] and a choice of law (English) clause;[104]
(2) the "Members' Agent's Agreement" which contained choice of forum (England), arbitration and choice of law (English) clauses; and
(3) the "Managing Agent's Agreement" which contained choice of forum (England), arbitration and choice of law (English) clauses.[105] In most of the Lloyd's cases, each individual was required to travel to London to execute these contracts.[106] The issue confronting the courts was whether the Choice Clauses were valid in light of the anti-waiver provisions of the US securities laws.

With the exception of the Ninth Circuit's initial decision in *Richards v. Lloyd's of London*,[107] each of the federal circuit courts that decided the Lloyd's cases upheld the validity of the Choice Clauses. In *Richards*, the Ninth Circuit found that the Choice Clauses operated to affect the very waivers which the "precise terms" of the anti-waiver provisions are meant to prohibit and, accordingly, found the Choice Clauses to be void.[108] The Ninth Circuit criticised the

---

101 *Id.*
102 To become a Name, a person was required to demonstrate that he met a means test – that he had a net worth of approximately $170,000 (*Roby*, 996 F.2d at 1357).
103 Paragraph 2.2 of the agreement stated that "[e]ach party irrevocably agrees that the courts of England shall have exclusive jurisdiction to settle any dispute and/or controversy of whatsoever nature arising out of or relating to the Member's membership of, and/or underwriting of insurance business at Lloyd's ..." (*Haynsworth*, 121 F.3d at 959–60).
104 Paragraph 2.1 of the agreement provided that "[t]he rights and obligations of the parties arising out of or relating to the Member's membership of, and/or underwriting of insurance business at, Lloyd's and any other matter referred to in this Undertaking, shall be governed by and construed in accordance with the laws of England" (*Id*).
105 *Roby*, 996 F.2d at 1357–8.
106 *See*, eg, *Bonny*, 3 F.3d at 158; *Roby*, 996 F.2d at 1357. In *Richards v. Lloyd's of London*, however, the plaintiffs executed the General Undertaking in the US (*Richards*, 107 F.3d at 1425).
107 107 F.3d 1422 (9th Cir. 1996), *rev'd en banc*, 135 F.3d 1289 (9th Cir. 1997), *cert. denied*, 119 S.Ct. 365 (1998) (Richards).
108 *Richards*, 107 F.3d at 1426.

"majority rule" courts for enforcing judicial discretion to find, and to decide, a policy issue in an area where Congress had already made the applicable policy decision.[109] Congress had specifically enacted anti-waiver provisions in the US securities laws and, therefore, the court reasoned, the anti-waiver provisions themselves render the Choices Clauses void. In addition, the Ninth Circuit disagreed with the "majority rule" courts that the remedies available to the US plaintiffs under English law were ample.[110]

However, in an *en banc* decision, the Ninth Circuit withdrew its initial *Richards* opinion and held that the Choice Clauses were indeed valid, thus resolving the conflict that had existed between it and the "majority rule" courts.[111] In upholding the validity of the Choice Clauses, the courts applied the "reasonableness" test developed by the US Supreme Court in *The Bremen v. Zapata Off-Shore Co.*[112] Under *The Bremen*, forum selection and choice of law clauses are presumptively valid where the underlying transaction is fundamentally international.[113] The presumption of validity may be overcome, however, by clearly showing that the clauses are "unreasonable" under the circumstances:

(1) if their incorporation into the agreement was the result of fraud, undue influence or overwhelming bargaining power;[114]
(2) if the selected forum is so "gravely difficult and inconvenient that [the plaintiff] will for all practical purposes be deprived of its day in court";[115]
(3) if the fundamental unfairness of the chosen law may deprive the plaintiff of a remedy;[116] or
(4) if the clauses contravene a strong public policy of the forum state.[117]

The Lloyd's courts found that the US plaintiffs were neither fraudulently induced into agreeing to the forum selection, choice of law

---

[109] *Id.*
[110] *Id* at 1429–30.
[111] 135 F.3d 1289.
[112] 407 US 1 (1972).
[113] *See* also *Scherk*, 417 US 507; *Mitsubishi Motors v. Soler Chrysler-Plymouth*, 473 U.S. 614 (1985); *Carnival Cruise Lines, Inc v. Shute*, 499 US 585 (1991), *on remand*, 934 F.2d 1091 (9th Cir. 1991).
[114] *Bremen*, 407 U.S. at 14–15.
[115] *Id* at 18.
[116] *Id* at 12–13.
[117] *Id* at 15.

or arbitration clauses nor were they inconvenienced by lit gating in London since they found it convenient enough initially to travel there.[118] Rather, the courts deemed the real question to be whether, by allowing Lloyd's to avoid liability for putative violations of the US securities laws, important US policies aimed at prospectively protecting American investors by requiring full and fair disclosure from issuers would be contravened.[119] Unanimously, the courts determined that, in the circumstances of the Lloyd's cases, no such US policy would be undermined. The US Supreme Court had recognised that uncertainty as to applicable law and the forum for disputes is likely to exist in transactions involving parties in two or more countries.[120] The ability to decide in advance on an acceptable forum for disputes is therefore an essential element of international commercial transactions, without which such transactions would lack predictability and orderliness.[121]

With respect to the application of US securities laws in particular, the courts cautioned against a hasty expansion of jurisdiction to extraterritorial transactions. For example, while noting the important function of US securities laws to protect investors in the US markets, the Fifth Circuit warned in *Haynsworth* that "[t]o insist on the application of American securities law where the laws of the parties' agreed-upon forum meet this concern would be the very height of the parochialism that *The Bremen* condemned".[122] Moreover, the courts concluded that English law provided the US plaintiffs with substantive and just remedies.[123]

Personal jurisdiction

Personal jurisdiction over foreign broker dealers
Pinker v. Roche Holdings Ltd
In *Pinker v. Roche Holdings Ltd*,[124] the US Court of Appeals for the Third Circuit clarified the standards for personal jurisdiction over

---

118 See *Bonny*, 3 F.3d at 160; *Roby*, 996 F.2d at 1363.
119 See *Bonny*, 3 F.3d at 161; *Roby*, 996 F.2d at 1364.
120 *Haynsworth*, 121 F.3d at 962 (citing *Scherk v. Alberto-Culver Co*, 417 U.S. 506, 516 (1974), *reh'g denied*, 419 US 885.
121 See *Richards*, 135 F.3d at 1293.
122 See *Haynsworth*, 121 F.3d at 966.
123 See *Bonny*, 3 F.3d at 161; *Roby*, 996 F.2d at 1366; *Haynsworth*, 121 F.3d at 966, 969.
124 292 F.3d 361 (3d Cir. 2002) ("*Pinker*").

foreign sellers of securities to American investors. The Third Circuit joined five other Circuit Courts in holding that federal courts should apply a "national contacts" test in cases under the federal securities laws. The *Pinker* Court applied the test and held that Roche Holdings Ltd had sufficient contacts with the United States as a whole to warrant assertion of personal jurisdiction by plaintiffs.

Pinker involved a securities fraud class action against Roche Holdings Ltd, a Swiss corporation with its principal place of business in Switzerland, which sponsored ADRs that were actively traded by American investors. Plaintiffs contended that they purchased ADRs at an artificially inflated price because of misrepresentations by the company regarding the competitiveness of the vitamin market at a time when the corporation's subsidiaries were engaged in a worldwide conspiracy to fix vitamin prices. The US District Court hearing the matter dismissed the Complaint. One of the grounds for dismissal was lack of personal jurisdiction.[125]

The Third Circuit reversed. The *Pinker* Court held that in performing its due process, minimum contacts analysis, it could consider contacts with the United States as opposed to analysing only state contacts. The *Pinker* Court referenced the nationwide service of process afforded under the securities laws as support for considering contacts with the United States as a whole as opposed to just the forum. The *Pinker* Court stated that "[w]e think that by sponsoring ADRs that are actively traded by American investors, Roche purposely availed itself of the American securities market and thereby evidenced the requisite minimum contacts with the United States to support the exercise of personal jurisdiction by a federal court".[126] Roche's ADRs were not traded on US exchanges and, as a result, Roche was not subject to the Exchange Act's reporting requirements. However, in compliance with Exchange Act Rule 12g3-2(b), Roche did have to provide materials it was required to prepare pursuant to regulations in its home country.

The Third Circuit took judicial notice of the fact that sponsored ADRs, such as Roche's, "require the issuer to deposit shares with

---

[125] The Complaint was also dismissed for failure to adequately plead reliance. The Third Circuit also reversed this portion of the decision.
[126] *Pinker*, 292 F.3d at 367.

an American branch of a depositary and to enter a deposit agreement with the ADR holders defining the rights of the ADR holders and the corresponding duties of the issuer".[127] The *Pinker* Court held that Roche's activities subjected it to US jurisdiction.

Therefore, by sponsoring an ADR, Roche took affirmative steps purposefully directed at the American investor. The aim of sponsoring an ADR, after all, is to allow American investors to trade equities of a foreign corporation domestically. Roche, therefore, clearly took "action" – sponsoring an ADR in a deliberate attempt to solicit American capital – "purposefully directed toward the [the United States]".[128]

The Court equated Roche's sponsorship of ADRs to an "active marketing of its equity interests to American investors", and held that "[a] foreign corporation that purposefully avails itself of the American securities market has adequate notice that it may be haled into an American court for fraudulently manipulating that market".[129]

In response to Roche's argument that it should not be subject to personal jurisdiction because the ADRs were not traded on an American exchange, the Court noted that the Complaint alleged that Roche was traded on the OTC market and that the average daily trading volume of the Roche ADRs was about 25,000 shares.[130]

Greenlight Capital Inc v. Greenlight (Switzerland) SA, 04 Civ. 3136 (SDNY 2005) (*Greenlight Capital*)

Greenlight Capital involved a trademark dispute between two investment advisory firms that both used the Greenlight name. Greenlight (Switzerland) is a corporation organised under Swiss law and based in Geneva, Switzerland. Despite the fact that Greenlight (Switzerland) was a foreign company that claimed it had never had a place of business in New York or been licensed to do business in the jurisdiction, the court concluded that it had personal jurisdiction. The Greenlight Capital Court based its finding of jurisdiction on the company's securities transactions and on its beneficial ownership of substantial quantities of securities registered pursuant to

---

[127] *Id* at 371.
[128] *Id* at 371 (internal citations omitted).
[129] *Id* at 371–372.
[130] *Id* at 372.

the Exchange Act. The Greenlight Capital Court held that "[i]t can certainly be said that Greenlight (Switzerland) transacts business in New York where, during a six-year period, as part of its regular business as an investment advisor... it has made repeated purchases of stock traded on the NASDAQ in sufficient volume to trigger the reporting requirements of Rule 13d-1".[131] The *Greenlight Capital* Court held that the Greenlight (Switzerland) transactions "suffice to confer jurisdiction in this case where all of [plaintiff's] claims stem directly from this activity" (*Id*).

Personal jurisdiction over foreign individuals
SEC v. Alexander, No. 00 Civ 7290 (SDNY 14th August 2001);
SEC v. Alexander, No. 00 Civ 7290 (SDNY 20th May 2003)
(*Alexander*)
The *Alexander* case illustrated that there are some lengths to which US courts will not go in construing contacts sufficient to subject a defendant to personal jurisdiction in the United States.

The *Alexander* Court ruled that an Italian mother charged with insider trading based on a tip from her daughter, a corporate executive, did not have the minimum contacts with the United States to make personal contacts fair and reasonable. The *Alexander* Court dismissed Gianna Toffoli, a 65-year-old non-English speaking resident of Italy, from the SEC's civil suit. The Court noted that the insider trading allegations at issue arose from a single transaction, initiated in Italy and involving the securities of an Italian company. The court said that Ms Toffoli did not know that her stock sale would be accomplished by the sale of ADRs listed on the NYSE. The Court also noted that the amount of loss avoided, US$20,250, was far below the amount found to have been sufficient to support jurisdiction in previous cases.

The SEC alleged that Ms Toffoli's daughter, the manager of public and investor relations at Italian eyewear company Luxottica Group SpA, tipped her about Luxottica's plans to make a tender offer for US Shoe, which owned LensCrafters. US Shoe was traded on the NYSE. When Luxottica did in fact make the offer, Luxottica's share price fell 20%. Ms Toffoli avoided this loss by selling shares of Luxottica through her Italian bank. Luxottica's ADRs are registered with the SEC and traded on the NYSE.

---

[131] *Greenlight Capital*, 2005 US Dist. LEXIS 2, at 12-13 (SDNY 3rd January 2005) (Baer, J.).

The Court explained that not every case where there is a causal connection between an action abroad and an ultimate injury to American investors has the minimum contacts necessary to show that the trader reasonably should have anticipated being haled into a US court.

In May 2003, the SDNY dismissed SEC charges against another defendant in the case. Penelope Afouxenide was a relief defendant who allegedly received illegal profits from her husband's insider trading in US Shoe prior to the Luxottica hostile tender offer. The SDNY held that the "SEC's allegations ... are not sufficient to demonstrate the requisite minimum contacts with the United States on the part of Defendant Afouxenide to support personal jurisdiction". The SDNY denied the motion of Ms Afouxenide's husband, Constantine Spyropoulos, to dismiss on similar grounds.

In its suit,[132] the SEC alleged that Spyropoulos received inside information concerning Luxottica's efforts to acquire US Shoe from defendant Adrian Alexander who, in turn, had received the information from defendant Belli. The SEC alleged that Spyropoulos used Afouxenide's brokerage account to illegally purchase shares of US Shoe Corp., then sold those shares after the tender offer announcement for a profit of US$117,175. Defendants Afouxenide and Spyropoulos did not contest that the trades occurred, but argued that they did not violate American securities laws.

The Defendants maintained that all of the US Shoe trades were carried out in Greece by telephone through Politis, of the Greek brokerage firm Iris SA and executed using Afouxenide's brokerage account in Greece. The Defendants asserted that both were Greek citizens, although Spyropoulos was also a US citizen, that they did not own any property in the United States, that they do not have any business contacts, bank accounts or brokerage accounts in the United States and that their trips to the United States were limited to trips to obtain medical treatment in 1991 and 1993 and to a family vacation in 2001.

In declining to dismiss charges against Spyropoulos, the Court noted that "[his] alleged activity would have created a near certainty that shareholders in the United States would be adversely affected" and that "the trading at issue here was not insignificant" (*Id*). With

---

[132] *SEC v. Alexander*, 2003 WL 21196852 (SDNY 20th May 2003).

respect to Ms Afouxenide, the Court noted that there were "no allegations that Defendant Afouxenide engaged in insider trading, or even that [she] traded securities at all" (*Id*). The Court observed that "[p]laintiff seeks only to have Defendant Afouxenide disgorge any alleged illegal profits earned through trading in the brokerage account maintained in her name".

Forum non conveniens

DiRienzo v. Philip Services Corp., 232 F.3d 49 (2d Cir. 2000); *aff'd in part on reh'g*, 294 F.3d 21 (2d Cir. 2002), *cert. denied*, *Deloitte & Touch LLP v. DiRienzo*, 2002 US LEXIS 8477 (18th November 2002) (*DiRienzo*)

In *DiRienzo*, the Second Circuit found that an action against Canadian corporation Philip Services was properly brought in the United States. The *DiRienzo* Court reversed a dismissal based on *forum non conveniens*, holding that where the corporation had conducted road shows in the US, owned American companies, derived profit from American activities and its shares were owned by American investors, it was properly sued in American courts.

Plaintiffs in a direct action and an uncertified class action brought suit against the directors and officers of a Canadian corporation in bankruptcy and other defendants, alleging federal securities fraud and related state law claims. The fraud claims were based on allegedly fraudulent misrepresentations regarding the income and value of Philip during a three-year period between 1995 and 1998. The SDNY dismissed both cases on the grounds of *forum non conveniens*. The *DiRienzo* Court concluded that the SDNY erred in both actions by giving less deference to plaintiffs' choice of forum and by failing to accord proper significance to the choice of a US forum by American plaintiffs. The *DiRienzo* Court held that the lower court's analysis was infected by that court's failure to appreciate the significance of the interest of the United States in deciding these matters, which arose out of the sales of defendant foreign metal processing company's securities in the United States.

The Second Circuit noted that the defendant, Philip Services Corporation, had its principal offices in Hamilton, Ontario, but owned 15 American companies and maintained facilities in 12 states. Its American efforts generated 70% of its corporate revenue. To raise money, the company sold securities in both the United

States and Canada. By the end of 1996, 60% of the company's 70 million shares were held by US investors. The company promoted the stock via road shows, press releases and filing financial reports with the SEC. When extensive litigation was commenced in different states and in Canada regarding the alleged securities fraud, the American suits were transferred by the Judicial Panel on Multi-District Litigation to the SDNY.

In analysing the SDNY's *forum non conveniens* findings, the *DiRienzo* Court held that the district court erred by finding that the local interest factor weighed heavily in favour of litigation in Ontario. The *DiRienzo* Court held that the district court "failed to acknowledge as a factual matter that many of the plaintiffs' securities transactions were conducted entirely in the United States, by Americans, in American dollars, on American stock exchanges". In response to the SDNYs conclusion that "parties who choose to engage in international transactions cannot expect always to bring their foreign opponents into a US forum" – the Court noted that the majority of plaintiffs had bought shares on the NYSE or NASDAQ and relied on statements filed with the SEC. The Court distinguished the case from others in which it had affirmed *forum non conveniens* dismissals, noting that *DiRienzo* "does not involve Americans who sought out involvement with a foreign forum. It was Philip who came to them by registering its stock on American exchanges, filing statements with the SEC, and conducting the bulk of its business – including multiple corporate acquisitions – in the United States".

The *DiRienzo* Court also recognised that "there is a strong public interest favouring access to American courts for those who use American securities markets. The fraud on the market theory itself illustrates investors' reliance on accurate and complete information. For securities markets to function efficiently, securities fraud law must be clear and enforceable". Moreover, the United States has its own interest in enforcing its securities laws.

Substantive rights – Fifth Amendment assertions
The evolution of international assistance has created the anomalous circumstance that, notwithstanding the fact that assistance is sought in a US civil case and no US criminal case could arise, a defendant may face foreign prosecution based upon his testimony.

The ability to invoke the Fifth Amendment to the US Constitution was severely limited by the US Supreme Court in such a case.

In *United States v. Balsys*,[133] the US Supreme Court declined to extend the Fifth Amendment's protection against self-incrimination to cases where the only threat of prosecution is by a foreign government. Taken at its extreme, this limitation of rights under the Fifth Amendment may be quite significant and would seem out of harmony with cases holding that the right to counsel, and other rights, attach at the moment of confinement, even if the defendant is a foreign national charged in the United States. However, it is important to view the US Supreme Court's ruling in the context of the facts of the case, which involved the investigation of Nazi war crimes. In *Balsys*, the Department of Justice subpoenaed Aloyzas Balsys, a resident alien and suspected Nazi war criminal, to testify about his wartime activities and his immigration to the United States. Balsys relied on the Fifth Amendment in refusing to respond to the Department of Justice's subpoena. In particular, he asserted his Fifth Amendment privilege against self-incrimination because he feared prosecution by Lithuania, Israel and Germany in connection with the matters at issue. Significantly, Balsys could claim no fear of US prosecution, as the statute of limitations had run on the charge of misrepresentation in his immigration application and there was no other basis for charges in the United States.[134]

The District Court originally hearing the case had granted the US Department of Justice's petition to enforce the subpoena, but the Second Circuit vacated that ruling, holding that a witness with a real and substantial fear of prosecution by a foreign country may assert the Fifth Amendment privilege against self-incrimination even if there is no valid fear of prosecution in the United States.[135] The US Supreme Court granted certiorari in order to resolve a split among the circuit courts,[136] and held that concern solely with

---

133 *US v. Balsys*, 524 US 666, 118, S.Ct. 2218 (1998) ("*Balsys*").
134 *Id* at 2221.
135 *Id* at 2222.
136 *See US v. Gecas*, 120 F.3d 1419 (11th Cir. 1997), *cert. denied* 118 S. Ct. 2365 (1998) (en banc) (holding that privilege cannot be invoked based on fear of foreign prosecution); *US v. Under Seal*, 794 F.2d 920 (4th Cir.) (same); *cert. denied sub nom. Araneta v. US*, 479 US 924 (1986); *In re Parker*, 411 F.2d 1067 (10th Cir. 1969) (same), *vacated as moot*, 397 US 96 (1970); *US v. Balsys*, 119 F.3d 122 (2d Cir.), *cert. granted* 188 S.Ct. 755 (1997) (allowing assertion of the privilege).

foreign prosecution is beyond the scope of the self-incrimination clause.

In making its decision, the *Balsys* Court focused on the issue of whether a criminal prosecution by a foreign government is a "criminal case" under the Fifth Amendment.[137] Concluding that it is not, the *Balsys* Court emphasised the potential consequences of an expansion of the clause to cover threat of foreign prosecution. Ordinarily, the *Balsys* Court reasoned, prosecution of criminals is not significantly hindered by assertion of the privilege against self-incrimination with respect to potential US prosecution, because US prosecutors have the discretion to grant immunity, thereby removing the threat of prosecution and requiring parties to testify. However, the scope of the immunity must be as broad as the privilege in order to be effective. Because the United States clearly may not grant immunity from prosecution by foreign governments, the Court concluded that the likely result of an expansion of the privilege would be the loss of crucial testimony in US criminal cases.[138]

Under the *Balsys* ruling, an individual subpoenaed in the United States in respect of securities transactions would not be able to assert the privilege against self-incrimination based solely on a fear of prosecution in another country, in the absence of a valid fear of prosecution in the United States. Therefore, such a person could be faced with a choice between contempt in the United States for refusing to respond to the subpoena, on the one hand, and prosecution abroad, on the other. In light of the globalisation of the markets, as discussed above, and the participation by many individuals and firms in the securities markets of more than one country, the *Balsys* Court's decision could impact on international securities law enforcement.

It is important to note, however, that the *Balsys* Court left open the possibility of revisiting the issue in the future. Specifically, the *Balsys* Court recognised the importance of cooperative conduct between the US and foreign governments in the enforcement of criminal laws.[139] Although the *Balsys* Court concluded that such cooperation does not at this time rise to a level that would justify

---

137 *Balsys*, 118 S.Ct. at 2222.
138 *Id* at 2234–35.
139 *Id* at 2235.

expanding the privilege, the *Balsys* Court stated that "[i]f it could be said that the United States and its allies had enacted substantially similar criminal codes aimed at prosecuting offenses of international character, and if it could be shown that the United States was granting immunity from domestic prosecution for the purpose of obtaining evidence to be delivered to other nations as prosecutors of a crime common to both countries, then an argument could be made that the Fifth Amendment should apply based on fear of foreign prosecution simply because that prosecution was not fairly characterised as distinctly 'foreign'".[140] With increasing cooperation in the international enforcement of securities laws and the movement toward consensus on the substance of such laws, the opening left by the *Balsys* Court could prove significant in cases relating to securities law matters.

RECENT SEC ASSERTIONS OF JURISDICTION
Jurisdiction over foreign broker–dealers
Non-US broker–dealers controlled by US registered broker–dealers
SEC v. Zahareas, 272 F.3d 1102 (8th Cir. 2001) (*Zahareas*)
In *Zahareas*, the US Court of Appeals for the Eighth Circuit clarified the definition of "control" under the Exchange Act and provided useful pointers for brokers seeking to provide finder and other services not requiring registration to US-based brokers.

Defendant John Tuschner was the former president and CEO of Tuschner & Company, a broker–dealer registered with the SEC. The SEC alleged that Tuschner & Company "controlled" Defendant Nicholas Zahareas in a series of transactions, thereby aiding and abetting Zahareas in becoming an "associated person" of a US securities broker in violation of a barring order and US federal securities law. Defendant Zahareas was a US citizen previously barred from trading US securities by the SEC, and permanently enjoined from committing future violations of the federal securities laws anti-fraud provisions. He was the president and majority

---

[140] *Id*. In his dissenting opinion, Justice Breyer, with whom Justice Ginsburg joined, also stressed the concept of "cooperative internationalism". In particular, he emphasised that, in recent decades, the US has "dramatically increased its level of cooperation with foreign governments to combat crime" (*Id* at 2243). In support, he cited the numerous mutual legal assistance treaties, extradition treaties and the similar agreements the US has entered into with foreign governments (*Id*).

shareholder of defendant Euroamerican Securities, SA, a brokerage and financial consulting firm doing business in Athens, Greece.

In 1996, Tuschner and Tuschner & Company reached an agreement with Zahareas whereby Zahareas would recruit Greek citizens to purchase certain securities in an IPO for which Tuschner & Company was serving as underwriter. The agreement called for Zahareas to be paid a fee of 8% of the total revenues generated by the IPO. Tuschner testified that he considered the payment to be a "foreign finders fee". This "finders fee" was paid into the account of Zahareas' wife in Greece.

Following the IPO, Zahareas established Euroamerican Securities (Euroamerican) and continued to refer Greek investors to Tuschner & Company. Tuschner & Company supplied Zahareas with the paperwork necessary to open an account, which he completed and returned. All paperwork to establish accounts and engage in trading came from Tuschner & Company. During the course of the parties' relationship, Tuschner & Company authorised its trader to accept orders directly from Zahareas. Zahareas received monthly reports noting the trades in which Euroamerican was involved and the commission due to Euroamerican. Euroamerican received 75% of the gross charges to each customer as compensation.

In September 1997, Tuschner testified before the SEC that he had ceased doing business with Zahareas and Euroamerican. However, as of December 1997, the Greek accounts had not been formally transferred away from Euroamerican, nor had the customers been notified of any termination of relationship between Tuschner & Company and Zahareas.

The US District Court for the District of Minnesota found that Zahareas associated with Tuschner & Company and that Tuschner aided and abetted in the association. That court issued a preliminary injunction enjoining the association. After the preliminary injunction was affirmed on appeal, the parties brought cross motions for summary judgment. The District Court granted the SEC's motion for summary judgment and for permanent injunction with regard to Defendant Tuschner. The District Court found that Zahareas, a banned agent, was controlled by Tuschner and was an "associated person", that Tuschner was aware of the ban and that he therefore violated the Securities Exchange Act of 1934.

The Eighth Circuit reversed the District's Court's grant of the SEC's motion for summary judgment holding him liable under Section 20(e) of the Exchange Act. The court concluded that the SEC failed to show that Zahareas was "controlled by" Tuschner under the plain language of Exchange Act Section 3(a)(18). The court remanded for entry of judgment in favour of Tuschner.

The *Zahareas* Court held that the "dispositive issue is whether Zahareas was 'controlled by' Tuschner". Section 3(a)(18) of the Exchange Act defines an "associated person" as follows:

> "Any partner, officer, director, or branch manager of such broker or dealer (or any person occupying a similar status or performing similar functions), any person directly or indirectly controlling, controlled by, or under common control with such broker or dealer, or any employee of such broker or dealer."

The *Zahareas* Court noted that Zahareas was not an employee of Tuschner, and that Zahareas controlled his own employees and performed his own consulting work with his own clients. This court refused to accept the District Court's holding that Zahereas was a controlled person simply because Tuschner & Company controlled access to shares of the IPO, stating that "[t]o hold that a refused buyer becomes an 'associated person,' whenever an underwriter does not sell to that buyer, would expand the scope of liability under [Section 3(a)(18)] beyond recognition".

Nor did the *Zahareas* Court agree with the District court's finding that Tuschner controlled the "means and manner of performance" of Zahareas by virtue of the fact that Tuschner provided paperwork to Zahareas for Greek investors to complete. The Eighth Circuit noted that the SEC "has pointed to no precedent in which providing and verifying paperwork amounts to 'control'" under Section 3(a)(18).

Finally, the Eighth Circuit disagreed with the district court's acceptance of the SEC's alternate theory that Zahareas was a Tuschner & Company representative in all but name, holding that the district court "departed from the express language of the statute" in finding that the term "associated person" was equivalent to a registered representative.

In responding to the SEC's argument that it should employ a general policy analysis, the Eight Circuit said that it recognised that "[f]or over 60 years, Congress has carefully limited the federal securities laws to the domestic shores of the United States". The court noted that "[d]espite being granted some authority by the statute, the SEC never enacted a rule or regulation applicable to transactions with foreign brokers such as those between Tuschner and Zahareas". The court explicitly referenced the 1989 release adopting Rule 15a-6 and the related Concept Release[141] as an example of the SEC's adherence to a territorial approach. In the Concept Release (and as discussed more fully in Chapter 7), the SEC stated that it "uses a territorial approach in applying the broker–dealer registration requirements to the international operations of broker–dealers. Under this approach, all broker–dealers physically operating within the United States . . . would be required to register as broker–dealers".

The *Zahareas* Court noted that the territorial approach was "based at least in part on avoiding the jurisdictional entanglement between US securities laws and European securities dealers". The court stated that: "Here, Zahareas's customers were all European; Zahareas made no sale to an American customer. The transaction with Tuschner was at arms-length. Indeed, European financial consultants and securities brokers would be quite surprised to learn that they were "controlled by" an American broker simply by selling an IPO using the broker's forms. Moreover, the SEC all but ignores the European and Greek securities laws in pursuit of its novel application of US laws".

The SEC filed a Petition for Rehearing and for Rehearing en Banc, which was denied on 6th February 2002 (*SEC v. John M. Tuschner*, No. 00-3047, 2002 US App. LEXIS 1813, at 1 (8th Cir. 6th February 2002)).

Jurisdiction over foreign broker–dealers for sale of unregistered securities
State Bank of India and Citibank, NA, Litigation Release 2001–139 (19th November 2001)
On 19th November 2001, the SEC issued a cease-and-desist order against the State Bank of India (SBI) and Citibank, NA (Citibank).

---

141 Exchange Act Release 27017 (18th July 1989).

SBI and Citibank consented to entry of the order directing both SBI and Citibank to cease violating Sections 5(a) and (c) of the Securities Act. The Order was issued pursuant to the finding that SBI and Citibank violated federal securities laws by selling "Resurgent India Bonds" (RIBs) in the United States without filing a registration statement with the SEC.

The Order finds that between 5th and 24th August 1998 SBI directly, and through the marketing efforts of a subsidiary and Citibank, raised approximately US$532 million in the United States by selling RIBs to non-resident Indians and entities owned or controlled by non-resident Indians. Of that amount, Citibank sold approximately US$160 million of the bonds.

SBI is the largest commercial bank in India, with offices in five major US cities. In July 1998, SBI entered into agreements with Citibank and others to act as "brokers" to seek subscriptions from eligible investors in the United States and abroad. Also in July 1998, SBI appointed "collecting banks", including SBI New York and Citibank, to act as regional centres where applications would be collected, processed and forwarded to SBI.

In SBI's pre-offering announcement, the RIBs were described as five-year denominated instruments carrying interest rates as high as 8%, transferable outside of India and giftable within India. The announcement stated that only non-resident Indians and their affiliates could purchase the RIBs and that the offering would be used mainly for infrastructure development in India.

In the United States, SBI and Citibank's NRI Services division conducted marketing, specifically targeting about one million non-resident Indians living in the United States, many of whom were also US citizens. Marketing efforts included mass mailings and cold calls. The marketing campaign featured the name "Resurgent India Bond" and frequently used the terms "bond[s]" and "investments" and other terms commonly associated with securities offerings. Citibank's marketing materials also touted similarities between RIBs and government bonds.

The Order found that RIBs are securities and that SBI and Citibank violated Sections 5(a) and (c) of the Securities Act by offering and selling the RIBs when the offering of such securities was not registered with the SEC, and ordered that the companies cease-and-desist from committing such violations.

Jurisdiction over foreign issuers and nationals for violation of US anti-fraud and disclosure standards

The ease of global dissemination of information in the Internet age has led to an increased concern on the part of US authorities regarding the impact on US investors of statements made by foreign issuers. Courts have been willing to interpret the "conduct and effects" test broadly enough to encompass actions against foreign issuers in this context. Two cases, *In the Matter of Eric John Watson* and *In the Matter of E ON AG*, demonstrate the SEC's efforts to expand its reach in this area.

In the matter of Eric John Watson, Administrative Proceeding 3010621 (Exchange Act Release 44934 (15th October 2001))[142]

The *Watson* proceeding is noteworthy because the SEC asserted jurisdiction over foreign activity by a foreign employee of a foreign subsidiary where the parent corporation was traded on the US markets. This matter resulted in the issuance of a consent order requiring Watson to cease-and-desist from violating Section 10(b) and Rule 10b-5 of the Exchange Act. The SEC alleged that Watson, a New Zealand citizen, misled US Office Products (USOP) in connection with the company's 1997 acquisition of McCollam Printers, Ltd, a New Zealand company. USOP was listed on NASDAQ at the time of the conduct in question. Watson was the CEO of Blue Star Group, Ltd, a subsidiary of USOP located in New Zealand, and President of USOP's International Division.

The SEC alleged that Watson targeted McCollam Printers as a potential acquisition for USOP without disclosing that he had purchased shares of McCollam or that he and two associates were continuing to purchase. Using nominee and foreign accounts, Watson and his associates purchased over two million shares of McCollam, which they then sold after the announcement that USOP had offered to purchase McCollam. The purchases and the sales all took place in New Zealand. The group realised profits of approximately US$533,000. The SEC found that Watson's actions had the effect of defrauding USOP and its shareholders.

---

142 Mann represented Watson in connection with this proceeding.

In the matter of E.ON AG, Administrative Proceeding 3-10318 (Exchange Act Release 43372 (28th September 2000))

In this matter, the SEC asserted jurisdiction over a foreign private issuer of securities in the United States for misleading foreign conduct in connection with the German company's denials of ongoing merger negotiations. These denials were disseminated in Germany and in the United States. The SEC took the position that where a foreign issuer avails itself of US markets, it must adhere to US securities laws, regardless of laws of the issuer's residence.

The SEC alleged that during July and August of 1999, senior management of the German industrial holding company E.ON AG directed the release of press information denying merger negotiations. Contrary to the press releases, significant merger negotiations were ongoing and the merger was ultimately finalised. At the time the misleading press releases were issued, the company was known as Veba AG. The information was disseminated in Germany and in the United States, where Veba's ADRs traded on the NYSE. The SEC alleged that Veba AG expected that US investors would learn of its denials of ongoing merger negotiations.

Veba AG claimed that it had issued the press releases because it was concerned that it would not be able to gain support for the merger from government and labour entities if news of the negotiations was spread. In rejecting Veba AG's position, the SEC articulated its view as to disclosure practices for foreign issuers where there is a divergence or conflict between the securities laws of the issuer's residence and the United States:

> "The Commission recognises that disclosure practices and laws regarding the existence of merger negotiations may differ in other jurisdictions. Where jurisdictional requirements are met, however, there is no safe harbor for foreign issuers from violations of the anti-fraud provisions of the US federal securities laws . . . When a foreign issuer voluntarily avails itself of the opportunities in the US capital markets, it must adhere to the US federal securities laws."[143]

---

[143] Exchange Act Release 43372 (28th September 2000).

SEC v. TV Azteca SA de CV, Azteca Holdings, SA de CV, Ricardo Salinas Pliego, Pedro Padilla Longoria, and Luis Echarte Fernandez, Civil Action No. 1:05-CV-00004 (DDC) (Filed 4th January 2005); Litigation Release 19022 (4th January 2005) (Azteca)

The SEC brought civil fraud charges against Azteca SA de CV (TV Azteca), a Mexican issuer with ADRs trading on the NYSE, its parent company, Azteca Holdings, SA de CV, and three current and former TV Azteca officers and directors. The SEC alleged that the defendants took elaborate steps to conceal a related-party transaction engaged in by Ricardo Salinas Pliego (Salinas), the chairman of the board of directors and controlling shareholder of TV Azteca since 1993. Salinas was also the CEO and chairman of the board of directors of Azteca Holdings from 1997 until April 2004. The SEC also alleged that Salinas and Pedro Padilla Longoria sold millions of dollars of TV Azteca stock while Salinas' alleged self-dealing went undisclosed.

The *Azteca* matter is the first foreign issuer case that highlights two significant aspects of SOX in the enforcement context. First, when the company disregarded the advice of counsel regarding US law, the US counsel resigned pursuant to Section 307 of SOX. Second, in this case, along with the *Hollinger* matter discussed below, the SEC is seeking, in part, an order barring director/officer defendants of this foreign issuer from serving as officers or directors of any publicly-held company with securities trading in the United States. The SEC sought the bar against Salinas and Pedro Padilla Longoria (Padilla). Salinas is the controlling shareholder of TV Azteca. The Salinas family indirectly owns and controls Azteca Holdings, which beneficially owns 55% of the outstanding stock of TV Azteca, and as a result, it appears, irrespective of the bar, has and would continue to have "control" of the company.

The question posed by the case is, notwithstanding the fact that the conduct, if it occurred in the United States, would draw the same pleas by the SEC for sanctions, are the sanctions responsive here? Secondly, given the fact that the shareholders are predominantly Mexican and that the board of directors is elected pursuant to Mexican law, can the United States "pre-empt" Mexican law and bar a person from serving as an officer or director of a foreign private issuer? If not, are there more appropriate and reasonable remedies that both redress the wrong and protect US investors? These same issues apply to the SEC's action against Black and Radler and

Hollinger, Inc, discussed below. Note that due to his status as the controlling shareholder, Salinas could still take action that was detrimental to US investors, but outside the purview of the SEC.

The self-dealing alleged by the SEC relates to the purchase of debt owed by a TV Azteca subsidiary to a third party. Salinas was a director of the subsidiary and president of the subsidiary during the relevant time period. The SEC alleged that a company secretly co-owned by Salinas purchased from a third party at a steep discount approximately US$325 million of indebtedness owed by the subsidiary to the third party. According to the Complaint, at the time Salinas purchased the indebtedness, he was aware that the subsidiary was in negotiations with another telephone company that would provide cash to the subsidiary sufficient to pay off the full amount indebtedness that Salinas had purchased at a discount. Three months after the purchase of the indebtedness, Salinas profited by US$109 million upon the subsidiary's repayment of the debt at full value.

According to the Complaint, TV Azteca and its management failed to disclose and in some instances falsely denied Salinas' involvement in the transactions. The SEC alleged that, while TV Azteca disclosed the transactions, it did not reveal that Salinas was involved in the debt purchase and profited from the purchase, despite advice from US counsel that the transactions were material, reportable conditions under US federal securities laws. US counsel ultimately informed TV Azteca that it was resigning consistent with its obligations under Section 307 of SOX.

The SEC also alleged that Salinas, Padilla and Echarte intentionally withheld information from and lied to the directors of TV Azteca about Salinas' connection to the transactions and that Salinas and Padilla fraudulently executed false SOX certifications. In the Complaint, the SEC cited an e-mail sent by Echarte to Salinas and Padilla following a December 2003 *New York Times* article discussing the resignation of counsel. In the e-mail, Echarte noted: "The damage is done and the situation that we didn't want to explain openly is now in the hands of the public". TV Azteca issued a press release in January 2004 confirming that Salinas owned half of the third-party purchaser of the indebtedness.

In the SEC litigation release in this matter, the Head of Enforcement for the SEC's Fort Worth, Texas office noted the cooperation between the SEC and the Comision Nacional Bancaria y de Valores (CNBV), stating "[e]nhanced global cooperation among securities regulators has significantly changed the ways in which the SEC investigates and prosecutes conduct that crosses international borders... geographic boundaries will not serve to protect those who seek to defraud investors".

SEC v. Conrad Black; F David Radler; and Hollinger, Inc, Civ. No. 04 CO 3761 (N.D. Ill. 2004);
Litigation Release 18969 (15th November 2004)
The SEC filed an enforcement action against Hollinger International's former Chairman and CEO, Conrad Black, former Deputy Chairman and COO, F David Radler, and Hollinger, Inc, a Canadian public holding company controlled by Black. Black is a British citizen with residences in London, England, Palm Beach, Florida and Toronto, Canada. According to the Complaint, Black's personal holding company, The Conrad Black Capital Corporation, owns 65.1% of The Ravelson Corporation Limited, a private Canadian corporation which directly and indirectly owns approximately 78% of Hollinger, Inc's stock. Black is the Chairman and CEO of Ravelson.

In its Complaint, the SEC alleges that Black and Radler, along with Hollinger, Inc, fraudulently diverted assets from Hollinger International Inc and concealed their self-dealing from shareholders. Hollinger International, Inc is a US public company and a subsidiary of Hollinger, Inc.

The SEC Complaint alleges that Black, Radler and Hollinger, Inc defrauded shareholders by engaging in a series of related-party transactions by which Black and Radler diverted to themselves, other corporate insiders and Hollinger, Inc approximately US$85 million of the proceeds from Hollinger International's sale of newspaper publications through what were described as "non-competition" payments. In addition, Black and Radler allegedly caused the sale of certain newspaper publications at below-market prices to another privately-held company owned and controlled by them, including the sale of one publication for US$1.

According to the Complaint, Black authorised the investment of US$2.5 million of Hollinger International's funds in a venture capital fund, with which he and two other directors of Hollinger

International were affiliated, without obtaining approval from the Audit Committee for the investment.

The Complaint alleges that Black and Radler misled Hollinger International's Audit Committee regarding the related-party transactions and misrepresented and omitted to state material facts regarding the transactions in Hollinger International's filings with the Commission.

The SEC is seeking an injunction from future violations of the US federal securities laws, disgorgement, civil penalties, a bar against. Black and Radler from serving as an officer or director of a public company, and the imposition of a voting trust upon the shares of Hollinger International held directly or indirectly by Black and Hollinger, Inc.

The attempt to impose a voting trust on the shares of Hollinger International held directly or indirectly by Black and Hollinger, Inc represents another approach to the issue raised in *TV Azteca*, wherein a controlling shareholder could still act to the detriment of investors despite being barred from acting as an officer or director. Query, why did the SEC seek the imposition of a voting trust on the shares of Hollinger International held by Black and Hollinger, Inc, but not the shares of TV Azteca held by Salinas? Was it because Hollinger International is a US public company? Because Hollinger, Inc is a Canadian company? What standards does the SEC apply in deciding what is the appropriate remedy?

SEC v. Koninklijke Ahold NV (Royal Ahold), Civil action no. 04-1742 (DDC 2004); *SEC v. A Michiel Meurs and Cees van der Hoeven,* Civil action no. 04-1743 (DDC 2004); *SEC v. Johannes Gerhardus Andreae,* Civil action No. 04-1741 (DDC 2004); *In the matter of Ture Roland Fahlin,* Administrative proceeding 3-11707; Litigation Release 18929 (13th October 2004) (*Royal Ahold*)

The SEC filed a Complaint alleging fraud and other federal securities violations against Ahold on 13th October 2004. Named in the Complaint were Royal Ahold, a Dutch company, and three of its former top executives. In addition, the SEC brought an administrative proceeding against a former member of Royal Ahold's supervisory board and audit committee.

In its Complaint, the SEC alleged that US Foodservice, Royal Ahold's wholly-owned US subsidiary, fraudulently inflated promotional allowances and that Royal Ahold improperly consolidated joint ventures through fraudulent side letters. According to the SEC, these actions, along with other accounting errors and irregularities, caused Royal Ahold's net income, operating income and net sales to be materially overstated from 2000 through to 2002.[144]

The Complaint alleged that US Foodservice overstated promotional allowances by at least US$700 million for 2001 and 2002 and that US Foodservice executives provided or assisted in providing Royal Ahold's independent auditors with false and misleading information regarding the allowances. According to the SEC, the US Foodservice executives persuaded personnel at major vendors to falsely confirm overstated promotional allowances to the auditors in connection with year-end audits.

With respect to the improperly consolidated joint ventures, the SEC alleged that Royal Ahold fully consolidated several joint ventures in its financial statements despite owning no more than 50% of the voting shares and despite the fact that the joint venture agreements called for joint control by Royal Ahold and the other partners. Royal Ahold provided its auditors with side letters to the joint venture agreements which purported to verify that Royal Ahold controlled the joint ventures. However, after executing the side letters, Royal Ahold executed additional side letters that rescinded the earlier side letters.

According to the SEC, Meurs signed all but one of the side letters regarding control and rescission. The Complaint alleged that he knew that auditors were relying on the letters regarding control but were unaware of the letters regarding rescission.

The SEC alleged that Van der Hoeven co-signed one of the rescission letters and was at least reckless in not knowing the auditors were unaware of its existence.

The SEC alleged that Andreae signed the side letters regarding control and rescission for ICA, Royal Ahold's Scandinavian joint venture, and knowingly or recklessly concealed the existence of the rescission letter from the auditors. Fahlin signed side letters on

---

[144] In connection with the US Foodservice allegations, the SEC filed a Complaint on 27th July 2004 against Michael Resnick, Mark P Kaiser, Timothy J Lee and William Carter (SEC Litigation Release 18797 (27th July 2004)).

behalf of one of Royal Ahold's partners in one of the joint ventures. He then became a member of Royal Ahold's supervisory and audit committee and learned that the auditors were relying on side letters such as the one he had signed regarding control, yet he took no action.

In settling the matter while neither admitting nor denying the allegations in the Complaint, Royal Ahold consented to an order enjoining it from future securities laws violations. Van der Hoeven and Meurs agreed to be similarly enjoined and to be barred from serving as an officer or director of a public company. Fahlin consented to an order directing him to cease-and-desist from causing any violations of the US federal securities laws. Andreae has not settled.

The SEC noted in its litigation release that it did not seek penalties in this matter because the Dutch Public Prosecutor's Office requested that the Commission refrain from seeking penalties because of potential double jeopardy concerns under Dutch law. In addition, the SEC noted the company's cooperation with regulators, proactive investigative approach and prompt remedial actions.

SEC v. Royal Dutch Petroleum Company; "Shell" Transport and Trading Company, plc, Civ. No. H-04-3359 (SDTX 2004); Litigation Release 18844 (24th August 2004)

On 24th August 2004, the SEC reached a settlement with Royal Dutch Petroleum Company and Shell Transport and Trading Company, plc (collectively Shell) in connection with the alleged overstatement of reported proved hydrocarbon reserves. Royal Dutch Petroleum Company is a Dutch corporation with its headquarters in the Netherlands and Shell Transport and Trading Company is an English corporation with headquarters in London.

Shell agreed to consent to a cease-and-desist order finding violations of the anti-fraud, internal controls, record-keeping and reporting provisions of the US federal securities laws and by paying US$1 disgorgement and a US$120 million penalty. In addition, Shell agreed to commit an additional US$5 million to develop and implement a comprehensive internal compliance program. In agreeing to the settlement, Shell neither admitted nor denied the factual allegations of the SEC Complaint.

The SEC Complaint alleged that Shell overstated proved reserves reported in 2002 by 4.47 billion barrels of oil equivalent, and that Shell overstated the standardised measure of future cash-flows by approximately US$6.6 billion.

According to the SEC, for the years 1998–2002, Shell materially misstated its reserves replacement ratio, an important performance indicator.

The SEC alleged that Shell's overstatement of proved reserves and its delay in correcting the overstatement were the result of its desire to create and maintain the appearance of a strong reserves replacement ratio, the failure of its internal reserves estimation and reporting guidelines to conform to SEC requirements, and the lack of effective internal controls over the reserves estimation and reporting process. The SEC also alleged that Shell rejected warnings regarding the overstatement of the reserves and attempted to manage potential exposure by delaying the de-booking of improperly recorded proved reserves until new proved reserves were found to offset the impact of the de-booking.

SEC v. ACLN, Ltd; Abderrazak "Aldo" Labiad; Joseph J H Bisschops; Alex de Ridder; Pearlrose Holdings International SA; Emerald See Marine, Inc; Scott Investments SA; BDO International (Cyprus); Minas Ioannoud; and Christakis Ionnau (Defendants); and Scandinavian Car Carriers A/S; Pandora Shipping, SA; Sergui, Ltd; Westbound Developments Corp.; Maverick Commercial, Inc; and DCC Limited (Relief Defendants), Civ. No. 02 CIV 7988 (SDNY 2002); Litigation Release 17776 (8th October 2002); Litigation Release 18888 (16th September 2004)

This matter involved the filing of a civil injunctive action in the SDNY against ACLN, Ltd, a Cyprus corporation operating from Antwerp, Belgium that shipped used cars to North and East Africa. ACLN's common stock was traded on NASDAQ and on the NYSE until 18th March 2002, when it was de-listed following an SEC trading suspension.

The SEC's Complaint alleged that those that controlled ACLN, Labiad the company's former President, Bisschops the company's former CEO and de Ridder the company's former COO, used the company to perpetrate a financial fraud that resulted in losses of hundreds of millions of dollars to US investors. The Complaint also named three offshore corporations through which the Commission claims the three engaged in improper stock transactions, the company's former auditors BDO International and two BDO Cyprus partners,[145] and six relief defendants. The Complaint alleged that from 1998 through to 2001, Labiad, Bisschops and de Ridder caused ACLN to misrepresent its revenues and income, fabricate a new car sales operation that never existed and claim ownership of assets that did not exist or that it did not own. The SEC claimed that ACLN did not own the largest physical asset on its balance sheet, a car-carrier vessel, and that it significantly inflated the value of the vessel. The Complaint cites the company's financial statements for the nine-month period ending 30th September 2001 as an example of misrepresentation, claiming that ACLN claimed to have bank deposits of over US$117 million at a time when its actual balance was less than US$2 million.

The SEC alleged that BDO International (Cyprus), the company's auditors, furthered the scheme "by failing to conduct even the most basic audit procedures that would have detected ACLN's financial fraud and forgery of bank account statements".[146]

According to the SEC, Labiad, Bisschops and de Ridder sold over US$80 million in ACLN stock at inflated prices as a result of the scheme.

On 13th September 2004, the SEC entered into a settlement agreement with defendants ACLN, Labiad and relief defendant Scandinavian Car Carriers requiring the disgorgement of approximately US$27.6 million from various accounts frozen in Europe. The Court's order requires that Labiad disgorge the equivalent of US$332,222 held in bank accounts in Monaco, that ACLN disgorge approximately US$3.3 million that the SEC repatriated from the Netherlands to the United States in 2003, and that Scandinavian Car Carriers disgorge approximately US$24 million from its bank account in Denmark.

Pursuant to the settlement, Labiad consented to an order permanently barring him from acting as an officer or director of any public company whose securities are registered with the Commission,

---

[145] BDO International and the two audit partners at BDO Cyprus entered into a settlement agreement with the SEC. This agreement is reviewed in the first section of this chapter discussing the SEC's assertion of jurisdiction over foreign auditors.
[146] SEC Litigation Release 17776 (8th October 2002). *See* the first section of this chapter.

and enjoining him from future violations of the US federal securities laws. ACLN consented to an order enjoining it from future violations of the US federal securities laws, and consented to the entry of a Commission order revoking the registration of its securities.

The SEC worked with agencies of several governments in investigating this matter and so as to freeze approximately US$45 million in bank accounts in Denmark, the Netherlands, Luxembourg and Monaco.[147]

SEC v. Lernout & Hauspie speech products, NV, Civ. No. 02CV01992 (DDC); SEC Litigation Release 17782 (10th October 2002); See SEC Litigation Release 18014 (4th March 2003); Administrative proceeding file 3-11054

The SEC filed a civil injunctive action against Lernout & Hauspie Speech Products, NV (L&H), which had headquarters in Ieper, Belgium and in Massachusetts. L&H traded on NASDAQ and NASDAQ Europe. On 28th February 2003, the US District Court for the District of Columbia entered the permanent injunction, thereby enjoining L&H from violating the anti-fraud, reporting, books and records and internal controls provisions of the federal securities laws. In its Complaint, the SEC alleged that L&H, which operated as a developer, licensor and provider of speech and language technologies, engaged in fraudulent schemes designed to inflate its reported revenue and income. According to the SEC, these fraudulent schemes lead to the end of L&H as an operating company and the loss of at least US$8.6 billion in market capitalisation, affecting investors in Belgium, the United States and elsewhere. The company filed for bankruptcy reorganisation in the United States and Belgium and is currently in liquidation proceedings in both jurisdictions.

---

[147] In its announcement of the action, the SEC acknowledged the assistance of, *inter alia*: INTERPOL; the Belgian Judicial Authorities, including the Office of the Investigating Judge, Antwerp Court, the Prosecuting Officer for Financial Crimes – Antwerp, and the Belgian Federal Police – Money Laundering Unit – Antwerp; the Danish Financial Supervisory Authority; the Danish Ministry of Justicy; the Danish Public Prosecutor for Serious Economic Crime; the Luxembourg Commission de Surveillance du Secteur Financier; the Tribunal de Premiere Instance de Monaco; the Banking, Insurance, and Securities Commission of Norway; the Netherlands Authority for the Financial Markets; the Netherlands Public Prosecution Service, Criminal Assets Deprivation Bureau; and the UK Financial Services Authority.

The SEC's Complaint details a list of alleged misconduct, including the following:

❑ improperly recognising over US$60 million in revenue from transactions with two Belgian entities that were formed for the specific purpose of engaging in transactions with L&H so that L&H could recognise revenue from its own research and development activities. L&H subsequently acquired the two companies on terms that repaid the amounts the companies had paid to L&H, plus a substantial profit. The SEC characterised these transactions as disguised loans that should not have been recognised as revenue;
❑ creating a series of "Language Development Companies" that the company then treated as new customers. According to the SEC, L&H established the private companies and secured funding for them. Many of the companies were incorporated in Singapore, although there were not actual operations there. The managing director of many of the Singapore companies was a Belgian national associated with L&H. L&H allegedly claimed over US$100 million in revenue from licensing fees and prepaid royalties it claimed were obtained from these customers. The company did not disclose the true nature of these companies, nor did the L&H disclose the fact that funds obtained from these companies were subject to material conditions imposing significant liabilities on L&H;
❑ improperly recognising approximately US$175 million in sales revenue between September 1999 and June 2000 from its Korean sales operations. The sales recognised by the company were allegedly subject to written and oral side agreements that did not appear in the contract files. Some of these side agreements provided that L&H would not collect licensing fees unless the customer generated sufficient revenue from the L&H software to cover the fees. L&H then engaged in a series of transactions with Korean banks designed to hide the uncollectible receivables by making it appear that the receivables had been factored to the banks on a non-recourse basis when in fact side agreements with the banks provided that L&H secured the debts. The SEC characterised these agreements as "fully secured loans from the banks to L&H Korea, rather than sales of receivables from L&H Korea to the banks";

❑ paying down its own receivables by arranging for third parties to purchase the licensing agreements from original customers. The third parties received loans collateralised by L&H Korea but not reflected on the company's books and used the proceeds to pay L&H Korea through the original customers.

In pursuing the L&H matter, the SEC worked with the Belgian Ministry of Justice pursuant to the provisions of the MLAT in effect between the United States and Belgium, and with the Jersey Attorney General.

On 4th March 2003, L&H consented to the entry of an order revoking the registration of its common stock. In its Order, the Commission found that L&H included materially false and misleading information in its financial statements and its Annual Reports for the calendar years 1996–1999 and in its Quarterly Reports for the first quarters of 2000.

SEC v. Vivendi Universal, SA, Jean-Marie Messier, and Guillaume Hannezo, 03 CV 10195 (SDNY 23rd December 2003); Litigation Release 18523 (24th December 2003)

On 24th December 2003, the SEC filed a settled enforcement action against Vivendi Universal, SA (Vivendi), its former CEO, Jean-Marie Messier, and its former Chief Financial Officer (CFO), Guillame Hannezo. Vivendi is a French company with its corporate headquarters in Paris. Its ADRs trade on the NYSE. Messier was a French citizen who resided in the City of New York. Hannezo was a French citizen who resides in Paris, France, but resided in New York, New York from mid-2001 through to at least July 2002. Pursuant to the settlement, Vivendi agreed to a US$50 million penalty and Messier agreed to relinquish his claim to a €21 million severance package he negotiated prior to his resignation from Vivendi. In addition, Messier and Hannezo agreed to pay disgorgement and civil penalties that totalled approximately US$1.26 million. Messier and Hannezo consented to officer and director bars of ten and five years, respectively.

In its Complaint, the SEC alleges that Vivendi, Messier and Hannezo violated federal securities laws by disguising Vivendi's cashflow and liquidity problems, improperly adjusting accounting reserves to meet EBITDA targets and failing to disclose material financial commitments. The SEC Complaint alleges the following specific conduct.

- during 2001 and the first half of 2002, Vivendi issued misleading statements that falsely portrayed Vivendi's liquidity and cash-flow as "excellent" and "strong". These statements were authorised by Messier, Hannezo and other senior executives.
- in order to meet earnings targets, Vivendi made improper accounting adjustments that raised EBITDA by approximately €59 million during the second quarter of 2001 and by €10 million during the third quarter of 2001.
- Vivendi failed to disclose future financial commitments regarding two of its subsidiaries. The Commission alleged that had Vivendi disclosed the commitments in its SEC filings and in meetings with analysts, questions would have been raised about the company's ability to meet its cash needs.
- Vivendi, Messier and Hannezo failed timely to disclose all of the material facts about the company's investment in a fund that purchased a 2% stake in a Polish telecommunications company in which Vivendi already held a 49% stake.

This case marked the first successful litigation pursuant to Section 1103 of the Sarbanes–Oxley Act of 2002. The SEC moved the District Court to order Vivendi to place the funds in escrow and the Court granted the motion on 24th September 2003.

In its litigation release, the SEC acknowledged the assistance of the Autorite' des Marches Financiers, formerly the Commission des Operations de Bourse.

SEC v. Parmalat Finanziaria SpA, 03 CV 10266 (SDNY 29th December 2003); SEC Litigation Release 18527 (30th December 2003); SEC Litigation Release 2065 (28th July 2004)

In December 2003, the SEC charged Parmalat Finanziaria SpA (Parmalat) with securities fraud. In its Complaint, the SEC alleged that from August through November to 2003, Parmalat fraudulently offered US$100 million of unsecured Senior Guaranteed Notes to US investors by materially overstating the company's assets and materially understating its liabilities. The offering failed after Parmalat's auditors raised questions about certain

Parmalat accounts. In support of its allegations, the SEC cited Parmalat's 19th December 2003 press release, in which the company acknowledged that the assets in its 2002 audited financial statements were overstated by at least approximately US$4.9 billion. The SEC further alleged that Parmalat falsely stated to US investors that it had used "excess cash balances" to repurchase corporate debt securities worth approximately US$3.6 billion when in fact the "excess cash balances" did not exist.

On 28th July 2004, the SEC filed an amended Complaint. Parmalat consented, without admitting or denying the allegations in the Complaint, to the entry of a final judgment settling the matter. In its amended Complaint, the SEC alleged that Parmalat used a variety of strategies, such as entering into fictitious loan agreements, assigning debt and uncollectible receivables to nominee entities, using nominees to disguise intercompany loans and falsely describing the sale of certain receivables, that caused the company to overstate its level of cash and marketable securities by approximately €3.95 billion (US$4.9 billion) and to understate its debt by approximately €7.9 billion. In addition, the SEC alleged that, between 1997 and 2003, Parmalat SpA transferred approximately €350 million to businesses owned and operated by Tanzi family members.

In consenting to the settlement, Parmalat agreed to be permanently enjoined from violating Section 10(b) of the Exchange Act and Rule 10b-5 thereunder, as well as Section 17(a) of the 1993 Act. Parmalat also agreed to adopt changes to its corporate governance structure. The changes agreed upon in the settlement include: adopting by-laws providing for governance by a shareholder-elected board of directors, the majority of which will be independent and serve finite terms; delineating the duties of the board of directors in the by-laws; adopting a Code of Conduct for directors; adopting an insider-dealing Code of Conduct; and adopting a Code of Ethics. In addition, the by-laws will require that the positions of chairman of the board of directors and managing director be held by two separate people. Finally, Parmalat consented to the continuing jurisdiction of the US District Court to enforce the provisions.

In its Litigation Release, the SEC acknowledge the assistance of Consob.

Insider trading

Insider trading issues in many respects inaugurated the SEC's international enforcement initiatives. Over 20 years later, insider trading cases are still a force in the exploration of jurisdictional issues and the establishment of the SEC's evolving position regarding assertion of jurisdiction. The rise of complex international brokerage and banking systems promises that this area will continue its role as a primary motivator in the development of SEC policy as it pertains to jurisdiction. The examples below reflect some of the issues that arise in investigating and litigating such cases.

SEC v. Jorge Eduardo Ballesteros Franco, et al, 01 CV 3872 (SDNY); Litigation Release 16991 (8th May 2001); Litigation Release 17035 (13th June 2001)

This matter relates to an insider trading action brought against eight Mexican nationals and the entities through which they traded. The SEC alleged that Jose Luis Ballesteros Franco, the former director of Nalco Chemical Company (Nalco) tipped his four sons and his brother about an impending merger between Nalco and a French company. One of the sons then allegedly tipped Carlos Minvielle, who then tipped his father, Eugenio Minvielle. The defendants purchased a total of 260,000 Nalco shares, at the time worth approximately US$9.8 million, prior to the merger.

The SEC alleged that the Ballesteros family utilised offshore trusts held in different names, as well as trustees located in the Isle of Jersey, along with offshore nominee companies, to execute the purchases. The Ballesteros family also used four different brokerage firms with accounts in both Switzerland and the United States.

On 9th December 2002, the US District Court for the Southern District of New York entered a final judgment against Juan Pablo Ballesteros pursuant to a settlement between Ballesteros and the SEC.[148] The judgment ordered Ballesteros to pay a penalty of US$106,403.75. He had previously paid an identical amount in disgorgement as well as prejudgment interest as part of an earlier settlement. He was convicted on 27th February 2002 of insider trading and was sentenced on 4th June 2002 to 15 months imprisonment, a US$40,000 fine and two years of supervised release.

---

148 SEC Litigation Release 17897 (17th December 2002).

On 21st October 2003, the US District Court for the Southern District of New York entered a final judgment against Jorge Eduardo Ballasteros, the former Chairman of Grupo Mexicano de Desarrollo, SA.[149] Jorge Eduardo Ballasteros was the brother of Jose Luis Ballasteros Franco. The Complaint in this matter alleged that, after receiving the tip from his brother regarding the impending merger, Jorge Ballesteros directed the purchase of 153,300 Nalco shares through two offshore companies, Gianni Enterprises Limited and Sagitton Limited that were owned by family trusts. The Commission alleged that after the 28th June 1999 public announcement concerning the merger, Jorge Ballesteros directed that the Nalco stock be sold, resulting in illegal profits of US$2,271,109.

The final judgment was entered pursuant to a settlement between Ballasteros and the SEC. Without admitting or denying the allegations in the Commission's Complaint, Jorge Ballesteros consented to the entry of the judgment, which directs him to pay a penalty of US$2,573,875. In light of the settlements with Jorge Ballasteros and with the estate of Jose Luis Ballasteros, the Commission filed a notice voluntarily dismissing its claims against the corporate and trust vehicles through which Jorge Ballesteros traded.

In a related matter, the SEC filed a civil injunctive action against another Mexican businessman and a company owned by his family in the British Virgin Islands.[150] In *SEC v. Pablo Escandon Cusi and Lori LTD*, the SEC alleged that Escandon was also tipped by Jose Luis Ballesteros as to the Nalco merger. The Complaint alleges that Escandon, the Chairman and CEO of Nadro SA de CV, Mexico's second largest pharmaceutical distributor, purchased 50,000 shares of Nalco stock through the brokerage account of Lori Ltd, a company owned by the Escandon family and incorporated in the British Virgin Islands. After the merger was announced, Escandon and Lori Ltd sold their shares and realised a profit of US$776,725.

The parties entered into a settlement agreement whereby Escandon and Lori Ltd consented to pay a total of US$1,716,546,

---

149 SEC Litigation Release 18441 (3rd November 2003).
150 *SEC v. Pablo Escandon Cusi and Lori LTD*, 02 CV 0971 (SDNY) (filed 7th February 2002). *See* Litigation Release 17356 (7th February 2002).

representing disgorgement of US$776,725, prejudgment interest in the amount of US$163,096 and a penalty of US$776,725. In the course of its investigation, the SEC received assistance from, *inter alia*, the Swiss Federal Office of Justice and the Jersey Financial Services Commission.

The SEC has also reached a settlement agreement in *SEC v. Hugo Salvador Villa Manzo and Multinvestments, Inc*, Civil Action No. 02CV1766 (SDNY 2002).[151] The SEC had alleged that Villa, the Chairman and part owner of a Mexican public company that indirectly owns Multinvestments, Inc, directed Multinvestments to purchase 50,000 shares of Nalco based on a tip from Jose Luis Ballesteros. Multinvestments realised approximately US$558,750 from the transaction. Pursuant to the settlement, the court entered an order enjoining Villa from future violations of the anti-fraud provisions of the securities laws. The court also ordered Villa and Multinvestments, Inc to pay US$1,503,471.83 representing US$558,750 in disgorgement, US$106,596.83 in prejudgment interest as well as a civil penalty of US$838,125.

Villa also settled a related administrative proceeding with the SEC. The settlement agreement bars him from associating with any broker dealer or investment adviser. See *In the Matter of Hugo Salvador Villa Manzo*, Administrative Proceeding File No. 3-10763 (24th April 2002).

SEC v. Alejandro Duclaud Gonzalez de Castilla, et al, 01
Civ. 3999 (SDNY); Litigation Release 16997 (11th May 2001)
The defendants in this matter were Mexican nationals with access to offshore accounts. The SEC alleged that the individuals and the offshore entities through which they traded had engaged in insider trading related to the purchase of CompUSA, Inc stock prior to the announcement of Grupo Sanborns, SA de CV's acquisition of CompUSA. The lead defendant, Alejandro Duclaud, was a partner in a law firm that represented Grupo Sanborns in the negotiations leading up to the acquisition. The Defendant, along with his family members, purchased approximately 750,000 shares of CompUSA prior to the announcement of the acquisition and sold those shares shortly after the announcement. The defendants' allegedly realised

---

[151] *See* Litigation Release 17356 (7th February 2002).

approximately US$4 million in profits from the transactions. An interesting aspect of this case is that while the SDNY granted the SEC's request for a preliminary injunction freezing the assets of the defendants in an amount equal to four times the alleged profits of the scheme, it denied the request for a preliminary injunction against future violations of the federal securities laws. The court relied on the fact that the defendants lived abroad and used offshore trading accounts in making its finding that there was a danger that the defendants might transfer assets beyond the jurisdiction of the United States absent the preliminary injunction.[152]

On 8th February 2002, Judge Robert Sweet granted defendants' motion for summary judgment as to the SEC's allegations of securities law violations related to the purchase of CompUSA stock. The court did permit the SEC to add claims related to the purchase of stock of another company.[153] In granting the motion for summary judgment, the court found that there was no evidence that the defendants had come into possession of material non-public information and that there existed widespread public speculation regarding the acquisition of CompUSA prior to the purchases by the defendants. The court also found that the SEC failed to establish the existence of a tipper and therefore could establish neither a duty to a tipper nor a breach of such duty.

In granting the SEC's motion to amend its Complaint, the court found that the motion to amend would result in a new cause of action based on purchases related to SBC Communications Inc's acquisition of an interest in Prodigy, but that the allegations based on the purchases of stock in El Globo, Inc would not constitute a separate cause of action. The court found that the allegations and evidence before it "established that:

(i) El Globo stock trades on the Mexican Bolsa;
(ii) the defendants who are alleged to have traded in the stock are all Mexican citizens residing in Mexico; and
(iii) the El Globo transaction took place entirely in Mexico, is governed by Mexican law, and is subject to the jurisdiction of the

---

[152] *SEC v. Gonzalez de Castilla, et al*, 145 F.Supp. 2d 402 (SDNY 2001).
[153] *SEC v. Alejandro Duclaud Gonzalez de Castilla, et al*, No. 01-3999, 2002 US Dist. LEXIS 1899 (SDNY 11th February 2002).

Mexican authorities".[154] The court therefore found that there was no basis for subject matter jurisdiction. The court stated that the allegations related to El Globo "do not constitute the basis for a cause of action but simply, potentially, . . . evidence of intent" under the Federal Rules of Evidence.

On 19th December 2002, the SEC entered into a settlement agreement with Alejandro Duclaud Gonzalez de Castilla, Rodrigo Igartua Baranda and their respective offshore trusts with regard to the Prodigy trades. According to the amended Complaint, Duclaud's firm represented Prodigy's owner in the SBC transaction. Duclaud allegedly tipped his friend, Ignacio Guerrero Pesqueira,[155] and his brother-in-law, Igartua, about the impending purchase by SBC of a large interest in Prodigy. The Complaint alleges that in the month preceding the 22nd November 1999 announcement of SBC's purchase, Guerrero and Igartua purchased 59,100 shares of Prodigy through offshore trusts, then sold the shares at a substantial profit and transferred US$148,300 to Duclaud's offshore trust as a "kickback".[156]

Pursuant to the settlement agreement, the defendants consented to the judgments without admitting or denying the allegations. The court permanently enjoined the defendants from violating the anti-fraud provisions of the federal securities laws and ordered Duclaud to pay US$182,895 in disgorgement and prejudgment interest, as well as a US$57,105 civil penalty. Igartua was ordered to pay US$25,375 in disgorgement and interest, as well as a US$7,925 penalty.

SEC v. Leon Levy, et al, 3-04-CV-0351 (NDTX);
Litigation Release 18584 (20th February 2004)
This matter involved an action against six Panamanian residents who allegedly purchased the stock of iDial Networks, Inc while in the possession of material non-public information concerning iDial's 23rd August 2003 merger with GlobalNet, Inc.

In its Complaint, the SEC alleged that Levy and Abecassis were present as consultants to iDial at iDial–GlobalNet merger

---

154 *Id* at 47.
155 Guerrero settled his matter with the SEC in May of 2001. Litigation Release 16997 (11th May 2001).
156 SEC Litigation Release 17903 (19th December 2002).

negotiations in Panama. After obtaining material, non-public information, Levy allegedly opened a brokerage account with a Texas-based broker and purchased 12,500,000 shares of iDial. According to the SEC, Levy and Abecassis then tipped friends and family members, who combined to purchase an additional 24,050,000 shares of IDial prior to the announcement of the merger.

The SEC filed an emergency action on 24th February 2004 seeking an accounting, an asset freeze, an order prohibiting the destruction or alteration of documents, expedited discovery and a repatriation order. The court granted the emergency relief.

Jurisdiction over foreign auditors and foreign affiliates
Auditor independence – Moret Ernst & Young
On 27th June 2002, the SEC announced a settled enforcement action against the Dutch accounting firm Moret Ernst & Young, now known as Ernst & Young Accountants, with regard to its relationship with a Dutch company.[157] This action is the first auditor independence case brought against a foreign audit firm. It also resulted in the first civil penalty imposed for an alleged auditor independence violation. The SEC censured the Dutch auditor for engaging in "improper professional conduct" with the meaning of Rule 102(e) of the SEC's Rules of Practice and ordered it to take certain remedial steps to avoid future independence problems. In addition, the company agreed to pay a US$400,000 civil penalty. Moret consented to the order without admitting or denying the SEC's findings.

The SEC's Order alleged that, from 1995 through to 1997, Moret audited financial statements of Baan Company, NV, a business software company with headquarters in the Netherlands whose stock was quoted on NASDAQ. According to the SEC, consultants affiliated with Moret had joint business relationships with Baan during this time, including projects designed for the Moret affiliates and Baan to jointly implement software products for third parties and to develop faster software implementation tools. The Moret affiliates and Baan also engaged in joint marketing efforts emphasising their "partnership", and Baan used Moret consultants as subcontractors and temporary employees in

---
[157] *See* 27th June 2002 press release 2002–95 at www.sec.gov/news/press/2002–95.htm.

servicing Baan clients. The SEC alleged that Moret consultants billed Baan approximately US$1.9 million from the joint business relationships during the period 1995–1997. Baan disputed approximately US$328,000 of this amount, which the SEC alleged further impaired Moret's independence as an auditor.[158]

In commenting on the fact that Moret was a foreign auditor, Paul Berger, an Associate Director of the SEC's Division of Enforcement, stated that "Auditor independence has no geographic limitations. Regardless of location, auditors have a fundamental obligation to ensure their independence. Investors have a right to expect that any audit firm, foreign or domestic, has no improper business ties to its audit client".

In the Matter of BDO International, Minas Ioannou and Christakis Ioannou, Administrative Proceeding File No. 3-10947; SEC Exchange Act Release 46880 (21st November, 2002).
This matter related to the SEC's action against ACLN,[159] BDO International and the two audit partners named as respondents. Pursuant to the settlement agreement, the respondents neither admitted nor denied the SEC's allegations related to their conduct. The respondents consented to a judgment permanently enjoining them from committing or aiding and abetting violations of the US securities laws and agreed to disgorgement of all audit and other fees received from ACLN. Minas Ioannou and Christakis Ioannou were suspended from appearing before the SEC.

The Complaint alleged that BDO International (Cyprus) was an accounting firm with its primary address in Cyprus. It is the Cyprus member firm of BDO International, a worldwide network of professional accounting and consulting firms. Minas Ioannou was then Managing Partner of BDO International (Cyprus) and the managing partner on the ACLN engagement. As such, he signed BDO International's audit reports with regard to ACLN. Christakis Ioannou was a certified accountant at the firm and the engagement manager on the ACLN engagement. The SEC alleged that neither had any training or experience in applying US GAAS.

---

[158] The SEC also alleged that Moret's US affiliate, Ernst & Young, lacked independence from Baan and that Ernst & Young performed audit work with regard to Baan upon which Moret relied in its 1997 external audit of Baan.

[159] This case is discussed below in this chapter.

The Complaint alleged that BDO International was not independent from ACLN and that its audits of ACLN were not conducted in accordance with GAAS. Specifically, the SEC claimed that the entity that prepared ACLN's records was owned and managed by BDO International employees, including one who worked on the ACLN audit, and other family members of BDO International partners. In addition, the SEC alleged that the financial statements audited by BDO International were not prepared in conformity with GAAP. The SEC claimed that the audit reports were false and misleading with respect to statements regarding the BDO International's independence and compliance with GAAS and the conformity of the ACLN financial statements with GAAP. The Complaint alleged that the respondents knew or were reckless in not knowing that the audit reports were false and misleading, and that they did not independently verify information provided by ACLN. As a result, ACLN was able to submit false invoices and bank records, overstate the revenue from its used car business and further overstate its revenue by relying on a new car sales line of business, accounting for over 50% of its revenue, that did not exist.

In the matter of Moore Stephens Chartered Accountants (UK) and Peter D Stewart, FCA, SEC Litigation Release 18695 (5th May 2004)

In an example of the potential for reciprocal discipline among regulators in auditor oversight cases, on 5th May 2004, the Investigation Committee of the Institute of Chartered Accountants in England and Wales (Institute) announced that Consent Orders had been issued against the firm of Moore Stephens Chartered Accountants (UK) and Peter D Stewart, FCA, a partner of Moore Stephens. In its litigation release, the SEC described the action as the first known disciplinary action brought by the Institute based on a Complaint by the Commission. The SEC described the Institute's action as the result of cross-border cooperation between the Commission and the Institute on this auditor oversight matter.

In the Institute matter, Moore Stephens consented to an order of a severe reprimand, a fine of £35,750 and the payment of costs. Stewart consented to an order that included a reprimand, a fine of £3,000 and costs.

The conduct giving rise to the disciplinary action, and upon which the SEC's own action was based, related to the issuance of a report on the consolidated financial statements of the Cronos Group,[160] for the year ended 31st December 1996, which stated that Moore Stephens Chartered Accountants had conducted its audit in accordance with GAAS in the United States, when, according to the SEC, this was not the case.

According to the SEC's litigation release regarding the US enforcement action, Stewart, the engagement partner on the audit, and two other auditors engaged in improper professional conduct within the meaning of Rule 102(e)(1(ii) of the Commission's Rules of Practice.[161] The SEC alleged that Moore Stephens UK became the auditors of Cronos after Arthur Andersen UK resigned when it failed to receive support for a US$1.5 million disbursement by the company, was denied access to the results of a corporate investigation into related party transactions, and after Cronos' board refused to investigate the US$1.5 million payment, forged and false confirmations and other related-party transactions.

The SEC alleged that Harbor, another Moore Stephens auditor on the engagement, learned from Arthur Andersen what had caused it to resign, but subsequently received a different explanation as to what caused the resignation from Stefan Palatin, then the Chairman and CEO of the Cronos Group. Nevertheless, Moore Stephens UK accepted the engagement. The SEC alleged that Stewart and the other Moore Stephens UK accountants chose to accept management's representations regarding the issues that had caused Arthur Andersen's resignation and to "audit around" the issues rather than question them.

In agreement to settle the SEC matter, Stewart, Harbor and another Moore Stephens accountant consented to the entry of an order pursuant to Rule 102(e) without admitting or denying the underlying factual allegations. As part of the agreement, Stewart consented to an order barring him from appearing or

---

160 According to the SEC, the Cronos Group was a Luxembourg holding company with headquarters in England until 1999 and in San Francisco, California after 1999. During the relevant time period, the Cronos Group was a foreign private issuer.

161 See *In the Matter of Peter D Stewart, FCA, John L Harbor, FCA, and David Chopping, ACA*, Administration Proceeding File 3-10820; Exchange Act Release #46157 (2nd July 2002).

practicing before the Commission; Harbor and the other Moore Stephens auditor were censured.

SARBANES–OXLEY

SOX carries the promise of significant expansion of jurisdiction over foreign private issuers in the US market, as well as US and foreign audit firms conducting audits for such issuers. SOX has resulted in massive rule-making efforts by the SEC and the newly created PCAOB. The result of these efforts is a drastic transformation of the regulatory landscape with respect to anti-fraud measures and the manner in which the accounting profession is regulated.

Potential impact on non-US issuers

In addition to Complaints from the international regulatory community regarding the expansion of jurisdiction resulting from SOX, this act is causing non-issuers to re-evaluate the desirability of participating in the world's largest capital market. While it is unlikely that the implementation of SOX will result in a mass exodus from the US markets, some foreign issuers have indicated that the new regulations will cause them to reconsider listing on American exchanges.[162] The SEC is currently evaluating whether to grant exemptions to foreign issuers with regard to certain of the SOX requirements that conflict with the local law of the issuer's home jurisdiction.[163]

Potential impact on foreign audit firms and foreign affiliates of US audit firms

The requirements of SOX will change virtually every aspect of the auditor/client and auditor/affiliate relationship. The provisions of SOX are discussed in other chapters, but key points are noted below.

Applicability to certain foreign firms
Firms preparing audit opinions. Any non-US public accounting firm that prepares or furnishes an audit report with respect to any issuer

---

[162] *See*, eg, "SEC's Exemption Gets Some Praise", *The Wall Street Journal*, 13th January 2003, at C16, reporting that "German auto maker Porsche AG announced that it was no longer considering a listing on the New York Stock Exchange, citing conflicts with Sarbanes–Oxley".

[163] As of the publication of this outline, the SEC has proposed a number of modifications to the law where there were conflicts with rules in foreign jurisdictions. The proposals are subject to a 30-day comment period and could be altered before becoming final.

is subject to SOX in the same manner as a public accounting firm that is organised and operates under the laws of the United States. This includes the requirement that the firm register with the PCAOB. In addition, the PCAOB is empowered to determine that a foreign public accounting firm, or a class of firms, that does not issue audit reports nonetheless plays such a substantial role in the preparation and furnishing of such reports for particular issuers that it is necessary or appropriate to subject the foreign public accounting firm to the requirements of SOX and related SEC and PCAOB rules.

Associated persons. Section 102 of SOX provides that a registering accounting firm must obtain consents from associated persons of the registering firm. The required consent includes an agreement by the associated person to provide testimony and documents upon request by the PCAOB. The PCAOB rules provide that, in circumstances where non-US laws preclude the firm from providing certain information or consents, the firm may submit a legal opinion to that effect in lieu of providing the information as part of the PCAOB registration application (see PCAOB Rule 2105). Note that SOX Section 106 does not contain a similar exception.

Production of audit workpapers

As noted above, the production of client information and audit workpapers may be illegal in some jurisdictions, regardless of whether the audit firm obtains a client's consent.

Consent to production

Consent by foreign firms. SOX Section 106 deems certain foreign accounting firms to have consented to the production of their audit workpapers for the PCAOB or the SEC in connection with any investigation, and to be subject to federal court jurisdiction for enforcement of any request to produce those papers, if the firm issues an opinion or otherwise performs material services upon which a registered public accounting firm relies in issuing all or part of any audit report or any opinion contained in an audit report.

Consent by domestic firms. A US-registered public accounting firm that relies upon the opinion of a foreign public accounting firm in issuing all or part of any audit report or any opinion contained in an audit report is deemed:

❑ to have consented to supplying the audit workpapers of that foreign public accounting firm in response to a request for production by the PCAOB or the SEC; and
❑ to have secured the agreement of that foreign public accounting firm to such production, as a condition of its reliance on the opinion of that foreign public accounting firm.

Maintenance of audit documentation. Section 103(a)(2)(A)(i) of SOX requires that the PCAOB adopt a standard that registered public accounting firms "prepare, and maintain for a period of not less than 7 years, audit work papers, and other information related to any audit report, in sufficient detail to support the conclusions reached in such report". Consistent with that provision, the PCAOB has issued Auditing Standard No. 3 – *Audit Documentation.* The stated purpose of the rule is to enhance oversight by enabling a full and fair recreation of the entire audit. Part 18 of Auditing Standard No. 3 requires that audit documentation supporting the work performed by other auditors (including auditors associated with other offices of the firm, affiliated firms or non-affiliated firms), must be retained by or be accessible to the office issuing the auditor's report. The initial version of the proposed rule would have required that non-US audit workpapers for audits of US issuers be shipped to the United States. The final rule instead followed the Proposed Amendment to Interim Auditing Standards, which requires that auditors at the US firm's office that is signing the audit opinion retain or have access to the audit documentation[164] so that it can review, *inter alia*, the documentation of other auditors, including affiliated firms, who audit a subsidiary, an affiliate or a division of the SEC issuer.

Continuing challenges

US and foreign regulators continue to negotiate regarding potential exemptions and modifications to SOX provisions with respect to foreign audit firms. In the event that these negotiations do not lead to a mutually satisfactory implementation of SOX, foreign audit firms, and indirectly foreign issuers, face the possibility that the lack of cooperation in asserting global standards could lead to a morass of intersecting and sometimes contradictory regulation.

---

164 *See* the PCAOB's Appendix A to Auditing Standard No. 3: Background and Basis for Conclusions, Multi-Location Audits and Using the Work of Other Auditors §§A60–A67.

THE FOREIGN CORRUPT PRACTICES ACT: ENFORCING CORPORATE INTEGRITY

With the accelerating pace of internationalisation, an ever-growing number of companies engaged in foreign markets are also raising capital in the US public markets and thus are subject to US disclosure requirements, including the FCPA. The growth has occurred both in the number of US companies investing in operations abroad and through foreign companies raising capital in the US markets. In the latter category, over 500 foreign companies from 36 countries have entered the US public securities market since the beginning of 1992, bringing the total to more than 800.

The Commission has responded to the demand for access to the US market by simplifying procedural requirements and removing technical barriers to entry. At the same time, however, as discussed below, it has redoubled its efforts to enhance the integrity of the US markets. Thus, the SEC is increasing its scrutiny of the foreign operations (and associated disclosures) of both domestic issuers and foreign companies filing reports with the Commission.[165] The application of one of the SEC's most effective weapons for requiring full and fair disclosure by foreign and domestic companies alike, the FCPA, is a powerful tool in the era of multi-national corporate initiatives.

Revelations stemming from a 15th July 2004 report of the Senate Permanent Subcommittee on Investigations concerning the activities of Riggs Bank have focused regulators on the relationships between several US oil and energy companies and government officials in Equatorial Guinea and Nigeria. The investigations of these relationships raise questions regarding the propriety of payments in the form of land purchases and leases, scholarships for relatives of officials who were studying abroad and lucrative services contracts for relatives of officials. Moreover, additional revelations of possible charges involving three former executives of Lucent for payments in Saudi Arabia, and an investigation of Halliburton for payments in Nigeria, evidence increased prosecutorial interest in this area.

---

[165] Marketplace: "If you must pay a bribe, don't let it distort accounting", Norris, *The New York Times*, 22nd November 1996, D6:1.

Background

The FCPA has two substantive prongs: the anti-bribery provisions and the books and records provisions.

The Anti-Bribery (or foreign payments) provision tends to be the part of the FCPA to which most attention is paid. It makes it illegal to make payments directly or indirectly to foreign officials, officials of foreign political parties or any other person acting as a conduit for payments to foreign officials or political parties, for the purpose of obtaining or retaining business.[166]

The Books and Records provisions, under Section 13 of the Exchange Act, although less well-known, give the SEC a far more potent and easily applied tool for requiring full and fair disclosure. The Books and Records provisions require companies who file reports with the SEC to maintain records that accurately reflect transactions and the nature and quantity of corporate assets and liabilities.

Accounting/books and records provisions and rules

Sections 13(b)(2)(A) and (B), the accounting provisions of the Exchange Act, are designed to provide assurances that corporations make and keep their books, records, and accounts in a fashion that will enable them to fulfil their disclosure obligations.

Section 13(b)(2)(A)

This section requires issuers to "make and keep books, records, and accounts, which, in reasonable detail, accurately and fairly reflect the transactions and dispositions of the assets of the issuer".

Rule 13(b)(2)-1 provides that "[n]o person shall, directly or indirectly, falsify or cause to be falsified, any book, record, or account".

Rule 13(b)(2)-2 provides that "no director or officer shall, directly or indirectly, make or cause to be made a materially false or misleading statement, or omit to state, or cause another person to omit to state, any material fact necessary in order to make statements made, in light of the circumstances under which such statements were made, not misleading to an accountant in connection with (1) any audit or examination of the financial statements of the issuer required to be made pursuant to this subpart, or (2) the

---

[166] *See* 15 USC. §§78dd-1 (Exchange Act §30A) and 78dd-2.

preparation or filing of any documents or report required to be filed with the Commission".[167]

Section 13(b)(2)(B)[168]

This section requires issuers to devise and maintain a system of internal accounting controls aimed at providing assurances that such issuers have reliable financial information from which to prepare financial statements and other disclosure documents.

One purpose of internal controls is to enable a company to detect and prevent illicit payments to foreign officials by being capable of highlighting irregularities which conceal disguised payments.[169] Such a system, for instance, would detect payments made through conduits by verifying (or assuring that there has been verification of) the value of consulting services received relative to the amount paid. Where a bribe is made and unaccounted for, this provision can provide an almost automatic enforcement vehicle, or charging as a separate offence, for any situation where there are indications of an accounting irregularity and/or an illegal foreign payment. It is therefore vital that companies demonstrate their commitment at the highest levels to the implementation of effective controls to assure accurate books and to prevent illegal foreign payments.

The 1988 FCPA Amendments

The amendments to the FCPA in 1988 (1988 Amendment) created a new criminal standard for application of the books, records and

---

[167] Although there is a materiality requirement in Rule 13(b)(2)-2, the SEC specifically rejected such a standard for Rule 13(b)(2)-l. *See* Exchange Act Release 15570 (15th February 1979) (citing a "concern that a limitation concerning 'material' falsity would unduly narrow the scope of the Rule and result in an unwarranted diminution of investor protection"). Obviously, those responsible for generating the sorts of records that are eventually incorporated into a company's financials should be made aware of the scope of their liability.

[168] Section 13(b)(2)(B) provides that the issuer must maintain a system of internal accounting controls sufficient to provide reasonable assurances.

[169] In enforcing Section 13(b)(2)(B), the Triton case, discussed *above*, explained: With respect to the requirements of (2)(II), any payment or gift, or the authorisation of the payment of any money or the giving of anything of value, to: (a) any foreign official; (b) any foreign political party or official thereof or any candidate for foreign political office; or (c) any person, while knowing that all or a portion of such money or thing of value will be given, directly or indirectly, to any foreign official, to any foreign political party or official thereof, or to any candidate for foreign political office, shall be recorded in sufficient detail to permit a determination of whether such payment or gift is prohibited by Section 30A(a) of the Exchange Act, excepted by Section 30A(b) of the Exchange Act, or is subject to an affirmative defence under Section 30A(c) of the Exchange Act.

internal accounting provisions of the statute applicable to persons or entities that knowingly falsify a book or record, or knowingly circumvent or fail to implement a system of internal accounting controls. With regard to subsidiaries, domestic or foreign, where a company has an equity interest of 50% or less, the FCPA requires only that the company use its "good faith" efforts to influence the subsidiary to maintain adequate internal controls. Such efforts would create a presumption of compliance by the company.

Jurisdiction
The SEC
The SEC has broad civil enforcement power over "issuers" (companies with a class of securities registered pursuant to Section 12 of the Securities Act or which are required to file reports with the SEC under Section 15(d) of the Exchange Act), their directors, officers, employees, agents and shareholders where acting on behalf of the issuer. The SEC can prosecute officers and directors who are not US citizens, nationals or residents; officers and directors of foreign issuers thus become liable in the United States for the FCPA violations of the company merely by virtue of their employment by an "issuer". The expansiveness of the SEC's jurisdiction is intended to increase the pressure on management – whether foreign or US nationals – to take the necessary steps to implement augmented internal controls systems. The SEC can enforce both the books and records/internal control and the anti-bribery provisions against these parties.

If the Commission determines that there have been violations of these provisions of the Exchange Act, it may file a civil action in US federal district court to seek an injunction against further violations of the statute and a penalty. Moreover, where fraud is involved, the court may bar a person from acting as an officer or director of a public corporation. With respect to the books, records and internal controls provisions of the Exchange Act, the Commission can also bring an Administrative Enforcement Proceeding and issue an agency order directing compliance with those sections of the law.

The Department of Justice
The DOJ has jurisdiction to bring criminal proceedings for knowing violations of the anti-bribery provision against the same

entities as the SEC and additionally to bring civil or criminal proceedings against "domestic concerns" (those who are not "issuers"), their officers, directors, employees, agents or shareholders (acting on behalf of the concern). Of course, the potential for individual and corporate criminal liability only increases the pressure on management to implement effective controls and employee education programs.

Accounting requirements and practices for companies under the FCPA

By mandating certain accounting practices, the FCPA adds a powerful weapon to the SEC's enforcement arsenal, the purpose of which is the deterrence of illegal payments and the assurance that shareholder disclosures remain accurate. Recent SEC enforcement activity illustrates the two-track approach that the SEC will take to addressing disclosure requirements for foreign payments under the FCPA. The fact that an independent auditor is not able to detect a bribe, or that there may be difficulties encountered in prosecuting a particular scheme for the ultimate payment of a bribe, does not mean that those who make questionable payments go unpunished. Corporate officials face not only potential criminal charges for paying bribes, but also charges for maintaining inaccurate corporate books and records and inadequate internal accounting controls which permitted illegal payments – even those unbeknownst to management – to be made. For these reasons, the spectre of an enforcement action under the books and records provisions of the FCPA should cause management to create committees not only to undertake searching one-time reviews but also to periodically re-review internal controls systems and employee education, and to deal quickly and appropriately with any issues that arise.

Corporate record keeping

The purpose of the corporate record-keeping provisions is to create a duty in a company's management to ensure that the company's books and records are accurate and that its annual financial statments can be prepared and independently audited. Moreover, management is charged with developing accounting control systems to ensure that the company has the ability to record economic events, safe-guard assets and conform transactions to management's authorisation. Management may find it appropriate or effective to issue special guidelines to employees dealing with accounting for all company transactions. Judgment should be exercised in designing systems of accounting controls that are appropriate, eg, to the company's size, the diversity of company operations, the degree of centralisation of financial and operating management and the amount of contact by top management with day-to-day operations. These issues should be revisited regularly to address the effectiveness of the implementation and the possible need for adjustment to changing circumstances. Indeed, most public companies have concluded that an independent audit committee of the board of directors can play a role in providing oversight to management's efforts to create and maintain effective internal accounting controls. To facilitate this process, management may wish to seek assistance from accounting and auditing literature or from consultants.

Role of management and boards
Imposing the corporate record-keeping obligations (to maintain accurate books and records and to implement effective internal controls) on companies does not necessarily require boards of directors or senior management to be involved in the minutiae of recording and accounting for every transaction that the companies may make. However, such obligations probably do require both management and boards to monitor and evaluate the adequacy of companies' books, records and internal accounting controls. While requirements to maintain accurate books and records and an adequate system of internal accounting controls does not mean that the management and board will be liable for every small, isolated error or irregularity, a system that permits frequent breaches and is unable to uncover or remedy those breaches in a timely fashion should be the subject of immediate management and board attention.

The auditor's role
The internal accounting controls that public companies are required to maintain under the Exchange Act are always considered by independent auditors in doing an audit. For example, US GAAS requires auditors to understand a company's internal control structure in planning and performing an audit. Auditors must

also provide advice to management regarding whether the internal accounting controls devised by management are adequate.[170]

Additionally, auditors are required to design their audits to provide reasonable assurance of detecting errors or irregularities (intentional misstatements) that are material to the financial statements, including illegal acts such as bribery. When risk factors indicate, auditors should make appropriate inquiries of management concerning a company's compliance with laws against bribery. The SEC has adopted a rule that makes it illegal for corporate management and directors to lie to or mislead its internal accountants or external auditors in any way in connection with the preparation of any report required to be filed with the SEC.

Recent legislation – deputising the auditor

Perhaps one of the most important developments since the passage of the FCPA is the recent congressional enactment of legislation that imposes expanded obligations on auditors in connection with their review of corporate financial statements. Among other things, the Private Securities Litigation Reform Act of 1995 (Litigation Reform Act) amended the Exchange Act to require auditors to report in a timely manner certain uncorrected illegal acts that have a material effect on the financial statements, which may include the payment of bribes, to the board of directors of issuers.[171] The provision further requires the company, or if the company fails to do so then the auditor, to provide information regarding the illegal act to the SEC. By requiring the auditor to inform on his client, subjecting him to penalties if he should fail, this legislation extends US generally accepted auditing standards that require auditors only to report illegal acts to a company's management. Essentially, the Litigation Reform Act mandates third-party oversight of corporate management. Moreover, the requirement that these irregularities be reported to the SEC enables the SEC potentially to begin its own investigation more quickly than might otherwise be possible.

---

170 A recent amendment to Regulation S-X authorises the SEC to supplement an auditors' duties under GAAS.
171 *See* Litigation Reform Act, tit. iii, Publ. L. No. 104–67 (adding section 10A to the Exchange Act).

In March 1997, new rules implementing the reporting requirements in Section 10A of the Exchange Act became effective.[172] The rules stipulate the required contents for the company notices and auditors' reports filed with the SEC under the amended Section 10A. The notice to the Commission (to be made to the Office of the Chief Accountant) must identify the company and the auditor, state the date the auditor made its report to the board regarding the illegal act and provide a summary of the auditor's report to the board. The required summary must describe the act and the potential impact of that act on the registrant's financial statements.

In response to commentary received during the comment period, the rule explicitly provides that the Section 10A notice and report are to be treated as exempt under FOIA in the same fashion as the SEC's investigative records because they are intended to assist the SEC in its enforcement efforts. (Previously, the rule had only provided that the reports were to be treated as non-public.) The SEC has acknowledged the importance of preserving the confidentiality of these reports to protect its own ability to investigate, the issuers' right to a fair adjudication, the issuer's privacy interests as well as the confidential source. The information itself, however, is not entirely shielded from disclosure since the rule does not affect an issuer's obligation to file Forms 8-K or N-SAR. While the confidential, FOIA-exempt treatment is important, it bears emphasising that these auditor reports are being furnished directly to the enforcement division.

Recent SEC FCPA enforcement actions
Montedison SpA[173]

On 21st November 1996, the SEC instituted a civil enforcement action against Montedison SpA (Montedison), an Italian company, alleging violations of the Exchange Act's anti-fraud provision and the FCPA books and records provisions. This was the first case the SEC had ever brought against a foreign private issuer of securities in the United States. Montedison, an Italian corporation with headquarters in Milan, had interests in the agro-industry, chemical, energy and engineering sectors. Since July 1987, ADRs of the

---

172 *See* 17 C.F.R. §§210.1-02 and 240. 10A- 1.
173 *SEC v. Montedison,* Civ. Action No. 1:96 CV 02631 (RWR) (DDC).

company's common stock have been listed on the NYSE. The ADRs are registered under Section 12(b) of the Exchange Act and Montedison filed reports with the SEC pursuant to Section 13(a) of the Exchange Act. It filed annual reports with the SEC on Form 20-F.

In its Complaint, the SEC alleged that Montedison violated the anti-fraud provisions of the Exchange Act by engaging in a fraudulent scheme to materially misstate its financial condition and results of operations on its books and records and in its reports filed with the Commission and disseminated to the investing public. According to the Complaint, the scheme began in approximately 1988 and operated through to the first half of 1993. The Complaint alleges that the scheme was designed to conceal hundreds of millions of dollars of payments that, among other things, were used to bribe politicians in Italy and other persons. Moreover, the scheme concealed losses of at least US$398 million. As a result, Montedison's assets allegedly were materially overstated on its books and records and in its financial statements for its 1988, 1989, 1990 and 1991 fiscal years.

The SEC's Complaint alleged two examples of Montedison's fraudulent conduct: the "Exilar Loan" and the "ENIMONT Affair". According to the Complaint, the Exilar Loan was a fraudulent accounting entry used to disguise and aggregate as an asset on the company's balance sheet numerous questionable payments or bribes that had been made from at least December 1988 through to May 1993. In the latter half of 1993, Montedison determined that the Exilar loan was uncollectible and took a write-down in the amount of 435 billion lire (approximately US$272 million, at US$1 to 1,600 lire) for the company's 1992 fiscal year. The Complaint alleges that the ENIMONT Affair involved fraudulent accounting entries that overstated real estate values to disguise numerous bribes on the company's books and records from at least 1990 through to 1992. The fraudulent entries resulted in a write-down on the company's 1993 financial statements of 202 billion lire (approximately US$126,250,000).

The Complaint alleged that the fraudulent conduct continued undetected for several years because of a "seriously deficient internal control environment at Montedison". The Complaint notes that Montedison's internal controls "were so deficient that, according to Montedison, neither the company itself, nor its auditors, have been able to reconstruct precisely what occurred and who was responsible". The fraudulent conduct was discovered after new management was appointed when Montedison disclosed that it was unable to service its bank debt. Many members of the former senior management responsible for the fraud were convicted by Italian criminal authorities and were sued by the company.

In its Complaint the Commission requested that the court:

(i) enter findings that Montedison violated Exchange Act Sections 10(b), 13(a), 13(b)(2)(A) and 13(b)(2)(B) and Rules l0b-5, 12b-20 and 13a-I thereunder;
(ii) grant a permanent injunction restraining and enjoining Montedison from violating such provisions; and
(iii) order Montedison to pay a civil penalty pursuant to Exchange Act Section 21(d)(3).

While the prosecution of an Italian company for payments presumably made by Italian employees to Italian officials may appear to be an aggressive jurisdictional posture by the SEC, it is actually fairly conservative. Section 13 imposes penalties on issuers for submitting inaccurate financial records to the SEC and for maintaining an inadequate system of controls which permits those inaccuracies. As an issuer which has exploited the US markets, Montedison was submitting false reports to the SEC and causing the false information to be disseminated. It remains possible, though considerably more tenuous, that the SEC could prosecute a company like Montedison and its officials under the foreign payments provision, which proscribes any "use of the mails or any means of instrumentality of interstate commerce" to make an illegal payment. Apparently, the SEC was unwilling to test the question whether the use of the capital markets and the issuance of a report in the United States inaccurately reflecting an illegal foreign payment was a sufficient "use" of the means of interstate commerce to support the application of Section 30A to conduct occurring and having effect wholly outside the United States. Potentially, the SEC could attempt the prosecution of a foreign company or even foreign officers or directors of a foreign issuer under such circumstances in the future.

In a March 2001 Litigation Release,[174] the SEC announced that, pursuant to a settlement agreement, the company was ordered to

---

[174] Litigation Release 16948 (30th March 2001).

pay a civil penalty of US$300,000 for violating the anti-fraud, financial reporting and books and records provisions of the US federal securities laws. The company was acquired by Compart, SpA in late 2000 and its ADRs were delisted. Compart then changed its name to Montedison. No securities of Compart are listed for sale by US stock exchanges.

The Triton case[175]
In February 1997, Triton Energy Corporation (Triton Energy), a US company, entered into a settlement acknowledging violations of the anti-bribery, books and records and internal control provisions. Simultaneously, two former senior officers of Triton Energy's subsidiary, Triton Indonesia, Inc (Triton Indonesia), Richard L McAdoo and Philip W Keever, also consented to the entry of orders concerning these offences (the two consented to an order enjoining future violations of the foreign payments provision).

The Commission's Complaint alleges that during the years 1989 and 1990, McAdoo and Keever authorised numerous improper payments to Roland Siouffl, Triton Indonesia's business agent. Siouffl acted as an intermediary between Triton Indonesia and Indonesian government agencies. It was alleged that, in authorising these payments, McAdoo and Keever knowingly or recklessly disregarded the high probability that Siouffi either had or would pass them along to Indonesian government employees for the purpose of influencing their decisions affecting the business of Triton Indonesia. The Complaint alleges that these payments were made in violation of the FCPA. According to the Complaint, McAdoo and Keever, together with other Triton Indonesia employees, also concealed these payments by falsely documenting and recording the transactions as routine business expenditures. The Complaint states that Triton Energy did not expressly authorise or direct these improper payments and misbookings.

During the relevant time period, the SEC alleged that Triton Energy failed to devise and maintain an adequate system of internal accounting controls to detect and prevent improper payments by Triton Indonesia to government officials and to provide reasonable

---

[175] *SEC v. Triton Energy Corporation, et al,* Civ. Action No. 1:97, C000401 (RMLT) (DDC 27th February 1997).

assurance that transactions were recorded as necessary to permit preparation of financial statements in conformity with generally accepted accounting principles. In particular, the Complaint alleges that Triton Indonesia recorded other false entries in its books and records, including, eg, falsely documenting and recording case payments totalling US$1,000 per month to clerical employees of the Indonesian national oil company made for the purpose of expediting payment of monthly crude oil invoices.

Simultaneous with the filing of the Complaint, Triton Energy consented, without admitting or denying the allegations, to the entry of a Final Judgment that permanently enjoined it from violating the books and records and internal controls provisions of the Exchange Act, and ordered Triton Energy to pay a US$300,000 penalty. In its press release announcing the settlement the SEC noted that its acceptance of the settlement was based upon its consideration of the fact that the violations occurred under former management and that certain remedial actions have been implemented by the current board of directors and senior management. Keever consented, without admitting or denying the allegations, to the entry of a Final Judgment that permanently enjoined him from violating the foreign corrupt practices and books and records provisions of the Exchange Act and ordered Keever to pay a US$50,000 penalty.

As part of these proceedings, the SEC also instituted cease-and-desist proceedings against former employees of Triton Energy, David Gore, Robert Puetz, William McClure and Robert P Murphy. These proceedings were based upon those individuals' conduct in connection with the improper payments and misbookings. The SEC found that, as a result of the falsely documented payments and other false entries, Triton Indonesia maintained books and records that did not accurately or fairly reflect the underlying disposition of assets. It also made a finding that Murphy, Triton Indonesia's Controller, knowingly participated in creating and recording false entries in Triton Indonesia's books and records. According to the Order, McClure, Triton Indonesia's Commercial Manager, failed to assure that the entries prepared by Murphy accurately reflected the underlying transactions. The Commission's Order also found that Gore, formerly Triton Energy's President and a director, and Puetz, formerly Triton Energy's Senior Vice-President of Finance and CFO, each received information indicating that Triton Indonesia was engaged in conduct that was potentially unlawful, but took no action to initiate an investigation of the serious issues raised by Triton Energy's internal auditor.

Without admitting or denying the Commission's findings, the respondents each consented to the entry of a cease-and-desist order. McClure and Murphy consented to cease-and-desist from committing or causing any violation of, and committing or causing any future violation of, the books and records provision of the Exchange Act. Gore and Puetz consented to cease-and-desist from committing or causing any violation of, and committing or causing any future violation of, the foreign payments provision of the Exchange Act. In addition, Gore, Puetz, McClure and Murphy consented to cease-and-desist from causing any violation of, and causing any future violation of, the record-keeping provision of the Exchange Act.[176] Unlike the Montedison case, the illegal payments (made to an intermediary to obtain favourable tax and regulatory treatment) were recorded as expenses albeit mischaracterised as legitimate expenses, so that the overall financial condition was not misstated. Although this is a more conventional exercise of jurisdiction than the Montedison case (a US company was prosecuted for the conduct of its employees – apparently all American nationals – in foreign subsidiaries) it is notable as only the fourth prosecution by the SEC under the foreign payments provision.

SEC v. International Business Machines Corporation, 00 CV 03040 (USD.C.), Litigation Release 16839 (21st December 2000);
In the matter of International Business Machines Corporation, Administration proceeding 3-10397(Exchange act Release 43761/AAER Release 1355 (21st December 2000))

In this matter, the foreign subsidiary of International Business Machines Corporation (IBM) went to great lengths to conceal the illicit payments made to foreign officials from IBM, including the creation of false invoices and other documentation. Nevertheless, the SEC pursued IBM for violations of the books and records provisions of the FCPA. The matter ultimately settled with the filing of a

---

176 *See In the Matter of David Gore, Robert Puetz, William McClure, and Robert P. Murphy,* Administrative Proceeding 3-9262 (27th February 1997).

consent cease-and-desist order and a settled civil action. IBM agreed to pay a penalty of US$300,000.

The Complaint alleged that IBM's wholly-owned foreign subsidiary, IBM-Argentina, SA, made approximately US$4.5 million in payments to bank officials in its efforts to secure the contract to modernise a government-owned bank. The contract was worth US$250 million. Senior management at IBM-Argentina subcontracted with Capacitacion Y Computacion Rural, SA and paid the subcontractor US$22 million. The US$4.5 million in illicit payments came from that US$22 million.

This case, as well as the *Chiquita Brands International* matter discussed below, demonstrate that corporations can incur liability under the FCPA without knowledge of the underlying misconduct. Indeed, the books and records and internal controls provisions of the FCPA permitted findings against IBM and Chiquita in circumstances where the subsidiaries actively concealed evidence of illicit payments from the parents.

In the matter of Chiquita Brands International, Inc, Administration Proceeding File 10613 (Exchange Act Release. 44902/AAER Release 1463 (3rd October 2001)); *SEC v. Chiquita Brands International, Inc,* 01 CV 02079 (DDC), Litigation Release 17269/AAER Release 1464 (3rd October 2001)

In October 2001, the SEC and Chiquita Brands International, Inc, entered into a settled cease-and-desist order and settled a civil action related to a payment to foreign customs officials in Columbia. This case demonstrates the importance of internal controls as a tool for corporations to protect themselves from liability under the FCPA, and also the importance of prompt, remedial action when potential violations are uncovered. The illicit payments at issue in this matter were made by CI Bananos de Exportacion SA (Banadex), a wholly owned, foreign subsidiary of Chiquita Brands International, Inc (Chiquita). The parties agreed, and the administrative order reflected, that Banadex acted without the knowledge or consent of any Chiquita employees outside of Colombia and that the subsidiary's conduct was in violation of the policies of both Chiquita and Banadex.

According to the order, Banadex made payments in 1996 and 1997 totalling US$30,000 to local customs agents in an effort to have two prior citations for customs violations ignored so that Banadex could renew its license to maintain incoming inventory awaiting inspection at its Colombia port facility. If the prior citations had resulted in a denial of Banadex' renewal application, the company would have incurred a cost of approximately US$1 million to replace the holding facility. Banadex identified the payments as discretionary payments on its books and records. The initial payment was identified on the company's books as a maritime donation. The second payment was identified as relating to a maritime agreement. Both of these characterisations were false.

When Chiquita became aware of questionable books and records entries relating to 1996, it conducted an internal investigation which ultimately resulted in the termination of Banadex employees responsible for the payments.

The civil penalty in this case, US$100,000, is reflective of Chiquita's proactivity, including the thorough investigation, remedial measures and overhaul of the subsidiary's internal controls.

In the matter of American Bank Note Holographics, Inc, Administration Proceeding File 3-10532 (Exchange Act Release 7994/Exchange Act Release 44563/AAER Release 1422 (18th July 2001); *SEC v. American Bank Note Holographics, Inc*, 01 CV 6453 (SDNY), Litigation Release 17068A/AAER Release 1425A (18th July 2001); *SEC v. Morris Weissman, et al*, 01 CV 6449 (SDNY), Litigation Release 17068A/AAER Release 1425A (18th July 2001); *SEC v. Joshua C Cantor, 03-CV 2488 (SDNY), Litigation Release 18081 (10th April 2003)*

This matter relates to illicit payments made to Saudi Arabian officials through a Swiss bank account in an effort to secure a contract to produce holograms for the Saudi Arabian government. According to the Complaint, the then chairman and CEO Morris Weissman and the then executive vice-president and general manager Joshua Cantor directed an employee of American Bank Note Holographics, Inc to wire approximately US$239,000 to the Swiss account to serve as a bribe for one or more Saudi officials. The corporation then recorded the US$239,000 payment as a consulting fee.

The company discovered and questioned the transaction during its audit process and instituted an internal investigation. At the conclusion of the investigation, the corporation terminated the responsible officers and notified the SEC of the circumstances.

Without admitting or denying the SEC's findings, American Bank Note Holographics agreed to an order to cease-and-desist from violating the FCPA's anti-bribery provisions and books and records and internal control provisions. The corporation also agreed to a US$75,000 penalty in the civil action.

On 10th April 2003, the Commission filed a settled action against Joshua C Cantor. The Complaint underlying the action included the FCPA violations described above, as well as significant financial fraud allegations.[177] Without admitting or denying the allegations in the Complaint, Cantor consented to an order permanently enjoining him from violating and/or aiding and abetting violations of the anti-fraud, reporting, record-keeping, internal controls and lying to auditors provisions of the federal securities laws, as well as from violating the FCPA. In addition, Cantor consented to a ten-year prohibition from acting as an officer or director of a public company.

SEC v. Eric Mattson, et al, Civ. No. H-01-3106 (SDTX), Litigation Release17126/AAER Release 1445 (12th September 2001); *SEC v KPMG Siddharta Siddharta & Harsono, et al,* Civ. No. H-01-3105 (SDTX), Litigation Release 17127/AAER Release 1446 (12th September 2001); *In the matter of Baker Hughes Incorporated,* Administration proceeding 3-10572, Exchange Act Release 44784/AAER Release 1447 (12th September 2001)

This matter gave rise to an injunctive action filed jointly by the SEC and the Department of Justice, the first such jointly filed action. The illicit payment was a bribe to a local tax official in Indonesia intended to lead the official to lower a tax assessment for an Indonesian company, PT Eastman Christensen, from US$3.2 million to US$270,000. Baker Hughes was the beneficial owner of PT Eastman Christensen. The Complaint alleged that Eric Mattson and James W Harris, respectively the former CFO and the former controller of Baker Hughes, authorised the payment of a US$75,000 bribe to the local tax official after its accountant, KPMG-Siddharta Siddharta & Harsono (KPMG-SSH), informed them that the official was demanding the payment. The Complaint also alleged that

---

177 On 6th August 2003, following a jury trial before the S.D.N.Y, Morris Weissman was convicted of conspiracy, securities fraud, falsifying books and records and making false statements to auditors. *See* Litigation Release 18283 (12th August 2003).

Baker Hughes' FCPA advisor advised Harris that such a payment would violate the anti-bribery provisions of the FCPA.

The jointly filed injunctive action was filed against KPMG-SSH. The SEC and the Department of Justice alleged that KPMG-SSH made the payment to the official and created a false invoice to conceal the payment in which it characterised the payment as one for services rendered. KPMG-SSH and its partner, Sonny Harsono, consented to a permanent injunction prohibiting future violations of the FCPA's anti-bribery, books and records and internal controls provisions.

Baker Hughes also consented to a permanent injunction prohibiting future violations of the FCPA's anti-bribery, books and records and internal controls provisions. The injunction related to Baker Hughes also included illicit payments to agents in Brazil and India authorised by senior management in 1995 and 1998.

Eric Mattson and James Harris moved to dismiss the charges. In addition to maintaining that they did not engage in the conduct alleged, they argued that the favourable tax treatment did not satisfy the "obtain or retain business" prong of the FCPA.[178] See the discussion of American Rice, *infra*. Relying on *United States v. Kay*, the court held that the payments did not violate the FCPA because they did not help Baker Hughes "obtain or retain business". The SEC appealed the decision to the US Court of Appeals for the Fifth Circuit. Pursuant to the Commissions unopposed motion filed on 13th July 2004, the Fifth Circuit Court of Appeals, on 14th July 2004, dismissed the appeal filed by the Commission and the litigation in this matter was concluded.[179]

SEC v. BellSouth Corporation, 02-CV-013 (ND GA), Litigation Release 17310 (15th January 2002)

On 15th January 2002, the SEC filed a settled civil action in federal court. Pursuant to the settlement agreement BellSouth agreed to pay a US$150,000 civil penalty. In its Complaint, the SEC alleged that BellSouth violated certain provisions of the FCPA. The SEC alleged that BellSouth violated the books and records and internal

---

[178] *SEC v. Mattson*, No. 01-CV-3106 (SDTX 11th September 2001). The argument that seeking favourable tax treatment does not satisfy the "obtain or retain business" prong of the FCPA is discussed *above*.
[179] Litigation Release 18863 (1st September 2004).

controls provisions of the Exchange Act. The matter stemmed from payments made by BellSouth's Venezuelan and Nicaraguan subsidiaries.

According to the Complaint, between September 1997 and August 2000, former senior management of BellSouth's Venezuelan subsidiary, Telcel, CA, authorised payments totalling approximately US$10.8 million to six offshore companies and improperly recorded the disbursements in Telcel's books and records, based on fictitious invoices, as services received. Telcel's internal controls failed to detect the unsubstantiated payments for a period of at least two years. As a result of theses failures, BellSouth was unable to reconstruct the circumstances surrounding the payments and could not identify the recipients of the payments.

The Complaint also alleged that, between October 1998 and June 1999, BellSouth's Nicaraguan subsidiary, Telefonia Celular de Nicaragua, SA's ("Telefonia"), improperly recorded payments to the wife of the Nicaraguan legislator who was the chairman of the Nicaraguan legislative committee with oversight of Nicaraguan telecommunications. The alleged improper payments related to BellSouth's purported efforts to accomplish the repeal by the Nicaraguan legislature of a foreign ownership restriction in effect in the telecommunications industry. BellSouth owned 49% of Telefonia and had an option to purchase an additional 40%. The foreign ownership restriction prohibited foreign companies from acquiring a majority interest in Nicaraguan telecommunications companies.

According to the Complaint, in October 1998, Telefonia retained the wife of a Nicaraguan legislator to provide regulatory and legislative services, including lobbying for the repeal of the foreign ownership restriction. The legislator, whose wife Telefonia retained, chaired the legislative committee with jurisdiction over the foreign ownership restriction. The legislator's wife had no legislative experience, although she did have experience in the financial and operational aspects of the telecommunications industry. BellSouth International knew that payments to the lobbyist could implicate the FCPA, yet a BellSouth International attorney approved the payments.

The Complaint alleges that the legislator drafted the text of a proposed repeal of the foreign ownership restriction and held hearings on the issue. In May 1999 BellSouth terminated the lobbyist, providing her with a severance payment in June 1999. Total payments to the lobbyist amounted to US$60,000. In September 1999, the legislative committee referred the proposed repeal to the Nicaraguan National Assembly. In December 1999, the Assembly voted to repeal the restriction and BellSouth exercised its 40% option in June 2000, thereby increasing its ownership interest in Telefonia to 89%.

On 15th January 2002 the SEC issued a related, settled cease-and-desist order against BellSouth finding violations of the books and records provisions and the internal controls provisions of the Securities Exchange Act of 1934. The Order cites BellSouth's cooperation with the SEC and the several remedial measures undertaken by BellSouth, including disciplining and terminating various employees. The Order also notes that BellSouth has initiated an enhanced compliance program.

United States v. Kay, 200 F. Supp. 2d 681 (SDTX) (18th April 2002); *SEC v. Murphy,* H-02-2908 (SDTX); Litigation Release 17651 (1st August 2002); Litigation Release 18925 (7th October 2004) (*American Rice*)

The *American Rice* case constituted a significant challenge to the broad interpretation afforded the "obtain or retain business" element of the FCPA. The criminal indictment against former corporate officers Douglas Murphy and David Kay was dismissed by the US District Court for the Southern District of Texas (SD Texas) on the grounds that the FCPA did not apply to bribes to gain better tax treatment. The DOJ appealed the decision and the SEC pursued civil remedies against Murphy and Kay in a parallel proceeding alleging the same conduct. The US Court of Appeals for the Fifth Circuit (Fifth Circuit) reversed the lower court decision and substantially adopted the government's position.

The SEC enforcement matter.[180] In July 2002, the SEC filed suit in SD Texas against two former officers of American Rice Co, Inc who allegedly authorised more than US$500,000 in bribery payments to Haitian officials. The SEC alleged that Douglas Murphy and David

---

[180] The Complaint in this matter is available at www.sec.gov/litigation/Complaints/comp17651.htm.

Kay authorised payments during 1998 and 1999 in order to reduce American Rice's import taxes by approximately US$1.5 million. American Rice was a public company with headquarters in Houston, Texas.

The SEC alleged that Murphy was American Rice's president and one of its directors, and Kay was the company's vice-president of Caribbean operations, during the relevant period. According to the Complaint, Kay directed an American Rice employee to prepare false shipping records and underreport the tonnage of rice arriving on certain vessels. Customs officials in Haiti used the false records to clear the vessels through customs. At Kay's direction, American Rice employees paid cash bribes to customs officials after the vessels cleared customs. Kay allegedly directed the American Rice controller in Haiti to record the payments as routine business expenditures in order to conceal the nature of the payments. The Complaint alleges that American Rice employees made at least 12 bribery payments totalling approximately US$500,000 in order for the company to avoid US$1.5 million in import taxes.

The Commission charged that Murphy was aware of the bribery scheme but took no action to stop the payments and that Lawrence Theriot, formerly the Caribbean operations consultant for American Rice, allegedly assisted Kay and Murphy by monitoring the bribery scheme and exploring alternative arrangements.

On 30th January 2003, American Rice, Joseph A Schwartz, Jr, Joel R Malebranche and Allen W Sturdivant consented to the issuance of an order requiring that they cease-and-desist from committing or causing any future violations of the Securities Exchange Act of 1934. The Order included a finding that Schwartz, the former controller for Haitian operations, and employees Malebranche and Sturdivant had participated in a scheme to bribe Haitian customs officials in violation of the FCPA. The order included a finding that American Rice had violated the books and records component of the FCPA.

On 30th December 2004, Lawrence Theriot settled the SEC matter without admitting or denying the underlying factual allegations. Theriot agreed to pay an US$11,000 civil penalty and to be enjoined from future FCPA violations.

The criminal matter. The SD Texas dismissed the indictments against Murphy and Kay on the grounds that the challenged payments were not covered by the FCPA because they were not made to obtain or retain business in Haiti. In ruling on the defendants' motion to dismiss for failure to state an offence, the court held that neither the language of the FCPA nor the legislative history supported the Government's argument that the FCPA encompassed payments made to reduce customs duties or tax obligations. Defendants argued that the alleged payments to Haitian officials, if made, could not have been for the purpose of obtaining or retaining new business, since American Rice had already established its business in Haiti. Instead, the payments, if made, were made to reduce customs duties and taxes on incoming goods. The government responded that Defendants' payments to reduce customs duties "were essential for [American Rice] to be able to conduct business in Haiti and, thus, the payments constituted prohibited payments made to retain business.[181] In holding that "Congress has considered and rejected statutory language that would broaden the scope of the FCPA to cover the conduct in question here", the court noted that Congress considered and rejected two bills that would have broadened the scope of the Act's prohibited activities. The House bill prohibited corrupt payments to foreign officials used to influence "any act of decision of such foreign official in his official capacity".[182] The Senate bill prohibited any payments made for the purpose of "obtaining or retaining business . . . or directing business to, any person or influencing legislation or regulations of [the foreign government]…".[183] The court noted that Congress rejected these proposals in favour of the "obtain or retain business" language, and referenced the 1977 Conference Committee Report that stated that "the purpose of the payment must be to influence any act or decision of a foreign official (including a decision not to act) or induce such official to use his influence to affect a government act or decision so as to assist an issuer in obtaining, retaining or directing business to any person".[184] The court also noted that Congress rejected subsequent efforts to amend the "obtain or retain business" language.

---

181 *US v. Kay*, 200 F.Supp.2d at 682.
182 *Id* at 684, citing H.R. 3815, 95th Cong. §2 (1977).
183 *Id*, citing S. 305, 95th Cong. §103 (1977).
184 *Id*, citing H.R. Conf. Rep. No. 95–831, at 12 (1977).

The Fifth Circuit's decision. The Fifth Circuit reversed the lower court decision, rejecting the argument that, as a matter of law, the challenged payments were not covered by the FCPA because they were not made to obtain or retain business. While agreeing with the lower court that the scope of the business nexus element contained in the statute was not explicit, the Court stated that the legislative history of the statute demonstrated that "Congress meant to prohibit a range of payments wider than only those that directly influence the acquisition or retention of government contracts or similar commercial or industrial arrangements".[185] The Court held that payments to reduce taxes or customs duties *could be* illicit payments subject to the FCPA if they were made to assist in obtaining and retaining business. The Court rejected the government's position that payments to reduce taxes or customs duties were, as a matter of law, made to assist in obtaining or retaining business, holding instead that the government must show that the payments were made to assist a defendant in obtaining or retaining specific business. In addition, *the Court held that the indictment must explain "the nexus between reduced taxes and obtaining identified business opportunities and retaining identified business opportunities"* (emphasis added).

Resolution of the criminal matter. Following the Fifth Circuit's decision to reverse the lower court's order to dismiss and to remand for consideration of what additional allegations might have to be included in the indictment, the matter was indicted and the case proceeded to trial. On 6th October 2004, Kay and Murphy were found guilty following the trial of violating the FCPA.[186] Murphy was also convicted of obstruction of justice in connection with the SEC investigation.

The ramifications of American Rice. While the decision to reverse the lower court decision in American Rice is technically limited to the Fifth Circuit, the Court's decision to uphold the government's expansive view of the business nexus prong will have a significant impact on the enforcement climate going forward. The decision supports the view that almost any payment *intended to influence* a foreign government official could fall under the Act if the foreign

---

[185] *US v. Kay*, No. 02-20588 at 22 (5th Cir. 4th February 2004).
[186] *See* Litigation Release 18925 (7th October 2004).

government official's decision could have a positive impact on the company's business.

An additional impact of the reversal in *United States v. Kay* is that it upheld the US' image in the international regulatory system. A decision that activities such as bribing foreign officials to obtain beneficial tax treatment are not covered by the Act would potentially have placed the United States in violation of the Organisation for Economic Cooperation and Development Convention on Combating Bribery of Foreign Offical in International Business Transactions (OECD Convention). The OECD Convention provides that members will criminalise payments made to foreign officials "in order to obtain or retain business or *other improper advantage in the conduct of international business*" (OECD Convention, art. 1(1)) (emphasis added).

While the government recovered from the lower court decision holding that payments to reduce taxes or customs duties were not payments made to assist in obtaining or retaining business, it is important to note that the American Rice case ultimately resulted in a higher burden in indicting and ultimately prevailing in FCPA cases. The requirement that the government demonstrate that the payments were made to assist a defendant in obtaining or retaining specific business, and the requirement that the indictment explain the nexus between reduced taxes and obtaining identified business opportunities and retaining identified business opportunities, are not insignificant hurdles for the government. Indeed, it may be that the SEC's decision to file an unopposed motion to dismiss its appeal in *SEC v. Eric Mattson*, discussed above, was due in part to the increased burden imposed by *United States v. Kay*.[187]

SEC v. Syncor International Corporation, Case No. 02CV02421 (USD.C., DDC 10th December 2002); United States v. Syncor Taiwan, Inc, Case No. 02-CR01244 (C.D. Cal.), SEC Litigation Release 17887 (10th December 2002)
On 10th December 2002, the SEC filed two settled enforcement proceedings, a Complaint and an administrative order, charging Syncor International Corporation (Syncor) with violating the FCPA. In addition, Syncor entered a guilty plea in the criminal matter.

---

[187] *See SEC v. Eric Mattson,* Litigation Release 18863 (1st September 2004.).

The SEC charged Syncor with violating the anti-bribery provisions of the FCPA as well as the books and records and internal controls provisions of the FCPA. Pursuant to its agreement, Syncor consented to a final judgment requiring it to pay a US$500,000 civil penalty and to the issuance of the administrative order. As part of its agreement, Syncor was required to retain an independent consultant to review and make recommendations concerning the company's FCPA compliance policies and procedures.

The SEC alleged that Syncor's foreign subsidiaries in Taiwan, Mexico, Belgium, Luxembourg and France made a total of at least US$600,000 in illicit payments to doctors employed by hospitals controlled by foreign authorities. The motive for the payments, according to the SEC, was to obtain or retain business with them and with the hospitals. The SEC alleged that the payments, which began in the mid-1980s, where made with the knowledge and approval of senior officers of the relevant Syncor subsidiaries, and in some cases with the knowledge and approval of Syncor's founder and chairman of the board. According to the Complaint, the payments were improperly recorded as promotional and advertising expenses.

The SEC noted in its Litigation Release that the settlement arrangement was affected by Syncor's full cooperation with the Commission staff. The SEC also noted that Syncor brought the matter to the attention of the SEC and the DOJ promptly upon becoming aware of the problem when notified by another company conducting due diligence in anticipation of a merger with Syncor.

In the criminal matter, Syncor Taiwan, Inc, a subsidiary of Syncor, agreed to plead guilty to one count of violating the anti-bribery provision of the FCPA and to pay a US$2 million fine. According to the DOJ, Syncor Taiwan made payments amounting to at least US$344,110 between 1st January 1997 and 6th November 2002 in order to obtain and retain business from hospitals owned by the legal authorities in Taiwan. The payments were allegedly authorised by the company's board chairman while in the Central District of California, and paid in cash in Taiwan via hand-delivered, sealed envelopes.[188] In addition, the DOJ alleged Syncor Taiwan made at least US$113,007 in illicit payments to physicians

---

188 *See* US Department of Justice Release 02-CRM-707 (10th December 2002).

employed by hospitals owned by the legal authorities in Taiwan in exchange for patient referrals to Syncor Taiwan's medical imaging centres.

While the nature of the alleged activity in the *Syncor* matter clearly qualifies as conduct for the purpose of obtaining and retaining business, the case is significant in two respects. First, the case demonstrates the intent of US authorities to aggressively pursue allegations of FCPA violations in the wake of the District Court decision in *American Rice*. Second, it demonstrates that, at least in the short term, *American Rice* has not altered the approach of the SEC or the DOJ in taking an expansive view of the scope of the statute. The alleged recipients of the payments from Syncor and its subsidiaries were doctors at hospitals run by government agencies. The SEC and the DOJ treated these recipients as "foreign officials, officials of foreign political parties, or any other person acting as a conduit for payments to foreign officials or political parties" designated by the statute.[189] Because both the civil and criminal matters were negotiated to resolution, the interpretation of the statute as covering payments to doctors working in hospitals operated by government agencies was not challenged.

In the matter of Schering Plough Corp., Litigation Release 49838 (9th June 2004); *SEC v. Schering-Plough Corp.,* 04CV00945 (PLF) (DDC) (9th June 2004)

On 9th June 2004, the SEC filed a settled Complaint and administrative order. The SEC alleged violations of Sections 13(b)(2)(A) and 13(b)(2)(B) of the Exchange Act. The findings contained in the administrative order described Schering-Plough's alleged violations of the books and records and internal controls provisions of the FCPA, through certain payments made by Schering-Plough Poland (SP Poland) to influence decisions made by a Polish governmental official. SP Poland, with headquarters in Warsaw, Poland, is a branch office of Schering-Plough Central East AG, which is a wholly owned subsidiary of Schering-Plough.

According to the SEC, SP Poland paid 315,800 zlotys, approximately US$76,000, to the Chudow Castle Foundation, to induce the

---

[189] While the allegations resolved through the SEC settlement and the guilty plea related to these recipients, both enforcement authorities alleged that Syncor made similar payments to doctors at private facilities.

Director of the Foundation to influence the purchase of Schering-Plough's pharmaceutical products within the Silesian Health Fund. The Chudow Castle Foundation was a charitable organisation whose mission was to restore castles and other historic sites in the Silesian region of Poland. The founder of the Foundation was the Director of the Selesian Health Fund, one of 16 regional government health authorities in Poland. The administrative order describes a series of payments by SP Poland to the Chudow Castle Foundation between February 1999 and March 2002. The administrative order states that some of the payments were structured in such a way as to conceal the nature of the payments and that the payments were made without the knowledge or approval of any Schering-Plough employee in the United States. According to the SEC, the SP Poland oncology unit manager provided false medical justifications for most of the payments on the documents he submitted to the company's finance department. All the payments to the Foundation were classified by SP Poland in its books and records as donations; however, the SEC's findings stated that, while the payments were made to a bona fide charity, they were made to influence the Director with respect to the purchase of Schering-Plough's products and were viewed as "dues" SP Poland was required to pay for assistance from the Director.

The SEC found that Schering-Plough's policies and procedures for detecting possible FCPA violations by its foreign subsidiaries were inadequate in that they did not require employees to conduct any due diligence prior to making promotional or charitable donations to determine whether any government officials were affiliated with proposed recipients. The SEC found that Schering-Plough should have been alerted to the FCPA issues related to SP Poland's payments to the Chudow Castle Foundation because:

(1) the Foundation is not a health care related entity, yet still received payments;
(2) the magnitude of the payments in relationship to Schering-Plough's budget for such donations;
(3) the apparent structuring of payments by the unit manager, which allowed him to exceed his authorisation limits; and
(4) the Director was the founder and Chairman of the Foundation and also a Polish government official with the ability to influence

the purchase of SP Poland's products by hospitals within the Silesian Health Fund.

Without admitting or denying the allegations in the Complaint, Schering-Plough consented to the entry of a final judgment by the Court that required the company to pay a US$500,000 civil penalty. Pursuant to the settled administrative order, Schering-Plough, without admitting or denying the findings contained in the Order, consented to the requirement in the Order that it cease-and-desist from committing or causing any violations and any future violations of Sections 13(b)(2)(A) and 13(b)(2)(B) of the Exchange Act, and agreed to a series of undertakings, including the following:

- to retain, within 30 days of the issuance of the Order, an independent consultant to review and evaluate Schering-Plough's internal controls, record keeping and financial reporting policies and procedures as they relate to FCPA compliance;
- to require that the independent consultant issue a report within 150 days after being retained, recommending policies and procedures reasonably designed to ensure compliance with the FCPA. The report is to be provided to the SEC at the same time it is issued to Schering-Plough;
- to adopt all recommendations in the report within 60 days of receiving the report, unless the independent consultant agrees to an alternative policy, procedure or system proposed by Schering-Plough;
- to require that the independent consultant enter into an agreement that provides that the independent consultant not enter into any professional relationship with Schering-Plough or its affiliates for a two-year period following the completion of the report.

SEC v. ABB Ltd, 04CV1141 (RBW) (DDC) (6th July 2004), Litigation Release 18775 (6th July 2004)

On 6th July 2004, the SEC filed a settled enforcement action in the US District Court for the District of Columbia charging ABB Ltd (ABB) with violating the anti-bribery, books and records and internal accounting controls provisions of the FCPA. Two of ABB Ltd's affiliates were charged by the DOJ in parallel criminal proceedings.

The SEC's allegations. ABB Ltd is a global provider of power and automation technology with headquarters in Zurich, Switzerland.

In its Complaint, the SEC alleged that ABB's US and foreign-based subsidiaries doing business in Nigeria, Angola and Kazakhstan offered and made illicit payments totalling over US$1.1 million to government officials in the three countries. The SEC alleged that that the payments occurred over a five-year period, from 1998 through to early 2003. The SEC alleged that the payments were made with the knowledge and approval of certain management-level personnel at the relevant ABB subsidiaries and that at least US$865,726 of the payments were made after ABB became a reporting company in the United States in April 2001. The SEC charged that ABB improperly recorded the payments in its accounting books and records and lacked any meaningful internal controls to prevent or detect such payments.

Nigeria. The SEC alleged that, from 1998 through to 2001, employees of Vetco Gray US and Vetco Gray UK provided cash and gifts to officials of the National Petroleum Investment Management Service (NAPIMS), the Nigerian state-owned agency responsible for overseeing Nigeria's investment in petroleum exploration and production. The SEC alleged that the payments were intended to influence NAPIMS' consideration of Vetco Gray Nigeria's bids on oil and gas projects in Nigeria. According to the Complaint, the majority of the payments related to the Bonga Oil Field Project, and were made through an intermediary and characterised as consulting payments rendered by the intermediary's companies. The SEC alleged that other related payments were made in the United States by an employee of Vetco Gray US.

Angola. The SEC Complaint alleged that ABB made similar illicit payments to officials of Sonangol, the Angolan state-owned oil company. The payments were made to Sonangol engineers who had responsibility for the technical evaluation of bids submitted to Sonangol, and were issued in the form of three separate training trips sponsored by ABB from 2000 to 2002. The SEC alleged that the three trips included two trips to the United States and Brazil and one trip to Norway and the UK. For each trip, ABB's Vetco Gray US and UK subsidiaries paid all the travel, meals, lodging and entertainment expenses of the Sonangol engineers, and provided them with cash spending money of US$120–200 per day. The Complaint alleged that Angola's gross annual per capita income was US$710.

The Complaint alleged that ABB employees undertook to hide the true nature of the payments by funnelling the payments through friends of the employees, who were then reimbursed by other companies related to the Vetco Gray subsidiaries. The SEC charged that the "per diem" payments were made despite a warning from one of the in-house attorneys at an ABB US subsidiary in 2000 that the payments were a "red flag" and a potential "violation of the FCPA".

Kazakhstan. The SEC Complaint alleged that in April 2001, Vetco Gray US and ABB Kazakhstan Ltd entered into a wellhead supply contract, and a related service contract, with TengizChevroil (TCO). TCO was a joint venture that was 20% owned by Kazakhstan's state oil company, KazMunaiGas. The SEC alleged that, in December 2001, ABB Kazakhstan began making payments to Kazakhstan companies owned by ABB Kazakhstan's former sales manager, who was at the time a government official employed in the country's state-owned oils and gas companies. The SEC alleged that six payments were made to five separate entities owned by the official and that the payments were made for the purpose of obtaining or retaining business. The Complaint charges that the payments were made pursuant to sham contracts for purportedly legitimate consulting services related to the maintenance of drilling equipment, but that no such services were actually performed. The payments were allegedly documented with phoney invoices, and improperly recorded as ordinary business expenses, to mislead ABB's auditors.

The resolution. Simultaneously with the filing of the SEC Complaint, and without admitting or denying the findings in the final judgment, ABB consented to the entry of a final judgment enjoining it from future violations of the FCPA and requiring ABB:

- to pay US$5.9 million in disgorgement and prejudgment interest;
- to pay a US$10.5 million penalty, which would be deemed satisfied by two of its affiliates' payments of criminal fines totalling the same amount in parallel criminal proceedings brought by the DOJ; and
- to retain an independent consultant to review the company's FCPA compliance policies and procedures.

The SEC noted in its litigation release announcing the settlement that ABB's decision to alert the SEC Staff and the DOJ to the misconduct, along with its cooperation with the SEC Staff during the course of the investigation, contributed to the nature of the settlement. Specifically, the SEC stated that the decision to allow ABB's US$10.5 million penalty obligation to be deemed satisfied by its affiliates payments in the criminal proceedings was based upon the company's cooperation.

The parallel criminal proceedings. In the criminal proceedings, the DOJ filed FCPA charges against ABB Vetco Gray, Inc, an ABB subsidiary located in Houston, TX, and ABB Vetco Gray UK, Ltd, based in Aberdeen, Scotland. Both subsidiaries entered guilty pleas in the US District Court for the Southern District of Texas. Each subsidiary agreed to plead guilty to two counts of violating the FCPA anti-bribery provisions. Each subsidiary agreed to pay one half of the US$10.5 million in criminal fines related to the conduct.

In the matter of Monsanto Co, Administration Proceeding 3-11789; Litigation Release 50978 (6th January 2005)

On 6th January 2005, Monasanto consented to an order requiring that it cease-and-desist from future violations of the FCPA, pay a US$500,000 penalty and take certain remedial actions. This matter related to alleged violations of the FCPA stemming from Monsanto's operations in Indonesia.

The SEC's allegations. According to the SEC's Order, in 2002 a senior Monsanto manager responsible for certain activities in the Asia Pacific region authorised and directed an Indonesian consulting firm to make an illegal US$50,000 payment to a senior Indonesian Ministry of Environment official. The purpose of the payment was to influence the official to repeal an unfavourable decree requiring an environmental impact study before authorising the cultivation of genetically modified crops.[190] In order to fund the US$50,000 payment, the senior Monsanto manager caused a consulting firm employee to create false invoices in the amount of US$66,000, which would total the US$50,000 payment plus the tax consequences of the consulting firm reporting the payment as consulting fee income. The consulting firm provided the US$50,000 to the Indonesian official, then invoiced Monsanto for US$66,000.

---

190 Despite the payment, the decree was not repealed.

The SEC also alleged that, from 1997 to 2002, Monsanto inaccurately recorded or failed to record in its books and records approximately US$700,000 of illegal or questionable payments made to various Indonesian government officials. According to the SEC, the US$700,000 was derived from a bogus product registration scheme undertaken by Monsanto's Indonesian affiliates. Monsanto's Indonesian affiliates used nominees to inflate sales of the company's pesticide products through over-invoicing and fictitious sales. The funds resulting from these efforts were used to make illicit payments to Indonesian government officials and their families, including payment for the purchase of land and construction of a house in the name of the wife of a senior Ministry of Agriculture official.

According to the SEC, Monsanto did not become aware of improprieties at its Indonesian affiliates until March 2001. This was in part due to efforts at the affiliates to mask the payments and in part due to Monsanto's failure to conduct internal audits of its Indonesian affiliates.

The resolution. Without admitting or denying the SEC's factual findings, Monsanto consented to an order requiring it to cease-and-desist from future violations of the FCPA's anti-bribery and books and records and internal control provisions. In addition, the company agreed to a series of undertakings, including the retention of an independent consultant to review the company's FCPA compliance policies and procedures and prepare a report for submission to Monsanto's Board of Directors and the SEC. In addition, the agreement requires the company to adopt the independent consultant's recommendations unless it can demonstrate that the recommendations are unduly burdensome and can propose an alternative action.

The SEC noted in its litigation release announcing the settlement that Monsanto's remedial actions and cooperation with the SEC Staff influenced its decision to accept the settlement agreement.

The parallel criminal proceedings. In the criminal proceedings, Monsanto entered into a deferred prosecution agreement in the US District Court for the District of Columbia. The company agreed to a US$1 million fine and to various remedial undertakings consistent with those in the SEC matter. The DOJ agreed to dismiss the criminal information after three years if Monsanto fully complies with the terms of the deferred prosecution agreement.

SEC v. The Titan Corporation, No: 05-0411 (DDC) (1st March 2005), Litigation Release 2204 (1st March 2005)
On 1st March 2005 the SEC announced the filing of a settled enforcement action charging The Titan Corporation (Titan), a California-based military intelligence company, with violating the anti-bribery, internal controls and books and records provisions of the FCPA.

The SEC's allegations. According to the Complaint, Titan paid more than US$3.5 million to its agent in Benin, Africa during the period of 1999 through to 2001. The agent was known at the time by Titan to be the President of Benin's business advisor. The SEC alleged that Titan failed to conduct any meaningful due diligence into the background of the agent and failed to assure that the services alleged to be performed by the agent were in fact performed.

According to the SEC, in 2001 approximately US$2 million was funnelled through the agent, at the direction of a senior Titan officer located in the United States, to the election campaign of Benin's then incumbent President and to reimburse the agent for the purchase of T-shirts with the President's picture and instructions to vote for him. Titan allegedly made the payments to assist the company in its development of a telecommunications project in Benin and to obtain the Benin government's consent to an increase in the percentage of Titan's project management fees for the project. The SEC alleged that the senior Titan officer directed that these payments be falsely invoiced by the agent as consulting services and that the payments be broken into small increments and spread out over time. In addition, the SEC alleged that, from 1999 to 2003, Titan improperly recorded payments in its books and records and directed agents to falsify invoices submitted to Titan.

The Complaint stated that Titan falsified documents that enabled its agents to under-report local commission payments in Nepal, Bangladesh and Sri Lanka and falsified documents presented to the US government by under-reporting payments on equipment exported to Sri Lanka, France and Japan. In addition, the Complaint alleged that Titan paid a World Bank Group analyst in cash to assist Titan in its project in Benin and paid a Benin government official approximately US$14,000 in travel expenses from 1999 to 2001.

With respect to internal controls, the SEC alleged that Titan never had a formal company-wide FCPA policy, failed to implement an

FCPA compliance program, disregarded or circumvented the limited FCPA policies in effect, failed to maintain sufficient due diligence files on its foreign agents and failed to have meaningful oversight over its foreign agents.

The resolution. Without admitting or denying the allegations in the Complaint, Titan consented to the entry of a final judgment permanently enjoining it from future violation of the FCPA and requiring that Titan:

(1) pay US$15.479 million in disgorgement and prejudgment interest;
(2) pay a US$13 million penalty, which will be deemed satisfied by Titan's payment of criminal fines of that amount in the parallel criminal proceeding; and
(3) retain an independent consultant to review the company's FCPA compliance and procedures and adopt and implement the consultant's recommendations.

The Report of Investigation (21(a) Report). The SEC also issued a 21(a) Report in this matter, to provide guidance regarding potential liability under the federal securities laws stemming from false or misleading disclosures in merger and other agreements. The SEC did not charge Titan under this theory, but noted that Titan represented in merger discussions with Lockheed Martin Corporation[191] that neither Titan nor any director, officer, agent or employee of Titan or its subsidiaries had taken any action that would violate the FCPA. In its 21(a) Report, the SEC alleged that this representation was publicly disclosed by Titan.

The SEC states in the 21(a) Report that when an issuer makes a public disclosure such as Titan's FCPA disclosure in the merger discussions with Lockheed Martin Corporation, it is required to "consider whether additional disclosure is necessary in order to put the information contained in, or otherwise incorporated into that publication, into context so that such information is not misleading". The SEC went on to say that the issuer cannot avoid the disclosure obligation "simply because the information published

---

[191] Merger negotiations were ongoing at the time Titan's conduct impacting on the FCPA came to light. The merger did not occur.

was contained in an agreement or other document not prepared as a disclosure document".

The parallel criminal proceedings. The US Attorney's Office for the Southern District of California and the DOJ Fraud Section brought criminal FCPA and tax charges against Titan. Titan entered a guilty plea before the US District Court for the Southern District of California on 1st March 2005. Titan pleaded guilty to one felony count of violating the anti-bribery provisions of the FCPA, one felony count for falsifying the books and records of Titan and one felony count for aiding and abetting in the filing of a false tax return. Titan agreed to pay a US$13 million fine.

IMPLICATIONS
Traditionally, when thinking about foreign corrupt practices, or the application of the FCPA, attention was focused solely on "domestic concerns" – in other words, individuals who are citizens, nationals or residents of the United States, or corporations, partnerships, associations, etc, which have their principal places of business in the United States or are organised under the laws of a state of the United States. The FCPA, however, has always provided the potential to reach beyond "domestic concerns" to foreign private issuers of securities in the United States. Internationalisation of the world's securities markets, and the equity provided by the US securities markets, have now brought that additional class of covered entities – foreign private issuers of securities – into US jurisdiction. Thus, whereas in the past focus has been principally on efforts of US companies to ensure that controls could be applied to their far flung operations, today, as increasing numbers of foreign corporations register their shares pursuant to the US securities laws, attention needs to be focused on the manner in which the operations of those foreign corporations are conducted.

As foreign companies are brought to the US markets, their investment bankers and advisors need to pay special attention from a due diligence standpoint to not only the corrupt payments issues, but also the controls issues, both with respect to corrupt payments and general accounting controls.

The SEC has demonstrated its commitment to enforcing both the accounting and the controls provisions against companies, be they foreign or domestic. Management should be especially vigilant of sweetheart deals. (What sorts of substantive services are "consultants" or brokers retained in foreign countries providing?) At bottom, however, the *Triton* and *BellSouth* cases underscore the importance of adequate internal controls since the company's US-based senior management would never have been in a position to detect or prevent the offences occurring in the distant Indonesian subsidiary in the former case or in Nicaragua with regard to the latter.

American employees working abroad need to be aware that, whatever the environment of the country in which they are operating, they are still subject to standards applicable in the United States. Conversely, foreign nationals working in foreign subsidiaries must be trained in and conditioned to abide by American standards for the conduct of business.

Investigation of offences under the FCPA by the SEC

On a worldwide basis, securities regulators have developed a successful multi-faceted approach to the enforcement and regulatory challenges posed by the internationalisation of the markets. While these understandings do not specifically include corrupt practices, they clearly include accounting and disclosure violations and thus it should be expected that the SEC will have the ability to obtain and provide assistance with respect to matters arising under the FCPA.

Cooperation among securities regulators to combat corruption

Recently, the SEC has successfully advocated a broad-based approach to fighting bribery in other international forums. In addition to efforts undertaken at the organisation for Economic Cooperation and Development to criminalise illicit payments, and at the Inter-American Convention Against Corruption, the SEC has been working with its regulatory counterparts to broaden cooperative efforts. At the encouragement of the SEC, the Council of Securities Regulators of the Americas (COSRA)[192] conducted a work plan to address ways that securities regulators can fight

---

[192] COSRA was formed in 1992 to strengthen cooperation among securities regulators within this hemisphere. Since its inception, COSRA has worked to develop principles for market development and oversight and to foster securities enforcement and regulatory cooperation within the region. Membership in COSRA is open to all securities regulatory authorities in the hemisphere.

foreign bribery. This work plan resulted in a Declaration on Combating Bribery in the Americas, which COSRA members signed in June 1996.

In connection with COSRA's implementation of the Summit of the America's Plan of Action for combating corruption, the organisation initiated a work program addressing the issue of illicit payments. Under this work program, COSRA members evaluated the approach to foreign bribery in place within their respective countries and the role securities regulators could play to further this approach. The work plan resulted in the signing, on 20th June 1996, of a Declaration on Combating Bribery in the Americas. By signing this Declaration, COSRA members state their intention to:

(1) develop and promote the effective enforcement of laws that address illicit payments by public companies;
(2) seek to ensure that independent auditors of public companies design appropriate audit procedures for the detection of illegal acts such as bribery; and
(3) provide mutual assistance in enforcing securities laws that relate to illicit payments, seeking to permit greater access to information for use by securities authorities during investigations and foster better communication among authorities investigating illicit payments.

Need for increased vigilance

It is a truism that as companies become increasingly international, their personnel and affiliates are constantly shifting from jurisdiction to jurisdiction. What may be legal in one jurisdiction may not be legal in another. Moreover, the expectations with respect to commissions or other payments may be very different from jurisdiction to jurisdiction. In the past, this has been an issue that was raised with respect to the legality of the actual payment. However, in today's era of internationalisation of markets and shifting of personnel between jurisdictions, the issue may actually be whether the conduct was legal in the country from which the activity emanated. Two examples of these issues follow below.

In many emerging markets, privatisation is just beginning to occur. Indeed some of the largest players in the market may not be private companies but rather might be public entities trading on behalf of the central bank or the government itself. People controlling such a portfolio are often government officials within the meaning of the FCPA. As do their private counterparts, these officials often receive soft dollars – be they monetary rebates or services – related to the amount of activity they generate for broker–dealers

A second illustration of this problem would occur where a trader of a large multi-national bank, who had operated in a jurisdiction where foreign corrupt practices are not yet outlawed, is transferred to a trading room in the United States. The employee may be fully aware of all of the operations and requirements of the multi-national bank for whom he or she works; however, he or she continues the activity, which was legal when it emanated from the non-US country where he or she was previously located. Thus, what may have been a legal payment of fees or sharing of a commission may be converted into a corrupt act using the means and instrumentalities of interstate commerce. What level of knowledge should be required for this conduct on the part of the bank's management?

Given the aggressiveness of the SEC's enforcement, companies should proactively evaluate their internal controls in order to assure their adequacy for this purpose. Indeed, it is advisable for companies that are conducting their international business from many locations to re-evaluate whether the controls they have in place are appropriate both for detecting and addressing foreign corrupt payment activity that could be subject to US jurisdiction.

CONCLUSION

The dynamic nature of the global securities markets has required regulators and courts to assess the effectiveness of existing regulatory schemes, and to develop new and creative measures to enhance market integrity and protect investors. Securities regulators will undoubtedly continue to explore their authority to investigate violations of the federal securities laws both by agreement and in foreign courts as the global markets expand and develop. Unquestionably, as world markets have evolved, the success of US regulators in achieving effective cooperation with foreign counterparts is chiefly related to the evolution of laws similar to our own countries in around the world. In fact, assistance now is sought from the SEC as often as the SEC seeks it. The greatest challenge for regulators will be to keep pace with rapidly evolving markets and dramatic advances in technology.

Ironically, the expansion of the regulation of markets worldwide and better cooperation is resulting in a limitation of the power of US regulators to act as *parens patrie* for the global marketplace. For the first time, the US courts have begun to re-evaluate the expansive interpretation of US jurisdiction. This limitation on the assertion of authority by the United States reflects the understanding that, in some circumstances, regulators in another jurisdiction may have a greater interest in enforcement against securities law violators and, more importantly, that sufficient regulatory protection exists in those jurisdictions to justify the reluctance of the SEC and the US courts to become involved. The recent enactment of SOX constitutes an attempt to return to the *parens patrie* role, but its reception by the international community may cause US regulators to re-evaluate its practical implementation.

9

Enforcement of US Securities Laws

Colleen P Mahoney
Skadden Arps LLP

THE SEC AND THE DIVISION OF ENFORCEMENT

The SEC was established in 1934 under the Exchange Act which, like the Securities Act, was motivated by the 1929 stock market crash. The SEC is the agency principally entrusted with the enforcement and administration of the federal securities laws. While the Commission itself is composed of five commissioners, the daily enforcement and administration of the securities laws is largely in the hands of the SEC Staff – in particular, the Division of Enforcement.

The SEC is divided into principal operating divisions of which the Division of Enforcement is one. Enforcement Staff members number approximately 350 at the SEC's Washington, D.C. headquarters, and another 600 or so in the SEC's five regional and six district offices around the country. These Staff members investigate possible securities laws violations and make recommendations to the Commission regarding enforcement actions. Only the five-person Commission, however, can authorise the bringing of an enforcement action or the settlement of an action.

In fiscal year 2004, the SEC initiated 635 enforcement actions in various program areas, including securities offering cases, issuer financial statement and reporting cases, broker-dealer cases, insider trading cases and market manipulation cases.[1] According to the 2003 SEC Annual Report, the first full year after

---

1   The 2004 SEC Annual Report has not yet been published. Information regarding fiscal year 2004 has been gleaned from various SEC documents.

the passage of SOX, the Commission obtained orders requiring defendants to disgorge illicit profits of approximately US$900 million and orders imposing approximately US$1.1 billion in civil penalties.

SUMMARY OF US FEDERAL SECURITIES LAWS LIKELY TO AFFECT FOREIGN INVESTORS AND MULTINATIONAL TRANSACTIONS

In order to discuss the international enforcement of the US securities laws, it is important to understand some of the most common obligations one has under those laws, the violation of which could lead the SEC to investigate and possibly to take enforcement action. This section of the chapter summarises materials previously discussed in this book, namely the registration requirements under the Securities Act, Regulation S and Rule 144A thereunder, as well as the Exchange Act and aspects of the FCPA, and describes the impact of these statutes on multinational transactions.

Registration under the securities act

The Securities Act prohibits the use of interstate commerce and the mails to sell securities unless a registration statement is in effect. The Securities Act also prohibits sending a prospectus that does not meet certain statutory requirements. "Interstate commerce" includes trade, commerce, transportation or any communication relating to securities between any foreign country and any part of the United States. The Securities Act's registration requirements therefore operate on all offerings made within the United States or where the United States' interstate commerce facilities are used.

Regulation S

Following a literal reading of Section 5 of the Securities Act, this act's registration requirement would apply in any case where interstate commerce was used. So, eg, any offering by a US issuer to foreign investors would trigger the Securities Act's registration requirements and have to be registered. Nonetheless, as a result of concern about the promotion of foreign investment in the United States, the SEC in 1964 issued a release stating that it would not take enforcement action for failure to register an offering made exclusively to foreign investors if the offering were made to prevent the distribution or redistribution of the offered securities in the United States or to US persons.[2]

Then in 1990, the Commission went further and adopted Regulation S. Regulation S provides a safe harbor for issuers, distributors and their affiliates, and for certain resales by other persons. To qualify for the safe harbor, sales must be made offshore and there can be no directed selling efforts in the United States. The transactions also must meet certain other criteria to maximise the likelihood that the shares come to rest offshore. These requirements were recently tightened to eliminate potential abuses. For example, the holding period to take advantage of the safe harbour was lengthened from 40 days to 1 year.

Rule 144A

At the same time it originally adopted Regulation S, the SEC also adopted Rule 144A.[3] This rule enables any issuer to effect a distribution to QIBs in the United States without having to register under the Securities Act. The theory was that large institutions (or QIBs) did not need the protection of Securities Act registration. Rule 144A exempts only resales; an exemption is still required for the initial sale by the issuer. The securities offered may not be of the same class as securities already listed on a US exchange, and publicity in the US must be limited. Rule 144A provides a safe harbour for foreign issuers wishing to reach a portion of the US market.

Reporting under the exchange act

The Exchange Act requires public companies to file periodic and other transaction related reports with the SEC containing certain financial information about the company, its officers and directors and its operations. Foreign issuers are required to file annual reports on Form 20-F; including financial statements reconciled to US GAAP each year. Foreign issuers also must submit interim reports on Form 6-K that includes information the company is required to make public under its own laws.

---

2 Securities Act Release 4708 (9th July 1964).
3 Securities Act Release 6862 (23rd April 1990).

Rule 15a-6

Section 15(a) of the Exchange Act provides that any broker-dealer using the US mails or interstate commerce facilities to carry out securities transactions must register as a broker or dealer with the Commission. Rule 15a-6, among other things, affords a safe harbor for non-US broker-dealers who simply execute unsolicited transactions or who solicit US persons who are major US institutional investors by furnishing them with research reports. The safe harbor also extends to foreign broker-dealers whose transactions are effected only through a US registered broker or dealer.

The Antifraud provisions of the US federal securities laws

Both the Securities Act and the Exchange Act have general antifraud provisions that prohibit fraud in connection with the offer, purchase or sale of any security. These provisions essentially prohibit the making of any materially false statement, the omission of a material fact or participation in any fraudulent, deceptive or manipulative scheme. These provisions are applied to a broad range of misconduct, including insider trading, financial fraud and market manipulation.

The Foreign corrupt practices act

As discussed in more detail in Chapter 8, the FCPA prohibits the bribery of foreign officials. However, payments for a "routine government action" are not prohibited. Moreover, it is a defense under the FCPA if a payment, gift, etc, is permissible under the written laws of the country where the payment is made or the gift is given. The FCPA also obliges issuers to maintain books and records that accurately reflect transactions and dispositions of the company's assets and to establish and maintain a system of internal accounting controls. The FCPA was amended in 1998 to implement the Convention of the OECD on Combating Bribery of Foreign Public Officials in International Business Transactions. Among other things, the amendments extend the jurisdictional reach of the FCPA to:

(1) US persons or entities acting outside the United States; and
(2) non-US persons acting within US territory. These changes add nationality-based and territorial-based jurisdiction-to-jurisdiction based on use of the mails or interstate commerce.

SARBANES–OXLEY
Adoption of SOX

The rash of significant financial restatements by well-known public companies and the continued decline in the securities markets prompted Congress to pass SOX the most significant securities legislation brought into force since the Exchange Act in 1934. SOX applies to all public companies that either have registered securities under Section 12 of the Exchange Act or are required to file periodic reports under Section 15(d) of the Exchange Act. SOX does not contain a general exemption for foreign private issuers.[4] SOX enacts a number of accounting and corporate governance reforms and directs the SEC to adopt additional regulations directed toward other areas of corporate reform.

All public companies have a host of new obligations under SOX including:

(1) the duty of the company's CEO and CFO to certify the company's financial reports;
(2) the duty of the audit committee of the board of directors to meet certain corporate governance criteria;
(3) the duty of the company to report material changes in its financial condition or operations in "real time;"
(4) the duty of management to create and disclose an internal controls report;
(5) the duty of the company to make disclosures concerning all material off-balance-sheet transactions; and
(6) the duty of the company to disclose whether it has adopted a code of ethics for senior financial officers. In addition, SOX prohibits a public company making loans to its officers (subject to important exceptions) and prohibits officers from trading securities during pension fund blackout periods. Finally, SOX requires that an executive repay to the company certain bonuses or other incentive-based compensation, as well as profits from the sale of the company's securities, if the company later has to restate a financial report due to misconduct.

---

[4] SOX does not apply to foreign private issuers that submit their information to the Commission under Rule 12g3–2(b) of the Exchange Act.

New forms of equitable relief available to the SEC

In any action brought or instituted by the SEC in federal court, SOX authorises the SEC to request, and a federal court to grant, "any equitable relief that may be appropriate or necessary for the benefit of investors."[5] In addition, whenever the SEC investigates a public company for possible violations of the securities laws, and it appears that it is likely that the company will make "extraordinary payments" to the company's directors, officers, partners, controlling persons, agents or employees, the SEC now has the ability to request that a federal court temporarily freeze those payments.[6] If a temporary order is entered, it can remain enforceable for up to ninety days.[7]

New criminal statutes and enhanced penalties

SOX creates several new criminal statutes and enhances the penalties for numerous other statutes. Two of the new criminal statutes are discussed above – the statutes prohibiting false CEO or CFO certifications of the company's financial statements and the destruction of accountants' work papers. The other new criminal statutes:

(i) prohibit improper influence on the conduct of audits;
(ii) prohibit retaliation against whistleblowers;
(iii) revise current prohibitions on the destruction of documents with the intent to frustrate federal investigations; and
(iv) expand current prohibitions on securities fraud.

Improper Influence on conduct of audits

SOX prohibits any officer or director of a public company or person acting at their direction from fraudulently influencing, coercing, manipulating or misleading any independent public or certified accounting firm for the purpose of rendering the financial statements materially misleading.[8] The SEC adopted final rules under this section of SOX that became effective on 26th June 2003.[9]

---

5   SOX Act, Section 305(b).
6   SOX Act, Section 1103(a).
7   Id.
8   SOX Act, Section 303(a).
9   SOX Act, Section 303(d). *See* Exchange Act Release 47890 (20th May 2003).

The new rules include examples of actions that could be seen as improperly influencing the auditor, including actions intended to coerce, manipulate, mislead, or fraudulently influence the auditor:

- to issue or reissue a report on the issuer's financial statements ie not warranted in the circumstances;
- not to perform audit, review or other procedures required by GAAP;
- not to withdraw an issued report; or
- not to communicate matters to an issuer's audit committee.[10]

Retaliation against whistle blowers
SOX places criminal liability upon anyone who takes any harmful action against a person with the intent to retaliate against that person for providing truthful information to a federal law enforcement officer relating to the commission or possible commission of any federal crime.[11] The maximum penalty for violation of this Section is ten years in prison and/or a fine.[12]

Document destruction
SOX imposes criminal sanctions upon anyone who knowingly alters, destroys, mutilates, conceals, covers up, falsifies, or makes a false entry in any record or tangible object with the intent to impede, obstruct, or influence the investigation of a federal agency or any bankruptcy case under Chapter 11 of the US Bankruptcy Code.[13] In order for the government to obtain a conviction under this statute, it need only prove that the destruction was "in relation to or contemplation of" a federal investigation or bankruptcy case, not that such an investigation or case was actually pending.[14] The maximum penalty for violation of this statute is twenty years and/or a fine.[15]

---

[10] *Id.*
[11] SOX Act, Section 1107.
[12] *Id.*
[13] SOX Act, Section 802.
[14] *Id.*
[15] *Id.*

New securities fraud statutes and penalties

SOX creates a new securities fraud statute, which provides criminal liability for anyone who executes a scheme or artifice to:

(1) defraud anyone in connection with any securities or
(2) obtain any money or property in connection with the sale of securities by means of false or fraudulent pretenses, representations or promises.[16] The maximum sentence under this provision is 25 years in prison and/or a fine. SOX also enhances the maximum penalties for willful violations of the securities laws by individuals by increasing the maximum term of imprisonment from ten to twenty years and increasing the maximum fines from US$1 million to US$5 million.[17] For anyone other than a natural person (eg, corporations), SOX increased the maximum fine from US$2.5 million to US$25 million.[18] SOX also increases the maximum penalties for a number of other statutes. For the mail and wire fraud statutes, SOX increases the maximum sentence from five to twenty years. For violations of ERISA, SOX increases the maximum penalty of imprisonment from one year to ten years, the maximum fine for natural persons from US$5,000 to US$100,000 and the maximum fine for non-natural persons from US$100,000 to US$500,000.[19] SOX also directs the United States Sentencing Commission to re-evaluate the Sentencing Guidelines in order to ensure that the Guidelines sufficiently reflect the serious nature of the offenses and penalties set forth in SOX.[20]

JURISDICTION

Generally

The extraterritorial reach of the US securities laws is clearly established. In order for the SEC, through the US courts, to apply the US securities laws to a foreign person or entity, a US court must have both subject matter jurisdiction and personal jurisdiction over the parties.

---

[16] SOX Act, Section 807.
[17] SOX Act, Section 1106.
[18] *Id.*
[19] SOX Act, Section 904.
[20] SOX Act, Section 905(b)(1).

Subject matter jurisdiction

US courts may hear and decide cases in connection with activities, even if occurring abroad, which have "substantial effects" in the United States. In analysing the jurisdictional reach of the federal securities laws, US courts, led by the Second Circuit, have developed and applied the "conduct" and "effects" tests. The Second Circuit has described these tests as follows:

> Under the 'conduct' test, a federal court has subject matter jurisdiction if the defendant's conduct in the United States was more than merely preparatory to the fraud, and particular acts or culpable failures to act within the United States directly caused losses to foreign investors abroad. Under the 'effects test,' subject matter jurisdiction exists where illegal activity abroad causes a 'substantial effect' within the United States.

Thus, US courts have found subject matter jurisdiction in cases brought by the Commission where either the illegal conduct has occurred in the United States or the illegal act occurred abroad but had a substantial harmful effect on US investors or securities markets.

Personal jurisdiction

For a court to exercise personal jurisdiction over a party, that party must have purposefully acted to create a "substantial connection" with the forum state.[21] Even if the transaction at issue involves allegedly harmful conduct that occurred entirely outside the United States, courts have found sufficient ties between foreign parties and the United States to warrant exercise of personal jurisdiction if sufficient "minimum contacts" exist to satisfy the due process clause of the US Constitution.

Under this standard, a non-US company that registers securities with the SEC and has them listed on the US securities exchanges is subject to the personal jurisdiction of the US courts for any matter arising out of that company's securities transaction because it has purposefully availed itself of the US market. The same principle applies to foreign companies that register with the SEC as non-resident broker-dealers or investment advisers.

---

21 *Burger King Corp. v. Rudzewicz*, 471 U.S. 462, 475 (1985).

SEC Investigations

The SEC has wide-ranging investigatory powers to review any conduct that could constitute a violation of the federal securities laws. Before the SEC initiates an enforcement action, the SEC Staff generally conducts an investigation to determine whether a violation of the securities laws occurred. This investigation may begin as an informal inquiry in which the Staff seeks voluntary cooperation from market participants and others in the form of document production and witness testimony. The Staff also may request that the Commission authorise a formal investigation that empowers the Staff to subpoena witnesses and to compel the production of records.

Obtaining documents without a subpoena

Under the federal securities laws, the SEC need not issue an investigative subpoena to obtain documents or records from "persons" registered with or regulated by the SEC. Such persons are obligated to make information and documents available whenever the SEC requests. For example, a non-resident broker-dealer who is registered with the Commission under Section 15(b) of the Exchange Act can be required to produce its books and records to the SEC without a subpoena. This rule has been interpreted to require the production of documents from a foreign branch office of a US registered broker-dealer or from a foreign broker-dealer registered and doing business in the US, wherever those documents may exist.

The SEC's subpoena power

The US securities laws give the SEC express investigative powers, including the power to issue subpoenas for documents and witnesses, to determine whether a securities law violation has occurred, is occurring or is about to occur. An investigative subpoena issued pursuant to a "formal order of investigation" from the Commission can require the production of documents from any person. However, service of the subpoena can only be properly effected inside the United States.

When the SEC serves a subpoena, it is not self-enforcing. However, the SEC can compel compliance by bringing an action in federal court seeking an order enforcing the subpoena. Once it is served in the United States, the party subpoenaed will be required to produce responsive documents, even those located outside the territorial confines of the United States. Similarly, a foreign resident who is served in the United States will be required to appear and give testimony in the United States.

It should also be noted that the Supreme Court has held that the SEC is under no obligation to notify the target or subject of an investigation when issuing a subpoena to a third party unless it is seeking the records of a customer of a financial institution.[22]

The Commission requires foreign brokers and investment advisers registered with the Commission to appoint the Commission as their agent for service of process in all matters arising out of the federal securities laws. In this way, the SEC can properly effect service of an investigative subpoena within the United States on foreign registered entities and persons.

Negotiating the scope of the subpoena

Sometimes the SEC's subpoenas are broad and burdensome. The recipient of the subpoena, whether an individual or a regulated entity, can discuss the breadth of the subpoena with the SEC Staff and try to negotiate a compromise. Often the Staff of the SEC will modify its request if it can be shown that not all of the requested documents are relevant to the investigation. It is possible to negotiate extensions of the deadline for complying with the subpoena, particularly if the documents are located in a foreign country.

After the documents have been produced and reviewed, the SEC will usually begin to take on-the-record testimony of witnesses. If you believe that you are the subject of the investigation, a meeting between your counsel and the Staff of the SEC is advisable prior to the testimony stage of the investigation. Counsel can then try to learn the focus of the SEC investigation, the Staff's view of the counsel's client and the legal theory underlying the Staff's case.

International enforcement cooperation

The SEC has an Office of International Affairs that provides assistance to the Enforcement Staff seeking evidence abroad and that assists foreign regulators in obtaining information from the US In 2003, the Staff made 309 requests to foreign regulators for

---

22 *SEC v. Jerry T. O'Brien, Inc.*, 467 U.S. 735 (1984).

enforcement assistance and responded to 344 requests for foreign assistance from foreign regulators.

Memoranda of Understanding

In its efforts to obtain foreign-based information to protect the US markets and investors, the SEC has worked to formalise its relationships with foreign securities regulators. To date, the SEC has entered into more than thirty-two MOUs with foreign countries' securities regulators, which establish procedures for sharing information and providing enforcement assistance in cases where key evidence exists outside of the United States borders. These MOUs cover most major foreign securities markets. Each MOU is individually negotiated with the foreign country's securities regulators and is designed to fit the circumstances prevailing in the particular market and the powers of the foreign regulator. In recent years, the SEC has entered into MOUs enabling it to request information in Egypt, Germany, Hong Kong, India, Portugal, Russia and South Africa.

As noted in Chapter 8, MOUs are generally non-binding agreements that state the parties' intent to exchange information and cooperate in securities violation investigations. However, they do not require signatory countries to provide information or cooperation, but rather form the framework for voluntary cooperation. Often, an MOU is the first step toward a binding agreement between two countries for mutual assistance, particularly in prosecuting criminal violations of the securities laws. The SEC has used MOUs to obtain evidence, particularly in insider trading investigations, where the subject is not a registered entity and, therefore, the SEC has difficulty effecting service of a valid subpoena in the United States.

Multilateral memorandum of understanding

In 2002, IOSCO created a Multilateral Memorandum of Understanding, the first global multilateral information-sharing arrangement among securities regulators.[23] The MOU provides for the exchange of basic information in investigating cross-border violations, including bank, brokerage, and client identification records. As of 25th April 2005, the IOSCO MOU had 32 signatories.

---

23 Copies of the IOSCO MOU can be accessed on IOSCO's website (www.iosco.org) or obtained from the IOSCO Secretariat.

US/UK memorandum of understanding
The MOU[24] entered into in 1991 between the SEC and the CFTC, on the one hand, and the SIB, on the other, is a good example of a typical MOU. The MOU covers broker-dealers, securities issuers, investment advisers, and clearing and transfer agents, as well as participants in the futures industry. It sets out a general framework for mutual assistance in enforcement matters, including providing access to information in the files of the requested authority, questioning or taking the testimony of persons designated by the requesting authority, obtaining specified information and documents from persons, and conducting compliance inspections or examinations, in each case with or without the participation of the requesting authority. Each authority can deny assistance on grounds of public interest, or where it finds that an assertion of jurisdiction would conflict seriously with and prejudice its sovereign interests.

In 1997, the SEC also signed an MOU with the Bank of England. This MOU is not an enforcement MOU, but rather a regulatory MOU which is designed to promote cooperation in the regulation of internationally active firms with new broker-dealer operations in the United States but which might operate in the UK as banks.

Other recent memoranda of understanding
In addition to the MOU with the Bank of England, the Commission signed MOUs with Germany and Portugal in 1997. The German MOU was signed by the new regulatory unit in that country, and it focuses on insider trading in the banking and brokerage sectors. The MOU with Portugal is particularly noteworthy, because Portugal changed its laws to enable it to more fully cooperate with other countries' requests for investigative help.

Mutual legal assistance arrangements
The US Government has also entered into MLATs with more than forty other counties. Although MLATs can only be used in investigating and prosecuting criminal matters, the SEC generally has been able to use these mutual assistance treaties in enforcing US

---

24   The SIB gave way to the FSA which, since 1st December 2002 and under the FSMA, is the sole regulator in the UK.

securities laws since all willful violations of the US securities laws may be prosecuted criminally. Unlike MOUs, compulsory measures must be applied to the assistance in gathering evidence if the offense is a crime in both countries that are subject to the MLAT, a concept known as dual criminality. The MLATs have been helpful to the SEC in acquiring documentary evidence from third parties outside of the United States who would otherwise be outside of the jurisdiction of US courts and thus outside of the subpoena power of the SEC.

Reciprocal authority
The SEC's power to strengthen international cooperation in enforcement of domestic securities laws was greatly enhanced by two pieces of federal legislation adopted by the Congress in 1988 and 1990.

First, Section 21(a)(2) of the Exchange Act permits the SEC, in its discretion, to conduct an investigation, including the use of its compulsory powers, on behalf of a foreign securities authority. In deciding how to exercise its discretion, the SEC is directed to consider "whether

(A) the requesting authority has agreed to provide reciprocal assistance in securities matters to the Commission; and
(B) compliance with the request would prejudice the public interest of the United States." Such assistance may be provided "without regard to whether the facts stated in the request would also constitute a violation of the laws of the United States." This permits the SEC to grant assistance to a foreign securities authority, regardless of whether there is an MOU, if it can obtain reciprocal assistance and receives all necessary confidentiality and use assurances. This facilitates the SEC's ability to demonstrate the value of international cooperation and to encourage the development of reciprocal assistance.

Second, Congress adopted ISECA, which among other things allows the SEC to sanction brokers, dealers or associated persons registered to do business in the United States who have been "found by a foreign financial regulatory authority to have . . . violated any foreign statute or regulation regarding transactions in securities." This provision allows the SEC to provide assistance to foreign authorities in punishing violators of securities laws and gives the SEC a mechanism for punishing securities violators in this country, even when the foreign country has not taken severe action against the offender.

POST-INVESTIGATIVE STAGE
The Wells submission
Following the Staff's investigation, the subject of the investigation usually has the opportunity to submit a written statement or brief videotape to the SEC, known as a "Wells submission". This submission, followed or coupled with settlement discussions, precedes the commencement of any enforcement action.

There is no "right" to file a Wells submission. Although the Staff's general practice is to give counsel an opportunity to file a Wells submission, there also are circumstances, such as emergency situations involving ongoing conduct or risk to investor assets, where the Staff will not provide a Wells notice and instead will seek Commission authorisation to obtain emergency relief in court.

The Wells submission can sometimes persuade the Staff to close an investigation without bringing an enforcement action or may persuade the Staff to modify the proposed charges. If the Staff decides to close the matter after a person receives a Wells notice, the Staff will send a letter advising the party that the Staff has concluded that it will not recommend that the Commission bring enforcement action. A similar letter will be sent to any party named in the formal order of investigation.

While it is unusual for the Staff or the Commission to close a case after a Wells is submitted, a Wells submission may convince the senior Staff or the Commission to negotiate an acceptable settlement. The Wells submission may persuade the SEC that a settlement offer that the defendant is prepared to accept, and which the Commission might otherwise reject, presents a palatable solution to a difficult case.

Settlement negotiations
In the event that the Wells Submission is unsuccessful in fully persuading the Commission to refrain from bringing an action, the Staff typically will give the party involved one last chance to settle

before the case is filed. If a settlement is reached at that point, an action is brought and simultaneously settled by a consent order. In that situation, the defendant has the advantage of negotiating with the Staff the wording of the Commission's order to which it will consent. Moreover, the defendant can consent to the Commission's findings and order without admitting or denying the factual allegations contained therein. As a practical matter, while the defendant cannot deny the allegations, the defendant often will issue a press release at the time of settlement stating that the case was settled in order to put the matter behind it and to get on with its business.

SEC ENFORCEMENT REMEDIES

The culmination of the Staff's investigation is the institution of an action to enforce the securities laws. Whether consented to or contested, an enforcement action can, among other things, impose substantial monetary penalties, suspend or bar securities professionals from the business, order the defendant to refrain from future violations and/or require review and implementation of new policies and procedures to ensure future compliance with US securities laws. The SEC's power and flexibility in enforcement cases have been greatly expanded in the last few years, particularly in light of the recent enactment of SOX.

Federal court actions
Injunctions and disgorgement
Injunctions in the securities laws context typically order defendants to stop violating the securities laws and to refrain from committing such violations in the future. Federal court actions seeking injunctions and other relief are considered the most serious remedy used by the SEC. An injunction will be granted where there has been a "proper showing" by the SEC that a person "is engaged or about to engage" in a violation of the law or is likely to violate the securities laws in the future. The failure to abide by an injunctive order can result in criminal fines and imprisonment. It should be further noted that one US Circuit Court of Appeals has held that there is no statute of limitations for a civil enforcement action for injunctive relief.[25]

---

25 *SEC v. Rind*, 991 F.2d 1486 (9th Cir. 1993).

In a typical injunctive action, the Commission also seeks an order requiring the payment of disgorgement, eg, the return of the defendant's ill-gotten gains or profit from the violation. The Commission also seek orders requiring the payment of prejudgment interest on the disgorgement.

The SEC does not litigate the majority of the cases; instead, it settles with the subjects of its investigations and enters consent decrees. The advantage to the investigated party is that it never admits or denies the allegations made. For the SEC, litigation expenses are minimised. More importantly, however, the defendant, in consenting to the decree, places itself in the position of being in contempt of a court order should it violate the consent order.

Penalties in insider trading cases
In 1984, the United States Congress gave the SEC, for the first time, the power to seek civil money penalties – up to three times the profit made or the loss avoided – for insider trading in the Insider Trading Sanctions Act (ITSA). In 1988, Congress further expanded the Commission's enforcement tools by passing ITSFEA. ITSFEA imposed specific responsibilities on broker-dealers and investment advisers to take steps to prevent illegal insider trading and authorised the imposition of very large monetary penalties on "controlling" persons if they failed to meet the newly imposed responsibilities.

Penalties for other violations
Both ITSA and ITSFEA provided new enforcement tools to the Commission, but only for insider trading violations. Insider trading cases, while well publicised, represent only a relatively small fraction (9% in 1998) of the enforcement cases brought by the Commission. The Securities Enforcement Remedies Act of 1990 (Remedies Act) provided much needed enforcement remedies for the vast majority of the SEC's cases. Under the Remedies Act, the SEC gained for the first time the power to seek civil money penalties from a court for every type of federal securities law violation.

The Remedies Act provided the Commission with the authority to seek civil penalties in a federal court against any person who violated the securities laws or the rules or regulations thereunder.

The size of the penalty depends on the type of misconduct involved. There are three tiers:

- the first tier provides for a maximum penalty of the greater of (1) US$6,500 for a natural person or US$65,000 for any other person, eg, corporations or other business entities or (2) the gross amount of pecuniary gain to the defendant resulting from the violation.
- the second tier provides, in cases where the violation involved fraud, deceit, manipulation, or reckless disregard of a regulatory requirement, for a maximum penalty of the greater of (i) US$65,000 for a natural person or US$325,000 for any other person, or (ii) the gross amount of pecuniary gain to the defendant resulting from the violation.
- the third tier provides, in cases where the violation involved (i) fraud, deceit, manipulation, or deliberate disregard of a regulatory requirement, and (ii) the violation directly or indirectly resulted in substantial losses or created a significant risk of substantial losses to other persons, for a maximum penalty of the greater of (i) US$130,000 for a natural person or US$650,000 for any other person, or (ii) the gross amount of pecuniary gain to the defendant resulting from the violation.

While the tiers provide some guidance about the range of permissible penalties, since the statute says that the penalties can be assessed "per violation" or for each transgression there is flexibility in calculating the appropriate amount. As indicated above, apart from penalties, the SEC seeks from wrongdoers disgorgement of any ill-gotten gains. If the defendant's assets are limited, the SEC will first seek disgorgement and try to return the disgorgement, if feasible, to the victims of the wrongdoing. If assets remain, the SEC will seek a penalty under the provisions listed above based on an analysis of the facts and circumstances of the case.

Officer and director bars
Federal courts can also bar individuals from serving as officers and directors if they have violated the antifraud provisions and demonstrated that they are unfit to serve as officers and directors of public companies. This so-called "officer and director bar" may be permanent or time-limited, but more often it is permanent. Before

SOX, the SEC could seek a bar where the corporate director or officer's conduct had been particularly egregious and has resulted in some personal profit (eg, the officer was involved in a financial fraud and engaged in insider trading).

As discussed above, SOX provided the SEC with authority to seek officer and director bars in administrative proceedings, and lowered the standard that the Commission must meet to obtain a bar from "substantial unfitness" to serve as an officer or director of a publicly held corporation, to simply showing that the officer or director is unfit to serve in such a role. Based on this lowered standard and the ability to proceed administratively to obtain an officer or director bar, it is likely that the Commission will seek such bars in a greater number of circumstances.

Administrative proceedings

While federal court actions are the Commission's most serious and traditional means of enforcing the federal securities laws, administrative proceedings are now the most common Commission means for addressing illegal conduct. Administrative proceedings are tried before administrative law judges. Generally, there is less opportunity for discovery by the respondent. Historically, administrative law judges have been viewed by the defense as being more likely to rule for the Commission Staff than a federal judge might be, given the same facts, but the SEC Staff has suffered several losses recently in administrative proceedings.

Administrative proceedings against regulated persons

The SEC can bring administrative proceedings against broker-dealers, investment advisers and other securities professionals. At the conclusion of the proceeding, the Commission can bar or suspend the professional or the firm and can order other relief such as a requirement that the firm review and modify its compliance procedures to prevent future violations. The Commission may also order disgorgement (payment of ill-gotten gain), interest and penalties.

Monetary penalties in administrative proceedings

The Remedies Act empowered the Commission to impose monetary penalties in administrative proceedings against broker-dealers, municipal securities, dealers clearing agencies, investment advisers, investment companies and individuals associated with these entities. The magnitude of the fines in administrative proceedings mirrors the three-tier structure for fines in court proceedings except that the Commission cannot impose a fine that exceeds the amounts specified in the tiers even if the defendant's gross pecuniary gain is greater.

Cease-and-desist proceedings
The Remedies Act also authorised the Commission to issue, in administrative proceedings, cease-and-desist orders against past, ongoing or threatened violations. Cease-and-desist orders may be entered against any person who is violating, has violated, or is about to violate the law, and against any other person that is, was or would be a "cause" of the violation, due to an act or omission the person knew or should have known would contribute to the violation. In addition to a cease-and-desist order, the Commission also may impose an order requiring the respondent to account for and disgorge illegal profits and pay interest, and to adopt procedures to prevent future violations. If a cease-and-desist order is violated, the SEC may seek civil penalties in federal court. Cease-and-desist orders provide the SEC with an attractive alternative to seeking injunctions in federal courts.

In emergencies, the Commission also has the power to issue *ex parte* temporary cease-and-desist orders against registered persons to stop ongoing illegal conduct by securities professionals and to safeguard investor assets.

Rule 102(e) proceedings

The SEC also has a rule, Rule 102(e), providing that the Commission may bring administrative proceedings against accountants, attorneys and other professionals who practice before the agency for violating the securities laws or for engaging in improper professional conduct. The rule is intended to protect the integrity of the SEC's processes by addressing problem professionals who play a key role in documents filed with the Commission and relied upon by investors. Rule 102(e) is used most commonly against accountants who fail to conduct an audit in accordance with GAAS and issue an opinion on financial statements that does not comply with GAAS. The SEC also brings proceedings under the rule against attorneys who have violated the securities laws, and are subject to an injunction, and who have practiced before the Commission or prepare documents filed with the Commission. A proceeding under this rule may result in a censure, a suspension of the professional or his firm, or a bar prohibiting future practice before the agency.

Other administrative proceedings

Finally, the Commission can institute proceedings to suspend the effectiveness of a registration statement (including the registration statement of a foreign company) that contains false and misleading statements, under Section 8(d) of the Securities Act.

Procedures in unsettled administrative cases

If the Commission chooses to bring a cease-and-desist proceeding rather than an action in federal court, the Commission must afford a respondent a hearing before an administrative law judge between one and four months after service of a notice instituting proceedings. In the order instituting proceedings, the Commission will specify the time period – either 120, 210 or 300 days from the date of service of the order – in which the hearing officer's initial decision must be filed with the Secretary.[26] The Commission may extend the time period for the issuance of an initial decision.[27]

Any adverse decision from an administrative law judge can be appealed to the full Commission, which considers anew all the evidence on the existing record and comes to its own determination without deference to the administrative law judge's ruling. If the Commission rules against the respondent, he or she can seek review in the United States Court of Appeals.

Other US regulatory action

The Commission is also authorised to refer matters to other federal, state or local authorities (including criminal authorities) or to self-regulatory organisations such as the NYSE or the NASD. It is important to note that a settlement with the SEC in an enforcement action does not bar, in the SEC's view, a criminal prosecution because the SEC

---

[26] 17 C.F.R. § 201.360 (2005).
[27] Id.

routinely insists that the settling party waive any right it may have to assert that the Commission's action bars a criminal prosecution under the double jeopardy clause of the US Constitution. The federal court in *US v. Marcus Schloss & Co.*[28] determined that a defendant in an SEC civil proceeding enters into a consent order explicitly recognising the absence of any bar to criminal proceedings arising out of the same conduct and cannot subsequently advance that civil decision as the basis for a double jeopardy claim. That court recognised the SEC's right to require the waiver.

While the federal securities laws provide for criminal sanctions (including fines and imprisonment) for willful violation, prosecution for such violations is not the province of the SEC but rather of the Department of Justice, typically through the local US Attorneys' Offices. The SEC investigates possible violations and refers them for prosecution.

RECENT ENFORCEMENT-RELATED REGULATORY INITIATIVES
The Commission's recent report on the importance of cooperation and self-policing

In October 2001, the Commission issued a significant report in which it stated its views on the importance of cooperation with the agency, and the role of "self-policing." That report (referred to as the Leon-Meredith Report, after the enforcement action to which it related) set forth the criteria the SEC will consider in determining whether, or how much, it will credit self-policing, self-reporting, remediation and cooperation in making enforcement decisions.[29] This guidance was released simultaneously with the SEC announcing it had settled a proceeding against a company employee, alleging inaccurate books and records and misstated periodic reports, but was taking no action against the company.[30]

The Leon-Meredith Report identifies four broad measures to be considered by the Staff in deciding whether and how to exercise its prosecutorial discretion: self-policing, self-reporting, remediation, and cooperation.

---

[28] 724 F. Supp. 1123, 1127 (S.D.N.Y. 1989).
[29] *See* Exchange Act Release 34-44969; Accounting and Auditing Enforcement Release 1470 (23rd October 2001). The Report may be found at www.sec.gov/news/litigation/investreport/34-44969.htm.
[30] *In the matter of Gisela de Leon-Meredith*, Exchange Act Release 44970 (23rd October 2001).

Self-Policing

The Leon-Meredith Report states the SEC will take into consideration policies and procedures a company has in place, prior to the discovery of misconduct, in its enforcement decisions. In this regard, the SEC will consider:

- whether the company had procedures in place intended to prevent and detect the misconduct;
- the reasons the procedures failed to prevent the misconduct;
- the "tone at the top": Did the misconduct arise from pressure to achieve specific results, or was there a tone of lawlessness set by those in control of the company;
- the nature of the misconduct;
- the position of the wrongdoer;
- the actions or inactions of senior personnel;
- the pervasiveness of the misconduct; and
- how and by whom the misconduct was uncovered.

In the Leon-Meredith matter, the SEC found significant that the violative conduct was limited to three employees of a company subsidiary. Senior personnel acted promptly, utilising the company's internal auditors to ascertain the nature and extent of Meredith's misconduct.

Self-Reporting

According to the Leon-Meredith Report, how and when the SEC and investors learn of wrongdoing, and a company's own actions after learning of potential wrongdoing, will influence whether and to what extent prosecutorial discretion will be exercised. The SEC will consider whether the company in question:

- promptly disclosed on its own initiative the wrongdoing and its impact to the investing public, to the SEC and the relevant self-regulatory organisation;
- demonstrates a commitment to learn the truth, fully and expeditiously;
- informs relevant persons, including its independent auditors, audit committee and Board of Directors; and
- undertakes a thorough, expeditious, and comprehensive review of the nature, extent, origins and consequences of the conduct.

In deciding not to institute an enforcement action against Seaboard, the SEC found significant the Company's speed and candor in disclosing the wrongdoing. The audit committee and full board were notified in a timely fashion, and the company disclosed to both the SEC and the public that its financial statements would have to be restated. The SEC found relevant that the price of Seaboard's stock did not decline after disclosure of the need to restate its financial statements, or the restatement itself. The SEC also noted that Seaboard quickly engaged counsel to conduct an internal investigation.

Remediation

Once a company confirms that misconduct has occurred, the SEC will take into consideration what steps are taken. For example, the following steps may be viewed favorably by the Staff in formulating an enforcement recommendation:

❑ disciplining or terminating culpable employees;
❑ changing or strengthening internal controls and procedures to prevent recurrence of the misconduct; and
❑ identifying the extent of damage to investors and other corporate constituencies and compensating those affected by the misconduct.

In the Leon-Meredith matter, the Staff looked favourably on Seaboard's swift and decisive actions. The Company terminated Meredith within 12 days of learning of the misconduct. Two employees responsible for supervising Meredith were also terminated. Seaboard strengthened its financial reporting processes to prevent a recurrence of such misconduct in the future. These steps included the development of a detailed closing process for the subsidiaries' accounting personnel, consolidating the subsidiaries' accounting functions under a Seaboard CPA, hiring additional qualified employees responsible for preparing the subsidiaries' financial statements, changing the subsidiaries' annual audit requirements, and vesting Seaboard's controller with supervisory responsibilities over the subsidiaries' reporting processes.

Co-operation

The fourth factor to be considered by the SEC in assessing an enforcement action against a company is the level of cooperation provided. The SEC will consider:

- ❏ whether the results of the company's review, as well as all relevant documentation, is shared with the Staff;
- ❏ whether information is disclosed to the Staff that was not requested and otherwise might not have been discovered;
- ❏ whether the information shared is thorough and reliable so that it may be used by the Staff to facilitate prompt enforcement action against those who may have violated the law;
- ❏ whether results of internal investigations are memorialised in a writing and shared with the Staff in a format that can be used by the Staff in an enforcement proceeding; and
- ❏ whether the company encouraged its employees to cooperate with the Staff's investigation and whether efforts were made to secure such cooperation.

In Leon-Meredith, the SEC found Seaboard's cooperation to be real and meaningful. The company provided the Staff with all information relevant to the underlying violations, including details of the internal investigation and notes and transcripts of interviews conducted. In this regard, the SEC found it significant that Seaboard did not invoke the attorney-client privilege, work product protection, or other privileges or protections with respect to any information uncovered in the investigation.

The SEC's "Cautionary Advice" regarding the use of "Pro Forma" financial information in earnings releases

In December 2001, the Commission issued a statement regarding the use by public companies of "pro forma" financial information in earnings releases.[31] A "pro forma" presentation of financial information refers to a presentation of earnings and results of operations on the basis of methodologies other than GAAP. While noting that "pro forma" financial information – eg, a presentation emphasising the results of core operations – may serve useful purposes, the Commission's statement expresses its concern that such presentations may be misleading if they obscure GAAP results. In light of that concern, the statement makes the following points:

- ❏ because "pro forma" financial information involves "selective editing" of GAAP results, "companies should be particularly

---

[31] See Exchange Act Release 45124 (4th December 2001).

mindful of their obligation not to mislead investors when using this information."

❏ the basis of any non-GAAP presentation should be clearly disclosed. Thus, if certain results are excluded, such as "unusual or nonrecurring transactions," the presentation "should describe the particular transactions and the kind of transactions that are omitted and apply the methodology described when presenting purportedly comparable information about other periods."

❏ attention must be paid to any material information ie omitted from a presentation. If "pro forma" results omit or obscure a result that would be material under GAAP (eg, by noting a "pro forma" profit in the case of a GAAP loss), "clear and comprehensible explanations of the nature and size of the omissions" are likely to be needed to avoid misleading investors.

❏ A non-GAAP presentation in an earnings release should generally be accompanied by a statement "in plain English" explaining how the disclosure "has deviated from GAAP and the amounts of each of those deviations." In this regard, the Commission's statement commends the earnings release guidelines jointly developed and issued by the Financial Executives International and the National Investor Relations Institute.

In the Commission's view, GAAP results are preferable, allowing investors to consistently track a company's financial results from year to year and to compare its performance with other companies. Accordingly, it is important to keep the Commission's statement on "pro forma" financial information in mind when making any financial statement disclosure that does not accord with GAAP.

"Cautionary Advice" regarding disclosure about critical accounting policies

In anticipation of future rulemaking, the SEC issued cautionary advice regarding disclosure about critical accounting policies.[32] The advice noted the SEC's view that companies' disclosure relating to accounting policies in the MD&A Section of reports filed with the SEC frequently could be enhanced. The release encourages public companies:

---

32 *See* Exchange Act Release 45149 (12th December 2001).

"to include in their MD&A this year full explanations, in plain English, of their "critical accounting policies," the judgments and uncertainties affecting the application of those policies, and the likelihood that materially different amounts would be reported under different conditions or using different assumptions."

The release proposes that companies adopt the following disclosure "regimen":

- company management and the auditor should pay particular attention to the company's "most critical accounting policies," and satisfy themselves that those policies have been properly selected, and are correctly applied and disclosed.
- MD&A disclosure should be closely reviewed to insure that it fully discloses the "critical accounting policies applied [by the company], the judgments made in their application, and the likelihood of materially different reported results if different assumptions or conditions were to prevail."
- the Audit Committee should be fully informed about the selection and application of critical accounting policies. The Audit Committee should review those policies, and the adequacy of the disclosure of those policies, prior to finalising and filing the annual report.

The release also suggests that if a company's management, Audit Committee or its auditor has any uncertainty about the application of specific GAAP principles, they should consult with the SEC's accounting Staff.

RECENT ENFORCEMENT CASES
Disclosure of merger negotiations

The Commission has historically maintained an enforcement focus on disclosure issues in the merger and tender offer context. The following case illustrates the SEC's continued attention to this area.

In the matter of E.ON AG, Exchange Act Release 43372 (28th September 2000)
E.ON AG (formerly Veba AG (Veba)), a German corporation, was charged by the SEC with violating the antifraud provisions of the

federal securities laws in connection with Veba's denials of merger negotiations with Viag AG. Veba made those denials after it had engaged in high-level discussions on the structure of the transaction, engaged investment bankers and legal advisors, and executed a confidentiality agreement. The company subsequently disclosed the discussions and consummated the merger with Viag AG.

At the time of the alleged violations, Veba's ADRs were listed on the NYSE and registered under the Exchange Act. Veba was based in Germany, but also had significant US operations.

Veba's denials were issued in both German and English and were carried in the *Wall Street Journal*, among other publications.

In its order, the Commission stated:

"The Commission recognises that disclosure practices and laws regarding the existence of merger negotiations may differ in other jurisdictions. Where jurisdictional requirements are met, however, there is no safe harbor for foreign issuers from violations of the antifraud provisions of the US federal securities laws. The Commission will not apply a different standard with respect to foreign issuers commenting on merger discussions or negotiations. When a foreign issuer voluntarily avails itself of the opportunities in the US capital markets, it must adhere to the US federal securities laws."

E.ON AG consented to an administrative judgment requiring it to cease-and-desist from committing or causing any violation and any future violation of the antifraud provisions of the US securities laws.

Financial reporting and disclosure

In the last several years, the Commission has increasingly focused on financial reporting and disclosure by public companies, both domestic and foreign. More specifically, the Commission has expressed concern about the adequacy of financial disclosures as well as companies using what the Commission perceives as "accounting gimmicks" that distort financial results. Questions, eg, have been raised about the extent to which issuers are using "special purpose entities" or "cookie jar" reserves to improve the appearance of financial statements or manage earnings. In addition, the Commission is focused on the taking of large charges in connection with restructurings or mergers to avoid future charges related to normal operating costs, among other things. The Commission also has placed additional emphasis on other disclosure issues.

The following cases illustrate the Commission's approach to these issues:

SEC v. Dollar General Corporation, et al, Litigation Release 19174 (7th April 2005)

On 7th April 2005, the SEC filed a settled enforcement action against Dollar General Corporation (Dollar General), a Tennessee-based discount retailer. Without admitting or denying the SEC's allegations, Dollar General consented to the entry of a final judgment permanently enjoining it from future violations of the antifraud, books and records, internal controls, and periodic reporting provisions of the federal securities laws, specifically, Section 17(a) of the Securities Act, Sections 10(b), 13(a), 13(b)(2)(A) and 13(b)(2)(B) of the Exchange Act and Rules 10b-5, 12b-20, 13a-1, 13a-11 and 13a-13 thereunder. As part of the settlement, Dollar General agreed to pay US$1 in disgorgement and a civil penalty of US$10 million, which the Commission expects will be distributed pursuant to the Fair Fund provisions of Section 308(a) of SOX.

The Commission alleged in its complaint[33] that, during its fiscal years 1998 through 2001, Dollar General engaged in fraudulent or improper accounting practices in violation of GAAP which ultimately resulted in a restatement of Dollar General's financial statements in January 2002 reducing the Company's pre-tax income by approximately US$143 million, or about 30 cents per share, over the restated period. The Commission alleged that Dollar General's misconduct included:

(1) intentionally underreporting at least US$10 million in import freight expenses for the Company's fiscal year 1999;
(2) engaging in an US$11 million sham sale of outdated, essentially worthless, cash registers in the Company's fiscal year 2000 fourth quarter;
(3) overstating cash accounts;
(4) manipulating the Company's reported earnings through the use of a general reserve or "rainy day" account;
(5) failing to maintain accurate books and records and filing inaccurate financial reports with the Commission; and
(6) failing to maintain adequate internal accounting controls.

---
33 A "complaint" in American law is what is referred to as a "statement of claim" in most Commonwealth common law countries. The French equivalent would be a "déclaration."

The Commission alleged that some of the fraudulent or improper accounting practices were effected by, or known to, former senior executives and accounting personnel, and were motivated in part by their desire to report earnings that met or exceeded analysts' expectations and to maintain employee bonuses. The SEC also charged the company's former CEO, President, CFO, Controller, and Accounting Manager with accounting fraud.

SEC v. Penthouse international, inc., et al,
Litigation Release 19048 (24th January 2005)
On 24th January 2005, the SEC filed a civil injunctive action against Penthouse International, Inc. (Penthouse), now known as PHSL Worldwide, Inc., a former officer of Penthouse, Charles Samel, and a Penthouse shareholder, Jason Galanis, charging them with accounting fraud, reporting violations and violations of the SOX certification rules. The Commission also instituted a settled cease-and-desist proceeding against Penthouse's former CEO, Robert C. Guccione.

The Commission alleged that Penthouse, Samel and Galanis engaged in accounting fraud and financial reporting violations at Penthouse in connection with the company's Form 10-Q for the quarter ended 31st March 2003. According to the complaint, Penthouse improperly included as revenue for that quarter US$1 million received as an up-front payment in connection with a five-year website management agreement. The SEC alleged that the payment should not have been recognised in that quarter because

(1) the agreement was not actually signed until the following quarter, and
(2) according to GAAP, the US$1 million payment should have been recognised as deferred revenue and amortised into income over the five-year life of the agreement. The inclusion of the US$1 million payment increased Penthouse's reported revenue by approximately nine per cent, from US$11,072,000 to US$12,072,000 and changed a quarterly net loss of US$167,000 to a purported net profit of US$828,000.

The Commission alleged that Penthouse's Form 10-Q was materially misleading in several other respects. For example, it bore an unauthorised electronic signature of Robert C. Guccione, Penthouse's principal executive officer and principal financial officer, and thus represented that Guccione had reviewed and signed it, and the accompanying SOX certification. According to the SEC, this representation was false, because Guccione had not seen or approved the filing of the Form 10-Q or the SOX certification. The SEC alleged that Penthouse's auditors and outside counsel also had not reviewed the filing, a fact that also was not disclosed in the filing.

The SEC also alleged that Samel and Galanis prepared and filed the false Form 10-Q, and they did so knowing or recklessly disregarding that Guccione had not seen or approved it, that Penthouse's auditor had not performed its required review of the Form 10-Q, and that it would be improper to include the US$1 million payment as revenue for the quarter ended 31st March 2003. According to the SEC, in two subsequent filings on Form 8-K that purported to correct misstatements in the 10-Q, Penthouse failed to disclose that Guccione had not reviewed, approved or signed the 10-Q or the attached SOX certification. The SEC alleged that, in one of these filings, Penthouse also misrepresented that the company's disclosure controls and procedures were adequate.

The SEC's complaint alleged that Penthouse and Samel violated, and Galanis aided and abetted violations of, Section 10(b) of the Exchange Act, and Rule 10b-5 thereunder. Further, the complaint alleged that Penthouse violated Section 15(d) of the Exchange Act and Rules 12b-20, 15d-11, 15d-13 and 15d-14 thereunder, that Samel and Galanis aided and abetted violations of Section 15(d) of the Exchange Act and Rules 12b-20 and 15d-13 thereunder, and that Samel also aided and abetted violations of Rule 15d-14. In its complaint, the Commission seeks permanent injunctions and civil penalties as to all of the defendants; and officer and director bars against Samel and Galanis. The litigation against Samel and Galanis is pending.

In the matter of the Walt Disney Company,
Exchange Act Release 50882 (20th December 2004)
On 20th December 2004, the Commission instituted settled enforcement proceedings against The Walt Disney Company (Disney), charging that, between 1999 and 2001, Disney failed to disclose certain related party transactions between the company and its directors which were required to be disclosed in its proxy statements

and annual reports filed with the Commission. The Commission also charged that Disney failed to disclose certain compensation paid to a Disney director.

In particular, the Commission alleged that Disney failed to disclose that the company employed three children of its directors, paying them annual compensation ranging from US$60,000 to US$150,000, and that the spouse of another director was employed by a subsidiary 50% owned by Disney and received compensation in excess of US$1 million annually. The Commission also alleged that Disney failed to disclose that it made regular payments to a corporation owned by a Disney director that provided air transportation to that director for Disney-related business purposes. The Commission further alleged that Disney failed to disclose that the company provided office and travel services valued at over US$200,000 annually to another Disney director.

Without admitting or denying the Commission's findings, Disney consented to the issuance of a Commission order requiring the company to cease-and-desist from committing or causing any violations and any future violations of Sections 13(a) and 14(a) of the Exchange Act and Rules 13a-1, 12b-20, and 14a-3(a).

SEC v. American International Group, Inc.,
Litigation Release 18985 (30th November 2004)
On 30th November 2004, the Commission filed a settled enforcement action against American International Group, Inc. (AIG) for violating the antifraud provisions and for aiding and abetting violations of the reporting and record-keeping provisions of the federal securities laws. The Commission action arose out of AIG's offer and sale of an alleged earnings management product. In its complaint, the Commission alleged that AIG developed, marketed, and, in the case of one public company – The PNC Financial Services Group, Inc. (PNC) – entered into transactions designed to enable the buyer of its product to remove troubled or other potentially volatile assets from its balance sheet, thereby allowing the company to supposedly avoid charges to its reported earnings from declines in the value of these assets. The Commission alleged that AIG was reckless in not knowing that the product it developed did not satisfy the accounting standards for removing the assets from a company's balance sheet.

According to the Commission's complaint, from at least March 2001 through January 2002, AIG, primarily through its wholly owned subsidiary, AIG-Financial Products Corp., marketed and sold to public companies a product known as C-GAITS. The Commission alleged this product consisted of AIG, for a fee, establishing a special purpose entity (SPE) to which the counter-party would transfer troubled or other potentially volatile assets and, in return, receive preferred stock in the SPE. The Commission alleged that AIG represented to prospective counter-parties that, under applicable accounting standards, the SPE would not have to be consolidated on the counter-party's financial statements and the counter-party would not have to record declines in the value of the transferred assets or the preferred stock as charges to its earnings. According to the complaint, independent auditors for some potential counter-parties raised issues about whether certain features of AIG's product could violate the accounting requirements for non-consolidation of SPEs. The Commission alleged that, with one exception, AIG did not inform other potential counter-parties of these issues.

In addition, the Commission's complaint alleged that AIG entered into three C-GAITS transactions through which PNC improperly sought to remove US$762 million in loan and venture capital assets from its balance sheet and, therefore, avoid charges to its income statement from declines in the value of these assets. The Commission alleged that, as a result, PNC made materially false and misleading disclosures about its financial condition and performance in filings with the Commission and in press releases. The Commission alleged that AIG was reckless in not knowing that the transactions with PNC did not satisfy the standards for non-consolidation by PNC.

In settling the Commission's action and related criminal charges by the Department of Justice, AIG agreed to pay US$126 million, consisting of a penalty of US$80 million, and disgorgement and prejudgment interest of US$46 million. In addition, AIG consented, without admitting or denying the allegations in the Commission's complaint, to the entry of a permanent injunction against violating, and aiding and abetting violations of, certain provisions of the federal securities laws. AIG also agreed to the appointment of an independent consultant to examine certain AIG transactions going back to the year 2000, including any transaction that was effected with the primary purpose of enabling a public company to achieve an accounting or financial reporting result. Further, AIG agreed to establish a Transaction Review Committee to review certain future transactions involving heightened legal, reputational or regulatory risk.

SEC v. Qwest communications international, inc., Litigation Release 18936 (21st October 2004); *SEC v. Nacchio, et al,* Litigation Release 19136 (15th March 2005)
On 21st October 2004, the Commission filed a settled enforcement action against Qwest Communications International, Inc. (Qwest), alleging that, between 1999 and 2002, Qwest fraudulently recognised over US$3.8 billion in revenue and excluded US$231 million in expenses as part of a scheme to meet optimistic and unsupportable revenue and earnings projections.

The Commission's complaint alleged that Qwest created the appearance of growth by engaging in one-time revenue generating transactions that the company publicly reported as recurring. The Commission's complaint also alleged that Qwest's accounting for such undisclosed one-time transactions was not in accordance with GAAP. The Commission's complaint further alleged that Qwest engaged in a variety of other conduct violative of the federal securities laws, including failing to disclose certain related party transactions, concealing the fact that the company improperly recognised US$112 million of revenue between 2000 and 2002, understating expenses, and engaging in the sale of unregistered securities.

Without admitting or denying the Commission's allegations, Qwest consented to a permanent injunction from future violations of the federal securities and the imposition of a US$250 million civil penalty to be distributed to defrauded investors pursuant to the Fair Funds provision of the SOX Act of 2002, and US$1 disgorgement. The terms of the settlement also require Qwest to maintain permanently a chief compliance officer.

On 15th March 2005, the SEC charged Joseph P. Nacchio, former co-chairman and CEO of Qwest, and eight other former Qwest officers and employees with fraud and other violations of the federal securities laws. In three separate but related civil actions, the Commission alleged that, between 1999 and 2002, the

Qwest defendants engaged in a multi-faceted fraudulent scheme designed to mislead the investing public about the company's revenue and growth.

According to the SEC's complaints, Nacchio and others made numerous false and misleading statements about Qwest's financial condition in annual, quarterly, and current reports, in registration statements that incorporated Qwest's financial statements, and in other public statements, including earnings releases and investor calls. As a result of that scheme, Qwest fraudulently recognised over US$3 billion of revenue and excluded US$71.3 million in expenses.

In addition to Nacchio, the Commission's complaints named former CFOs Robert S. Woodruff and Robin R. Szeliga, former COO Afshin Mohebbi, former executive vice president of wholesale markets Gregory M. Casey, former senior vice president of pricing and offer management Roger B. Hoaglund, former senior vice president of finance William L. Eveleth, former director of financial reporting James J. Kozlowski, and former senior manager of financial reporting Frank T. Noyes. The SEC's complaints seek injunctions, disgorgement of ill-gotten gains plus prejudgment interest, and civil penalties against all of the defendants, and officer/director bars against Nacchio, Woodruff, Szeliga, Mohebbi, Casey, and Eveleth.

The Commission's complaints alleged that, in Commission filings and other public statements, Nacchio, Woodruff, and Szeliga fraudulently characterised nonrecurring revenue from the one-time sales of capacity in the form of indefeasible rights of use (IRU) and equipment as recurring "data and Internet service revenues," thereby masking Qwest's declining financial condition and artificially inflating its stock price. According to the SEC, Qwest used such nonrecurring revenue to fill the gap between actual and projected revenue. The SEC alleged in its complaint that, over time, Qwest's dependence on such one-time transactions grew to the point that it was likened internally to an "addiction" and the non-recurring IRU and equipment sale transactions were likened to "heroin." Among other things, the Qwest executives' misrepresentations about Qwest's revenue sources allowed Qwest to maintain a stock price sufficiently high to complete its pending merger with US West, Inc. In addition, the Commission alleged that each of the defendants participated in the company's scheme to improperly recognise revenue on IRU transactions.

In the Matter of General Electric Co., Exchange
Act Release 50426 (23rd September 2004)
On 23rd September 2004, the SEC instituted a cease-and-desist proceeding against General Electric Company (GE) for allegedly failing to fully disclose the terms of Jack Welch's – GE's former CEO – retirement package. The retirement package, which GE and Welch agreed to in 1996, included as a principal benefit continued access to GE "facilities and services" comparable to those Welch received as CEO, including access to GE aircraft, cars, offices, apartments, and financial planning services. In his first year of retirement, Welch received approximately US$2.5 million in such benefits.

GE filed its agreement with Welch as an exhibit to its 1996 Form 10-K and incorporated it by reference as an exhibit in each subsequent Form 10-K until 2002, the year after Welch retired. However, neither these Forms 10-K, GE's other periodic reports filed during the years 1996–2002, nor GE's six proxy statements for the years 1997 through 2002 described or disclosed the type or nature of the benefits Welch would receive in retirement beyond stating that GE would provide him with lifetime access to GE facilities and services comparable to the access he enjoyed as CEO. As a result, according to the SEC, GE violated the proxy solicitation and periodic reporting provisions of the Exchange Act by filing annual reports and proxy statements that failed fully and accurately to disclose the "facilities and services" Welch would receive in retirement.

Without admitting or denying the Commission's findings, GE agreed to cease-and-desist from causing or committing any violations and any future violations of sections 13(a) and 14(a) of the Exchange Act and Rules 13a-1, 14a-3, and 14a-9.

SEC v. Computer Associates International, Inc.,
Litigation Release 18891 (22nd September 2004)
On 22nd September 2004, the Commission filed securities fraud charges against Computer Associates International, Inc. (Computer Associates) and three former top executives – Sanjay Kumar, former Chairman and CEO, Steven Woghin, former General Counsel, and

Stephen Richards, former Head of Sales. The Commission in its complaints alleged that from 1998 to 2000, Computer Associates' executives routinely held the company's books open for several days after the end of each quarter to improperly record revenue from contracts that were not executed until after the quarter ended. The Commission alleged that, as a result, Computer Associates prematurely recognised US$2.2 billion in revenue in fiscal years 2000 and 2001, and more than US$1.1 billion in revenue in prior quarters. Computer Associates was also charged with making material misrepresentations and omissions, through the individual defendants, about its revenue and earnings in SEC filings and other public statements.

Computer Associates reached a joint settlement with the Commission and the Justice Department. The settlement permanently enjoins Computer Associates from committing further violations of the anti-fraud, reporting, books and records, and internal control provisions of the federal securities laws, and requires the company to reform its corporate governance and financial controls and to appoint an independent examiner. Additionally, the settlement provides for a deferred prosecution agreement with the Justice Department, and requires Computer Associates to pay US$225 million in restitution to injured shareholders.

This settlement is noteworthy because Computer Associates was not required to pay a penalty to the Commission, which could then be distributed to injured shareholders under the Fair Funds provision of the SOX Act. Instead, Computer Associates' penalty was paid directly to injured shareholders.

Woghin, the former General Counsel, consented to a partial judgment imposing a permanent injunction against future violations of the anti-fraud, reporting, books and records, and internal controls provisions of the federal securities laws, and barring him for serving as an officer or director of a public company. The Commission's claims for disgorgement and civil penalties against Woghin, and all of its claims against the other individual defendants, are pending.

SEC v. Bristol-Myers Squibb Company,
Litigation Release 18820 (4th August 2004)
The Commission filed a civil accounting fraud action against Bristol-Myers Squibb Company (Bristol-Myers), a public company

engaged in the manufacturing, distribution and sale of pharmaceuticals and other related health care products.

The Commission alleged that, from the first quarter of 2000 through the fourth quarter of 2001, Bristol-Myers engaged in a fraudulent scheme to inflate its sales and earnings in order to create the false appearance that the company had met or exceeded its internal sales and earnings targets and Wall Street analysts' earnings estimates. The complaint alleges that Bristol-Myers inflated its results primarily by

(1) stuffing its distribution channels with excess inventory near the end of every quarter in amounts sufficient to meet its targets by making pharmaceutical sales to its wholesalers ahead of demand; and
(2) improperly recognising US$1.5 billion in revenue from such pharmaceutical sales to its two biggest wholesalers. In connection with the US$1.5 billion in revenue, Bristol-Myers covered these wholesalers' carrying costs and guaranteed them a return on investment until they sold the products. According to the complaint, Bristol-Myers recognised the US$1.5 billion in revenue upon shipment, contrary to GAAP.

The complaint further alleges that the company tapped improperly created divestiture reserves and reversed portions of those reserves into income to further inflate its earnings. In addition, the complaint alleges that, as a result of the channel stuffing, Bristol-Myers materially understated its accruals for rebates due to Medicaid and certain of its prime vendors, customers of its wholesalers that purchased large quantities of pharmaceutical products from those wholesalers.

Bristol-Myers, without admitting or denying the allegations, consented to a permanent injunction from future violations of certain anti-fraud, reporting, books and records and internal controls provisions of the federal securities laws. Bristol-Myers agreed to pay disgorgement of US$1, a civil penalty of US$100 million, and US$50 million into a fund for the benefit of its shareholders. Bristol-Myers also agreed to various remedial undertakings, including the appointment of an independent advisor to review, assess and monitor the company's accounting practices, financial reporting and disclosure processes and internal control systems.

SEC v. Halliburton Company, Litigation Release 18817 (3rd August 2004)

The Commission filed and settled a civil accounting fraud action against Halliburton Company (Halliburton) and its former controller, Robert Muchmore. The Commission also instituted separately settled cease-and-desist proceedings against Halliburton and Muchmore. In addition, the Commission filed an enforcement action against Halliburton's former CFO, Gary V. Morris, in the Southern District of Texas.

The Commission alleges in its complaints against Halliburton, Muchmore, and Morris that over six financial reporting periods, spanning approximately 18 months covering 1998 and 1999, Halliburton failed to disclose that it had changed its accounting practice as to the recognition of revenue on certain cost overrun claims from customers. The Commission alleged that Morris and Muchmore were responsible for the company's failure to disclose the accounting change in Halliburton's Commission filings. Additionally, the Commission alleged that Morris and Muchmore played key roles in the preparation and review of quarterly earnings releases and analyst teleconference scripts that included the inaccurate income figures. According to the Commission, Morris and Muchmore were, therefore, also responsible for the absence in the releases and scripts of any clarifying reference to the accounting change or its impact.

In settling with the Commission, Halliburton consented to cease-and-desist from committing or causing future violations of the federal securities laws, and to pay a US$7.5 million civil penalty. The Commission's order against Halliburton noted that the penalty, in part, reflects the Commission's view that there were unacceptable lapses in the company's conduct during the course of the investigation, which had the effect of delaying the production of information and documentation necessary to the Staff's expeditious completion of its investigation.

Muchmore settled with the Commission by consenting to an order requiring him to cease-and-desist from committing or causing future violations of the federal securities laws, and to pay a civil penalty of US$50,000.

SEC v. Lay, Litigation Release 18776 (8th July 2004)

On 8th July 2004, the Commission charged Kenneth Lay, the former CEO and Chairman of the Board of Directors of Enron Corporation (Enron), with violating, and aiding and abetting the violation of, the antifraud, periodic reporting, books and records, and internal control provisions of the federal securities laws. Simultaneous with the filing of the Commission's complaint, Lay was charged criminally by the Department of Justice's Enron Task Force.

According to the Commission's complaint, Lay, along with others at Enron, engaged in a wide-ranging scheme to defraud investors. The Commission alleged that during 2001, Lay, with specific knowledge of rapidly deteriorating performances of Enron's business units, made numerous false and misleading public statements about Enron's financial condition. The Commission claimed that Lay, as Enron's Chairman and CEO, had oversight of Enron's business units and supervised the senior executives and managers of these units, reviewed drafts of public filings and draft press releases, and participated in conference calls with investment analysts.

The Commission's complaint further alleged that Lay profited from the scheme to defraud by selling large amounts of Enron stock at prices that did not reflect its true value. The SEC alleged that these sales also occurred while Lay was in possession of material non-public information concerning Enron and generated unlawful proceeds in excess of US$90 million during 2001. Specifically, Lay sold over US$70 million in Enron stock back to the company to repay cash advances on an unsecured Enron line of credit. The complaint stated that, in addition, while in possession of material non-public information, Lay amended two program trading plans to enable him to sell an additional US$20 million in Enron stock in the open market. The Commission claimed that the proceeds from the sales constitute illegal gains resulting from his scheme to defraud. As a result of the alleged conduct, the Commission is seeking disgorgement of all ill-gotten gains, civil money penalties, a permanent bar from acting as a director or officer of a publicly held company, and an injunction against future violations of the federal securities laws.

SEC v. Skilling, Litigation Release 18582 (19th February 2004)
On 19th February 2004, the Commission charged Jeffrey K. Skilling, the former President, CEO and COO of Enron, with violating, and aiding abetting the violation of, the antifraud, periodic reporting, books and records, and internal control provisions of the federal securities laws. Simultaneous with the filing of the Commission's complaint, Skilling was charged criminally by the Department of Justice's Enron Task Force.

According to the Commission's complaint, Skilling and others improperly used reserves within Enron's wholesale energy trading business, Enron Wholesale, to manufacture and manipulate reported earnings; manipulated Enron's "business segment reporting" to conceal losses at Enron's retail energy business, Enron Energy Services; manufactured earnings by fraudulently promoting Enron's broadband unit, Enron Broadband Services; and improperly used special purpose entities and the LJM partnerships to manipulate Enron's financial results. In addition, the SEC alleged that Skilling made false and misleading statements concerning Enron's financial results and the performance of its businesses, and that these misrepresentations were also contained in Enron's public filings with the Commission. The Commission further alleged in its complaint that Skilling sold Enron stock while in possession of material, non-public information that generated unlawful proceeds of approximately US$63 million. As a result of the alleged conduct, the Commission's suit seeks disgorgement of ill-gotten gains, civil money penalties, a permanent bar from acting as a director or officer of a publicly held company, and an injunction against future violations of the federal securities laws.

SEC v. Causey, Litigation Release 18551 (22nd January 2004)
On 22nd January 2004, the Commission charged Richard A. Causey, the former Chief Accounting Officer of Enron, with violating, and aiding abetting the violation of, the antifraud, periodic reporting, books and records, and internal control provisions of the federal securities laws. Simultaneous with the filing of the Commission's complaint, Causey was charged criminally by the Department of Justice's Enron Task Force.

According to the Commission's complaint, Causey, and others, fraudulently manipulated Enron's merchant asset portfolio; improperly used "off-balance-sheet" special purpose entities; manipulated Enron's "business segment reporting" to conceal losses at Enron Energy Services; manipulated expenses to conceal losses at Enron Broadband services; and manipulated reserves in Enron's wholesale energy trading business to smooth earnings and conceal losses. The Commission's complaint further alleges that Causey, and others, made false and misleading statements concerning Enron's financial results and the performance of its businesses, which were also reflected in Enron's public filings. As a result of the alleged conduct, the Commission's suit seeks disgorgement of ill-gotten gains, civil money penalties, a permanent bar from acting as a director or officer of a publicly held company, and an injunction against future violations of the federal securities laws.

SEC v. Fastow, Litigation Release 18543 (14th January 2003)
On 14th January 2003, the Commission settled civil fraud charges against Andrew S. Fastow, the former chief financial officer of Enron. The Commission's complaint, filed on 2nd October 2002, alleges violations of the anti-fraud, periodic reporting, books and records, and internal control provisions of the federal securities laws. The Commission settled this action in coordination with the Department of Justice's Enron Task Force, which entered into a guilty plea with Fastow on related criminal charges. In resolving the parallel civil and criminal proceedings, Fastow agreed to serve a ten-year sentence, disgorge more than US$23 million and to cooperate with the government's continuing investigation.

The allegations in the Commission's complaint stems from Fastow's conduct relating to six transactions. Three of the transactions, RADR, Chewco, and Southampton were part of an alleged scheme to hide Fastow's interest in and control of certain entities in order to keep those entities off Enron's balance sheet. The complaint alleges that Fastow secretly nominated certain of the owners of these entities, funded certain of their investments through undisclosed loans, collected undisclosed fees, and demanded and received under-the-table payments.

Two of the remaining three transactions, the Nigerian barges and the Cuiba transaction, are alleged to have been sham sales – best described as asset-parking arrangements. In one of these sales, a sale of an interest in certain Nigerian barges to a financial institution, Fastow is alleged to have promised that the financial institution would be taken out of the investment and later arranged for an entity that he controlled to buy the financial institution's interest at a pre-arranged rate of return. The last transaction included in the complaint relates to an instance of backdating documents to avoid diminution in Enron's investment in the stock of a technology company. Fastow and others allegedly created documents that purported to lock in the value of Enron's investment in the technology company back in August 2000, when that company's stock was trading at its all-time high price.

SEC v. Gemstar-TV Guide International, Inc.,
Litigation Release 18760 (23rd June 2004)
The Commission filed a settled enforcement action against Gemstar-TV Guide International, Inc. (Gemstar), alleging that Gemstar improperly reported its highly touted interactive program guide licensing and advertising revenues in its financial statements from 1999 through 2002.

The Commission's complaint alleges that Gemstar materially overstated its revenues by nearly US$250 million through several means. First, Gemstar allegedly recorded revenue under expired, disputed, or non-existent agreements, and improperly reported this as interactive program guide (IPG) licensing and advertising revenue. Second, the Commission alleged that Gemstar recorded and reported revenue from a long-term agreement on an accelerated basis in contravention of GAAP and Gemstar's disclosed revenue recognition policy, which required the recording and reporting of such revenue ratably over the term of the agreement. Third, Gemstar allegedly inflated its IPG advertising revenue by improperly recording and reporting revenue amounts from multiple-element transactions. Gemstar's recording and reporting of this revenue was improper under GAAP because Gemstar could not determine the IPG advertising's fair value. Additionally, the Commission alleged that some of those improperly reported transactions included so-called "round-trip" transactions whereby Gemstar paid money to a third party that then used those funds to buy advertising from Gemstar. Fourth, the Commission alleged that Gemstar improperly recorded and reported IPG advertising revenue from non-monetary and barter transactions. Gemstar's recording and reporting of this revenue was not in accordance with GAAP because it did not meet the revenue recognition requirements for such transactions and because Gemstar could not properly establish the IPG advertising's fair value. Finally, the Commission's complaint alleges that Gemstar improperly reported certain revenues as IPG advertising revenues when in fact those revenues were derived from the sale of print advertising. Gemstar shifted revenues by invoicing advertisers for both IPG and print advertising, but recording the revenue only as IPG revenue.

Gemstar agreed to settle the case by, among other things, paying a US$10 million civil penalty. The Commission stated that, in assessing the penalty amount, it considered the scope and severity of Gemstar's misconduct, Gemstar's initial failure to cooperate in the Commission's investigation or undertake remedial actions, and Gemstar's significant cooperation and remediation following a change in senior management and restructuring of its corporate governance.

SEC v. Symbol Technologies, Inc.,
Litigation Release 18734 (3rd June 2004)
The Commission filed a civil accounting fraud action against Symbol Technologies, Inc. (Symbol), alleging that Symbol and its senior management inflated revenue, earnings and other measures of financial performance in order to create the appearance that Symbol had met or exceeded its financial projections.

The Commission's complaint alleges baseless accounting entries, artificial reduction of operating expenses, improperly recognised revenue and manipulation of inventory levels and accounts receivable data. The allegedly fraudulent accounting practices had a cumulative net impact of US$230 million on reported revenue and US$530 million on pre-tax earnings. In addition, the Commission claimed that certain members of senior management interfered with two internal investigations into accounting practices by discarding, sanitising, or withholding documents, and delayed the Commission's investigation.

As part of the settlement, Symbol agreed to pay US$37 million to injured investors and appoint an independent examiner to review its accounting practices. In assessing the penalty amount, the SEC considered the scope and severity of the fraud, initial efforts to cover up the misconduct and impede investigations, and the company's eventual cooperation and remediation. Importantly, the SEC levied penalties against Symbol, and not just the alleged individual wrongdoers, for "having created and fostered the environment in which the wrongdoing took place."

SEC v. Lucent Technologies, Inc.,
Litigation Release 18715 (17th May 2004)

The Commission filed a settled accounting fraud action against Lucent Technologies, Inc. (Lucent) and nine former and current officers. The Commission's complaint alleges that Lucent violated GAAP as a result of fraudulent and reckless actions by the individual defendants and deficient internal controls that led to numerous accounting errors by others. The Commission's complaint also alleges that, in a drive to realise revenue, meet internal sales targets and/or obtain sales bonuses, the individual defendants improperly granted, and/or failed to disclose, various side agreements, credits and other incentives (collectively "extra-contractual commitments") to induce Lucent's customers to purchase the company's products. According to the Commission, these extra-contractual commitments were made in at least ten transactions in fiscal 2000, and Lucent violated GAAP by recognising revenue on these transactions both in circumstances:

(a) where it could not be recognised under GAAP; and
(b) by recording the revenue earlier than was permitted under GAAP.

To settle the charges, Lucent consented to a permanent injunction against future violations of the anti-fraud, reporting, books and records and internal controls provisions of the federal securities laws. Lucent also agreed to pay a US$25 million penalty for failing to cooperate fully during the Staff's investigation and for actions the company took after the company reached a settlement agreement in principle with the Commission. Specifically, after the conclusion of the Commission's investigation, Lucent's former Chairman/CEO and its outside attorney spoke to a reporter about a transaction that was a subject of the Commission investigation.

Lucent's outside attorney characterised the transaction as a "failure of communication." The Commission found that Lucent's public statements undermined both the spirit and letter of its agreement in principle with the Staff not to deny the Commission's allegations.

Three of the individual defendants reached settlements with the Commission. These defendants agreed to permanent injunctions against future violations of the anti-fraud, reporting, books and records and internal controls provisions of the federal securities laws, and to pay civil penalties ranging from US$60,000 to US$110,000. In addition, one of the settling defendants agreed to be barred from acting as an officer or director of a public company for five years and another agreed to a three-year bar.

SEC v. Brightpoint, Inc., American International Group, Inc., Phillip Bounsall, John Delaney and Timothy Harcharik,
Litigation Release 18340 (11th September 2003)
The Commission filed a civil accounting fraud action against Brightpoint, Inc. (Brightpoint), American International Group, Inc. (AIG), two former officers of Brightpoint, and a former employee of Brightpoint. The Commission also instituted separately settled cease-and-desist proceedings against Brightpoint, AIG, one former Brightpoint employee and an AIG employee.

The Commission alleged that AIG, beginning in 1997, developed and marketed a "non-traditional" insurance product for the stated purpose of enabling public reporting companies to smooth earnings over a period of time, by creating the appearance of insurance, and an assumption of risk by AIG, when in fact AIG was simply accepting cash from the "insured" that would be refunded back. According to the complaint, AIG issued such a purported policy to Brightpoint, for the purpose of assisting Brightpoint to conceal US$11.9 million in losses in 1998. The alleged policy allowed Brightpoint to recognise an insurance receivable of US$11.9 million, when in fact all that occurred was a "round-trip" of cash.

The complaint further alleged that AIG and Brightpoint violated the antifraud provisions of the Exchange Act, as well as the reporting and books and records provisions, and that AIG aided and abetted Brightpoint's antifraud violation. Brightpoint and AIG consented to entry of a final judgment in settlement of the civil matter, as well as to a cease-and-desist order in the administrative proceeding enjoining the companies from further violations of the securities laws. As part of the settlement, AIG agreed to pay a US$10 million civil penalty and US$100,000 of disgorgement, and Brightpoint agreed to pay a US$450,000 civil penalty.

In the matter of Reliant, Inc. and Reliant Energy, Inc.,
Exchange Act Release 47828 (12th May 2003)
The Commission instituted a cease-and-desist proceeding against Reliant Resources, Inc. and Reliant Energy, Inc. (collectively referred to as Reliant), and simultaneously accepted Reliant's offer of settlement. Under the terms of the settlement, Reliant consented to entry of an order requiring Reliant to cease-and-desist from committing, or causing to be committed, further violations of the antifraud provisions, books and records provisions, and record keeping provisions of the securities laws.

The Commission found securities violations as a result of two distinct types of transaction. First, the Commission found that Reliant had violated the securities laws by taking part in "round trip" energy trades that were simultaneous buy and sell transactions that resulted in an equal amount of revenues and expenses for Reliant. The SEC found that these transactions were undertaken solely to increase volume at Reliant, and led to a material misstatement in Reliant's financial statements when accounted for on a gross basis. Second, the Commission found that Reliant took part in actions to shift earnings from the current period, where those earnings were coming in well above forecasted amounts, to future periods, where earnings were likely to come in below the forecasted amounts. These structured transactions created a smoothing effect on Reliant's earnings, which the Commission alleged created a material misstatement in Reliant's financial statements.

SEC v. HealthSouth Corporation and Richard M. Scrushy,
Litigation Release 18044 (20th March 2003)
The Commission filed charges in the United States District Court for the Northern District of Alabama against HealthSouth Corporation (HRC) and its Chief Executive Officer Richard M. Scrushy, alleging that HRC and Scrushy had violated the antifraud, reporting, and books and records provisions of the federal securities laws. The

complaint alleged that HRC had overstated its earnings since 1999 by US$1.4 billion. In addition, the complaint alleged that HRC had overstated its assets by US$800 million. The Commission later filed an amended complaint to allege that, since 1991, Scrushy sold at least 13,823,000 shares of HRC common stock for proceeds in excess of US$170 million, based upon his knowledge of HRC's actual financial results and the impact that disclosure of those results would have on the price of HRC's shares.

According to the complaint, HRC artificially inflated its earnings in order to meet Wall Street analyst expectations. The complaint alleged that, on a quarterly basis, HRC executives would present Scrushy with an analysis of HRC's actual earnings compared to Wall Street analyst expectations, and would be instructed by Scrushy to record false earnings to make up for any shortfall. HRC Executives would allegedly makeup those shortfalls by reducing a contra revenue account or decreasing certain expenses. To avoid detection, the executives would allegedly make a corresponding increase in HRC's assets or decrease in HRC's liabilities.

For the alleged violations, the complaint seeks permanent injunctions against HRC and Scrushy, civil money penalties from HRC and Scrushy, disgorgement of ill-gotten gains, and prejudgment interest thereon. The Commission likewise sought and received emergency relief freezing substantially all of Scrushy's assets, among other things. The freeze on Scrushy's assets was later lifted after a hearing on the matter.

HRC consented to the entry of an order by the court:

(1) requiring that the company place in escrow, under the Court's supervision, all extraordinary payments (whether compensation or otherwise) to its directors, officers, partners, controlling persons, agents, or employees, pursuant to the provisions of SOX;
(2) prohibiting the company and its employees from destroying documents relating to the company's financial activities and/or the allegations in the Commission's case against HRC or Scrushy; and
(3) providing for expedited discovery in the Commission's case.

In a related criminal action, a federal grand jury in the Northern District of Alabama indicted Scrushy on charges of conspiracy, mail fraud, wire fraud, securities fraud, making false statements, making a false certification of a financial statement, money laundering, obstruction of justice, perjury, forfeiture, and aiding and abetting. Scrushy's trial is currently pending.

SEC v. Dynegy Inc., Litigation Release 17744 (25th September 2002); In the matter of dynegy inc., Exchange Act Release 46537 (24th September 2002)

In this matter, the Commission asserted that Dynegy engaged in two different types of misconduct. First, the Commission's order found and the Commission's complaint alleged that Dynegy improperly disclosed and accounted for a US$300 million financing transaction involving special purpose entities (SPEs). Second, the Commission asserted that Dynegy issued materially misleading press releases regarding increases in trading activity on Dynegy's electronic trading platform.

The Commission alleged that Dynegy misled the investing public by failing to properly account for and disclose the closing of a financing arrangement that the company carried out with a group of SPEs. The Commission stated that Dynegy closed the SPE related transaction and reported the proceeds of the closing – US$300 million – as increases in its cash flow. The Commission explained that Dynegy's accounting failed to comply with GAAP and caused a materially misleading appearance of Dynegy's financial statements.

In addition, the Commission asserted that, in early 2002, Dynegy issued two misleading press releases announcing increases in trading traffic on Dynegydirect, the company's electronic trading platform, with corresponding increases in the revenues. The Commission stated that the press releases were misleading because the company failed to disclose that the increases in trading volume and revenue were largely the result of a series of "round-trip" or "wash" sales that Dynegy executed with trading partners. The Commission found that the "round-trip" trades lacked any economic substance and were executed for the purpose of inflating trading volume.

In settling the matter, Dynegy agreed to pay a US$3 million civil penalty and consented to the entry of a cease-and-desist order finding that the company engaged in securities fraud. The Commission explained in the litigation release announcing the settlement of this matter that the amount of the penalty reflected the Commission's dissatisfaction with Dynegy's failure to cooperate fully during the early stages of the investigation.

SEC v. Adelphia Communications Corp., Litigation Release 17627 (24th July 2002); Litigation Release 17837 (14th November 2002); Press Release 2005–63, (25th April 2005)

On 24th July 2002, the Commission announced the filing of a civil action in the United States District Court for the Southern District of New York against Adelphia Communications Corporation (Adelphia); its founder John J. Rigas; his three sons Timothy J. Rigas, Michael J. Rigas, James R. Rigas; and two senior executives at Adelphia, James R. Brown and Michael C. Mulcahey, in one of the largest financial fraud cases brought by the Commission to date. In its complaint, the Commission charged that Adelphia, at the direction of the individual defendants:

(1) fraudulently excluded billions of dollars in liabilities from its consolidated financial statements by hiding them in off-balance-sheet affiliates;
(2) falsified operations statistics and inflated Adelphia's earnings to meet analysts expectations; and
(3) concealed rampant self-dealing by the Rigas family, including the undisclosed use of corporate funds to purchase company stock and luxury condominiums.

The Commission's complaint charged the defendants with violations of the antifraud, periodic reporting, record keeping, and internal control provisions of the federal securities laws. The Commission sought a judgment ordering the defendants to account for and disgorge all ill-gotten gains, including all compensation received by the individual defendants during the alleged fraud, all property unlawfully taken from Adelphia by the individual defendants through undisclosed related-party transactions, and any severance payments related to the individual defendants' resignation from the company. The Commission also sought civil penalties and orders barring each of the individual defendants from acting as an officer or director of a public company.

On 14th November 2002, the Commission announced that Brown, the former vice-president of Finance at Adelphia, without admitting or denying the allegations in the complaint, consented to the entry against him of a permanent injunction against violations of Section 17(a) of the Securities Act, Sections 10(b) and 13(b)(5) of the Exchange Act, and Rules 10b-5, 13b2-1, and 13b2-2, and, as a control person, of Sections 13(a) and 13(b)(2)(A) and 13(b)(2)(B) of the Exchange Act and Rules 12b-20, 13a-1 and 13a-13, and a permanent officer and director bar. Brown also agreed to provide the Court with an accounting. The Commission's claims against Brown for disgorgement of ill-gotten gains, plus prejudgment interest, and a civil penalty remain pending.

On 25th April 2005, the SEC announced that it and the United States Attorney's Office for the Southern District of New York ("USAO") reached an agreement to settle the SEC's civil enforcement action and resolve the criminal charges against Adelphia and the Rigas family defendants. The USAO also announced that it had entered into a non-prosecution agreement with Adelphia and had settled forfeiture claims against Rigas family members.

Under the settlement agreement, which is subject to the approval of the District and Bankruptcy Courts for the Southern District of New York, the Rigas family members will forfeit in excess of US$1.5 billion in assets that they derived from the fraud, including the Rigas family's interests in certain cable properties. Upon the forfeiture of these assets, Adelphia will obtain title to those cable properties and will pay US$715 million into a victim fund to be established in the District Court in accordance with the non-prosecution agreement. Under the non-prosecution agreement, payment to the victim fund must occur at or around the time of Adelphia's emergence from Chapter 11 bankruptcy protection.

Also under the settlement agreement, Adelphia and the Rigas family members agreed to entry of permanent injunctions enjoining them from the antifraud, periodic reporting, and record keeping and internal control provisions of the federal securities laws. The individual Rigas family members further agreed to orders barring them from acting as officers or directors of a public company.

SEC v. WorldCom, Inc., Litigation Release 17588 (27th June 2002)
This matter is the result of an alleged massive accounting fraud perpetrated by the senior management of WorldCom, Inc. (WorldCom). On 27th June 2002, the Commission filed a complaint

alleging that WorldCom fraudulently overstated its income, before taxes and minority interests, by approximately US$3.055 billion in 2001 and US$797 million during the first quarter of 2002. The Commission's complaint further alleged that WorldCom falsely portrayed itself as a profitable business during 2001 and the first quarter of 2002 by fabricating reporting earnings. The Commission alleged that WorldCom did so by capitalising (and deferring) rather than expensing (and immediately recognising) approximately US$3.8 billion of its costs. The company transferred these costs to capital accounts in violation of GAAP. The Commission alleged that these actions were intended to mislead investors and manipulate WorldCom's earnings to keep them in line with estimates by Wall Street analysts.

The Commission's complaint sought:

(1) a permanent injunction;
(2) civil monetary penalties;
(3) a court order prohibiting WorldCom and its directors, officers, employees, and agents from destroying, altering or hiding relevant documents;
(4) a court order prohibiting WorldCom or its affiliates from making any extraordinary payments to any present or former officer, director or employee, including severance payments, bonus payments, or indemnification payments; and
(5) the appointment of a corporate monitor to ensure that documents are not destroyed and extraordinary payments are not made.

On 28th June 2002, based upon a joint agreement between the Commission and WorldCom, US District Court Judge Jed Rakoff entered an order, which among other things:

(1) directed WorldCom and its affiliates to preserve all items relating to WorldCom's financial reporting obligations, public disclosures required by the federal securities laws, or accounting matters;
(2) provided for the Court to appoint a Corporate Monitor having oversight responsibility with respect to all compensation paid by WorldCom for the purposes of preventing unjust enrichment as a result of the conduct alleged in the Commission's complaint

and to ensure that WorldCom assets are not dissipated by payments that are not necessary to the operation of WorldCom's business.[34]

On 1st November 2002, the Commission filed an amended complaint against WorldCom adding claims that WorldCom violated the antifraud and books and records provisions of the federal securities laws in connection with several securities offerings. The amended complaint also broadened the time period relating to the Commission's charges by alleging that WorldCom misled investors from at least as early as 1999 through the first quarter of 2002, and further stated that the company had acknowledged that during that period, as a result of undisclosed and improper accounting, WorldCom materially overstated the income it reported on its financial statements by approximately US$9 billion.

On 26th November 2002, the Commission announced that WorldCom consented, without admitting or denying the allegations in the Commission's complaint, to the entry of the judgment that settles part, but not all, of the Commission's action against WorldCom. The judgment:

(1) enjoins WorldCom from violating the antifraud, reporting, and the books and records and internal controls provisions of the federal securities laws;
(2) orders an extensive review of the company's corporate governance systems, policies, plans, and practices;
(3) orders an extensive review of the company's internal accounting control structure and policies;
(4) orders that WorldCom provide reasonable training and education to certain officers and employees to minimise the possibility of future violations of the federal securities laws; and
(5) provides that civil money penalties, if any, will be decided by the Court at a later date.

On 7th July 2003, Judge Rakoff approved the settlement of the Commission's claim for a civil penalty against WorldCom. Under the terms of the approved settlement, WorldCom was liable for a civil penalty of US$2.25 billion, but once the US Bankruptcy Court

---

[34] On 3rd July, US District Court Judge Jed S. Rakoff appointed former Commission Chairman Richard Breeden as the Corporate Monitor.

for the Southern District of New York approved WorldCom's reorganisation plan, the company was only obligated to pay the reduced sum of US$500 million in cash plus US$250 million in common stock of the reorganised company. Pursuant to the Fair Funds provision of SOX, the funds and stock paid as a result of the penalty will be returned to the shareholder victims of the company's fraud.

The Commission's action in WorldCom is significant for a number of reasons. First, the matter stands as the leading example of the Commission's new policy of "real time enforcement." WorldCom publicly announced its intentions to restate its financial results on 25th June 2002; the Commission filed its original complaint the next day. Second, it provides a glimpse into the Commission's efforts, in financial reporting matters, to quickly seek court intervention to prevent the destruction of documents and dissipation of corporate assets. Third, the SEC took the highly unusual step of ordering WorldCom to file a sworn statement under oath pursuant to Section 21(a) of the Exchange Act describing the events leading to the restatement.

In addition to the charges against the company, the Commission has brought civil actions against four former employees of WorldCom. The Commission has announced that its investigation is continuing.

In a related criminal action, a federal jury in New York City convicted Bernie Ebbers, WorldCom's former CEO, of securities fraud and filing false statements with securities regulators. Ebbers has received 25 years in prison.

In the matter of Trump Hotels & Casino Resorts, Inc.,
Exchange Act Release 45287 (16th January 2002)
This case is the Commission's first enforcement action charging that a company's use of "pro forma" earnings figures was misleading and violated the antifraud provisions of the securities laws.[35] The Trump Hotels & Casino Resorts, Inc.'s (Trump Hotels) press release at issue had disclosed earnings in a manner that did not conform to GAAP. The press release stated that net income and

---

35 The Commission previously issued "cautionary advice" on the use of "pro forma" financial information in earnings releases.

earnings-per-share figures excluded an US$81.4 million one-time charge. The release failed to disclose, however, that net income included a one-time gain of US$17.2 million. The SEC charged the undisclosed one-time gain was material because it represented the difference between positive and negative earnings, and between meeting analyst expectations and not meeting those expectations. The press release was alleged to be misleading because it implied that all one-time items were excluded (when in fact the one-time gain was included and only the one-time charge was excluded). In settlement, Trump Hotels agreed to cease-and-desist from violating the antifraud provisions of the Exchange Act.

Financial Fraud
The following are recent financial fraud cases involving either foreign issuers or conduct offshore.

In the matter of the Coca-Cola Company,
Exchange Act Release 51565 (18th April 2005)
On 18th April 2005, the SEC filed a settled administrative cease-and-desist proceeding against the Coca-Cola Company (Coke). The action related to Coke's alleged failure to disclose certain end-of-quarter sales practices in Japan used to meet earnings expectations, and misstatements in a Form 8-K concerning a subsequent inventory reduction.

According to the Commission, at or near the end of each reporting period between 1997 and 1999, Coke engaged in "channel stuffing" in Japan for the purpose of pulling sales forward into a current period. The channel stuffing, otherwise referred to as "gallon pushing", was accomplished by offering Japanese bottlers extended credit terms in order to induce them to purchase additional quantities of beverage concentrate. The Commission alleged that a bottler's inventory of concentrate purchased from Coke typically corresponds to the bottler's sales of finished product. Due to Coke's gallon pushing, however, Coke's Japanese bottlers' concentrate inventory levels increased at a rate more than five times greater than that of finished product sales. Coke's quarterly earnings per share increased approximately US$0.01 to US$0.02 as a result of the gallon pushing, and the practice made it likely that the bottlers would purchase less concentrate in future periods.

Despite these effects, Coke did not disclose its gallon pushing practice in its periodic reports filed with the Commission.

The SEC also alleged that Coke's 26th January 2000 Form 8-K disclosing, among other things, a worldwide concentrate inventory reduction planned for the first half of 2000 was false and misleading because it failed to disclose that more than US$0.05 of the estimated earnings impact resulting from the inventory reduction was attributable to an anticipated reduction of sales for Japan. The Commission also found the Form 8-K to be false and misleading because it improperly described:

(1) the time period during which Coke reviewed inventory levels;
(2) the Japanese bottlers' prior awareness of the inventory reduction; and
(3) the inventory reduction as a joint effort between Coke and its bottlers, when the inventory reduction was in fact solely a Coke initiative.

Significantly, in announcing this action, the SEC noted that Coke's accounting treatment for sales made in connection with gallon pushing was proper. The SEC also commended Coke for taking substantial steps, both prior to and during the SEC's investigation, to strengthen its internal disclosure review process to prevent future violations.

Without admitting or denying the Commission's allegations, Coke agreed to cease-and-desist from committing or causing any violations and any future violations of Sections 17(a)(2) and 17(a)(3) of the Securities Act and Sections 13(a) of the Exchange Act and Rules 12b-20, 13a-1, 13a-11, and 13a-13 thereunder.

SEC v. Time Warner, Inc., Litigation Release 19147
(21th March 2005); *In the matter of James W. Barge, et al,*
Exchange Act Release 34-51400 (21th March 2005)
On 21st March 2005, the SEC charged Time Warner Inc. (formerly known as AOL Time Warner) with materially overstating online advertising revenue and the number of its Internet subscribers, and with aiding and abetting three other securities frauds. The Commission also charged that the Company violated a Commission cease-and-desist order issued against America Online, Inc. on 15th May 2000 by artificially inflating its online advertising revenue and

the number of AOL subscribers, as well as its failure to consolidate AOL Europe's financial statements.

The Commission's complaint against Time Warner alleged, among other things, that beginning in mid-2000 and extending through 2002, the company employed fraudulent round-trip transactions that boosted its online advertising revenue to mask the fact that it also experienced a business slow-down. The SEC alleged that the round-trip transactions ranged in complexity and sophistication, but in each instance the company effectively funded its own online advertising revenue by giving the counterparties the means to pay for advertising that they would not otherwise have purchased. According to the SEC, to conceal the true nature of the transactions, the company typically structured and documented round-trips as if they were two or more separate, bona fide transactions, conducted at arm's length and reflecting each party's independent business purpose. Time Warner, however, delivered mostly untargeted, less desirable, remnant online advertising to the round-trip advertisers, and the round-trip advertisers often had little or no ability to control the quantity, quality, and sometimes even the content of the online advertising they received.

Several of the counterparties to the round-trip transactions were publicly traded companies. The SEC alleged that three of these counterparties improperly recognised revenue on the round-trip transactions and reported materially misstated financial results to their own investors. The Commission alleged that, as a consequence, the company aided and abetted the frauds of three public companies.

The SEC alleged that the company also artificially inflated the number of AOL subscribers in the second, third, and fourth quarters of 2001 so it could report to the investment community that it had met its new subscriber targets, an important metric the market used to evaluate AOL (both before and after its merger with Time Warner). According to the SEC, the company counted members from "bulk subscription sales" to corporate customers (for distribution to their employees) when the company knew that the memberships had not, and mostly would not, be activated.

In addition, the SEC alleged that, from March 2000 through January 2002, the company failed to properly consolidate the financial results of AOL Europe in its financial statements. AOL

Europe was originally a 50/50 joint venture between AOL and Bertelsmann. In March 2000, AOL entered into a contingent purchase agreement relating to Bertelsmann's interest in AOL Europe. According to the Commission's complaint, the agreement gave AOL broad and direct powers enabling it to control the operations and assets of AOL Europe, a fact that the company acknowledged in a letter to the European Commission (in the context of satisfying EC merger regulations). The SEC alleged that the company's failure to properly consolidate AOL Europe, as required by GAAP when one entity has a controlling financial interest in another entity, resulted in material misstatements of its financial results, including overstatements of operating income and free cash flow in 2000 and 2001, overstatements of net income in 2000, understatements of net losses in 2001, and understatements of total debt in 2000 and 2001.

Without admitting or denying the allegations in the complaint, Time Warner consented to the entry of a judgment that, among other things, ordered it to pay US$300 million in civil penalties. The judgment further ordered the company to comply with the Commission's 15th May 2000 cease-and-desist order against AOL; enjoined the company from violating antifraud, reporting, books-and-records, and internal control provisions of the federal securities laws; and enjoined the company from aiding and abetting securities fraud. As part of the settlement, Time Warner agreed to restate its historical financial results to reduce its reported online advertising revenues by approximately US$500 million (in addition to the US$190 million already restated) for the fourth quarter of 2000 through 2002 and to properly reflect the consolidation of AOL Europe in the company's 2000 and 2001 financial statements. The company also agreed to engage an independent examiner to determine whether the company's historical accounting for certain transactions was in conformity with GAAP.

In a separate administrative proceeding, Time Warner CFO Wayne H. Pace, Controller James W. Barge, and Deputy Controller Pascal Desroches consented to the entry of a Commission cease-and-desist order finding that they caused reporting violations by the company based on their roles in accounting for US$400 million paid to the company by Bertelsmann AG in two sets of transactions. The SEC alleged that, in 2001 and 2002, the company inflated its online advertising revenue in connection with transactions in which Bertelsmann paid US$400 million as consideration for amendments to a multi-billion-dollar contingent purchase agreement governing the company's purchase of Bertelsmann's interest in AOL Europe.

SEC v. Elan Corporation, Litigation Release
19066 (8th February 2005)
The Commission filed a settled civil enforcement action against Elan Corporation, plc (Elan), a pharmaceutical company headquartered in Dublin, Ireland, charging the company with violating the antifraud provisions of the federal securities laws by failing to disclose material information about the company's financial results in press releases and in periodic reports filed with the SEC. According to the Commission's complaint, Elan made public statements during 2000 and 2001 that it was generating record amounts of revenue, net income, and cash flow from drug sales and licensing activities. The complaint alleges that these statements were materially misleading because Elan failed to disclose, or inadequately disclosed, certain transactions that were critical to the company's purported success.

Specifically, the Commission alleged that Elan failed to disclose that substantial portions of its revenues were generated by selling partial royalty rights to some of its most important products and by selling off other drug product lines entirely, and "round-trip" transactions in which joint ventures, of which Elan was a partner, paid license fees to Elan using money that Elan had provided to the partners. In addition, the Commission's complaint alleged that Elan, facilitated a US$148 million artificial sale of certain joint-venture related securities between one of its off-balance sheet subsidiaries and a purchasing entity that Elan had created and Elan had paid US$1 million to participate in the transaction. The complaint alleged that Elan failed to disclose its relationship with the purchaser, that it was required to consolidate the purchaser under applicable accounting rules, that the purchaser did not negotiate the US$148 million purchase price, and that the claimed "estimated fair value" did not reflect what a willing buyer would pay to acquire the securities, which was substantially less than US$148 million. Subsequently, in September 2003, Elan restated its financial results due to this transaction, which reduced its 2001 net income by US$73.9 million, or 22%.

Elan, without admitting or denying the allegations in the Commission's complaint, consented to the entry of a final judgment that permanently enjoined the company from violating the antifraud, internal controls, and reporting provisions of the federal securities laws. Elan also agreed to pay US$1 in disgorgement and a US$15 million civil penalty, which will be distributed to investors harmed by the alleged violations.

In the matter of Teltran International Group, Ltd., Exchange
Act Release 45796 (22nd April 2002); *SEC v. Byron Robert Lerner,*
Litigation Release 17481 (22nd April 2002)

On 22nd April 2002, the Commission filed a complaint against Bryon Lerner, the CEO of Teltran International Group, Ltd. (Teltran), for intentionally causing the company to overstate its reported revenue in quarterly and annual filings made during 1999. Specifically, the Commission alleged that Teltran entered into a contract to acquire Channelnet Limited, a company based in the United Kingdom, on 15th July 1999. The transaction closed one month later. The Commission alleged that Lerner caused Teltran to record the transaction as having occurred on 1st June 1999. In addition, the Commission asserted that Lerner sold stock at a time when he knew the company was misrepresenting its revenues in its Commission filings.

Lerner settled the matter by consenting to the entry of an injunction from violating the antifraud and record keeping provisions of the federal securities laws. He also agreed to pay US$137,000 in disgorgement with pre-judgment interest. In a related administrative proceeding, Teltran consented to the entry of a cease-and-desist order finding that the company engaged in securities fraud and other securities violations.

In the matter of Boston Scientific Corp.,
Exchange Act Release 43183 (21st August 2000)

On 21st August 2000, the Commission entered an order pursuant to which Boston Scientific Corp. (Boston Scientific), without admitting or denying the Commission's allegations, agreed to a cease-and-desist from committing or causing any violations of

Sections 13(a), 13(b)(2)(A) and 13(b)(2)(B) of the Exchange Act and Rules 13a-1, 13a-13 and 12b-20 thereunder.

The Commission found that forty employees of Boston Scientific's Japanese subsidiary, and 143 independent distributors, participated in a scheme to inflate the subsidiary's sales figures. In 1997 and 1998 the Japanese subsidiary recorded thousands of false sales totaling more than US$75 million. The Japanese subsidiary submitted its false sales and earnings data to Boston Scientific, which then incorporated those figures in its consolidated financial statements. Managers at the Japanese subsidiary carried out the scheme by storing goods at leased warehouses and recording sales to the cooperating distributors. To mask the fact that the distributors never paid for the goods, the managers would issue them credits and recorded false sales of the same goods to other distributors. The Japanese subsidiary also falsely confirmed the sales to Boston Scientific's independent auditors.

Boston Scientific uncovered the fraud in the fall of 1998, after the implementation of a new a management information system at the Japanese subsidiary. Boston Scientific promptly notified the SEC and went public with its discovery of the accounting irregularities. In its order, the Commission found that Boston Scientific failed to accurately track accounts receivable, cash receipts and product returns.

In accepting the offer of settlement, which did not include fraud charges, the Commission acknowledged the remedial acts promptly undertaken by Boston Scientific and the cooperation afforded the Commission Staff.

SEC v. Garth H. Drabinsky, Myron I. Gottlieb, Robert Topol, Gordon C. Eckstein, Maria M. Messina, Diane J. Winkfein, D. Grant Malcolm and Tony Fiorino, Litigation Release 16022, (13th January 1999); Administrative Proceeding Files 3–9806, 9807, 9808 (13th January 1999)

The SEC filed a federal court action, alleging that former officers, directors, and members of the accounting staff of Livent Inc., a Canadian-based theater owner and producer of live theatrical entertainment, engaged in a multi-faceted and pervasive fraud spanning eight years between 1990 and 1998. The fraud, allegedly orchestrated by Livent's former chairman and CEO, and the company's former president and a director, had three main components: a multi-million dollar kickback scheme designed to misappropriate funds for personal use; the improper shifting of pre-production costs to fixed assets or other projects; and the improper recording of revenue for transactions that contained side agreements purposely concealed from Livent's outside auditors. The fraud involved multiple violations of the antifraud, books and records, and internal controls provisions of the federal securities laws, and resulted in at least seventeen false filings with the Commission that materially overstated the results of Livent's operations and its financial condition.

According to the complaint, Livent's former CEO manipulated income and operating cash flows with the active participation of several long-time associates, including Livent's former senior vice president of finance and administration, the company's former senior executive vice president and chief operating officer, several individuals in the company's accounting department, and Livent's former CFO and former Deloitte & Touche engagement partner for Livent's 1995 audit, among others.

The former CEO and president were not only charged by the Commission, but were charged in a criminal indictment with sixteen felony violations of the federal securities laws. They are contesting the charges. Two other senior participants also pleaded guilty to one felony count each, for violations of the federal securities laws.

The former senior vice president for finance and administration consented to a court order and administrative proceeding barring him from practicing before the Commission for five years. The Commission has entered three other administrative orders related to the conduct described in the complaint. Livent consented to an order directing the company to cease-and-desist from committing securities violations and to cooperate with the Commission; the former budgeting controller agreed to a cease-and-desist proceeding and a three-year bar from practicing before the Commission; and the former theater controller agreed to a three-year bar.

SEC v. Latin American Resources, Inc., John B. Lowy and Harold J. Glasband, Litigation Release 15802 (8th July 1998)
The Commission filed a complaint in federal court seeking injunctive relief against Latin American Resources, Inc. (LARI),

John B. Lowy, a principal stockholder and counsel to LARI, and Harold J. Glasband, LARI's CFO and a LARI director, and civil penalties against Lowy and Glasband for violating the antifraud provisions of the securities laws by knowingly and recklessly making material misstatements regarding the ownership and value of certain agricultural plantations in Brazil in an Information Statement filed with the National Association of Securities Dealers, Inc. by a New York brokerage firm, and in a July 1994 Registration Statement filed by LARI with the Commission.

In those documents, the Commission alleged, LARI falsely claimed that it owned certain Brazilian agricultural plantations, properties that comprised approximately 95% of LARI's assets at the time of the false filings, and dramatically overstated their value. Lowy was chiefly responsible for negotiating the purported Brazilian transactions and Glasband also participated, and they subsequently became aware of infirmities in the purported title to the Brazilian plantations and material inaccuracies in their valuations. The Commission also alleged that LARI violated annual and quarterly reporting requirements and requirements that issuers maintain proper books and records and internal accounting controls; that Lowy and Glasband directly or indirectly falsified LARI's books and records; and that Glasband made false and misleading statements and omitted material facts in statements to LARI's accountant in connection with the audit of LARI's financial statements.

With the filing of the complaint, LARI and Glasband consented to the entry of final judgments permanently enjoining them from violating the securities laws. Glasband also consented to pay a US$25,000 civil penalty. In addition, in a related proceeding, LARI's former auditor, Dennis Klein, consented to an order denying him the privilege of practicing before the Commission as an accountant.

In the matter of Ngai King Tak, Evelyn A. Wong and Haroutioun K. Aydjian, Exchange Act Release 38988 (28th August 1997)
Two Hong Kong residents and a US citizen provided false confirmations in connection with the audit of Jasmine Corp. The Company ultimately went bankrupt. They agreed to a cease-and-desist order.

SEC v. Alexandra Montgomery et al, Litigation Release 15419 (24th July 1997); Litigation Release 16975 (26th April 2001).

Montgomery was an officer and director of International Nesmont Industrial Corporation (Nesmont), a Canadian refiner and processor of precious metals. Its former officers allegedly engaged in a deliberate scheme to overstate the company's income and inflate its reported assets. They did so in part by allegedly including fake gold materials (in fact, brass bars made to look like gold bars) in inventory. The SEC filed a civil action against the former CEO, the CFO and the head assayer alleging violations of the antifraud, books and records, and reporting provisions. The SEC accused the CFO and her mother of insider trading.

The officers consented to the entry of final judgments permanently enjoining them from violating the antifraud and other provisions of the securities laws, and barring them from future service as officers or directors of any publicly traded company. The CFO and her mother were ordered to disgorge US$282,400 in illegal insider trading profits and to pay civil penalties. The head assayer was dismissed from the action following his death in 1999.

SEC v. Montedison SpA, Litigation Release 15164 (21st November 1996); Litigation Release 16948 (30th March 2001)

On 20th November 1996, the SEC filed a civil injunction action against Montedison SpA, in which it alleged that the Italian conglomerate, which until 2000 had ADRs listed on the NYSE, repeatedly falsified its US regulatory filings. In particular, the SEC claimed that the company materially misstated its financial position by hiding the misappropriation of approximately US$400 million, allegedly used by former corporate management to bribe Italian politicians. The SEC obtained assistance from the Italian CONSOB, which had conducted it own investigation into the matter.

In 2000, Montedison was acquired by Compart, S.p.A. and its ADRs were delisted. Compart thereafter changed its name to Montedison and agreed to a settlement on behalf of the former Montedison requiring the payment of a civil penalty of US$300,000.

Auditor Independence

At the same time it is focusing on accounting and disclosure by public companies, the Commission also has expressed concern about auditor independence ie, the requirement that the outside accounting firm be "independent" from the issuer whose financial statements it audits. In December 2000, the Commission passed new rules on auditor independence, limiting the non-audit services that may be provided by an independent auditor, and requiring additional disclosure on non-audit fees. The auditor independence rules have been codified by SOX. The Commission has also brought significant enforcement actions against major US accounting firms alleging that the firms violated the Commission's independence rules and/or caused violations of the issuer reporting requirements.

In the matter of Ernst & Young LLP,
Initial Decision Release 249 (16th April 2004)
This initial decision originated from public administrative proceeding initiated on 20th May 2002 by the Commission against Ernst & Young LLP (E&Y) alleging that E&Y violated the auditor independence requirements in connection with E&Y's audit of the financial statements of PeopleSoft, Inc. from 1994 through 1999 by jointly developing and marketing a software product with PeopleSoft.[36] According to the Commission's allegations, E&Y agreed to pay PeopleSoft a guaranteed minimum royalty of 15% to 30% from each sale of the resulting product, with a guaranteed minimum royalty of US$300,000. In addition, the Commission alleged that E&Y earned hundreds of million of dollars in consulting revenues from implementing PeopleSoft software for third parties pursuant to an "Implementation Partners Agreement" it had with PeopleSoft. E&Y allegedly coordinated and jointly marketed its implementation services with PeopleSoft, undertaking reciprocal endorsements of each other and providing links to each other's websites. E&Y and PeopleSoft also held themselves out as "business partners" of one another and shared customer information, customer leads, and "target accounts." The Commission's charged that E&Y violated Rule 2–02(b) of Regulation S-X and caused PeopleSoft to file reports with the Commission that failed to include independently audited financial statements as required.

---

36 See *In the Matter of Ernst & Young LLP*, Exchange Act Release 45964 (20th May 2002).

Significantly, the Commission sought to enforce the auditor independence requirements in the absence of any allegations that the audit work itself was flawed.

On 2nd July 2002, an administrative law judge dismissed the proceedings because the decision to issue the enforcement proceeding was made only by one SEC Commissioner – an action ie permitted only in limited circumstances, none of which was present in this matter.

On 23rd October 2002, the SEC ordered that the administrative proceeding be dismissed without prejudice, but nevertheless noted that the Commission, not an ALJ, has the authority to review action taken by a Commissioner as Duty Officer.[37]

On 13th November 2002, the SEC re-instituted its administrative proceeding against E&Y.[38] After an 11-day hearing, E&Y was found to have violated the independence requirements. The sanctions imposed against E&Y included a cease-and-desist order, disgorgement of US$1,686,500 plus pre-judgment interest, the requirement to retain and independent consultant to assure the Commission that E&Y's leadership is committed to, and has implemented policies and procedures that reasonably can be expected to remedy the violations. Significantly, the sanctions imposed also included suspending E&Y from accepting audit engagements for new Commission registrant audit clients for a period of six months.

In the matter of Grant Thornton LLP, Doeren Mayhew & Co. P.C., Peter M. Behrens, CPA, Marvin J. Morris, CPA, and Benedict P. Rybicki, CPA, Securities Act Release 8355 (20th January 2004)

On 20th January 2004, the Commission instituted public administrative proceedings pursuant to Rule 102(e) and cease-and-desist proceedings against Grant Thornton LLP (Grant Thornton) Doeren Mayhew & Co. P.C. (Doeren Mayhew), a Grant Thornton partner and two Doeren Mayhew directors for alleged misconduct in connection with their audit of MCA Financial Corporation's (MCA) financial statements for the fiscal year ended 31st January 1998. The Commission alleged that in connection with the 1998 MCA audit,

---

37 See *In the Matter of Ernst & Young LLP*, Administrative Proceeding 3-10786, Exchange Act Release 46710 (23rd October 2002).

38 See *In the Matter of Ernst & Young LLP*, Exchange Act Release 46821 (13th November 2002).

the respondents caused and aided and abetted MCA's violations of the antifraud and reporting provisions of the federal securities laws, violated or caused and aided and abetted violations of Section 10A of the Exchange Act and engaged in improper professional conduct.

The Commission alleged that the respondents, notwithstanding knowledge that MCA failed to disclose several million dollars of material, related party transactions in its 1998 annual financial statements, jointly issued a report containing an unqualified opinion on MCA's 1998 annual financial statements and consented to the inclusion of their report in MCA's offering materials. The Commission also alleged that the respondents failed to inform MCA's Board of Directors that MCA's financial statements omitted the material, related party transactions. The Commission further alleged that the respondents engaged in improper professional conduct by failing to adequately plan the 1998 MCA audit, not acting with sufficient skepticism in conducting the audit, and not obtaining enough evidence to support their conclusions.

On 5th August 2004, the respondents consented to the Commission's entry of an Order Making Findings and Imposing Remedial Sanctions without admitting or denying the Commission's findings. As part of the Order, Grant Thornton agreed to

(1) pay disgorgement and prejudgment interest of US$59,749;
(2) pay a penalty of US$1.5 million;
(3) be censured for its alleged conduct;
(4) require its entire professional staff to undergo fraud-detection training and provide at least US$1 million to fund such training; and
(5) suspend certain joint audits with other auditing firms for a period of five years.

Pursuant to the Order, Doeren Mayhew, which voluntarily discontinued conducting public audits as of 19th March 2003, agreed not to accept new public company auditing engagements for six months. In addition, Doeren Mayhew agreed that if it engages in audits of public companies after the expiration of six months, it would establish and implement certain policies and procedures specifically designed to improve the quality of its public company audit practice for a period of three years. Doeren Mayhew also was censured and required to pay disgorgement and prejudgment interest of US$115,126.86.

Pursuant to the Order, Morris, Behrens and Rybicki were denied the privilege of appearing or practicing before the Commission for periods of five years, three years and one year, respectively, from the entry of the Order.

SEC v. Kenneth Wilchfort and Marc Rabinowitz,
Litigation Release 18102 (24th April 2003)
On 24th April 2003, the Commission announced the filing of a complaint against Kenneth Wilchfort and Marc Rabinowitz, two partners of E&Y for aiding and abetting the non-fraud based securities violations of Cendant Corporation (Cendant) and a predecessor company, CUC International (CUC). The complaint alleges that Wilchfort and Rabinowitz, the E&Y partners responsible for providing audit services to Cendant and CUC, failed to detect, and take proper remedial actions against, Cendant and CUC's activities that caused their financial statements to violate GAAP. The complaint asserted that Wilchfort and Rabinowitz breached their duties as accountants when they failed to detect the improper accounting and issued unqualified audit opinions of Cendant and CUC's financial statements. The Commission explained that Wilchfort and Rabinowitz breached their duties despite the fact that Cendant and CUC provided them with false documents and lied to them.

Wilchfort and Rabinowitz settled the Commission's charges by consenting to the entry of injunctions against future violations of the reporting provisions of the federal securities laws. The defendants also consented to the entry of administrative orders suspending them from appearing and practicing before the Commission for at least four years.

In the matter of Moret Ernst & Young Accountants,
Exchange Act Release 46130 (27th June 2002).
In the first-ever auditor independence case against a foreign audit firm, the Commission instituted and settled an administrative action against Moret Ernst & Young Accountants (Moret), a Dutch accounting firm known as Ernst & Young Accountants.

As alleged in the Commission's order, Moret audited the financial statements of Baan Company, N.V. (Baan), a business software company headquartered in the Netherlands. Baan's stock was traded on the NASDAQ National Market for fiscal years 1995 through 1997. The Commission alleged that during the same period, Moret had joint business relationships with Baan that impaired Moret's independence as an auditor. Most of the joint business relationships were established to allow Moret to assist Baan in implementing its software products for third companies. According to the Commission's order, Moret billed Baan approximately US$1.9 million in connection with the joint business relationships.

The Commission found that Moret improperly used and relied on audit work performed by its affiliated firm in the United States, Ernst & Young LLP. At the time, Ernst & Young also lacked independence from Baan due to joint business relationships it had with Baan.

Moret, without admitting or denying the Commission's order, consented to the Commission's entry of a censure pursuant to Rule 102(e)(1) Moret was ordered to pay a civil penalty of US$400,000 and to comply with a number of remedial undertakings to develop, enhance and implement auditor independence policies and practices.

In the matter of KPMG LLP, Exchange Act Release 45272
(14th January 2002)
The Commission in this matter filed and simultaneously settled administrative proceedings against KPMG LLP (KPMG), alleging the accounting firm lacked independence from its client when it audited the client's financial statements at the same time it had substantial financial investments in the client. KPMG's audit client was AIM Funds (AIM), a family of mutual funds managed by AIM management. KPMG audited the financial statements of numerous AIM funds and portfolios.

In May 2000, KPMG invested US$25 million through SunTrust Bank in an AIM government money market fund. Unbeknownst to KPMG at the time of the investment, that AIM fund was one of the funds audited by KPMG. KPMG made significant additional investments in that fund, reaching a point where its account balance represented approximately 35% of KPMG's total invested surplus cash and constituted approximately 15% of the fund portfolio's net assets.

KPMG remained unaware that it had invested in its audit client, and that the particular portfolio was one of those it audited, until an AIM employee notified AIM management, which in turn notified KPMG in December 2000. KPMG immediately liquidated its investment in the fund and resigned from all of its AIM fund audit engagements. AIM retained another audit firm to reaudit the financial statements of the relevant portfolios.

The SEC's order noted that KPMG not only issued audit reports while its independence was impaired, but it "repeatedly confirmed its putative independence from the AIM funds," including the portfolio in which it had invested, during the period in which it was invested in that portfolio. The order stated "[t]his impairment of KPMG's independence occurred primarily because the firm lacked adequate policies or procedures to prevent or detect this independence problem and because the steps that KPMG personnel usually took before initiating similar firm investments were not taken here."

The SEC censured KPMG and required undertakings requiring the adoption and implementation of new policies and procedures, and additional training of relevant personnel.

The SEC's action in this matter is significant in that it censured the firm in a case where there were no showing of harm to investors, and no indication of any deliberate misconduct by the firm. The case highlights the importance of having adequate policies and procedures in place to prevent and detect violations.

In the matter of KPMG Peat Marwick LLP,
Exchange Act Release 39400 (19th January 2001)
The Commission in December 1997 instituted public administrative proceedings against KPMG Peat Marwick alleging that KPMG Peat Marwick lacked independence from one of its audit clients Porta Systems, Inc. (Porta), when it issued its audit report in connection with Porta's 1995 year-end financial statements.

In September 1995, KPMG Peat Marwick announced a strategic alliance with KPMG BayMark, L.L.C. (BayMark), a company designed to, among other things, provide non-audit services such as broker-dealer and turnaround services to KPMG Peat Marwick audit clients. BayMark was owned by its four individual principals. It received its start-up capital and working capital in the form of loans from KPMG Peat Marwick. Later in 1995, one of

BayMark's principals took on the role of interim president and COO of Porta, a financially troubled company that had engaged BayMark for turnaround assistance. KPMG Peat Marwick audited Porta's 1995 financial statements and prepared its audit report.

The Commission alleged that KPMG Peat Marwick lacked independence from its audit client Porta in both fact and appearance because of certain aspects of its alliance with BayMark, and the fact that KPMG Peat Marwick had loaned US$100,000 to each of the BayMark principals when BayMark was created, including the individual who would later become the interim president and COO of Porta.

The Commission also asserted that certain aspects of the alliance structure compromised KPMG Peat Marwick's independence from Porta because there was an identity of interest between KPMG Peat Marwick and BayMark, which had become an "affiliate" of an audit client.

KPMG Peat Marwick did not deny that a loan to an officer of an audit client was technically a violation of independence standards, but argued instead that the audit team that performed the audit was indisputably "in fact" independent because it had no knowledge of the details of the financial relationship between BayMark and KPMG Peat Marwick when it performed its audit work and issued its opinion.

KPMG Peat Marwick also argued that none of the allegations constitute violations of the independence rules, and, in fact, the key items of the alliance (the capital loans, the use of the KPMG initials and the royalty) had been disclosed in 1994 to the Office of the Chief Accountant (OCA) Staff members who, upon hearing about these structural elements in a face-to-face meeting, did not object to KPMG Peat Marwick's conclusion that it would be independent of BayMark's clients. KPMG Peat Marwick asserted that it entered into the alliance in the good faith belief that the OCA Staff had agreed that there was no independence problem.

KPMG Peat Marwick also asserted that it disclosed the key facts of the Porta engagement to the OCA in late 1995, including the fact that BayMark was running Porta, and believed in good faith that it had clearance to proceed with the audit of Porta while it modified the BayMark Alliance to address the Staff's concerns about the structure which were first raised in 1995.

The case was tried at a hearing before an Administrative Law Judge, and was thereafter dismissed by the Judge. On appeal, the Commission found that KPMG had violated the independence requirement in two aspects. First, the Commission held that KPMG's loan to the officer of KPMG's audit client, Porta, constituted an independence violation. The Commission also found that KPMG's receipt of royalty fees from BayMark was a contingent fee that violated the independence requirements. The Commission also held, however, that KPMG did not engage in improper professional conduct.

The Commission held that since KPMG was not independent, KPMG caused Porta to file its 1995 annual report in violation of Section 13(a) of the Exchange Act and Rule 13a-1 thereunder which requires such report to be certified by an independent public accountant. The Commission held that "negligence is sufficient to establish 'causing' liability under Exchange Act Section 21C(a), at least in cases in which a person is alleged to 'cause' a primary violation that does not require scienter."

Significantly, the Commission ordered KPMG to cease-and-desist from causing violations of the reporting provisions of the Exchange Act and from committing violations of the auditor independence requirements. The Commission reasoned that the seriousness of the violations, KPMG's failure to appreciate the seriousness of the violations, and the "forward-looking effect to be served by the cease and-desist order," warranted the order. The Commission noted in particular its conclusion that senior level employees at KPMG failed to undertake a reasonable inquiry that would have led them to discover the independence violations. KPMG is appealing to the US Court of Appeals.

Significance of KPMG Peat Marwick

The Commission's action against KPMG Peat Marwick represents the first contested case in which the Commission has sought a cease-and-desist order against an accounting firm directly in connection with an alleged violation of the Commission's independence rules. Before the Commission's action against KPMG Peat Marwick, auditors were alleged to have "caused" a registrant's violation of the independence rules, not to have directly violated the regulation. The action against KPMG Peat Marwick is significant because a direct violation of the independence rules gives rise to strict liability, unlike a claim of "causing" a reporting violation which requires a showing of, at a minimum, negligence.

The action against KPMG Peat Marwick is also noteworthy with respect to the Commission's allegation that KPMG Peat Marwick was a cause of Porta's violation of the Exchange Act. The Commission's allegation that KPMG Peat Marwick caused material misstatements in Porta's financial statements is premised solely on its allegation that the firm lacked independence from Porta. The Commission identified no accounting irregularities in Porta's 1995 financial statements. Porta was reaudited by another firm that issued an identical auditors report. The Commission has nevertheless alleged that Porta's 1995 financial statements were inaccurate because they falsely represented that they had been audited by an independent accountant. Accordingly, KPMG Peat Marwick could only have caused a violation of the Exchange Act's reporting provisions if in fact lacked independence from Porta.

In the matter of PricewaterhouseCoopers LLP,
Exchange Act Release 40945 (14th January 1999)
On 14th January 1999, the Commission instituted administrative proceedings against Price Waterhouse Coopers (PwC) and simultaneously settled the allegations that the firm had failed to comply with the applicable Commission independence rules.

Three types of conduct were involved:

(1) three professionals owned securities of publicly-held audit clients for which they provided professional services;
(2) five partners or their spouses owned securities or other financial interests in publicly-held audit clients for which those partners did not provide professional services;
(3) Coopers & Lybrand's (C&L) retirement plan (prior to and after its merger with Price Waterhouse) owned securities of publicly-held audit clients of C&L and, after the merger, of PwC.

In settlement of the charges, PwC agreed to a censure, and:

(1) to the appointment by the Commission of a person to conduct an internal review and report to the audit committee of the client any instances of professionals in the firm owning securities of the audit client,

(2) to adopt policies and procedures to assure compliance with applicable independence rules;

(3) and to create a US$2.5 million fund for programs to further awareness and education throughout the profession of the independence requirements for public accounting firms.

Aiding and Abetting Violations of the US federal laws

Following the collapse of Enron, the Commission charged certain investment banks that set up complex structured finance transactions for that company with aiding and abetting Enron's securities law violations. Those cases are summarised below.

Canadian Imperial Bank of Commerce,
Daniel Ferguson, Ian Schottlaender, Mark Wolf,
Litigation Release 18517 (22nd December 2003)
The Commission charged Canadian Imperial Bank of Commerce (CIBC) and three of its executives with aiding and abetting Enron's accounting fraud through a series of complex structured finance transactions over a period of years preceding Enron's bankruptcy. Simultaneously with the filing of the complaint, CIBC settled the action, agreeing to consent to entry of a final judgment against the Company. CIBC agreed to pay US$80 million in disgorgement, fees and penalties.

According to the complaint, the financings complained of involved purported transfers of assets from Enron to various off-balance sheet special purpose entities. Enron accounted for the asset transfers as sales in order to book earnings and operating cash flows, without reporting the associated debt on its financial statements. CIBC organised a syndicate of banks to provide the majority of the capitalisation of the special purpose entities with debt financing. CIBC also provided outside "at risk" equity that was required to validate the financing of certain qualified special purpose entities. According to the complaint, the supposedly "at-risk" equity necessary to qualify these special purpose entities was not actually "at risk," due to various agreements between CIBC executives and Enron executives.

According to the complaint, CIBC took part in all of these actions, despite concerns that Enron had "financially engineered" a large portion of its profits. According to the complaint, CIBC nonetheless desired to be included in Enron's elite tier of banks. CIBC earned US$18 million in fees from the fraudulent financing deals.

In the matter of Citigroup, Inc., Exchange Act Release 48230
(28th July 2003)
The Commission instituted cease-and-desist proceedings against Citigroup, Inc. (Citigroup), alleging that the Company had aided and abetted the violations of securities laws by Enron Corp. and Dynegy Inc., by creating various complex structured finance transactions intended to disguise the true nature of those transactions as loans from Citigroup to those entities. The Commission simultaneously accepted Citigroup's offer of settlement, consenting to a cease-and-desist order and the payment of US$120 million in disgorgement, fees and penalties.

According to the complaint, Citigroup took part in three types of activities that aided Enron's fraudulent activities. First, Citigroup allegedly took part in a transaction whereby Enron fraudulently generated US$500 million of cash flows from operating activities through the sale of US Treasury bills that were financed through a loan from Citigroup. Second, Citigroup allegedly assisted Enron in the sale of an interest in its pulp and paper businesses to a special purpose entity capitalised by Citigroup with a US$194 million loan and US$6 million in equity. In order to avoid the requirement that Enron consolidate this transaction on its financial statements, it was necessary that Citigroup retain the risk of loss with respect to he equity portion of the transaction. However, despite documentation that made it appear that Citigroup was taking on the risk from these transactions, Enron had provided oral representations that Citigroup would not lose anything in the transaction. Third, Citigroup allegedly took part in certain prepaid transactions, whereby Citigroup passed the risks of the transaction back to Enron through the use of a special purpose entity. Despite the lack of any transfer of risk, Enron treated these transactions as actual sales, thus increasing earnings and cash flows from operations. The complaint alleges that these activities aided and abetted Enron's antifraud violations.

With respect to Dynegy, Citigroup allegedly set up a complex structured finance transaction whereby Citigroup provided a US$300 million loan to Dynegy, which Dynegy then used to purchase discounted gas from an SPE which it sold for an immediate profit. Dynegy is now repaying the loan by paying above-market gas prices to the same SPE. According to the complaint, Citigroup knew that Dynegy was using the US$300 million loan proceeds to gain a US$79 million tax benefit based on the transaction as an actual sale, and that Dynegy was reporting the proceeds derived from the transaction as cash flows from operating activities, despite the fact that they were funded with debt. The complaint alleges that these activities aided and abetted Dynegy's antifraud violations.

SEC v. JP Morgan Chase & Co.,
Litigation Release 18252 (28th July 2003)
The SEC charged JP Morgan Chase & Co (JP Morgan) with aiding and abetting Enron's securities fraud. The complaint alleged that JP Morgan aided and abetted Enron's manipulation of its reported financial results through transactions that allowed Enron to report loans from JP Morgan as cash flows from operating activities. According to the complaint, the complex nature of these transactions served no business purpose other than to disguise the fact that the transactions were loans. JP Morgan simultaneously agreed to the filing of a consent and final judgment settling the action, enjoining JP Morgan from further securities violations, and requiring JP Morgan to pay US$135 million in disgorgement, penalties and fees.

According to the complaint, JP Morgan and Enron engaged in seven transactions between 1997 and 2001, which were intended to disguise loans from JP Morgan as commodity trades, thus achieving Enron's desired accounting and reporting objectives. According to the complaint, JP Morgan and Enron entered into "prepay" transactions, whereby JP Morgan would pay for a commodity up front, with delivery to occur on a separate date. However, unlike a normal prepay transaction which is treated as a sale, these transactions were designed in such a way that no commodity price risk ever passed to JP Morgan. This was accomplished through simultaneous trades between Enron, a counter party, and a special purpose entity sponsored by JP Morgan, which passed the price risk back to Enron. The Commission alleged that

JP Morgan knew that Enron was using these trades in order to disguise what was principally a loan transaction as a transaction involving actual earnings and cash flows from operating activities. According to the complaint, these actions assisted Enron in carrying out its securities fraud.

SEC v. Merrill Lynch & Co., Inc., Daniel H. Bayly,
Thomas W. Davis, Robert S. Furst, and Schuyler M. Tilney,
Litigation Release 18038 (17th March 2003)
The Commission charged Merrill Lynch & Co., Inc. (Merrill) and four of its former senior executives with aiding and abetting Enron Corporation's securities fraud. The complaint alleged that Merrill assisted Enron's earnings manipulation through two fraudulent year-end transactions in 1999. The transactions allegedly had the effect of overstating Enron's fourth quarter income in 1999 by US$60 million. Merrill consented to entry of a judgment simultaneously with the filing of the complaint.

The Commissions complaint alleged that, in December 1999, senior Enron executives approached Merrill with two transactions that they had designed. The first was allegedly an "asset-parking arrangement whereby Merrill bought an interest in Nigerian barges from Enron with the express understanding that Enron would arrange for the sale of the interest within six months at a specified rate of return. No risk was transferred as a result of this transaction, and Merrill knew that Enron was entering into the transaction for the purpose of recording US$28 million in revenue and US$12 million in pre-tax income.

In the second transaction, Merrill and Enron allegedly entered into two energy options contracts, one physical and one financial, that had the purpose and effect of increasing Enron's income by approximately US$50 million, despite the fact that trading under the options was not to begin for nine months, and Enron had told Merrill that it might want to unwind the transactions early. According to the complaint, Merrill knew that the transaction, which it believed to be a wash trade, would have significant impacts on Enron's reported results, bonuses and stock price. Merrill demanded a multi-million dollar fee for entering into the transaction.

The Commission found that Merrill's actions aided and abetted Enron's violations of the antifraud provisions, reporting provisions, and books and records provisions of the federal securities laws. Merrill settled the transactions by accepting entry of a permanent injunction against further securities violations, and by agreeing to pay US$80 million in disgorgement, penalties and fees.

Mutual funds

Another area toward which the SEC has directed substantial energy lately has been enforcement actions against mutual funds and traders. These cases have focused primarily on:

(1) sales practices;
(2) market timing activities; and
(3) late trading. Market timing refers to the practice of short term buying and selling of mutual fund shares in order to exploit inefficiencies in mutual fund pricing. Late trading refers to the practice of placing orders to buy or sell mutual fund shares after the close of the market at 4:00 p.m. EST, but at the mutual fund's net asset value, or price, determined at the market close. Several of the cases in this area have been brought in conjunction with criminal charges filed by the New York State Attorney General.

In the matter of Putnam Investment Management LLC,
Administrative Proceeding File 3-11868 (23rd March 2005)
On 23rd March 2005, the SEC instituted a settled administrative proceeding against Putnam Investment Management LLC (Putnam) alleging violations of Section 206(2) of the Advisers Act and Section 34(b) of the 1940 Act.

The SEC alleged in its administrative cease-and-desist order that Putnam failed to adequately disclose to the Putnam Funds' Board of Trustees and the Putnam Funds' shareholders the conflicts of interest that arose from its "shelf space" arrangements with broker-dealers that provided increased visibility within the broker-dealers' distribution systems. According to the Commission, from 2000 through 2003, Putnam Funds' distributor and affiliate, Putnam Retail Management Limited Partnership (PRM), entered into preferred marketing arrangements with more than 80 broker-dealers whereby the broker-dealers provided services designed to promote the sale of Putnam Funds. More than 60 broker-dealers allegedly received directed brokerage commissions from the

Putnam Funds' portfolio transactions. The SEC alleged that these arrangements were based primarily upon negotiated formulas relating to gross or net fund sales and/or the retention of fund assets.

The SEC further alleged that PRM did not use its own assets to pay for the services it received under the arrangements. According to the Commission, because the financial results of Putnam, PRM, and other affiliates were combined within consolidated financial statements, the entire Putnam organisation benefited from the use of fund assets to defray such expenses. Putnam allegedly did not adequately disclose this conflict of interest to the Putnam Board or the Putnam shareholders. According to the SEC order, neither the Putnam Funds' prospectuses nor Statements of Additional Information adequately disclosed that Putnam directed fund brokerage commissions to satisfy the negotiated preferred marketing arrangements.

Without admitting or denying the SEC's allegations, Putnam consented to an SEC order censuring the firm and ordering it to cease-and-desist from committing or causing any violations of Section 206(2) of the Advisers Act and Section 34(b) of the 1940 Act. Putnam also agreed to direct a senior level employee to implement and maintain policies with respect to

(1) its preferred marketing arrangements, including, among other things, the selection of broker-dealers that also sell fund shares, and
(2) its disclosures to the Putnam Board and Putnam shareholders. In addition, Putnam agreed to make a nominal disgorgement payment and pay a US$40 million civil penalty. Pursuant to the Fair Funds provision of the SOX Act, Putnam will distribute the penalty to the Putnam Funds in accordance with a distribution plan approved by the Commission.

In the matter of Citigroup Global Markets, Inc.,
Exchange Act Release 54145 (23rd March 2005)
On 23rd March 2005, the SEC instituted a settled cease-and-desist proceeding against Citigroup Global Markets, Inc. (CGMI) alleging that CGMI violated Section 17(a)(2) of the Securities Act and Rule 10b-10 of the Exchange Act by failing to provide important information to

customers relating to their purchases of mutual fund shares. The SEC coordinated its investigation with the NASD, which brought a separate enforcement action against CGMI for its sales of Class B shares. The SEC and the NASD both noted that the charges arose out of a broader investigation of mutual fund sales practices.

The Commission alleged two distinct disclosure failures at CGMI, which offered retail brokerage services under the Smith Barney trade name. First, the SEC alleged that CGMI did not fully disclose to its customers material information about its revenue-sharing program, known as the Tier Program. The SEC explained that, under the Tier Program, approximately 75 mutual fund complexes made revenue sharing payments to CGMI in exchange for access to or "shelf space" within CGMI's retail brokerage network. In addition, CGMI provided additional benefits to the mutual fund complexes that made higher revenue sharing payments, such as increased access to branch offices, greater agenda space at sales meetings, and visibility in CGMI's in-house publications and broadcasts. The SEC alleged that CGMI only offered and sold the funds of those mutual fund complexes that participated in the Tier Program. According to the SEC, this practice created a conflict of interest that CGMI failed to adequately disclose to its customers.

The SEC alleged a second disclosure failure related to CGMI's sale of Class B mutual fund shares in amounts aggregating US$50,000 or more. The SEC alleged that CGMI recommended and sold Class B shares to certain customers who, depending on the amount of their investment and the holding period, generally would have obtained a higher overall rate of return had they instead purchased Class A shares. As a result of the Class B purchases, CGMI received more in commissions than it would have if it had sold Class A shares of the same funds. According to the Commission, these customers could have benefited had they purchased Class A shares, because they would have qualified for breakpoints beginning at the US$50,000 level. The SEC alleged that CGMI's financial consultants, when recommending and selling Class B shares to customers, did not adequately disclose that:

(1) Class B shares were subject to higher annual fees that could have a negative impact on the customers' investment return; and

(2) once breakpoints become available beginning at the US$50,000 level, an equal investment in Class A shares could yield a higher return.

Without admitting or denying the SEC's allegations, CGMI consented to the entry of a cease-and desist order against committing or causing any violations of Section 17(a)(2) of the Securities Act and Rule 10b-10 under the Exchange Act. Section 17(a)(2) prohibits the making of materially misleading statements or omissions in the offer and sale of securities. Rule 10b-10 requires broker-dealers to disclose the source and amount of any remuneration received from third parties in connection with a securities transaction.

The SEC's order also imposed a censure and a US$20 million civil penalty against CGMI, and required CGMI to comply with certain undertakings. As part of those undertakings, CGMI will retain an independent consultant to conduct a review of CGMI's mutual fund sales practices. In addition, CGMI will offer affected customers the option of converting their Class B shares into Class A shares in such a manner that each customer is placed in the same financial position, based on actual fund performance, in which such customer would have been had the customer purchased Class A shares instead of Class B shares.

In the matter of Banc of America Capital Management, LLC, et al,
Exchange Act Release 51167 (9th February 2005); *In the matter of Columbia Management Advisors, Inc., et al,*
Exchange Act Release 51164 (9th February 2005)
On 9th February 2005, Bank of America (BOA) and FleetBoston Financial Corporation (Fleet) agreed to pay a total of US$675 million to settle market timing charges previously filed by the SEC against three BOA and two Fleet subsidiaries. The entities named in the SEC's enforcement action were:

(1) Banc of America Capital Management, LLC (BACAP), BOA's mutual fund advisory subsidiary;
(2) BACAP Distributors, LLC (BACAP Distributors), BOA's clearing firm;
(3) Banc of America Securities, LLC (BAS), BOA's broker dealer subsidiary;

(4) Columbia Management Advisors, Inc. (Columbia Advisors), a registered investment adviser that managed Columbia mutual funds for Fleet; and
(5) Columbia Funds Distributor, Inc. (Columbia Distributor), a registered broker-dealer that was the principal underwriter and entity responsible for selling the funds. The joint settlement was the result of BOA's acquisition of Fleet on 1st April 2004.

The SEC alleged that, from as early as July 2000 and continuing through July 2003, BACAP and BACAP Distributors entered into arrangements with two BAS clients that allowed them to engage in frequent short-term trading in at least 13 Nations Funds mutual funds, including international funds. According to the SEC, in connection with one of these arrangements, BACAP and BACAP Distributors received "sticky assets," long-term investments that were to remain in place in return for allowing the client to market time the funds. In addition, in 2002, the Board of Trustees of the Nations Funds approved a redemption fee on short-term trades in certain funds susceptible to timing, but simultaneously approved an exemption for one of these entities from the redemption fee. The SEC alleged that BACAP and BACAP Distributors failed to disclose the existence of these approved timing relationships, or the fact that one of these clients was being exempted from the redemption fee, in prospectuses and proxy statements issued to shareholders and potential shareholders. The Commission also alleged that BAS, a registered broker dealer, facilitated market timing and late trading by certain introducing broker dealers and a hedge fund at the expense of shareholders of Nations Funds and other mutual fund families.

With regard to Columbia Distributor and Columbia Advisors, the Commission alleged that, from at least 1998 through 2003, Columbia Distributor secretly entered into arrangements with at least nine companies and individuals allowing them to engage in frequent short-term trading in at least seven Columbia funds. According to the SEC, in connection with certain of the arrangements, Columbia Distributor and Columbia Advisors accepted so-called "sticky assets," long-term investments that were to remain in place in return for allowing the investors to actively trade in the funds. The SEC alleged that the special arrangements were never disclosed to long-term shareholders or to the independent trustees of the Columbia funds. In addition to trading made pursuant to specific arrangements, the Commission alleged that Columbia allowed or failed to prevent hundreds of other accounts from engaging in a practice of short-term or excessive trading, contrary to representations made in fund prospectuses that the funds did not permit short-term or excessive trading.

In the settlements, the BOA subsidiaries agreed to pay a total of US$375 million, consisting of US$250 million in disgorgement and US$125 million in penalties, and Columbia Advisor and Columbia Distributor agreed to pay a total of US$140 million, consisting of US$70 million in disgorgement and a civil penalty of US$70 million. The money will be distributed to the mutual funds and their shareholders that were harmed as a result of market timing and late trading in Nations Funds and Columbia Funds. The Commission also censured BACAP, BACAP Distributors, BAS, Columbia Advisor, and Columbia Distributor, and ordered them to undertake certain remedial actions to strengthen their oversight of compliance with the federal securities laws and cease-and-desist from further violations.

In its release announcing the settlements, the Commission said that it considered certain efforts voluntarily undertaken by BACAP, BACAP Distributors, BAS and the Nations Funds. Among other things, BAS voluntarily undertook to exit the unaffiliated introducing broker dealer mutual fund clearing business. The Nations Funds and the independent trustees also voluntarily undertook to implement certain election and retirement procedures that will result in the replacement of seven trustees by early 2005. The Governance Committee of the Board of Trustees of Nations Funds ("Board"), comprised entirely of independent trustees, is responsible for making recommendations to the Board on issues related to the composition and operation of the Board, including nominating replacements for these trustees.

In the matter of Gary L. Pilgrim, Securities Act Release 8505
(17th November 2004); In the matter of *Harold J. Baxter,*
Securities Act Release 8506 (17th November 2004);
In the matter of Pilgrim Baxter & Associates, Ltd.,
Administrative Proceeding File 3-11524 (21st June 2004)
On 20th November 2003, the Commission filed a civil injunctive action charging Gary Pilgrim, Harold Baxter and Pilgrim Baxter &

Associates, Ltd. (PB) with fraud and breach of fiduciary duty in connection with market timing of the PBHG Funds.[39] The New York Attorney General also filed a contemporaneous action in New York State Supreme Court.

The Commission's complaint alleged that in March 2003, both Pilgrim and Baxter approved market timing in several PBHG funds, including one fund managed by Pilgrim, by a hedge fund that Pilgrim had a substantial interest in. Neither Pilgrim nor Baxter disclosed Pilgrim's interest in the hedge fund, or that the hedge fund was permitted to engage in market timing. As a result of this undisclosed arrangement, the Commission alleged that the hedge fund realised profits in excess of US$13 million, US$3.9 million of which was Pilgrim's share. The Commission's complaint also alleged that Baxter provided non-public PBHG fund portfolio information to a close friend who was president of a registered broker-dealer. Baxter's friend relayed the non-public information to customers who in turn market timed the PBHG funds and exercised hedging strategies. The Commission's complaint further alleged that PB permitted numerous PBHG Fund investors to engage in short-term trading in contravention of PBHG Fund's four-exchange limitation. Based on this conduct, the Commission's complaint sought a permanent injunction, disgorgement, prejudgment interest, civil penalties, and to enjoin Pilgrim and Baxter from acting in certain positions with an investment company.

On 21st June 2004, the Commission filed a settled cease-and-desist proceeding against PB for the same conduct underlying the previously filed civil injunctive action. Under the terms of the settlement, the Commission's federal court action against PB was dismissed, and PB consented to the entry of an administrative order requiring PB to pay US$40 million in disgorgement and US$50 million in civil penalties. PB also consented to cease-and-desist from future violations of the federal securities laws, a censure, and to undertake a series of compliance and mutual fund governance reforms.

On 17th November 2004, Baxter and Pilgrim reached settlements with the Commission involving the dismissal of the district court

---

[39] *See* SEC v. Gary L. Pilgrim, Harold J. Baxter and Pilgrim Baxter & Associates, Ltd., Litigation Release 18474 (20th November 2003).

action, and the entry of a settled cease-and-desist proceeding. The settlement required Baxter and Pilgrim to each pay US$60 million in disgorgement and US$20 million in civil penalties. Baxter and Pilgrim also consented to orders to cease-and-desist from committing and/or causing violations of the federal securities laws, requiring them to cooperate in ongoing investigations, and to broad restrictions on any future employment in the securities industry.

In the matter of Strong Capital Management, Inc., et al,
Exchange Act Release 49741 (20th May 2004)
On 20th May 2004, the SEC filed a settled enforcement action against Strong Capital Management, Inc. (SCM), its founder and majority owner, Richard S. Strong, two affiliated entities and two other SCM executives, for allowing and, in the case of Richard Strong, engaging in undisclosed frequent trading in Strong mutual funds in violation of their fiduciary duties to the Strong funds and their investors.

The Commission alleged, among other things, that SCM entered into an express agreement with hedge fund manager Edward Stern allowing his hedge funds (the Canary hedge funds) to market time certain Strong funds, in order to obtain non-mutual fund business from Stern and his family. The SEC alleged that this agreement enabled the Canary hedge funds to make approximately 135 round trip trades in four Strong funds, realising gross profits of US$2.7 million from December 2002 to May 2003. Under SCM's policies and procedures, other shareholders would have been ejected from the Strong funds for engaging in similar trading.

The SEC also alleged that Richard Strong engaged in frequent trading in several Strong funds, including one fund he managed. According to the SEC, between 1998 and 2003, he engaged in several hundred such trades, making gross profits of US$4.1 million and net profits of US$1.6 million. The Commission alleged that SCM failed to disclose the arrangement with Stern, and Strong and SCM failed to disclose Strong's personal trading, to the Strong funds' Boards of Directors or shareholders. In fact, the Strong funds' prospectuses and SCM's policies and practices created the misleading impression that frequent trading of the kind practiced by Strong and the Canary hedge funds would not be allowed. The SEC further alleged that SCM provided the Canary hedge funds with the month-end portfolio holdings for the funds in which Canary traded before other shareholders could see the same information, to the possible detriment of the funds and their shareholders. According to the Commission, SCM's affiliated transfer agent, Strong Investor Services, Inc., and its affiliated broker-dealer, Strong Investments, Inc., facilitated SCM's violations by allowing the Canary hedge funds' frequent trading. The SEC also alleged that SCM executives aided and abetted SCM's and Strong's violations by approving the arrangement with the Canary hedge funds, and by failing, after learning of Richard Strong's frequent trading, to follow up on a directive to monitor the trading and ensure it stopped.

All parties consented to cease-and-desist orders and agreed to pay civil penalties to settle the SEC action. SCM agreed to pay US$40 million in disgorgement and US$40 million in civil penalties, and Strong agreed to pay US$30 million in disgorgement and US$30 million in civil penalties. In addition, the Commission barred Strong from association with any investment adviser, investment company, broker, dealer, municipal securities dealer or transfer agent. SCM and its two affiliates also consented to censures and undertook compliance and mutual fund governance reforms.

SEC v. Alliance Capital Management, L.P.,
Investment Company Act Release 26312A (15th January 2004)
The Commission instituted administrative cease-and-desist proceedings against Alliance Capital Management, L.P. (Alliance), a registered investment advisor. Simultaneously, the Commission accepted an offer of settlement whereby Alliance consented to the entry of an order requiring Alliance to cease-and-desist violating the securities laws, and requiring Alliance to pay US$250 million in civil penalties and disgorgement. The administrative order includes findings that Alliance violated various provisions of the Advisers Act of 1940 and the Investment Company Act of 1940, by negotiating market-timing arrangements related to the sale of various mutual funds. The Commission alleged that Alliance was involved in more than US$600 million in timing transactions all of which were undisclosed. The Commission's complaint alleges that these actions violated the antifraud provisions of the Advisers Act, proxy solicitation provisions of Exchange Act, and provisions of the Advisers Act requiring companies to institute policies and

procedures reasonably designed to prevent the misuse of material, non-public information.

SEC v. Mutuals.com, Inc., Connely Dowd Management, Inc., MTT FundCorp, Inc., Richard Sapio, Eric McDonald and Michelle Leftwich, Litigation Release 26255 (4th December 2003)
The Commission filed a civil injunctive action against Mutuals.com, Inc. (Mutuals.com), its CEO, and two broker-dealers for helping Mutuals.com's institutional investors and advisory clients carry out thousands of market timing arrangements and illegal late trades in shares of hundreds of mutual funds. The complaint further alleges that Mutuals.com took part in numerous actions intended to circumvent discovery of their actions, including forming and registering two additional broker-dealers through which they could carry out the illegal trades, changing account numbers for blocked customer accounts, using alternative registered representative numbers for representatives who were blocked from trading, using different branch identification numbers, switching clearing firms, and suggesting that customers use a third party tax-identification number or social security number. The Commission's complaint alleges that this conduct violated the antifraud provisions, the mutual fund pricing provisions, and the broker-dealer record keeping provisions of the Exchange Act, Securities Act, and Investment Company Act. The Commission seeks a permanent injunction, disgorgement, civil penalties, and pre-judgment interest.

SEC v. Invesco Funds Group, Inc. and Raymond R. Cunningham, Litigation Release 18482 (2nd December 2003)
The Commission filed a civil injunctive action against Invesco Funds Group, Inc. (IFG) and IFG's president, alleging that IFG fraudulently accepted investments from traders taking part in market timing activities. According to the complaint, IFG entered into these transactions knowing that they were detrimental to long-term investors. In addition, the complaint alleges that IFG failed to make any disclosures to investors that IFG was accepting these short-term trades. The Commission further alleges that these actions violated the antifraud provisions of the Exchange Act and the Securities Act, as well as provisions of the Investment Company Act prohibiting the filing of false and misleading registration

statements. The Commission seeks a permanent injunction, disgorgement, civil penalties, and pre-judgment interest.

In the matter of Putnam Investment Management, LLC, Investment Company Act Release 26255 (13th November 2003)
The Commission brought administrative cease-and-desist proceedings against Putnam Investment Management, LLC (Putnam). The Commission simultaneously accepted an offer of settlement from Putnam, consenting to the entry of an order requiring Putnam to cease-and-desist from committing further violations of the antifraud provisions, censuring Putnam for its activities, and requiring Putnam to pay restitution and a civil penalty to be determined at a future time. The Commission alleged that Putnam employees engaged in aggressive market timing transactions without disclosing to investors that such trading was taking place. In addition, the Commission alleged that Putnam lacked controls dedicated to detecting and deterring short-term trading by its employees.

In the matter of Steven B. Markovitz, Exchange Act Release 48588 (2nd October 2003)
The Commission brought an administrative cease-and-desist proceeding against Steven Markovitz (Markovitz), a hedge fund trader at Millennium Partners, L.P. Simultaneously, the Commission accepted an offer of settlement whereby Markovitz consented to the entry of an order requiring Markovitz to cease-and-desist from committing further violations of the antifraud provisions of the Securities Act and the Exchange Act, and barred Markovitz from association with any investment advisor, and from working in any capacity for an investment company or investment advisor. The Commission alleges that Markovitz violated the securities laws by taking part in late trading in shares of mutual funds offered by Millennium Partners. The Commission alleges that these actions violated the antifraud provisions of the Securities Act and Exchange Act, as well as aiding and abetting violations of certain mutual fund pricing provisions by the funds.

In the matter of Theodore Charles Sihpol III, Exchange Act Release 48493 (16th September 2003)
The Commission brought an administrative cease-and-desist proceeding against Theodore Charles Sihpol, III (Sihpol), formerly a

trader with Banc of America Securities LLC ("BAS"). The administrative complaint alleges that Sihpol violated the securities laws by taking part in late trading in shares of mutual funds offered by BAS. The Commission alleges that these actions violated the antifraud provisions, the mutual fund pricing provisions, and the broker-dealer record keeping provisions of the Exchange Act, Securities Act, the 1940 Act and the Advisers Act.

Selective disclosure and other analyst issues

Selective disclosure occurs when a company releases material non-public information, such as upcoming earnings information, to securities market professionals or major investors before disclosing the information to the public. The SEC perceives that there often is an unstated expectation that analysts receiving such information will "reward" the company by providing positive coverage. The SEC believes that those who receive this non-public information are given an advantage over others who learn of the information only upon a public disclosure by the company, leading to concerns about the integrity of our capital markets.

In October 2000, the Commission passed Regulation FD, which is intended to prohibit selective disclosure to the professional investment community and to encourage broad public disclosure. Foreign private issuers and foreign government issuers are not subject to Regulation FD. Under Regulation FD, when an issuer learns of an *unintentional* disclosure of material non-public information, the issuer must make *prompt* public disclosure of that information. The regulation provides that an issuer "learns" of a disclosure when a senior official knows (or is reckless in not knowing) that a disclosure of both material and non-public information has been made. "Prompt" disclosure means as soon as reasonably practicable, but no later than either 24 hours after discovery of the unintentional disclosure or prior to the commencement of the next day's trading on the NYSE, if later. When an issuer makes *an intentional* disclosure of material non-public information, the issuer must *simultaneously* make public disclosure of the same information.

SEC v. Flowserve Corporation and C. Scott Greer,
Litigation Release 19154 (24th March 2005)
On 24th March 2005, the SEC filed two settled enforcement proceedings charging Flowserve Corporation (Flowserve) with violating

Regulation FD and Section 13(a) of the Exchange Act. First, the SEC filed a federal injunctive action against Flowserve for violating, and C. Scott Greer, Flowserve's Chairman, President and CEO, with aiding and abetting Flowserve's violations of Regulation FD and Section 13(a). Second, the Commission issued an administrative order finding that Flowserve violated the same provisions, and Greer and the Company's Director of Investor Relations, Michael Conley, were each a cause of Flowserve's violations.

The action arose from a private meeting attended by Greer, Conley and analysts from four investment and brokerage firms. One of the analysts at the meeting asked a question about Flowserve's earnings guidance for the year. Notwithstanding Flowserve's policy requiring Greer and Conley to respond that the Company's guidance was effective at the date given and would not be updated until the Company did so publicly, Greer reaffirmed the earnings guidance and provided additional non-public information. Thereafter, one of the analysts in attendance at the meeting issued a report to the investment firms' subscribers stating that Flowserve reaffirmed its earnings guidance. The next day, Flowserve's stock experienced a 75% increase in trading volume and closed approximately 6% higher.

Without admitting or denying the Commission's charges, Flowserve and Greer consented to the entry of a final judgment in the federal lawsuit that requires the Company to pay a US$350,000 civil penalty and Greer to pay a US$50,000 penalty. Flowserve, Greer and Conley also agreed to the issuance of the Commission's administrative order. In announcing the settlement, the Commission cited the lack of cooperation Greer and Conley afforded the Commission Staff.

This action is notable because it is the first case filed by the SEC involving reaffirmation of earnings guidance. When Regulation FD was adopted, the SEC cautioned that non-public affirmation of earlier guidance would likely raise serious FD issues. It is also the first settled action against an investor relations officer for violating Regulating FD.

SEC v. Siebel Systems, Inc., et al,
Litigation Release 18766 (29th June 2004)
The Commission filed a civil action against Siebel Systems, Inc., charging violations of Regulation FD, Exchange Act Rule 13a-15

and a prior Commission cease-and-desist order involving violations of Regulation FD and pursuant to which Siebel had paid US$250,000. Two senior executives of Siebel were also charged with aiding and abetting these violations.

The Commission's complaint alleges that the senior executives disclosed material non-public information to institutional investors six months after Siebel consented to the Commission's prior cease-and-desist order. The Commission alleged that one of the senior executives violated Regulation FD by making positive comments about Siebel's business activity levels and transaction pipeline that materially contrasted with negative public statements Siebel had made about its business in the preceding weeks. The day after these alleged disclosures, the company's stock price closed approximately 8% higher than the prior day's close, and trading volume nearly doubled the average daily volume for the preceding year.

The case is currently pending and is the first SEC case alleging violation of Rule 13a-15, which requires issuers to maintain disclosure controls and procedures to ensure proper handling of information required to be disclosed in reports filed or submitted under the Exchange Act. The Rule also requires issuers to ensure that management has the necessary information to make timely disclosure decisions. The Commission seeks an order requiring Siebel to comply with the prior cease-and-desist order and imposing a permanent injunction, civil penalties and other equitable relief.

In the matter of Schering-Plough Corporation and
Richard J. Kogan, Litigation Release 18330
(9th September 2003)
On 9th September 2003, the Commission filed and simultaneously settled a civil action against Schering Plough Corporation (Schering) and its CEO, Richard Kogan, alleging violations of Regulation FD and the books and records provisions of the Exchange Act. At the same time, the Commission instituted cease-and-desist proceedings and simultaneously settled those proceedings, finding that Schering had committed or caused to be committed violations of Section 13(a) of the Exchange Act and

Regulation FD by selectively disclosing to Schering's four largest institutional investors material non-public information.

In its civil complaint, the Commission alleged that Kogan, in four different meetings with institutional investors, through a combination of spoken language, tone, emphasis and demeanor, disclosed negative and non-public information regarding Schering's earnings prospects for 2002 and 2003. Specifically, Kogan warned these investors that Schering was going to take a "hard hit" to earnings in 2003; that 2003 would be a "tough year" for Schering; and that 2003 would be a "very, very difficult year." In addition, Kogan warned investors that "the street" had not sufficiently lowered Schering's earnings estimates for the third quarter of 2002 in response to Schering losing its patent on the drug Claritin. In reaction to Kogan's warnings, each of these investors took part in larger volumes of sales than had previously been seen, and one of the investors downgraded Schering's stock from a "buy" to a "sell."

According to the complaint, because of the massive sell-off from these institutional investors, the price of Schering's stock fell 17% from 1st to 3rd October 2003. On 3rd October 2003, Kogan held a meeting with analysts and portfolio managers at Schering's headquarters, in which Kogan allegedly warned the analysts that 2003 was going to be a "real tough" year, and that Schering's earnings in 2003 were going to be "terrible." Later on that same day, after the close of markets, Schering issued a press release that projected earnings per share estimates for the third quarter of 2002 and for fiscal year 2003 that were materially below Wall Street analysts' estimates. The Commission alleged that Kogan's actions constituted a violation of Section 13(a) of the Exchange Act and of Regulation FD.

Pursuant to the settlement of the administrative proceeding, Schering consented to a cease-and-desist order requiring the Company to cease committing, or causing to be committed, violations of Section 13(a) and regulation FD. In addition, under the terms of the settlement in the civil action, Kogan agreed to pay a US$50,000 civil penalty for his role in causing Schering's violation of Regulation FD and Schering agreed to pay a US$1,000,000 civil penalty for its violation of regulation FD and Section 13(a).

In the matter of Raytheon Company and Franklin A. Caine, Exchange Act Release 46897 (25th November 2002); *In the matter of Secure Computing Corporation and John McNulty,* Exchange Act Release 46895 (25th November 2002); *In* the matter of Siebel Systems, Inc., Exchange Release 46896 (25th November 2002); *SEC v. Siebel Systems, Inc.,* Litigation Release 17860 (25th November 2002); *Report of Investigation in the matter of Motorola,* Inc., Exchange Act Release 46898 (25th November 2002).

On 25th November 2002, the Commission filed three settled administrative cases and issued one report of investigation finding violations of Regulation FD. Each of the matters involved a senior company official selectively disclosing material non-public information to an analyst or institutional investor group. The companies and individuals charged in the administrative proceedings settled the matters by consenting to cease-and-desist orders from causing or committing any future violations of Section 13(a) of the Exchange Act and Regulation FD. In addition, Siebel Systems, Inc. agreed to pay a civil penalty of US$250,000. These are the Commission's first and only filed enforcement efforts brought under Regulation FD.

The Commission also has grown concerned about the extent to which issuers become involved with analysts' projections about a company's expected performance. The following is an example of a case where the issuer's so-called "entanglement" in the analysts reports and projections resulted in the issuer's, in effect "adoption" of the estimates. The result was that the company was held liable for fraud for misstatements in the reports and the forecasts.

In the matter of Presstek, Inc., Exchange Act Release 39472 (22nd December 1997)

In this matter, the SEC initiated public administrative proceedings against Presstek, alleging disclosure and reporting violations of US securities laws in connection with false and misleading information generated by outside analysts and adopted, promoted and distributed by the company. Presstek consented to the entry of the SEC's findings and order enjoining it from further violations of the securities laws.

According to the Commission, from 1994 through 1996, Presstek, through its own statements and its widespread distribution of third-party reports, published false and misleading information concerning its sales and business prospects. In that regard, the Commission specifically alleged that

(i) Presstek issued a materially false and misleading press release;
(ii) Presstek distributed a highly promotional financial newsletter published by others that included earnings projections that materially exceeded Presstek's own non-public forecasts;
(iii) Presstek's senior management reviewed, edited, and distributed a research analyst's report which materially overstated Presstek's sales and earnings outlook; and
(iv) Presstek filed periodic reports with the Commission that did not accurately disclose adverse developments in its business relationship with Heidelberger Druckmaschinen, A.G., a German printing press manufacturer, that is the primary source of Presstek's revenue.

Many of these false and misleading disclosures occurred in November 1995, the Commission asserted, when the price of the company's stock was highly volatile because Presstek's business with Heidelberger had encountered difficulties. Although a recently introduced Heidelberger press that incorporated Presstek's technology had experienced substantial production delay causing a significant reduction in demand for Presstek equipment, Presstek touted the market acceptance of the new press, and citing "industry sources," falsely stated that Heidelberger had "sold" more than 500 of the presses. Presstek also did not disclose the existence of the technical problems delaying commercial production, that Heidelberger had informed Presstek that it should reduce its shipments, or the concomitant delay of sales to purchasers of Presstek's high profit margin consumable products used in the press. In addition, Presstek's Form 10-K for 1995, and its Forms 10-Q for the first three quarters of 1996, similarly failed to include in the MD&A section the necessary discussion of the material impact of the production delay on its operating results.

The Commission also alleged that in 1994 and 1995, Presstek distributed copies of a third party's financial newsletter that contained earnings projections that Presstek management knew, or was reckless in not knowing, far exceeded Presstek's own internal forecasts. Through such distribution, the Commission maintained, Presstek implicitly adopted the newsletter's erroneous forecasts.

The Commission further alleged that in November 1995, Robert Howard, Presstek's founder and chairman, reviewed the draft of a research analyst's report that substantially overstated Presstek's sales and earnings expectations eg, projecting sales of a particular Presstek product that were materially greater than Presstek's internal projections, and overstating projected sales of other Presstek products as well. Although Howard edited the analyst's report before it was published, he did not correct the erroneous sales projections, and Presstek subsequently distributed the report to investors for more than six months without disclaimer, in effect adopting and disseminating projections that were materially inconsistent with Presstek's non-public internal projections.

Additionally, the Commission has grown concerned about the integrity and objectivity of research by securities firms. SOX includes a provision requiring the Commission to promulgate rules addressing conflicts of interest affecting the integrity and objectivity of research by securities firms. The Commission thereafter promulgated Regulation AC. Regulation AC requires research reports to include certifications:

(i) that the report accurately reflects the research analyst's personal views; and
(ii) whether or not the analyst's compensation is related to the specific recommendations in the research. Below are examples of recent Commission actions in this area.

In the matter of Needham & Co., Inc.,
Exchange Act Release 50521 (25th August 2004)
On 25th August 2004, the SEC instituted a settled administrative proceeding against Needham & Co., Inc. (Needham) alleging violations of Section 17(b) of the Securities Act, Section 17(a) of the Securities Exchange Act, and Rule 17a-4 thereunder.

According to the SEC, Needham violated Section 17(b) of the Securities Act by failing to disclose to investors that it received payments in consideration for publishing research on four public companies. Specifically, on four occasions between 1999 and 2001, Needham received undisclosed payments ranging from US$75,000 to US$100,000 from other investment banking firms for research coverage of those firms' investment banking clients. For example, in January 2000, Needham was paid US$75,000 by the lead underwriter of Crossroads Systems, Inc.'s (Crossroad) IPO in consideration for Needham issuing a research report on Crossroad within 90 days of the IPO. The SEC alleged that Needham's failure to disclose the US$75,000 payment in violation of the federal securities laws deprived investors of information relating to the objectivity of the research.

The SEC also alleged that Needham violated Section 17(a)(1) of the Exchange Act and Rule 17a-4 thereunder by failing to preserve business-related internal e-mails for a period of three years. Between July 1999 and June 2001, Needham preserved only e-mails that were sent to individuals outside the firm, not internal e-mails. As a result, the SEC did not have access to these e-mails during its investigation.

Needham, without admitting or denying the SEC's allegations, agreed to cease-and-desist from committing future violations of Section 17(b) of the Securities Act, Section 17(a) of the Exchange Act, and Rule 17a-4 thereunder. Also, Needham agreed to pay a civil monetary penalty in the amount of US$700,000, and to:

(1) review its procedures regarding the preservation of its e-mails for compliance with federal securities laws and regulations and the rules of the NASD, and
(2) inform the SEC once the review is completed that it has established systems and procedures reasonably designed to achieve compliance with those laws, regulations, and rules. Lastly, Needham consented to be censured under Section 15(b)(4) of the Exchange Act.

SEC v. Bear, Stearns & Co. Inc.; SEC v. Jack Benjamin Grubman; SEC v. J.P. Morgan Securities Inc.; SEC v. Lehman Brothers, Inc.; SEC v. Merrill Lynch, Pierce, Fenner & Smith Inc.; SEC v. US Bancorp Piper Jaffray, Inc.; SEC v. UBS Securities LLC, f/k/a UBS Warburg LLC; SEC v. Goldman, Sachs & Co.; SEC v. Citigroup Global Markets Inc., f/k/a Salomon Smith Barney Inc.; SEC v. Credit Suisse First Boston LLC, f/k/a Credit Suisse First Boston Corp.; SEC v. Henry McKelvey Blodget; SEC v. Morgan Stanley & Co. Inc., Litigation Release 18438 (31st October 2003)

In 2003, the SEC and the Attorneys General of various states entered into a global settlement of alleged securities violations against 10 of America's largest investment banking firms and two individuals. The complaints alleged that the investment banking firms violated various analyst independence rules. Each investment banking firm agreed to a consent order that included Commission findings that the firm had taken part in some or all of the following fraudulent activities:

- maintaining inappropriate influence over research analysts, thereby creating conflicts of interest between the investment banking firms and the analysts that the investment firms failed to handle in an appropriate manner;
- inappropriately offering "hot" initial public offering allocations to favored customers;
- issuing fraudulent research reports;
- issuing research reports that were not based on principles of fair dealing and good faith and did not provide a sound basis for evaluating facts, contained exaggerated and unwarranted claims about the covered companies, and/or contained opinions for which there was no reasonable basis in violation of the NYSE and NASD rules; and
- providing payment for research without disclosing such payments in violation of the Exchange Act and the NYSE and NASD rules.

Pursuant to the terms of the settlement, the 10 firms agreed to pay a total of US$875 million in disgorgement and penalties, to be split between the SEC and the states. In addition, the settlement requires the firms to pay more than US$500 million into funds to promote independent research and investor education. The total of all payments under the settlement was roughly US$1.4 billion.

Insider trading

SEC v. Jun Singo Liang, Litigation Release 19049 (25th January 2005)
The Commission filed a settled enforcement action against Jun Singo Liang (Liang), a Chinese citizen and former executive of Chinese Internet technology provider NetEase.com, Inc. (NetEase), a Beijing-based company with offices in Newark, California. According to the Commission's complaint, shortly before NetEase was scheduled to release its financial results for the third quarter of 2003, Liang learned that the NetEase division he managed, which typically accounted for half of the company's revenue, was likely to report a significant revenue shortfall. Over the two trading days leading up to the scheduled announcement of the company's

financial results, Liang sold 47,000 shares of NetEase stock (which trades as ADRs on the Nasdaq National Market). The Commission's complaint alleges that Liang avoided losses of over US$700,000 by selling ahead of the company's announcement that it would fall short of industry analysts' revenue projections for the quarter.

Without admitting or denying the allegations in the Commission's complaint, Liang consented to the entry of a final judgment enjoining him from future violations of the antifraud provisions of the federal securities laws and barring him from serving as an officer or director of any publicly-held company with securities trading in the United States for a period of five years. Liang also agreed to pay disgorgement and prejudgment interest totaling US$731,169 and a civil penalty of US$355,129. In its release announcing the settled enforcement action, the Commission stated that it decided to seek a lower penalty than it might otherwise have pursued, because Liang voluntarily disclosed his trading activity to NetEase and to the Commission Staff.

SEC v. Eric I. Tsao, Litigation Release 18889 (14th September 2004)
In this matter, the SEC sued Eric I. Tsao, a former executive at MedImmune, Inc. (MedImmune), for illegal insider trading on three separate occasions between September 1999 and December 2001 after learning about potential business combinations between MedImmune and other public companies. The complaint alleged that Tsao purchased stock in each of the three public companies involved in discussions concerning potential business combinations with MedImmune, and on at least one occasion in MedImmune during the conduct of such discussions. The complaint further alleged that Tsao used nominee accounts located in Taiwan in the name of family members to carry out his trades.

Without admitting or denying the allegations, Tsao consented to the entry of a final judgment that permanently enjoins him from future violations of the federal securities laws, bars him from acting as an officer or director of a public company, requires him to disgorge US$146,850 in illicit profits, and US$24,758.30 in prejudgment interest, and orders him to pay a civil penalty in the amount of US$220,275 and a Remedies Act penalty of US$110,000. In a related criminal proceeding, Tsao pled guilty to one felony count of criminal insider trading and one felony count of perjury arising from false statements that Tsao made to the SEC Staff during the investigation.

Multinvestments, Inc., Litigation Release 17395 (6th March 2002); *SEC v. Pablo Escandon Cusi and Lori, Ltd.,* Litigation Release 17356 (7th February 2002); *SEC v. Jorge Eduardo Ballesteros Franco,* Litigation Release 17897 (17th December 2002); *SEC v. Jorge Eduardo Ballesteros Franco, et al,* Litigation Release 16991 (8th May 2001); Litigation Release 17035 (13th June 2001); *In the matter of Ricardo Ballesteros Gutierrez,* Exchange Act Release 44420 (13th June 2001)

In this matter, the SEC sued a former director of the Nalco Chemical Company (Nalco), his brother, his four sons and two family friends, all Mexican nationals, alleging that they engaged in illegal insider trading in the stock of Nalco prior to the announcement that Nalco was to be acquired by Suez Lyonnaise des Eaux, a French company. The complaint alleged the use of offshore trusts and brokerage accounts located in the US and Switzerland. The SEC charged the former director of Nalco tipped the others on the pending acquisition. The former director was subsequently killed in a car accident. His estate agreed to pay disgorgement and prejudgment interest in the amount of US$3,744,870 on behalf of all the family defendants. Several of the family members and the two family friends consented to a judgment requiring the payment of penalties and the entry of a permanent injunction against future violations of the securities laws.

The US Attorney for the Southern District of New York indicted the former Nalco director's brother and one son for conspiracy and violations of the securities laws. On 27th February 2002, the former director's son was convicted of one count of insider trading and sentenced to serve fifteen months in prison.

On 7th February 2002, the Commission filed another complaint related to this matter bringing an enforcement action against Pablo Escandon Cusi (Escandon) and Lori, Ltd., a company owned by Escandon's family. As in the related actions, the Commission alleged that a former Nalco director tipped Escandon about Suez Lyonnaise des Eaux's acquisition of Nalco.

The Commission asserted that Escandon and Lori, Ltd. realised a total of US$776,725 in illegal profits. The defendants settled the matter by agreeing to pay US$1,716,546, which represented disgorgement with prejudgment interest and a civil penalty levied against Escandon. Escandon and Lori, Ltd. also consented to the entry of injunctions against future violations of the antifraud provisions of the federal securities laws. In a related action brought on 17th December 2002, a son of the former Nalco director consented to the entry of an injunction against future violations of the antifraud provisions of the federal securities laws and agreed to pay approximately US$213,000 in civil penalties and disgorgement.

The Commission has finalised settlements in all of these actions. The Commission received more than US$10 million from settlements with more than 20 defendants involved in insider trading in Nalco's stock, including a recent US$2.5 million civil penalty against Jorge Eduardo Ballesteros Franco. The Commission intends to have the funds distributed to the victims of the fraud pursuant to the Fair Funds provisions of SOX.

SEC v. Lorraine Cassano, et al, Litigation Release 16161
(26th May 1999); Litigation Release 16848 (2nd January 2001)
In this action the SEC alleged that Lorraine Cassano, a secretary at IBM, learned of a secret IBM plan to take over Lotus Development Corporation, and tipped her husband, Robert Cassano. The SEC further alleged that Mr. Cassano tipped others, and the information ultimately spread through a network of relatives, friends, co-workers and business associates. The 25 individuals who were ultimately charged allegedly made profits of more than US$1.3 million. Sixteen of the defendants, including the Cassanos, settled the charges against them prior to or during trial and made payments for disgorgement, prejudgment interest and penalties. Two of the defendants stipulated to liability during trial. Of the remaining seven defendants, four were found liable for violations of the SEC regulations prohibiting insider trading in connection with a tender offer, and three were found not liable. Those six defendants who stipulated to liability or were found liable at trial were ordered to make payments for disgorgement, prejudgment interest and penalties.

SEC v. Halton Technologies, Ltd, Litigation Release 15893; (22nd September 1998); Litigation Release 15937 (16th October 1998)

In this matter, the SEC filed a complaint alleging that Halton, an Israeli entity, engaged in illegal insider trading shortly before an announcement that ADC Telecommunications, Inc. intended to acquire Teledata Communications Ltd., an Israeli firm, and obtained a temporary restraining order prohibiting Halton from obtaining or disposing of proceeds from the sale for a 10-day period.

According to the SEC's complaint, Halton, which is located in the same city where Teledata is headquartered, while in possession of material inside information about the acquisition, spent more than US$450,000 to purchase a total of 225 Teledata call options and 45,000 shares of Teledata common stock, and following announcement of the merger, its investment increased in value by more than US$300,000, or 66%.

In its application for a temporary restraining order, the Commission advised the Court that "absent an immediate order freezing the account, Halton will have little or no incentive to ever come forth or cooperate with the Court or the Commission's investigation . . ." Subsequent to entry of the freeze order, Halton contacted the Commission Staff, identified its principal, offered to cooperate with the Commission's investigation, produced documents requested by the Commission and brought its principal and others involved in Halton's decision to purchase Teledata securities to the United States to be deposed. Halton denied that it had any advance information that Teledata was to be acquired by ADC.

After reviewing the information provided by Halton and other evidence acquired in its investigation, the Commission concluded that the purposes of the temporary restraining order and asset freeze had been achieved and joined with Halton in a request that the complaint be dismissed, without prejudice. Halton represented to the Court that it would continue to cooperate with the Commission's investigation and consent to the jurisdiction of the Court for purposes of any action the Commission might commence. The court dismissed the complaint in accordance with the request.

SEC v. Roy Handojo, Litigation Release 15540 (24th October 1997)
Roy Handojo, a 25-year-old Indonesian national working as a visiting analyst at a US bank's New York office, allegedly engaged in insider trading. In slightly over a month, Handojo made profits of US$628,052 by purchasing shares of companies' stocks immediately before the public announcement of their acquisition of other companies, despite being a self-declared inexperienced investor. The SEC initially obtained a temporary freeze of Handojo's assets in his brokerage and bank accounts based on concern that he would leave the United States. The court also granted the SEC expedited discovery and other ancillary relief. Handojo ultimately consented to a court order enjoining him from violating the antifraud provisions of the Exchange Act. He also agreed to disgorge his profits from the illegal trading with interest, although the amount exceeding US$588,765.72 was waived based on his inability to pay.

SEC v. Abdul Ismail, Ong Congqin Bobby, and Lum Kwan Sung, Litigation Release 15442 (15th August 1997)
This insider-trading case involved three individuals who traded in a company that was to be acquired by a Singapore-based company just before the transaction was announced. All three defendants were foreigners living outside of the United States, but their buy orders were executed on the Pacific Stock Exchange. The SEC sought and obtained an asset freeze to prevent the defendants from removing the proceeds of their transactions beyond the jurisdiction of the federal court. One of the defendants, a London businessman, came forward and identified himself. The SEC subsequently concluded it did not have sufficient evidence to prosecute him and dismissed the case against him. The case against the other defendants is pending.

Broker-Dealer Record-Keeping and Reporting Requirements
SEC v. Banc of America Securities LLC,
Exchange Act Release 49386 (10th March 2004)
In this settled enforcement action, the Commission charged Banc of America Securities LLC (BAS) for violations of the record keeping and access requirements of the federal securities laws. The violations occurred during the Commission's investigation into whether

BAS improperly traded in securities in advance of issuing research concerning such securities.

The Commission's order found that BAS failed to preserve or produce certain requested records. Specifically, the Commission found that BAS willfully failed to produce compliance reviews, compliance and supervision records relating to the personal trades of a former senior employee of the firm, and electronic mail, including a requested electronic mail exchange pertaining to matters known to be under investigation. Under the terms of the settlement, BAS agreed to a censure, a US$10 million civil penalty, and consented to a cease-and-desist order. The significance of this matter is that the SEC charged BAS not in connection with the conduct under investigation, but for BAS' conduct during the Commission's investigation.

SEC v. Citigroup Global Markets Inc., f/k/a Salomon Smith Barney Inc.; SEC v. Credit Suisse First Boston LLC, f/k/a Credit Suisse First Boston Corporation, Litigation Release 18438 (31st October 2003)
As part of the global analyst settlement described above, the SEC also charged Salomon Smith Barney and Credit Suisse First Boston with violations of the broker-dealer record keeping and reporting requirements under Section 17(a) of the Exchange Act. The complaint alleged that by inappropriately "spinning hot IPOs" to favored customers, the investment banks had violated the securities laws, in addition to NYSE and NASD rules. As part of the global settlement, the firms consented to a final order, enjoining them from further violations of the securities laws, including section 17(a) of the Exchange Act.

SEC v. The Nikko Sec. Co. Int'l, Inc., Litigation Release 15861 (27th August 1998)
In this matter, the SEC filed a settled complaint in federal court against The Nikko Securities Co. International, Inc. (Nikko New York), alleging that Nikko New York, in connection with certain sales of its mortgage-backed securities (MBS) portfolio, violated the broker-dealer record keeping and reporting provisions of the federal securities laws and the terms of a prior order issued by the Commission requiring Nikko New York to comply with those same record keeping and reporting provisions. Nikko New York

consented to the entry of a final judgment directing Nikko New York to comply with the Commission's prior order and to pay a US$2.5 million civil penalty.

The complaint alleged that between August and November 1994, Nikko New York, by improperly using an internal interest rate forecast rather than the market's interest rate forecast, overstated the fair value of its MBS portfolio in its books and records and in reports filed with the NYSE; that Nikko New York sold the majority of the MBS portfolio to its London-based affiliate for at least US$17 million above fair value, improperly booked the entire transaction as trading proceeds and failed to report the US$17 million loss that would have been recognised had the securities been properly valued; and that in connection with the sale of a portion of the MBS portfolio by Nikko New York's London affiliate, two Nikko New York employees violated the antifraud provisions of the securities laws by misappropriating approximately US$842,000 from its London-based affiliate and falsified books and records to hide the illicit profits.

In a related settled cease-and-desist administrative proceeding, the Commission found that Nikko New York violated the broker-dealer record keeping and reporting provisions, and failed reasonably to supervise its employees with a view to preventing violations of the antifraud provisions and broker-dealer record keeping and reporting provisions of the securities laws. The Commission censured Nikko New York, and ordered the company to cease-and-desist from committing violations of the broker-dealer record keeping and reporting provisions and to appoint two unaffiliated directors to constitute an audit committee.

The Commission also found that three senior officers of Nikko New York during the relevant period – the chairman and CEO, the president and a senior vice president and general manager – each knew that Nikko New York's books and records relating to its MBS portfolio were inaccurate, but failed to take steps to correct them and in so doing willfully aided and abetted Nikko New York's violations of the broker-dealer record keeping and reporting provisions. The three officers settled the administrative and cease-and-desist proceedings by consent decree. Each of the three was suspended from associating with any broker or dealer for a period of six months, ordered to cease-and-desist from committing any violations of the broker-dealer record keeping and reporting provisions, and required to pay a US$50,000 penalty.

Regulation S
SEC v. Parnes, et al, Litigation Release 17865 (26th November 2002)
Litigation Release 16877 (31st January 2001)
In this case, the Commission filed a complaint against Ari Parnes and others, alleging they schemed to cause ImmunoGen to issue US$3.6 million of convertible debentures under Regulation S. The SEC alleged that although the debentures were nominally bought by five Panamanian companies with a post office box in Switzerland, the securities were in fact held by Parnes' attorney in New York and never left the United States. As part of a larger stock manipulation scheme, the defendants converted the Regulation S debentures into common stock, illegally distributing the securities and securing illegal profits. The Commission's complaint charges the defendants with securities fraud, and seeks penalties, disgorgement and a permanent injunction against future violations.

On 26th November 2002, the Commission announced that the US District Court for the Southern District of New York entered permanent injunctions against future violations by the defendants of the anti-fraud, registration, and other provisions of the federal securities laws. In addition, the court ordered the defendants to pay a total of US$890,000 in civil penalties, disgorgement, and prejudgment interest. The court also barred a broker involved in the scheme from association with any broker or dealer for a period of three years.

SEC v. William T. Craig and Scott R. Sieck,
Litigation Release 16056 (10th February 1999)
The Commission charged that Madison Group Associates, Inc. (Madison Group), a now defunct microcap entertainment company, issued stock to an offshore entity. Although this offering was purportedly conducted pursuant to Regulation S, the offshore entity was actually controlled by William Craig and Scott Sieck. Craig was the Chairman and CEO of Madison Group, while Sieck was a consultant to the company. Soon after the offshore entity received the Madison Group stock, it sold its shares into US

markets. The Commission charged that Craig and Sieck personally profited from their undisclosed role in this abusive Regulation S offering. Craig and Sieck were charged with other securities laws violations in connection with Madison Group. As a result of a settlement, Craig was permanently barred from serving as an officer or director of a publicly held company, and was permanently enjoined from committing further the antifraud provisions of the securities laws. Sieck agreed to an injunction, and a civil penalty of US$16,000.

SEC v. Jui-Teng Lin and Yuchin Lin,
Litigation Release 15869 (2nd September 1998)
In this complaint, the SEC alleged that Jui-Teng Lin (Dr Lin), the former president and CEO of LaserSight, Inc., and Yuchin Lin (Ms Lin), his wife and LaserSight's former bookkeeper, assisted by Ms Lin's brother, Kuo-chang Wong (Wong), diverted LaserSight corporate funds to themselves through certain "consulting" and other arrangements and concealed their interest in those transactions, and orchestrated a sham offshore transaction as part of a scheme to sell unregistered LaserSight stock in purported reliance on Regulation S.

According to the SEC, on several occasions in 1992, Ms Lin disbursed funds totalling about US$375,000 from LaserSight to two Taiwanese entities controlled by Wong, purportedly for consulting or other services. No services were provided and instead, in each instance, Wong initially deposited the funds into his personal bank accounts in Taiwan or Hong Kong, and then a short time later transferred them back to the Lins' personal bank account. The Lins subsequently used those funds to exercise LaserSight stock options. The Lins falsified LaserSight corporate records in carrying out these diversions and their non-disclosure, together with the non-disclosure of certain unauthorised loans, rendered three of LaserSight's 1993 quarterly reports and its 1993 annual report materially false.

In 1993 the Lins also carried out an elaborate sham to enable them to sell restricted LaserSight shares they owned without registration. As part of that sham, they purported to sell 160,000 LaserSight shares to KCC Group, an Antiguan entity, pursuant to Regulations S. Dr Lin had established KCC Group, installed Wong as its sole director and owner, and provided Wong with the funds KCC Group used to "purchase" the shares. After the "sale," Dr. Lin made false representations to an attorney to secure an opinion letter authorising the removal of the restrictive legend from KCC Group's shares. The Lins subsequently opened brokerage accounts in the name of KCC Group from which they directed the sale of the shares into the market. Dr Lin filed false ownership reports with the Commission disclosing that he had sold LaserSight stock to KCC Group when in fact he still retained beneficial ownership, and later failed to disclose that he had sold the shares when he ultimately gave up beneficial ownership.

Simultaneously with the filing of the complaint, Dr and Ms Lin consented to the entry of final judgments of permanent injunctions enjoining them from violating the securities laws, agreed to disgorge their wrongful gains from their sales of LaserSight stock together with prejudgment interest, and agreed to pay civil penalties of US$100,000 and US$50,000 respectively. In a related matter, the SEC issued a cease-and-desist order by consent against Wong finding that he was a cause of the Lins' violations of the antifraud and securities registration provisions.

In re GFL Ultra Fund Ltd.,
Securities Act Release 7423 (18th June 1997)
In this matter, a British Virgin Islands fund allegedly purchased for cash overseas securities that had been issued at substantial discounts and hedged some or all of those securities through short selling in the United States before and/or during the forty-day restricted period attempting to rely upon Regulation S. According to the SEC, the fund participated in 90 transactions involving the common stock of 47 issuers. Commissioner Steven Wallman dissented and wrote that the application of Regulation S to these transactions was unclear at the time of the conduct.

In the matter of Candie's, Inc. et al,
Securities Act Release 7263 (21st February 1996)
This matter involved four offerings of securities purportedly made in reliance on Regulation S. In all four offerings, the only liquid market for the securities was in the United States. In each instance, a large block of securities was sold at a substantial discount to the

prevailing market price in return for a short-term, unsecured promissory note. The respondents knew almost nothing about the foreign purchasers. In each instance, the securities were transferred to the newly opened accounts of the foreign purchasers with one of the defendants, a broker-dealer in New York. Shortly after the expiration of the forty-day restricted period of Regulation S, the securities were sold to US customers. In all four of the transactions, the foreign purchasers bore little market risk because they used the proceeds of the US sales to pay off their promissory notes. In essence, the foreign purchasers acted as mere conduits for the sale of unregistered securities in the United States. Pursuant to an offer of settlement, a consent order was entered whereby the defendants agreed to permanently cease-and-desist from committing or causing any violation and any future violation of Section 5 of the Securities Act, and one defendant was suspended from association with any broker, dealer, investment adviser, investment company or municipal securities dealer for a period of five months.

SEC v. Scorpion Technologies, Inc.,
Litigation Release 14814 (9th February 1996)
The SEC alleged that Scorpion Technologies falsified disclosures of its business operations and financial health through sham transactions. Approximately 20 million shares of the company's stock were issued in purported reliance upon Regulation S. The complaint alleges that this stock was issued to offshore purchasers at a discount from the market price. It was then sold to public investors in the United States without "coming to rest" in the hands of bona fide offshore purchasers. The SEC received assistance from authorities in the United Kingdom, Hong Kong and Guernsey in this case. In addition, the United States Department of Justice obtained an indictment against the participants for securities fraud and money laundering.

Offering frauds
SEC v. John F. Turant, Jr., et al,
Litigation Release 18351 (15th September 2003)
In this matter the SEC filed a complaint in federal court seeking an injunction, disgorgement, prejudgment interest and civil penalties against John F. Turant, Russ R. Luciano and four entities operated by them.

According to the SEC's complaint, the defendants raised approximately US$4.5 million from more than 100 investors in an offering fraud. The complaint alleged that the defendants promised investors returns from 20% to 40% in investments in two hedge funds for the purpose of day-trading securities. The complaint further alleged that of the US$4.5 million of investor funds raised, more than US$3.8 million was used for unauthorised purposes, including US$2.2 million to pay existing investors in the nature of a Ponzi scheme, and almost US$1 million for the defendant's personal use.

A default judgment against Turant was entered on 29th January 2004. The judgment permanently enjoins Turant from future violations of the federal securities laws and ordering Turant to pay a civil penalty in the amount of US$120,000, and disgorgement and prejudgment interest of US$1,742,118.62.

SEC v. Daniel T. Todt et al, Litigation Release 15771 (5th June 1998); Litigation Release 15775 (5th June 1998); Litigation Release 15797 (1st July 1998); Litigation Release 15960 (28th October1998); Litigation Release 16184 (10th June 1999); 16467 (9th March 2000)
In this matter, the Commission filed a complaint in federal court seeking emergency injunctive relief and civil penalties for violation of the federal securities laws in connection with an offer and attempt to sell forged and fictitious securities of a Japanese bank.

The Commission alleged in its complaint that beginning in March 1997, the defendants had been engaged in continuing offers and attempts to sell a fraudulent bank certificate purportedly issued by the Bank of Tokyo-Mitsubishi, Ltd. (Mitsubishi Certificate). The defendants allegedly participated in the fraudulent scheme to use the Mitsubishi Certificate to obtain millions of dollars for themselves, while invoking both "humanitarian" goals and the names of "official" entities, ranging from the Federal Reserve Bank to the United Nations Security Council, in an effort to make their scheme appear legitimate. The court granted the temporary relief and three weeks later, upon consent of the defendants, entered preliminary injunctive relief as to some defendants and permanent relief as to four others. In October 1998, the court entered a default judgment against one of the defendants, permanently enjoining him from violations of the securities laws and imposing a US$75,000 fine, which it deemed "appropriate given the fraudulent conduct – and the significant risk of substantial losses to" others. The court subsequently entered final judgment against the two remaining defendants, ordering each of them to pay civil penalties of US$200,000 and US$100,000, respectively.

SEC v. Rob Nite, Philip L. Thomas, and David V. Sims, Litigation Release 15472 (4th September 1997); Litigation Release 15667 (11th March 1998); Litigation Release 15938 (19th October 1998)

In this matter, the SEC filed a complaint in federal court in September 1997 against three Southern California businessmen alleging a multi-million dollar fraudulent investment scheme involving the fictional trading of securities purportedly issued by major international banks. According to the Commission, the defendants offered and sold to the public interests in a bogus program to trade the purported securities, amassing approximately US$3.7 million. The victims were promised astronomical returns on relatively small investments. (eg, returns of US$1 million per week for 40 weeks or US$40 million on investments of US$50,000 to US$150,000. The defendants did not invest the victims' funds, but instead misappropriated those funds for their own personal benefit, including donations to religious organisations, purchases of luxury automobiles and gifts to family members. The scheme, commonly referred to as a "prime bank" scheme, has been the subject of official warnings issued to investors by several federal agencies including the SEC and the Board of Governors of the Federal Reserve System. The Commission sought permanent injunctions against the defendants prohibiting further violation of the securities laws, disgorgement of the ill-gotten gains with interest and civil penalties.

In March 1998, defendants Thomas and Sims consented to entry of final judgments permanently enjoining future violations of the antifraud provisions of US securities laws. The Commission waived payment of disgorgement and did not assess civil penalties, based upon demonstrated inability to pay. Six months later, in September 1998, the court entered summary judgment against Nite, permanently enjoining him from future violations of the antifraud provisions of the federal securities laws and ordering him to pay US$3,678,500 in disgorgement and US$100,000 in civil penalties. At the time, Nite was incarcerated, awaiting trial for conspiracy to commit fraud, wire fraud, bank fraud and interstate transportation of stolen property, charges unrelated to the Commission's action.

SEC v. Terry Koontz, Zone Productions, Inc., et al,
Litigation Release 15892 (21st September 1998)
In this matter, originally filed under seal, the SEC obtained an emergency court order freezing the assets of ten defendants who were participating in a massive prime bank Ponzi scheme in which more than US$19 million was raised from more than 80 investors in 16 states.

The Commission alleged that beginning in August 1997, Terry Koontz, Jeffrey DeVille and Mykael DeVille recruited a network of salesmen on the East Coast to sell interests in an "international bank debenture trading program" named Private Pool LLC, falsely representing to investors that their funds would be invested in a 40-week bank debenture trading program through Koontz, an international bond trader affiliated with Barclays Bank, and secured by government bonds, and falsely promising a 1% weekly return. Instead, the complaint alleges, investor funds were deposited into a bank account controlled by Koontz, who dissipated at least US$9.9 million, including US$468,000 on automobiles, over US$250,000 on jewelry, US$650,000 on real estate and gratuitous transfers of over US$6.5 million to his wife and other defendants.

The Commission obtained an order temporarily restraining the fraudulent activities, freezing assets, prohibiting the acceptance of additional investor funds, requiring repatriation of funds transferred abroad and other relief.

SEC v. Michael D. Richmond, individually, Michael D. Richmond d/b/a Liberty Network, Royal Meridian International Bank, Meridian Monetary et al, Litigation Release 15813 (17th July 1998)

In this matter, the Commission filed a complaint in federal court alleging that the defendants were engaged in an on-going Ponzi scheme involving unregistered securities in the form of "International Certificates of Deposits" (CDs), and had obtained US$7.2 million from more than 185 investors in fourteen states.

According to the Commission, Michael Richmond orchestrated the scheme in which he used internet websites and a network of

Liberty sales agents to convince unsophisticated investors, including many elderly persons and widows, to liquidate annuities and other investments in order to purchase fraudulent securities issued by the Royal Meridian International Bank (RMIB).

The Commission alleges that the sales agents falsely guaranteed rates of return from 12% to 24%, and falsely represented that RMIB held 125% in cash reserves for each investment, that all investments would be secured by government bonds, that certain large investors would receive security interests in their investments, and that RMIB was a "fully-chartered" private, offshore bank, with offices in Canada, the Bahamas, Guernsey and Turks & Caicos. The Commission further alleges that RMIB is a shell with no offices and no apparent significant sources of revenue from which it can pay the guaranteed return except through the sale of additional fraudulent securities to unwitting investors, that investor funds, instead of being deposited with RMIB and secured and reinvested as represented, were being deposited into money market and bank accounts controlled by Richmond and used to repay other investors and for personal expenses incurred by the Richmond and others, and that only US$2.7 million remained available to repay defrauded investors.

The court issued a temporary restraining order prohibiting further violations of the securities laws and additional orders freezing assets, prohibiting the acceptance of additional investor funds, requiring an accounting of assets, and directing the repatriation of assets transferred abroad. On 22nd December 1998, two of the sales agent defendants consented to the entry of permanent injunctions against violations of the securities laws and orders of disgorgement. The Commission is seeking permanent injunctions against future violations, disgorgement and the imposition of civil monetary penalties against the remaining defendants.

SEC v. Christian Schindler, a/k/a "Rudy Gerner," Inter Capital Brokerage, Inc., Intercap Forex Brokerage, Inc., and Inter-Capital Brokerage U.S.USA. Inc, Litigation Release 15684 (26th March 1998)

In this matter, the SEC alleged in a complaint filed in federal court that Schindler, an Austrian national, and three of his companies perpetrated from the United States a multi-million dollar affinity fraud targeted primarily at German-speaking Europeans. According to the SEC, Schindler, who used "Gerner" as an alias, was convicted in Germany in 1995 of felony criminal fraud in the offer, purchase and sale of securities and commodities to investors, and is permanently enjoined from violating the antifraud and other provisions of the Commodity Exchange Act.

The complaint alleges that since late 1996, Schindler and his Intercap Companies, which were engaged in the solicitation, pooling and investment of customers' funds in the securities, commodities and foreign exchange markets, fraudulently obtained almost US$6 million from more than forty European investors, inducing them to make various investments in United States Treasury bonds, publicly-traded stock and stock in the Intercap Companies, through false and misleading statements concerning

(1) Schindler's identity, and his criminal and disciplinary history;
(2) the returns investors would obtain on their investments;
(3) the safety and liquidity of the investments offered;
(4) the types of investments defendants would make with investors' money; and
(5) purported troubles involving the SEC. According to the SEC, Schindler and the Intercap Companies then transferred the investors' funds overseas and diverted hundreds of thousands of dollars to their own benefit.

The court initially issued an emergency order temporarily restraining defendants from further violating the antifraud provisions of the federal securities laws, freezing defendants' assets, appointing a receiver and directing the defendants to repatriate assets transferred overseas. Ten days later, the court converted the restraining order to a preliminary injunction and appointed a permanent receiver. The suit is still pending.

MARKET MANIPULATION
SEC v. Surgilight, Inc., Jui-Teng Lin, Yuchin Lin and Aaron Tsai, Litigation Release 17469 (11th April 2002)

In this matter, the Commission charged Surgilight, Inc. (Surgilight), a laser eye surgery company, Jui-Teng Lin (Dr Lin), the former CEO of Surgilight, and two other individuals with manipulating the market for securities of Surgilight. The Commission alleged in its complaint that Dr Lin with the assistance of others, caused Surgilight to issue a series of false and misleading press releases touting

Surgilight's success in developing lasers to treat a common eye disorder. According to the complaint, at the same time Surgilight issued its press releases, Dr Lin used brokerage accounts held in the names of Taiwanese nationals to order hundreds of Surgilight securities transactions to create the appearance of an active and liquid market for Surgilight stock. The complaint states that the defendants moved the proceeds of the scheme, approximately US$1.7 million, through a series of bank accounts located in Taipei, Taiwan, and eventually returned the funds to a Surgilight bank account located in Orlando, Florida.

The complaint charges the defendants with violating the antifraud, registration, and other provisions of the federal securities laws. The Commission is seeking disgorgement of all ill-gotten gains with pre-judgment interest and civil penalties as well as a permanent officer and director bar against Dr Lin.

In a related matter, the US Attorney's Office for the Eastern District of New York indicted Jui-Teng Lin on securities fraud and money laundering charges. A jury convicted Jui-Teng Lin of the charges on 13th December 2002.

SEC v. Stephen Hourmouzis and Wayne Loughnan, Litigation Release 16705 (15th September 2000)

The Commission in this case sued two Australian residents, Stephen Hourmouzis and Wayne Loughnan, for their use of the Internet to tout the stock of Rentech, Inc. (Rentech), a Denver company. The complaint alleged the defendants sent e-mails into the United States and posted messages on Internet message boards. Those e-mails and messages included false statements about Rentech's patented technology, and predicted a 900% increase in the company's stock price. Rentech's stock price doubled as a result of the touting, and the defendants sold their stock at a profit. The defendants were subject to a judgment for securities fraud and ordered to disgorge their profits after they failed to respond to the complaint.

SEC v. Miko Leung (a/k/a Leung Ming Kang) and Sit Wa Leung, Litigation Release 15631 (29th January 1998)

In this matter, the Commission filed a complaint in federal court against Miko Leung (Miko), the former chairman and president of MTC Electronic Technologies, Inc. (MTC) and his brother Sit Wa

Leung (Sit Wa), alleging that the defendants engaged in a false disclosure and accounting fraud scheme that culminated in a "pump and dump" stock manipulation, and unjustly enriched themselves by more than US$16 million by selling MTC stock, including approximately 1.5 million shares they had stolen. The Commission is seeking permanent injunctions, disgorgement, civil penalties and officer and director bars against both defendants.

According to the Commission, between 1990 and 1993, MTC falsely claimed that it had developed a telecommunications business in China that generated millions of dollars in revenues, and deceived its independent accountants by providing them with false documentation in support of fictitious sales. After disseminating false information, Miko and Sit Wa sold MTC stock through nominee accounts they controlled. In addition, the Commission alleged, between February and August 1992, Miko induced MTC's board to issue below market options on 1.52 million MTC shares ostensibly to be used as incentives for MTC employees, then stole and fraudulently exercised those options and deposited the MTC shares in nominee brokerage accounts that they controlled. The defendants later sold MTC stock shares at artificially inflated prices, realising illegal profits of US$12.1 million on the stolen shares and another US$4 million on other shares, and subsequently laundered the proceeds of their illegal securities transactions through a series of bank accounts worldwide, primarily nominee accounts that they controlled.

In a related matter, the Commission issued a cease-and-desist order against Ronald W. Driol regarding violations of the antifraud provisions of the federal securities laws. Driol consented to the order in which the Commission found that Driol played an indispensable role in facilitating the sale of the stolen options stock by placing Hong Kong Bank of Canada's signature guarantee on the share certificates issued in the names of existing and prospective MTC employees, and in transferring the proceeds of the stock sale from the nominee brokerage accounts to other nominee bank accounts.

In the matter of voucher investment fund RUSS-INVEST, Securities Act Release 7294 (21st May 1996)

On 21st May 1996, the SEC instituted administrative proceedings against this Russian investment fund for making an unregistered public offering of securities and failing to register as an investment company. The action was based on RUSS-INVEST's solicitation of US investors in a half-page advertisement in *The New York Times*. The SEC made its first request to, and received substantial assistance from, the Russian Federal Commission for the Securities Market. The action, which resulted in a cease-and-desist order against RUSS-INVEST, was entered pursuant to an offer of settlement from the firm.

Conclusion

The SEC's expanded enforcement powers and its initiatives to gain greater cooperation from foreign governments and foreign securities regulators have dramatically increased the SEC's presence around the world. All firms with any contact with the US securities markets should be familiar with the US securities laws and should be aware that their conduct may well be within the reach of the SEC's enforcement effort.

Index

A
AAER Release
 1425A 585
 1445 586
 1446 586
 1464 584
Accounting and Auditing
 Enforcement Release 1470 630
Accounting for Contingencies
 216, 251
Accounting Research Bulletin
 (ARB) 216
"Accredited Investor" 132–5, 417
Administrative Proceeding File
 3-11524 691
 3-11868 686
 3-9262 583
"Adopted Amendments" 149,
 154–5, 157–60, 175, 207, 394
"Advisers Act" 3, 5, 8, 137, 335,
 337, 341–1, 368–9, 418, 449–50,
 686–7, 694, 697
 Rule 206(4)-2 under the 347
 Rule 206(4)-6 under the 347
 Rule 206(4)-7 under the 348
Advisers Act Release
 1897 343
 1943 347
Aircraft Carrier Release 174–5,
 177
Alberta Securities Commission
 (ASC) 520
"All Holders/Best Price Rule"
 282, 307
alternative trading systems (ATSs)
 444

Amendments to Regulation S 147,
 150–2, 154, 168
American Depositary Receipt
 (ADRs) 81, 115
American Stock Exchange
 (AMEX) 19
amicus curiae 6, 285
Anti-money Laundering 373, 402,
 463–4, 474
Article 11 of Regulation S-X 189,
 230
Asian Regional Committee of the
 International Organisation of
 Securities Commissions
 (Asian IOSCO) 487
"Asset Test" 374, 384
Audit Committee 18, 50, 51, 73,
 183, 219, 222, 236, 241, 244–6,
 256–65, 267–9, 271, 274, 277,
 303–4, 388, 390, 392–5, 399, 549,
 551, 576, 613, 615, 631–2, 635,
 681, 712
"audit committee financial
 expert" 259–60, 262–3, 390,
 393
"audit partner" 50, 264, 268–9,
 271, 395
Auditor engagement duties
 264
average daily trading volume
 (ADTV) 454

B
Banc of America Capital
 Management, LLC (BACAP)
 689

725

Banc of America Securities, LLC (BAS) 689, 697, 710
Bank of England 480, 497, 499, 501–3, 621
Banque Paribas case 523, 527
"benefit plan investors" 380–1
"Breheny Speech" 301, 308
"Bright Line/Formalist Test" 307–8
British Columbia Securities Commission (BCSC) 506
brochure rule 344
Broker–Dealer Registration 542
broker–dealer "lite" rules 503

C
Canadian Imperial Bank of Commerce (CIBC) 682
Capital Formation and Regulatory Processes 85
capital lease obligations (FASB SFAS 13) 215
Case-by-Case Option 197
Category 2 of Regulation S 167
certificates of deposit (CDs) 9
Chinese Walls 444
Code of ethics 390, 396, 558, 613
Comision Nacional Bancaria y de Valores (CNBV) 548
Comissao do Mercado de Valores Mobiliàrios of Portugal (CMVM) 490
Commodities Trading Futures Commission (CFTC) 13
Commodity Exchange Act (CEA) 13
Commodity Futures Modernization Act 13
"Comprehensive fashion" 170
"conduct and effects" approach 352, 356–7
Conduct of bids 310, 313–14
"controlled foreign corporation" (CFC) 375
"cookie jar" 636
"cooling-off" period 40–1, 113, 269–71

Coopers & Lybrand's (C&L) retirement plan 681
"Corporate Financing Rule" 114–15
Council of Securities Regulators of the Americas (COSRA) 605
Critical accounting policies 47, 50, 199, 218–21, 275, 395, 634–5
Cross-Border Tender Offers 281, 283, 295
customer identification programs (CIPs) 464–5
"CyberForce" group 5

D
definitions of security 8, 10
Department of Justice (DOJ) 7
Depository Trust Company (DTC) 364
"directed selling efforts" 39, 96, 100, 141, 165, 168, 170, 175, 286, 294, 416, 611
"disclosure controls and procedures" 244–8, 254, 277, 387–8, 390, 392–3, 396, 639
"distribution compliance period" 142–7, 154–6
"distribution participants" 108–9, 132, 452, 455, 460–1
Division of Corporation Finance 4, 64, 75, 177–8, 191, 239, 241, 276

E
earnings before interest and taxes (EBIT) 230
earnings before interest, taxes, depreciation and amortisation (EBITDA) 226
earnings information 233, 697
earnings per share (EPS) 64
Effects of Regulation S amendments 157
"equitable price" 310–12
"ERISA plan" 380–3
Europe and Overseas Commodity Traders, SA (EOC) 523–4

INDEX

European Union (EU) regulations 281
"excess cash balances" 558
Exchange Act Release
  §30A 572
  22214 80
  27017 407, 542
  28899 446
  34-44969 630
  34-47890 272
  34-51400 664
  35057 347
  37940 347
  38067 451
  38672 420
  38732 459
  39400 678
  39472 701
  40760 445
  40945 681
  43183 668
  43372 81, 545, 635
  44420 707
  44970 630
  45149 634
  45272 677
  45287 662
  45796 668
  45908 435
  46130 676
  #46157 567
  46421 336
  46537 657
  46685 52
  46895 105, 701
  46896 105
  46897 105, 701
  46898 105, 701
  48230 683
  48493 696
  48588 696
  49386 710
  49741 693
  50426 644
  50521 703
  51164 689
  51167 689
  51238 83
  51427 106
  51523 449
  54145 687
Exchange Act Rule
  12g3-2(b) 531
  13a-15(f) and 15d-15(f) 277
  15a-6 135, 335
  16b-3 398
  3b-2 272
  13a-14 and 15d-14 243, 247
  13a-14(d) and 15(d)-14(d) 250
  13(b)(2)-(7) 236
Exchange Release 46896 701
exchange-traded funds (ETFs) 398

F

"factual business information" 34–5, 107
"family resemblance" test 10
FASB Statement
  No 5 216, 251
  No 107 223
  No 119 223
FIA MOU 480, 500–1
"FIN 45" 208–210, 216
Financial Crimes Enforcement Network (FinCEN) 373, 464, 470, 472, 475
Financial Intermediaries Managers and Brokers Regulatory Association 497
"financial reporting oversight role" 270, 395
Financial Services
  Act of 1986 496
  and Markets Act 2000 2, 361
  Authority (FSA) 2
"first-time adopter" 52, 193, 195–6
FOCUS Report 412
foreign personal holding company 374
"foreign private issuer" 16–18, 39, 46, 48, 51, 55, 98–9, 115–18, 141, 170, 173–6, 184, 186–9, 192–6, 198, 215, 222, 224, 226, 248–9, 258, 262, 275, 290, 294–5, 298, 545–6, 567, 578

"Foreign shell bank" 466–7, 469
Forum of European Securities Commissions 486
FPHC income 374
"fraud act" 3
"Free-Riding and Withholding Interpretation" 114, 340
"free-writing prospectus" 34
Freedom of Information Act (FOIA) 76
"frustrating action" 317, 321, 324
"FSMA" 2, 361–2, 621
"fulcrum fee" 345
"fullest mutual assistance" 492
"FundSettle" 372
"furnish" versus "file" 233
Futures Industry Association MOU 500

G

General Securities Principal (Series 24) 434
generally accepted accounting principles (GAAP) 49
Genesis of Regulation S 136
German Takeover Act 324
Global Minerals 512–15
Gramm–Leach–Bliley Act 3, 13–14
"Greenlight Capital" 532–3
gun-jumping 25, 29, 34, 40–2, 92, 95, 177

H

Howey test 10–11
"Hybrid Test" 307–8

I

IFRS Option 196
Independence Standards Board (ISB) 52
Initial Decision Release 249 673
initial public offers (IPOs) 30
Insider Trading Sanctions Act (ITSA) 625
Insolvency Regulation 328, 330
"Integral Part/Functionalist Test" 307

"integration doctrine" 180
interactive program guide (IPG) 651
"internal control over financial reporting" 74, 244–6, 249–55, 276–80, 305–6
Internal Revenue Service (IRS) 376
International Business Machines Corporation (IBM) 583
International Financial Reporting Standards (IFRS) 17
International Organisation of Securities Commissions (IOSCO) 17, 486–7
International Securities Enforcement Cooperation Act (ISECA) 486
International Series 662 492
International Series Release
323 496
331 492
806 496
932 492
1104 490
1124 491
IS-116 490
Interpretative letters 6
"investment adviser" 266, 333, 335–7, 341–3, 345–7, 354–60, 369, 380–1, 406, 411, 413, 417–19, 421–3, 449, 561, 690, 694, 716
Investment Advisers Act of 1940 3
Release 2333 358–9, 369
Release 2376 342
Investment Advisers Registration Depository (IARD) 343
"investment company" 3, 20, 135, 290, 294, 335, 337, 342, 345, 351, 360, 362–3, 365–6, 374, 385, 387–98, 407, 419, 452, 457, 692, 694–6, 716, 723
Investment Company Act of 1940 3, 694
Investment Company Act Release 16044 398

INDEX

25722 387
25914 389
25915 394
26001 394
26312A 694
Investment Management
  Regulatory Organisation
  (IMRO) 480, 496–7, 499
"Issuer Information" 38, 45
"Issuer Safe Harbour" 140–1, 158, 416

J
Japanese Financial Services
  Agency (Japan FSA) 493
Jersey Financial Services
  Commission (FSC) 495
Johnson–Shad accord 13

K
KPMG-Siddharta Siddharta &
  Harsono (KPMG-SSH) 586

L
Legended certificates 156
"Leon-Meredith Report" 630–1
Litigation Reform Act 3, 89, 223, 426, 577
Litigation Release
  2065 557
  2204 602
  14814 716
  15164 580, 672
  15419 672
  15442 710
  15472 718
  15540 710
  15631 722
  15771 717
  15775 717
  15802 670
  15813 719
  15832 60, 276
  15861 711
  15869 714
  15892 719
  15893 709
  15937 709

16022 669
16056 713
16161 708
16705 722
16839 583
16848 708
16877 713
16948 580, 672
16991 559, 707
17068A 585
17126 586
17127 586
17269 584
17310 587
17356 707
17395 707
17469 721
17481 668
17588 659
17627 658
17744 657
17782 554
17837 658
17860 701
17865 713
17897 707
18038 685
18044 655
18081 585
18102 676
18252 684
18330 699
18340 654
18351 716
18438 704, 711
18482 695
18517 682
18523 556
18527 557
18543 650
18551 649
18715 653
18734 652
18760 651
18766 698
18775 597
18776 648
18817 647

729

Litigation Release (*continued*)
  18820 645
  18844 551
  18863 587, 593
  18889 706
  18891 644
  18925 589, 592
  18929 549
  18936 642
  18969 548
  18985 640
  19022 546
  19048 638
  19049 705
  19066 667
  19136 642
  19147 664
  19154 105, 697
  19174 637
  19243 64
  26255 695
Lloyd's of London cases 526
London Stock Exchange (LSE) 334
long-term debt (FASB SFAS 47) 215

M
Management's Discussion and Analysis (MD&A) 47, 276
"material variable interest" 209
"Materiality Guidance" 234
"Matters Relating to Independent Accountants" 263
Memoranda of Understanding (MOUs) 479
Monetary Authority of Singapore (MAS) 492
Morgan Stanley
  India Securities Pvt Ltd (MSISL) 412
  letter 411
  no-action letter 192
multi-jurisdictional disclosure system(MSDS) 231
Municipal Securities Rule Making Board 7
Mutual Legal Assistance Treaties (MLATs) 479

"mutual recognition" or "reciprocal regulation" 137

N
NASAA model regulation 423
NASD conduct Rule
  2710 114
  2110–1 114
NASD Regulation, Inc (NASDR) 7
NASD Rule
  2210(b)(2) 434
  2210(d)(2)(A) 435
  2711 434–7
  2711(b) and (c) 435
  2711(c) 435
  2711(h) 435–6
  2711(h)(2) 436
  3011 464
  4460(b)(1) 112
NASD's PORTAL system 163
National Association of Securities Dealers Automated Quotation system (NASDAQ) 7
National Association of Securities Dealers, Inc (NASD) 7
National Petroleum Investment Management Service (NAPIMS) 598
New York Stock Exchange (NYSE) 7, 15
no-action letter 6, 158, 192, 350–2, 368, 409–11, 417, 458
"non-accredited investors" 132, 134
"non-GAAP financial measure" 53, 225–7, 229–34, 305
North American Securities Administrators Association (NASAA) 422
NYSE Rule
  312(g) 115
  445 464

O
off-balance-sheet arrangement 208, 210–11, 213
Office of Foreign Asset Control (OFAC) 65

Office of the Chief Accountant (OCA) 679
"officer and director bar" 626, 659, 722
open-ended investment companies (OEICs) 362
operating leases (FASB SFAS 13) 215
Operation of Regulation S 137
Outline of Regulation S 139
over-the-counter (OTC) markets 3
Overview of Rule 144A 161

P
"passive foreign investment company" 20, 374
Patriot Act 373, 402, 463–4, 466–7, 473–8
Patriot Act §312(a) 473
PCAOB
  Release 2003–007 185
  Rule 2105 569
"pecuniary interest" 337
"PFIC rules" 20, 374–6
PIPE (private investment in public equity) transactions 179–81
Preliminary Note 2 to Regulation S 147
Press/media policy 286
PriceWaterhouseCoopers 681
"principal market" 152–5, 459
"Private Offerings, Resales and Trading through Automated Linkages" 164
Private Securities Litigation Reform Act 3, 89, 577
"Proposed Amendments" 150–7, 454, 459
Public Company Accounting Oversight Board (PCAOB) 50, 183
Public Utility Holding Company Act of 1935 (PUHCA) 3, 5
"purchase obligation" 215
Purchaser and distributor agreements 156
Purchaser certifications 156

"purchaser representative" 133

Q
Qualified institutional buyers (QIBs) 18
"qualifying electing fund" (QEF) 376
"Qwest" 642–3

R
Regulation A 131, 305
Regulation Analyst Certification (Regulation AC) 97, 101, 434, 439–42, 703
Regulation D Rule 501 134
Regulation FD 102–5, 107–8, 181, 228–9, 234, 289, 697–701
Regulation M 96, 108–10, 402, 451–4, 456, 459–63
Regulation S
  flexibility 145
  on Form 8-K 149
"Remedies Act" 625, 627–8, 706
"Resale Safe Harbour" 140, 144–5, 159
"restricted securities" 129–34, 138–9, 145, 155, 158–61, 164–5, 179, 294, 339, 416, 425
"Resurgent India Bonds" (RIBs) 543
Rule 10A-3 under the Exchange Act 256
Rule 10b-5 Exchange Act 229, 426
Rule 10b-5 of the Exchange Act 180, 247, 508, 544
Rule 14d-10 of the Exchange Act 282, 307
Rule 14d-9(d) under the Exchange Act 170
Rule 152 of the Securities Act 180
Rule 155 under the Securities Act 177
Rule 15a-6 under the Exchange Act 165, 405
Rule 2–01 of Regulation S-X 263
Rule 3–10 of Regulation S-X 190
Rule 3–20 of Regulation S-X 187
Rule 3a-1 under the 1940 Act 363

Rule 3a-2 under the Act 363
Rule 3b-16 under the Exchange Act 446
Rule 501(a)(1) of Regulation D under the Securities Act 407
Rule 501(a)(2) of Regulation D 407
Rule 501(a)(7) of Regulation D 407
Rule 504 of Regulation D 133
Rule 505 of Regulation D 133
Rule 506 of Regulation D 133–5
Rule 802 of the Securities Act 292, 294, 298
Rule 901 of Regulation S 139
Rule 901 or 903 under Regulation S 155, 164
Rules 13e-3 and 13e-4, Regulation 14D and Rules 14e-1 and 14e-2 of the Exchange Act 290
Rules 504 and 505 of Regulation D 131

S

"sale of business" controversy 2, 10
Sarbanes–Oxley Act
  Section 303(a) 614
  Section 303(d) 614
  Section 305(b) 614
  Section 1103(a) 614
  Section 1106 616
  Section 1107 615
Schedule B of the Securities Act 163
"scienter" 80, 83, 426, 680
seasoned issuer 23, 26, 34, 36, 70–1, 98, 192
SEC enforcement matter 589
SEC International Series Release No. IS-1129 489
SEC Litigation Release
  16997 563
  17172 516
  17776 553
  17887 593
  18441 560
  18797 550

SEC Staff Accounting Bulletin 99 (SAB 99) 63
SEC under Rule 12g3–2(b) of the Exchange Act 18
Securities Act (Section 2(1)) 8
Securities Act of 1933 1–3, 247, 443
Securities Act Release
  4708 137, 611
  6711 199, 275
  6791 275
  6835 201, 206, 275
  6862 136, 611
  6863 136, 416
  7053 166
  7190 149
  7263 715
  7294 723
  7314 85
  7386 223
  7392 152
  7423 715
  7470 169
  7516 90, 288, 379
  7637 58
  7759 92
  7801 50
  7856 94, 379
  7878 190
  7881 102
  7919 264
  7983 57
  8040 47, 218, 275
  8056 206
  8098 48, 199, 275
  8176 53, 225, 233, 275
  8177 260–1
  8182 207, 275
  8183 51, 264
  8193 101
  8220 256
  8238 243, 249–50, 252
  8350 199, 276
  8355 674
  8392 249
  8400 232
  8400A 232
  8505 691
  8506 691

8518 191
8523 121
8545 249
8567 52, 53, 192
8591 23
Securities Act Rule 135c 148
Securities Act Rules 901 to 905 139
Securities Act Safe Harbour 170, 174
Securities Act
  Section 17(b) 39
  Section 8 or Section 8A 26
Securities and Exchange Board of India (SEBI) 491
Securities and Exchange Commission 1, 4, 465, 481, 492, 494, 515–516, 518, 521, 527
Securities and Futures Commission (SFC) 497
Securities and Investments Board (SIB) 496
Securities Association Limited 497
Securities Exchange Act of 1934 1, 3, 540, 589–590
"seed money" 165, 381
self regulatory organizations (SROs) 114, 256, 403, 418, 442, 459, 486, 493
"Series 24 Principal" 434
"Shields Plan" rights 458
small business investment companies (SBICs) 389
"specially designated nationals" (SDNs) 65
"statutory insiders" 336

T
The Foreign corrupt practices act 20, 83, 571, 612
Tender Offer Safe Harbour 173–174
Triton case 573
Trust Indenture Act of 1939 3

U
UK Companies Act 3
UK Takeover Panel 290, 321
UNCITRAL Model Law 329–330
unit investment trusts (UITs) 387
Unitary Filing of Suspicious Activity and Blocking Reports 472
United Nations Commission on International Trade Law's (UNCITRAL) 329
unseasoned issuer 24, 34, 37, 42, 45, 93
US Court of Appeals 519, 523, 530, 539, 587, 589, 680
US federal agency 1
US federal securities laws 1–4, 9, 11, 13–14, 17, 21, 63, 75, 135, 137, 168, 170, 174, 183–184, 336, 451, 523, 545, 547, 549, 551, 554, 581, 610, 612, 636
US GAAP Condensed Information Option 197
USA Patriot Act of 2001 402

W
Williams Act 174